S. Haykin

Introduction to Computer Architecture

Second Edition

Harold S. Stone, Editor
University of Massachusetts

Tien Chi Chen
IBM San Jose Research Laboratory

Michael J. Flynn
Stanford University

Samuel H. Fuller
Digital Equipment Corporation
Maynard, Massachusetts

William G. Lane
Department of Computer Science
California State University, Chico

Herschel H. Loomis, Jr.
University of California, Davis

William M. McKeeman
University of California, Santa Cruz

Kay B. Magleby
Bell Northern Research
Palo Alto, California

Richard E. Matick
IBM Watson Research Laboratory
Yorktown Heights, New York

Richard Sites
Digital Equipment Corporation
Maynard, Massachusetts

Thomas M. Whitney
Apple Computer Inc.
Cupertino, California

 SCIENCE RESEARCH ASSOCIATES, INC.
Chicago, Henley-on-Thames, Sydney, Toronto

A Subsidiary of IBM

The SRA Computer Science Series

William A. Barrett and John D. Couch, *Compiler Construction: Theory and Practice*
Marilyn Bohl and Arline Walter, *Introduction to PL/1 Programming and PL/C*
Mark Elson, *Concepts of Programming Languages*
Mark Elson, *Data Structures*
Peter Freeman, *Software Systems Principles: A Survey*
C. W. Gear, *Introduction to Computer Science: Short Edition*
Philip Gilbert, *Software Design and Development*
A. N. Habermann, *Introduction to Operating System Design*
Harry Katzan, Jr., *Computer Systems Organization and Programming*
Henry Ledgard and Michael Marcotty, *The Programming Language Landscape*
James L. Parker and Marilyn Bohl, *FORTRAN Programming and WATFIV*
Stephen M. Pizer, *Numerical Computing and Mathematical Analysis*
Harold S. Stone, *Discrete Mathematical Structures and Their Applications*
Harold S. Stone, *Introduction to Computer Architecture, Second Edition*

Acquisition Editor	Alan W. Lowe
Project Editor	James C. Budd
Production	Greg Hubit Bookworks
Compositor	Typographic Service Co.
Illustrator	John Foster

Library of Congress Cataloging in Publication Data

Main entry under title:

Introduction to computer architecture

(SRA computer science series)
Bibliography: p.
Includes index.
1. Computer architecture.   I.   Stone, Harold S.,
1938–
QA76.9.A73I57   1980   621.3819'5   79-27493
ISBN 0-574-21225-6

Acknowledgments

We wish to acknowledge the following for their permission to reprint the materials listed:

Courtesy of Fairchild Camera and Instrument Corporation: figure 3-1*a*

Courtesy of Texas Instruments, Inc.: figures 3-1*b* and 3-3

Printed in the United States of America.

10   9   8   7   6   5   4

Foreword

A number of years ago Edsger Dijkstra kindly provided a foreword to a book describing an Algol 60 translator and run time system that a colleague, Lawford Russell, and I had written. In his foreword, Dijkstra stated that it was important that such books be read by computer designers as well as language implementors. Similarly, I believe that this present book deserves a wide readership, which should certainly include students with a serious interest in system software, as well as any would-be computer architects. The perspective that it gives on present-day computers, and on how their designs have evolved and are likely to continue to evolve, will be as valuable to such a readership as the solid technical detail it gives of current practices in computer architecture.

In fact, at the time Dijkstra made these comments the term "computer architecture" was, I believe, yet to be coined. When it was first used it seemed to many of us that it implied somewhat unjustifiably, or at least prematurely, a successful concern for such qualities as simplicity and elegance, as well as practicability, in computer design. Yet there was a need for a term to cover the task of designing the external functional aspects of a computer which constitute the interface, or abstraction, that it provides to programmers and users. Moreover since then, as books such as this indicate, much progress has been made in developing the subject and gaining a greater understanding of useful design trade-offs, to the point where the use of the term "computer architecture" is as appropriate as it is well established.

It has been said that one of the major ways in which the task of computer design differs from that of programming is that, over the years, the computer designer will be reimplementing a basically similar abstraction from ever-changing primitives, while a programmer will be using what to him or her are constant primitives to produce a sequence of perhaps wildly differing abstractions. Yet there is much that can be learned from a study of different computer architectures. For example, as this book shows so clearly, microprocessor designers would do well to study the past evolution of minicomputer designs, since even though slavish copying of past solutions is usually inappropriate, so too is their blind and perhaps not always expert reinvention. The other side of the coin, the problems that the computer designer has of coping with rapid technological change, is equally well covered in the book. It does this both by providing admirable general syntheses of particular design problems, such as that of exploiting synchro-parallelism, and also up-to-date discussions of topical problems, such as the use of microprocessors in the construction of large-scale computers, and the impact of current LSI design constraints.

In summary, the editor and his colleagues have produced a most valuable book which will, despite its title, serve not just as an introductory text but also as a handbook to current trends in computer architecture.

B. Randell

Instructor's Preface
to the Second Edition

This text is intended as a first book in computer architecture for computer science or computer engineering programs. The presentation carries the student from an elementary overview through a detailed discussion of the various fundamental aspects into several specialized and advanced topics. Part I is suitable for a one-semester course for juniors and seniors. Part II is a natural extension of Part I suitable for a second semester for juniors and seniors or as a stand-alone course for first-year graduates. The text is highly modular, and the instructor can easily construct a semester course by drawing from selected chapters throughout the text. The subjects from chapter to chapter tend to be independent of each other, and the chapters themselves are written to require few, if any, prerequisites from prior chapters.

Readers familiar with the first edition will find the second edition to be a major revision of the earlier material. A new chapter on operating systems ties together architectural considerations with techniques for executive control of computers. The earlier material on calculators, which then was the high-technology area for large-scale integration, has been dramatically revised to create a chapter on microprocessors, thus bringing the book on target with the major innovations in the low end of computers. Other chapters that have changed extensively between editions are those on minicomputers, memories, input/output systems, stack machines, and pipelined computers. The two editions share a common structure and a common set of authors, so that patterns of teaching developed for the text in the past few years can be retained for the present edition.

The book is designed to satisfy two types of needs. One need is for the student who wishes to understand the subject of computer architecture because of interests in computer science but who does not wish to learn how to build a computer. This student has generally taken at least one course in programming computers, perhaps in a high-level language, and preferably has learned some of the more intimate details about computers, perhaps through a course in assembly language. This student has not had switching theory and logic design and does not have experience reading logic diagrams or designing digital circuits. This student will be quite comfortable with the text. Only in a few places in the early chapters is there mention of elementary hardware such as logic gates. If the student has used AND or OR instructions in programs, there should be no difficulty with this material. The detailed hardware material that does exist in the book is suitable as an introduction to hardware for students without this background.

The second type of student may have had experience in switching theory and logic design but very little programming experience. For this student the book is sprinkled with selected fragments of programs to illustrate specific concepts of computer architecture. In understanding these examples, the student becomes more conversant with software as well as computer architecture.

This text carries numerous examples of architectural features that have been designed to support specific software functions. In particular, Chapter 12 on operating systems emphasizes how architecture design interacts with and simplifies operating systems. To design computer architectures that simplify or eliminate program functions is possible only if the computer architect has a strong background in both logical design and programming. Material is provided to strengthen a student in both these areas without presuming extensive knowledge in either. University curricula should ideally reflect the intent of this text by providing programs that bridge the two parts.

One of the important features of the book is the inclusion of extensive problems within or at the end of each chapter. They do not require access to a computer but often involve the programming of fragments of a computer program. Students should be encouraged to write and debug such program fragments on a real computer, and preferably on several different computers.

Because computer technology is changing so rapidly, one of the pitfalls of any textbook in this area is the inclusion of material that eventually becomes obsolete. This text, in going into its second edition, deals with the problem of obsolescence by focusing on trends and observing the reasons for these trends. Where several competitive techniques for design exist, the text explores each technique and indicates the relative advantages and disadvantages under varying design constraints. Consequently, the student is told more than what is recent practice in the industry. Rather the student is told how architectural considerations will change in time as the underlying device technology evolves.

This editor's experience with the first edition of the text was one in which the basic reading material was constant from year to year but the problem sets underwent vast changes. For design-oriented questions, acceptable answers for 1975 constraints became poor and eventually unacceptable by 1980. The most successful questions to make students aware of the changes taking place were those questions that created totally artificial and realistic constraints and asked for designs that satisfied the constraints as given. The questions stimulated the students to isolate the fundamental concepts of a chapter and to apply these concepts in a context quite foreign from the one in which the concept was first described. Such exercises help prepare the student for future years in which the student must apply basic course material in a computing milieu markedly different from the present one.

Term projects constitute another way that students can make use of basic ideas exposed in this book. With microprocessors both inexpensive and in great supply, a student has the opportunity to put together a complete working computer system, from basic hardware to a small executive control program.

Before closing this preface, I wish to thank Steve Mitchell, whose inspiration led to the development of this text. He conceived the idea, outlined its form, and brought together the coauthors for the first edition. My role as editor was greatly simplified by the coauthors themselves, each expert in his own area, yet frequently contributing to other chapters and the book as a whole through exchange of information and helpful critiques. Thanks are also in order to George Miller, Amar Mukhopadhyay, Myron Calhoun, Bruce Barnes, Martha Sloan, and Samuel Fuller, whose critical comments helped shape the first edition and whose influence is still evident in this edition. The second edition drew on many more people, including Bob Safran, Alan Lowe, and particularly Greg Hubit, technical editor, whose red pencil brought order and structure to the anarchy of the draft material. Only through the intense efforts of the people named here and many others unnamed could a project of this complexity reach fruition.

Harold S. Stone
Amherst, Massachusetts

Contents

PART I

Basic Computer Architecture

CHAPTER 1

Introduction

Harold S. Stone

The study of computer architecture is the study of the organization and interconnection of components of computer systems. Computer architects construct computers from basic building blocks such as memories, arithmetic units, and buses. From these building blocks the computer architect can construct any one of a number of different types of computers, ranging from the smallest hand-held pocket calculator to the largest ultra-fast super-computer. The functional behavior of the components of one computer is similar to that of any other computer, whether it be ultra-small or ultra-fast. By this we mean that a memory performs the storage function, an adder does addition, and an input/output interface passes data from a processor to the outside world, regardless of the nature of the computer in which they are embedded. The major differences between computers lie in the way the modules are connected together, the performance characteristics of the modules, and the way the computer system is controlled by programs. In short, computer architecture is the discipline devoted to the design of highly specific and individual computers from a collection of common building blocks.

The plan of this text is to take the reader through the central topics of computer architecture, starting with the most general topics to lay the foundation for further reading and leading to more specialized topics involving such areas as the design of the memory and input/output systems and the design of high-speed computers. In this chapter, we present the most elementary aspects of computer design as a brief preparation for what lies ahead. Here we cover a simplified machine architecture as a case study, and, in the course of the design exercise, we expose the several areas that are treated in each of the chapters to follow.

This book is organized into two parts. Part I consists of Chapters 1 through 6 and contains the core introductory material for a good foundation in computer architecture. Part II starts with Chapter 7 and focuses on several specialized topics in depth, carrying them through recent research developments.

In Chapter 2, we investigate computer arithmetic and data representations. The algorithms are given in sufficient detail to make hardware implementation straightforward. Also treated are representations of structures of data as well as the representation of individual numbers.

Chapter 3 treats the design of a microprocessor, the computer-on-a-chip. Microprocessors have already changed the entire nature of the computer industry since their first appearance early in the 1970s. Where computers were once formidable in size and cost, the microprocessor is dwarfed by a thumbnail, and costs but a few dollars. Products are now commonplace that could not exist without this invention. Such things as the hand-held calculator, sophisticated automotive control systems, and intelligent typewriters are all a direct outgrowth of this device. Chapter 3 serves as an introduction into the early history of microprocessors, their general functional characteristics, internal architecture, and innovative applications.

Chapter 4 begins a series of chapters on conventional computer architecture. In this chapter, we discuss minicomputers, and then follow with chapters on memories and input/output systems. Together, these three chapters contain the material necessary to master the structure of conventional computers.

Minicomputers are used as the example of conventional computers, primarily because minicomputers of today are full-fledged computers in every sense of the word, but they are physically smaller and cost less than their largest counterparts. Minicomputers need not be less powerful than a full-scale computer, and indeed, many minicomputers available today are every bit as powerful as the largest scientific computers of many years ago. The severe cost and size constraints on minicomputers often dictate that the minicomputer be designed with just the bare essentials of functional hardware. Consequently, the architecture of these machines lacks frills and luxuries, resulting in designs of great simplicity and comprehensibility. As such, they make excellent vehicles for the initial study of computers.

Chapters 5 and 6 deal with the subjects of computer memories and input/output, respectively. Both of these chapters are relevant to a variety of advanced types of computers because the differences in memories and input/output systems across the range of computers is small when compared to the differences in processors and in the organization of the system modules. The chapters treat the variations that exist from system to system.

After Chapter 6, we begin Part II and investigate machine architectures emerging in the 1970s. Chapter 7 discusses computers based upon a pushdown stack architecture. Such computers appeared in the early 1960s, but relatively few of these computers were installed as compared to the more conventional register-structured computer. Early examples of such machines include the KDF-9 and the Burroughs B-5000. The stack machines have interesting properties that lead to efficiencies of operation, and these are studied in the chapter. The particular advantages of stack machines in some environments, specifically for implementing subroutine calls and parameter passing, have led to a large increase in their popularity today.

High-speed computation has been an area in which advances have generally been attributed to both computer architecture and inherently faster components, and future improvements are likely to be due to architecture rather than raw speed. High-speed computers have deviated from conventional computers to attain greater computational ability, and the speed increase is due mainly to replication of computational hardware to form vector processors, multiprocessors, and pipeline computers. The descriptions of these various types of computers appear in Chapters 8 and 9.

Microprogramming is a hardware implementation technique that is the central theme of Chapter 10. Microprogramming refers to the technique of using a programmed "inner" computer to perform the various control functions required for each instruction in the repertoire of an "outer" computer. Microprogramming uses control programs stored in a separate high-speed control memory to replace wires, flip/flops, and logic gates of a "hard-wired" implementation of the control function. Microprogramming was used as an implementation technique for several of the computers designed in the infancy of computer design in the early 1950s, but it then fell into disuse because of low performance relative to other implementation methods. It became increasingly popular in the middle of the 1960s with the introduction of the IBM System/360. The smaller machines in this series made heavy use of microprogramming because this was the most economical way to implement the large instruction repertoire required for the computer. The faster and more expensive machines in the series also made use of microprogramming, but specialized high-speed logic replaced microprogrammed functions of the smaller machines. In recent years, microprogramming has bloomed into an area of wide interest because of the ease of emulation of different computers and the possibility of tailoring a computer to specific applications to attain greater efficiency.

Chapter 11 explores methods for evaluating the performance of computer systems to enable the computer architect to determine how well his computer system design meets his design goals. The analysis methods include mathematical methods that model the computer system according to principles of queueing theory, event-driven simulation models that predict behavior by crude imitation of the computer system in a realistic environment, and experimental techniques that measure the behavior of the actual system in real working conditions. Each of these techniques is useful, but each has its own weaknesses. Use of a combination of all three techniques is required to guarantee accurate prediction of behavior.

The last chapter, Operating Systems, addresses the major interactions between computer architecture and executive software systems. Executive programs known as *operating systems* have evolved almost in parallel with the computers themselves. For first generation computers these executive programs were merely collections of common input/output programs and math libraries that saved users the burden of rewriting these tricky and complex functions. Eventually operating systems incorporated the ability to sequence different user jobs through a computer system, one job at a time, and by the early 1960s, several jobs could be in various stages of computation concurrently on one machine because of sophisticated control algorithms embedded in operating systems. Time-sharing made interactive access possible, with several dozen users simultaneously plugging away at their respective consoles while ever more complex operating systems juggled the myriad program streams to enable one computer to serve all comers. Chapter 12 investigates just what these operating systems do that impacts the design of the computer itself, and where the computer design should evolve to provide better support for executive functions.

Returning to this introductory chapter, we discuss the simplified conventional computer in the next section, and, in a later section, we explore several issues that are the subject of the chapters sketched above.

1-1. ARCHITECTURE OF AN EARLY COMPUTER

In this section, we examine a highly idealized and simplified computer to serve as a point of departure for material in the remainder of the book. To place this material in a historical context, the machine we describe follows the general description of one of the earliest computers. A paper by Burks, Goldstine, and von Neumann [46] detailed the organization of this computer, and was remarkable in the thoroughness and insight the authors displayed. The influence of the proposal was considerable. Almost all of the computers designed and constructed in the next decade embodied many of the ideas in the proposal. This type of machine is often called a *von Neumann machine* to credit the contribution of John von Neumann to its development. The proposed machine was eventually constructed and run successfully in the early 1950s, but it was not the first computer constructed nor was it the first von Neumann computer to run successfully. Wilkes in England and later Eckert and Mauchly, with the aid of von Neumann's ideas, completed similar machines before von Neumann's reached completion. They generally share the credit for the construction of the first modern electronic computers [Rosen, 69].

Figure 1-1 shows the general structure of the computer proposed by Burks et al. The memory consists of $4096 = 2^{12}$ words, with each word containing 40 bits. Each word is identified with a unique address in the range $0 \leq x \leq 4095$. The proposal by von Neumann and his colleagues called for the storage medium to be a cathode ray storage tube. A particular word is read from this memory by presenting a 12-bit address to the memory address register (identified in the figure as the M register) together with a READ control signal. The selected word is copied from memory and appears somewhat later in the memory data register, denoted S in the figure. Von Neumann anticipated a

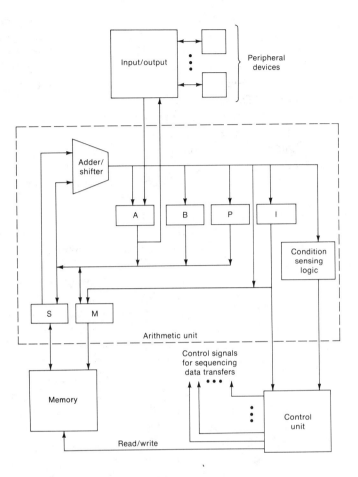

Figure 1-1   Block diagram of a simplified computer

memory access time from 5 to 50 microseconds in his design, which was quite ambitious for his time. It was roughly a decade before memories with this access time were made widely available through the development of magnetic core technology. Today, of course, with improved core technology and integrated-circuit memory technology that is gradually supplanting magnetic cores, memories with access times below .5 microsecond are common.

To write data into the memory, a datum is placed into the S register, the address of the datum is placed in the M register, and a WRITE signal is generated. The memory responds to this signal by copying the datum in the S register into the word selected by the M register. The read and write modes of memory operations described by von Neumann are common to almost all present-day computers.

Returning to Figure 1-1, we see that data manipulation is done in the arithmetic unit portion of the computer. This portion consists of an adder/

shifter, an accumulator register (the A register) and an accumulator extension (the B register). Addition and subtraction make use of the adder and the A register. Multiplication requires both shifting and addition, and produces a double-length result from two 40-bit operands. The product of a multiplication is captured in the A and B register pair with the most significant bits in A and the least significant in B. Division can be done with the hardware given in the figure using an algorithm similar to the familiar algorithm for decimal division.

The control unit shown in Figure 1-1 is the functional unit that forces the memory and arithmetic unit to perform the sequential steps of an algorithm. Von Neumann and his colleagues were well aware of ways of stating an algorithm as a sequence of elementary actions, each elementary action executable by the computer. A computation is done by presenting each step of the algorithm in encoded form to the control unit, which then generates signals that cause the arithmetic unit and memory to perform the necessary actions. The von Neumann machine was among the first to embody the notion that instructions can be stored in the same memory as the data. In this way, instructions can be removed and rewritten into memory much like data, thereby making it possible to change from program to program quite easily. Computers with this property are called *stored-program* computers. As an added property of this instruction storage method, instructions are indistinguishable from data, so they may be manipulated just as data are manipulated. The interpretation of a 40-bit pattern as an instruction or a datum depends on the state of the machine when the item is fetched from memory. If the state of the machine dictates that the item should be passed to the control unit, then the item is interpreted as an instruction. If, on the other hand, the item is transferred to the A register, it is treated as a datum.

The 1946 proposal contains a great insight concerning the use of instructions as data. Special instructions were incorporated in the computer repertoire that modify just the address portion of an instruction. In this way, programs could modify their own instructions during program execution so that a single instruction could be made to operate on many different data. This tended to reduce the memory requirements for programs. This concept was embodied in most computers through the early 1960s when it finally fell into disfavor. By then, much more elaborate and powerful mechanisms to attain the same functional capability had come into use, and these do not suffer from disadvantages of self-modification of instructions. Nevertheless, von Neumann's original idea has been extremely influential, even if not implemented as he originally intended.

Since instructions were stored in the same 40-bit words in which numbers were stored, Burks et al. proposed an instruction encoding compatible with the data format. The encoding is shown in Figure 1-2. Each instruction occupies 20 bits, with two instructions stored in one word. Each 20-bit instruction contains two fields—an 8-bit operation code that determines the function performed, and a 12-bit address of an operand.

At this point in our discussion, some of the architectural decisions in the

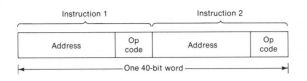

Figure 1-2 Instruction encoding for the von Neumann computer

design become apparent. The instruction encoding, the size of the instruction repertoire, the precision of the data representation, and the size of memory are all interrelated. The 40-bit word length gives sufficient precision and numeric range to be useful over a reasonably large class of problems. Longer word lengths increase the cost of the computer, without necessarily giving useful additional numerical precision for typical calculations. A shorter word length might have been possible from the point of view of numerical precision but the instruction encoding would be severely hampered if the word length were shorter. Hence, 40 bits is reasonable for each datum. Instructions with fewer than 20 bits have less room either for the operation code or for the address, and if either is shortened the computer is severely restricted in power. If, on the other hand, a single instruction is stored per word because a word is too short to contain two instructions, there are too many bits to specify all of the instructions that could be implemented in von Neumann's machine within the economic constraints of the times. Consequently, some memory is wasted in the instruction encoding.

Within a decade, memories with 2^{15} words became prevalent, so that address fields quickly expanded to 15 bits. Likewise address-modification functions such as indexing and indirection were incorporated into the instruction encoding, with the result that one instruction was encoded in as many as 36 bits, and numeric data representations were made equal in length to the length of a single instruction.

Several representative instructions appear in Table 1-1. We also introduce a notation in this table that we follow throughout this text. Machine registers are denoted by their names such as A or B, and memory locations are denoted by the name MEMORY followed by a bracketed expression whose value gives the address of the item in memory. The ALGOL symbol ":=" denotes data flow, and indicates that the value of the expression on the right of the symbol is moved to the register or memory location named on the left. For example, the instruction LOAD X has the effect of copying the contents of a designated memory location into the A register. In the example shown in the table, the contents of MEMORY[X] are moved into the A register, where X is an address in the range $0 \leq X \leq 4095$. Reversing the right side and the left side of the ALGOL-like notation yields MEMORY[X] := A which is a "store" instruction that copies the contents of A into the location X of memory. Note how MEMORY[X] denotes a numeric operand

TABLE 1-1. Typical Instructions for a von Neumann Computer

Instruction	Example	Action
Load	LOAD X	A := MEMORY[X];
Store	STORE Y	MEMORY[Y] := A;
Load negative	LNEG Z	A := − MEMORY[Z];
Load absolute value	LABS W	A := ABS(MEMORY[W]);
Add	ADD X	A := A + MEMORY[X];
Subtract	SUB Y	A := A − MEMORY[Y];
Multiply	MUL Z	A := A × MEMORY[Z];
Divide	DIV W	A := A / MEMORY[W];
Branch (left)	BRAL X	P := X, LEFT INSTRUCTION;
Branch (right)	BRAR Y	P := Y, RIGHT INSTRUCTION;
Branch positive (left)	BPOSL X	**if** A ≥ 0 **then** P := X, LEFT INSTRUCTION;
Branch positive (right)	BPOSR Y	**if** A ≥ 0 **then** P := Y, RIGHT INSTRUCTION;
Store address (left)	STADL X	MEMORY [X], LEFT ADDRESS := A;
Store address (right)	STADR Y	MEMORY [Y], RIGHT ADDRESS := A;
Shift (left)	SHL	A := 2 × A;
Shift (right)	SHR	A := A ÷ 2;

value when it appears on the right of ": =", while it names the destination of a data move when it appears on the left of ": =". This is in keeping with the conventions of most programming languages.

We see from the table that the von Neumann machine could load the A register with the true or negative value of an operand, or with its absolute value. Also, it could add, subtract, multiply, or divide two numbers, one in the A register and one in a designated memory cell.

Two branch instructions and two conditional branch instructions have been included. In each case the two forms of an instruction are used to select between the left and right instructions that lie in a single word. The use of the P register in these instructions is explained below.

Address modification in this computer is done by replacing the address part of an instruction with a new address. The two instructions that modify addresses are again identical except that they modify the left and right instruction-address fields, respectively. When an address is modified by one of these instructions all other bits in the word are unmodified.

The shift instructions give the programmer access to the hardware for the shift operation, which has to be there to do the multiplication and division. In this example the left shift doubles the numerical value stored in the A register, and the right shift halves that value.

This completes the discussion of the basic instructions of the von Neumann computer. At this point we can touch upon the design of the control unit and describe how the execution of an instruction takes place. In this machine the sequence of steps during execution of a single instruction depends only on the 8-bit operation code of the instruction. The memory address determines the operand of the instruction but does not affect the individual steps in the instruction execution sequence.

The control unit makes use of two registers, P and I, that respectively contain the address of the next instruction to be executed and a copy of the instruction currently in execution. The P register is actually 13 bits in length rather than 12 for it must contain 12 bits to identify a memory address and an additional bit to identify the left or right instruction in the word at that address.

Instruction execution involves the following steps:

1. Read the next instruction into the I register. The address of the instruction is contained in the P register.
2. Update the P register to specify the instruction immediately following the instruction just read.
3. Decode the 8-bit operation code. The decoder output has one output line for each instruction in the computer repertoire. An output line is energized by the decoder if and only if the instruction contains the corresponding operation code.
4. Generate a sequence of data transfers and numerical operations that constitute the execution of the instruction. The sequence of actions may include reading or writing of memory, transfers of data to and from registers, transfers of data through the adder/shifter for numerical processing, or a change of the value of the P register if the instruction is a branch instruction.

At the close of the last step, the instruction is fully executed. The control unit then returns to Step 1 to execute the next instruction, and continues to repeat the execution of instructions until it stops because of the execution of a HALT instruction or because of a console switch action that forces a halt.

There are various ways of constructing the control unit, and we leave a full discussion of its internal structure to Chapters 3, 4, and 10. Its functional behavior, however, can be determined almost completely from the instruction encoding and the registers and data-transfer paths in the remainder of the computer.

The last portion of the computer shown in Figure 1-1 is the input/output unit. The von Neumann proposal was probably less influential on future computer designs in this area than in other areas, but the proposal authors still had sufficient vision to foresee some powerful notions of input/output.

Perhaps the most tantalizing notion is the graphical output they proposed. The Selectron tube, being a cathode ray tube, glowed in positions in which 1 bits were stored and did not glow where 0 bits were stored. By forcing patterns of ones (1s) and zeros (0s) in memory, the programmer could display graphical output on the Selectron tube. Of course, cathode ray output is quite common today, and it bears some resemblance to the Selectron input/output available to von Neumann, but rarely is such a tube used as a memory and as an input/output device simultaneously.

Other input/output media proposed included teletypewriter and an auxiliary magnetic wire memory, which is suggestive of tapes, drums, and disks available today. Data flow for input/output came through the A register to the input/output unit and from there to the peripheral units. Input/output was controlled by the program on a word-by-word basis. For example, to output a data array, each array element had to be loaded into the A register and transmitted to the input/output unit, with each step of this sequence controlled by instructions in the program. There was no capability for overlapping input/output with computation in the proposed machine, primarily because of the high cost of hardware at that time. Nevertheless, early computer designers including the von Neumann team recognized that overlapped input/output and computation was essential for efficient use of a computer. Buffering of input/output to permit this overlap was added to computers while they were still in their infancy.

Now that we have treated the overall design of the von Neumann machine, in the next section we shall reconsider the important aspects of its design and indicate how they have evolved in the past three decades.

1-2. TRENDS IN COMPUTER ARCHITECTURE SINCE VON NEUMANN

The previous section suggests four areas in which we can focus our discussion. They are the:

1. Arithmetic unit
2. Control unit
3. Memory
4. Input/output unit

In this section we give a brief view of how the von Neumann computer has evolved to today's computers in each of these areas.

Arithmetic Unit

The von Neumann computer had an arithmetic unit consisting of an adder and a shifter, each fairly rudimentary. By the late 1950s it was common to include multiplier hardware, fast adders, fast shifters, and, in some instances, hardware for automatic floating-point arithmetic, in order to attain higher computation speed. Division then, as now, is seldom done with hardware specialized to division. It is more common to use an interative algorithm which in turn uses multipliers, adders, and shifters.

By the middle of the 1960s and reaching into the present, the main deviation from the basic design of an arithmetic unit as presented by Burks et al. has been in ultra-high-speed computers. Such computers typically use many different arithmetic units, or a single unit timeshared to do parts of many different computations simultaneously. In extreme cases as many as 64 full arithmetic units are combined in one computer as, for example, in the ILLIAC IV computer. Computers consisting of many independent arithmetic units are typically known as *parallel* or *array* computers. Chapter 8 covers various ways of constructing computers of this general class. Computers in which some fast portion of the arithmetic processor can service several computations in different phases at a single time are generally known as *pipeline* computers. These are described in some detail in Chapter 9.

With the rapid development of integrated circuit technology there came the possibility of doing low-speed computation at minimum cost. Early microprocessors had 4-bit arithmetic units embedded within them, and could do arithmetic on longer operands serially, 4 bits at a time. By the end of the 1970s, arithmetic units on microprocessors expanded to 16 bits, and included some capability for multiplication and division as well as the minimal set of operations which include addition, subtraction, and a few other operations. Arithmetic units on separate chips were introduced in the middle of the 1970s to enhance the arithmetic capability of the microprocessors. As microprocessors developed that could do more and more of the operations found in the peripheral arithmetic chips, so the peripheral chips too became even more powerful. Today chips exist that can do such things as signal processing, floating-point arithmetic, and a variety of transcendental functions.

The algorithms for performing some of the complex arithmetic operations, such as multiplication and division, appear in Chapter 2 together with a discussion of techniques for dealing with negative numbers.

Control Unit

The control unit presents the most interesting challenge for computer architects today because it includes the design of the instruction repertoire, the instruction encoding, and the hardware implementation of the instructions. The control unit is a critical architectural feature of a computer, since it strongly influences the ultimate cost and performance of the machine.

We briefly review the evolution of the design of control units since von Neumann by examining the following areas:

1. Effective-address calculations
2. Instruction repertoire
3. Instruction encoding
4. Control-unit implementation

Von Neumann, his colleagues, and other early computer designers recognized the need to have one instruction operate on many different data during a calculation. Some computations require a thousand, a million, or even a billion repetitions of a sequence of instructions on different data. It is essential to use a single copy of the instructions for that iteration rather than a different copy for each iteration to eliminate the need to construct and store all of those instructions. The capability to reuse an instruction on different data was built into the von Neumann machine by including instructions that modify the address portion of an item resident in memory. The item modified could be an instruction, and once modified the original form of the modified instruction was lost. Typical iterative loops contained instructions to modify one or more instructions in the loop in preparation for the next repetition of the loop.

The process of instruction modification was both costly in time and error-prone. Moreover, because the instructions were physically changed, a program could not easily be restarted from its beginning at any time during a computation. Restart procedures required a fresh copy of the program to be loaded into memory to begin a computation. This greatly hindered program checkout and debugging.

Automatic address-modification techniques were introduced soon after the construction of the first computers. These entailed the use of special registers known then as *b-boxes*, and now as *index registers*, to hold the incremental changes of the addresses in instructions. Let REG[1], REG[2], ..., REG[N] denote a set of registers that are part of the arithmetic unit, and let ADDR denote the integer encoded in the address portion of an instruction. Then the operand of that instruction is found at MEMORY[ADDR] when no indexing occurs, and at MEMORY[ADDR + REG[INDEX]] when REG[INDEX] is selected as an index register. In many computers the index register is specified by a small field in each instruction. A zero value in this field denotes no indexing, and a nonzero value identifies the index register to be used for indexing. The operand address produced by indexing or by any other address modification is called the *effective address* of the instruction.

Note that the operand address of an instruction may be quite different from the value of ADDR, and that the instruction itself is not altered in memory by the indexing operation. Indexing alters the effect of the instruction without changing the instruction. While indexing is perhaps among the most frequently implemented address-modification methods, it is only one of several in use in present computers. For this brief summary we mention another method known as *indirection*, for which the operand address is not ADDR but is found in MEMORY[ADDR], and the operand of the instruction is in MEMORY [MEMORY[ADDR]]. Thus with indirection what would normally be an operand for an instruction becomes the address of the operand.

Computers with both indexing and indirection can combine the methods in either of two ways. *Pre-indexing* does the indexing and then the indirection to give an effective address of MEMORY[ADDR + REG[INDEX]]. *Post-indexing* does the indirection and then the indexing to yield an effective address of the form MEMORY[ADDR] + REG[INDEX]. The more operations done in a single address modification operation, the more specialized is the use of that modification. For example, post-indexing is very useful in the context of a subroutine with an array parameter. The array is to be accessed through an indirect address, and the subroutine computes indices for accesses to array elements. Post-indexing is ideal for this because the address of an array element is obtained by adding the index to the address obtained from an indirect reference. Similar examples exist to show the usefulness of pre-indexing. Perhaps post-indexing is the more useful of the two methods if one had to decide between them, but the designer should make such a decision only after a thorough study of the intended applications of the computer.

This brings us to the next subject of this section, the instruction repertoire. The instruction repertoire of the early computers typically contained fixed-point arithmetic instructions, boolean and shift instructions, and a few primitive instructions for controlling the instruction sequence.

Second-generation computers had much larger instruction sets for more flexibility and power. These computers fell into two broad categories: business computers and scientific computers. Business data-processing computers were typically character oriented and had extensive capability for manipulating variable-length data. Data operations were generally character replacements, or character comparison for sorting and merging, or fixed-point arithmetic. Arithmetic was slow in this type of computer because it was generally done serially by character, and often done decimally rather than in radix 2. The other class of computer at this time was the scientific computer. It had extensive floating-point arithmetic capability, but operated on data of fixed precision. It had very little capability for dealing with variable length strings of characters, and did not have decimal arithmetic, although such operations obviously could be performed through programming at a relatively high cost in computing time. The most prevalent computer series of this type was the IBM 709, 7090, and 7094 series. Toward the end of the second generation the distinction between business data processing and scientific computing tended to fade. Large scientific users often performed computations involving sorting, merging, and character manipulation on variable length data, which were previously classed as business functions. Likewise business applications made use of sophisticated forecasting and inventory control programs which in turn relied heavily on operations typical of scientific computing. Beginning in the middle 1960s manufacturers combined both kinds of functions into one computer.

The major obstacle in the way of having a single general-purpose computer for both business and science was cost. As the number of instructions in a computer repertoire grew so did the cost of its control unit, which in turn materially affected the cost of the machine to the user. New device technologies and new design techniques brought hardware costs down dramatically in the middle 1960s, thereby making it possible to construct a general-purpose computer to satisfy all users. As computers moved into the third generation, instruction repertoires soon encompassed many different types of instructions designed for a large variety of functions. The number of elementary instructions has now increased from a few dozen in the early computers to over a hundred, and in a few instances to over two hundred. Arithmetic instructions account for a small portion of these repertoires. Newer functions include instructions for subroutine entry and exit, environment changing, status recording, and memory protection. Even the one-chip microcomputer of the late 1970s can perform upwards of one hundred different elementary instructions.

Current trends in the design of instruction repertoires seem to be aimed in two divergent directions. On the one hand there is the trend to use instructions that are powerful, that do macro or functional high-level operations. Contrary to this is the trend to make use of primitive instructions to attain a high level of flexibility. The flexibility is achieved at the cost of lower computation speed and some wasted memory space for instruction storage. A recent trend that incorporates both power and flexibility is the trend to develop microprogrammed computers whose instructions can easily be altered by the user while executing a program. High-level functions can then be inserted into the repertoire for a short time and removed sometime later. Thus speed and flexibility are both high while the cost is held low. A few microprogrammed computers have essentially no instruction repertoire, and are said to be *soft machines*. These machines have to be provided with instruction sets for the microprogram to interpret when each program is run. Chapter 10 describes these soft machines and other topics related to microprogramming.

Let us turn to the third of the topics mentioned above for the control unit, the evolution of instruction encoding. Von Neumann's computer exemplifies the essence of simplicity in instruction encoding, since each instruction is composed of only two fields, one for the operation and one for an address. Since that time the number of addresses per instruction has evolved considerably. Von Neumann's computer is a *one-address* computer because each instruction contains one address field. Most instructions for von Neumann's computer have either two or three operands, so that some operands in the one-address instruction format are implicit. To be specific consider the instructions

LOAD X

ADD Y

The LOAD instruction has two operands, a source, in this case MEMORY[X], and a destination, which in this case is a machine accumulator A. The destination address A is not explicitly encoded; it is implicitly encoded because A is the unique destination of the LOAD instruction. The ADD instruction has three operands, two source operands which in this example are A and MEMORY[Y], and one destination, which in this case is A. Again the A is not explicitly encoded as the source and destination operand.

The one-address computer was popular through the second generation of computers, but it is becoming less and less common as computers become less expensive and more powerful. By the beginning of the 1960s it became feasible to use multiple accumulators in a processor because hardware costs were dropping rapidly. A computer at that time might have eight or sixteen accumulators instead of a single one. Thus the destination register of the LOAD instruction cannot be encoded implicitly since it might be any of the accumulators. Consequently, the instruction encoding is forced to include an explicit encoding of the destination of the LOAD. The instruction encoding in assembly language might be LOAD 1,X which means copy MEMORY[X] into accumulator REG[1]. In this example at least two addresses per instruction must be designated. But since the register in question is only one of a small number of registers, its field may be encoded in a very few bits.

To encode a three-operand instruction such as ADD Y, we can choose to make one of the source operands the same as the destination operand, so that again only two address fields are required to specify three operands. Thus the instruction may take the form ADD 2,Y which means compute the sum of REG[2] and MEMORY[Y] and store the result into REG[2].

Many computers now use the two-address format because it represents a reasonable compromise in the use of extra memory for instruction encoding to obtain extra flexibility. Of course, since typical arithmetic instructions have three operands, one might be tempted to increase the number of address fields per instruction to three to achieve greater flexibility, but except for some special cases, three-address instructions generally result in more bits expended for instruction encoding. The relatively good encoding efficiency obtained with two-address formats has biased computer designers to favor two-address instructions over three-address instructions. The major exception to this rule is the class of high-speed computers that execute instructions in parallel or out of sequence when conditions permit. For example, to evaluate the expression $A \times B + C \times D$, one can use the sequence of instructions

$$
\begin{aligned}
&\text{LOAD } 1,A \\
&\text{LOAD } 2,B \\
&\text{MUL } 1,2,3 \\
&\text{LOAD } 4,C \\
&\text{LOAD } 5,D \\
&\text{MUL } 4,5,6 \\
&\text{ADD } 3,6,7
\end{aligned}
$$

The first two instructions are two-address instructions that load REG[1] and REG[2] with operands A and B, respectively. The MUL 1,2,3 instruction forms their product and stores the result in REG[3], because our convention is to use the third address to denote the destination operand. Note that while these operations are going on, the next three operations could proceed concurrently, because they involve a totally separate set of registers. Some computers can actually execute these sequences concurrently, the most notable example of this being the CDC 6600.

Having proceeded from one-address to two-address and then to three-address instructions, one might expect the next advance in machine encoding to be four-address instructions. Actually, zero-address instructions have become more popular for arithmetic instructions and may eventually find wide acceptance. For these instructions the three operands are specified implicitly, and need not be explicitly encoded in address fields. A complete discussion appears in Chapter 7.

The trend today is to have many different instruction formats in a single computer to provide maximum flexibility with a minimum waste of memory arising from the encoding scheme. Thus an instruction with three operands may well have all three addresses specified if this makes sense for the contexts in which the instruction is used. Instructions with fewer operands may have fewer address fields, and when operands are specified implicitly, address fields are omitted from the instruction format. One consequence of this encoding practice is that instructions need not all be the same length. Good encoding schemes encode the most often-used instructions with the shortest-length codes. The great variety of instruction formats within a single computer makes the classification of computers by address format somewhat meaningless today, although such a classification was once possible and meaningful.

The last topic of interest with respect to the control unit concerns the various methods of implementation that have been used during the evolution of computers. Early computer designers recognized the need for modularity in the physical construction of computers. Therefore the natural basic building blocks they used were NAND/NOR logic gates and flip/flops, which in turn were fabricated from discrete resistors, capacitors, and vacuum tubes. Minimum cost implementations entailed minimizing the number of logic gates. Second-generation computers used transistors in place of vacuum tubes, with some simplification in the structure of the logic gates, but the ground rules for designs were similar to those used previously. Registers were relatively expensive during this period, so that multiple registers were found mainly in high-speed computers whose users were willing to pay a premium for speed.

During the early 1960s several developments in device technology led to revolutionary changes in the logic devices available and to dramatic decreases in the cost per logic function. The logic devices at this time were fabricated on flat films deposited on a silicon substrate. The resulting silicon chip contained several active transistors, not just a single transistor; yet the cost of fabricating a chip was approximately equal to the cost of fabricating a single transistor using previous fabrication techniques. The new technology was essentially a batch-fabrication technology.

This new technology had a major impact on computer design, and then on computer architecture. The cost of batch-fabricated devices can be held low if many copies of a chip are produced. And whether the chip contains 10 transistors, 100 transistors, or even 10,000 transistors, the cost of producing that chip is approximately the same, so that the designer can tap the extra capability available in complex chips at essentially no cost. In the late 1960s technology had advanced to the point where registers, arithmetic units, and memories each appeared on chips and were produced in high volumes.

Unfortunately, unstructured logic in control units is not naturally iterative and repetitive, so that it did not lend itself to the high-volume production required for successful use of integrated-circuit technology. During this period designers frequently turned to microprogrammed implementations of control units, which are memory intensive and therefore were well adapted to the capabilities of integrated-circuit technology.

With the emergence of microprocessors in the early 1970s the whole picture changed completely. The microprocessor is an entire arithmetic and control unit, a complete computer except for memory and I/O. Control logic plus all registers and arithmetic units are integrated into one chip. Since each chip is a functional device with a large variety of uses, it can be manu- factured in quantities high enough to bring the cost down to a few dollars. This is what von Neumann might have paid for a single vacuum tube out of the several thousand in his computer. Yet microprocessors today, by any measure, are many times as powerful as von Neumann's machine.

With entire processors on a chip, and today with entire computers (memory and I/O included) on the same chip, one might believe that computer archi- tecture issues are dead. Quite the contrary: the microprocessor is but one more building block available to computer designers that was not available in prior decades. Between 1970 and 1980, the revolution in semiconductor technology had changed the whole picture for computer architecture. Where once a single processor was shared among all tasks, it is now feasible and desirable to dedicate microprocessors to specific tasks. The concept of a single master control has given way to distributed control in a federated sys- tem of processors. Many of the changes evoked by microprocessors and some inkling of the changes yet in store are described in Chapter 3.

This brings us to the end of the brief history of control-unit design. Let us now turn our attention to other portions of the computer.

Memory

Since von Neumann's proposal, three types of memories have come into popular use as the primary memory of a computer. In the 1950s primary memories were principally rotating drums. Magnetic drums have an inherent rotational latency. If the item accessed is not under the read head of a drum at the time the access request is issued then the request is not granted until the item eventually reaches the read head, and the computer remains idle until the access occurs. The late 1950s saw the introduction of second-generation computers with magnetic-core primary memories. These machines were sub- stantially faster than their predecessors because such memories have random- access capability; that is, any item can be fetched from memory in a fixed time span that is independent of the previous memory reference. The third type of memory in use is the most recently introduced. This is integrated- circuit memory. Like magnetic-core memories, integrated memories are random-access memories, but they are 2 to 10 times faster than core memo- ries today, and improving in speed with each new advance in integrated circuits. During the transistion period as integrated memories became competitive with core memories, most computers used cores exclusively, then combinations of core and integrated circuit. By the middle of the 1970s, integrated memories dropped below the cost of core memories, and the tide had turned. Just as magnetic-drum/main memories had been replaced by core memories in the late 1950s, so have core memories been replaced by integrated memories. Rotating magnetic memories, primarily disks, are still in use today as auxiliary memory, but even here they may be supplanted by integrated memories as technology continues to advance.

The organization of primary memory today is essentially as von Neumann envisioned. Items have unique physical addresses, and accesses are made by address. The advances in memory architecture since von Neumann's time have been primarily in two related areas:

1. Memory hierarchies consisting of high-speed first-level storage together with much larger and slower second-level and third-level storage appear to the program as a single large memory whose speed is nearly equal to first-level storage. Frequently used items tend to reside in the fastest memory of the hierarchy and automatically drift to the slower parts of the hierarchy when frequency of use diminishes.

2. Several independent programs can run in the same computer system simultaneously, each using a completely separate set of memory locations. Memory address facilities simplify the problem of allocating memory to the individual programs, and guarantee that one program cannot interfere with another program. In some instances, specified data or program segments are permitted to be shared by two or more programs.

Rather than deal with these topics in great detail here, we mention that the first of the two is called *virtual memory,* and is covered in Chapter 12. The second describes a situation known as *multiprogramming,* and the address translation facilities are essential for its support. One method for achieving the functional behavior mentioned above is to use a technique called *paging.* It is described in both Chapters 8 and 12. The use of paging for sharing of information appears in Chapter 12.

The major emphasis on memory architecture in this text is at the device and memory-organization level. This material has received relatively little attention in the computer architecture literature and merits thorough coverage in an introductory text. The bulk of the material on memories appears in Chapter 5.

Input/Output

The first computers were extremely slow by today's standards, but even at their speeds they were much faster than the input/output devices available for them. Almost from the beginning of the development of computers, designers worked out methods for buffering input/output so that input/output could be done concurrently with computation. By the second generation of computers, input/output for high-speed computers was done by functionally independent modules known as *data channels* or *direct memory access* (DMA) *channels*. These devices do arithmetic computations and access memory, much like the arithmetic processor of a computer. For high-speed computers, the need for faster input/output led to full-fledged processors being dedicated to input/output in support of other processors that are dedicated to numerical computation. The CDC 6600, which appeared in the middle of the 1960s, is an extreme example of this notion because it has ten stored-program input/output processors to service a single ultra high-speed central processor.

Recent advances in input/output architecture have generally been in the regularizing of the input/output system, so that all devices are treated more or less uniformly with respect to the hardware interface and with respect to the software for operating the devices. The use of a single bus for both memory and input/output devices permits input/output devices to be accessed as if they were special locations in memory. This is one method for forcing all devices to fit a uniform pattern, and it has been used successfully in several computers, most notably the DEC PDP-11 minicomputer series. Microprocessors have also been used in the input/output interface of various peripheral devices. In this way all interfaces can be identical in hardware structure, yet they can be specialized to particular input/output devices by changing the program loaded in the microprocessor interface. The most common designs for input/output systems are treated in Chapter 6, and a related discussion of programming considerations for input/output appears in Chapter 4. Among the notable advances in input/output systems since von Neumann is the use of an interrupt system to control input/output. This is described in both Chapters 4 and 6.

1-3. WHAT LIES AHEAD

The trends for the future are clear from the trends of the last several years. Manufacturers will strive to make faster computers, smaller computers, and less expensive computers as long as new developments in device technology can support these advances. To give a coherent view of what lies ahead, we review several trends in computer architecture and project them forward.

The first trend concerns the notion of sharing and multiple use of a processor. Part *a* of Figure 1-3 depicts a stand-alone computer as per the von Neumann concept. High costs forced this type of machine to be shared among hundreds of users in a community of users because no one user could afford the luxury of having such a machine dedicated to his particular problem. Time-sharing was a pioneering concept introduced at MIT in the early 1960s. This type of system, as shown in part *b* of Figure 1-3, permits many users to

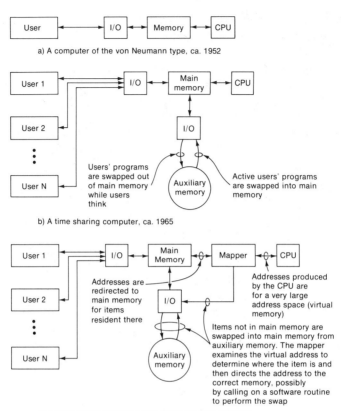

a) A computer of the von Neumann type, ca. 1952

b) A time sharing computer, ca. 1965

c) A time-sharing computer with virtual memory, ca. 1972

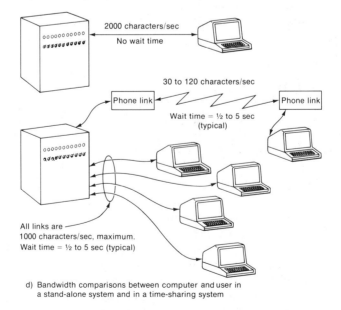

d) Bandwidth comparisons between computer and user in a stand-alone system and in a time-sharing system

Figure 1-3 The evolution of time-sharing systems

access one computer simultaneously. It depends strongly on the slowness of human interactions as compared to the speed of the computer, so that while one user is thinking, his program is swapped out of the computer system to auxiliary memory, and a program for an active user replaces it. Because of the increased productivity which this type of system gave the programmer through close interaction with a computer, the notion of time-sharing must be one of the landmarks in the history of computing. It is still in widespread use, perhaps to the detriment of the bulk of time-sharing users because of advances that provide even better alternatives today than time-sharing.

Originally time-sharing provided a means for distributing the costs of computation over many users, and users typically were charged only for their share of machine cycles. Already by the late 1960s, processor costs had dropped so dramatically that there was very little economic benefit in sharing a processor among several users, solely for the machine cycles. But memory costs remained high, and users had need for memories of sufficiently large size that they had to share this cost. Time-sharing systems continued to be justifiable as a means to share memory costs over several users. The shift from sharing processor costs to sharing memory costs came almost unnoticed to time-sharing users. As memory demand became the overriding factor, new systems in the late 1960s and early 1970s were developed with elaborate memory-mapping mechanisms, as indicated in part *c* of Figure 1-3, that permitted several users to share a common large physical memory while each user program operates on what appears to be a gigantic virtual memory. The number of simultaneous users per time-sharing system climbed from 10 to 100 in this period, with the 100-user systems requiring very powerful high-end machines. Each new machine announcement brought forth more sophistication in sharing and ever more elaborate mechanisms for protection to prevent unauthorized sharing of data and to insure the integrity of the system.

By the middle of the 1970s the microprocessor introduced a dramatic new perturbation into the economics of time-sharing systems. The microprocessor, when dedicated to an individual user in a highly interactive environment, provides a tool that enhances the user's productivity well beyond the productivity available under a time-sharing system. When the user's productivity is the dominant cost, the most cost-effective alternative is to organize the system to minimize this cost. Because microprocessors are so inexpensive, and memory costs are dropping equally rapidly, if not today then certainly in the near future each can have a dedicated-computer system on the same basis that one has a typewriter, telephone, or filing cabinet. Part *d* of Figure 1-3 indicates some of the prevailing economics that suggest why time-sharing systems are not cost-effective in terms of sharing the cost of processor and memory. The two systems shown are a time-sharing system, in which each user communicates to a central computer over a link that runs at a maximum speed of about 1000 characters per second, and a dedicated computer that achieves an instantaneous rate of about 2000 characters per second. Although the dedicated computer has about twice the maximum communication speed of the time-shared computer in this example, the maximum speed is only part of the story.

Because of sharing, there are delays introduced in the time-sharing system not present in the dedicated system. The user may not be aware of these delays, but they are there nevertheless. Perhaps they are as little as 1 second in many instances, and climb to several seconds per transaction when the time-sharing system is heavily loaded. Though each delay is insignificant in itself, the time is lost time that cannot be recaptured. The result is that the time-sharing user may have to spend four hours doing what the dedicated-system user can do in two hours or one hour. The differences are extremely dramatic for those time-sharing systems in which the user-communication link is limited to 120 characters per second (high-speed phone link) or to 30 characters per second (low-speed phone link). With a telephone link of this type, productivity drops extraordinarily low as compared to the dedicated system, and the user pays the communication charges as well.

This argument suggests that the future will bring a proliferation of dedicated computers, each with approximately the memory capacity and speed of what a user had available only through time-sharing a decade ago.

This is not the whole answer. Time-sharing will still exist, in all likelihood, but for other reasons. Systems can evolve into centralized hosts with distributed satellites, as in part *a* of Figure 1-4, or into totally distributed systems without a centralized host, as in part *b* of Figure 1-4. The purpose of connecting machines together is to give recognition to the notion that these machines share information, and the system then becomes an information utility. Information has value, and is a genuine commodity. In a computer system that information may be corporate records, the latest release of a new computer language, the daily newspaper, the university library catalog and perhaps the books themselves, or today's advertisements for the local shopping mall. No one user can afford to expend the effort to recreate large amounts of information. Each user must therefore tap a pool of information. The major difference between the information utility of Figure 1-4 and the time-sharing machines of Figure 1-3 is that the information utility is designed to transfer information to a computer dedicated to user interaction where the user can operate on the data with high efficiency. The time-sharing system interacts with the user directly, and this contributes to the inefficiency of the system.

Moving to other trends, consider the impact of the microprocessor on the design of a user system. Figure 1-5 contrasts two approaches, again bearing some resemblance to the time-sharing development. The first approach, shown in part *a*, is the conventional one used on most computer systems through the mid-1970s. The central processor controls all input/output in this system, with some of the detailed actions of data transfers done by direct-memory access (DMA) channels. In part *b* of Figure 1-5, we see the effects of the microprocessor evolution. Here, each I/O device has its own processor dedicated to serving that device. Tasks that once were relegated to the central processor and competed for its resources are now done concurrently in a relatively simple dedicated system. This reduces the complexity of both central processor software and the I/O device software. This is but one way to take

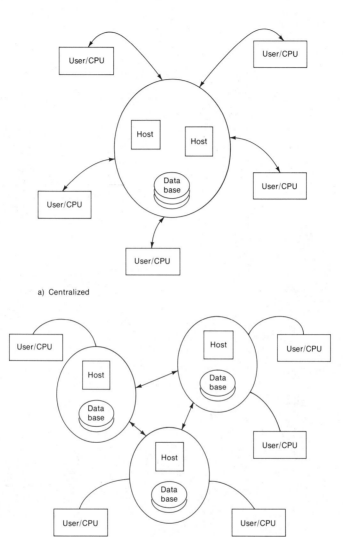

a) Centralized

b) Distributed

Figure 1-4   An information utility

advantage of the microprocessor to increase performance and decrease the software development effort.

Finally we come to issues of reliability. Computers are very complex devices, even when built from a handful of chips. When failures occur, it takes a good deal of sophistication to identify that a failure has occurred and to diagnose the precise problem. With the number of computers in use changing from 30,000 in the mid-1960s to in excess of 30 million in the mid-1980s,

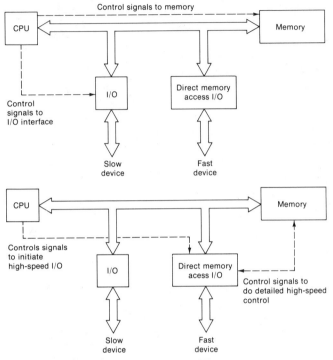

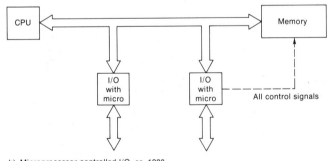

a) Conventional low- and high-speed control, ca. 1970

b) Microprocessor controlled I/O, ca. 1980

Figure 1-5 Input/output control structures

we have to recognize that there are not enough people who can be engaged in servicing computers to support the needs of the 1980s. There must be another way, and indeed there is. Present and future generations of computers must have built-in diagnosis, some self-correcting hardware, and some means of enabling the user to assist in the service process. Again the ubiquitous microprocessor provides a solution. Already computer manufacturers have incorporated diagnostic microprocessors in their systems to log errors, to identify permanent and transient-type failures, to diagnose faulty components, and to provide means for remote diagnosis if needed over telephone links to central service facilities. Reliability and ease of repair will be a major thrust in computer systems of the 1980s.

In closing this introduction we wish to call the reader's attention to the literature on computer architecture. Bell and Newell [71] and Siewiorek, Bell, and Newell [80] have collected several important papers of the 1950s, 1960s, and 1970s, including descriptions of several computers that appeared during these years. Many of the design techniques, trends, and innovations in computer architecture hinted at in this introduction appear in the orginal in these collections. A fairly extensive set of citations to other original source material appears in the bibliography of these books.

CHAPTER 2

Data Representation

Herschel H. Loomis, Jr.

2-1. IMPORTANCE OF DATA REPRESENTATION

One of the powers of the digital computer is its versatility of application to problems in a variety of fields. In making such application, the way in which data to be operated upon is represented in the computer is important. Early numerical applications of modern computers used a binary representation of numbers which had a fixed radix point and a limited, fixed number of significant digits. Since that early beginning, computer words have been interpreted in a variety of ways: as alphanumeric text in business applications; as floating point (scientific notation) numbers for greater programming ease and problem-solving flexibility in numerical analysis; and as arrays of light intensities representing an image of the planet Jupiter in an unmanned fly-by, to name just a few.

In all these examples, the fundamental unit of information is the binary digit, called the *bit*. Higher-order structures made up of these bits vary widely from example to example. In fact, the difference between a "good" computer program and a "poor" one is often the way in which these higher order structures are put together and interpreted.

In this chapter, we will describe a number of data representations in use and explore several of their characteristics to indicate how to select the best representation for a particular problem.

We will consider information from several different points of view. The most basic aspect examined concerns the representation in nondecimal radices such as octal, binary, hexadecimal, and the representation of alphanumeric characters. Next we consider the composites of the basic units, such as the *computer word,* which corresponds to a physical unit of information in the computer. Then we examine how words are put together in more complex structures such as arrays or lists. Throughout this discussion, we consider the relation between these interpretations and the physical characteristics of the computer implied by these interpretations.

Throughout all of this discussion, one very important point must be kept in mind: the meaning of a set of data depends on the interpretation of the bits that represent the data in memory.

2-2. NUMBERS

Fixed Radix-point Numbers

Numbers in Various Bases   One of the major advances of civilization was the development of the positional number system, which is quite different from the nonpositional system used by the early Romans. In the positional system, each digit position has a value called a *weight* associated with it. To obtain the value of such a number, each digit value is multiplied by the weight of its position, and then all such products are summed. We can formally represent such a number and its numerical value as shown in Equation 2-1:

$$X = X_{n-1} X_{n-2} \cdots X_0 . X_{-1} \cdots X_{-m}$$
$$V(X) = \sum_{i=0}^{n-1} X_i R^i + \sum_{i=-1}^{-m} X_i R^i \qquad (2\text{-}1)$$

(Integer   (Fractional
portion)   portion)

where $V(X)$ denotes the numerical value of X.

The point between X_0 and X_{-1} is the so called *radix point* and separates the integer (whole number) portion of the number from the fractional portion.

Normally, some constraints are placed upon the values that X_i may assume, that is:

$$0 \leq X_i < R$$

(Some number systems, such as the signed-digit system proposed by Avizienis [64], allow other values, but those systems are rarely used.)

The value R associated with such a system is called the *radix* or *base* of the number system. Various common values of R are in use. When R is 10 we have the standard *decimal system,* the one in which most of us carry out day-to-day computations. Base 2 systems are called *binary* and form the foundation for all electronic computer systems in current use. Other commonly used systems are ones which have a power of 2 as the base, such as base 8 or *octal,* base 16 or *hexadecimal.* These systems are used because they are simply related to the binary system.

The binary system is the fundamental system used by all electronic computer systems known to the author, because electronic devices that operate in more than two states are difficult to achieve. Theoretical studies have been made of systems having a fundamental base larger than base 2, in particular of the *ternary* or base 3 system, although no practical application of this theory has yet been made.

Working with numbers in different bases requires the *conversion* of numbers from one base to another, which involves performing some arithmetic. Normally in such a conversion, the arithmetic is performed in the familiar base. Because of this, conversion from a familiar base to a foreign base involves algorithms different from those used to convert from a foreign base to the familiar one.

Conversion of integers from a foreign base to the familiar base is relatively simple; it involves substitution of the appropriate values into the integer portion of Equation 2-1.

$$V(X) = \sum_{i=0}^{n-1} X_i R^i$$

For example,

$$V(3507_8) = 7 + 0(8) + 5(8^2) + 3(8^3) \qquad \text{(arithmetic base 10)}$$
$$= 1863_{10}$$

The subscript signifies the base.

$$V(110110_2) = 0 + 1(2) + 1(2^2) + 0(2^3) + 1(2^4) + 1(2^5)$$
$$= 54_{10}$$
$$V(110.111_2) = 0 + 1(2) + 1(2^2) + 1(2^{-1}) + 1(2^{-2}) + 1(2^{-3})$$
$$= 6.875_{10}$$
$$V(.325_6) = 3(6^{-1}) + 2(6^{-2}) + 5(6^{-3})$$
$$= (.578703703\ldots\ldots\ldots)_{10}$$

In the last example note that some numbers that are exact in one radix representation cannot be represented exactly in a finite number of digits in some other base. This occurs when the reciprocal of the foreign base itself cannot be represented in a finite number of digits in the familiar base.

Equation 2-1 can also be used when the familiar base is other than 10.

Example 2-1: Convert 31_{10} to base 2.   (arithmetic base 2)

$$V(31_{10}) = [1 + 3\,(10)]_{10}$$
$$= [1 + (011)\,(1010)]_2$$
$$= [1 + (11110)]_2$$
$$= 11111_2$$

Conversion to a foreign base can be accomplished using the following methods, one for integer, the other for fractional numbers.

Consider the integer number in some familiar base R' and consider how to compute its base R representation using arithmetic in base R'.

$$V(X) = X_0 + X_1(R) + X_2(R^2) + \cdots + X_{n-1}(R^{n-1})$$
$$\text{(arithmetic base } R')$$

Divide $V(X)$ by R yielding

$$V(X)/R = \frac{X_0}{R} + [X_1 + X_2(R) \cdots + X_{n-1}(R^{n-2})]$$

$$= \frac{X_0}{R} + Q_1$$

The portion in brackets, Q_1, is the quotient of the division operation, and since X_0 is less than R, X_0 is the remainder. Note that the remainder gives X_0, and the quotient Q_1 can be used to compute the remaining X_is. Thus, in general, we have

$$Q_i/R = \frac{X_i}{R} + [X_{i+1} + \cdots + X_{n-1}(R^{n-2-i})] = \frac{X_i}{R} + Q_{i+1}$$

This suggests a repeated process of division by R where each remainder yields a digit of the representation, and each successive quotient is the dividend of the next step. The process terminates when a quotient of 0 is produced.

Example 2-2:   Convert 63_{10} to base 5.   (arithmetic base 10)

$$63/5 = \frac{3}{5} + 12 \qquad\qquad X_0 = 3$$

$$12/5 = \frac{2}{5} + 2 \qquad\qquad X_1 = 2$$

$$2/5 = \frac{2}{5} + 0 \qquad\qquad X_2 = 2$$

$$63_{10} = 223_5$$

Example 2-3:   Convert 1863_{10} to base 8.   (arithmetic base 10)

$$1863/8 = \frac{7}{8} + 232 \qquad\qquad X_0 = 7$$

$$232/8 = \frac{0}{8} + 29 \qquad\qquad X_1 = 0$$

$$29/8 = \frac{5}{8} + 3 \qquad\qquad X_2 = 5$$

$$3/8 = \frac{3}{8} + 0 \qquad\qquad X_3 = 3$$

$$1863_{10} = 3507_8$$

The conversion of fractional numbers likewise proceeds from an interpretation of the fractional portion of Equation 2-1. Let X be such a fractional number.

$$V(X) = \frac{X_{-1}}{R} + \frac{X_{-2}}{R^2} + \cdots + \frac{X_{-m}}{R^m}$$

Multiplying $V(X)$ by R yields

$$R \times V(X) = X_{-1} + \frac{X_{-2}}{R} + \cdots + \frac{X_{-m}}{R^{m-1}} = X_{-1} + F_1$$

Now, $R \times V(X)$ has an integer part, namely X_{-1} and a fractional part. Multiplying F_1 by R yields

$$R \times F_1 = X_{-2} + \frac{X_{-3}}{R} + \cdots + \frac{X_{-m}}{R^{m-2}} = X_{-2} + F_2$$

In general,

$$R \times F_j = X_{-(j+1)} + \frac{X_{-(j+2)}}{R} + \cdots + \frac{X_{-m}}{R^{m-(j+1)}} = X_{-(j+1)} + F_{j+1}$$

The process terminates when (and if) a fractional part of 0 is achieved.

Example 2-4:   Convert $.63671875_{10}$ to hexadecimal. *

$$16 \times (.63671875) = 10.1875 \qquad X_{-1} = 10 \text{ or A}$$
$$F_1 = .1875$$
$$16 \times (.1875) = 3.0 \qquad X_{-2} = 3$$
$$F_2 = 0$$

so the process terminates and

$$.63671875_{10} = .A3_{16}$$

---

*Note that symbols for hexadecimal digit values of 10 through 15 are represented by the symbols A through F, respectively.

Example 2-5: Convert $.5125_{10}$ to base 8.

$$8 \times (.5125) = 4.1 \qquad X_{-1} = 4, F_1 = .1$$
$$8 \times (.1) \quad = 0.8 \qquad X_{-2} = 0, F_2 = .8$$
$$8 \times (.8) \quad = 6.4 \qquad X_{-3} = 6, F_3 = .4$$
$$8 \times (.4) \quad = 3.2 \qquad X_{-4} = 3, F_4 = .2$$
$$8 \times (.2) \quad = 1.6 \qquad X_{-5} = 1, F_5 = .6$$
$$8 \times (.6) \quad = 4.8 \qquad X_{-6} = 4, F_6 = .8$$

A repetition of a previously arrived at fractional part has occurred $(F_2 = F_6)$, so the conversion process does not terminate. Therefore the result is:

$$.5125_{10} = (.4063146\overline{6314}\ldots\ldots)_8$$

where the 6314 digits repeat indefinitely.

Finally, in connection with the conversion to a foreign base, note that mixed numbers are converted by separating the number into its integer and fractional parts and converting each separately and then combining the result.

The binary system currently is firmly established as a fundamental system for representing data in electronic digital computers. It is however inconvenient to represent large binary numbers in positional binary because of the large number of digits required. Consider the 24-bit binary integer number.

$$(010011001111000001011010.)_2 = (5{,}042{,}266)_{10}$$

We can group the bits in groups of b bits, and each b-bit group can be considered as a digit of a radix 2^b representation of the number. For example, if $b = 3$, our number becomes

$$(010,011,001,111,000,001,011,010.)_2$$

$$\text{or } (23170132)_8$$

This is the octal system, and is seen to be three times as economical in positions. Also, octal numbers are easier to remember for short periods of time than are binary numbers. If $b = 4$, we have the hexadecimal representation, and in our example,

$$(0100,1100,1111,0000,0101,1010.)_2$$

becomes

$$(4CF05A)_{16}$$

While all computers use the binary system internally, programmers use either octal or hexadecimal for convenience. They tend to use octal for machines whose word lengths are multiples of 3 bits and hexadecimal for machines whose word lengths are multiples of 4 bits.

Earlier in this section, the question of foreign radix arithmetic was raised and the method was discussed as being unwieldy for human use in radix conversion. Nevertheless, computers generally operate in a radix system that is either binary or some other power of 2, and the rules for doing arithmetic in these systems become important when one designs logic circuits for the performance of arithmetic. We consider the rules for simple arithmetic in the next section.

PROBLEMS

1. Convert the following numbers from the indicated base to the decimal system:
   a) 15.21_6
   b) 15.21_8
   c) 1101.101_2
   d) $AF.3_{16}$

2. Convert the following numbers from the decimal system to the designated base:
   a) 78_{10} to hexadecimal
   b) 105_{10} to ternary (base 3)
   c) $.5625_{10}$ to binary
   d) 33.51_{10} to base 5
   e) $.05_{10}$ to binary

3. Convert 23170132_8 and $4CF05A_{16}$ to decimal to demonstrate their equivalence to the binary number 010011001111000001011010.

4. Convert 7352.7_8 to hexadecimal.

Rules for Simple Arithmetic   In order to define the rules for arithmetic in a foreign radix, we make use of the basic relation that the result of an operation on two numbers represented in radix R must have the same value as the result of the same operation on the radix 10 representation of the same numbers. Thus we can define digit addition tables for the various systems as shown in Figure 2-1. Since the operation of addition is *commutative* ($x+y = y+x$, for all choices of x,y), the portion of the base 8 and 10 tables below the diagonal is not shown.

Base 2

+	0	1
0	0	1
1	1	10

Base 3

+	0	1	2
0	0	1	2
1	1	2	10
2	2	10	11

Base 8

+	0	1	2	3	4	5	6	7
0	0	1	2	3	4	5	6	7
1		2	3	4	5	6	7	10
2			4	5	6	7	10	11
3				6	7	10	11	12
4					10	11	12	13
5						12	13	14
6							14	15
7								16

Base 10

+	0	1	2	3	4	5	6	7	8	9
0	0	1	2	3	4	5	6	7	8	9
1		2	3	4	5	6	7	8	9	10
2			4	5	6	7	8	9	10	11
3				6	7	8	9	10	11	12
4					8	9	10	11	12	13
5						10	11	12	13	14
6							12	13	14	15
7								14	15	16
8									16	17
9										18

Figure 2-1   Addition tables for various bases

One can easily verify that these tables follow the rule stated above for constructing foreign radix arithmetic rules. For example, we note: $(2 + 3)_4 = 11_4$ corresponds to $(2 + 3)_{10} = 5_{10}$ and $11_4 = 5_{10}$.

Likewise:

$$(8 + C)_{16} = (14)_{16} \text{ corresponds to } (8 + 12)_{10} = 20_{10} \text{ and } 14_{16}$$
$$= 16 + 4 = 20_{10}.$$

Next, let us apply our knowledge of addition of n-digit numbers in the decimal system to infer some general rules for adding n-digit numbers in any radix. We note that whenever the sum in a given digit position exceeds 9 (radix $- 1$), we keep the least significant digit of the sum in the current digit position and generate a *carry* into the next digit position, as we work in the number from least significant to most significant portions of the number. We show the carries as ones (1s) and zeros (0s) above the column to which they are added. As examples consider

Radix 10:
```
          1 1 1 0    Carries
          5 1 7 3
        + 2 8 4 7
        ─────────
          8 0 2 0
```

Radix 2:

$$\begin{array}{r} 1\ 1\ 1\ 1\ 1\ 0\ 1\ 0 \\ \hline 1\ 0\ 1\ 1\ 1\ 0\ 1 \\ +\ 0\ 1\ 0\ 0\ 1\ 0\ 1 \\ \hline 1\ 0\ 0\ 0\ 0\ 0\ 1\ 0 \end{array}$$ Carries

Radix 16:

$$\begin{array}{r} 1\ \ 0\ 1\ 0 \\ \hline A\ \ 1\ 3\ F \\ +\ 2\ F\ 9\ 3 \\ \hline D\ 0\ D\ 2 \end{array}$$ Carries

Subtraction, or the minus $(-)$ operation, can be similarly determined using individual tables for each digit and a *borrow* which propagates from least to most significant digit. Figure 2-2 shows subtraction tables for radix 2, 8, and 10. The form of these tables is such that the less significant digit represents the difference and the more significant, if a 1, represents a borrow. When subtracting multidigit numbers, one way to deal with the borrow is to use it to decre-

Radix 2   Subtrahend

Minuend $-$ 0   1

$\downarrow$ 0 | 0   11

1 | 1   0

Radix 8
Subtrahend $\rightarrow$

Radix 10
Subtrahend $\rightarrow$

Minuend

$-$	0	1	2	3	4	5	6	7
0	0	17	16	15	14	13	12	11
1	1	0	17	16	15	14	13	12
2	2	1	0	17	16	15	14	13
3	3	2	1	0	17	16	15	14
4	4	3	2	1	0	17	16	15
5	5	4	3	2	1	0	17	16
6	6	5	4	3	2	1	0	17
7	7	6	5	4	3	2	1	0

$\downarrow$

$-$	0	1	2	3	4	5	6	7	8	9
0	0	19	18	17	16	15	14	13	12	11
1	1	0	19	18	17	16	15	14	13	12
2	2	1	0	19	18	17	16	15	14	13
3	3	2	1	0	19	18	17	16	15	14
4	4	3	2	1	0	19	18	17	16	15
5	5	4	3	2	1	0	19	18	17	16
6	6	5	4	3	2	1	0	19	18	17
7	7	6	5	4	3	2	1	0	19	18
8	8	7	6	5	4	3	2	1	0	19
9	9	8	7	6	5	4	3	2	1	0

Note: Entry in table is either borrow and difference or just difference.

Figure 2-2 Subtraction tables for various bases

ment the minuend in the next digit position before applying the table to find the difference and borrow. Note the following examples:

	Radix 10	Radix 2	Radix 8
Borrows	0 0 1 0 0	0 1 0 0 0 1 1 0	1 1 1 0 0
Minuend	2 5 1 9	1 0 1 1 1 0 0	2 7 1 5
Subtrahend	− 1 4 2 8	− 0 1 0 1 0 0 1	− 2 7 3 4
Difference	1 0 9 1	0 1 1 0 0 1 1	$\cdots\,$ 7 7 7 6 1

In the example for radix 8, we note that a borrow is generated by the most significant digit subtraction, a direct consequence of the fact that the subtrahend is greater than the minuend and we therefore expect a negative result. In fact, we humans normally rearrange the problem to subtract the smaller from the larger and then affix a minus sign to the result. Some computers may in fact handle the situation in this way. However, there are other ways to represent and operate on negative numbers; some of these ways are covered in the next section.

PROBLEM

Using A and B for the digit values 10 and 11 respectively, construct an addition table for the duodecimal system (radix 12). Perform the addition in radix 12 of the following pair of numbers:

$$10A_{12} + BB1_{12}$$

Negative Number Representation   The most familiar way for dealing with negative numbers is by means of the *signed-magnitude* representation. In this representation, $-b$, where b is a string of digits forming a fixed-point number, is that number which, when added to b, forms the sum 0. In other words, $-b$ is the *additive inverse* of b. Now we have a mechanism for dealing with the case where a larger positive number is subtracted from a smaller positive number: Invert the order of subtraction and affix a minus sign to the difference.

TABLE 2-1. ADDITION OF SIGNED-MAGNITUDE NUMBERS

B	C	$b:c$	$B + C$	Operation Required	Case #
b	c	don't care	$b + c$	addition	1
$-b$	$-c$	don't care	$-(b + c)$	addition	2
b	$-c$	$b > c$	$b - c$	subtraction	3
b	$-c$	$b < c$	$-(c - b)$	subtraction	4
$-b$	c	$b < c$	$c - b$	subtraction	5
$-b$	c	$b > c$	$-(b - c)$	subtraction	6
b	$-c$	$b = c$	0	subtraction	7
$-b$	c	$b = c$	0	subtraction	8

The presence of so-called negative numbers now increases the number of cases we must consider in developing rules for handling addition. To examine the various cases, let B and C be the numbers to be added and b and c be magnitudes of these numbers, respectively, as shown in Table 2-1. Note that the operation is commutative.

Treating negative numbers in this way means that we need both an adder and a subtractor, together with some input switching and testing, to permit the eight basically different cases of Table 2-1 to be implemented. Figure 2-3 shows the use of subtractors and adders to produce an adder that will properly treat signed-magnitude numbers. In the system there presented we use a 1 in the

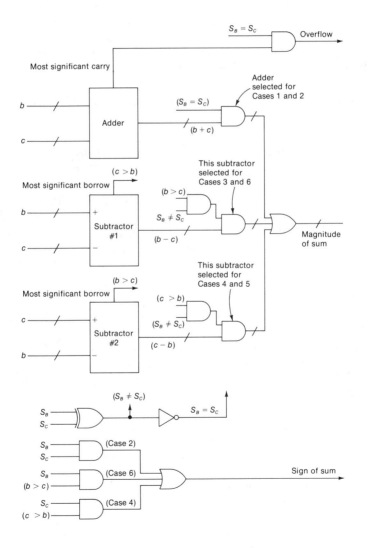

Figure 2-3 Signed-magnitude adder

sign position to mean "minus." The adder makes use of three-component binary subcircuits, an adder and two subtractors. In cases 1 and 2, the signs of the operands are the same and therefore the magnitude of the result is the sum of the magnitudes of the operands. The sign of the result is provided by the (case 2) gate. If the signs of B and C differ, we need to form the difference of the magnitudes, with the smaller being subtracted from the larger. Since we do not know in advance which difference to form, we form both and examine the most significant borrow. If the borrow is a 1, it means that the larger was subtracted from the smaller in that subtractor and hence the result of the other subtractor is the proper difference. Thus, in cases 3 and 6, the borrow from subtractor 2 signals $b > c$ and therefore the output $(b - c)$ of subtractor 1 is selected as the magnitude. In cases 4 and 5, the borrow from subtractor 1 selects the output of subtractor 2.

The sign of the result is determined for each of the three possible negative sign-producing cases, cases 2, 4, and 6.

Finally, in cases 7 and 8, none of the three magnitude-selection gates is enabled, so a zero magnitude is the output, the correct value for these cases. The sign is 0 (plus).

Some economies can be effected in the signed-magnitude adder of Figure 2-3 by eliminating one of the two subtractors. Let us eliminate subtractor 2. But then, how are cases 4 and 5 computed? We simply notice that subtractor 1 is producing the two's complement of the correct difference, so the magnitude of the result could be obtained in these cases by adding a following circuit which converts the two's complement of the difference into the actual difference.

Two other ways of representing negative numbers that do not require the special-case handling of the signed-magnitude method are the radix-complement (RC) and the diminished radix-complement (DRC), or digit-complement, methods.

To develop the *radix complement,* assume that we have an n-digit, radix R number. An n-digit, radix R number can have any one of R^n possible values and hence has a representation in R^n. If a positive number b is to be represented, so long as $b < R^n/2$, its n-digit, radix R representation is used. To represent $-b$, we use instead $R^n - b$ as the representation.

Using this system, let us examine the result of forming the sum of b and $-c$, as shown in Table 2-2.

In Table 2-2 we see two cases explored. If $b \leq c$, then $R^n - (c - b)$ is less than R^n, and the result is still negative, as shown in Example 2-6.

TABLE 2-2. THE SUM OF b AND $-c$ IN RADIX COMPLEMENT

B	C	$b:c$	$B + C$	Sign of Result
b	$R^n - c$	$b > c$	$R^n + (b - c)$	Positive
b	$R^n - c$	$b \leq c$	$R^n - (c - b)$	Negative

Example 2-6: If $R = 10$, $n = 3$, find $053 - 101$ by the radix-complement method.

$$053 + (10^3 - 101) = 053 + (899)*$$
$$= 952$$
$$= (10^3 - 48)$$
$$(53 - 101 = -48)$$

If $b > c$, then $R^n + (b - c)$ is greater than or equal to R^n, and this fact is signalled by the generation of a carry out of the nth digit position of the adder. An n-digit adder normally ignores this carry, since it adds modulo R^n. Thus all multiples of R^n are ignored, leaving only $(b - c)$.

Example 2-7: If $R = 10$, $n = 3$, find $101 - 053$ by the radix-complement method.

$$101 + (10^3 - 053) = 101 + (947)$$
$$= 1048$$

but we ignore the 1 in the 10^3 column since our addition is modulo 10^3, so our result is 048.

Because the most significant digit of the number carries the information about sign, we will slightly change the interpretation of the most significant digit to permit more convenient representation and evaluation of negative numbers. We add the nth digit or sign, which can contain only a 0 or a 1, and we do our addition there modulo 2. Now we are able to generalize our positional number to the radix-complement method. Let us allow a sign, n integer digits, and, for simplicity, allow no fractional digits $(m = 0)$. We use a comma to separate the sign from the rest of the number.

$$X_n, X_{n-1} \ldots \ldots X_0$$
$$0 \leq X_n \leq 1, 0 \leq X_i < R \quad \text{for } 0 \leq i < n.$$

How do we evaluate such a number? If $X_n = 0$, that is, if the number is positive, it is no different from the previous value as found in Equation 2-1.

Let x be the magnitude of a number; let X be its signed, radix-complement representation and $\widehat{X}$ its $n - 1$ digit representation. Consider the representation of $-x$.

$$V_{RC}(X) = -x$$
$$\text{but } V(\widehat{X}) = R^n - x \quad \text{and } X_n = 1.$$

---

*$X_n \geq R/2$ is frequently interpreted to mean the number is negative, and hence in radix-complement form.

Therefore we must assign $V(X_n)$ to be $-R^n$, and we have

$$V_{RC}(X) = (-X_n R^n) + \sum_{0}^{n-1} X_i R^i \tag{2-2}$$

Thus, the digit weight of the sign is negative in radix complement. Applying this to our previous examples, and adding a sign digit, we find:

$$V_{RC}(1,899) = -1000 + 800 + 90 + 9 = -101$$
$$V_{RC}(0,101) = -0 + 100 + 1 = 101$$

Thus, in summary, we see that there are two ways for determining the sign of the number being represented. We can allow the most significant digit its full range of R values (0 to $R - 1$), interpreting values greater than or equal to $R/2$ as meaning that the entire number is a radix-complement representation of a negative number and interpreting values less than $R/2$ as meaning that the entire number is positive. This is the result of applying the radix-complement technique. The other way is to treat the sign digit as a binary digit regardless of R, interpreting a 1 as meaning that the rest of the number is a radix-complement representation of a negative number and a 0 as meaning that the rest of the number is positive. Both methods are in use, although the second method has the advantage that a simple evaluation-expression exists for numbers irrespective of sign. Also, the first method is awkward when R is odd, although there are no odd radices in common use. Finally, note that both methods are the same if $R = 2$, the most important case.

There is an area of possible confusion in terminology because of the fact that the term *radix complement* is used both for a number system and for the result of an operation performed on numbers. When we speak of an entire number system as the radix-complement system, we are referring to a system in which both positive and negative numbers can be represented. So if we desire to represent the number 105 in the signed ten's complement system ($R = 10$, $n = 3$), we obtain the number 0,105. If however, we desire to represent -105, we first take the ten's complement of 105 and affix a 1 for the sign digit, obtaining 1,895. Thus the radix-complement system is capable of representing both positive and negative numbers. On the other hand, when we speak of the radix complement of a number, we are referring to the result of an operation performed on the number, A, equivalent to subtracting A from R^n. So the radix complement of 105 is 895, and that of 895 is 105. When we represent these numbers in the signed, ten's complement system, we obtain 0,105 for $+105$ and 1,895 for -105. In the decimal system, the radix complement is called *ten's complement* and in the binary system, *two's complement*.

Now let us examine a variation of the radix-complement method, the *diminished radix-complement* or *digit-complement*, method. This variation is designed to make the conversion from positive to negative numbers easier than with the radix-complement method. The ith digit of the diminished radix complement of a number, x, is $R - 1 - X_i$. The sign of the number is positive if the number is less than $\frac{1}{2} R^n$. As before, the sign can be indicated by a separate binary sign digit, in which case the sign digit of the diminished radix complement of the number is $1 - X_n$. For example, let $R = 10$, $n = 3$, $m = 0$ and assume a binary sign digit:

$$DRC(0053) = 1,946$$

$$DRC(0931) = 1,068$$

$$DRC(0000) = 1,999$$

One criterion that the negative number system must fulfill is that the sum of X and the representation of minus X must be a representation of 0.

Thus, $X + DRC(X) = Z$ such that $V_{DRC}(Z) = 0$. Now let us take a number X and add to it its DRC. For the least significant digit, $X + (R - 1 - X_0) = R - 1$, with no carry. Then, for each $i > 0$, we find the ith digit sum is $X_i + (R - 1 - X_i) = R - 1$, generating no carry. Finally, with no carry into the sign, $X_n + (1 - X_n) = 1$. Thus the representation of the sum of a number and its diminished radix complement is $1, (R - 1)(R - 1) \ldots (R-1)$, which is one representation of the number 0, that is, the diminished radix complement of 0. Therefore, if we compare the radix complement of a number and its diminished radix complement, we note that the DRC is one less than the RC in the least significant digit position, or $RC(X) - 1 = DRC(X)$. Thus, we can state that the value of the general signed, diminished radix-complement number is given by the following expression:

$$V_{DRC}(X) = X_n(-R^n + 1) + \sum_{i=0}^{n-1} X_i R^i \tag{2-3}$$

Applying this to the previous examples for $n = 3$, $m = 0$, $R = 10$ yields

$$V_{DRC}(1,946) = (-10^3 + 10^0) + 900 + 40 + 6$$
$$= -53$$
$$V_{DRC}(1,999) = (-10^3 + 10^0) + 900 + 90 + 9$$
$$= 0$$
$$V_{DRC}(0,053) = 0 + 50 + 3$$
$$= 53$$

Finally, as a result of Equation 2-3 we now have a simpler method for taking the radix complement of a number than performing R^n minus the number. We form the diminished radix complement (digit complement), and add a 1 in the least significant digit position.

Be careful here also to avoid confusion between the diminished radix-complement *system*, in which both positive and negative numbers can be represented, and the diminished radix-complement *operation* on a number, which produces a representation of the negative of the original number.

Now let us leave the general case and look specifically at the binary case, treating first the *two's-complement* or radix-complement representation. Later we will consider the diminished radix complement, which is called the *ones' complement*. We assume that the leading digit, X_n, is the sign digit. Addition falls into four basic categories, each of which should be examined: 1) both summands positive, 2) both negative, 3) one positive and one negative with the negative one greater in magnitude, and finally, 4) one positive and one negative with the positive greater than or equal in magnitude to the negative.

Case 1. Both positive, that is, $B = 0, b; C = 0, c$.

  a) $b + c < 2^n$ implies that the result is representable.
  b) $b + c \geq 2^n$ generates a carry into sign bit, which is an *overflow* condition.

Case 2. Both negative, that is, $B = 1, (2^n - b); C = 1, (2^n - c)$.

  a) $b + c \leq 2^n$ implies that

$$(2^n - b) + (2^n - c) = 2^{n+1} - (b + c) \geq 2^n$$

  and hence the addition generates a carry into the sign-bit position, preserving a sign of 1, and also generating a carry out of the sign-bit position.

  b) $b + c > 2^n$ implies that

$$(2^n - b) + (2^n - c) = 2^{n+1} - (b + c) < 2^n$$

  and hence the addition generates no carry into the sign-bit position, causing an apparent sign change, which is an *overflow*.

Case 3. One positive, one negative, that is, $B = 1, (2^n - b); C = 0, c; b > c$;

$$c + 2^n - b = 2^n - (b - c) < 2^n$$

  and hence no carry occurs into the sign bit and the result is negative.

Case 4. Same as case 3 except $b \leq c$.

$$c + 2^n - b = 2^n + (c - b) \geq 2^n$$

  and a carry occurs into the sign bit, yielding a positive result.

Example 2-8: $R = 2, n = 5, m = 0.$

Case 1. *a*) 0 0 0 1 1 0 0 ← Carries (shown above the column to which
$\qquad$ 0 1 0 0 1 0. $\quad$ (+18) $\quad$ they are added)

$\qquad$ + 0 0 0 1 1 1. $\quad$ (+7)
$\qquad$ $\overline{0\ 1\ 1\ 0\ 0\ 1.}$ $\quad$ (+25) $\qquad$ No overflow.

$\qquad$ *b*) 0 1 1 1 1 0 0 ← Carries
$\qquad$ 0 1 0 0 1 0. $\quad$ (+18)

$\qquad$ + 0 0 1 1 1 1. $\quad$ (+15)
$\qquad$ $\overline{1\ 0\ 0\ 0\ 0\ 1.}$ $\quad$ (+33) $\qquad$ Overflow, 33 > 32. Note sign
$\qquad\qquad\qquad\qquad\qquad\qquad\qquad$ change.

Case 2. *a*) 1 1 0 0 0 0 0 ← Carries
$\qquad$ 1 1 0 0 1 0. $\quad$ (−14)

$\qquad$ + 1 1 1 0 0 1. $\quad$ (−7)
$\qquad$ $\overline{1\ 0\ 1\ 0\ 1\ 1.}$ $\quad$ (−21) $\qquad$ No overflow.

$\qquad$ *b*) 1 0 0 0 1 0 0 ← Carries
$\qquad$ 1 1 0 0 1 0. $\quad$ (−14)

$\qquad$ + 1 0 0 0 1 1. $\quad$ (−29)
$\qquad$ $\overline{0\ 1\ 0\ 1\ 0\ 1.}$ $\quad$ (−43) $\qquad$ Overflow, 43 > 32. Note sign
$\qquad\qquad\qquad\qquad\qquad\qquad\qquad$ change.

Case 3. $\quad$ 0 0 0 0 0 0 0 ← Carries
$\qquad$ 1 1 0 0 1 0. $\quad$ (−14)

$\qquad$ + 0 0 1 1 0 1. $\quad$ (+13)
$\qquad$ $\overline{1\ 1\ 1\ 1\ 1\ 1.}$ $\quad$ (−1) $\qquad$ No carry out of sign, no sign
$\qquad\qquad\qquad\qquad\qquad\qquad\qquad$ change.

Case 4. $\quad$ 1 1 1 0 0 0 0 ← Carries
$\qquad$ 1 1 1 0 0 1. $\quad$ (−7)

$\qquad$ + 0 0 1 0 1 0. $\quad$ (+10)
$\qquad$ $\overline{0\ 0\ 0\ 0\ 1\ 1.}$ $\quad$ (+3) $\qquad$ Carry out of sign, sign change.

Note that overflow is also detectable by observing that the carry into the sign-bit position differs from the carry out of the sign-bit position.

The *ones'-complement* number system has a similar set of categories and, additionally, the question of a correction in certain cases enters the picture. The need for this correction can be seen from the fact that the negative ones' complement must have an additional 1 added to obtain its value (see Equation 2-3); so if two negative numbers are added, the sum will be off by 2 × 1. Thus some correction is needed in the addition process.

Case 1. The same as for two's complement.

Case 2. $B = 1, (2^n - b - 1); C = 1, (2^n - c - 1).$

    a) $b + c < 2^n$ implies that

$$2^n - b - 1 + 2^n - c - 1 = 2^{n+1} - (b + c) - 2 \times 1$$

This result will not be the correct ones' complement unless a correction is added to the least-significant-bit position:

Then $2^{n+1} - (b + c) - 2 + 1 \geq 2^n$
$$\uparrow$$
$$\text{correction}$$

and a carry is generated into the sign-digit position. Also a carry is generated out of the sign-digit position. There is no overflow.

    b) $b + c \geq 2^n$ implies that

$$2^n - b - 1 + 2^n - c - 1 + 1 =$$
$$2^{n+1} - (c + b) - 1 < 2^n$$
$$\uparrow$$
$$\text{correction}$$

Thus no carry is generated into the sign digit but a carry is generated out of the sign digit.

Case 3. $B = 1, (2^n - b - 1); C = 0, c; b \geq c.$
$$c + 2^n - b - 1 = 2^n - (b - c) - 1 < 2^n$$

No carry is generated into the sign bit and no carry is generated out of the sign bit. The result is negative and no correction need be made.

Case 4. $B = 1, (2^n - b - 1); C = 0, c; b < c.$
$$c + 2^n - b - 1 = 2^n + (c - b) - 1 \geq 2^n$$

Thus a carry is generated into the sign bit and causes a sign change to a positive number. Also a carry then propagates out of the sign bit. Since the sign is now positive, 1 must be added as a correction to make the result look like $2^n + (c - b)$ which is congruent modulo 2^n to $c - b$, the desired result.

Now the question arises, how do we effect the correction needed in cases 2 and 4? Note that in both these cases the carry out of the sign bit is 1, and in cases where no correction is needed that same carry is 0. Thus the correction needed is simply to use the carry out of the sign as the carry into the least significant bit. This correction is called the *end-around carry*.

Example 2-9: $R = 2, n = 0, m = 3.$

Case 2. *a)*

```
    ⌒‾‾‾‾‾⌒
  ⓵ 1  1  1̂ 1  ← Carries
    1 .0 1  1    (−0.500)
 + 1 .1 1  0    (−0.125)
   ‾‾‾‾‾‾‾‾‾‾
    1 .0 1  0    (−0.625)     End-around carry.
```

b)

```
    ⌒‾‾‾‾‾⌒
  ⓵ 0  1  1̂ 1  ← Carries
    1 .0 0  1    (−0.750)
 + 1 .0 1  1    (−0.500)
   ‾‾‾‾‾‾‾‾‾‾
    0 .1 0  1    (−1.250)     Overflow. End-around carry.
```

Case 3.

```
    ⌒‾‾‾‾‾⌒
  ⓪ 0  1  1̂ 0  ← Carries
    1 .0 1  1    (−0.500)
 + 0 .0 1  1    (+0.375)
   ‾‾‾‾‾‾‾‾‾‾
    1 .1 1  0    (−0.125)     No end-around carry.
```

Case 4.

```
    ⌒‾‾‾‾‾⌒
  ⓵ 1  1  0̂ 1  ← Carries
    1 .0 1  0    (−0.625)
 + 0 .1 1  0    (+0.750)
   ‾‾‾‾‾‾‾‾‾‾
    0 .0 0  1    (+0.125)     End around carry.
```

To conclude our discussion of the specifics of addition of the various forms of binary numbers, we finally consider the simple hardware realizations of these addition algorithms.

The basis for the simple parallel adder is the *1-bit full adder,* which is the implementation of the addition rules for a single bit position. This logic circuit accepts two inputs from the appropriate bits of the addend and augend and one input from the carry generated by the next-less-significant-bit addition. Its outputs are the sum bit for this bit position and the carry into the next-more-significant-bit position.

A *two's-complement adder* can be obtained by connecting several adders of the kind just described, with the carry into the least significant bit set at 0 and the carry out of the most significant bit ignored (except perhaps for overflow protection). The *ones'-complement adder* is formed similarly, except that the carry input to the least significant bit is connected to the carry output of the most significant bit (end-around carry). Part *a* of Figure 2-4 shows a symbol for a full adder along with its truth table. The connection of six of these adders to form a 6-bit two's-complement adder is shown in Part *b* of Figure 2-4 along with labelling of each signal line to correspond to the two's-complement adder example, case 4 [$(−7) + (+10)$]. Part *c* of Figure 2-4 shows four full adders connected to form a ones'-complement adder. The signal lines in this figure are labelled to correspond to the example of case 4 [$(−0.625) + (0.750)$].

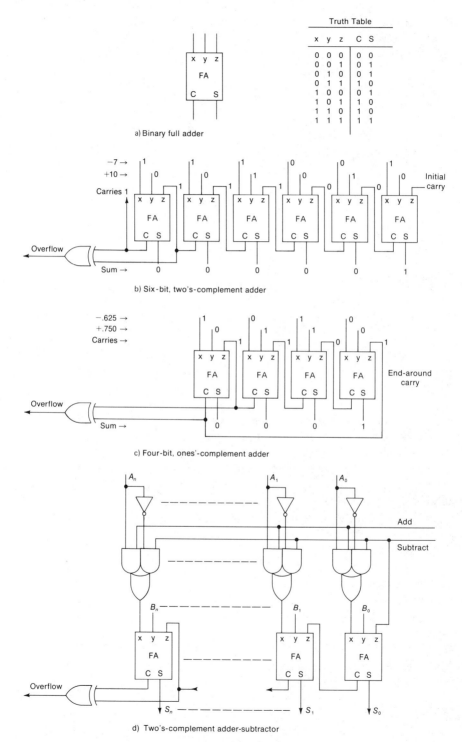

a) Binary full adder

Truth Table

x	y	z	C	S
0	0	0	0	0
0	0	1	0	1
0	1	0	0	1
0	1	1	1	0
1	0	0	0	1
1	0	1	1	0
1	1	0	1	0
1	1	1	1	1

b) Six-bit, two's-complement adder

c) Four-bit, ones'-complement adder

d) Two's-complement adder-subtractor

Figure 2-4 Binary adders

Finally, in Part *d* of Figure 2-4, we show the circuit for a *two's-complement adder-subtractor*. When Add = 1 (and Subtract = 0), we form the sum of *A* and *B*. When Subtract = 1 (and Add = 0), we form the sum of *B*, the ones' complement of *A*, and 1 (added via the carry into the least significant bit). Thus we see that, in this case at least, the add-1 operation required as a part of forming the two's complement is easily handled if an adder is involved.

We have examined three different ways of treating negative numbers, the signed-magnitude method, the radix-complement (RC) method, and the diminished radix-complement (DRC) method. We have seen how each relates to the operations of addition, sign conversion, and evaluation, and we have seen simple implementation of two's- and ones'-complement adders.

With respect to addition, the signed-magnitude method is most difficult to implement, with DRC being considerably simpler, and RC the simplest since it lacks the end-around carry.

For the process of negation, sign and magnitude seems the simplest, DRC is next, with RC being most expensive. In practice, the difficulties with signed-magnitude addition outweigh its advantages and it is not used as commonly as the RC or DRC method.

PROBLEMS

1. Give in your own words two different methods to find the radix complement of a number.

2. Express the following *magnitudes* as negative numbers in 1) signed-magnitude; 2) signed diminished radix complement; and 3) signed radix-complement form, using as the radix that which the number is given in. The most significant digit is to be a binary sign digit.
   a) 153_{10} ; $n = 3$
   b) 101101_2; $n = 6$
   c) 28.35_{10} ; $n = 2$
   d) $.7725_8$; $n = 0$
   e) $.AA10_{16}$; $n = 0$

3. Find the indicated value (the leading digit is a binary sign digit):
   a) $V_{SM}(1,9053_{10}) =$
   b) $V_{DRC}(1,9053_{10}) =$
   c) $V_{RC}(1,9053_{10}) =$
   d) $V_{RC}(0,A.5F_{16}) =$
   e) $V_{DRC}(1,752_8) =$

4. What happens when two negative RC numbers are added together where the sum of the magnitude equals R^n?

5. Convert $V(A) = +1953_{10}$ and $V(B) = +785_{10}$ to 4-digit hexadecimal positive numbers and perform the following operations in the system indi-

cated. Check your results by operating in the decimal system and comparing the results.

a) $A + B$ SM
b) $A - B$ RC
c) $B - A$ RC
d) $A - B$ DRC

6. a) Develop the truth table for a binary full subtractor that has these inputs: m, the minuend bit; s, the subtrahend bit; and r, the borrow input; and that produces two outputs: d, the difference bit; and b, the borrow output to the next-more-significant bit.

   b) Show the structure of a subtractor for two 5-bit binary magnitudes, constructed from the full subtractors specified in part (a).

More Arithmetic   Three arithmetic operations are examined in this section: those of shifting, multiplication, and division of binary numbers (base 2). These topics could be treated in more generality, but the complexity of the treatment does not appear to be justified in view of the preponderance of the binary system.

First, we consider *shifting*. Our intuition tells us that a left shift corresponds to multiplication by a power of 2. Let us therefore multiply Equation 2-1 by 2^p and interpret the result.

$$2^p V(X) = \sum_{i=0}^{n-1} X_i 2^{i+p} = \sum_{j=p}^{n-1+p} X_{j-p} 2^j = \sum_{j=p}^{n-1} X_{j-p} 2^j + \sum_{j=n}^{n-1+p} X_{j-p} 2^j \quad (2\text{-}4)$$

Thus we find the original ith bit of the word associated with the 2^{i+p} value bit position, or the original X_i has to be moved to the $i + p$ position. The following table shows this for $n = 5, m = 0$:

Bit No.	4	3	2	1	0	·
Before	X_4	X_3	X_2	X_1	X_0	·
After 3 left	X_1	X_0	—	—	—	·

Thus, a shift left of p places is effectively multiplication by 2^p, provided the bits lost off the most significant end are all 0 (otherwise an *overflow* condition results), and further provided that 0s are shifted into the p least significant bit positions. Figure 2-5 shows the basic 1-bit shift for signed-magnitude numbers.

Division by 2^p yields the following modification to Equation 2-1:

$$2^{-p} V(X) = \sum_{i=0}^{n-1} X_i 2^{i-p} = \sum_{j=-p}^{n-1-p} X_{j+p} 2^j$$

or

$$2^{-p} V(X) = \sum_{j=0}^{n-1-p} X_{j+p} 2^j + \sum_{j=-p}^{-1} X_{j+p} 2^j \quad (2\text{-}5)$$

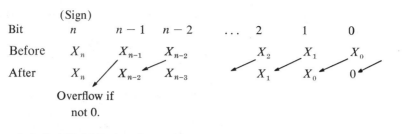

Overflow if
not 0.

a) Left shift, 1 bit, signed magnitude

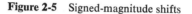

b) Right shift, 1 bit, signed magnitude

Figure 2-5 Signed-magnitude shifts

The second part of the expression contains those bits which are "shifted off" the right end of the number, and correspond to the remainder when $V(X)$ is divided by 2^p. The p most significant bits of the resulting word must be 0.

Thus with signed-magnitude representation, a left shift of p bits corresponds to multiplication by 2^p, with overflow a result if any of the p most significant bits of X are 1. A right shift corresponds to taking the quotient of the original word and 2^p, if dealing with integer representations.

When dealing with signed ones'-complement or two's-complement number systems, the sign bit enters into the operation in a direct way. Figure 2-6 shows how two's-complement numbers are shifted.

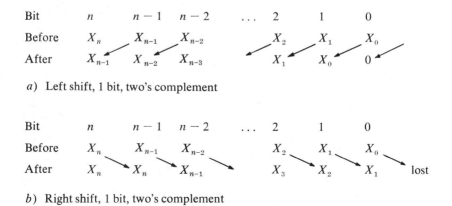

a) Left shift, 1 bit, two's complement

b) Right shift, 1 bit, two's complement

Figure 2-6 Two's-complement shifts

Let us first consider a left shift of the negative number X by p bits, by simple application of Part a of Figure 2-6 p *times*. As long as bits X_n through X_{n-p} are all 1, then the original number has a value of at least $-2^n + 2^{n-1} + \cdots + 2^{n-p} = --2^{n-p}$. Therefore we would expect no information to be lost by a left shift of p bits; that is no overflow occurs. If this condition exists, then a p-bit left shift of a negative number in two's-complement form corresponds to multiplication by 2^p.

In a right shift of p bits (see Part b of Figure 2-6), the sign bit must be maintained, to preserve the sign of the word. Information shifted off the right end of the word is lost, causing the value of the shifted word to be less than or equal to the value of the original word divided by 2^p, or equal to $\lfloor V_{2C}(X)/2^p \rfloor$.* When X is positive, this is the normal quotient, but when X is negative, it has a slightly different interpretation.

Example 2-10: $R = 2, n = 15, m = 0; X_{15}X_{14}X_{13} \cdots X_1X_0$.

Signed Magnitude: Same as positive numbers in two's complement.

Two's Complement:

	15 14 13 12	11 10 9 8	7 6 5 4	3 2 1 0
Positive numbers:				
$+1123_{10}$	0 0 0 0	0 1 0 0	0 1 1 0	0 0 1 1
Shift right 3 or 140 = $\lfloor 1123/8 \rfloor$	0 0 0 0	0 0 0 0	1 0 0 0	1 1 0 0
Shift left 4 or 17968 = (16 × 1123)	0 1 0 0	0 1 1 0	0 0 1 1	0 0 0 0
Shift left 5 with overflow (looks like negative number)	1 0 0 0	1 1 0 0	0 1 1 0	0 0 0 0
Negative numbers:				
-1123_{10}	1 1 1 1	1 0 1 1	1 0 0 1	1 1 0 1
Shift right 3 or − 141 = $\lfloor -1123/8 \rfloor$	1 1 1 1	1 1 1 1	0 1 1 1	0 0 1 1
Shift left 4 or − 17968 = (−1123 × 16)	1 0 1 1	1 0 0 1	1 1 0 1	0 0 0 0
Shift left 5 with overflow (looks like positive number)	0 1 1 1	0 0 1 1	1 0 1 0	0 0 0 0

The examples just shown illustrate one result of the lack of symmetry in positive and negative numbers in the two's-complement system. Note that the value of 0000 0100 0110 0011 after shifting right 3 places is $\lfloor 1123/8 \rfloor$

---

*$\lfloor Z \rfloor$ means the largest integer less than or equal to Z. This is commonly called the "floor" function of Z.

or 140 whereas the value of 1111 1011 1001 1101 after a 3-bit right shift is $\lfloor -1123/8 \rfloor$ or -141. This latter result, since humans divide in signed-magnitude form, is not the quotient of -1123 and 8. As a consequence, shifting right by p bits and converting to the two's-complement value does not yield the same result as converting to the two's complement, then shifting right by p bits. This lack of consistency in results when interchanging the order of some operations can create serious problems because it may not be expected by the user and may create errors that are difficult to find.

The effect of shifting in the ones'-complement system is easier to understand because the negative of a number is simply its bit-by-bit complement. Thus if a positive number is shifted right by p bits, this corresponds to taking the integer part of the original number divided by 2^p, provided 0s are shifted from the sign bit X_n into X_{n-1}. Then to obtain a similar result for negative numbers, we shift right by p bits, shifting 1s from X_n into X_{n-1}.

When shifting positive numbers left, if we do not shift a 1 into the sign bit and if 0s are shifted into the least significant bit position, then a p-bit shift corresponds to multiplication by 2^p. For negative numbers, no overflow occurs if we do not shift a 0 into X_n, and we must shift 1s into the least-significant-bit position. Figure 2-7 (on the following page) shows the basic 1-bit shift operation for ones'-complement numbers.

Example 2-11: $R = 2, n = 15, m = 0; X_{15}X_{14} \cdots X_1X_0.$

Ones' Complement:

	15 14 13 12	11 10 9 8	7 6 5 4	3 2 1 0
Positive numbers:				
$+2880$	0 0 0 0	1 0 1 1	0 1 0 0	0 0 0 0
Shift right 3 $360 = \lfloor 2880/8 \rfloor$	0 0 0 0	0 0 0 1	0 1 1 0	1 0 0 0
Shift right 7 $22 = \lfloor 2880/128 \rfloor$	0 0 0 0	0 0 0 0	0 0 0 1	0 1 1 0
Shift left 3 $23040 = 2880 \times 8$	0 1 0 1	1 0 1 0	0 0 0 0	0 0 0 0
Negative numbers:				
-2880	1 1 1 1	0 1 0 0	1 0 1 1	1 1 1 1
Shift right 7 $-22 = -\lfloor 2880/128 \rfloor$	1 1 1 1	1 1 1 1	1 1 1 0	1 0 0 1
Shift left 3 $-23040 = 2880 \times 8$	1 0 1 0	0 1 0 1	1 1 1 1	1 1 1 1

In summary, then, positive numbers are treated the same in all three number systems. A right arithmetic shift of p bits shifts 0 into X_{n-1}, and produces $\lfloor V(X)/2^p \rfloor$. A left arithmetic shift of p bits shifts 0 into X_0 and produces $2^p \times$

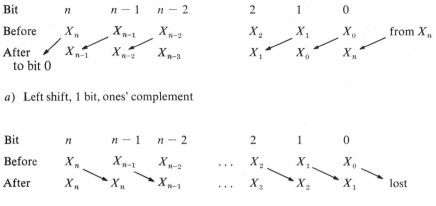

a) Left shift, 1 bit, ones' complement

b) Right shift, 1 bit, ones' complement

Figure 2-7   Ones'-complement shifts

$V(X)$ so long as X_n is not changed; that is, so long as no overflow occurs.

Negative signed-magnitude numbers are treated as if the number were positive, and the sign bit does *not* participate in the shift. An arithmetic right shift of negative two's-complement numbers involves shifting the sign (X_n) into X_{n-1}, preserving the sign and a p-bit shift produces $\lfloor V_{2C}(X)/2^p \rfloor$. A right shift of negative ones'-complement numbers is performed in the same way, but the result is $-\lfloor |V_{1C}(X)|/2^p \rfloor$. A left shift of a two's-complement number involves shifting 0s into X_0, whereas for ones' complement, X_n, the sign is shifted into X_0. The result is the same in both cases, however, so long as no overflow occurs: $V(X) \times 2^p$.

We observe, therefore, that shifting right a negative number in two's-complement form causes truncation towards the smaller value algebraically, while shifting right a number in ones'-complement form causes truncation towards the smaller *magnitude*. Thus the effect of shifting negative numbers in the ones'-complement system is the complement of the effect of shifting positive numbers, a desired result, whereas shifting negative numbers in the two's-complement case is not symmetrical with respect to the positive number case.

Shifting is frequently accomplished in computers by means of a *shift register*. A simple left-and-right-shift register constructed from delay-type flip/flops is shown in Figure 2-8. The dashed AND gate on the $X_0 D$ input is included to shift in the sign on left shift of ones'-complement numbers. For two's-complement numbers, that gate is eliminated, as is the OR gate on the same flip/flop, so that 0 is shifted into X_0 on a left shift. The sign bit of the shift register remains unchanged for left or right shift in either number system, so it has no inputs connected to it. In practical systems, shifting would be just one of several functions given such a register. In particular, loading of the register must also be accomplished. The gating to accomplish that function is not shown in Figure 2-8.

Next, in our consideration of arithmetic, we move to the process of *multiplication*. We consider the process as applied to signed-magnitude, two's-complement, and then ones' complement numbers.

Signed-magnitude multiplication is easiest to perform and to understand because the signs and the magnitudes can be treated separately. Thus the sign of the product is minus if either (but not both) the multiplier or the multiplicand is negative. Otherwise, the sign of the product is positive. Let us next consider the magnitude of the product. Let $\hat{B}$ be the magnitude portion of B, the multiplier, and $\hat{C}$ the magnitude for C, the multiplicand. Using Equation 2-1 and the requirement that the value of the product of $\hat{B} \times \hat{C}$ must be the product of the values, we obtain Equation 2-6.

$$V(\hat{B} \times \hat{C}) = V(\hat{B}) \times V(\hat{C}) = \left(\sum_{i=-m}^{n-1} B_i 2^i \right) \times \left(\sum_{i=-m}^{n-1} C_i 2^i \right)$$

$$= \sum_{i=-m}^{n-1} \left(B_i 2^i \times \left(\sum_{j=-m}^{n-1} C_j 2^j \right) \right) \qquad (2\text{-}6)$$

Equation 2-6 concerns the value of the product and the value of $\hat{B}$, $\hat{C}$. Let us for the moment move into the realm of binary arithmetic and see what operation *in binary* on $\hat{B}$ and $\hat{C}$ in Equation 2-6 might be related to:

$$\hat{B} \times \hat{C} = \sum_{i=-m}^{n-1} B_i \times (2^i \times (\hat{C})) \qquad (2\text{-}7)$$

Equation 2-7 suggests that if these operations are carried out properly, then Equation 2-6 will hold. But $(2^i \times \hat{C})$ simply represents an arithmetic left

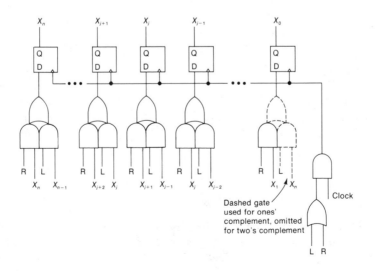

Figure 2-8   Shift register structure

shift of i bit positions, assuming no overflow or truncation. Since B_i is either 1 or 0, if B_i is 1, $B_i \times (2^i \times (\hat{C}))$ corresponds to the selection of the appropriate shifted value of $\hat{C}$, and if B_i is 0, that shifted value of $\hat{C}$ is ignored. To produce the summation, the selected shifted values of $\hat{C}$ are added together.

The following simple example will illustrate how this multiplication is accomplished in steps similar to the steps of multiplication humans are familiar with.

Example 2-12: Multiply 01101 by 10111 (13_{10} by 23_{10}).

$$9 \ 8 \ 7 \ 6 \ 5 \ 4 \ 3 \ 2 \ 1 \ 0 \leftarrow \text{Bit position}$$

$$
\begin{array}{llll}
& 0 \ 1 \ 1 \ 0 \ 1 & (\hat{B}) \\
& 1 \ 0 \ 1 \ 1 \ 1 & (\hat{C}) \\
\hline
& 0 \ 1 \ 1 \ 0 \ 1 & 2^0 \times C_0 \times \hat{B} \\
& 0 \ 1 \ 1 \ 0 \ 1 & 2^1 \times C_1 \times \hat{B} \\
& 0 \ 1 \ 1 \ 0 \ 1 & 2^2 \times C_2 \times \hat{B} \\
& 0 \ 0 \ 0 \ 0 \ 0 & 2^3 \times C_3 \times \hat{B} \\
& 0 \ 1 \ 1 \ 0 \ 1 & 2^4 \times C_4 \times \hat{B} \\
\hline
& 0 \ 1 \ 0 \ 0 \ 1 \ 0 \ 1 \ 0 \ 1 \ 1 & \hat{B} \times \hat{C}
\end{array}
$$

Value of $\hat{B} \times \hat{C}$ is 299_{10} which equals 13×23.

To implement a multiplication algorithm in iteration on i, we will use bit i of the multiplier to gate the multiplicand (shifted i places left) into the partial product accumulator. Because overflow and truncation can occur in shifting, destroying the simple arithmetic significance of the shift, attention must be paid to allowing the proper number of bits to appear in the partial products and developing sum as it develops. Consider numbers with n integer bits and m fractional bits, that is, $X_{n-1} X_{n-2} \cdots X_0 . X_{-1} \cdots X_{-m}$. The smallest representable number is 2^{-m}, and the product of two such numbers is 2^{-2m}; hence the product must have provision for $2m$ fractional digits. The largest representable number is $2^n - 2^{-m}$ in this system and the product of two such numbers is

$$2^{2n-1} - 2^{-2m} < 2^{2n} - 2 \cdot 2^{n-m} + 2^{-2m} < 2^{2n} - 2^{-2m}$$

Thus $2n - 1$ integer bits are insufficient, and $2n$ bits are sufficient to represent the product. This is a satisfying result, since we probably recall a rule of thumb that suggests that the product of 2 p-digit numbers is a $2p$-digit number (the sign bit doesn't count). Our product has the form

$$P_{2n-1} \, P_{2n-2} \cdots P_1 \, P_0 \, . \, P_{-1} \cdots P_{-2m}$$

Thus, the process of multiplying 2 $(m + n)$-bit numbers is as follows:

1. Set $i = -m$, set $\hat{P}(-m) = $ all zeros $(2n + 2m$ bits).
2. Extend the word of $\hat{C}$ by adding $n + m$ bit positions of zeros at the more significant end of the word, producing $\hat{C}(-m)$.
3. If $B_i = 1, \hat{P}(i + 1) = \hat{P}(i) + \hat{C}(i)$, else $\hat{P}(i + 1) = \hat{P}(i)$
4. $i = i + 1$, shift $\hat{C}(i)$ one bit left to produce $\hat{C}(i + 1)$
5. If $i = n$, go to 6, else go to 3.
6. $\hat{P}(n)$ contains the $2n + 2m$-bit product.

In this algorithm, the $\hat{P}(i)$ corresponds to the accumulating sum of the partial products, the selected $\hat{C}(i)$. In normal hand multiplication, we would write down the appropriate partial products in correct registration and then add them all up to obtain the product, as we did in Example 2-12. Usually a computer does this in an accumulating register, adding partial products one at a time to the developing product.

Example 2-13: $n = 5, m = 0$.

	9 8 7 6 5 4 3 2 1 0	← Bit position
B:	0 - - - - 0 1 1 0 1	$V(B) = 13$
C:	0 - - - - 1 0 1 1 1	$V(C) = 23$
$\hat{C}(0)$	0 0 0 0 0 1 0 1 1 1	
$\hat{P}(0)$	0 0 0 0 0 0 0 0 0 0	
$+\hat{C}(0)$	0 0 0 0 0 1 0 1 1 1	
$\hat{P}(1)$	0 0 0 0 0 1 0 1 1 1	
$+0$		
$\hat{P}(2)$	0 0 0 0 0 1 0 1 1 1	
$+\hat{C}(2)$	0 0 0 1 0 1 1 1 0 0	
$\hat{P}(3)$	0 0 0 1 1 1 0 0 1 1	
$+\hat{C}(3)$	0 0 1 0 1 1 1 0 0 0	
$\hat{P}(4)$	0 1 0 0 1 0 1 0 1 1	
$+0$		
$\hat{P}(5)$	0 1 0 0 1 0 1 0 1 1	$V(\hat{P}) = 299 = 13 \times 23$

Example 2-14: $n = 0, m = 4.$

$B:$	.0 1 0 1	$V(B) = .3125$
$A:$	.1 1 0 1	$V(C) = .8125$
$\hat{C}(-4)$	. 0 0 0 0 1 1 0 1	
$\hat{P}(-4)$	. 0 0 0 0 0 0 0 0	
$+\hat{C}(-4)$	. 0 0 0 0 1 1 0 1	
$\hat{P}(-3)$	. 0 0 0 0 1 1 0 1	
$+0$		
$\hat{P}(-2)$	. 0 0 0 0 1 1 0 1	
$+\hat{C}(-2)$	. 0 0 1 1 0 1 0 0	
$\hat{P}(-1)$	. 0 1 0 0 0 0 0 1	
$+0$		
$\hat{P}(0)$	. 0 1 0 0 0 0 0 1	$V(\hat{P}) = .25390625$
		$= (.3125) \times (.8125)$

Multiplication of signed two's-complement numbers could be treated in a similar fashion; that is, by converting to magnitudes, multiplying, and then recomplementing the result if negative. There are also direct ways to handle the operation without explicitly recognizing that either positive or negative numbers are involved. One such method for two's-complement multiplication is discussed here.

We will proceed from the expression for the two's-complement value of the number $B_n B_{n-1} \cdots B_0 . B_{-1} \cdots B_{-m}$, where B_n is the sign bit, to represent the product of two numbers, B and C:

$$V_{2C}(B \times C) = V_{2C}(B) \times V_{2C}(C) = \left[(-B_n 2^n) + \sum_{i=-m}^{n-1} B_i 2^i \right]$$

$$\times \left[(-C_n 2^n) + \sum_{j=-m}^{n-1} C_j 2^j \right]$$

$$= (-B_n 2^n) \times \left[(-C_n 2^n) + \sum_{j=-m}^{n-1} C_j 2^j \right]$$

$$+ \sum_{i=-m}^{n-1} B_i 2^i \times \left[(-C_n 2^n) + \sum_{j=-m}^{n-1} C_j 2^j \right]$$

$$(2\text{-}8)$$

Interpreting Equation 2-8 as we did Equation 2-6 in light of our knowledge of two's complement arithmetic operations, we can deduce that

$$B \times C = -B_n \times (2^n \times C) + \sum_{i=-m}^{n-1} B_i \times (2^i \times (C))$$

where B is in full two's-complement representation. Now if we use arithmetic shifts to obtain the product of 2^i and C, properly allowing the requisite digits to be added so that overflow and truncations do not occur, and add or not to the partial product depending or whether or not B_i is equal to 1 for i from $-m$ to $n - 1$, we will account for all but the sign of B. Finally, *subtracting 2^nC* (add -2^nC) from the partial product takes proper account of the effect of the sign bit.

The number of bits required in the final product is $2n + 2m + 1$, and is more than needed to handle positive numbers, since a bit is needed for the sign. This is sufficient to deal with all cases but that of multiplying two values of -2^n together, whose product, 2^{2n} is greater than $2^{2n} - 2^{-m}$, the largest representable positive number. This special case must be detected by a specific test and an overflow signaled if it occurs. However, this is related to the basic difficulty with the two's complement system that one representable number (-2^n) has no representable negative $(+2^n)$.

The algorithm for multiplication based on the foregoing is as follows:

1. Set $i = -m$, set $\hat{P}(-m) = $ all 0s $(2n + 2m + 1$ bits).
2. Extend C into $\hat{C}(-m)$ by copying $n + m$ sign bits (C_n) at the more significant end of the word.
   (Note: This yields $2^{-m}C$ in a word where

$$n' = 2n \quad \text{and} \quad m' = 2m.)$$

3. Use the ith multiplier bit, B_i, to form the next partial product, $\hat{C}(i)$, then accumulate:

   If $B_i = 1$, form $\hat{P}(i + 1) \leftarrow \hat{P}(i) + \hat{C}(i)$, else $\hat{P}(i + 1) \leftarrow \hat{P}(i)$.

4. $i \leftarrow i + 1$ and form $\hat{C}(i + 1)$ by shifting $\hat{C}(i)$ 1 bit left.
5. If $i = n$ go to 6, else go to 3.
6. If the sign of the multiplier is 1, subtract the multiplicand from the accumulated product:

   If $B_n = 1$, form $P(n + 1) \leftarrow \hat{P}(n) - \hat{C}(n)$, else $\hat{P}(n + 1) \leftarrow \hat{P}(n)$.

7. $\hat{P}(n + 1)$ contains the $2n + 2m + 1$-bit, signed, two's-complement product.

Example 2-15: $n = 4$, $m = 0$; B negative, C positive.

Step		8 7 6 5 4 3 2 1 0	← Bit position
	B:	1 0 1 1 1 .	$V_{2C}(B) = -9$
	C:	0 1 1 0 1 .	$V_{2C}(C) = +13$
2	$\hat{C}(0)$	0 0 0 0 0 1 1 0 1 .	$V_{2C}(\hat{C}(0)) = +13$
1	$\hat{P}(0)$	0 0 0 0 0 0 0 0 0 .	
3	$+ \hat{C}(0)$	0 0 0 0 0 1 1 0 1 .	
	$\hat{P}(1)$	0 0 0 0 0 1 1 0 1 .	
3	$+ \hat{C}(1)$	0 0 0 0 1 1 0 1 0 .	
	$\hat{P}(2)$	0 0 0 1 0 0 1 1 1 .	
4	$+ \hat{C}(2)$	0 0 0 1 1 0 1 0 0 .	
3	$\hat{P}(3)$	0 0 1 0 1 1 0 1 1 .	
	$+ 0$	0 0 0 0 0 0 0 0 0 .	
3	$\hat{P}(4)$	0 0 1 0 1 1 0 1 1 .	
6	$- \hat{C}(4)$	1 0 0 1 1 0 0 0 0 .	
	(+ two's comp.)		
7	$\hat{P}(5)$	1 1 0 0 0 1 0 1 1 .	$V_{2C}(\hat{P}(5)) = -117$
			$= (-9) \times (+13)$

Direct implementation of the foregoing algorithm would require a $2n + 2m + 1$-bit shift register to hold the shifting multiplicand $C(i)$, a $2n + 2m + 1$-bit adder and a $2n + 2m + 1$-bit product register. A slight rearrangement of Equation 2-7 yields:

$$B \times C = -B_n \times (2^n C) + \sum_{i=-m}^{n-1} 2^{-(n-i)} (B_i \times (2^n C)) \qquad (2\text{-}9)$$

This form suggests that for each bit of the multiplier that is a 1, the multiplicand is added to the most significant end of the developing product and the product is shifted right as more significant bits of the multiplier are considered.

When adding the multiplicand into the most significant end of the partial product, overflows can develop in the addition if a large-magnitude multiplicand is used and two successive multiplier bits are 1. To prevent this overflow information from being lost, an extra most-significant bit is added to C, the adder, and P. The final result will be taken from the $2n + 2m + 1$ least significant bits of P, and the overflow will have disappeared unless the case of $-2^n \times -2^n$ is encountered.

The algorithm is as follows:

1. Set $i = -m$ and set $P(-m) = 0$.
   (P has sign, $2n + 1$ integer bits, including an extra integer-guard bit,

and $2m$ fractional bits. $\widehat{C}$ is the multiplicand with only one bit of sign extension to $n + m + 2$ bits.)

2. Use the ith multiplier bit to form the next partial product and accumulate: If $B_i = 1$, form $\widehat{P}(i + 1) \leftarrow 2^{-1}\widehat{P}(i) + \widehat{C}(i)$, else $\widehat{P}(i + 1) \leftarrow 2^{-1}\widehat{P}(i)$.
3. $i \leftarrow i + 1$.
4. If $i = n$ go to 5, else go to 2.
5. If the sign of the multiplier is 1, subtract the multiplicand from the shifted, accumulated product: If $B_n = 1$, $\widehat{P}(n + 1) \leftarrow 2^{-1}\widehat{P}(n) - C(n)$, else $\widehat{P}(n + 1) \leftarrow 2^{-1}\widehat{P}(n)$.
6. $\widehat{P}(n + 1)$ contains the $2n + 2m + 1$-bit, signed, two's-complement product.

Figure 2-9 shows a block diagram of a realization of this algorithm, and Example 2-16 illustrates the operation of this realization. Initially, the $n + m + 1$ most significant bits of $\widehat{P}$ are cleared and the multiplier is inserted in the $n + m + 1$ least significant bits. Note the presence of the extra bit to avoid loss of information in the overflow case. Note also that even though this guard bit is needed at step $i = 1$, the final result is only $2n + 2n + 1$ bits and no overflow appears. The least significant bit of the $\widehat{P}$ register contains the bit of the multiplier being examined and controls whether $\widehat{C}$ or 0 is added to the feed-back, shifted, accumulated product. The final step, when bit n of the multiplier, the sign, is in the least significant position of the product register, is to *subtract* $\widehat{C}$ from the shifted, accumulated product by selecting the subtract function of the adder/subtractor.

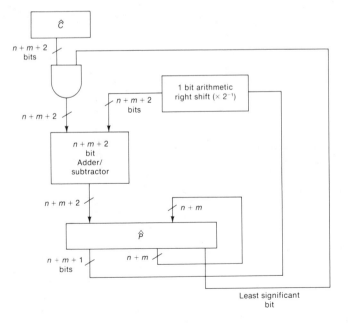

Figure 2-9 Block diagram of a two's-complement sequential multiplier

Example 2-16: $n = 4, m = 0$; B negative, C positive

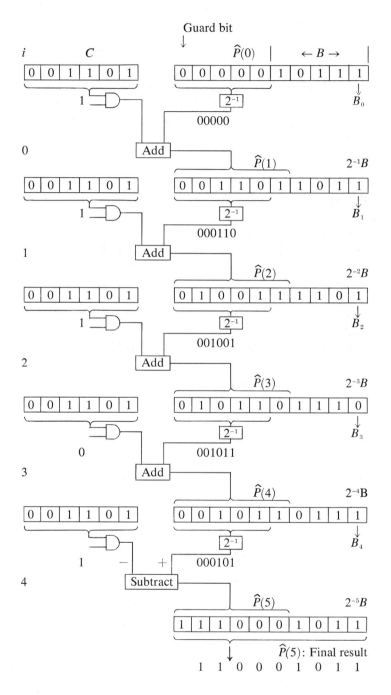

$$V_{2c}(\widehat{P}(5)) = -117 = (-9) \times (+13)$$

The realization shown in Figure 2-9 is a considerable improvement over the realization suggested by Examples 2-13 and 2-14, in that an adder of about $\frac{1}{2}$ the width required in those examples is needed and the multiplicand need not be stored in a double-length shift register.

The subtraction operation in step $i = n$ can be easily accomplished by forming the ones' complement of the multiplicand, using that as one input to the adder, and adding a 1 to the least significant bit of the adder by forcing a carry into the least significant adder bit.

Direct computation of the product in the two's-complement case requires $n + m + 1$ additions. Conversion of the operands to signed magnitude, then performing signed-magnitude multiplication and conversion back to two's complement if the product is negative, requires a conversion of operands, $n + m$ additions, and a conversion of result. Because the two's complement conversion involves an addition of 1 in the least significant bit, the latter method really involves $n + m + 2$ additions, and may therefore be slightly slower than the direct computation method.

A similar analysis will yield a similar algorithm for the direct multiplication of 2 ones'-complement numbers, although a more complex correction is required if the multiplier is negative. In that case a direct implementation of the multiplier requires, in the worst case, $n + m + 2$ additions. For this reason, and because forming the ones' complement is simple, it may be preferable to compute the ones'-complement product by converting to magnitudes, multiplying ($n + m$ additions), and then determining the product sign and recomplementing the product magnitude if the sign is negative.

In this portion of this chapter, we have presented multiplication algorithms for signed-magnitude and two's-complement number systems. Other algorithms are presented in the books by Chu [62] and Hwang [78] and in the paper on arithmetic by MacSorley [61].

The final arithmetic process which we will treat in this chapter is *division*. Rather than follow the previous pattern of developing algorithms for signed-magnitude, two's-complement, and ones'-complement schemes, we shall treat only the signed-magnitude method. Normally, division is formulated on the basis of integer divisor and dividend yielding an integer quotient and remainder. This interpretation is consistent with the Euclidian division algorithm, presented in Equation 2-10. Other interpretations of the numbers involved are possible, but are not common and will not be treated here. An integer Y divided by an integer D has an integer quotient Q and remainder R defined by:

$$\frac{Y}{D} = Q + \frac{R}{D} \qquad (2\text{-}10)$$

where normally $0 \leq R < D$.

We will first develop an algorithm for division that corresponds to the usual human technique for division. This algorithm is illustrated by Example 2-17 on the following page.

Example 2-17: Divide $D = 00110$ (6_{10}) into $Y = 10011$ (19_{10}).

```
              8 7 6 5 4 3 2 1 0 ← Bit position
                      0 0 0 1 1    Operation
  0 0 1 1 0 |0 0 0 0 1 0 0 1 1    Trial divisor = 2⁴D.
    −   0 0 1 1 0                  Subtract 2⁴D.
```

$$Y = 19_{10} \qquad D = 6_{10} \qquad Q = 3_{10} \qquad R(0) = 1_{10}$$

	Operation
$-\ \ 0\ 0\ 1\ 1\ 0$	Subtract $2^4 D$.
$1\ 1\ 0\ 1\ 1\ 0\ 0\ 1\ 1$	Negative, so restore by
$+\ \ 0\ 0\ 1\ 1\ 0$	adding back $2^4 D$; $Q_4 \leftarrow 0$.
$R(4)\ \ 0\ 0\ 0\ 0\ 1\ 0\ 0\ 1\ 1$	
$-\ \ \ \ 0\ 0\ 1\ 1\ 0$	Subtract $2^3 D$.
$1\ 1\ 1\ 1\ 0\ 0\ 0\ 1\ 1$	Negative, so restore by
$+\ \ \ \ 0\ 0\ 0\ 1\ 1\ 0$	adding back $2^3 D$; $Q_3 \leftarrow 0$.
$R(3)\ \ 0\ 0\ 0\ 0\ 1\ 0\ 0\ 1\ 1$	
$-\ \ \ \ \ \ 0\ 0\ 1\ 1\ 0$	Subtract $2^2 D$.
$1\ 1\ 1\ 1\ 1\ 1\ 0\ 1\ 1$	Negative, so restore by
$+\ \ \ \ \ \ 0\ 0\ 1\ 1\ 0$	adding back $2^3 D$; $Q_2 \leftarrow 0$.
$R(2)\ \ 0\ 0\ 0\ 0\ 1\ 0\ 0\ 1\ 1$	
$-\ \ \ \ \ \ \ \ 0\ 0\ 1\ 1\ 0$	Subtract $2^1 D$.
$R(1)\ \ 0\ 0\ 0\ 0\ 0\ 0\ 1\ 1\ 1$	Positive, so $Q_1 \leftarrow 1$.
$-\ \ \ \ \ \ \ \ \ \ 0\ 0\ 1\ 1\ 0$	Subtract $2^0 D$.
$R(0)\ \ \ \ \ \ \ \ \ \ 0\ 0\ 0\ 0\ 1$	Positive, so $Q_0 \leftarrow 1$.

Check: $Y = 19_{10}$ $D = 6_{10}$ $Q = 3_{10}$ $R(0) = 1_{10}$

$$\frac{19}{6} = 3 + \frac{1}{6}$$

One disadvantage of this method is the restoration required when we subtract too much from the current remainder. Fortunately, there is a technique of binary division called *nonrestoring,* which eliminates the extra steps. To see the basis for this method, consider that we have just subtracted $2^j D$ from $R(j + 1)$, producing a negative result. At the next step, we add $2^{j-1} D$ to $R(j)$. Now

$$R(j - 1) = R(j + 1) - 2^j D + 2^{j-1} D$$
$$= R(j + 1) - (2^j - 2^{j-1})D$$
$$= R(j + 1) - 2^{j-1} D$$

But, that is precisely the remainder we would have if we were to subtract $2^j D$ from $R(j)$, discover the negative result, restore by adding back $2^j D$, and then subtract $2^{j-1}D$. Thus, subtraction of $2^j D$ and then addition of $2^{j-1}D$ is equivalent to subtraction of $2^j D$, restoration by adding $2^j D$, and then subtraction of $2^{j-1}D$.

The difference between the restoring and nonrestoring algorithms is illustrated in Figure 2-10. Part *a* of Figure 2-10 shows the development of the partial remainder as successive trial divisors are subtracted and then added back if restoration is needed. Part *b* of Figure 2-10 shows the course of partial remainder development for the same numbers operated upon using the nonrestoring method. Note that the negative partial remainder values of -77, -29, and -5 all appear in both algorithms, as do the remainders of $+7$ and $+1$. Thus in this example, at least, the nonrestoring algorithm converges to the same final solution as the restoring algorithm does.

The nonrestoring method is next informally presented and illustrated by example, then analyzed, formally stated, and illustrated by other examples. We consider the case where $m = 0$, Y is the dividend, D the divisor, Q the quotient and $R(j)$ the jth partial remainder, Y, D, and Q have n bits, and are unsigned. The process is as follows:

1. Increase the number of digits in the dividend by $n - 1$ zeros, producing the initial partial remainder, and place the divisor below the extended dividend, aligning the leftmost digits. This establishes the first trial division as $2^{n-1}D$.
2. Subtract the trial divisor from the partial remainder.
3. If the result is positive, enter a 1 in the appropriate quotient bit. If the result is negative, we really should not have subtracted, so enter a 0 in the appropriate quotient bit.
4. If the partial remainder is positive, shift and subtract the trial divisor; if the partial remainder is negative, shift and add the trial divisor. Repeat step 3.

The final step in the operation, either adding or subtracting $2^0 D$, will not be corrected by subsequent operations to effect the equivalent of a restore operation if the final remainder is negative, so some special correction will be needed.

Let us analyze the meaning of the quotient bits and relate them to Equation 2-10.

$$R(n - 1) = Y - 2^{n-1}D \text{ always}$$

$$R(j - 1) = R(j) - 2^{j-1}D \text{ if } Q_j \text{ is 1}$$

$$R(j - 1) = R(j) + 2^{j-1}D \text{ if } Q_j \text{ is 0}$$

$$\text{or } R(j - 1) = R(j) + (1 - 2Q_j)2^{j-1}D$$

Combining these equations successively yields

$$R(0) = Y - \left[2^{n-1} - \sum_{j=1}^{n-1} (1 - 2Q_j)2^{j-1} \right] D$$

$$= Y - \left[2^{n-1} - \sum_{j=1}^{n-1} (2^{j-1}) + \sum_{j=1}^{n-1} Q_j 2^j \right] D$$

$$= Y - \left[\sum_{j=1}^{n-1} 2^j Q_j + 2^0 \right] D$$

Thus $R(0) = Y - Q \times D$ provided a 1 is inserted into bit Q_0, to account for the 2^0 appearing in the equation for $R(0)$. Therefore, the final step of the algorithm is as follows:

5. $Q_0 \leftarrow 1$, end.

The following example illustrates the method with the same numbers as Example 2-17.

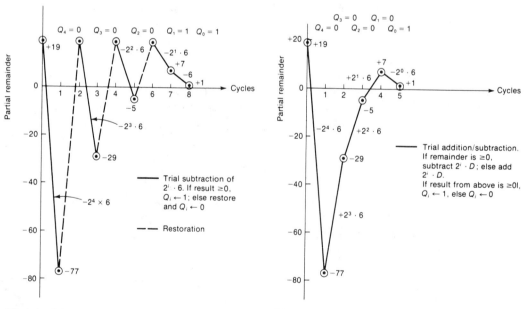

a) Restoring division, $19 \div 6$

b) Nonrestoring division, $19 \div 6$

Figure 2-10   Restoring and nonrestoring division

Example 2-18: Divide $D = 00110$ (6_{10}) into $Y = 10011$ (19_{10}). All negative numbers are signed magnitude.

	4 3 2 1 0 ← Bit position			
	0 0 0 1 1	*Step*		*Operation*

0 0 1 1 0 $\overline{\lvert0\ 0\ 0\ 0\ 1\ 0\ 0\ 1\ 1}$		1		Trial divisor $= 2^4 D$.
$-$ 0 0 1 1 0 0 0 0 0		2		Subtract $2^4 D$.
$R(4) -$ 1 0 0 1 1 0 1		3		Negative, so $Q_4 \leftarrow 0$.
$+$ 0 0 1 1 0 0 0 0		4		Shift and add $2^3 D$.
$R(3) -$ 1 1 1 0 1		3		Negative, so $Q_3 \leftarrow 0$.
$+$ 0 0 1 1 0 0 0		4		Shift and add $2^2 D$.
$R(2) -$ 0 0 1 0 1		3		Negative, so $Q^2 \leftarrow 0$.
$+$ 0 0 1 1 0 0		4		Shift and add $2^1 D$.
$R(1) +$ 0 0 1 1 1		3		Positive, so $Q_1 \leftarrow 1$.
$-$ 0 0 1 1 0		4		Shift and subtract $2^0 D$.
$R(0) +$ 0 0 1		5		$Q_0 \leftarrow 1$.

Check: $Y = 19_{10}$ $D = 6_{10}$ $Q = 3_{10}$ $R(0) = 1_{10}$

$$\frac{19}{6} = 3 + \frac{1}{6}$$

The method just presented still suffers from one shortcoming: It does not always leave a remainder that is nonnegative, the conventional situation in the implementation of the Euclidian division algorithm as shown in Equation 2-10. The modifications necessary to remove this shortcoming and to make the algorithm more suitable for hardware implementation are incorporated in the following algorithm for nonrestoring division of positive integers:

1. Extend the dividend by $n - 1$ digits, producing the initial partial remainder, $R(n)$, and place the divisor below the extended dividend, aligning the leftmost digits. This establishes the first trial divisor as $2^{n-1}D$. Set $j = n - 1$.

2. Subtract the trial divisor from the partial remainder.

3. If the result, $R(j)$, is positive, enter a 1 in the least-significant quotient bit. If the result is negative, enter a 0.

4. Shift the remainder and quotient 1 bit left, producing $2 \times R(j)$.

5. If the result, $R(j)$, is positive, compute $R(j - 1) = 2 \times R(j) - 2^{n-1}D$. If $R(j)$ is negative, compute $R(j - 1) = 2 \times R(j) + 2^{n-1}D$.

6. Set $j = j - 1$.
7. If $j > 0$, go to step 3; else go to step 8.
8. If $R(0)$ is negative, compute $R'(0) = R(0) + 2^{n-1}D$ and set $Q_0 = 0$, else, set $Q_0 = 1$.
9. End.

Step 8 checks for a negative remainder and makes the appropriate correction to the remainder (actually a restore operation) and to the quotient. Recall that at the end of step 8 the correct quotient is obtained by forcing a 1 in Q_0. Hence if no correction to $R(0)$ is needed, step 9 simply sets the necessary 1 into Q_0. If, however, restoration of the remainder is necessary by adding $2^{n-1}D$ to $R(0)$, 2^0 must be subtracted from Q, in effect changing Q_0 from 1 to 0.

Example 2-19: Divide $D = 00111$ (7_{10}) into $Y = 01111$ (15_{10}) for $n = 5$. All negative numbers are in two's-complement form.

D	R	Q	Step	Operation
4 3 2 1 0	9 8 7 6 5 4 3 2 1 0	4 3 2 1 0	*Step*	*Operation*
0 0 1 1 1	0 0 0 0 0 0 1 1 1 1	- - - - -	1	
-2^4D	1 1 1 0 0 1		2	Subtract 2^4D
$R(4)$	1 1 1 0 0 1 1 1 1 1	- - - - 0	3	
$2 \times R(4)$	1 1 0 0 1 1 1 1 1 -	- - - 0 -	4	Shift left
$+2^4D$	0 0 0 1 1 1	- - - 0 -	5	Add 2^4D
$R(3)$	1 1 1 0 1 0 1 1 1 -	- - - 0 0	3	
$2 \times R(3)$	1 1 0 1 0 1 1 1 - -	- - 0 0 -	4	Shift left
$+2^4D$	0 0 0 1 1 1	- - 0 0 -	5	Add 2^4D
$R(2)$	1 1 1 1 0 0 1 1 - -	- - 0 0 0	3	
$2 \times R(2)$	1 1 1 0 0 1 1 - - -	- 0 0 0 -	4	Shift left
$+2^4D$	0 0 0 1 1 1	- 0 0 0 -	5	Add 2^4D
$R(1)$	0 0 0 0 0 0 1 - - -	- 0 0 0 1	3	
$2 \times R(1)$	0 0 0 0 0 1 - - - -	0 0 0 1 -	4	Shift left
-2^4D	1 1 1 0 0 1	0 0 0 1 -	5	Add -2^4D
$R(0)$	1 1 1 0 1 0 - - - -			No shift performed
$+2^4D$	0 0 0 1 1 1	0 0 0 1 0	8	Add 2^4D
$R'(0)$	0 0 0 0 0 1 - - - -	0 0 0 1 0		

Check: $Y = 15_{10}$ $D = 7_{10}$ $Q = 2_{10}$ $R'(0) = 1_{10}$

$$\frac{15}{7} = 2 + \frac{1}{7}$$

Several things in this example are worthy of mention:

1. An extra bit is included in R and in $2^{n-1}D$ so that the most significant bit can be used to tell whether the remainder is positive (0) or negative (1).

2. Subtraction is accomplished by adding the two's complement of $2^{n-1}D$.

3. Negative remainders are in two's complement form.

4. There are always sufficient unused bits at the right end of the remainder register for all but one of the quotient bits.

Now, let us consider a simple hardware realization of a division algorithm. Figure 2-11 shows the hardware structure required to realize the algorithm for nonrestoring division. Example 2-20 illustrates the operation of this hardware.

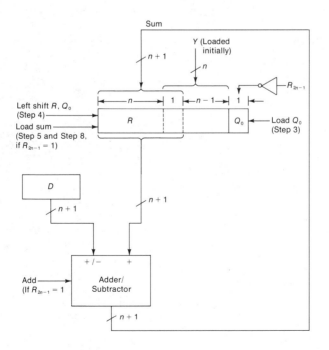

Figure 2-11 Nonrestoring divider structure

Example 2-20: $n = 5; D = 00101\ (5_{10}); Y = 11000\ (24_{10}).$

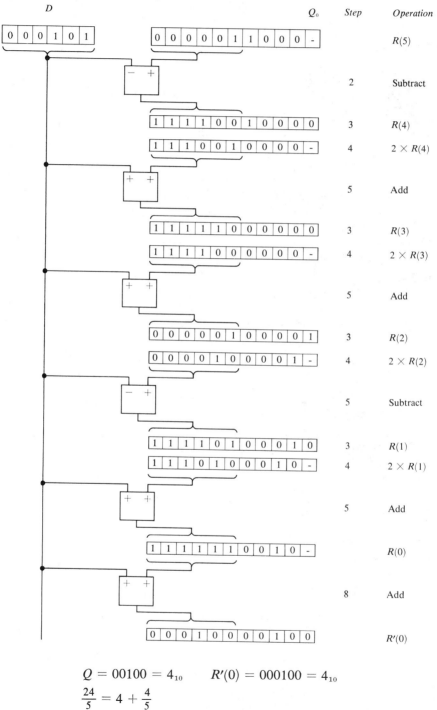

$$Q = 00100 = 4_{10} \qquad R'(0) = 000100 = 4_{10}$$
$$\frac{24}{5} = 4 + \frac{4}{5}$$

There exist direct methods for dividing signed two's and ones' complement numbers; however, they tend to require no fewer steps (add/subtracts) than converting to signed-magnitude and then employing the algorithm just discussed.

PROBLEMS

1. We are working with binary numbers containing 15 information bits plus 1 sign bit, of the form: $X_{15}X_{14} \cdot \ldots . X_0$.
   a) Two's-complement negative numbers:
      1) Represent B and C, where $V_{2C}(B) = 2583_{10}$ and $V_{2C}(C) = -2583_{10}$.
      2) Shift B and C 5 bits right arithmetically and evaluate results.
      3) Shift B and C 3 bits left and evaluate results.
      4) Comment on the results of 2 and 3.
   b) Repeat part a for the ones'-complement system.

2. Multiply the following numbers in the indicated systems. Check your results. The most significant bit in all cases is the sign.
   a) $(0.320_8) \times (1.510_8)$ in signed-magnitude $(n = 0, m = 9)$
   b) $(01101110_2) \times (10011001_2)$ in two's complement $(n = 7, m = 0)$
   c) $(FF0A_{16}) \times (003F_{16})$ in two's complement $(n = 15, m = 0)$
   Hint: Convert all numbers to binary before proceeding.

3. Carry out the division algorithm for the following set of unsigned numbers, $n = 6$, and check the results:
   a) $D = 010000$ $Y = 001110$
   b) $D = 111001$ $Y = 100111$
   c) $D = 000100$ $Y = 101011$

Other Number Representations

In addition to the simple binary representation studied in the previous section, other codes are used to represent numbers in certain circumstances. Sometimes decimal numbers are represented by using a 4-bit binary code for each digit. Nonweighted codes are also used. These are codes in which the value of a number cannot be expressed as a sum of weighted digit values such as in Equations 2-1, 2-2, or 2-3. Finally, extra digits can be added to provide error detecting or correcting capability.

The most straightforward of the decimal codes is the *Binary-Coded Decimal* representation. In this representation, each digit is represented by a conventional 4-bit binary number. Thus, each 4-bit digit can take on the value 0000 to 1001. Values larger than 1001 are not allowed since they correspond to values greater than or equal to $R = 10$. As an example, the 4-digit BCD version of the number 5830 is represented as

$$X_{33} \; X_{32} \; X_{31} \; X_{30} \qquad X_{23} \; X_{22} \; X_{21} \; X_{20} \qquad X_{13} \; X_{12} \; X_{11} \; X_{10} \qquad X_{03} \; X_{02} \; X_{01} \; X_{00}$$

| 0 | 1 | 0 | 1 | | 1 | 0 | 0 | 0 | | 0 | 0 | 1 | 1 | | 0 | 0 | 0 | 0 |

Arithmetic involving BCD representation of numbers is based primarily on the rules of decimal arithmetic and secondarily on performing binary operations on the digits themselves. For example, the addition of two n-digit BCD numbers involves for each digit, the addition of the binary versions of the digits and the 1-bit decimal carry into the digit. If the sum is 1001 or less, the decimal carry out of that digit is 0 and the binary sum is the BCD version of the sum digit. If the sum is 1010 or greater, a decimal carry out of 1 is generated and the decimal sum is generated by subtracting 1010 (10) or by adding 0110 modulo 16.

Another commonly used code is the *excess-three code*. In this case a normal decimal digit is represented by the binary code for the digit plus 3. Thus, 0_{10} has code 0011, 6_{10} is 1001, and 9_{10} is 1100. This code has the advantage that the negative of a number in this representation is easily related to its ones' complement. A more practical advantage appears when addition of two excess-three numbers is considered. If the codes for two digits and a decimal carry into the digit are all added together, the binary value of the sum is 6 greater than the actual sum; 0110 corresponds to 0_{10} and 1111 to 9_{10}. Thus, if the sum is 16 or greater, a decimal carry is needed and the sum is corrected by adding 3. Otherwise the sum is corrected by subtracting 3 or by adding 13 modulo 16.

Another basically binary code which finds some application is a so-called Gray code. This is a code whose characteristic is that if you arrange the code representations in numerical order of their value, adjacent code words differ in one and only one bit position. Table 2-3 shows one such code for four bits. The next code word in sequence is obtained by changing one bit in the least significant position which yields a new code word.

One very important application for such codes is in mechanical-to-binary encoders such as shaft encoders, which give a binary representation of some parameter such as angle. For example, in the case of the shaft encoder, if a normal binary code were used, at some point, a transition between 0001111 and

TABLE 2-3. Sixteen-Value Gray Code

Value	Code	Value	Code
0	0000	8	1100
1	0001	9	1101
2	0011	10	1111
3	0010	11	1110
4	0110	12	1010
5	0111	13	1011
6	0101	14	1001
7	0100	15	1000

TABLE 2-4. CODE FOR A 36-ELEMENT GRAY CODE SHAFT ENCODER

Angle (degrees)	Code	Angle (degrees)	Code	Angle (degrees)	Code	Angle (degrees)	Code
0-10	000000	90-100	001101	180-190	110000	270-280	111101
10-20	000001	100-110	001111	190-200	110001	280-290	111111
20-30	000011	110-120	001110	200-210	110011	290-300	111110
30-40	000010	120-130	001010	210-220	110010	300-310	111010
40-50	000110	130-140	001011	220-230	110110	310-320	111011
50-60	000111	140-150	001001	230-240	110111	320-330	111001
60-70	000101	150-160	011001	240-250	110101	330-340	111000
70-80	000100	160-170	011000	250-260	110100	340-350	101000
80-90	001100	170-180	010000	260-270	111100	350-360	100000

0010000 must be made. Since the angle may vary continuously, the point of transition must occur exactly at the same place for each bit or else some code such as 0000100 representing a drastically different angle may be spuriously generated. Table 2-4 shows a code suitable for a shaft encoder with 10-degree resolution.

Other codes for the representation of numbers have been devised with specific purposes in mind. One important purpose, especially for data held in auxiliary storage media, is for detection and correction of errors. These codes involve the use of parity checks or other redundant data with which the validity of the information can be determined. A complete description of this topic is beyond the scope of this chapter, so we mention in passing codes for correction of single errors [Hamming, 50] and codes for correction of errors in arithmetic units [Massey and Garcia, 72]. In each type of code some patterns of 0s and 1s correspond to valid data and other patterns to data contaminated by errors. The idea is that any highly probable error will change a valid datum into a pattern that is invalid, and validity can be easily checked. The Hamming codes can detect combination of two random changes, and can correct any single random change. The arithmetic codes are similar except that the changes produced by an error in a carry circuit are additive and affect the entire carry chain rather than a single bit. The interested reader should consult the references for more information.

PROBLEMS

1. Present a formal algorithm for the addition of two n-digit, excess-three numbers, using as the basic operation the binary addition of two 4-bit numbers.

2. Devise a 1-digit multiplication table in BCD. Show the partial product as a 2-digit BCD number.

3. By trial and error, construct a Gray code to encode a shaft into 16 sectors.

Word Size

The size of a word, the unit of information containing the representation of a number, is usually fixed by physical constraints for a particular computer system. Thus, selection of a word size of b for a computer causes the fixed-point number to have b significant bits. Sometimes, however, it is desired to have operations and data be defined for a higher degree of significance. One way to accomplish this is to define a class of double-word arithmetic instructions, where each number is represented by two standard words. One physical word contains the less significant half and the other word contains the more significant half. One application of this can be seen in multiplication, where the product of two n-bit words produces a $2n$-bit product. This multiplication of two single words produces a double word. The programmer must decide or must equip the program to decide how to round the result back to n bits or whether to carry on the calculations in double words. The decision to discard significant bits normally has to be made at some level of significance, for if we choose to carry double words as our standard, the product of two double words yields a quadruple word, and so on.

Also, there are operations that reduce the level of significance of a result. For example, the difference of two nearly equal large numbers has many fewer significant digits than either number. To cope with this problem of increasing and decreasing significance during the course of a computation, a variable word length can be used. This word length normally is some multiple of the actual physical word length. Thus we might address the least significant end of a number, encountering first a number which specifies the number of words which make up the number. The arithmetic then proceeds reading successive physical words until the specified number of words are processed. This scheme on the face of it would appear to be quite reasonable; however, problems involved with detection of the sign of the number and the position of the radix point may make the whole process more cumbersome than the result justifies [Avizienis, 64]. Instead, what is commonly done is to allow for two degrees of significance for numbers and to then use whichever one is justified to meet the particular needs of the program.

Another problem with the fixed radix-point and fixed word-size representations is overflow in addition and multiplication. Overflow prevention requires proper scaling of the values throughout the program and the detection of overflow to signal an incorrect result. The most common solution to the problem is to use the computer equivalent of scientific notation, *floating-point numbers*, which are treated in detail in the next section of this chapter.

Floating-point Numbers

A floating-point number is similar to the familiar scientific notation that allows human representation of very large or very small numbers. The number consists of two parts—a signed, fixed-point (usually fractional) part often called the *mantissa* and a part called the *exponent*. In scientific notation the exponent is the power of 10 by which the mantissa is multiplied to produce the true value of the number. In floating-point representation the same relation holds except the exponent is the power of the radix of the representation.

Types of Floating-point Representation   There exists a large number of possible variations in the way that floating-point numbers are represented, such as variation in radix, treatment of exponent and matissa signs, and word size. Rather than treat all possible variations in general, we consider only those few in common use and try to call attention to some general principles as they emerge in this treatment.

The simplest type is the one used by the Burroughs B-5500, where both the mantissa and the exponent are in signed-magnitude form. An example of this type of number follows, where the radix is 8 and numbers are shown in their octal representation.

Sign	Sign of exponent	Exponent	Mantissa
(1 bit)	(1 bit)	(6 bits)	(39 bits)
0	0	03	0000000000053

which converts to $53_8 \times 8^3 = 53{,}000_8$ or $5 \times 4096 + 3 \times 512 = 22{,}016_{10}$.

Many other types of representation exist; Table 2-5 shows the characteristics of some of the commonly used representations, based on a word whose bits are numbered starting with bit 0 at the left-hand end.

The proposed standard is worth some special mention; illustrated in Table 2-5 is the normalized nonzero version of the standard [Coonen, 79].

The unusual part of this representation is that any number with a nonzero exponent representation must be nonzero in value and hence is in normalized form. In this form, there is an assumed 1, called the *hidden bit,* in the bit position just to the left of the actual mantissa. This provides an effective 24-significant-bit mantissa stored in 23 bits. The IBM base-16 system has a worst case of only 21 significant bits when the high-order hex digit is 0001. The proposed standard thus supplies almost a full decimal digit of precision more than the IBM system's worst case. On the other hand, the proposed standard's exponent range is approximately $10^{\pm 38}$, while the IBM system provides a range of approximately twice that, $10^{\pm 76}$.

There are several characteristics of floating-point words to consider, a primary one being the lack of uniqueness of representation; for example 5.3×10^1 is the same number as 0.53×10^2, yet it has these two different representations (and others). This characteristic makes comparison of numbers difficult and consequently floating-point numbers are usually represented in normalized form, where the mantissa is always represented with a nonzero most significant digit. (Thus our first example, showing a Burroughs floating-point number, is not normalized.) Another advantage of normalization is that the maximum number of significant digits is retained in the representation. To see

TABLE 2-5. FLOATING NUMBER SYSTEMS

	Proposed Standard (Normalized)	IBM System 360, 370	Burroughs B-5500	Control Data 6000, 7000 Series
Bits used:	0–31	0–31	1–47	0–59
Radix:	2	16	8	8
Radix point:	Before first bit (with assumed 1 to left)	Before first digit	After last digit	After last digit
Mantissa				
Sign position	0	0	1	0
Value position	9–31	8–31	9–47	12–59
Representation	Signed magnitude, fractional, normalized with most significant 1 assumed	Signed magnitude	Signed magnitude	Ones' complement of *entire word*
Exponent				
Sign position	—	1	2	1
Value position	1–8	1–7	3–8	1–11
Representation	Value + 127 (a nonzero number must have a nonzero representation)	Value plus 64	Signed magnitude	*Value + 1024 if ≥ 0; Value + 1023 if < 0.
Range of value	−126 to 127	−64 to +63	−63 to +63	−1023 to +1023

* An exponent of 1777_8 is possible; it corresponds to -0 exponent and denotes an "indefinite" operand.

this advantage, consider the following example involving the addition of two 5-digit floating-point decimal numbers:

Unnormalized: Add $.00700 \times 10^0$ and $.00020 \times 10^{-2}$.
Aligning the number with the smaller exponent and adding yields:

$$.00700 \times 10^0$$
$$.00000 \times 10^0 \quad \text{(2 shifted off right end of number)}$$
$$\overline{.00700 \times 10^0}$$

Normalized: Add $.70000 \times 10^{-2}$ and $.20000 \times 10^{-5}$.
Aligning the number with the smaller exponent and adding yields:

$$.70000 \times 10^{-2}$$
$$.00020 \times 10^{-2}$$
$$\overline{.70020 \times 10^{-2}}$$

Therefore, in the normalized case, we preserve the full five digits of significance in contrast to the effective three digits of significance in the specific unnormalized example.

The proposed standard goes one step farther and assumes in the normalized case that the most significant bit is always 1 and does not explicitly include that bit in the representation, thus giving it one more bit of precision.

Example 2-21: For the decimal number -53851_{10} the signed-magnitude representation in various systems is:

Hexadecimal	$-$ D 2 5 B
Binary	$-$1101 0010 0101 1011
Binary	$-$001 101 001 001 011 011.
Octal	$-$ 1 5 1 1 3 3 .
Binary scientific	$-1.101\ 001\ 001\ 011\ 011\ 000\ 000 \times 10^{15}$ $(10_2 = 2_{10})$

Hexadecimal scientific	$-.\text{D25B} \times 10^{+4}$	$(10_{16} = 16_{10})$
Octal scientific	$-.151133 \times 10^{+6}$	$(10_8 = 8_{10})$

Bit positions	0 1234567	8901 2345 6789 0123 4567 8901
IBM representation	1 1000100	1101 0010 0101 1011 0000 0000
Bit positions	0 12345678	901 234 567 890 123 456 789 01
Standard representation	1 10001110	101 001 001 011 011 000 000 00

Zero is an important number to be represented. In all of the example systems shown, it is represented by a 0 exponent field, plus a 0 mantissa. When the exponent is 0 in the case of the standard representation, a most significant *1* is *not* assumed. Example 2-22 shows the value of zero in the IBM and standard system.

Example 2-22:

IBM representation:

Bit positions	0 1234567	8901 2345 6789 0123 4567 8901
	0 0000000	0000 0000 0000 0000 0000 0000

Standard representation:

Bit positions	0 12345678	901 234 567 890 123 456 789 01
	0 00000000	000 000 000 000 000 000 000 00

Example 2-23: For the decimal number $+.011718750$, the signed-magnitude representation in various systems is:

Hexadecimal	+ 0 3
Binary	+.0000 0011
Binary	+.000 000 110
Octal	+ 0 0 6
Binary scientific	$+1.1 \times 10^{-7}$
Hexadecimal scientific	$+.3 \times 10^{-1}$

Bit positions	0 1234567	8901 2345 6789 0123 4567 8901
IBM representation	0 0111111	0011 0000 0000 0000 0000 0000
Bit positions	0 12345678	901 234 567 890 123 456 789 01
Standard representation	0 01111000	100 000 000 000 000 000 000 00

Floating-point numbers represent a much wider range of values than do fixed-point numbers. For example, the largest IBM floating-point number is approximately 1×16^{63} whereas the smallest normalized nonzero positive number is approximately 1×16^{-64}.

Arithmetic Floating-point arithmetic is relatively simply performed in the cases of multiplication and division, since the mantissa and exponents can be treated separately. However, in addition and subtraction, the exponents of the two numbers must be made equal by "unnormalizing" the number with the smaller exponent. In any of the cases overflow conditions and underflow conditions must be watched and treated properly to obtain correct results.

Let us consider multiplication and addition in some detail. First, though, we adopt some simple conventions:

> B,C refer to the binary words.
> $m_r(B)$ refers to the representation of the mantissa of B.
> $m(B)$ refers to the value of the mantissa of B.
> $e_r(B)$ refers to the representation of the exponent of B.
> $e(B)$ refers to the value of the exponent of B.

The multiplication procedure is as follows:

1. Form the double-length product $m(P) = m(B) \times m(C)$.
2. Form the sum $e(B) + e(C) = e(P)$.
3. Zero detection:
   a) If $m(B)$ or $m(C)$ is 0: force $m(P)$ to be 0 and $e(P)$ to be most negative value. (Force P to be true zero.)
4. Normalize the double-length product.
5. Special cases for normalized result:
   a) If $e(P)$ produced an overflow when formed and $e(P) > 0$: force $m(P)$ to be 0 and $e(P)$ to be largest positive exponent.
   b) If $e(P)$ produced an overflow bit and $e(P) < 0$: force $m(P)$ to be 0 and $e(P)$ to be most negative exponent.
6. Round the product to the appropriate word size, renormalizing if necessary.

The above algorithm is deficient in the respect that it treats all cases of underflow by forcing the result to be zero. It is possible that a product may suffer underflow when it is normalized, but an unnormalized representation may exist without underflow, i.e., $e(P) = 0$, representing the most negative exponent. Representing such a number is possible with the proposed standard by assuming that any number with $e_r = 0$ (most negative exponent) is unnormalized and that there is no hidden bit in the mantissa when $e_r = 0$.

The process for division is similar, but will not be covered in detail.

Example 2-24:

1. Form the product of B and C (using IBM 360 representation):

```
Bit position      0   1234567   8901 2345 6789 0123 4567 8901
           B = 1    0100011   1010 0101 1000 0011 0000 0000
           C = 0    0011000   0001 0000 0000 0000 0000 0000
```

$$m(B) = -.A58300_{16} \qquad\qquad e_r(B) = 43_8$$
$$e(B) = e_r(B) - 100_8$$
$$= -35_8$$
$$m(C) = .10000_{16} \qquad\qquad e_r(C) = 30_8$$
$$e(C) = -50_8$$
$$m(P) = m(B) \times m(C) \qquad e(P) = e(B) + e(C)$$
$$= -.0A5830_{16} \qquad\qquad = -105_8 < -100_8$$

Normalize:
$$m(P') = -.A58300_{16} \qquad\qquad e(P') = -106_8$$

Case 5b occurs, hence force $P'' = 0$.
$$m(P'') = 0 \qquad\qquad e(P'') = -100_8$$
$$e_r(P'') = 000_8$$

```
Bit position      0   1234567   8901 2345 6789 0123 4567 8901
        P'' = 0    0000000   0000 0000 0000 0000 0000 0000
```

2. Form the product of B and C (using IBM 360 representation):

```
Bit position      0   1234567   8901 2345 6789 0123 4567 8901
           B = 1    0100011   1010 0101 1000 0011 0000 0000
           C = 1    1101000   0001 0000 0000 0000 0000 0001
```

$$m(B) = -.A58300_{16} \qquad\qquad e_r(B) = 43_8$$
$$e(B) = -35_8$$
$$m(C) = -.100001_{16} \qquad\qquad e_r(C) = 150_8$$
$$e(C) = 50_8$$
$$m(P) = m(B) \times m(C) \qquad e(P) = e(B) + e(C)$$
$$= .0A5830A583_{16} \qquad\qquad = 13_8$$

Normalize:
$$M(P') = .A5830A583_{16} \qquad\qquad e(P') = 12_8$$

Round to 6 digits:
$$m(P'') = .A5830A_{16} \qquad\qquad e(P'') = 12_8$$
$$e_r(P'') = 112_8$$

```
Bit position      0   1234567   8901 2345 6789 0123 4567 8901
        P'' = 0    1001010   1010 0101 1000 0011 0000 1010
```

3. Form the product of B and C (using the proposed standard):

Bit position   0   12345678   901 234 567 890 123 456 789 01
$\quad\quad B = 0$ 10001111   011 000 000 000 000 000 000 00
$\quad\quad C = 1$ 01111010   111 000 000 000 000 000 000 00

$$m_r(B) = +.30_8 \qquad\qquad e_r(B) = 217_8$$
$$m(B) = +1.30_8* \qquad\qquad e(B) = e_r(B) - 177_8$$
$$= 20_8$$

$$m_r(C) = -.70_8 \qquad\qquad e_r(C) = 172_8$$
$$m(C) = -1.70_8* \qquad\qquad e(C) = -5_8$$
$$m(P) = m(B) \times m(C) \qquad e(P) = e(B) + e(C)$$
$$m(P) = -2.45_8 \qquad\qquad e(P) = 13_8$$
$$= -10.100\ 101_2$$

Normalize:

$$m(P') = -1.010\ 010\ 100_2 \qquad e(P') = 14_8$$
$$= -1.224_8$$
$$m_r(P') = -.224_8 \qquad\qquad e_r(P') = 14_8 + 177_8 = 213_8$$

Bit position   0   12345678   901 234 567 890 123 456 789 01
$\quad\quad P' = 1$ 10001011   010 010 100 000 000 000 000 00

Figure 2-12 shows the basic structure of a hardware realization of a floating-point multiplier. The basic parts of this multiplier are a signed integer adder, an integer multiplier, a shifting unit for normalization, and a simple adder to perform the round operation.

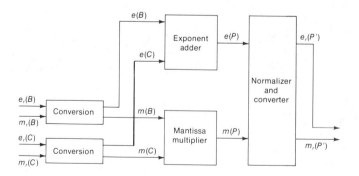

Figure 2-12   Floating-point multiplier structure

---

*Recall that there is an assumed most significant 1 bit associated with the value of normalized standard numbers.

The addition procedure is as follows (assume $e(B) \leq e(C)$):

1. Set $e(S) = e(C)$.
2. Form $e(C) - e(B)$ and shift $m(B)$ right by that number of digits. (Alignment)
3. Form $m(S) = m(B) + m(C)$.
4. If $m(S) = 0$, then set $e(S) =$ most negative exponent; else normalize for overflow or cancellation and adjust $e(S)$ if necessary.
5. Round $m(S)$ and if overflow shift and adjust $e(S)$.
6. Test for exponent overflow or underflow and if necessary set correct result.

Example 2-25:

1. Add B and C (using IBM representation):

Bit position   0   1234567   8901 2345 6789 0123 4567 8901

$$B = 1 \quad 1000000 \quad 1010\ 0101\ 0011\ 1000\ 0000\ 0000$$
$$C = 0 \quad 1000000 \quad 1010\ 0101\ 0111\ 1010\ 1111\ 1111$$

$m(B) = -.A53800_{16}$	$e(B) = 0_8$	$e_r(B) = 100_8$
$m(C) = +.A57AFF_{16}$	$e(C) = 0_8$	$e_r(C) = 100_8$
$m(S) = .0042FF_{16}$	$e(S) = 0_8$	

Normalize:

$$m(S') = .42FF00_{16} \qquad e(S') = -2_8 \qquad e_r(S') = 76_8$$

Bit position   0   1234567   8901 2345 6789 0123 4567 8901

$$S' = 0 \quad 0111110 \quad 0100\ 0010\ 1111\ 1111\ 0000\ 0000$$

2. Add B and C (using standard representation):

Bit position   0   12345678   901 234 567 890 123 456 789 01

$$B = 1 \quad 01111100 \quad 001\ 001\ 010\ 000\ 000\ 010\ 000\ 00$$
$$C = 1 \quad 10000010 \quad 111\ 111\ 111\ 110\ 001\ 101\ 000\ 01$$

$m_r(B) = -.11200200_8$	$e_r(B) = 174_8$
$m(B) = -1.11200200_8$	$e(B) = -3_8$
$m_r(C) = -.77761502_8$	$e_r(C) = 202_8$
$m(C) = -1.77761502_8$	$e(C) = 3_8$

Align and add:

$m(C) = -001.111\ 111\ 111\ 110\ 001\ 101\ 000\ 01$	$e(C) = 3_8$
$m(B') = -000.000\ 001\ 001\ 001\ 010\ 000\ 000\ 01$	$e(B') = 3_8$
$m(S) = -010.000\ 001\ 000\ 111\ 011\ 101\ 000\ 10$	$e(S) = 3_8$

Overflow has occurred in addition, so normalize by shifting $m(S)$ right.

$$m(S') = -001.000\ 000\ 100\ 011\ 101\ 110\ 100\ 01 \qquad e(S') = 4_8$$
$$= -1.00435642_8$$
$$m_r(S') = -.00435642_8 \qquad\qquad e_r(S') = e(S') + 177_8 = 203_8$$

Bit position   0   12345678   901 234 567 890 123 456 789 01
$$S' = 1 \quad 10000011 \quad 000\ 000\ 100\ 011\ 101\ 110\ 100\ 01$$

The first of the previous examples shows how a loss of significance can occur when two opposite-signed, nearly equal-magnitude numbers are added. The second illustrates how the case of an overflow in addition is handled.

Figure 2-13 shows the structure of a floating-point adder built from shift registers and a signed-magnitude adder.

Rounding in floating-point systems is a tricky operation to implement in a numerically acceptable manner. Although such rounding is not particularly expensive in hardware or in time, nearly all computers built in the seventies round improperly and introduce biases that are quite detectable. The following three rules should prevail for any reasonable rounding scheme and are incorporated in the proposed floating-point standard.

1. If the true result of an operation is representable within the floating-point format, then the true result is delivered.
2. If the true result is not representable, then it should be rounded up or rounded down to the nearest representable number.
3. In case the true result is exactly halfway between two representable numbers, the tie should be broken by a rounding scheme that is unbiased. The proposed standard requires that the round be done to the nearest "even" number, that is, round so that the last bit of the mantissa is a 0.

Floating-point numbers when implemented in a computer system are a tremendous help to the programmer; for now there is no need to be concerned with a large number of special error cases which can regularly occur in fixed-point arithmetic. Instead, one need only worry about the case of overflow and underflow in the very unlikely cases where the extremes in exponents are reached and about whether or not sufficient precision has been used to avoid the effects of loss of significance in addition.

PROBLEMS

1. Illustrate the operation of floating-point multiplication for the following two numbers in standard representation:

Bit positions: 0   12345678   901 234 567 890 123 456 789 01
$$B = 1 \quad 00000011 \quad 000\ 000\ 000\ 000\ 000\ 000\ 001\ 01$$
$$C = 0 \quad 10001011 \quad 000\ 000\ 000\ 000\ 000\ 000\ 010\ 00$$

Give the result in standard form.

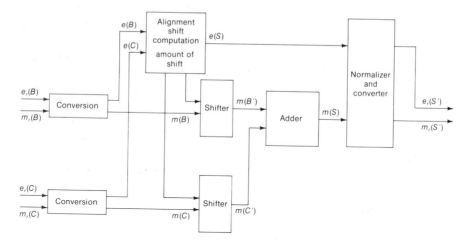

Figure 2-13 Floating-point adder structure

2. Illustrate the operation of floating-point addition for the two numbers of Problem 1.

3. *a)* State the algorithm for floating-point division, in a manner similar to that given in this section.

   b) Illustrate B/C where $m(B) = +7531_8$, $e(B) = +25_8$ and $m(C) = -653_8$, $e(C) = +37_8$.

4. To implement rounding in a floating-point unit, the proposed standard suggests that the floating-point unit have 3 bits to the right of the least significant bit of the mantissa. These bits catch the bits that determine if the result is to be rounded up or down. The first 2 of these bits are the 2 bits of the true result that fall beyond the precision of the result mantissa. They are called the *guard bit* and *round bit,* in moving from higher to lesser significance. The last bit is called the *sticky bit,* and it is 1 if *any* bit beyond the round bit in the true result is a 1; otherwise it is 0.

   a) Assume that the guard, round, and sticky bit are correctly set after each operation. Show how to implement the three rounding rules by observing their values.

   b) Show how to set the guard, round, and sticky bits in the course of a floating-point addition.

   c) Repeat part (*b*) for floating-point multiplication.

2-3. CODES FOR CHARACTER REPRESENTATION

As was mentioned earlier, computers are used for processing information in many kinds of situations, not restricted to simple arithmetic involving numbers. Sorting and classifying text information, parsing statements in a computer language (what a compiler does), information retrieval—these are all examples of applications where the computer processes information consisting of letters, numbers, punctuation, and special symbols. Two considerations associated with this type of data emerge: 1) the coding or representation in bits of each desired symbol, and 2) the method of packing character codes into physical computer words to make efficient use of storage.

The first task in selecting a code for character information is to establish a set of desired symbols to be represented. A set of 64 possible code words, for example, is sufficient to represent 26 letters, 10 digits, and 28 special symbols (such as * / + − @ % #), punctuation (. , : ; ! ?), and functions (tab, space, change color, and so on). For these 64 codes we require 6 binary bits, and in the early days of computer usage this field length was universally accepted for character representation. Computers such as the IBM 7094 have a word size of 36 bits, dividing nicely into six 6-bit characters. This 6-bit character code is sometimes called the *BCD code* since it is a logical extension of the 4-bit BCD code discussed earlier. Table 2-6 shows this code. Six-bit codes are also in use in the CDC 6000 series and 7600 machines.

In spite of its widespread use, the 6-bit code has become insufficient for many computer applications. For example, it does not permit the expression of upper and lower case letters, nor can Greek symbols be included, to mention a few of the limitations. To avoid some of these limitations, a standard character size of eight bits was proposed and two different standard 8-bit character sets are currently in use: ASCII (American Standards Committee on Information Interchange) was developed as the standard code for the data communications and computer industries and EBCDIC (Extended Binary Coded Decimal Interchange Code) was developed by IBM. Table 2-6 also shows the portion of these codes corresponding to those characters represented in BCD. To distinguish the 8-bit character from its 6-bit predecessor, the 8-bit character is usually called a *byte*. In an excess of cuteness, it has even been suggested that 4-bit digits be called "nibbles," since two of them make up a byte. As a consequence of the change to an 8-bit standard code, most current computers (the CDC 6000 series and 7600 computers are exceptions) now have a word size which is a multiple of 8 bits. In fact most minicomputers are 16-bit machines, and the first two microprocessors had word sizes of 4 and 8 bits.

At this point, it is appropriate to emphasize an important point made earlier: most computers store information as binary bits packed into words of fixed size. What in fact these bits mean depends on how they are used. They may be a collection of 8-bit characters; they certainly are treated as such if transmitted to a line printer by the input/output system. They may be integer numbers, and are so processed when sent to the integer adder. They may be computer instructions, and are interpreted this way by the computer control section. Sometimes it is difficult to make a decision as to what the information represents and, in fact, sometimes the interpretation of words may change during a computation.

TABLE 2-6. Six-bit bcd code and a Portion of the 8-bit ascii and ebcdic codes

Character	BCD code	EBCDIC code	ASCII code
blank	110 000	0100 0000	0010 0000
.	011 011	0100 1011	0010 1110
(	111 100	0100 1101	0010 1000
+	010 000	0100 1110	0010 1011
$	101 011	0101 1011	0010 0100
*	101 100	0101 1100	0010 1010
)	011 100	0101 1101	0010 1001
—	100 000	0110 0000	0010 1101
/	110 001	0110 0001	0010 1111
'	111 011	0110 1011	0010 1100
,	001 100	0111 1101	0010 0111
=	001 011	0111 1110	0011 1101
A	010 001	1100 0001	0100 0001
B	010 010	1100 0010	0100 0010
C	010 011	1100 0011	0100 0011
D	010 100	1100 0100	0100 0100
E	010 101	1100 0101	0100 0101
F	010 110	1100 0110	0100 0110
G	010 111	1100 0111	0100 0111
H	011 000	1100 1000	0100 1000
I	011 001	1100 1001	0100 1001
J	100 001	1101 0001	0100 1010
K	100 010	1101 0010	0100 1011
L	100 011	1101 0011	0100 1100
M	100 100	1101 0100	0100 1101
N	100 101	1101 0101	0100 1110
O	100 110	1101 0110	0100 1111
P	100 111	1101 0111	0101 0000
Q	101 000	1101 1000	0101 0001
R	101 001	1101 1001	0101 0010
S	110 010	1110 0010	0101 0011
T	110 011	1110 0011	0101 0100
U	110 100	1110 0100	0101 0101
V	110 101	1110 0101	0101 0110
W	110 110	1110 0110	0101 0111
X	110 111	1110 0111	0101 1000
Y	111 000	1110 1000	0101 1001
Z	111 001	1110 1001	0101 1010
0	000 000	1111 0000	0011 0000
1	000 001	1111 0001	0011 0001
2	000 010	1111 0010	0011 0010
3	000 011	1111 0011	0011 0011
4	000 100	1111 0100	0011 0100
5	000 101	1111 0101	0011 0101
6	000 110	1111 0110	0011 0110
7	000 111	1111 0111	0011 0111
8	001 000	1111 1000	0011 1000
9	001 001	1111 1001	0011 1001

Figure 2-14 shows how character information stored internally in ASCII code, using 16-bit words, would be transmitted to a terminal and displayed on the screen.

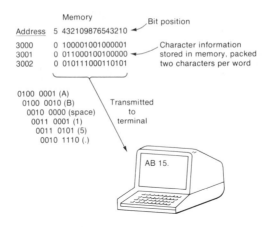

Figure 2-14   Character storage and output

PROBLEM

Assume that a computer program has read in the 5 decimal digits of an integer starting with the most significant in J(5) and ending with the least significant in J(1). Each digit is in EBCDIC Code and is right justified. Write a FORTRAN program to produce the binary integer representation of the number in a variable N. Assume only digits 0 through 9 are allowed.

2-4. DATA STRUCTURES

The physical considerations which govern a computer structure also impose constraints on the way in which data is organized for use by the computer. We have already seen how the basic elements of data representation (bits, digits, and characters) are related to the interpretation of information in a computer word. Additionally, we have seen that nonnumerical interpretations are possible. To compound the problem, the physical resource of main memory is expensive, too expensive to be large enough to service the storage needs of large programs. Recourse is then had to cheaper storage such as tape, disk, or drum. The different characters of these storage media force a hierarchical approach to data management. At one extreme, the programmer is forced to deal explicitly with each type of memory, performing the detailed exchanges of information between working memory and bulk storage. On the other hand, so-called *virtual* schemes have been implemented which automatically manage the transfer of needed blocks of data between bulk storage and working storage, making the programmer think that he has unlimited, virtual, main memory. Here he or she has traded programming simplicity for operating-system complexity and degradation of system performance. All of these issues are important to the design of computers and to their intelligent use; they are, however, the proper subject of later chapters. In the balance of this section, we deal with the various types of higher-order structures from the point of view of ease of manipulation for various classes of problems.

Basic Consideration

We consider here several different types of data structures. Each type has a particular advantage for applying the computer to certain classes of problems. For example, data may be presented to a computer in one order, but it may be desired to process it in a different order, depending on other inter-relationships of the data. One may then have the choice of sorting the data first before processing to establish new interrelationships, or one may set up a more complex cross-reference scheme. The ultimate decision depends on the details of the problem and the performance requirements. We make no conclusions regarding the use of these schemes, but merely present these schemes and show some of their applications. Also, some of these schemes are automatically embodied in programs produced by certain compilers, and certain specialized languages are used to facilitate use of particular data structures. In some cases, the use of special classes of data structures may be actually built into the hardware. In the remainder of this section, we describe arrays, and sparse arrays, and briefly mention some higher-order data structures.

Arrays

Arrays (or subscripted variables) are a basic storage mode for all high-level languages. They are advantageous when implementing algorithms in which the position arrangement of data is important. An example of an array used in a FORTRAN program is shown in Figure 2-15. This program segment shows the type of index computation for which arrays are well suited.

Array storage has several drawbacks including the need for a fixed pre-declared size (in some languages at least), and the need for a fixed word size for the elements of the array. The advantages are that many problems, particularly numerical analysis problems, have solutions that are easily understood and specified through the manipulation of arrays. This fact also has given rise to the development of hardware to process arrays automatically for improved processing performance. Chapters 8 and 9 treat such developments in detail.

Sparse Arrays and Scatter Tables

In some cases, the range of indices for an array is large, and only a small percentage of the elements of the large array is actually used. In such cases, storage of the entire array can be wasteful of memory space. One common way to solve this problem is to store only those elements actually needed, finding them by means of an *index*, sometimes called a *scatter table*. Figure 2-16 shows the scheme of using an index to find 1 of 100 actual elements stored in a

```
        DIMENSION A(10,10),B(10,10),C(10,10)
        .
        .
C       CALCULATE MATRIX PRODUCT C OF A*B
        DO 10 I=1,10
           DO 10 J=1,10
              Z=0.
              DO 9 K=1,10
9                Z=Z + A(I,K)*B(K,J)
10            C(I,J)=Z
        .
        .
        END
```

Figure 2-15 Example of a FORTRAN program using arrays

1,000,000 element vector. The subscript of the desired element is the key used to find the proper index entry, which in turn either contains the desired data or points to the desired data. The index is searched until KEY(J) matches the desired key. Several methods for finding the desired index can be used: simple search, binary search, or hash-code computation.

Simple search is the easiest to program but the most time consuming for search. Whenever an entry is desired, the index is searched from the beginning until either the desired entry is found or the index is exhausted.

Binary search is more complex to program and requires that the index be sorted each time an entry is added, but is much less time consuming than the previous type. The average length of search for simple search is proportional to one-half the index length whereas the maximum length of search for the binary search is proportional to the logarithm base 2 of the index size.

In the binary search, the index is in numerical order of keys. The first look at the table is at the middle word; if the key is less than the midpoint index,

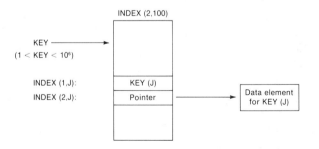

Figure 2-16 Scatter storage scheme

the desired value is in the upper half. If greater, the desired value is in the lower half. If equal, the desired index is found and the search terminates. The next step is to search the portion known to contain the value (if it is included in the index) by dividing it in half and examining the middle index entry. Thus the region of interest is halved at each step, giving rise to the $\log_2 N$ dependency of maximum search length.

The *hash-code* method of indexing is slightly more complex than the binary search algorithm but appears to be the most economical in time required for entry, deletion, and recovery of items from a sparse array. Morris presents some different methods of hash coding and contrasts their differences [Morris, 68].

In the hash-coding scheme, a function is used to compute an index, J, based on the key word which is the actual name of the entry. Various functions can be used, but they usually have the one desirable feature of producing differing hash codes for closely similar key words. Thus, for example, in Figure 2-16, if the hash code for 953,252 were 53, then 953,252 would be placed in INDEX (1,53) and a pointer to the 953,252 element of the array would be placed in INDEX (2,53). Other keys are often used, such as the coded representation of names.

One problem can arise in the use of hash-coding techniques. By its very nature, a hash code must map some number of keys into one hash code, and although efforts are taken to reduce the likelihood of two keys having the same code, as the index fills up the likelihood of a collision increases. Several schemes for handling a collision are possible, the simplest being: If a collision occurs (same hash code, different key), look in adjacent index locations for the desired key or for an empty position to put the desired key.

In general, hash-coding schemes require more programming effort than simple search techniques, but the savings in search time usually justify the use of the method, if many references are to be made to the data.

Stacks and Queues

Stacks and queues are extremely useful data structures when data is to be accessed in an order directly related to the order in which entries were made. The *stack* or *push-down-stack* is a *last-in, first-out* structure. One important application of stack structures is for the storing of arguments and return points in recursive procedures. Some compilers and interpreters construct stacks automatically when a recursive procedure is encountered. Stacks are directly implemented in a number of computers such as the Digital Equipment Corporation PDP-11, and a number of microprocessors have directly implemented stack operations. Some computers go beyond just having stacks directly implemented to the point where stacks are such an important part of the computer that the fundamental architecture of the computer becomes different. Chapter 7 treats such computers in detail.

A *queue* is a *first-in, first-out* data structure, used extensively in handling requests for service in a computer environment.

We will leave detailed discussion of stacks and queues until later chapters.

This has been a somewhat brief look at some of the important types of data structures. For a more thorough treatment of the subject, the reader is referred to the specific references given, or to a good general text on data structures such as Knuth [68], or Stone [72].

2.5. SUMMARY

This chapter has presented a study of the techniques of data representation. The properties, representation, and arithmetic involving different number systems were considered in substantial detail. Nonnumerical representations were next considered, and finally the higher-order data structures of arrays and stacks were treated. Specific implications of data-representation considerations on hardware will appear in all of the later chapters.

CHAPTER 3

Microprocessor Architecture

Thomas M. Whitney

3-1. INTRODUCTION

Throughout history there have occurred key technological discoveries that cause dramatic changes in the way people work and live. The invention of the printing press, the manufacture of steel, the steam engine, and the telephone are some events which would be included on such a list. In the past 100 years, the pace of discoveries of this magnitude seems to be accelerating; in just 30 years we have gone from the discovery of the transistor to the ability to mass fabricate tens of thousands of interconnected transistors in a single series of processing steps. This recent technological advance, called LSI for Large Scale Integration, has made possible the microprocessor or "the computer on a chip." Although it is too early to have a historical perspective, it is probable that the microprocessor will be included on future lists of discoveries that have reshaped our social and environmental existence. Just as the gasoline engine permitted low cost and portable mechanical power to be placed wherever needed, the microprocessor has permitted low cost and portable computational power to be distributed throughout the home and industry. The impact has only begun to be felt.

It is not possible to be involved with science or engineering today without having some contact with microprocessors. However, every person probably has a different idea of what one is. A microprocessor could literally be defined as a "small processor" for a computer, but a more restricted definition actually has become accepted: A microprocessor is a single integrated circuit that contains an arithmetic logic unit as well as control capability for memory and input/output access. Microprocessors are components used to build microcomputers. Usually the microprocessor must be combined with other integrated circuits to complete the microcomputer, although in some architectures so much memory and I/O control capability resides within the single large-scale integrated circuit that the terms microprocessor and microcomputer become synonymous.

Since microprocessors have arithmetic logic units, input/output ports, and memory, how do they differ from "ordinary" computers, and why have a special chapter devoted to them? In many ways, the design of microprocessors is identical to that of larger machines. The key difference is the concern and knowledge the architect must have of integrated circuit design and manufacturing constraints. The three primary constraints, not encountered in traditional computer architecture are:

1. size of the integrated circuit die
2. circuit power dissipation
3. total number of input/output pins on the integrated circuit package.

These constraints will be discussed in this chapter as various design alternatives are compared.

Should microprocessor architects come from backgrounds in device physics and semiconductor processing, or from computer science and architecture? Although an ideal background combines aspects of both, the current state of the art is such that most of the features of large machines are being gradually incorporated into microprocessors as technology permits denser circuits. It is probably easier for the hardware and software designers of minicomputers to learn some aspects of the component industry than for component designers to really understand computer architecture. Evidence that this is in fact taking place is seen by examining changes in the instruction sets of microprocessors from a historical point of view.

This chapter will concentrate on the building blocks and concepts of microprocessor architecture. The technology for microprocessors is changing so rapidly that a textbook discussing specific vendor implementations or part numbers might be considered obsolete before it is published. In Section 3-2 we will briefly discuss microprocessor history, examining its roots in calculator development and the driving forces behind lower cost and higher performance. Section 3-3 discusses the relationship of architecture to intended usage, the unique technological constraints on microprocessor design, and the importance of software as a starting point for architecture. Section 3-4 categorizes the types of microprocessors. Section 3-5 describes fundamental microprocessor structure, concentrating on the design trade-offs involving bus architecture and the use of I/O pins.

Section 3-6 describes microprocessor implementations, including control techniques for sequential logic and basic principles for the arithmetic logic unit, for memory and for input/output control. In the final section some trends in technology that will affect future architecture are discussed along with present and future application areas.

In a single chapter it is not possible to cover many interesting and related topics on microcomputers. For instance, we have not tried to deal in depth with many aspects of instruction-set design, high-level versus assembly-language programming, or development tools, nor in particular with the plethora of peripheral integrated circuits available for special- and general-purpose I/O, interrupt control, and direct memory access. For these topics the reader is referred to other chapters of this book or to one of the several textbooks dedicated to microcomputers [Peatman, 77; Klingman, 77]. Ideally, a course taught from this book would be followed by an entire course on microprocessors, in which a specific microprocessor could be studied in detail from literature supplied by the vendor, and accompanied by a corresponding laboratory course.

3-2. HISTORY OF MICROPROCESSORS

Microprocessor products have been one of the major driving forces for the development of large-scale integration due to the significant economic payoff from denser, lower-cost, and lower-power circuits. Prior to the transistor the logical operations that comprise a computer were executed by the cheapest, fastest, most reliable technology available: relays in the forties, vacuum tubes and transistors in the fifties. The largest computers of the early 1960s contained over a half million discrete diodes and transistors.

The significant revolutionary step was the invention of the planar transistor in the late 1950s. With this method of fabrication, all transistor electrodes could be brought to one surface. By a batch process of alternating impurity diffusions through "masks" on thin silicon wafers and etching unwanted areas, thousands of planar transistors could be made at the same time. Equally important, these transistors could be connected together by the deposition of metal through additional masks to form circuits and thus logic gates and memory. Parts *a* and *b* of Figure 3-1 show an integrated circuit wafer and chip.

The first integrated circuits of the early 1960s contained a few logic gates and were called SSI (small scale integration). Later, as processing techniques improved, hundreds and thousands of gates (medium scale, MSI and large scale, LSI) were built into a single "chip" of silicon.

Integrated circuits made it possible to continue a decrease in the cost of electronics that goes back through several generations of technology. Figure 3-2 shows the approximate cost of logic devices from tubes through the projected cost of very large-scale integration. This graph shows logic cost decreasing an order of magnitude every five years, or about 36.9% per year. Tubes for a dollar in 1955, discrete transistors for a dime in 1960, and 10,000 transistors in one integrated circuit for $10 in 1975 are all on the curve. It now seems clear that 100,000 transistors for $10 (VLSI or very large-scale integration) is readily achievable in 1980.

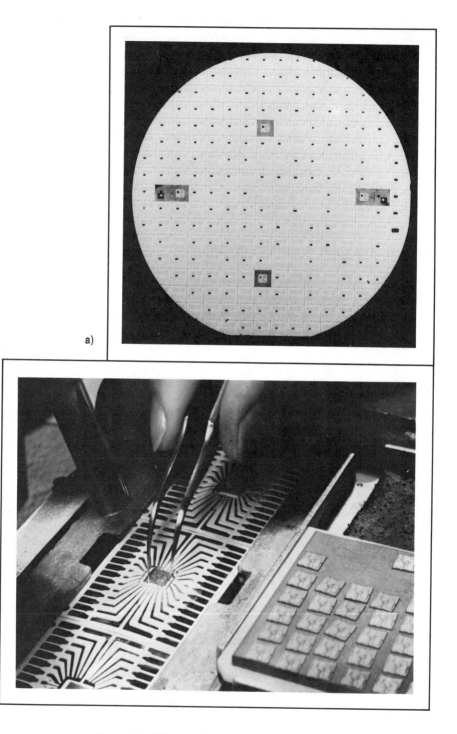

a)

b)

Figure 3-1 Silicon wafer and integrated circuit die

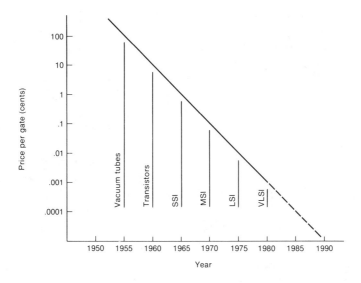

Figure 3-2 Costs of logic gates for different technologies

The history of microprocessors is rooted in the history of calculators. It was 1963 before the price of transistors made electronic calculators practical. Prior to that, transistor logic could not compete with levers, springs, gears, and motors where speed of execution was not the overwhelming design criterion. The early electronic calculators filled the product gap between the most powerful $2000 rotary calculators and the $20,000 smallest computers.

In October 1965, the electronics industry was excited by the announcement of the VICTOR 3900, the first metal-oxide semiconductor, large-scale integrated circuit (MOS/LSI) calculator. It cost $1825 and contained 29 integrated circuits with 21,000 integrated transistors. Unfortunately, like Charles Babbage's Difference Engine of 1823, the technology was not quite ready. The low yield of the MOS circuits prevented the machine from ever being marketed.

The idea was too "right" to be dormant long, however, and in 1967 Japan's Hayakawa Electric (now Sharp Company) introduced a manufacturable integrated-circuit calculator. It contained 50 integrated circuits, 43 discrete transistors, 200 germanium diodes, an 8-digit display, consumed 6 watts, and weighed 6 pounds. The era of integrated-circuit calculators had arrived, and it progressed much faster than most American calculator manufacturers thought possible.

In 1970 Electronic Arrays Company introduced a set of six "standard" calculator integrated circuits. Prior to this, calculator circuits were custom designed by a semiconductor company for one calculator manufacturer. These standard circuits, the precursors of today's microprocessors, made it much easier for anyone to be in the calculator business.

Other general processor chip sets (4–6 circuits) were available at this time from Fairchild, Rockwell, and National. These sets shared a serial, 4-bit approach to processing which was indicative of their intended use in sophisticated calculators.

The first true microprocessor is generally attributed to an effort started at Intel in 1969. Under contract to Busicom, a Japanese calculator company, a 4-bit CPU, the Intel 4004, was designed on a single chip. It contained about 2000 transistors. Coupled with memory and external I/O, the processor could be used in a variety of generalized applications.

Figure 3-3 shows the rapid progress made in integrated circuits for 4-function calculators during this period. The number of integrated circuits required to build a simple calculator went from 40 to 4 to 1 in about a 3-year period.

The 4-bit microprocessor of 1970 was followed by the 8-bit microprocessor in 1973 and some early 16-bit single-chip processors in 1976.

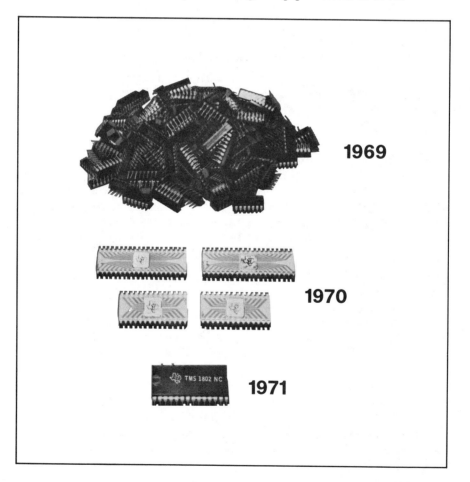

Figure 3-3   Integrated circuits required for a 4-function calculator over a 3-year period

Although calculators provided the initial incentive and financial backing for microprocessor development, it was not long before instrument and computer peripheral designers discovered what could be accomplished with low-cost, programmable, digital logic. The chip set of the HP-35 handheld scientific calculator, introduced in 1972, soon appeared in other Hewlett-Packard instruments such as an integrating gas chromatograph, a surveying instrument, and an oscilloscope. Gradually, more and more analog circuitry was replaced by digital logic, and microprocessors were accepted as the new "tool" of the digital designer.

The impact has been much more than mere replacement of previous functions at a lower cost and with greater reliability, although these are very important results. Programmable logic, as represented by microprocessors, allows entirely new features to be implemented. Microprocessors are not used to drive an analog meter in an instrument display; rather, an accurate, fast digital readout can be provided. This is the significant message of the microprocessor, a completely new component for creative product designers.

It is interesting to compare the history of microprocessors with the history of mainframes and minicomputers. As various technological constraints of circuit density, power dissipation, and pins per package are removed, the features and instruction sets of microprocessors tend toward those capabilities found useful in the larger machines. In this respect we can predict the future for microprocessor architecture. However, the freedom of much lower cost, lower power and thus product size, and increased reliability challenge the architect to make a fresh approach—to find some unique contribution for this new generation of devices.

3-3. DESIGN CONSIDERATIONS

Microprocessor design, as with all engineering design, involves complex multiparameter trade-offs. As always, the design is driven by the market for the product, i.e., by the requirements of the users. Before getting into the actual structure and implementation of microprocessors, some general design considerations will be discussed.

Software Considerations

Microprocessors (and all computers) are useful because they solve real computational and control problems. To apply a microprocessor the user must express the problem in terms of data structures and algorithms and then relate this description to the hardware capabilities of the machine, i.e., he/she must write a program. A reasonable design approach for the architect is to determine those functions most often needed by the intended user and to optimize the hardware accordingly. Functions not provided in direct hardware can be implemented as sequences of instructions in software. Determining what is to be placed in hardware and what will be executed as software/firmware extensions is a fundamental job of the microprocessor architect.

Microprocessor programmers have "rediscovered" the value of high-level languages. Many of the same arguments that raged for mainframe computers and minicomputers regarding the advantages of assembly language for execution speed and minimum memory requirements versus high-level languages for minimized development time and structured programming are being heard again.

Much has been written on "language-directed" machine design, in which the machine architecture is optimized to execute a particular language well [Bass, 76; McKeeman, 67; Allison, 77]. However, a machine which is a good vehicle for assembly language may not be a good target for a specific compiler. In any case, we can probably learn a lot about what microprocessors will be asked to do by studying the run-time representation of compiled programs.

An interesting study by Peuto and Shustek [77] showed that the types of instructions executed by programs on an 8080 microprocessor and on an IBM 370 do not vary significantly. This reinforces an earlier study by Knuth [71] that nearly 70% of all expressions in FORTRAN are simple moves of one variable to another, that most expressions had but one operator, and that 40% of all additions were increments by one. This indicates that a giant step toward a good microprocessor design can be made by doing the *fundamental* operations simply and rapidly.

Another approach to instruction set design comes from examining the operating system requirements for multi-tasking, a common type of environment for microprocessors [Rothmuller 76, 79]. System functions are necessary to permit semi-independent tasks to share a single processor via a first-come, first-served or a priority structure. The interrupt-intensive environment common in microprocessor control applications is indicative of these needs. Thus languages and operating systems requirements provide a good basis for machine design. The following concepts are important considerations in the design of an instruction set, and hence in the overall design of the microprocessor.

1. *Data types and structures*—Few applications operate on only one data size, such as a byte. In any case, addresses must be manipulated, bits tested, and fields moved within words. It is always necessary to form aggregates of primitive data types, such as words, vectors, arrays, linked lists, etc. Instruction and hardware support to handle these variable quantities can contribute greatly to microprocessor performance.

2. *Operators*—Included in capabilities must be arithmetic as well as logical (AND, OR, XOR, NOT) operators.

3. *Address and storage management*—Even the simplest of programs eventually needs some dynamic storage capability, if only to put items on a stack. Block-structured languages require dynamic tree structures, and mechanisms for reentrant code are sometimes useful. These addressing requirements do not map well onto the page-based, linear address space of many calculator, controller, and standard micropro-

cessor families. Multiple pointers, index registers, segment registers and base registers can facilitate high-level language implementation. If straightforward assembly-language programming will be most common, some of these features may get in the way.

4. *Control Structures*—Relational expressions and operators ($<$, $\leq$, $=$, $\neq$, $\geq$, $>$) are necessary to control program flow. Instructions are needed for unconditional jumps, and for conditional jumps which test various data types and status conditions for program branching.

5. *Task synchronization and process handling*—Hardware support for saving the machine state under task/switching is important for real-time control. All data movement could be thought of as interprocess message transfers, including external interrupts.

6. *Protection and exception handling*—The software/hardware trade-off that the architect faces is usually left to software when testing for exceptional conditions (for example arithmetic overflow, stack overflow/underflow, index out of range). Such checks consume considerable programmer time and errors are easily made. If it is assumed important to know when an exceptional condition has occurred, then it is helpful to have mechanisms at the hardware level to identify, report, and help recover from them.

Technological Considerations

Tempering the desire of microprocessor architects to meet the user's needs are the three particular constraints of semiconductor technology:

1. Die Size A semiconductor wafer and a microprocessor die (or chip) were shown in parts *a* and *b* of Figure 3-1. The cost of a microprocessor is about one half in the chip and one half in the packaging. The chip cost is proportional to "yield," the number of working chips on a wafer. Obviously if a die is made smaller, more dies per wafer are possible. But the yield improvement of reduced die size is much more than proportional to the number of potentially good dies per wafer. Yield (Y) is related to defect density (D) or "flaws" on a wafer and chip area (A) by the exponential formula $Y = ke^{-DA}$ [Murphy, 64], where k is a proportionality constant. Figure 3-4 shows the yield for various-sized microprocessors for defect densities in the 10 to 20 per square centimeter range, which is typical of today's semiconductor processes. Under these conditions a 10% increase in die size can result in a 50% reduction in yield!

Example 3-1: Consider a microprocessor with an area of 25 square millimeters (i.e., about 200 mils per side). What would be the effect on chip yield of increasing each linear dimension by 10%, assuming a defect density of 20 defects per square centimeter?

Solution: From Figure 3-4, the yield for an area A of 25 mm^2 and defect density D of 20 is about 4%. Increasing the area to 30.25 (5.5 $\times$ 5.5) mm^2 decreases the yield to about 2.8%.

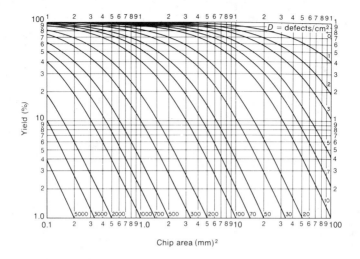

Figure 3-4   Semiconductor chip yield

Thus the secret to low cost in a microprocessor is high yield per wafer. Chip size is related to the amount and type of logic on the chip and the amount of interconnection required between elements. As technology advances, we are able to squeeze more total gates and memory elements in a given geometry. The successful microprocessor architect must be able to relate the importance of potential architectural features to the amount of silicon area their implementation will require. The architect must also choose between different ways of implementing the same logic or control function, keeping in mind chip area, performance, and power dissipation.

Figure 3-5 and Table 3-1 from Shima [78] show the evolution in chip performance and characteristics for one family of microprocessor, the Zilog Z8000. It evolved from the Intel 8008 and 8080 and the Zilog Z80, and the Z80A (a shrunken version of the Z80). Using the performance measure of Figure 3-5, the Z8000 achieves a two-order-of-magnitude improvement in a period of 7 years since the 8008.

2. Power Dissipation   One of the fundamental measures of computer performance is instruction execution speed. Unfortunately for microprocessor architects, high speed usually means high power. Semiconductor packages have limitations on power dissipation, varying from about one watt for plastic packages to two watts for ceramic packages. Semiconductor reliability is adversely affected by heat, so there is a strong incentive to keep the components within their rated specifications.

Within a given technology at a specific maturity point, minimum gate delays are not a parameter the architect can control. However, the total gates per die may be limited by power dissipation. By knowing the layout rules for the integrated circuit, the architect may trade power dissipation for speed and

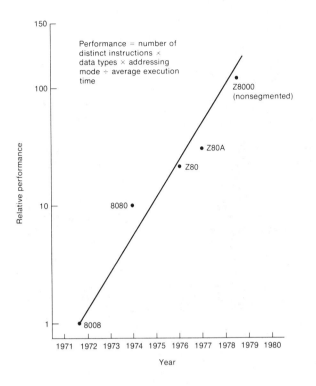

Figure 3-5 Performance over time for a microprocessor family

density. Figure 3-6 suggests the interrelationship of these three factors. By making a device larger, the density is less but switching speed increases. By making a device slower, power is saved. If power dissipation is increased, the density must be decreased. As with all engineering design, several factors must be simultaneously traded off to achieve an optimal design.

TABLE 3-1. COMPARISON OF MICROPROCESSOR CHARACTERISTICS

	8080	Z80	Z80A	Z8000
Date of initial production	1974	1976	1977	1978
Power consumption (W)	1.2	1.0		1.5
Number of transistors	4800	8200		17,500
Number of gates	1600	2733		5833
Chip size (mm²)	22.3	27.1	22.4	39.3
Density (gates/mm²)	72	101	122	148
Number of distinct instructions*	34	52		81
Combination of number of distinct instructions and data types*	39	60		149
Combination of number of distinct instructions, data types and addressing modes*	65	128		414

*The numbers represent a conservative counting method. The user sees much larger number of instructions in assembly-language notation.

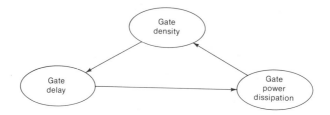

Figure 3-6 Interrelationship of density, delay, and power in integrated circuit design

Figure 3-7 shows the technological improvements in speed-power product (gate delay in nanoseconds times power dissipation in milliwatts equals speed-power in picojoules) from the first microprocessor, with predictions for the future. As can be seen, this rapid decrease is expected to continue during the next few years.

3. Package Leads Half of the microprocessor cost is package-related, and the number of pins or leads is proportional to the cost. In addition, certain package sizes have become standardized in the industry; to be nonstandard for a high volume part would be prohibitively expensive. Thus the designer has to arrange the architecture of the microprocessor and the related micro-computer system so that the proper number of signals leave the chip. For early designs, 18- and 24-pin packages were the largest available. This led to the concept of multiplexed data and address buses. With 40-pin packages, more flexibility and larger addresses became feasible. Still larger packages are now becoming more common.

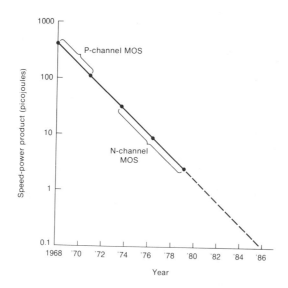

Figure 3-7 Speed-power product of microprocessors versus time

The first multichip calculator designs used serial communication lines for addresses and data between chips, partly to save pins and partly to save bus space within chips [Whitney, 72, 75]. The large-computer designer has to be concerned about printed circuit board space and interconnection, but with a hundred or more pins per circuit board, the architecture will rarely have to relinquish a desirable feature due to lack of interconnectability; the microprocessor architect, on the other hand, is frequently so restrained.

With this background in design considerations, the next section shows the types of microprocessors that have evolved as a result.

3-4. TYPES OF MICROPROCESSORS

Minicomputers of the 1960s were often classified by the number of bits in a word. The PDP-8 from Digital Equipment Corporation, with its 12-bit word, was most common until the 16-bit length became a standard. Following this background, many attempts have been made to try to classify microcomputers by their word length. But where should one measure word length? Some microprocessors manipulate 4-bit, 8-bit and 16-bit quantities internally and may have an 8-bit or a 16-bit path to memory. Microprocessors tend to be very irregular in their instructions for data manipulation, so that word size is not a conclusive classification parameter.

It is equally difficult to count registers. Some registers can be used with only part of the register instructions; others may not be accessible to software at all.

There *are* two factors that are reasonable measures of a microprocessor's power: addressing modes and I/O capability. Early microcomputers were intended for dedicated control applications; assembly-language programming (and in some cases, machine-language programming) was all that was ever intended. As the demands for higher-level languages appeared, the addressing mechanisms proved to be wholly inadequate. Multiple index registers, base registers, pointers, and stack mechanisms were developed, all symmetrically used by all instructions, to provide flexibility that equates to processing power.

The I/O area is a critical distinguishable characteristic of microprocessors. Some microprocessors are designed to work smoothly with vendor-supplied peripheral support circuits, but not so smoothly otherwise. Some are oriented to the standard world of off-the-shelf transistor-transistor logic circuits. Some single-chip microcomputers have self-contained memory and can control a number of direct-I/O signal lines sufficient for many applications. The number of interrupt levels, and the time and technique used to respond to each is also a significant separating feature.

To classify microprocessors we choose five categories, although a good case could be made for more or less.

1. Calculator-Game/Toy   The emphasis for these low-end microprocessors is *low cost*. Often bit-serial BCD arithmetic is emphasized for small packages

(18 or 24 pins) and some dedicated I/O lines such as for keyboard input or display output.

Internal memory consists of a few registers, probably a fixed number of BCD characters long, plus sufficient internal read-only memory (ROM) to get most jobs done and still keep the cost down. Processing speed is slow to save on battery power, but sufficient for the applications. The chip is a self-contained microcomputer with the goal being to use as few additional components as possible in the final product. From one point of view, the game or toy is simply a fancy package for the integrated circuit.

2. Single-chip Controller   These parts share the goals of the game/toy class for low cost and few external discrete or integrated-circuit parts. In fact, they may be used in more sophisticated calculators and games. Their main application is as peripheral controllers. Many have programmable internal timers to allow time-outs and eliminate the need for external one-shot circuits. Register flexibility is more general than for calculators, a random-access-memory (RAM) array is usually included, and the microprocessor is typically 8-bit oriented. More internal ROM is used than for category 1 (1K bytes minimum).

Some designs are planned to attach external RAM and ROM. The key advantages of single-chip microprocessors are the ability to directly control external I/O devices with only a single chip.

3. Midrange Standard   These 8-bit microprocessors first appeared in the early 1970s and quickly found their way into a wide variety of computer terminals, peripherals, instrument controllers, and home and small business computers. They are characterized by having all ROM and RAM external to the microprocessor chip except for a few internal scratch-pad and working registers.

Some internal 16-bit instructions exist, primarily for address manipulation since memory is byte oriented. Multiple-level vectored interrupts are typical, with various masking options. Microcomputers are constructed with the use of external LSI chips to control serial communication lines, flexible discs, and general I/O ports, to set priority interrupt levels, and to provide direct memory access (DMA). These microprocessors have been and are the dominant factor in the market.

4. High Performance   This class of microprocessor primarily evolved from the midrange standard class; most vendors offer an instruction-set "compatible" version. High-performance microprocessors are characterized by their rich instruction sets with much more uniformity of addressing modes than was technologically possible during the development of their midrange fathers and grandfathers. This class is primarily 16-bit oriented with 8-bit, 4-bit, and single-bit instructions as subsets. Addressing goes beyond 64K bytes. Sophisticated vectored-interrupt structures exist for 64 to 256 devices. Hardware multiply and divide assistance is present, sometimes for floating-point as well. General performance easily pushes these microprocessors into the mini-computer range.

A last distinguishing characteristic is the built-in capability to support multiple-processor configurations.

5. Bit-slice   There are many applications where the high density MOS (metal-oxide-semiconductor) microprocessors do not have the speed to compete with bipolar technology. Bit-slice microprocessors are designed to match the speed of bipolar medium-scale-integration with the design ease and flexibility of microprocessors.

In one sense, bit-slice microprocessors do not belong in this classification at all since they do not fit our definition of a microprocessor (i.e., one chip with all the ALU functions). Bit-slices are 2- or 4-bit pieces of an ALU that can be connected together end-to-end to form a CPU of N-bits. Extra bipolar circuits are used to form a microcomputer, and microprogrammed control is typically utilized. Instruction-execution speeds an order of magnitude better than with MOS microprocessors can be obtained, but at a much higher cost. The designer has a large degree of flexibility in setting up I/O and memory control and in the definition of the microprogrammed instruction set. Design with these parts is nearly the same as with conventional MSI logic.

A summary of the five microprocessor categories is provided in Table 3-2.

TABLE 3-2. Categories of Microprocessors

	Applications	Capacity	Characteristics
1. Calculator/ Game/Toy	4- to 8-function calculators; games; toys	No external ROM or RAM; few internal registers; no general purpose interrupts; 4 bits	Lowest cost; bit-serial, BCD arithmetic; small packages; limited I/O; few external components
2. Single-chip Controller	Complex games/ toys; peripheral controllers; simple instruments; timers; home appliances; automobiles	Internal ROM and RAM; limited expand-ability; 8 bits; multiple I/O ports; simple interrupts	Low cost; low power with battery back-up; single package oriented
3. Midrange Standard	Programmable calculators, instru-ments, terminals; peripherals; home computers; appliances; industrial control	8-bit data, 16-bit addresses; multiple internal registers; stack addressing; several vectored interrupts	Many extra chips typically required; external ROM/RAM
4. High Per-formance	Complex terminals; minicomputers; industrial data acqui-sition and control; communication processors	Basically 16-bit oriented; address >64K byte; multiple vectored maskable interrupts; stack instructions	Enhanced instruction set; hardware multiply/divide
5. Bit-slice	High-speed data acquisition; disc controllers; high speed peripherals	2- or 4-bit slices cascaded to form N-bit processors	High speed; many chips for micro-computer

PROBLEMS AND DISCUSSION QUESTIONS

3-1. Large-scale integration has brought many advantages to system design, but has also required new related technologies and design approaches to be developed. List and discuss some of these.

3-2. Is there any end to the logarithmic decrease in the cost of gates shown in Figure 3-2? If so, what is it and when might it be expected to take effect?

3-3. Since many products are built from the same building blocks, i.e., off-the-shelf integrated circuits, what distinguishes one product from another? Take CRT terminals as an example.

3-4. Early minicomputers and microcomputers were "hardware driven," i.e., specified by logic designers, whereas later minicomputers and micro-processors have been largely software driven, i.e., specified by language and operating system personnel. Discuss why this change has occurred.

3-5. Why is it that the types of instructions executed on an 8080 micro-processor and a mainframe computer do not vary significantly?

3-6. Using Figure 3-4, estimate the yield on a chip 5.2 mm by 6.1 mm if the process used has a defect density of 10 defects per square cm.

3-7. Discuss the logic behind the performance measure for microprocessors used in Figure 3-5, i.e.,

$$\text{Performance} = \frac{\text{no. of instructions} \times \text{data types} \times \text{addressing modes}}{\text{average execution time}}$$

How might you modify this measure?

3-8. What category of microprocessors might you select for each of the following applications?
   a) Microwave oven
   b) Flexible disk drive controller
   c) Hard disk drive controller
   d) Graphics terminal
   e) Automobile control system
   f) Electronic typewriter
   g) Digital voltmeter

3-5. MICROPROCESSOR STRUCTURE

A microprocessor contains all the elements of the von Neumann computer described in Chapter 1 except for memory and input/output, which generally are implemented separately and attached to the microprocessor over buses, thus forming a microcomputer. As technology progresses both memory and I/O are gradually merging onto the chip as in today's calculator and game/

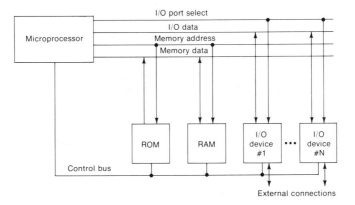

Figure 3-8   General microcomputer structure

toy microprocessor types. To appreciate the architectural alternatives possible in microprocessor design, we begin with a general treatment of microcomputer structure.

General Structure

Figure 3-8 shows the most general microcomputer structure.

The microprocessor's role in life, like the conventional computer described in Chapter 1, is to execute a program. This involves fetching instructions from memory, accessing data and storing the results of operations in memory, and controlling input/output operations. The coordination of these data transfers is done by appropriate lines in the control bus.

The control and bus lines necessary for memory operations are shown in Figure 3-9. MEM READ and MEM WRITE indicate whether data is to be placed *on* the data bus (READ) or clocked *from* the data bus into memory

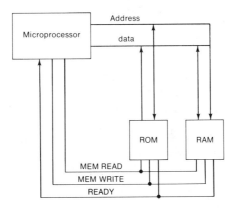

Figure 3-9   Microprocessor memory operations

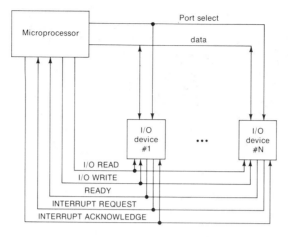

Figure 3-10 Microprocessor I/O operations

(WRITE). In either case the address bus specifies the location affected. The READY signal notifies the microprocessor that the operation has been completed.

The I/O bus works in a similar way as indicated in Figure 3-10. Direction of data movement on the data bus is specified by the I/O READ and I/O WRITE signals; READY signifies the completion of the operation. The I/O device is selected by the PORT SELECT bus, which is like an address bus for I/O devices. Since there are generally only 64 to 256 I/O ports, the port select bus need be only 6 to 8 lines wide. Two other control lines are required in practical systems; INTERRUPT REQUEST signals the micro- processor that an I/O device is ready for service. Since I/O devices operate asynchronously from the rest of the system, the microprocessor continues operation until it reaches a point where it can handle the I/O device, and then issues INTERRUPT ACKNOWLEDGE. Various methods of interrupt processing are practical, as described later.

Multiplexed Buses

Examining Figure 3-8 through 3-10, we see that typical requirements for pins on the microprocessor are those listed in Table 3-3.

TABLE 3-3. MICROPROCESSOR PIN REQUIREMENTS

Memory address	16 (or more)
Memory data	8 or 16
I/O port select	6 to 8
I/O data	8
Memory control	3
I/O control	5
Total pins	40–50

The table gives a total of 40–50 desired microprocessor pins, without consideration of power, clocks, and other specific purposes not yet discussed. Since our earlier discussion indicated that cost is related to pin count, we must find some way of reducing the number of pins by sharing functions. Integrated circuit packages come in "standard" sizes, such as 16, 24, 40, and 64 pins, so the incentive is high to reduce pin count to one of these critical numbers.

Figures 3-9 and 3-10 indicate the similarity of the structures of the memory operations and I/O operations. By multiplexing the data and addressing functions for each on one set of wires the number of pins can be significantly reduced. This is shown in Figure 3-11.

In this structure only one address bus is provided and one data bus. An additional control signal, MEM/$\overline{\text{IO}}$, signifies whether the present operation is for memory or for I/O. This is the most common form of bus multiplexing, and almost all microprocessors use it to some extent.

The bus structure of Figure 3-11 facilitates a common feature of most computer systems called Direct Memory Access (DMA). Many I/O transfers from or to memory are too fast for standard microprocessor instruction cycles. DMA is a provision for directly reading or writing to memory from I/O without passing the data through the processor. Since the memory and address buses of Figure 3-11 are the same, a direct path for these transfers is provided. The control for DMA transfers must come from the I/O device itself. The I/O device requests DMA service by use of the BUS REQUEST line, thus disabling the microprocessor while the transfer takes place. When a BUS REQUEST is received by the microprocessor, it continues for a few clock times until it reaches a point at which it can suspend itself, then notifies the DMA device to proceed by sending BUS ACKNOWLEDGE. The DMA

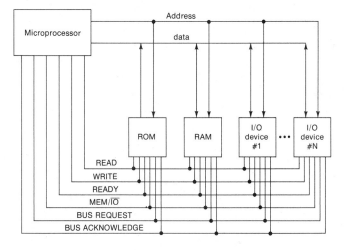

Figure 3-11 Microprocessor structure with multiplexed buses

device then manages the address and data buses as if it were the microprocessor. A typical DMA interface must have registers for the starting memory address, the length of the data transfer (typically given in number of bytes), and a byte counter.

Another important use of the BUS REQUEST line is in multiple microprocessor systems. Two or more microprocessors can share the same buses and memory with contention handled by the BUS REQUEST and BUS ACKNOWLEDGE lines.

Even the pin reduction possible with Figure 3-11 may not be sufficient for some microprocessors, particularly as data buses increase to 16-bits, and address buses beyond 16 bits. Again applying the principle of multiplexing, we can combine the address and data buses into one bus, with a control signal designating whether the current information on the bus is address or data. A new requirement for either address or data latches or buffers (i.e., registers), external to the microprocessors, emerges however, since the address information and data bus information must both be present when a memory or I/O read or write operation is performed. Such latches may be separate integrated circuits or built into the I/O peripheral controller circuitry. The latches are enabled by the ADD/DATA control signal as shown in Figure 3-12. This method slows down the microprocessor by forcing two bus cycles for a memory or I/O operation that requires only one bus cycle when no multiplexing of address and data is used.

One additional multiplexing method is possible. This is to use the microprocessor data bus as a status and partial control bus to/from the microprocessor. A separate control signal specifies when the bus contains status information that then must be latched into an external register. The 8080

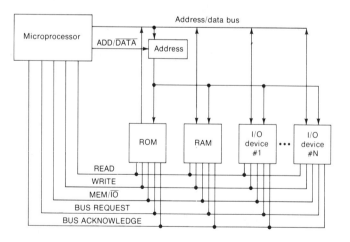

Figure 3-12 Multiplexed address and data bus

family of 8-bit microprocessors are the most common devices that use this technique. Typically, special large-scale-integrated circuits are provided by the vendor to match external register requirements to the particular multiplexing methods implemented by the microprocessor.

With this overview of bus structures behind us we can now proceed to the internals of the microprocessor. Table 3-4 provides a summary of the typical bus control signals that the microprocessor's internal logic is required to generate. A good exercise is to study the signals used by an actual microprocessor from technical literature supplied by the vendor.

TABLE 3-4. TYPICAL MICROPROCESSOR CONTROL BUS SIGNALS

Signal	Microprocessor Type	Function
MEMORY READ	OUTPUT	Reads one n-bit word from memory to data bus as specified by address.
MEMORY WRITE	OUTPUT	Writes one n-bit word from data bus to memory as specified by address.
READY	INPUT	Indicates valid memory or I/O data on data bus in response to READ, or acceptance of memory or I/O data in response to WRITE.
WAIT	OUTPUT	Indicates microprocessor has gone into "wait" state pending response from memory or I/O.
REFRESH	OUTPUT	Address bus contains a memory refresh address; used with dynamic RAMs.
BUS REQUEST	INPUT	Requests processor to suspend bus operations. May be used as a DMA request.
BUS ACKNOWLEDGE	OUTPUT	Indicates microprocessor compliance with bus request.
INTERRUPT REQUEST	INPUT	Indicates a device wishes to interrupt the microprocessor.
INTERRUPT ACKNOWLEDGE	OUTPUT	Indicates that interrupting device should place identifier on data bus.

3-6. INTERNAL DESIGN

Microprocessor designers face technological constraints of die size, power limitations, and pin count. The appropriate architectural circuit design techniques to minimize the effect of these constraints varies with the purpose of

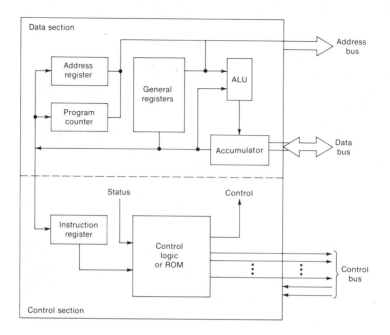

Figure 3-13 Hypothetical microprocessor block diagram

the microprocessor and the technology available. In this section we explore some fundamental requirements of microprocessor architecture and the particular methods that are typically employed.

General Structure

Figure 3-13 shows a block diagram for a hypothetical microprocessor. It is divided into a lower control section and an upper data section. For purposes of this discussion the microcomputer bus structure of Figure 3-11 has been selected, with multiplexed memory and I/O buses.

The data section contains address registers, the program counter, other registers which will be discussed in more detail later in this section, and the arithmetic logic unit (ALU). The control section provides instruction decoding and timing information to the remainder of the microprocessor. It must maintain status information, both from inside the chip and from the outside world. Techniques for implementing these control signals are a major topic of this section.

Fundamentally there are only three types of data manipulated by the microprocesser:

1. *Instructions.* Instructions are bit sequences that are decoded in the ALU and I/O portions of a system to direct data transfers and operations.

They are stored in external (in this example) ROM or RAM and are sequentially brought into the microprocessor instruction register according to the program flow. As with other types of computers, microprocessors go through FETCH and EXECUTE cycles, which may be overlapped (pipelined) for greater throughput.

2. *Addresses.* Addresses point to the location in memory or an I/O device where other elements of information are stored.

3. *Data, or operands.* Operands represent numeric, logical, or alpha information which is to be operated on by the microprocessor.

Control Section

The microprocessor combines the instruction in the instruction register with timing signals, internally generated status conditions, and external inputs to generate a set of data-transfer, ALU, and external-control signals. We prefer to consider the design of a control sequence as similar to writing a computer program. The designer has in mind instructions, addresses, and operands stored in registers, the connecting paths between them, and the list of internal signals or commands that transfer the data and perform logical operations. Simply stated, it is only necessary to devise a correct sequence of commands to meet the specific requirements. Hence we approach control from the point of view of a flowchart, and then examine alternate ways to obtain hardware implementations of the flowchart.

Control-unit design is rooted in the techniques of classical sequential-machine design. One way of representing the classical sequential machine is shown in Figure 3-14. It is composed of storage elements, or memory (sometimes called the state), and combinational-logic elements, with feedback from the storage outputs back to the input. We will be concerned only with synchronous or clocked systems, in which the memory transitions all occur in response to a clock. In asynchronous systems, the moment of transition of a memory element may be dependent upon a completion signal from another part of the system.

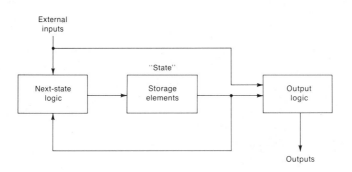

Figure 3-14 Classical sequential machine

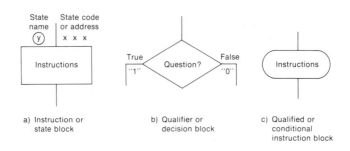

a) Instruction or
state block

b) Qualifier or
decision block

c) Qualified or
conditional
instruction block

Figure 3-15   Flowchart symbols

In discussing control we refer back to the classical sequential machine to place the different design methods in context.

Flowchart   A flowchart is a graphic representation of the definition or solution of a problem or sequence of events in which symbols are used to represent operations, data, or decisions. It is a valuable tool that aids the designer in organizing his requirements, whether it be a computer program or a digital system control sequencer. For our purposes in control design, we can think of the flowchart as representing the next-state function and output function for a sequential machine. We examine how a design requirement for a sequential machine, once specified by a flowchart, can be implemented directly in different hardware configurations.

Many different types of flowcharts exist. We use three different symbols as shown in Figure 3-15.

The *instruction block,* sometimes called a *state block,* is represented by a rectangle. Inside are placed instructions, often represented by mnemonics. A state block has a state name, often a letter, and a state code or address. The instructions correspond to the outputs in the sequential machine of Figure 3-14.

The *qualifier,* or *decision, block* is shown as a diamond and is used to represent branching in a sequence. Only one qualifier may be used in each block, and the next path followed is dependent upon whether the answer to the "question" asked by the qualifier is true or false. Qualifiers are also called status signals and correspond to the external inputs in Figure 3-14.

The *qualified,* or *conditional-instruction block* is represented by an oval; it always follows a decision block in a flowchart. Inside are written instructions that are *dependent* upon the qualifier in the preceding qualifier block. Some examples will help to clarify how these symbols are used.

The first example (part *a* of Figure 3-16) shows a simple state transition in which no qualifiers are tested. The machine makes the transition from State A where instructions I1 and I2 are executed, to State B where instructions I1 and I3 are executed.

In part *b,* the qualifier Q1 is tested; if true, the "1" path is followed and the next state is D where I4 is executed. If Q1 is false, or in the "0" logic state, the next machine state is E where no instructions are executed. Note that Q1 is tested while the machine is in state C and at the same time instructions I2 and I4 are active. The decision block is *always* associated with a state block.

The term *Algorithmic State Machine* (ASM) chart is used by Clare [73] to distinguish the fact that a state block and a decision block are executed simultaneously as opposed to a conventional program flowchart in which each block is executed sequentially. In flowcharts we will always draw a state block and a decision block touching to represent this important difference.

The third example (part *c*) uses the conditional instruction block. The two conditional instructions, I1 and I2, are both associated with state E. If Q2 is true, I1 is active in state E, if false, I2 is active. In either case, the next state is F.

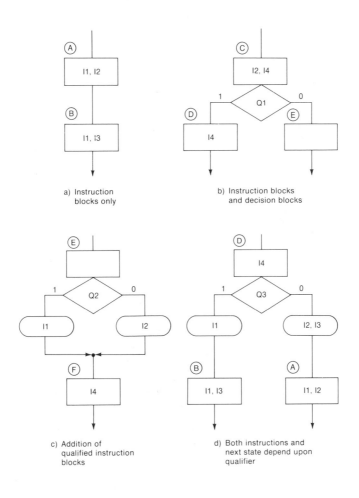

Figure 3-16   Uses of flowchart symbols

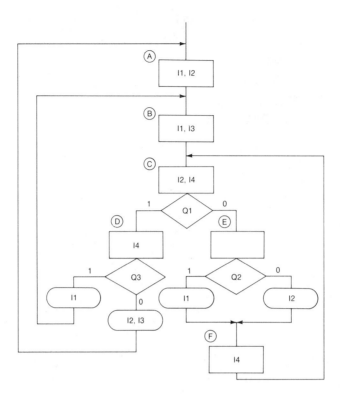

Figure 3-17 Flowchart for 6-state sequential machine

The final example in Figure 3-16 (part *d*) combines examples of parts *b* and *c*. Both the next state and some of the instructions are dependent upon Q3.

Figure 3-17 combines the segments of Figure 3-16 into a complete six state flowchart for a sequential machine with three external inputs, that is, qualifiers Q1, Q2, and Q3, and four outputs, instructions I1 through I4.

It is necessary to tie the concept of "state" to the principle of synchronous operation. In a synchronous sequential machine the memory elements are changed only in response to a clock signal and all change at once. This change corresponds on the flowchart to movement to the next state block. In fact, each state is represented in hardware by a state code or address realized by memory elements. Thus if the machine is "in" state C, the next clock signal moves the machine to either state D or E depending upon input Q1. Q1 is associated with state C because it is tested during the state C period of time.

Example 3-2:   Represent a 3-bit Gray code counter by a flowchart. If an input *x* is true, the counter is to go through only the first 4 states. An output Z1 is required at binary counts 2 and 6 and at count 3 if *x* is active, and an output Z2 at counts 1, 3, 5, 7.

Solution: We let each state code correspond to the binary number for that state as shown in the illustration. Remember that in a Gray code only one variable changes at each state transition.

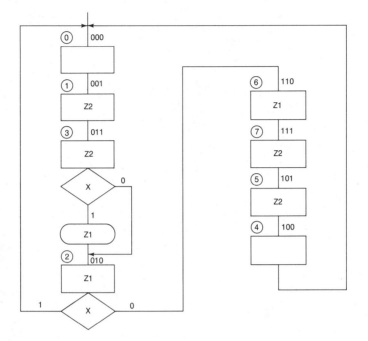

Counter-Decoder Control Methods   A commonly used control technique is the use of a multiphase clock, implemented with a counter and decoded outputs as instructions. Synthesis procedures for counters are covered in basic courses on sequential circuit design and are not explained here. Clare [73] explains the procedures in a manner tied closely to the other material of this chapter.

Figure 3-18 shows a 4-phase clock. By logically ANDing the clock signals with qualifier inputs, instructions can be activated sequentially. Figure 3-19 shows a generalized control unit for a digital system. Note the correspondence to the classical sequential machine of Figure 3-14. The block called external memory represents the registers and single flip/flops present in the system. Some of the outputs from these memory elements are returned to the counter input logic to determine the next state. These are examples of qualifiers appearing on flowcharts.

The counter can be designed to count in any manner required; the modulo 4 counter of Figure 3-18 is a simple example. In most systems it is inefficient always to proceed through 4 phases. By proper design of the input logic the counter can vary its sequence. As in most digital system designs, the trade-off is between speed and cost; the variable counter provides higher system speed, but costs more than the simple, fixed, multiphase clock.

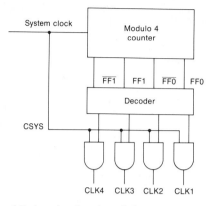

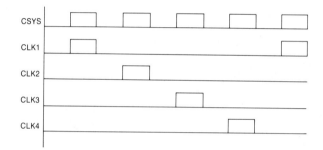

a) Hardware for a four-phase clock

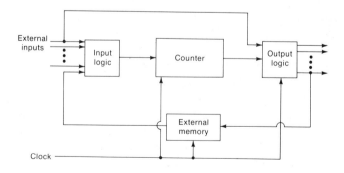

b) Timing signals for a four-phase clock

Figure 3-18   Hardware and timing signals for a 4-phase clock

Figure 3-19   Controller implemented with a counter and logic

Example 3-3: Implement the flowchart of Example 3-2 using clocked D-type (Delay) flip/flops.

Solution: Since there are eight states, we need three state flip/flops. The first step is the construction of a next-state and output table:

Present State				Input	Next State			Output	
	F3	F2	F1	x	F3	F2	F1	Z1	Z2
0	0	0	0	—	0	0	1	0	0
1	0	0	1	—	0	1	1	0	1
3	0	1	1	0	0	1	0	0	1
3	0	1	1	1	0	1	0	1	1
2	0	1	0	1	0	0	0	1	0
2	0	1	0	0	1	1	0	1	0
6	1	1	0	—	1	1	1	1	0
7	1	1	1	—	1	0	1	0	1
5	1	0	1	—	1	0	0	0	1
4	1	0	0	—	0	0	0	0	0

The excitation function for delay flip/flops is particularly simple since the output follows the input after each clock signal. The inputs D1, D2, D3 are therefore equivalent to the next state. The solution is shown in Karnaugh maps for the three inputs and the two outputs.

This example may seem trivial. Actually all the principles of counter-gate control-method design are embodied in it.

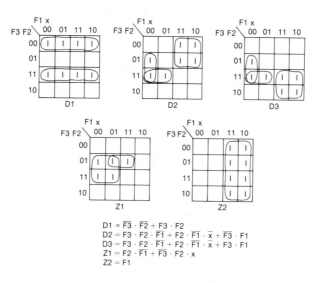

$$D1 = \overline{F3} \cdot \overline{F2} + F3 \cdot F2$$
$$D2 = F3 \cdot F2 \cdot \overline{F1} + F2 \cdot \overline{F1} \cdot \overline{x} + \overline{F3} \cdot F1$$
$$D3 = F3 \cdot F2 \cdot \overline{F1} + F2 \cdot \overline{F1} \cdot \overline{x} + F3 \cdot F1$$
$$Z1 = F2 \cdot \overline{F1} + \overline{F3} \cdot F2 \cdot x$$
$$Z2 = F1$$

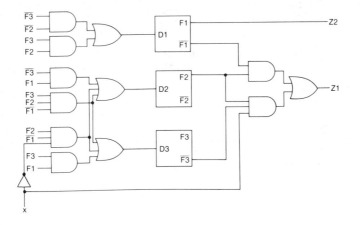

Solution: Example 3-3

Read-Only Memory Based Methods   The greatest change in recent years in control unit design has been the increased use of Read-Only Memory, or ROM. The advantage of read-only memory has been known since the earliest computers but the costs were prohibitive until the advent of integrated circuits. Actually the third generation IBM 360 computers used read-only memory extensively, but at an increased cost over conventional counter-gate or random logic design. Some of these increased costs were regained in other benefits such as flexibility and ease of design change.

The simplest way to think of a read-only memory is as an array of OR gates. Each output from the memory can be selected by several of the input or address lines. Associated with the memory is a decoder which is an array of AND gates. Figure 3-20 shows the two parts of a read-only memory. An address consists of an n-bit code, which can select one of 2^n words in memory

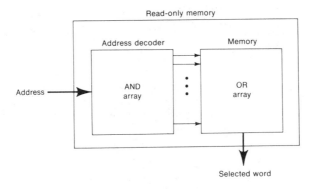

Figure 3-20   Read-only memory as an AND-OR array

when fully decoded. Words consist of fixed-length bit strings that are set or programmed at the time of manufacture and are not intended to be altered during machine operation, hence the term "read-only." However, depending upon the technology that implements the memory, there may be ways to change the stored patterns, either electrically or manually, but always at a speed slower than the speed of access.

To illustrate the use of read-only memory as an AND-OR array, we can implement a pair of simple 3-variable Boolean equations.

Example 3-4: Implement the following two equations in a 3-input, 2-output ROM.

$$X = \overline{B}C + ABC$$
$$Y = AC + AB\overline{C}$$

Solution: We can expand the two equations to become

$$X = (A + \overline{A})\overline{B}C + ABC = A\overline{B}C + \overline{A}\overline{B}C + ABC$$
$$Y = A(B + \overline{B})C + AB\overline{C} = ABC + A\overline{B}C + AB\overline{C}$$

Now consider C to be the least-significant bit of a binary address. Then X is true for addresses 101, 001, 111 or 5, 1, 7 and Y is true for 7 or 5 or 6. The diagram shows connections for these lines.

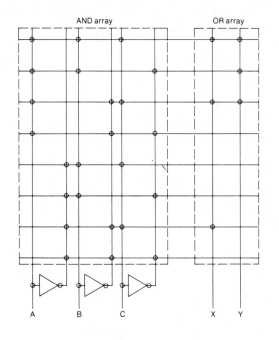

Solution: Example 3-4

In this example the 3 inputs are fully decoded in 8 lines. However, no outputs are required for addresses 0, 2, 3, 4, so part of the decoder can be deleted. This concept forms the basis of the programmable logic array, described in the following text.

The programmable logic array (PLA) is simply a partially decoded read-only memory. The term *programmable logic array* is perhaps inappropriate since all read-only memories are programmable in some manner and are also logic arrays. By convention a programmable logic array has come to mean a read-only memory with n inputs and less than 2^n words, in which both AND and OR arrays are programmed [Reyling, 74].

In a programmable array, the address is made up of two types of inputs: 1) the state inputs as fed back from the memory elements of the sequential machine, and 2) qualifier or status inputs from throughout the digital system. Logical combinations of the next state and status inputs are ANDed in the decoder portion of the PLA to form "product terms." Groups of product terms are ORed together to form the outputs or instructions from the PLA, just as example 3-4 is implemented.

The programmable logic array may be implemented as a part of an integrated circuit, such as the control section for a microprocessor, or it may be fabricated as a separate component. A programmable logic array made by Hewlett-Packard for in-house use is an integrated circuit with 8 state flip/flops within the circuit, 16 status inputs, 72 product terms, and 30 outputs. This circuit is shown in Figure 3-21. One of the disadvantages of this type of separate integrated circuit is the large number of leads: 46 are required plus power and clock inputs. When realized as an internal part of an integrated circuit, the inputs and outputs do not all require connection to the outside world, and this disadvantage is eliminated.

The National Semiconductor PLA (part No. DM 7575) has 14 inputs, 8 outputs, 96 allowable product terms, and no internal state flip/flops. The

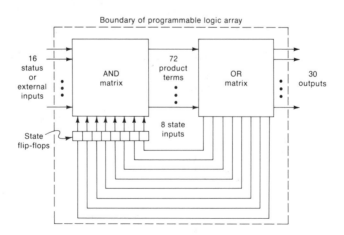

Figure 3-21 Block diagram of an integrated programmable logic array

circuit is provided in a 24-pin dual in-line package.

When implemented with integrated circuits, the determination of a connection in the AND and OR matrices is specified by a single masking operation. This allows one basic circuit design to be customized or programmed at little incremental expense.

Example 3-5:   Implement the counter of Example 3-2 with a PLA.

Solution: The equations from the solution to Example 3-3 are repeated here:

$$D1 = \overline{F3} \cdot \overline{F2} + F3 \cdot F2$$

$$D2 = \left\{ F3 \cdot F2 \cdot \overline{F1} \right\} + \left\{ F2 \cdot \overline{F1} \cdot \overline{x} \right\} \begin{array}{l} \dotplus \overline{F3} \cdot F1 \\ \\ \dotplus F3 \cdot F1 \end{array}$$

$$D3 = $$

$$Z1 = F2 \cdot \overline{F1} + \overline{F3} \cdot F2 \cdot x$$

$$Z2 = F1$$

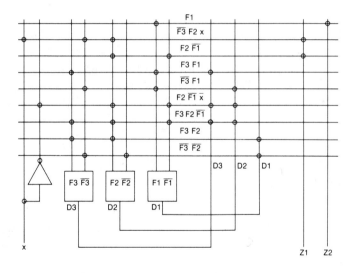

Solution: Example 3-5

The solution (see illustration) has 4 inputs (x, D3, D2, D1), 9 product terms, and 5 outputs. Note that product terms appearing in more than one output can be shared, just as AND gates are shared in Example 3-2. In this simple example the Z2 output can be eliminated by taking Z2 directly from F1. This also eliminates one product term. Another trick is to form Z2 from the product term $\overline{F3} \cdot F1$ and F3 · F1, that is, $Z2 = F1 = \overline{F3} \cdot F1 + F3 \cdot F1 = (\overline{F3} + F3) = F1$.

One other important point should be mentioned. In Example 3-3 we used Karnaugh maps to simplify the logic equations; this reduces the number of gates and the number of inputs per gate to lower the cost of implementations. In the AND matrix of Example 3-5, all connection points are available and there is no need to minimize the logical equations, except to reduce the number of products to fall within the capacity of the PLA.

Microprogramming Microprogramming is the term applied to the use of read-only memory for the implementation of the control function in a digital system. In some digital systems, RAM is used for this function. The commonly used term is then *Writable Control Store* (WCS). Programming is required as part of this technique since techniques analogous to computer programming are used, such as stored instructions, subroutines, conditional branches, and program description by flowcharts. It is "micro" in the sense that a more detailed control of the hardware of the machine is implied than with higher-level programming. Chapter 10 contains a detailed description of microprogramming. Most small and medium-sized computers and many large ones use microprogramming for the control. Since calculators and microprocessors are also increasing their use of this technique we introduce it here, but only in its simplest form and in relation to other microprocessor control techniques.

In the classical sequential machine in Figure 3-14, there are two logic sections: one to decode the next state and the other to determine the appropriate outputs. There are two types of inputs to the logic: external and present state. In a programmable logic array, the next-state logic and the output logic are combined into a single AND-OR (that is, decoder-memory) array. The user customizes or programs both the decoder and the memory. This has the advantage that most or all of the logic system can be realized in one low-cost part, or in one portion of the microprocessor.

However, a system typically has many external inputs, corresponding to various status conditions and special flip/flops, but fewer than all combinations of external inputs are required as product term lines. The programmable logic array of Figure 3-21 has a total of 24 inputs so that $2^{24} = 16,777,216$ product terms are possible, yet only 72 are built into the array. A standard read-only memory cannot be used efficiently as a programmable logic array for this reason. A memory with ten address inputs would have 1024 words which correspond to product terms, but typically less than 10% of these would be used with the programmable-logic-array approach to logic design.

A fully decoded read-only memory is more widely manufactured because of the optimum usage of pins and because of its application to microprogramming. Microprogramming is a method for efficiently using low-cost read-only memory for most of the logic of the system. In Figure 3-22 the total logic of a microprogrammed system has been separated into two parts. All dependence upon external inputs is concentrated in gate logic shown as "next-state logic." The system outputs are implemented by read-only memory and thus depend

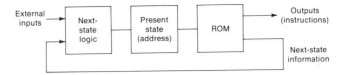

Figure 3-22 Microprogramming model of a sequential machine

only upon the present state of the system as represented by the address input to the memory. External inputs help select the next address, but are not part of the address itself, as in a programmable logic array.

In any digital system there are some instruction lines that are never active simultaneously, that is, they are mutually exclusive. Two examples of such signals would be the commands to the arithmetic logic unit and the selection of data for a bus. In the first example, an arithmetic logic unit may have capability to add, subtract, invert, and so on, but it can only do one of these at a time. In the second example, several registers may have access to a bus, but only one can be connected at a time. A group of 2^n mutually exclusive outputs can be encoded into n lines to narrow the width of a microprogrammed word. An external decoder is then required, but the additional decoder cost is less than the additional ROM cost. The decoder, however, adds a time delay which may be objectionable in some high-speed systems.

Determining a microprogramming word format is similar to selecting a word format for the assembly language of a computer. Wider words with two or more possible next addresses provide flexibility, but at the cost of additional ROM. Some typical formats are considered in the following text.

In many microprograms, most of the time the next address is one more than the present address. In this instance a simple implementation is for the ROM address register to be a counter. When a branch is to be made, an address is forced into the counter from the output of the memory. Figure 3-23

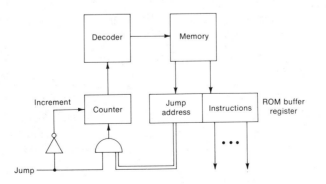

Figure 3-23 Microprogrammed control implementation—2-field word format

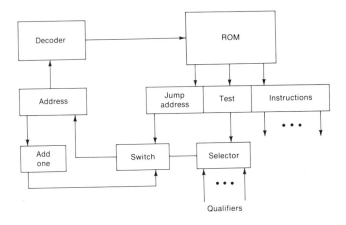

Figure 3-24 Microprogrammed control implementation—3-field word format

shows this implementation. The word format for this example has only two fields, one for the jump address and one for instructions. If the jump line is true the jump address is loaded into the counter (address register), otherwise the counter is incremented.

A modification of Figure 3-23 is to perform the increment operation by an adder and gate the incremented address and the jump address into a switch, the output to be selected by a branch signal.

Figure 3-23 makes no provision for the generation of the jump signal. The most common technique is to add a third field to the word format called the *test field*. At each state of the machine one qualifier is selected as the jump signal, or if no branch is required the jump signal is forced false. Figure 3-24 shows an implementation with these added features. The switch, selector, and adder are all part of the next-state logic implemented with gates. Compare Figures 3-22 and 3-24 to see the correspondence.

Another common word format is the two-address format. The two possible next addresses are included in the read-only memory output. This provides greater flexibility since either of two addresses can be selected at each state, but at added cost since the ROM word becomes wider. Part *a* of Figure 3-25 shows this format.

One last format is worthy of mention. The size of read-only memory is determined by the number of words and the width of each word. A technique to keep the width small is to use a variable word format. With two different formats, one bit of each word is used as a format indicator. As shown in part *b* of Figure 3-25, Format 1 has all but the format bit used as instruction bits, as indicated by the left-most bit equal to 1. Format 2 has two fields, a test and a jump address, and the format indicator is 0. With Format 2, the control lines are all disabled. With Format 1 the next address is assumed to be 1 more than the present address.

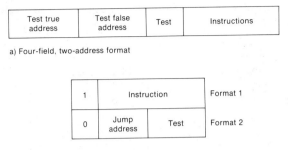

a) Four-field, two-address format

b) Variable format

Figure 3-25   Two types of word formats

Variations and combinations of these formats are possible. More discussion of their relative merits is contained in Chapter 10. In general, wider words result in a faster machine, but at an added cost.

The type of flowchart drawn for an algorithm or sequential machine is necessarily related to the type of implementation. With a programmable array it is possible to test more than one qualifier per state and to implement conditional outputs. Conditional outputs are not allowed in a microprogrammed approach since the ROM output lines are not conditioned by the external or qualifier inputs. All requirements can still be implemented by microprogramming, but a corresponding flowchart must be used. To test two qualifiers in one microstep with microprogramming, two test fields are necessary in the word format and, in general, there must be provision for branching four ways. This is so costly that a restriction to a single qualifier per state time is generally made.

The address of a ROM word corresponds to the state code on a flowchart. A state is described by the contents of a ROM word. Generally it includes instructions to be executed, the qualifier to be tested, if any, and the next state choices.

Example 3-6:   Redraw the flowchart of Figure 3-17 and implement it with microprogramming, using the two-address format of Figure 3-25, part *a*.

Solution: (illustrated on the following page)

False addr.	True addr.	Test	Inst.			
xxxx	xxxx	xx	I4	I3	I2	I1

There are ten states, so a 4-bit address is required. The four qualifier conditions (Q1, Q2, Q3, and "no test") can be encoded into 2 bits. The complete memory map is shown below.

Qualifier Encoding		Address Assignment		Memory Map						
				false	true	qual	I4	I3	I2	I1
no test	00	A	0000	0001	0001	00	0	0	1	1
Q1	01	B	0001	0010	0010	00	0	1	0	1
Q2	10	C	0010	0100	0011	01	1	0	1	0
Q3	11	D	0011	0111	0110	11	1	0	0	0
		E	0100	1001	1000	10	0	0	0	0
		F	0101	0010	0010	00	1	0	0	0
		G	0110	0001	0001	00	0	0	0	1
		H	0111	0000	0000	00	0	1	1	0
		I	1000	0101	0101	00	0	0	0	1
		J	1001	0101	0101	00	0	0	1	0

The removal of the conditional outputs is accomplished by the addition of four states. The specific physical situation would have to be examined to see if the desired system behavior is still represented. For instance, in the original

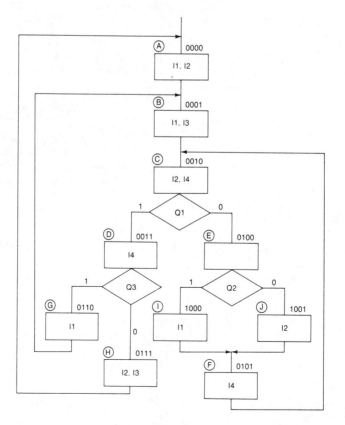

Solution: Example 3-6

flowchart, in state D the instruction I1 is active *at the same time as* I4 if Q3 is true. In Example 3-6, I1 becomes active in state G and I4 is no longer active. The ultimate acceptance of this revision depends upon what I4 and I1 actually do. It may be necessary, for instance, to carry I4 over into state G to obtain equivalence.

Hardware Implementation   Having completed a general discussion of control implementation, we can observe how some of these methods have been actually implemented in practice. Figure 3-26 shows a 1-chip microprocessor (TI-TMS 1802) designed for calculator or game/toy use. It uses PLAs in three places to control the output decoding, timing, and general control. In many situations it is more conservative of chip area and interconnections to have one PLA drive another, rather than to have one large array.

A microprocessor circuit that uses both the counter-decoder control method and a small microprogrammed control unit is shown in Figure 3-27. This circuit was used in the early Hewlett-Packard hand-held calculators (for more information see Whitney [72, 75]). Decoding off the system counter is used both for timing signals to the rest of the circuit and to decode keyboard drivers and multiplex keyboard inputs. A microprogrammed ROM controller, organized 58 words by 25 bits, controls the flow of data throughout the remainder of the circuit. Note that some of the outputs from the timing decoder are qualifier inputs to the microprogrammed control.

The more common use of microprogramming is with bit-slice microprocessors. The subject of microprogramming is treated extensively in Chapter 10 of this text.

The different control methods each have their particular advantages and disadvantages. The speed of discrete-counter logic dictates its use for critical timing and control circuits where speed is the primary criterion. But discrete logic lacks flexibility. A small change in the definition of one instruction implemented with discrete logic could cause major changes in chip layout.

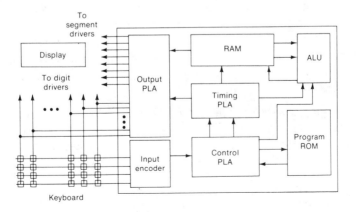

Figure 3-26   Use of PLA control technique in a 1-chip microprocessor

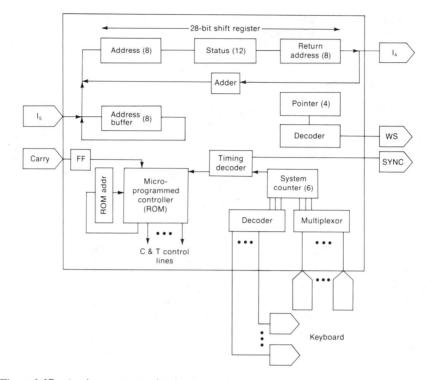

Figure 3-27   A microprocessor circuit using both counter-decoder and microprogramming control methods

Consequently higher-level functions that are not as time-critical but require some flexibility are implemented with PLAs. This technique also achieves high functional density on the chip due to the packing densities achievable from ROMs. The large number of inputs and outputs is not a constraint if the PLA is entirely internal to the chip. Microprogramming is frequently bypassed in favor of PLAs internal to microprocessors because of speed. Also, the generality and power of microprogramming, with multiple next addresses, etc., cannot be as effectively utilized internal to a chip as can be done in the external implementation of a computer instruction set.

Data Section

The microprocessor data section (see Figure 3-13) is not unlike that found in minicomputers and earlier mainframe computers. A program counter stores the current instruction or operand address and can be incremented or combined arithmetically through the ALU with one of several registers. Early single-accumulator microprocessors have now largely given way to multiple-accumulator designs; in some microprocessors an entire bank of registers may be treated equally as accumulators.

Perhaps the real key to microprocessor flexibility is in the register bank.

Generally these are separated into groups with special functions as follows:

1. *Accumulator*. Stores operands before and after arithmetic and logical processing steps; has a direct input to the ALU.
2. *Register File*. General purpose registers used for scratch-pad storage of operands, data, and addresses; usually as wide as the available addresses; provide local high-speed storage for nonmemory reference instructions.
3. *Base registers*. A base register is used to store a starting or ending address for a segment of code or data. It provides a method for program relocatability; i.e., all memory references in a program can be relative to the base address which is all that must be modified if the code or data is moved. Generally an index register is added to the base register to provide an absolute address. Segment or page registers provide a similar function.
4. *Index Registers*. Useful as an index to an array of data or a sequence of instructions. When used with a base address, the address in the index register provides a displacement which can be easily incremented or decremented by special instructions. Also useful to implement program loops.
5. *Pointers*. Pointers are often used to designate the top of a stack. Stacks are typically implemented in external RAM so that the length may grow without restriction (except by the total amount of RAM), although some microprocessors have internal stacks that provide much faster operation. A full discussion of the uses of stacks is contained in Chapter 7. Microprocessors tend to use stacks in their more rudimentary form for saving subroutine or procedure-call return addresses and parameters, and for saving the machine state during interrupt processing.
6. *Status Register* (also called the flag register or the condition-code register). One-bit fields are used to store special states or alarm conditions such as ALU carry, arithmetic overflow/underflow, stack overflow/underflow, accumulator zero, parity error, interrupt enabled. These bits can be tested by conditional jump instructions for branching control.

A key factor in the overall processing power of a microprocessor is the ALU. Flexibility in selecting input operands and in designating a destination address can save many machine cycles. Again, the richness of the instruction set for arithmetic and logical operations may decide if a desired operation can be performed in one machine cycle or two or three. Most microprocessors provide for decimal-adjust logic to correct for binary-coded-decimal (BCD) arithmetic.

Sometimes an alternate arithmetic unit is dedicated to address modification. In designs with multiple index, base, and pointer registers, as much arithmetic activity may be necessary on addresses as on operands.

The software view of the data section is most easily expressed by the *programming model*. The programming model shows those registers available to the programmer through the standard instruction set. The programming

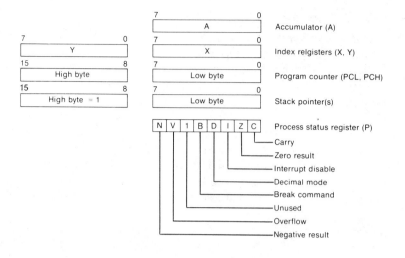

Figure 3-28   Programming model for the 6502 microprocessor

model for a typical midrange microprocessor (6502) is shown in Figure 3-28.

The processor status register, P, can be thought of as an array of individual flip/flops or flags. The programmer must study the instruction set to become familiar with the full range of operations that are possible.

Most of this description could as easily apply to traditional computers as to microprocessors. The differences relate to the discussion earlier in this chapter on chip area, power dissipation, and pins. Multiple internal data paths, such as a rich set of sources and destinations for ALU operands, consume valuable chip area, not only for the metal lines themselves, but for the gating required into and out of the ALU.

The critical-path delay in a processor is often through the ALU. The microprocessor architect can decide to speed up this path by using larger integrated-circuit devices to implement critical gates, but at the expense of chip area and power dissipation. Is it better to add metal lines and gates to provide a direct path to the ALU for some register, to add a new instruction which moves the accumulator to this register directly, or to leave out both and decrease the critical ALU execution time by 10%? These are the kinds of trade-offs which require a combination of integrated-circuit *and* computer-architecture knowledge not necessary in conventional computer design.

I/O Section

The microprocessor I/O interface has several unique qualities. The microprocessor manages I/O in much the same way as memory: identification information, in the form of addresses, is sent out on the address bus, control signals are activated on the control bus, and data flows in or out on the data bus. Two basic types of I/O systems exist in microprocessor-based systems: [Wakerly, 77].

1. *Memory-mapped I/O*. I/O operations are treated exactly the same as memory operations. Certain addresses within the memory address space are reserved for I/O. There are no special I/O instructions or control lines. Each device or port must be organized as a set of registers, "memory locations," that respond to read and write commands. This type of I/O is used in the PDP-11 family of minicomputers.
2. *Isolated I/O*. With this method, special I/O input and output instructions are used. A separate port may be needed with some devices to initiate and stop operation. This I/O system, with a separate I/O bus is used in the Hewlett-Packard 2100 family of minicomputers.

The advantages of the memory-mapped I/O are that all memory reference instructions may also be used for I/O, but at the expense of more complex decoding at each device. The isolated I/O method uses shorter and faster instructions but usually requires more control signals from the processor.

One factor which tends to distinguish memory and I/O operations in microcomputers is the relative difference in data-transfer and response times of the two types of operations. Electromechanical devices respond in terms of milliseconds or seconds, whereas the memory may be able to cycle as fast as the microprocessor instruction time. To synchronize I/O operations, "ready" and "wait" signals of some type are usually provided on the control bus. Memory can also use these signals to implement asynchronous memory, thus permitting slower (and cheaper) or faster (and more expensive) memory to be used on the same system.

One of the more important uses for microprocessor based systems is in "real-time" control. These applications are characterized by unpredictable external events, unsynchronized to the processor clock. To interact with these events, microcomputers are provided with interrupt-handling systems. Most microprocessors have very simple interrupt systems at the chip level but provide for external circuitry to add capability.

Interrupt systems can be polled or vectored. In a polled system, a software program interrogates each I/O device, according to some preset priority, to determine which device requested service. The priority can be "maskable," i.e., modified according to the state of the microprocessor system. In a vectored system, the interrupting device will provide an address or pointer to the system indicating its identity. The microprocessor in response to an interrupt will enter an interrupt-service routine.

Some commonly used interrupt-service routines are (in increasing order of complexity):

1. Execute a subroutine jump to a fixed location in memory.
2. Execute a subroutine jump to the address contained in a fixed location in memory (jump indirect).
3. Execute a subroutine jump to an address provided by the interrupting device (vectored interrupt).

4. Execute a subroutine jump to the address contained in a table in memory, where the index into the table is provided by the interrupting device.
5. Execute an instruction provided by the interrupting device.

   In each case, the subroutine jump may be a special "interrupt subroutine jump" instruction in which the processor state (registers, program counter, status information) is saved, usually on a stack. Methods 3, 4, and 5 are all examples of vectored interrupts.

   Almost all microprocessors provide external peripheral integrated circuits to assist in the typical I/O functions such as interrupt handling and direct memory access (DMA). The best way to become familiar with these important devices is from the integrated circuit catalog of the vendor, since they vary widely between microprocessor families and over time.

PROBLEMS AND DISCUSSION QUESTIONS

3-9. You are responsible for the architecture of a 40-pin microprocessor. Four pins are already allocated to power and clock. You have 36 pins available to perform your functions. The following are the constraints your design must satisfy:

Address bus	16 lines
Data bus	8 lines
Read/Write	1 line
I/O port address	8 lines
Internal status	6 lines
Bus control	2 lines
Interrupt control	2 lines
Memory control (READY, GO)	2 lines

   a) Show a method for meeting the design objectives by multiplexing address and data on the same set of lines. You may multiplex other signals, but you must share address and data lines. If you multiplex any lines you must also work out a method for distinguishing the present use of the lines. This may require more pins.
   How many cycles are required for a memory READ?
   For a memory WRITE?

   b) Show a different design in which you multiplex I/O port addresses with memory addresses.
   How many cycles for a READ?
   How many cycles for a WRITE?

   c) Change the solution for (b) to the situation in which you use memory-mapped I/O. Does this require more or fewer pins?
   How many cycles for a READ?   for a WRITE?

d) Comment on which of the three designs you find to be the best overall solution to the design problem, and why.

3-10. You are faced with problem 3-9, but in this case the parameters have changed. They are:

Address bus	24 lines
Data bus	16 lines
I/O port address	8 lines
Internal status	8 lines
Bus control	2 lines
Interrupt control	2 lines
Memory control	2 lines

a) Work out a way of meeting the design objectives, multiplexing where possible and where necessary under the assumption that you have 40 pins.
b) Repeat and create a design for a system with 48 pins.
c) Analyze your two designs for interfacing with the microprocessor and indicate where and how the 48-pin design leads to higher performance than the 40-pin design. (The 48-pin design cannot be lower performance than the 40-pin design unless you really goofed up your design.)

3-11. Implement a BCD subtractor with counters. Draw a flowchart for your design.

3-12. Write a flowchart for a key-debounce routine. Consider transient noise, leading-edge bounce, and trailing-edge bounce. Also consider that the user may want to push the same key twice in succession.

3-13. Is there any purpose in minimizing the number of logical equations implemented in a PLA? Does the answer depend upon the technology used?

3-14. Design a traffic light controller for a 4-way intersection using
a) a PLA;
b) microprogrammed control.
Include left-turn lanes on one of the streets. Draw a flowchart to specify your design.

3-15. Design a digital machine to play the game Blackjack (or Twenty-one), using a microprogrammed controller. Define the necessary hardware qualifiers and control signals; show a flowchart. The external appearance of the machine should be a slot to accept cards and three lights labeled STAND, HIT, and BROKE.

3-16. Suggest several uses for the unused status bit in the programming model for the 6502 microprocessor of Figure 3-28.

3-7. TECHNOLOGY AND TRENDS

It has been estimated [Faggin, 78] that 45,000 gates will be integrated on a single chip in 1985, about ten times the number necessary to build a standard 8-bit microprocessor. It is reasonable to ask the question, "What will all that logic be used for?"

One approach is to duplicate today's mini- and maxi-computer architectures, or to continue to add functions to current microprocessors, maintaining a degree of instruction-set compatibility to protect the software investment of a generation of users. This approach will undoubtedly be followed simply because of the evolutionary nature of the data-processing industry. Architectural creativity is, to some degree, stifled along this development path.

However, low-cost processing power suggests another opportunity which might be considered a revolutionary approach [Faggin, 78]. This approach builds upon parallel-processor architectures, as outlined in Chapter 8. Given the already existing fact that a complex CPU can be purchased for a few dollars, it seems logical to devise a structure to use multiple processors to provide more total processing power than any single unit. To utilize this concept effectively, several problems must be solved.

Perhaps the most critical problem in parallel processing is the software operating system. For some applications with predefined, partitionable tasks, a set of equal processors can be coordinated to operate efficiently. The general case is much more difficult and will require a joint hardware/software effort to effect a smooth running system. Some of the 45,000 gates can be used to assist in this endeavor.

The second area to be understood is a means of interprocessor communication. Again a coordinated hardware/software design is needed, such that messages can be transmitted with minimum contention for bus time, and with a priority system which is dynamically modified according to the demands of real-time data processing.

Several examples of innovative use of microprocessors appear in the remainder of this section. These examples suggest some of the possibilities available and should help stimulate thinking to other imaginative microprocessor applications.

The section on the implementation of control logic lists the several classical methods for implementing control logic available prior to the introduction of microprocessors. Microprocessors are themselves controllers, and as such can be used as yet another way of implementing control logic. Given any handful of digital components that produce timing and control signals as per some algorithm specification, that same handful can be replaced by a microcomputer, perhaps by a single device, provided that the performance of the microprocessor is high enough to meet the timing requirements. Instead of dealing with flip/flops, gates, counters, PLAs, and ROMs, the designer instead uses a standard microprocessor and programs it for the specific application. Osborne [76, 77, 78] elaborates this idea in great detail by examining a controller for a printer designed originally with discrete logic, and then shows that same controller implemented with each of three distinct microprocessors. Each logic gate of the original controller is simulated by specific instructions in a control program for the microprocessor implementations.

The advantage of this approach is that the controller can be built with a fixed amount of hardware, namely with a microcomputer, yet the flexibility and capabilities of the controller are open-ended. They depend on the program and not directly on the microprocessor hardware except for the size of memory. One basic controller can be designed, built, and tested, and then inserted into a system to perform many different functions depending on the software loaded with the controller.

Often these design techniques lead both to reduced costs and to the availability of more functions within a controller. The major constraint on the design technique is performance; high-speed applications must often resort to the conventional techniques because microprocessor-based implementations are typically limited by the basic clock cycle of memory, which is as much as 10 times slower than clock cycles in a hard-wired logic implementation. Cost reductions in microprocessor implementations are sometimes illusory because the cost of the software development for such an implementation cannot be ignored, and may be much higher than anticipated. Nevertheless, the idea of using microprocessors to replace hardware control circuitry is valid and has to be in the repertoire of design approaches available to the engineer.

Another application of microprocessors is illustrated in Figure 3-29. The figure shows two different computers, completely disconnected, in part *a*. Our objective is to be able to execute instructions for both computers in such a way that, on one computer system, we can execute two different instruction sets. In this way we can tap existing programs without reprogramming. Part *b* of Figure 3-29 shows one way this is done today, namely with a "hybrid" computer that has two modes of operation—one for each instruction set. This practice is especially important when users are converting from one computer system to another, and has been used extensively by IBM when converting from the 7000 and 1400 series computers to the System 360 series. Several other manufacturers have found this to be an extremely effective means for smoothing the conversion process.

Microprocessors have led to another means for achieving the goal of Figure 3-29, part *b*. A possible alternative using microprocessors is shown in part *c*. Here we have one microprocessor for each instruction set. Control passes back and forth between the micros as the applications change. For example, micro *A* may be able to execute existing user applications, and micro *B* may be the new microprocessor with advanced software tools and enhanced capabilities. The user develops new programs to run on *B*, and executes old programs on *A*. *A* and *B* need not even run simultaneously in this system. That is, when *A* is executing, *B* might well shut down, and conversely, since the performance of the system may not be a serious issue and the cost of an idle microprocessor is negligible.

A related question is the problem of how to deal with interrupts in a computer system, and to do so as quickly as possible. As we shall see later

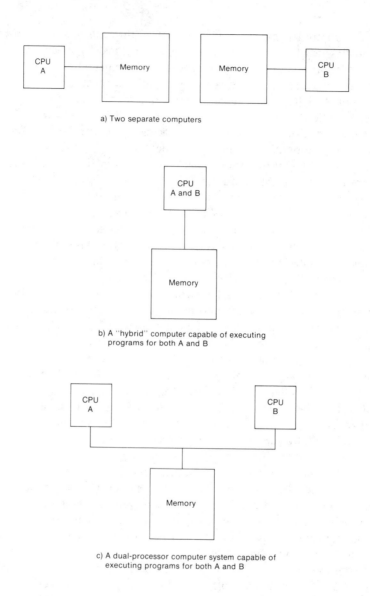

a) Two separate computers

b) A "hybrid" computer capable of executing
programs for both A and B

c) A dual-processor computer system capable of
executing programs for both A and B

Figure 3-29   Three different ways of executing programs for two types of processors

(Chapters 4 and 6), external devices can interrupt processors, that is, force a processor to suspend its present execution and take up execution in a program that services the external device. Control returns to the interrupted program when the service program completes its action. Unfortunately, interrupts have a good deal of overhead associated with them because before the service program can take control, the registers in use by the interrupted program must be copied into memory, to be copied back again later when the service program completes. This permits a subsequent return to the point of interruption without damaging the interrupted program by the action of the interrupt. The overhead is the penalty paid in order to use a single processor for two purposes. In the 1950s, hardware was much too expensive to permit other alternatives. By the 1960s and 1970s, additional hardware in the processor had helped reduce the overhead associated with interrupts, mainly by providing several sets of registers. In this way, when an interrupt occurs, the service routine uses a private set of registers and does not need to save and restore the registers of the interrupted program.

Figure 3-30 shows another way of handling interrupts available today. Instead of allocating a set of registers to a service routine, allocate an entire microprocessor. Radoy and Lipovski [74] describe an early version of this idea in the context of high-performance parallel systems, but it clearly has wider applicability today. This idea tends to reduce interrupt latency, but it also tends to simplify program structure. Timing problems in real-time programs are among the most difficult and costly problems to eliminate in a computer system, with a good deal of the difficulty due to the unpredictability of points of interruption. The system in Figure 3-30 is much simpler to program, and might well be implemented without interrupts whatsoever. Consequently, the cost of software development may well be significantly lower by dedicating a microprocessor to each device than by trying to service each device through a single processor. Like the system in part *c* of Figure 3-29, the system in Figure 3-30 need not permit more than one processor to execute at a time, and it could still be an effective system. That is, when an interrupt for a device is honored, its corresponding micro then turns on and all others shut down. At the conclusion of the service routine, the interrupted micro resumes execution.

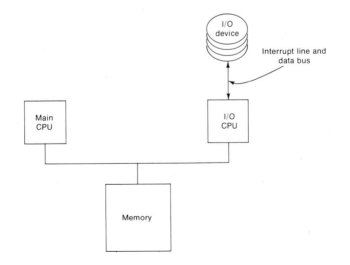

Figure 3-30 A dual-processor system with interrupts fielded by a dedicated processor

The examples in this section suggest that the microprocessor is more than just an inexpensive computer. While it indeed can and will replace computers in conventional applications, it also creates a whole new set of opportunities and challenges that have not existed before.

Architectural solutions for one generation's technology become obsolete in another generation. New challenges emerge for the innovative engineer with the appropriate tools—integrated circuit design, computer architecture, and computer science—and with the perspective and imagination to integrate these tools into new products. Microprocessor architecture remains a rich area for the application of the creativity of a new generation of designers.

CHAPTER 4

Introduction to Minicomputers

K. B. Magleby

The rapid growth of the minicomputer and microcomputer industry is one of the most remarkable developments during the last two decades. Both technical and economic considerations must be examined to explain why this industry developed.

This chapter begins with a definition of minicomputers from a practical and economic point of view. The development of minicomputers over a period of time is closely linked with the technological changes that took place concurrently. The general trends in the development are covered in the early part of the chapter, and specific important advances, such as microprogramming, are covered in more detail later in the chapter. Minicomputer discussion focuses on several areas. First we present the minicomputer processor structure to show the major components. Next comes a discussion of the interface with memory and input/output devices, with the notion of bus structure emerging as a principal idea in tying together the various components of a minicomputer. Design considerations are treated in Sections 4-3 and 4-4, which investigate the instruction repertoire and effective-address calculation mechanisms of typical minicomputers. The PDP-11 and HP 2116/21MX computers serve as case studies to show how various design questions have been settled in actual practice. Performance, in particular, has been a central issue in design, and the case studies reveal several parameters that strongly influence the trade-off in cost and performance.

The various addressing modes that are used in minicomputers have a major impact on system performance for a given application. These address modes are defined and the benefit of each alternative is given, together with examples of existing minicomputer implementations. The characteristics of the input/output system of a minicomputer determine how effectively the system will work with a variety of external devices. The latter part of the chapter treats various input/output systems.

Techniques for performance evaluation give the designer tools to select a given set of alternatives for a particular application. These techniques also give the user tools to select the particular minicomputer structure that best satisfies his needs. Several performance analysis techniques are defined and illustrated with examples. The chapter closes with a number of system applications that illustrate the use of minicomputers.

4-1. DEVELOPMENT OF MINICOMPUTERS

Economic Factors

Minicomputers as we know them today first became an important part of the computer community about 1965, when economic and technical factors combined to make small, dedicated processors attractive for a large number of applications. By almost any definition that excludes cost, most early computers would, by today's standards, be classified as minicomputers. Taking cost into account, minicomputers have become that amount of computing power that can be provided for less than $50,000. Classifications such as computing power, memory size, system configuration, etc., fail to distinguish the salient features of the minicomputer from their larger, more expensive counterparts. As costs diminish in time, minicomputers become more powerful. The power of today's minicomputer exceeds the power of large-scale computers of a decade ago, and a large-scale computer of today may be only as powerful as a minicomputer of the next decade.

The minicomputer industry has grown from essentially no sales in 1965 to over one billion dollars annual sales in 1978, and is continuing to grow at the rate of 20% to 30% per year. What have been the economic and technical factors that have produced this remarkable industry? What distinguishes a minicomputer from other classes of computers? What applications have contributed to the rapid growth of minicomputer sales?

In the early days of computing, computer designers found that computing cost was minimized by designing large computing systems. There was a large cost for input/output equipment, memory interfaces, and basic control logic, all of which represented fixed overhead, independent of computing power. To take advantage of these expensive modules, hardware and software systems were organized in such a way as to share the computer over a large number of concurrently executing computing tasks. By the early 1960s the cost of computing hardware had been reduced by advanced semiconductor technology to such extent that hardware costs were no longer the major cost elements in providing a solution. Data acquisition and display, programming costs, and real-time requirements now assumed a major role. The computer could be dedicated to a specific task even if it were not utilized 100% of the time.

One of the first successful minicomputers, the PDP-8, was introduced by Digital Equipment Corporation (DEC). This computer had the same command structure as an earlier computer offered by DEC, the PDP-5, but was about ⅓ the size, ½ the cost, and 3 times as fast. While only about 100 PDP-5s were sold, over 10,000 PDP-8s have been sold. Clearly, the PDP-8 provided the right match of computing to a large number of applications. Shortly after the introduction of the PDP-8 a number of other manufacturers introduced minicomputers that were also quite widely used. These included the Hewlett-Packard 2116, the Varian 620, the Data General NOVA, and others.

The features that are usually used to classify a computer as a minicomputer are as follows:

1. Size
2. Computational power
3. Cost
4. Application

Most minicomputers are part of systems dedicated to a specific task. The physical size of the computer is normally less than ½ a conventional 19″ × 6′ equipment rack. Often the system must be portable, and both physical size and weight are important. While some of the early computers had the same computational power as the minicomputers of the late 1960s, the former occupied hundreds of square feet and were certainly not portable.

Computational power is not as easily defined as the horsepower of an engine, but certain figures of merit have been established which are indications of computational power. The primary figures of merit that determine computational power are word length and memory speed. Given a fixed instruction-set effectiveness, these two features determine the rate at which a computer solves problems. The available memory size often determines the size of a problem that a computer can tackle, but not the rate at which the computer solves the problem, and hence is not a useful factor in determining computational power. The generally accepted computational power of a minicomputer implies a word length of 16 bits or less and a memory cycle time of about 1 microsecond.

Perhaps the most significant factor in the rapid growth of the minicomputer industry is system cost. When computers are very expensive, the efficient use of the machine is the most important economic consideration. The users must stand in line, and cannot be allowed to sit at the console and think while the machine stands idle. As the machine costs drop, the salary of the user becomes more significant, and efficient use of his time becomes important enough to allow the machine to stand idle for periods of time. This cost threshold was reached in the mid-1960s when the cost of a computing system with minimum input/output capability and enough memory to perform a variety of useful work (about 4K 16-bit words) dropped below $25,000. Today this threshold is higher due to inflation and other economic factors.

The proper size, computational power, and cost determine when it is practical to use a minicomputer for a given application. The key factor that makes a minicomputer so attractive for a large number of applications is the ability to dedicate the machine to a given job or group of jobs. Usually data are collected and processed as they are generated "in real time" as opposed to being gathered, encoded, and run at the convenience of the computer in "batch mode." Often, since data are available in real time, results of analysis of current data can be used to control the external system and minimize the amount of data that is collected and analyzed. As an example, a minicomputer system was used to analyze the structure of crystals in real time in less than half the time required by a computer with 50 times the computational power operating in batch mode. The minicomputer controlled the position of the crystal and analyzed only useful data, and thus did not need to make 100 readings in order to determine which one reading was significant.

Table 4-1 summarizes the characteristics of a typical minicomputer.

TABLE 4-1. A Typical Minicomputer

Feature	Requirement
Size	Less than ½ of a 19" × 6' equipment rack
Power	16-bit word 1 μsec cycle time
Cost	Less than $25,000 for a 32K system with minimum I/O
Application	Dedicated to one or a group of related jobs

Technical Factors

The improved performance at low cost was made possible by a number of significant technical advances. Early computers used vacuum tubes for logic elements and had limited memory capacities. Later, rotating-drum memories served as the main working memory, and discrete transistors and diodes served as logic elements. A significant improvement in performance occurred when the drum memory was replaced by magnetic-core memories. The first minicomputers became possible when the logic elements were produced using integrated circuits and low-cost core-memory systems were developed. This occurred about 1965. From the early 1970s, large-scale integration has made solid-state memories more economical than core memories with a factor of from 2 to 5 improvement in performance. The use of microprocessor technology adds another factor of from 2 to 5 improvement in performance.

For each technology, computer designers found a different system structure to be optimum. Early minicomputer designers minimized the number and size of solid-state storage registers and simplified the logic structure, thereby limiting the richness of the instruction repertoire. This placed a burden on software development. With large-scale integration the cost of logic decreased, and arrays of storage registers were available at low prices. In the early 1970s minicomputers were developed with extensive command structures and several multipurpose registers. Large-scale integration also made read-only memories and associated microprocessors economically attractive in place of

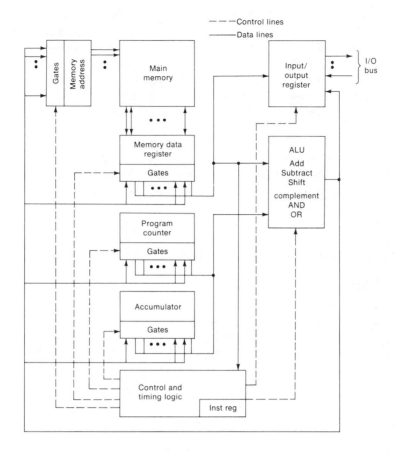

Figure 4-1 Early minicomputer structure

the fixed logic that earlier minicomputers used to implement command structures. This led to microprogrammed processors in which microcode stored in a read-only memory implements the command structure, as per the discussions in Chapters 3 and 10.

Figures 4-1 through 4-3 give the major block diagram of a minicomputer for each technology. In Figure 4-1, a typical integrated circuit contains a J-K flip/flop or four 2-input AND gates. The central processing unit, excluding main memory and input/output control, requires about 400 integrated circuits. In Figure 4-2, a typical large-scale integrated (LSI) circuit is a 16-bit flip/flop array or an 8-bit arithmetic and logic unit (ALU) with more functions than the ALU shown in Figure 4-1. The control and timing is still done with fixed logic, but up to 4 times as many gates are included in a single circuit such as a 4-bit decoder. The central processing unit is reduced to about 100 LSI circuits. Figure 4-3 gives the block diagram of a microprocessor-based computer in which the microprogramming replaces the fixed logic to implement the control function.

As the technology used by computer designers developed, corresponding advances were being made in the development of software for minicomputers. Early minicomputer manufacturers supplied only a symbolic assembler and a few utility routines such as a symbolic editor and a simple math library. This placed a heavy burden on the user to develop his own operating system as well as solve his basic programming tasks in a primitive language. By 1967 minicomputer suppliers had developed compilers that could operate in the restricted core memories used in most minicomputers (4K or 8K 16-bit words). By 1970 most suppliers offered several compilers, e.g., ALGOL and FORTRAN, and interpreters such as BASIC. During this same time, simple operating systems were developed which greatly simplified the task for the user. By 1970 the minicomputer user had most of the conveniences offered to the large computer user.

The development of powerful programming aids greatly accelerated the usage of minicomputers in a diverse range of applications. The following list gives some applications where minicomputers are commonly used.

- Real-time instrument systems
- On-line control systems
- Data communication controllers
- Engineering problem solving
- Production control and scheduling
- Data acquisition systems

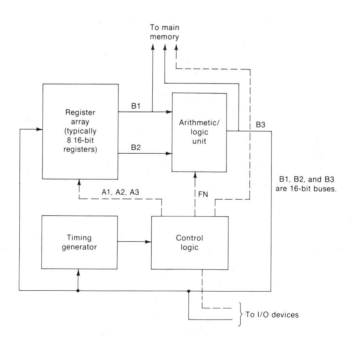

Figure 4-2   Minicomputer structure using integrated circuits

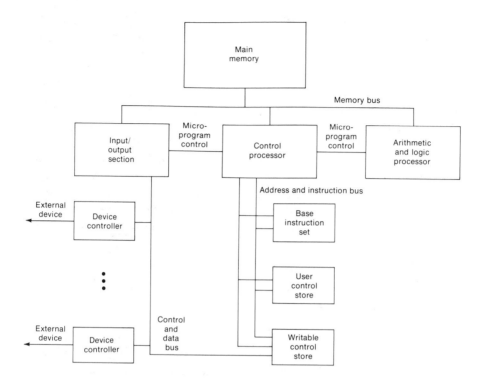

Figure 4-3   Minicomputer implementation

4-2. MINICOMPUTER STRUCTURE

Basic Elements

The major functional elements in a minicomputer are the input/output system, the processor, and the main memory. The structure of a minicomputer is the way in which these elements are interconnected. Interconnections between the major components usually consist of parallel data paths for each bit in the computer's word and a number of data paths for signals that control interelement data transfer. This collection of signals is called a *bus*. Before describing the various bus structures, we give a brief description of the functional elements themselves. The input/output system and memory system are subjects of full chapters in this text, and the processor structure has been described earlier in this chapter and in Chapter 3.

The Input/Output System   The input/output system provides the interface between the peripheral devices on the one hand and the processor and memory on the other. The major functions performed by the input/output system are to:

- Control input/output devices
- Buffer data
- Format data
- Provide processor with status information.

The Processor   The processor controls the data transfer between the basic elements, executes the commands that modify the data or control program execution, maintains system status, and controls the sequence and timing of instruction execution. The basic elements of the processor are data and instructions registers, arithmetic and logic unit, and system control logic.

The organization of the processor is more important in determining system cost/performance than any other minicomputer system consideration. The parameters that a system designer uses to determine processor organization are as follows:

1. Internal bus structure
2. Register structure and function
3. Arithmetic and logic unit function
4. Instruction set
5. System timing

Figure 4-4 gives a block diagram of a typical processor showing the basic elements of the processor. The register block contains the general-purpose registers accessible to the programmer as well as the system registers, such as the program counter, auxiliary registers used in computation, and stack pointers. The instruction is usually held in a register contained in the control logic while it is being decoded.

The processor buses, B1, B2, and B3, are single-direction buses that contain one line for each bit in the word length of the processor. The register block can gate the contents of any register onto B1 or B2, and load any register from B3. The register to be gated onto or loaded from a bus is given by addresses A1, A2, and A3 from the control logic. A typical control cycle

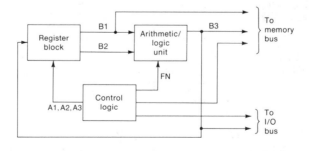

Figure 4-4   Basic processor block diagram

begins by placing the contents of two different registers on B1 and B2 terminals, with the results of an operation then being loaded back into one of the registers. Interconnection to the outside buses is done via B1, B3, and lines from the control logic. A1, A2, and A3 select either an external bus or a register in the register block.

The arithmetic and logic unit accepts the two input buses, B1 and B2, and performs the function given by the FN code from the control logic. The results of the function are available for transfer to an external bus or a processor register via B3. Typical functions performed by the arithmetic and logic unit are:

Minimal Functions	Extended Functions
ADD	SUBTRACT
LOGICAL AND	SHIFT RIGHT 2
LOGICAL OR	SHIFT LEFT 2
EXCLUSIVE OR	SHIFT RIGHT 4
SHIFT RIGHT	SHIFT LEFT 4
SHIFT LEFT	COMPARE
ROTATE RIGHT	INCREMENT
ROTATE LEFT	DECREMENT

Note: Shift operations drop the bit shifted out of the register and insert a 0 into the opposite end of the register. Rotate operations insert the bit shifted out of the register into the opposite end.

The control logic and timing unit contains the sequence-control logic that determines the basic phase that the processor is executing. The processor typically has the following phases:

1. Instruction *fetch* — read the next instruction to be executed from the main memory location given by the contents of the program counter.
2. Instruction *execute* — perform the functions indicated by the instruction that has been fetched in Phase 1.
3. *Indirect* — if the instruction uses indirect addressing, the indirect phase is needed to get the address of the operand.
4. *Interrupt* — this phase is entered if an external device has requested an interrupt.

Figure 4-5 gives the sequence of the various phases that can occur.

The control logic decodes the instruction and provides the proper signals to the other units to execute it. An ADD instruction, which adds two registers and places the results in a third, is executed by sending the appropriate operand addresses to the register blocks and sending the ADD function code to the arithmetic and logic unit.

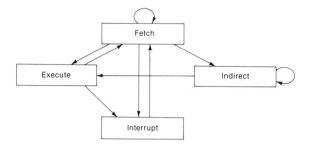

Figure 4-5   Sequence control

There are five different classes of instructions that may be included in any minicomputer's instruction list. These classes are:

1. *Memory-reference instructions* — instructions for which one of the operands is contained in the main memory.
2. *Register-reference instructions* — instructions that perform operations on the contents of a single register.
3. *Register-register instructions* — instructions that perform operations between two registers.
4. *Input/output instructions* — those instructions that transfer data to or from an input/output device or control some function of the input/output device.
5. *Macroinstructions* — complex instructions that typically take several main memory cycles; these instructions may involve several main memory locations and several registers.

A more detailed description of each instruction type is given in the instruction repertoires section (4-3) of this chapter.

The Main Memory   Chapter 5 gives a detailed description of memory systems. The memory system of most modern minicomputers is currently a random-access, solid-state memory. The main memory holds data that can be moved to or from either the processor or the input/output system directly. The data transfer, in either case, is controlled by the processor.

The main memory contains a data buffer, an address register, and a data storage array. Data and address information is transferred from either the processor or the input/output system via a memory bus. The same bus can be used for both address and data by identifying different processor cycles for each type of transfer.

The width of the various buses that interconnect the major system elements is one of the major elements that determines system costs. Minicomputer designers minimize the bus width and use various address-extension techniques to increase the size of main memory that can be addressed. These techniques are discussed in detail in Section 4.4.

Bus Structures

All minicomputer organizations can be classified by the basic bus structure that interconnects the major elements of the system. The three types of bus structures are:

1. Single-bus structure
2. Compatible-input/output-bus structure
3. Multiple-bus structure

Each type is described in more detail in the following text.

To evaluate the performance of a bus structure, the following parameters are defined:

1. *Programmed input/output data rate* — the rate of input or output that can be accomplished via the processor under program control.
2. *Interrupt-processed input/output data rates* — the speed that processing of input/output data can be accomplished via the processor under interrupt control.
3. *Direct-memory-access speed* — the rate that data can pass from an input/output device directly to memory.
4. *Memory-bus data rate* — the speed of the bus that interconnects the main memory and processor.
5. *Input/output-bus data rate* — the speed of the bus that connects the input/output devices to the processor.
6. *System overloading* — a condition that occurs when a task cannot be performed by a major element because the bus is busy.
7. *System overhead* — any activity that is required to accomplish data transmission between two major elements of the system, but which is not part of the data transmission.

Single-Bus Structure The simplest system organization is to have a single bus that interconnects system elements, as shown in Figure 4-6. A typical assignment of signal lines in the bus is also shown. These lines may be directional, that is, duplicated for signals in each direction.

In a single-bus system, the data-transmission protocol between any two elements of the system is identical. A typical protocol is as follows:

1. The element that is to initiate action signals the bus controller via the bus-request line.
2. When the bus is free, the bus controller signals the waiting element via the bus-available line.
3. The element takes control of the bus and signals all other elements via the bus-busy line that the bus is unavailable.
4. The element requests or transmits data via the data lines to the element identified on the module-address bus.
5. The destination element indicates that it has received the data via the

data-received line.
6. Steps 4 and 5 are repeated until the data transfer is complete.
7. The initiator signals the bus controller that it has completed the transfer by clearing the bus-busy line.

Since the protocol is identical for all elements, data can be transferred between any pair of elements. This makes it possible for two input/output devices to communicate with each other without processor control or for input/output devices to send or receive data directly to or from the memory. Programmed input/output is accomplished by a data transfer from an input/ output device to the processor and then a transfer from the processor to memory.

The bus speed must be fast enough to allow the processor-memory communication to take place at speeds limited by the memory elements. Since the bus must be long enough to interconnect all elements of the system and each interconnection adds capacity on the lines, each element must have relatively expensive low-impedance drivers to drive the bus. Input/output controllers

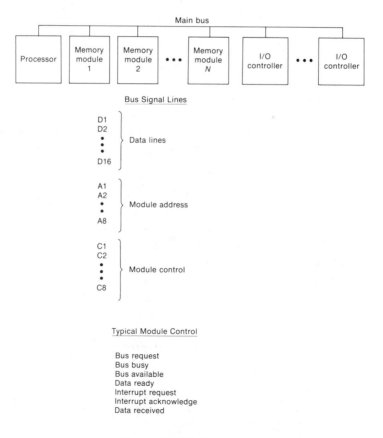

Figure 4-6 Single-bus structure

must be fast enough to operate at the same data-transfer rate as the processor-memory rate, which may add to the cost of the controllers.

An analysis of some of the parameters defined for a single-bus structure follows.

Programmed input/output data rate. The best way to determine the fastest input/output rate possible under program control is to write a benchmark program using a typical command structure for a minicomputer and to estimate the running time. An assumed assembly language is used with a description of the function of each instruction. (For a more detailed description of assembly language, refer to Stone [72].) The following is an example of such a benchmark with the estimated running time:

			Number of Cycles	
READ	SDS	N	1	*(Skip if data-ready flag set)* Test device N to see if data-ready flag is set. If set, skip next instruction.
	JMP	* − 1	1	*Jump* back to previous instruction and loop until flag is set.
	LIA	N	1	*(Load input into accumulator)* Load data from device N into accumulator.
	STA	M,I	3	*(Store, indirect)* Store data into the memory location given by the contents of memory location M.
	INC	M	3	*(Increment)* Increment memory location M.
	ISZ	CTR	3	Increment and test CTR for zero *Note:* CTR must be initialized to $(-L)$, where L is length of record to be read.
	JMP	READ	1	Repeat reading until L reads occur.
		Total cycles	13	

At the maximum input/output rate the JMP * − 1 instruction would not be executed; so the maximum data rate would be 1/12 CT, where CT is the memory-cycle time. Thus, for a 1 microsecond memory the maximum data rate is about 83,000 words per second.

Interrupt-processed input/output rate. Again, a simple benchmark program is the best way to estimate the maximum data rate for an interrupt processor. Assume the main program is running when an interrupt occurs and hardware diverts the computer to begin processing the interrupt in the interrupt-service routine. The service routine is as follows:

		Cycles	
		2	At least two cycles are expended honoring the interrupt to store the former program counter before entering the service routine.
STA	T1	2	Save contents of accumulator in memory location T1.
LIA	N	1	Load data from device N into accumulator.
STA	M,I	3	Store data into memory location given by contents of memory location M.
INC	M	3	Increment memory location M.
LDA	T1	2	Restore accumulator.
ISZ	CTR	3	Increment and test CTR for zero. *Note:* CTR must be initialized to $-L$, where L is length of record to be read.
RTI		2	Return from interrupt.
	Total cycles	18	

At least two cycles are typically used to divert the execution of the processor to the service routine. These normally are one cycle for storing the program counter of the interrupted routine and one cycle to load a new program counter for the service routine. Thus, at least 18 cycle times are required per datum transferred. Again, for a 1 microsecond memory the maximum data rate is $10^6/18$ or about 56,000 words per second.

Direct-memory-access (DMA) input/output rate. Direct memory access refers to a hardware controller for routing data directly between memory and an input/output device without requiring intervention by the processor to control each datum transferred. This is discussed in more detail in Chapter 6.

In a single-bus structure, the direct-memory-access data rate is limited by the memory-cycle time and the bus speed. For a 1 microsecond memory and a system with a bus-cycle time of less than 1 microsecond, the maximum input/output rate is 1 million words per second. Few peripheral devices require input/output rates approaching this speed. Also, when the rate exceeds 500,000 words per second, the DMA channel uses every bus cycle, and the processor must suspend operation.

Memory-bus speed. To gain a performance advantage over other bus structures, the memory bus should be at least twice as fast as the main memory. This allows one DMA transfer to take place in one memory module while the processor accesses another memory module without degrading system performance. Thus, for a 1 microsecond memory, a 500 nanosecond bus-cycle time is required. Systems exist that do not conform to this guideline, and system performance is then limited by the bus speed.

System overloading. In a system that does not meet the memory-bus speed requirement described previously, system overloading can occur. For example, a system with a bus speed of 1 microsecond and a 1 microsecond memory cycle time suffers a 50% rate reduction in program execution if data is transferred from one input/output device to another at a rate of 500,000 words per second.

System overhead. The input/output method that usually has high overhead is interrupt-processed data. In the benchmark interrupt-service program, the 2 cycles required to divert execution to the interrupt service routine plus the 4 cycles to save and restore the register plus the 2 cycles to return to the main program all represent system overhead. In this the overhead is 8 out of 18 cycles or 44%. Other types of interrupt systems may require many cycles to determine which device is requesting service or the device priority.

For low-data-rate devices, programmed input/output can have high overhead, since the processor must wait for the external device.

Relative merits of single-bus structure. The single-bus structure offers a single type of interface for all system modules. All module controllers can be almost identical. Since the processor can address peripheral devices in the same way that memory locations are addressed, no special input/output instructions are needed. This provides a powerful input/output-instruction set. Due to the universal nature of addressing modules on the bus, device-to-device data transfers are straightforward.

Since the bus must be physically long enough to interconnect all the system elements, it is generally expensive to make it extremely fast. Its speed can be a limiting factor in system performance.

Compatible-Input/Output-Bus Structure The compatible-input/output-bus structure uses two buses to interconnect system modules. The input/output bus is similar to the single bus and is used to connect the processor and direct-memory-access modules to the various peripheral devices. A second bus is added to interconnect the processor and direct-memory-access units with the memory modules. Figure 4-7 gives a block diagram of a compatible input/output bus structure.

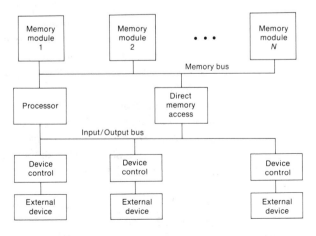

Figure 4-7 Compatible-input/output-bus structure

The peripheral devices can communicate with each other via the input/output bus, and can communicate with either the processor or DMA unit. A single device interface can operate either under programmed input/output or via the DMA channel since a compatible communication protocol is used. The device interface does not need to know whether the processor or the DMA unit is responding to its input/output requests.

The centralized direct-memory-access unit simplifies the device interface requirements and lowers interface hardware costs. This unit performs packing and unpacking of characters into words and contains the starting address of the memory locations holding data to be transferred, the block length, and the address of the next word in memory to be accessed.

Since there are two buses, the memory bus can be physically short, permitting a low-cost high-speed bus, while the longer input/output bus can be slow. Typically, the input/output bus is 2 to 4 times slower than the memory bus.

The evaluation of the basic parameters is as follows.

1. *Programmed input/output data rate* — same as for the single bus structure.

2. *Interrupt-processed input/output data rate* — same as for the single-bus structure.

3. *Direct-memory-access data rate* — typically ½ to ¼ of the memory speed, since the input/output bus is typically slower; for a 1 microsecond memory the DMA rate is 250,000 to 500,000 words per second.

4. *Memory-bus cycle time* — should be at least half the main memory-cycle time to allow processor access to one memory module while the DMA unit is accessing another without degrading system performance; for 1-microsecond memory the memory-bus cycle time should be less than 500 nanoseconds.

5. *Input/output-bus speed* — determined by the data rate required for the fastest peripheral devices. Typically, from ½ to ¼ the speed of the main memory is fast enough to provide for the transfer rate required by a disk memory, which usually is the fastest peripheral device used in a minicomputer system. Disk-memory transfer rates are usually below 4,000,000 bits per second, which requires a 250,000-word-per-second transfer rate for a 16-bit minicomputer.

6. *System overloading* — Data can be transferred between input/output devices without affecting processor execution. The memory bus need only be tied up during transfers between input/output devices and memory, and then for less than 1 memory cycle, since the memory bus can be fast. System overloading usually does not occur with this bus structure.

7. *System overhead* — As with the single-bus structure, the system overhead for interrupt-processed data is about 44% or higher depending on the type of interrupt system used.

Examples   *Example of a single-bus minicomputer.*   The PDP-11 manufactured by the Digital Equipment Corporation is an outstanding example of a single-bus minicomputer. The PDP-11 uses a "Unibus" consisting of 56 signal lines to interconnect all system modules. Each module interface to the Unibus has a module address and intermodule communication can take place between any two modules (see Chapter 6 for the signal assignments and communications protocol for the Unibus).

Example of a compatible-bus minicomputer.   The HP 2100/1000 series minicomputers use a compatible-bus structure. The architects of this minicomputer family optimized the system structure to allow interface with a variety of devices with a minimum-cost device controller. The basic input/output bus has a standard device interface on the bus side of the device controller. Device controllers are designed on a single card with an edge connector on two sides; one connector plugs into the bus and the other receives a cable to interconnect to the device. The device can make data transfers via program control or DMA. The type of transfer is determined by the system programmer; this allows the system programmer to intermix programmed input/output and DMA transfers with a given device to optimize timing vs. system-overhead considerations in a real-time system.

Multiple-Bus Structure   This is a common minicomputer structure. A typical multiple-bus minicomputer is shown in Figure 4-8. A separate input/output

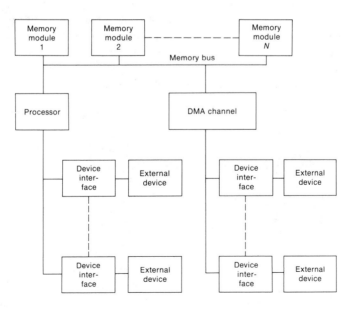

Figure 4-8   Multiple-bus structure

bus is used for each input/output method. A programmed input/output bus is used for devices that use interrupt processing or programmed input/output. A DMA bus is used for devices that transfer blocks of data to or from memory. The speed of these buses corresponds to the required data transfer rate for each method of input/output.

Each device interface is preassigned to a particular input/output method, and it is not possible for a single device to operate using both programmed input/output and DMA. This restriction allows the system designer to optimize the signaled protocol for each bus.

Most of the basic parameters are the same as those for the compatible input/output bus. DMA data transfer rate is typically faster, approaching the speed of main memory, since the added bus speed does not affect the speed or cost of the programmed input/output bus. System overloading is also less likely to occur than with either of the other two bus structures.

The XDS Sigma 3 is an example of a computer that uses a *multiple-bus structure*.

4-3. INSTRUCTION REPERTOIRES

The various kinds of instructions that may be included in a microcomputer's instruction list have already been enumerated in our discussion of processor organization (Section 4-2). The selection of an instruction repertoire for a minicomputer is the area that provides the minicomputer architect an opportunity to optimize the system performance for a given type of application. Since the word length is limited, the architect must make efficient use of all the bits in the various instruction formats. The instructions which reference memory contain fields to determine the command and identify the operand. Because of the limited word length, a variety of address modes is used to give an extended address to allow larger main memories to be efficiently accessed.

Memory-reference Instructions

A typical word format for the following reference class of instructions is as follows:

Operation Code	Register	Address Mode	Displacement
4	2	2	8

The number under each field indicates the number of bits in the field. This instruction format is the most difficult to establish since a critical trade-off between three basic parameters must be performed. These parameters are:

1. instruction power, that is, the number of bits in the operation-code field;

2. addressing power, that is, the number of bits in the address-mode field; and
3. address range, that is, the number of words addressable by the displacement field.

The following text includes a more detailed description of each field.

Operation-Code Field   Since the instructions included in this class reference memory, typical operations involve one memory location and one register. Two exceptions to this rule are typically included in the memory-reference class. They are the increment memory location and jump instructions.

Typical operation codes are:

ADD	COMPARE
SUBTRACT	MULTIPLY
LOAD REGISTER	DIVIDE
STORE REGISTER	INCREMENT MEMORY
AND	DECREMENT MEMORY
OR	JUMP
EXCLUSIVE OR	JUMP TO SUBROUTINE

Register Field   One of a number of registers in the register block shown in Figure 4-4 may be selected as one of the operands that is involved in the instruction. This field determines which register is selected. In some minicomputers, only one register is involved in memory-reference instructions, and this field is omitted. For those instructions that do not reference a register, that is, increment and jump instructions, this field has no meaning and can be decoded to indicate which instruction is specified.

Address-Mode Field   The displacement field can be interpreted in several ways. The address mode field is used to specify how the displacement field is to be used in computing the effective address of the second operand of the instruction. There are a number of different address modes that have been used in minicomputers, including direct addressing, indirect addressing, indexed addressing, and relative addressing. These are described in detail in Section 4-4.

Displacement Field   This field gives the displacement from a memory location. The location itself is determined by the address mode used to find the address of the second operand. The displacement is either a positive integer or a signed integer. Often the address-mode field must be interpreted to determine if the displacement field is used as a positive integer or a signed integer. For example, in direct addressing the displacement is usually a positive integer, while in relative addressing from the program counter the displacement is usually a signed integer.

Register-reference Instructions

Register-reference instructions operate on a single register. Typical instruction format is as follows:

Class Code	Register	Operation	Parameter
4	3	5	4

The class code specifies that this instruction is a register-reference instruction. Other class codes indicate input/output instructions, register-register instructions, and macro instructions.

The register field specifies which register in the register block is being referenced. In the example shown here, up to eight of the registers in the register block may be referenced by this type of instruction.

The operation field is decoded to indicate what function is to be performed on the register. In this example, up to 32 different operations may be specified. Typical operations for register-reference instructions are given in Table 4-2.

The parameter field is used as a constant that can be loaded into the register, added to the register, or subtracted from the register; it can also specify the number of times to shift or rotate the register.

Many variations exist in this class of instructions, but the same typical operations are performed.

TABLE 4-2. REGISTER-REFERENCE INSTRUCTIONS

Clear register
Complement register
Increment register
Decrement register
Skip if register is 0
Shift register N bits to right
Shift register N bits to left
Rotate register N bits right
Rotate register N bits left
Clear bit N
Set bit N
Complement bit N
Skip if bit N is 0
Skip if bit N is 1
Rotate register and carry N bits right
Rotate register and carry N bits left
Arithmetic shift right N bits
Arithmetic shift left N bits
Long shift right N bits (two adjacent registers shifted)
Long shift left N bits
Load register with N
Add N to register
Subtract N from register

Note: N is given by the parameter field.

Register-Register Instructions

Register-register instructions involve two of the registers in the register block. One method of achieving this class of instructions is to assign the first n main-memory locations to refer to the n registers in the register block. Then the operations specified in the memory-reference class can also be performed between registers. This method, however, makes the first n main memory locations inaccessible. A more common method of implementing this instruction is shown in the following instruction format:

Class Code	Register 1	Register 2	Operation
4	3	3	6

As with the register-reference commands, the class code specifies the instruction as a register-register type. The two register fields give the registers to be operated upon. Note that if both register fields specify the same register, a register-reference command results, that is, an instruction that references only one register. The operation field defines the function to be performed on the two registers. With this format, there is a simple implementation using the structure shown in Figure 4-4. Usually the result of the operation replaces one of the operands, say register 2. Then the three addresses in A1, A2, A3 become register 1, register 2, register 2. The FN in Figure 4-4 is derived directly from the operation field for many of the instructions. Typical operations for this class of instructions are given in Table 4-3.

This class of instructions in some minicomputers has been extended to function as memory-reference instructions or memory-memory instructions by interpreting the contents of the named register as the address of the operand rather than the operand. In this case the format of the instruction becomes:

Class Code	Mode	Register 1	Mode	Register 2	Operation
2	2	3	2	3	4

The mode field specifies how to interpret the register field. Typical mode specifications are:

1. Direct—use the contents of the register as an operand.
2. Indirect—use the contents of the register as the address of the operand.
3. Indirect, increment—use the contents of the register as the address of the operand and increment after use.
4. Decrement, indirect—decrement the contents of the register and use the contents as the address of the operand after decrementing.

The increment and decrement modes make processing arrays much more efficient. Incrementing the register after its use and decrementing the register before its use simplifies the implementation of a push-down stack operation.

TABLE 4-3. REGISTER-REGISTER INSTRUCTIONS

Operation	Definition
ADD	Add the two registers—result in register 2
AND	Logical AND the registers—result in register 2
OR	Logical OR—result in register 2
XOR	Exclusive OR—result in register 2
COMP	Compare—skip next instruction if equal
MPY	Multiply—result in register 2
DIV	Divide—result in register 2
SHIFT	Linked shift of the two registers
ROTATE	Linked rotate of the two registers
MOVE	Transfer the contents from register 1 to register 2
XCHANG	Exchange the contents of the two registers

Input/Output Instructions

Input/output instructions transfer data between the computer and external devices and control the operations of these devices. A typical instruction format is as follows:

Class Code	Device-Select Code	Register	Operation
2	8	3	3

The class code specifies the input/output class of instructions. The device-select code identifies which external device is being addressed. The device-select code usually is sent directly to an external bus that allows external device controllers to detect that they are being accessed. The operation field specifies the action being taken. Typical external-device interfaces contain two flip/flops to indicate the status of the external device. (See Chapter 6 for more detailed descriptions of programmed input/output.) Figure 4-9 gives a simplified device interface.

A typical transfer of data is accomplished via the following sequence:

1. Data are transferred from a processor register to the device register by gating the data onto the data bus and the desired external-device selector code onto the select-code bus.
2. The busy flip/flop is set to signal to the external device that a datum is ready.
3. The device accepts and processes the datum and sets the done flip/flop.
4. The device control logic clears the busy flip/flop and the processor can send more data.

To perform these functions, the typical input/output instructions are as given in Table 4-4.

TABLE 4-4. INPUT/OUTPUT INSTRUCTIONS

Operation	Definition
LIR	Load data into register
MIR	Inclusive OR data into register
OTR	Output data from register
STB	Set busy flip/flop
SBS	Skip next instruction if busy flip/flop is set
STD	Set done flip/flop
SDS	Skip next instruction if done flip/flop is set
CLB	Clear busy flip/flop
CLD	Clear done flip/flop

Macroinstructions

Macroinstructions are the more complex instructions that are typically implemented using a read-only control memory. They usually take several main-memory cycles and may involve several registers and memory locations. Typically they have a one-word format for those operations relating to the registers and a two-word format for those operations that reference memory. The typical one-word format is:

Code Class	Register 1	Register 2	Operation
2	3	3	8

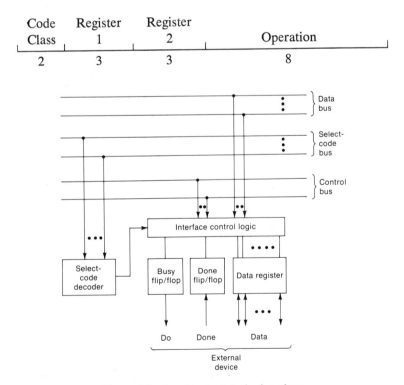

Figure 4-9   Input/output-device interface

The typical two-word format is:

Class Code	Register	Mode	Operation
2	3	3	8

Address
16

The various fields are interpreted in essentially the same way as their corresponding fields are interpreted in other instructions. Some typical macroinstructions are given in Table 4-5.

TABLE 4-5. Macroinstructions

Operation	Definition
One-Word Format	
FLT	Convert the number contained in the two registers to a floating-point number
FIX	Convert the number contained in the two registers to a fixed-point number
BCD	Convert the number contained in the two registers to binary
Two-Word Format	
FMPY	Floating-point multiply
FADD	Floating-point add
FSUB	Floating-point subtract
FDIV	Floating-point divide
FLOAD	Load two registers with contents of successive memory locations
FSTORE	Transfer contents of two registers to successive memory locations

Overview of Command Structures

During the preceding discussion we have indicated that all the instructions except the memory-reference instructions are specified by a class code. How does the minicomputer determine that a memory-reference instruction is specified? There are two methods used to separate instruction types:

1. Reserved operation-code method
2. Class-code method

The reserved operation-code method reserves some of the operation codes of the memory-reference class to specify the other classes. This is the method used in the typical instruction formats given previously to separate instruction types. Table 4-6 summarizes the instruction formats using the reserved operation-code method.

TABLE 4-6. RESERVED OPERATION-CODE METHOD

Format	Instruction Class
Operation Code | Register | Mode | Displacement	Memory reference (Operation code 0000 not used)
Class Code 0000 | 00 | Device-Select Code | Register | Operation	Input/output
Class Code 0000 | 01 | Register 1 | Register 2 | Operation	Register-register
Class Code 0000 | 10 | Register | Operation | Parameter	Register reference
Class Code 0000 | 11 | Register 1 | Register 2 | Operation	Macroinstruction

The class-code method uses a separate fixed-length class-code field to specify the different instruction types. This uses some of the bits in the memory reference instruction to specify its class, but uses fewer bits in the other instruction types. This method usually results in a poor balance between the memory-reference class and the other instruction types. An example of the class code method is shown in Table 4-7.

TABLE 4-7. CLASS-CODE METHOD

Format	Instruction Class
Class Code 00 | Operation Code | Register | Mode | Displacement	Memory reference
Class Code 01 | Operation Code | Mode | Register 1 | Mode | Register 2	Register-register
Class Code 10 | Operation Code | Register | Operation Code | Parameter	Register reference
Class Code 11 | Operation Code | Device-Select Code	Input/output

4-4. ADDRESS MODES

Perhaps the most important feature that distinguishes minicomputers from advanced calculators and conventional computers is the method of determining the address of the operand in the memory-reference class of instructions.

Due to the short word length, the number of bits in the address field is limited. As mentioned earlier, the word length is limited to minimize system cost. Various techniques have been developed to extend the effective address field. While most of them are described here, no single minicomputer uses all of these modes. Controversy exists among computer designers over the relative merit of each mode, and selection of the set of address modes to be included in a given machine is often one of the most difficult tasks of the designer.

Definitions   To indicate the address calculation that the address mode specifies, the following definitions are helpful:

- Effective address (EA)—the address that results from the address mode calculation; the EA is the absolute address in memory of the operand.
- Contents of a given memory location (MEMORY [X])—the contents of memory location X, where X represents an integer address.
- Displacement (D)—the contents of the displacement field of the instruction.
- Register contents (REG [1])—the contents of register 1; the value of the program counter is denoted as PC, and the value of the stack pointer is denoted as SP.

Address Range   The address range of a particular address mode is defined as the number of words in main memory that can be addressed. Since the address range is usually a power of 2, often the range is given as a multiple of 1024 (2^{10}), and K is used to mean 1024. Thus an address range of 4K indicates that the particular address mode has a 12-bit address and can address 4096 words.

The displacement field in the memory-reference instruction format given in Section 4-3 has eight bits. This has an absolute range of 256 words that can be addressed directly. Some method of address-range extension is needed to provide a useful number of main-memory locations that can be addressed. The register or memory location used to contain the other elements of the address calculation about to be described is usually the same length as a computer word. Thus, in a 16-bit computer, most other addressing modes have a range of 2^{16} or 64K.

The program counter and other registers contain 16 bits, so the relative address modes can also address up to 64K words.

Description and Objectives of Address Modes

Typical Address Modes   Minicomputers may reference memory by using any of the following address modes:

1. *Direct addressing*—The displacement field specifies the absolute address of the operand. No other register is used and no computation performed.

$$EA := D$$

2. *Indirect addressing*—The displacement field or the result of some address computation gives the memory location that contains the address of the operand.

$$EA := MEMORY [D]$$

3. *Indexed addressing*—The displacement field is added to or subtracted from an index register, IR, that may be automatically incremented after each operation. Indexed addressing is useful for manipulating arrays or blocks of data.

$$EA := D + REG [IR]$$

4. *Relative addressing*—The effective address is obtained by adding the displacement field to one of the other registers in the computer. Typical registers that are used are:

- *Program counter*—used in relative jump instructions or to set up parameters to be passed to subroutine.

$$EA := D + PC$$

- *Base register*—used in programs where the base register BASE contains the starting address of the segment assigned to the data or instruction being referenced.

$$EA := D + REG [BASE]$$

- *Stack pointer*—used to reference a push-down stack location other than the top of the stack.

$$EA := D + SP$$

The effective address can be computed by other techniques such as stack addressing and dynamic memory mapping, described next.

Stack Addressing   The use of last-in, first-out stacks (push-down stacks) can add significant power to the address capability of minicomputers. Instructions that operate with stacks reference either a register or a memory location for one operand and the top of the stack for the other. As data are loaded onto the stack, a stack pointer that indicates the top of the stack is automatically incremented to point to the new top of the stack. Operations that use the top of the stack as an operand automatically increment the stack pointer. Some operations use the top two elements of the stack as operands, leaving the result as the top of the stack. The use of stacks allows reentrant subroutines and can reduce the running time of arithmetic operations.

Reentrant subroutines are used to avoid the need for a separate copy of common programs used by several different main programs that are running under interrupt control. As a simple example, assume that two interrupt-service routines reference the same subroutine (see Figure 4-10). The lower-

Lower-Priority Service Routine
_____

MEMORY LOCATION	INSTRUCTION	COMMENTS
	Instruction 1	
	Instruction 2	
	.	
	.	
	.	
100	JSB SUM	
	.	Jump to sum subroutine; store return address in top of stack location which will contain sum.
	.	
	.	
	ANSWER	
	.	
	.	
	.	
	Last instruction of service routine	

Higher-Priority Service Routine
_____

	Instruction 1	
	Instruction 2	
	.	
	.	
	.	
300	JSB SUM	
	.	Jump to sum subroutine; store return address in top of stack.
	.	
	ANSWER	
	.	
	.	
	.	
	Last instruction of service routine	

Figure 4-10   Two interrupt service routines

priority interrupt-service routine is executing the common subroutine (see Figure 4-11) when the higher-priority interrupt occurs. The sample code in Figures 4-10 and 4-11 indicates how the use of a stack simplifies reentrant programming.

The higher-priority interrupt occurs when the lower-priority service routine is executing SUM. The arrow in Figure 4-11 indicates the instruction being executed when the higher-priority interrupt occurs. Figure 4-12 traces the contents of the stack.

The remaining part of the service routine may use the stack, but it returns the stack to the last condition shown before it returns to the lower-priority service routine.

The SUM subroutine evaluates: SUM = AB + CD + EF + GH

SUM	PUSH	AC	Push down present accumulator value.
	PUSH	A	Push A onto stack.
	MPS	B	Multiply top of stack by B; leave product on top of stack.
	PUSH	C	Push C onto stack.
	MPS	D	Multiply top of stack by D; leave product on top of stack.
	ADT		Add the top two elements on the stack; leave sum on top of stack.

Higher-priority interrupt occurs here.

	PUSH	E	
	MPS	F	
	ADT		
	PUSH	G	
	MPS	H	
	ADT		
	POP	A,I	Store top of stack (SUM) in address given by contents of accumulator.
	INA		Increment accumulator.
	LDA	S	Load accumulator from top of stack.
	RTI		Return to main program location by popping return address off stack.

Figure 4-11 Common subroutine

TOS→ AB + CD ACCUM RET. ADDRESS₁	Contents of stack when higher-priority interrupt occurs; the integer 1 indicates first entry into subroutine.
TOS→ RET. ADDRESS₂ AB + CD ACCUM RET. ADDRESS₁	Contents of stack when higher-priority service routine enters SUM.
TOS→ AB + CD + EF + GH RETURN ADDRESS₂ AB + CD ACCUM RET. ADDRESS₁	Contents of stack after SUM for higher-priority routine is calculated.
TOS→ AB + CD ACCUM RET. ADDRESS₁	Contents of stack after higher-priority service routine exits SUM.

(TOS = Top of stack)

Figure 4-12 Stack contents

In the interrupt example, the return address for interrupts can be saved on the stack. The last instruction in the interrupt-service routine is a return from interrupt, which retrieves the return address from the stack. The return addresses may also be stored elsewhere, depending on the structure of the particular computer.

Dynamic-Memory Mapping In 16-bit minicomputers with multilevel indirect addressing, the maximum address length for a word is 15 bits, which provides a range of 32,768 words. As the cost of memory has dropped and the size of problems that minicomputers have been applied to has increased, the address range has needed to be expanded. One way of extending this range is through a mapping mechanism explained here. Maps of this type have been implemented in many different minicomputers. This example is drawn from the HP 1000 computer family.

In the basic instruction set, the memory-reference commands have the following format:

Direct/ Indirect	Operation Code	Zero/ Current	Relative Word Address
1	4	1	10

The 16-bit effective address obtained as an indirect address or via another address extension is interpreted as follows:

Direct/ Indirect	Page Address	Relative Word Address
1	5	10

The dynamic-memory mapping system converts the 5-bit page address to a 10-bit page address, thereby extending the address range from 32 pages of 1024 words to 1024 pages of 1024 words. The extension is accomplished as follows:

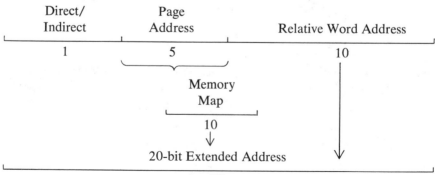

The memory mapping is accomplished with 32 registers of 12 bits in length. The 5-bit page address specifies one of the 12-bit memory-map registers. Ten of the 12 bits give the address extension and the remaining 2 bits are used for memory protection.

Examples of Address-Mode Implementations

Two minicomputers whose basic architecture uses very different address modes are the HP 2116 and the PDP-11. The PDP-11 architecture was determined when the cost of logic and registers had become less than it was when the HP 2116 command structure was chosen. As a result, the basic PDP-11 has more machine registers and a more elaborate address structure than the basic HP 2116. When microprogramming was added to the HP 2116 at a later date, the command structure was extended to include other address modes. The basic command structure and the later evolution of the HP 2116 are described in Section 4-5.

The PDP-11 command structure provides a good contrast to that of the HP 2116. The basic PDP-11 uses a single-bus structure to interconnect the processor, memory, and input/output devices. The processor contains eight 16-bit general registers, which may be used as accumulators, index registers, program counter, or stack pointers. There is also a central-processor status register that contains information about the priority of the program being executed and the conditions resulting from the last instruction that was executed.

The various address modes used in the PDP-11 are listed and described in the following paragraphs.

Single-Operand Addressing The PDP-11 instruction word contains a 10-bit operation code and a 6-bit address field. The address field comprises a 3-bit address-mode field and a 3-bit register field. The instruction format is as follows:

Operation	Addresses	
	Mode	Register
10	3	3

The mode field specifies the following address modes.

0. Direct   The operation is performed on the contents of the specified register.

           OPERAND := REG [R]

1. Indirect   The specified register contains the address of the operand. (EA denotes *effective address*.)

           EA := REG [R]

2. Autoincrement	The specified register contains the address of the operand. The register is incremented after the instruction is executed.

$$EA := REG [R]; REG [R] := REG [R] + 1$$

3. Autoincrement Indirect	The contents of the address location given by the specified register determines the address of the operand. The register is incremented after the instruction is executed.

$$EA := MEMORY [REG [R]]; REG [R] := REG [R] + 1$$

4. Autodecrement	The specified register is decremented and used as the address of the operand.

$$REG [R] := REG [R] - 1; EA := REG [R]$$

5. Autodecrement Indirect	The specified register is decremented. The contents of the memory location given by the contents of the specified register is the address of the operand.

$$REG [R] := REG [R] - 1; EA := MEMORY [REG [R]]$$

6. Indexed	The specified register is used as an index register. Its contents are added to the next word following the instruction to obtain the address of the operand. (PC denotes *program counter.*)

$$EA := MEMORY [PC] + REG [R]$$

7. Indexed Indirect	The contents of the specified register are added to the word following the instruction. The memory location given by the result contains the address of the operand.

$$EA := MEMORY [MEMORY [PC] + REG [R]]$$

These address modes have many interesting uses. The autoincrement and autodecrement instructions facilitate stack processing. The combination of the autoincrement mode stepping forward after the operand address is determined and stepping backward before the address is obtained in the autodecrement mode makes stack operations automatic. Elements within the stack can be addressed via indexed addressing.

General register 7 is used as a program counter. By using the indexed-address mode with register 7 in the register field, addressing relative to the program counter is obtained. The autoincrement mode with register 7 uses the word following the instruction as the operand (immediate addressing). The autoincrement indirect mode with register 7 uses the word following the instruction as an absolute address.

Double-Operand Addressing   The instruction format for double-operand addressing is as follows:

Operation	Source Address		Dest. Address	
	Mode	Register	Mode	Register
4	6		6	

The modes for these instructions are the same as for the single-operand instructions. The operations available are as follows:

Double-Operand Instructions
_____
MOVE
ADD
SUBTRACT
COMPARE
BIT SET
BIT CLEAR
BIT TEST

Single-Operand Instructions
_____
CLEAR
INCREMENT
DECREMENT
NEGATE
TEST
COMPLEMENT
ADD CARRY (FOR MULTIPLE-PRECISION ROUTINES)
SUBTRACT CARRY (FOR MULTIPLE-PRECISION ROUTINES)
ROTATE RIGHT
ROTATE LEFT
SWAP BYTES
ARITHMETIC LEFT SHIFT
ARITHMETIC RIGHT SHIFT

Branch Instructions   The PDP-11 branch-instruction format allows the programmer to test the results of the last operation and branch on the outcome of the test. The processor-status register bits are as follows:

Z	Set if result is zero
N	Set if result is negative
C	Set if a carry resulted
V	Set if an overflow occurred

The branch-instruction format is as follows:

Operation Code	Offset
8	8

The offset is multiplied by two and added to the program counter if the branch condition is satisfied. The branch instructions are as follows:

UNCONDITIONAL
BRANCH ON EQUAL—TESTS Z BIT—EQUAL TEST
    FOLLOWS A COMPARE INSTRUCTION
BRANCH ON NOT EQUAL—TESTS Z BIT—FOLLOWS A
    COMPARE INSTRUCTION
BRANCH ON MINUS—TESTS N BIT—BRANCH IF SET
BRANCH ON PLUS—TESTS N BIT—BRANCH IF CLEAR
BRANCH ON CARRY SET/CLEAR—TESTS C BIT—BRANCH
    IF SET/CLEAR
BRANCH ON OVERFLOW SET/CLEAR—TESTS V BIT—
    BRANCH IF SET/CLEAR
BRANCH ON LESS THAN ZERO
BRANCH ON GREATER THAN OR EQUAL   } TESTS
BRANCH ON LESS THAN OR EQUAL   LOGICAL
BRANCH ON GREATER THAN   COMBI-
BRANCH ON LESS THAN   NATIONS
BRANCH ON HIGHER   OF Z, N,
BRANCH ON LOWER OR SAME   C, V
BRANCH ON HIGHER OR SAME

Jump Instructions   The jump-instruction formats are as follows:

Jump

	Destination Address	
Operation	Mode	Register
10	3	3

Jump to Subroutine

		Destination Address	
Operation	Register	Mode	Register
7	3	3	3

The program counter is stored in the specified register and control is transferred to the destination address. The old contents of the specified register are automatically stored in the processor stack to facilitate nested subroutines. There is no limit to the number of nesting levels.

Return from Subroutine

Operation	Register
13	3

This instruction loads the specified register into the program counter and then loads the top of the processor stack into the specified register.

Input/Output Operations Since the PDP-11 is a single-bus structure, input/output registers are addressed as memory locations. A block of memory locations (usually high-order addresses) is reserved for input/output registers. A typical input/output device will have a data register and a status register. As an example, the paper-tape-reader status register is interpreted as follows:

Out of Tape	Busy	Done	Interrupt Enable	Enable Read
15	11	7	6	0

These bits may be read or set by instructions that address the memory location reserved for the paper-tape status register.

The Uses of Various Address Modes

Direct Addressing This is the most efficient method of addressing an operand when it is within range of the instruction. Typical range of the memory-reference instructions is less than 1024 words. Often some method of address-range extension is needed.

Indirect Addressing The main uses of indirect addressing are address-range extension, array operations, and subroutine return. Since the indirect address is a full-length word, the address range is typically 32K or 64K, depending on whether the computer allows multilevel indirect addressing.

A typical use of indirect addressing would be to find the sum of an array of numbers. The following assembly-language program using the HP 2116 instruction set illustrates how it can be done.

```
START   ADA  PTR, I      Add the nth array element.
        ISZ  PTR         Increment element address.
        ISZ  CTR         Increment array length counter and test to
                            see if done.
        JMP  START       Return to start if not done.
        STA  SUM         Store the sum.
         :
         :
        PTR              Starting address of array.
         :
         :
CTR                      Number of words in array.
```

Using the PDP-11 instruction set, the array operation could be done as follows:

MOV XBASE, R4	Point R4 to array.
CLR SUM	Clear sum to zero.
LOOP ADD @ (R4) + , SUM	Add array element to memory location of sum. Addressing is autoincrement indexed.
CMP R4, LASTX	Compare next array element with ending address.
BLT LOOP	If low continue loop.
⋮	⋮
XBASE	Base address of X.
LAST	Last address in X.
SUM	Sum word.

Indirect addressing is useful in returning from a subroutine. The HP 2116 subroutine call stores the return address in the first memory location of the subroutine and starts execution in the next memory location. Typical subroutines are as follows:

START 0
————————————— ⎫ Reserved for return address
————————————— ⎬ Body of subroutine
————————————— ⎭ Return to calling program
JMP START, I

This method is not used on more modern computers because the subroutines for this method are modified and cannot be stored in ROM.

Indexed Addressing The primary use of indexed addressing is for array operations. The array operation in the previous example could be performed using indexed addressing as follows:

LDX ELS	Load index register with number of elements of array.
NEXT LAX ARY	Load A with array element. (Adds the X register to ending address of array to get operand address.)

ADA SUM   Adds the previous sum to the current element.
STA SUM   Stores the current sum.
DSX   Decrements the X register and skips the next in-
                 struction if zero.
JMP NEXT

Relative Addressing   Typically used to address elements relative to a program counter or stack pointer. Addressing relative to the program counter is used in jump instructions to set up loops. Addressing relative to the stack pointer is used to obtain elements other than the top of the stack.

Stack Addressing   The use of stack addressing is illustrated in Section 4.4.1.

4-5. THE EVOLUTION OF MINICOMPUTER STRUCTURES

Most minicomputers in use today had their original architecture defined in the mid-1960s, when the technology used to implement the structure was significantly different from that of today. As new technology was introduced and the command structures were enhanced, the basic command structure was nevertheless retained to insure that the original software would run on the enhanced computer.

The evolution of the Hewlett-Packard family of minicomputers is a good example of how this evolution took place. The HP 2116 was the first member of the family. The basic command structure was defined in 1965 when integrated circuits were just becoming available. The cost of logic to implement the basic commands was a major consideration at the time the command structure was being defined. As solid-state technology advanced, however, it became economically feasible to use microprogramming to implement the structure. With the lowered cost of logic, many enhancements to the command structure could be added, which significantly improved the performance of the computer.

Base Instruction Set

A block diagram of the HP 2116 is shown in Figure 4-13. The basic structure is a compatible input/output bus. The processor has two arithmetic/logic registers, a program counter, memory data and address registers, and a 1-bit extend register. The arithmetic and logic unit performs add, INCLUSIVE OR, EXCLUSIVE OR, complement, and shift functions. The control and timing unit determines which register to gate onto the R or S processor bus, the function the arithmetic and logic unit performs, and the register that receives the result. The time sequence of these events is determined by the timing generator. In the original implementation, the processor was partitioned as a 4-bit slice, with four bits of each register, a 4-bit processor, and

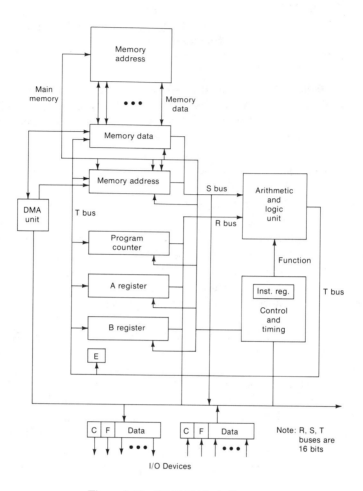

Figure 4-13   HP 2116 block diagram

associated logic on a printed circuit card. The control and timing unit and input/output control were on separate printed circuit cards. A typical integrated circuit contained a J-K flip/flop or four 2-input logic gates. The processor used approximately 500 of these integrated circuits. The main memory was a 4096 × 16 core-memory module. The basic unit could use two memory modules to provide an 8K memory.

The base instruction set of the HP 2116 has three types of instructions. They are the memory-reference group, the register-reference group, and the input/output group. The reserved operation-code method is used to define each group.

Memory-Reference Instructions   The memory-reference instruction format is as follows:

Direct/ Indirect	Operation Code	Registers A/B	Zero/ Current	Relative Word Address
1	3	1	1	10

The first bit specifies direct or indirect addressing; the next three bits specify the operation code (operation code 0 is reserved to define other instruction groups); the next bit either determines the register involved in operations between memory and the register or is decoded as an extension of the operation code for those instructions not involving register selection; the remaining 11 bits determine the memory location.

The memory is divided into pages of 1024 words each. Page 0 is called the base page and can be referenced from any other page. The page containing the instruction is the current page. The first six bits of the address are the same as the first six bits of the instruction and the last ten bits are given by the address field of the instruction. A memory map is shown in Figure 4-14. Since page 0 is available from any other page, it is used for common data or as pointers to other pages by using indirect addressing.

The memory-reference class of instructions has the following operation codes:

000	Reserved to specify other instruction groups.
0010 AND	Performs an AND between memory and the A register.
0100 XOR	Performs an EXCLUSIVE OR function between memory and the A register.
0110 IOR	Performs an INCLUSIVE OR function between memory and the A register.
0011 JSB	Jump to subroutine. Stores program counter in memory and jumps to next location.
0101 JMP	Jump to location given by address.
0111 ISZ	Increment memory location and skip next instruction if the result is 0.
100 I/O ADA/ADB	Add the contents of memory to the A or B register.
101 I/O CPA/CPB	Compare A or B to memory and skip next instruction if not identical.
110 I/O LDA/LDB	Load memory into the A or B register.
111 I/O STA/STB	Store the A or B register contents in memory.

Register-Reference Instructions　The register-reference instructions have two formats as follows:

An instruction on page 5 can access the shaded pages

Figure 4-14   A memory map

Shift/Rotate Group

0 000 A/B 01	Operation Code	CLE	1	SLA/B	Operation Code
7	3	1	1	1	3

The operation codes are:

A/BLS	Shift left.
A/BRS	Shift right.
RA/BL	Rotate left.
RA/BR	Rotate right.
A/BLR	Rotate left with extend bit.
A/BRR	Rotate right with extend bit.
A/BLF	Rotate left four bits.

The operations are executed from left to right in sequence. For example, the rotate left four bits instruction in both operation-code fields would rotate the register eight bits. Between the two operation-code executions the extend bit can be cleared and the selected register can be shifted left.

Alter/Skip Group

0 000 A/B 1	OP Code	SEZ	SSA/B	SLA/B	INA/B	SZA/B	RSS
6	4	1	1	1	1	1	1

The operation codes are:

CLA/B	Clear the register.
CMA/B	Complement the register.
CCA/B	Set the register to all 1s.
CLE	Clear the extend bit.
CME	Complement the extend bit.

CCE	Set the extend bit.
SEZ	Skip if extend bit is 0.
SSA/B	Skip on sign of register.
SLA/B	Skip on least bit of register.
SZA/B	Skip if register is 0.
INA/B	Increment register.

The last 6 bits of the instructions have specific interpretations. Any combination of these operations can be performed in a single instruction. For example, a two's complement instruction would be a combination of complement and increment instructions. A combination of INA and SZA would be the same as an ISZ instruction referring to the A register.

Input/Output-Instruction Group The input/output instructions have the following format:

1 000 A/B 1	Hold/Clear	Operation Code	Select Code
6	1	3	6

Each input or output device interface has a control bit, a flag bit, and a data register. The select code is used to select one of up to 64 input/output devices. The operation codes are:

HLT	Halt.
STF	Set flag.
CLF	Clear flag.
SFC	Skip if flag is clear.
SFS	Skip if flag is set.
MIA/B	Merge data into A/B register.
LIA/B	Load data into A/B register.
OTA/B	Output the A/B register.
STC	Set control bit.
CLC	Clear control bit.

The set and clear control instructions do not use a register, so the register-select bit is used to extend the operation code. Device-select code 0 is reserved for master-interrupt control. The control bit either enables or disables the interrupt system.

The merge instruction is useful for packing partial-word data under software control. For example, two 8-bit characters can be packed by a LIA instruction followed by an ALF,ALF instruction (rotate left eight places) and a MIA instruction on the next input cycle.

Table 4-8 summarizes the command structure.

TABLE 4-8. BASE INSTRUCTION SET FOR HP 2116

15	14 13	12	11	10	9	8	7	6	5	4	3	2	1	0
D/I	AND	001	0	Z/C	←				Memory Address					→
D/I	XOR	010	0	Z/C										
D/I	IOR	011	0	Z/C										
D/I	JSB	001	1	Z/C										
D/I	JMP	010	1	Z/C										
D/I	ISZ	011	1	Z/C										
D/I	AD*	100	A/B	Z/C										
D/I	CP*	101	A/B	Z/C										
D/I	LD*	110	A/B	Z/C										
D/I	ST*	111	A/B	Z/C										

15	14 13	12	11	10	9	8	7	6	5	4	3	2	1	0
0	SRG	000	A/B	0	D/E	*LS		000	†CLE	D/E	‡SL*	*LS		000
			A/B	0	D/E	*RS		001		D/E		*RS		001
			A/B	0	D/E	R*L		010		D/E		R*L		010
			A/B	0	D/E	R*R		011		D/E		R*R		011
			A/B	0	D/E	*LR		100		D/E		*LR		100
			A/B	0	D/E	ER*		101		D/E		ER*		101
			A/B	0	D/E	EL*		110		D/E		EL*		110
			A/B	0	D/E	*LF		111		D/E		*LF		111
			NOP	000				000						000

15	14 13	12	11	10	9	8	7	6	5	4	3	2	1	0
0	ASG	000	A/B	1	CL*	01	CLE	01	SEZ	SS*	SL*	IN*	SZ*	RSS
			A/B		CM*	10	CME	10						
			A/B		CC*	11	CCE	11						

15	14 13	12	11	10	9	8	7	6	5	4	3	2	1	0
1	IOG	000		1	H/C	HLT		000	←		Select Code			→
				1	0	STF		001						
				1	1	CLF		001						
				1	0	SFC		010						
				1	0	SFS		011						
			A/B	1	H/C	MI*		100						
			A/B	1	H/C	LI*		101						
			A/B	1	H/C	OT*		110						
			0	1	H/C	STC		111						
			1	1	H/C	CLC		111						
				1	0	STO		001		000			001	
				1	1	CLO		001		000			001	
				1	H/C	SOC		010		000			001	
				1	H/C	SOS		011		000			001	

15	14 13	12	11	10	9	8	7	6	5	4	3	2	1	0
1	EAG	000	MPY**	000		010				000			000		
			DIV**	000		100				000			000		
			DLD**	100		010				000			000		
			DST**	100		100				000			000		
			ASR	001		000			0	1					
			ASL	000		000			0	1			number		
			LSR	001		000			1	0		←	of		→
			LSL	000		000			1	0			bits		
			RRR	001		001			0	0					
			RRL	000		001			0	0					

15	14 13	12	11	10	9	8	7	6	5	4	3	2	1	0
1	FLT PT	100		101			00	FAD		000		0		000	
								FSB		001					
								FMP		010					
								FDV		011					
								FIX		100					
								FLT		101					

Notes		
* = A or B, according to bit 11.	†CLE	Only this bit is required.
D/I, A/B, Z/C, D/E, H/C coded 0/1.	‡SL*	Only this bit and bit 11 (A/B as
**Second word is Memory Address.		applicable) are required.

Extended Instruction Group The original architecture of the HP 2116 reserved a group of instructions for the extended arithmetic unit option and future instruction enhancements. This group was also intended as a means of calling software realizations of instructions that could be implemented with hardware for faster execution. The instruction format is as follows:

1 000 A/B 0	Operation Code
6	10

The first group of instruction enhancements was provided by the extended arithmetic unit which could be added to the HP 2116 or HP 2115 computers. This consisted of two logic cards containing about 120 integrated circuits that plugged into the computer mainframe. The instructions were chosen to speed up the routines that performed integer multiply/divide and floating-point operations. They consist of six variable-length linked rotate and shift instructions using both the A and B registers. The instruction format is as follows:

1 000 00	Operation Code	Number of Shifts
6	6	4

The results of these enhancements on the HP 2116 instruction times are summarized by Table 4-9.

TABLE 4-9. ENHANCEMENT OF HP 2116 WITH EXTENDED
ARITHMETIC UNIT (EAU)

Operations	Execution Time with EAU/ Execution Time without EAU (msec)
Integer multiply	.019/1.15
Integer divide	.021/.310
Floating multiply	.344/.750
Floating divide	.448/1.5
Floating square root	3.94/6.45

Microprogramming's Impact on the HP 2116 Architecture

The cost restraints on logic were removed when the cost of read-only memory dropped below optimized fixed-logic costs. In addition, the cost of fixed registers also dropped dramatically. Memory costs were dropping at the same time, with core memory being replaced by solid-state memory. This removed many of the software restraints that were placed on the early software-development teams. Compilers that had to be constrained to 4K memory systems could be enhanced and run in larger memory.

A block diagram of the HP 21MX computer is shown in Figure 4-15. The graceful evolution of the basic system structure is apparent. This foresight is

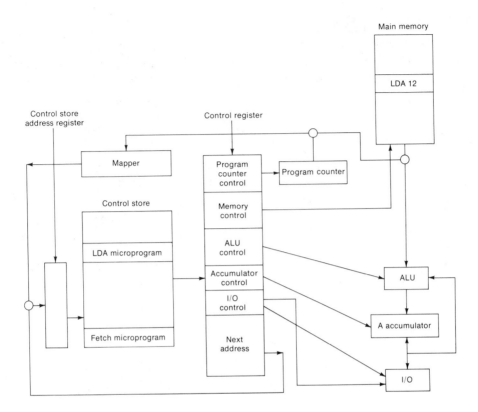

Figure 4-15   Microprogram control structure in the HP 21MX

not unique to the HP series of computers, as demonstrated by the evolution of the Data General computers. In both cases, the architects were aware of the cost trends and made wise choices of system/command structures in order to optimize performance over an extended time period.

The new element introduced by microprogramming was the microinstruction format. This chapter's author remembers the many extended discussions regarding microinstruction word length and system cost. The HP 21MX series designers made a good choice relative to future logic costs at the time the architecture was determined.

The function of the microprogrammed logic unit is to replace the fixed-logic portion of the computer, which is the sequence, timing, and control circuits of the HP 2116. The three logic printed-circuit boards were replaced by a read-only memory and associated control logic. At the same time, the instruction set was enhanced and total costs were reduced.

Extended Instruction Set

Using microprogramming, the instruction set of the Hewlett-Packard family was extended to include a number of more complex instructions. These instructions use the macro-call instruction format that was originally intended for software implementation of complex instructions. These instructions use two additional registers, X and Y, which function as index registers. These instruction formats are summarized in Table 4-10. The meanings of the instructions are as follows:

SAX/SAY/SBX/SBY	Store the A or B register in the memory location given by adding the contents of the X or Y register to the operand address of the instruction. The operand address is the contents of the memory location following the location of the instruction.
CAX/CAY/CBX/CBY	Copy the contents of the A or B register into the X or Y register.
LAX/LAY/LBX/LBY	Load the A or B register in the memory location given by adding the contents of the X or Y register to the operand address of the instruction.
STX/STY	Store the contents of the X or Y register in the memory location given by the operand address of the instruction.
CXA/CYA/CXB/CYB	Copy the contents of the X or Y register into the A or B register.
LDX/LDY	Load the X or Y register from the memory location given by the operand address of the instruction.
ADX/ADY	Add the contents of the memory location specified by the operand address to the X or Y register.
XAX/XAY/XBX/XBY	Exchange A or B registers with X or Y registers.
ISX/ISY/DSX/DSY	Increment or decrement the X or Y register and skip the next instruction if the result is 0.
JLY	This instruction is used to enter a subroutine. Jump to a memory location given by the address portion of the instruction. Load the return address into the Y register.
JPY	Transfer control to the address given by adding the contents of the Y register to the contents of the memory location specified by the operand address of the instruction.

The extended instruction group also contains instructions for bit, byte, and word operation. Floating-point arithmetic operations are also included.

TABLE 4-10. EXTENDED INSTRUCTION SET FOR HP 21MX

	15	14	13	12	11	10	9	8	7	6	5	4	3	2	1	0
SAX/SAY/SBX/SBY	1	0	0	0	A/B	0	1	1	1	1	1	0	X/Y	0	0	0
CAX/CAY/CBX/CBY	1	0	0	0	A/B	0	1	1	1	1	1	0	X/Y	0	0	1
LAX/LAY/LBX/LBY	1	0	0	0	A/B	0	1	1	1	1	1	0	X/Y	0	1	0
STX/STY	1	0	0	0	1	0	1	1	1	1	1	0	X/Y	0	1	1
CXA/CYA/CXB/CYB	1	0	0	0	A/B	0	1	1	1	1	1	0	X/Y	1	0	0
LDX/LDY	1	0	0	0	1	0	1	1	1	1	1	0	X/Y	1	0	1
ADX/ADY	1	0	0	0	1	0	1	1	1	1	1	0	X/Y	1	1	0
XAX/XAY/XBX/XBY	1	0	0	0	A/B	0	1	1	1	1	1	0	X/Y	1	1	1
ISX/ISY/DSX/DSY	1	0	0	0	1	0	1	1	1	1	1	1	X/Y	0	0	I/D
JUMP INSTRUCTIONS	1	0	0	0	1	0	1	1	1	1	1	1	///	0	1	0

JLY = 0
JPY = 1

	15	14	13	12	11	10	9	8	7	6	5	4	3	2	1	0
BYTE INSTRUCTIONS	1	0	0	0	1	0	1	1	1	1	1	1	0	///	///	///

LBT = 0 1 1
SBT = 1 0 0
MBT = 1 0 1
CBT = 1 1 0
SFB = 1 1 1

	15	14	13	12	11	10	9	8	7	6	5	4	3	2	1	0
BIT INSTRUCTIONS	1	0	0	0	1	0	1	1	1	1	1	1	1	///	///	///

SBS = 0 1 1
CBS = 1 0 0
TBS = 1 0 1

	15	14	13	12	11	10	9	8	7	6	5	4	3	2	1	0
WORD INSTRUCTIONS	1	0	0	0	1	0	1	1	1	1	1	1	1	1	1	///

CMW = 0
MVW = 1

The Evolution of Minicomputer Families

Since minicomputers are constrained by cost, they necessarily have limitations in power and versatility imposed by the cost constraint. With the rapid decrease in component cost experienced by integrated-circuit technology, features that are too expensive to include in a minicomputer at one time become quite feasible to incorporate several years later. Thus minicomputers have evolved continually over the past two decades to incorporate sophisticated and powerful extensions as hardware costs diminished. We have indicated just a few of these for the HP 2116. In this section we trace the typical evolution experienced by a minicomputer family to indicate how the evolution might proceed in the future. The microcomputer is in a very real sense reliving this same evolution, so that minicomputer history provides a model for the future microcomputer industry.

Basic system: no frills
> 16-bit word.
> Fixed-point arithmetic.
> Discrete logic or small-scale integrated circuits.
> Magnetic core memory, 32K words maximum.

First extension: extended instructions
> Floating-point instructions.
> Additional registers plus additional instructions other than floating-point instructions.
> 32-bit and 64-bit data formats are included.

Second extension: microprogrammability
> Instructions implemented in ROM can be altered easily to extend the instruction set.
> A special RAM memory is incorporated to replace ROM for instructions that can be changed dynamically.

Third extension: large memory
> Memory mapping and memory protection is incorporated to provide 1 million or more words of main memory.
> Additional instructions are included to control the mapping process, and to provide a privileged mode for an executive control program.

Fourth extension: performance enhancement
> Special high-speed buffer memory, high-speed arithmetic units, and other hardware facilities are incorporated to boost processor performance.

Fifth extension: evolution to a new family
> A new family of computer is introduced that eliminates problems caused by constraints on the old family that are no longer valid because of new technology.
> The new family may be partially compatible with the old family, but not fully compatible. Software must be easily transportable in some fashion from old family to new family.

The software for microprocessors also is evolving along the same lines as minicomputer software. First, only machine language or assembly-type languages were used to program microprocessors. As the hardware becomes more advanced, higher-level software is being developed to allow the user to prepare programs more efficiently.

With the introduction of a new family the evolution process begins anew. Readers can trace this evolution in several minicomputer families such as the HP 2000 (HP 2116, HP 2100, HP 21MX, HP 1000), PDP-11 (Model 20, Model 10, Model 34, Model 45, Model 70, VAX), and Data General NOVA (NOVA, ECLIPSE, M-600). The evolution is just beginning for the microprocessors as the second and third generation micros appear. Consider the evolution of the 8000 series (8008, 8080, Z-80, 8086, Z-8000) and 6800 series (6800, 6802, 6809, 68000) to observe how this process is moving. Presently, microprocessors are in various stages of extending instruction sets and memory size. On-chip floating-point arithmetic was not available at the end of the 1970s, but floating-point peripheral chips did appear early in the 1980s.

4-6. INPUT/OUTPUT SYSTEMS

Chapter 6 gives a detailed discussion of input/output systems, both for minicomputers and larger computing systems. In this section the input/output problem and solution for the minicomputer is summarized and the reader is referred to Chapter 6 for more details.

In minicomputer systems, performance is usually sacrificed to obtain lower cost. The system designer has a trade-off for performance versus cost in the input/output system. In this system a minimal hardware interface with external devices can be used, with many of the functions of the device controller performed either via software or by a more expensive high-performance controller. In most cases, minicomputer designers place a greater burden on software implementation of controller functions. Perhaps the only exception to this rule is in the interrupt system provided by minicomputer designers. Since many of the applications of minicomputers are in real-time systems, interrupt response time is an important parameter in evaluating minicomputers.

Types of Input/Output Systems

There are three types of input/output systems presently used to transfer data from peripheral devices and the main memory. These are:

1. Programmed input/output
2. Direct memory access
3. Interrupt-processed input/output

These methods are defined earlier in this chapter (Section 4-2) and are described in detail in Chapter 6. A short classification of interrupt systems and the relative merits of each type of interrupt system is presented here.

There are basically four types of interrupt systems:

1. Single-priority, polled
2. Single-priority, vectored
3. Multi-priority, polled
4. Multi-priority, vectored

Single-Priority Polled Interrupt Systems In a single-priority polled minicomputer system, the interrupt-request input is the INCLUSIVE OR of all of the interrupt requests of the external devices. No hardware assistance is provided in determining which device is requesting service, or, in the case of simultaneous interrupts, which device is most important. These latter tasks must be determined via software by polling the devices with instructions that sample each device individually. While this saves in hardware cost, system performance is greatly degraded since a high system overhead is incurred in performing the device-recognition and priority-determination functions.

Single-Priority Vectored Interrupt Systems In single-priority vectored interrupt systems, the interrupt system also has an INCLUSIVE OR for all device-interrupt requests; in addition, a device-select-code bus is included to allow the device requesting service to identify itself. If another device requests service before the first request is granted, the processor receives the interrupt request, but the second device is inhibited from placing its select code on the bus until acknowledgment is sent to the first device indicating that the processor has its request. In most minicomputers, the select code forces the processor to take its next instruction from a memory address derived from the select code. In some computers, however, the processor polls all requesting devices for their codes, determines priority, and starts to service the device with highest priority. As in the first case, if another device of lower priority requests service, the higher priority service routine is interrupted until the processor determines the priority of the new request. System overhead is greatly reduced, but high-priority devices may still be interrupted for short periods by low-priority devices and thus degrade overall system performance.

Multi-Priority Polled Interrupt Systems In a multi-priority polled interrupt system, the device interrupts are combined via an INCLUSIVE OR gate. The devices are arranged in an apriori priority arrangement with the highest-priority devices "closest" to the processor. The lower-priority devices must be inhibited from interrupting while higher-priority devices are being serviced. One method is to use an interrupt-request chain that passes through each device interface. If a device is granted an interrupt it breaks the chain and this inhibits lower-priority devices from requesting an interrupt. This is shown in Figure 4-16. When an interrupt is posted, the processor must poll the devices to determine which device caused the interrupt.

Multi-Priority Vectored Interrupt Systems This is the most powerful interrupt system used in minicomputer systems. Its implementation is essentially a

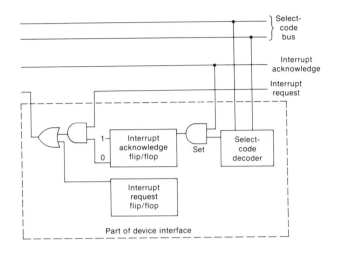

Figure 4-16 Device interface for multipriority interrupt system

combination of the two previously described systems. The external devices are arranged in order of their priority along the input/output bus. The priority chain is as shown in Figure 4-16. When the interrupt-acknowledge flip/flop is set, the acknowledged device puts its select code on a select-code input bus to indicate to the processor which device caused the interrupt. This select code then forces the processor to an address for that select code, where the processor initiates a service routine for that device.

Evaluation of Input/Output Methods

Table 4-11 evaluates the relative merits of each type of interrupt system with respect to several important criteria.

TABLE 4-11. Interrupt System Summary

	Response Time	System Overhead	Maximum Data Rate	Cost
Single-priority, polled	Slow	High	Low	Low
Single-priority, vectored	Fast	High	Moderate	Moderate
Multi-priority, polled	Slow	Moderate	Low	Low
Multi-priority, vectored	Fastest	Low	High	High

4-7. PERFORMANCE ANALYSIS

Benchmark Programs

The most common method of comparing the performance of different computer architectures is to write sample programs of typical operations to determine the execution time of these operations. If one is evaluating various

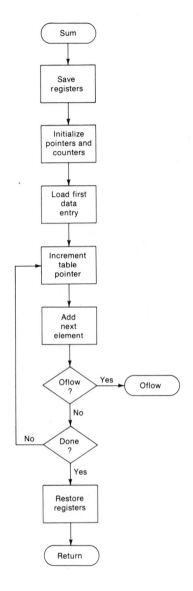

Figure 4-17 Flowchart for benchmark program

computers for use considerations, actual instruction times would be used. For architecture comparisons, a fixed logic speed is used and the number of machine cycles (memory references) is determined.

As an example of the use of benchmark analysis, the instructions of the HP 2116 series and the PDP-11 are compared. The benchmark program chosen is the addition of a group of numbers, checking to see if an overflow occurs after each addition; if an overflow occurs, branch to an alarm routine. A flowchart of the program is given in Figure 4-17.

The assembly-language program using the HP 2116 instruction set is as follows:

CALLING SEQUENCE

JSB SUM		
LENGTH		Length of table
TABLE ADDRESS		
RESULT		
NEXT INSTRUCTION		

No. of Cycles				
	SUM	NOP		
2		STA	TEM	Save A register contents.
3		LDA	SUM,I	Get length of table.
2		STA	LENGTH	
2		ISZ	SUM	
3		LDA	SUM,I	Get table address.
2		STA	POINTER	
2		ISZ	SUM	
3		LDA	POINTER,I	
2	LOOP	ISZ	POINTER	
3		ADA	POINTER,I	
1		SOC		Test for overflow.
—	× length	JMP	OFLOW	
2	of table	ISZ	LENGTH	Increment and test length.
1		JMP	LOOP	
3		STA	SUM,I	Store results.
2		ISM	SUM	Set return address.
2		LDA	TEM	Restore A register contents.
2		JMP	SUM,I	Return.

$28 + 9 \times$ length of table

TEM	0
LENGTH	0
POINTER	0

The same program using the PDP-11 instruction set is as follows:

CALLING SEQUENCE

JSR R5 SUM
LENGTH
TABLE ADDRESS
RESULT

No. of
Cycles

Cycles	Label	Op	Operands	Comment
2	SUM	MOV	R1, −(SP)	
2		MOV	R2, −(SP)	Save R1–R3.
2		MOV	R3, −(SP)	
2		MOV	(R5)+, R1	Load R1 with table length.
2		MOV	(R5)+, R2	Load R2 with table address.
2		MOV	(R5)+, R3	Load R3 with address of result.
3	LOOP	ADD	(R2)+, (R3)	Add the nth element.
1	× length	BVS	OFLOW	Check for overflow.
1	of table	INC	R1	Increment counter.
1		BNE	LOOP	
2		MOV	(SP)+, R3	
2		MOV	(SP)+, R2	Restore R1–R3.
2		MOV	(SP)+, R1	
2		RTS	R5	

20 + 6 × length of table

The JSR R5 SUM instruction stores the contents of R5 on the stack and then loads the program counter into R5 before transferring control to the subroutine. The RTS R5 instruction loads R5 into the program counter and restores R5 from the stack. As an example in determining the number of cycles for an instruction, consider the ADD (R2)+, (R3) instruction. One memory reference is needed to get the instruction, a second memory reference is needed to get the next element in the table, and a third memory cycle is used to store the result.

The power of the PDP-11 addressing modes is illustrated in this example. The choice of the benchmark program can influence the outcome of this method of analysis. Also, the assumption that the cycle time is the same may not be true as the instruction logic becomes more complex.

Input/Output System Analysis

To evaluate the performance of an input/output system, the parameters for bus structures given in Section 4-2 need to be determined. The example of the benchmark program given in that section should be evaluated with each command structure. The relative importance of each of the parameters depends on the use intended for the minicomputer. For example, a machine capable of fast interrupt-response time would be of little value if it was intended to be used with a keyboard printer as the main input/output device. Interrupt-response time, however, could be the most important parameter in evaluating the performance of a minicomputer to be used in a real-time system.

As an example of using benchmark techniques, consider the programmed input/output example given in Section 4-2. The command structure used in that example is that of the HP 2116. To compare the relative speed of the PDP-11 command structure the same program is as follows:

No. of
cycles

5	LOOP	BIT	DEV,FLG	Test to see if flag set.
1		BEQ	READ	Branch back if flag not set.
5		MOV	DEV,LOC	Transfer data from device to memory.
4		INC	*−1	Increment memory location address.
2		INC	CTR	Increment CTR (CTR = number of elements to be read).
1		BNE	LOOP	Branch to loop if CTR $\neq$ 0.

18

The PDP-11 uses a single-bus structure with a block of memory locations reserved for input/output devices. The memory-reference class of instructions is used to address input/output devices.

In a similar way, the other parameters listed in Section 4-2 can be evaluated for each structure to be evaluated. The relative importance of each parameter depends upon the intended use of the minicomputer.

Performance Trade-offs

In the design of any minicomputer system the designers must evaluate the relative importance of several factors. These include:

- Cost
- Arithmetic speed
- Logical-operating speed
- Memory addressing
- Array-processing speed
- Program compactness
- Input/output capability
- Real-time requirements

Since the word length of the instruction is limited, the designer cannot optimize all of the above parameters in a single design. The range of applications intended for the minicomputer determines the relative importance of each parameter. For example, a minicomputer to be used in a stand-alone word processor would emphasize logic operations, array processing, and cost. A minicomputer intended for real-time data acquisition would emphasize input/output capability, real-time response, arithmetic speed, and cost. Using the techniques given in this section and the parameters in Section 4-2, the reader can evaluate his design or an existing design for the use he intends for a minicomputer application.

4-8. SOME APPLICATIONS OF MINICOMPUTERS

As the cost of minicomputers has decreased, the number and range of applications where minicomputers are economically attractive has become more and more extensive. The boundary between the minicomputer and the microprocessor has become blurred. The basic techniques described in this chapter tend to apply both to advanced microprocessor applications as well as minicomputers. A few classic uses of minicomputers are described in the following sections.

Real-Time Instrumentation System

The rapid growth of the minicomputer market is due to the many different applications that can benefit from dedicated real-time computation. A typical example is an instrumentation system which is designed to characterize a device or subsystem. Such a system is shown in Figure 4-18.

Typical applications for a system of this type range from production testing of printed circuit boards to checkout of the complete electronic system of a fighter aircraft on the flight line. In the printed circuit-board testing application, programmable signal sources simulate the inputs normally supplied to the device from the other parts of the system. Under program control, the parameters of the signal sources such as level, frequency, and rise time are varied to determine sensitivity to parameter variations. For complete printed circuit boards, manual parameter sensitivity testing is costly and is normally not performed. When the device does not give the correct response, the computer enters into a diagnostic mode to provide the test technician with enough data

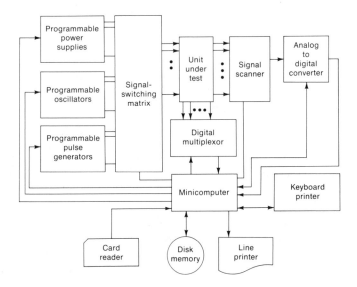

Figure 4-18 Real-time instrumentation system

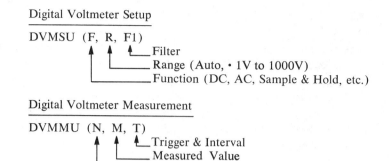

Figure 4-19   Measurement commands

to locate the faulty components. Upon completion of the testing, a report is printed giving the major test results, which can be used as production records. These results are also stored and can be analyzed by the computer to give statistical trends to help production management control production quality.

To assist in writing programs to control the system and analyze the data, an extension of the BASIC programming language is used. Commands are added that specify a given signal type with certain parameters to be applied to a given input pin on the printed circuit board. The BASIC compiler generates the necessary instructions to set up the programmable signal sources and the signal-switching matrix to accomplish the application of the desired signal to the specified input pin. A sample command to set up a measurement is shown in Figure 4-19.

Computing Data-Acquisition System

Data-acquisition systems are the simplest type of instrumentation system. An elementary data-acquisition system converts data from a number of inputs to a form suitable for printing by an output recorder. In more complex systems, some processing of the raw data is done, and the operation of the system may be controlled to some extent by the data.

Because it can easily carry out complex programs, and because its programs can be changed easily, an instrumentation computer in a data-acquisition system makes control of the system extremely flexible. It also provides rapid, local data processing, thereby eliminating the loss of time inherent in remote data processing.

A typical computing data-acquisition system is used, for example, in testing jet engines. The analog inputs are physical parameters, such as pressure, temperature, fuel flow, and engine speed, and the computer outputs are operating parameters, such as efficiency and power. The computer not only provides immediate results to help the operator set up the test, but also controls some portions of the test, thereby making the checkout more automatic.

Figure 4-20 is a block diagram of the system, illustrating its use in jet

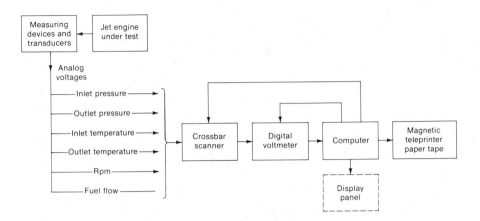

Figure 4-20   Computer-controlled acquisition system

engine testing. Surprisingly, this computing system costs little more than a less flexible noncomputing system capable of performing some, but not all, of the same tasks.

Microwave Network Analyzer System

A block diagram of a network-analyzer system including an instrumentation computer and a network analyzer is shown in Figure 4-21. This system

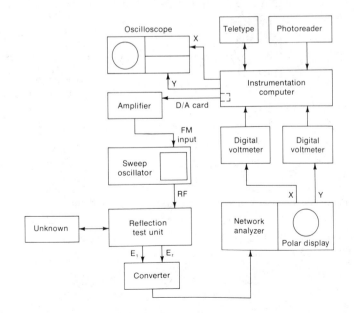

Figure 4-21   Computer-controlled network analyzer

measures the reflection coefficient of an unknown device as a function of frequency, then calculates impedance, admittance, standing wave ratio, return loss, and mismatch loss. Residual errors in the system are measured with a calibrating short in place of the unknown, and the computer automatically subtracts these errors from the measurements. The refined results are stored in the computer memory and displayed on the oscilloscope. The network analyzer provides a Smith Chart display of the raw data.

PROBLEMS

4-1. For a 16-bit general-purpose computer of your design:
   a. List the types of instructions and give basic instruction formats.
   b. For the input/output type of instructions, give a complete list and coding of those instructions.
   c. Give a block diagram of a typical input/output interface.

4-2. Draw a block diagram of a microprogrammed machine and give the microcode to implement the input/output instructions given in the answer to problem 4-1.

4-3. A minicomputer uses a push-down stack to provide for reentrant programs. The computer's compiler uses a left-to-right scan for arithmetic functions. The computer's command list includes the following operations between the top of the stack and memory:

LDS A —Load the top of the stack with the contents of memory location A and push the previous contents of the stack down.

STS B —Store the top of the stack into memory location B and pull the remaining contents of the stack up.

ADS C —Add the contents of memory location C to the top of the stack.

SBS D —Subtract the contents of memory location D from the top of the stack.

MPS E —Multiply the top of the stack by the contents of memory location E.

DVS F —Divide the top of the stack by the contents of memory location F.

The computer also has the following commands which operate on the top two elements in the stack and leave the result in the top of the stack; the remaining elements are pulled up after the arithmetic operation is complete.

$$\text{ADT, SBT, MPT, DVT}$$

For the equation

$$Y = A[(BC + EF) + 6]$$

    a. Give the coding to evaluate the equation and indicate the contents of
the stack after each operation.

    b. If the coding given in *a* is reentered three times, what is the minimum
number of words on the stack that must be reserved?

4-4. A computer has the following memory-reference instruction format:

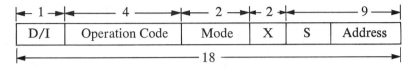

The address is a two's complement signed number.

The address modes are as follows:

    D/I—Direct or indirect
    MODE
        0—Absolute
        1—Relative to data-base register
        2—Relative to program counter
        3—Immediate
    X
        0—No indexing
        1—Relative to IR-1
        2—Relative to IR-2
        3—Relative to IR-3

The registers have the following lengths:

    Index register—8 bits
    Program counter—16 bits
    Base register—14 bits

The indirect address is interpreted as follows:

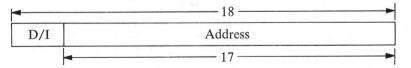

For each of the following address modes give the equation to compute
the effective address, and sketch a memory map to give the number of
words and relative location that can be addressed:

    a. Direct, absolute, no indexing
    b. Direct, absolute, indexed

    c. Direct, relative to program counter, no indexing
    d. Direct, relative to program counter, indexed
    e. Direct, relative to data-base register, no indexing
    f. Direct, relative to data-base register, indexed
    g. Direct, immediate, no indexing
    h. Direct, immediate, indexing
    i. Indirect, absolute, no indexing
    j. Indirect, absolute, indexed
    k. Indirect, relative to program counter, no indexing
    l. Indirect, relative to program counter, indexed
m. Indirect, relative to data-base register, no indexing
    n. Indirect, relative to data-base register, indexed
    o. Indirect, immediate, no indexing
    p. Indirect, immediate, indexed

For the immediate modes, give the range of the operand that can be addressed. Use the following symbols:

EA	—Effective address which results after address computation
A	—Address given in instruction
DB	—Data-base register contents
PC	—Program-counter contents
IR	—Index-register contents
MEMORY [N]	—Contents of memory-location N

4-5. Two computers A and B have the following interrupt systems:

Computer A—When an interrupt occurs, computer A completes the next instruction in the current program; it then stores the program-counter contents in memory location 0 and executes a JUMP INDIRECT with memory-location 1 containing the indirect address.

Computer B—When an interrupt occurs, computer B completes the current memory cycle; it then executes the contents of the memory location given by the device-select code. For multicycle instructions, the program counter contains the location of instructions whose execution was interrupted. For single-cycle instructions, the program counter contains the location of the next instruction to be executed.

For each computer, determine the minimum interrupt-response time (the time from the occurrence of an interrupt until the interrupt-service routine is started) and maximum data-transfer rate under interrupt processing. Assume that direct and indirect addressing capabilities and the following instructions are included in the computer's instruction set:

JSB N —Jump subroutine; stores contents of the program counter in memory location N and starts execution at location N + 1;

JMP   —Unconditional jump to location N.

CPA   —Compare register A to EA, skip if not equal.

LXA   —Load index-register 1.

LXB   —Load index-register 2.

SXA   —Store index-register 1.

SXB   —Store index-register 2.

Register Reference

Class Code	Register	Operation
5	2	9

The operations are:

CLR   —Clear register.

CMR   —Complement register.

SRR   —Shift right.

SLR   —Shift left.

RRR   —Rotate right.

RRL   —Rotate left.

SRZ   —Skip if register is 0.

SLZ   —Skip if LSB is 0.

SMZ   —Skip if MSB is 0.

SRN   —Skip if register is not 0.

SLN   —Skip if LSB is not 0.

SMN   —Skip if MSB is not 0.

Input/Output

Class Code	Register	Operation Code
5	2	9

Class

The operation codes are:

LIA   —Load input/output data into A.

LIB   —Load input/output data into B.

OTA   —Output register A to input/output register.

OTB   —Output register B to input/output register.

STF   —Set flag on input/output device.

CLF   —Clear flag on input/output device.

SFZ	—Skip if input/output flag is 0.
SFN	—Skip if input/output flag is not 0.
STC	—Set control bit.
CLC	—Clear control bit.
SCZ	—Skip if control bit is 0.
SCN	—Skip if control bit is not 0.
LIA $N^{H/C}$	—Load into accumulator the contents of device N data, and either hold or clear the device flag.
OTA $N^{H/C}$	—Output to device N the contents of the accumulator, and either hold or clear the device flag.
STC N	—Set control bit and start device action.
CLC N	—Clear control bit and idle device.
SFS N	—Skip if flag on device N is set.
SFC N	—Skip if flag on device N is clear.
LDA N	—Load accumulator from memory location N.
STA N	—Store accumulator into memory location N.

4-6. Draw a block diagram for three different bus structures. For each, list its advantages and disadvantages.

4-7. Draw a block diagram of a microprogrammed processor and give a format for the control-memory instructions.

4-8. A computer has the following instruction format:

Memory Reference

D/I	Operation Code	Mode	Address
1	4	3	8

The address modes are:

000—Direct/indirect
001—Relative to base register
010—Relative to program counter
011—Immediate, data is in address field
100—Index register 1, automatically increment
101—Index register 2, automatically increment
110—Index register 1, no change
111—Index register 2, no change

The operation codes are:

ADA	—Add to register A.
ADB	—Add to register B.

ISZ   —Increment, test memory, skip if 0.
JMP   —Jump to effective address (EA).
JSB   —Save program counter in EA, jump to EA + 1.
LDA —Load register A.
LDB —Load register B.
STA —Store register A.
STB —Store register B.

Notes: The computer sets control bit to start device or signal that data is read for device.

The device sets flag to interrupt computer or signal that data is ready for computer.

a. Write an input/output service routine which:
1. Saves the contents of the registers used.
2. Reads an 80-character record from device (8-bit characters).
3. Tests for an alarm condition and branches to subroutine if alarm character 11110000 is detected.
4. Compares each character for a match in a table of 20 characters. Stores in Table 1 if a match is found, in Table 2 if no match.
5. Restores registers.

b. Write a version of the program and determine the execution time in cycles for the following addressing modes:
1. Direct/indirect only.
2. Direct/indirect, relative to a base register, and relative to the program counter.
3. Direct/indexed only.
4. Any combination which gives the shortest execution time.

c. For each program determine the number of memory locations used and the execution time in cycles.

CHAPTER 5

Memory and Storage

Richard E. Matick

The architecture of memory and storage is a topic so vast and poorly defined that a general approach would bypass the underlying reasons for the seemingly complex systems encountered in practice. For that reason, this chapter is aimed at providing the student with a fundamental understanding of the various storage devices, their technology, and the methods of organization which are the basic principles required for dealing with storage architecture in the real world. This chapter attempts to show how the organization of various memory systems evolves from the fundamental requirements of storage and retrieval. In some cases the details of device hardware are included also, in order to provide a more complete understanding. The terms *storage* and *memory* are often used interchangeably to mean the online storage system.

5-1. PROCESSOR VERSUS MEMORY SPEED

All mathematical computations, either mental, mechanical, or electronic, require a storage system of some kind, whether the numbers be written (stored) on paper, in our brain, on the mechanical cogs of a gear, as holes in paper, as electronic circuits, or any other. In fact, the minimum storage requirements of any computing or calculating system are:

1. An internal storage, capability for temporarily holding the numbers to be processed, the intermediate results, and the final answer
2. External storage for holding the input numbers to be processed
3. External storage for permanent (or semi-permanent) recording of answers for further use.

TABLE 5-1. PROCESSOR AND MEMORY PARAMETERS FOR VARIOUS COMMERCIAL COMPUTERS

Computer	Year Delivered	Main Memory Capacity	Word Size (bits)	Main Memory Cycle Time (μs)	Processor Cycle Time (μs)	Address Size (bits)
IBM 650 (drum main)	1954	1-2 K words	60 5 bits/digit	4.8 max. rotation	7.8 μs/pulse but serial by digit	20 (4 decimal digits)
IBM 704	1955	4-32 K' words	36	12	12	15
IBM 7090	1960	32 K' words	36	2.2	2.2	15
IBM 7030 Stretch	1961	16-256 K' words	64	2.1	0.6	18
CDC 6600	1964	32-128 K' words	60	1.0	0.1	18
Univac 1108	1965	64-256 K' words	36 (6 Char.)	0.75	0.125	18
IBM 360/75	1965	256-1024 K' bytes	64 (8 bytes)	0.75	0.195	24
RCA Spectra 70/55	1966	64-512 K' bytes	32	0.84	—	16
IBM 360/85	1969	512-4096 K' bytes + 16-32 K' cache	128	0.96 (0.08 cache)	0.08	24
CDC 7600	1969	64-512 K' words	60	0.275	0.0275	30
IBM 360/195	1971	1-4 M' bytes + 32 K' cache	128	0.756 (cores) 0.054 (cache) 0.162 effective storage	0.054	24
Burroughs B7700	1972	128-1024 K' words	48	1.5	0.0625	20
Univac 1110	1972	131-1024 K' words 32-256 K' plated wire	36 (6 Char.)	1.5 (core) .52 write, .38 read, plated wire	0.075	24
IBM 370/168	1973	1-8M' bytes +16K' cache	64	0.4 0.08 cache	0.08	24
Amdahl 470V/6	1975	1-8M' bytes +16K' cache	32 [8]	0.2 0.032 cache	0.032	24
Cray 1	1976	1M' words	64	0.05	0.0125 (pipelined)	
IBM 370/3033	1978	4-8M' bytes +64K' cache	64	0.4 0.058 cache	0.058	24

where K = 1000, K' = 1024, M' = K'K'

In some cases, 1 and 3 or 2 and 3 are the same medium, but not always. The power of a computer or calculator is dependent to a large extent on the size and speed of its associated storage capabilities, both internal and external. Thus, it is not surprising that the development of storage has played a significant role in the development of calculators and computers.

The major problems of computer design and architecture have shifted away from the central processor per se toward other areas in which memory and storage are a significant part. In the early years of computers, the processor and storage were the main preoccupation of hardware designers. They were faced with improving both the raw speed of the central processing unit and the speed of memory since there was little difference between these two. In addition, there was little memory needed or available even on large systems. For instance, the first large scientific computer, the IBM 704, had a basic machine cycle time of $12\mu s$, and a main-memory cycle time of $12\mu s$. The machine cycle time was dictated by the main-memory cycle time, and the basic logic and memory-device speeds were comparable. As technology progressed, however, logic speed increased greatly while memory speed at reasonable costs increased much less, relative to logic. The result was a large gap, measured in orders of magnitude between logic delay and memory cycle time. For example, the IBM System 370 Model 3033 has a logic delay of 4–5ns per stage, a basic machine cycle time of 58ns and a main memory (integrated circuit) of $0.4\mu s$ cycle time;* the CDC 7600 computer has a basic cycle time of 27.5ns and a main memory of $0.275\mu s$; the Cray I has a processor cycle time of 12.5ns and a semiconductor main memory of 50ns.

Thus, processor cycle times and logic delays have improved dramatically, while main memory has improved at a much slower rate, leaving a significant gap. This discrepancy in speed can be seen in Table 5-1, where some of the important parameters are plotted for several of the larger commercial computers. A comparison of the columns for main-memory cycle time and processor cycle time shows the latter improving much more than the former. In fact, the difficulty with main memory can be seen even more dramatically by plotting main-memory cycle time versus year, as in Figure 5-1. This shows that main-memory cycle time is approaching a lower limit. It is, of course, possible to further increase the speed of main memory, but the difficulties arise in two ways—first, it is necessary to introduce new technologies, which are more expensive; second, the size of main memory required on a given system has increased dramatically (see Table 5-1, third column), which in itself tends to increase the cycle time just by increasing the array-propagation delay. Technology is faced with the need to decrease the cost per bit while increasing speed or decreasing cycle time, a rather formidable task. This chapter attempts to put the various storage technologies into perspective in order to show the

---

*The gap between logic and main memory is bridged by a 64K-byte cache memory paged out of main memory.

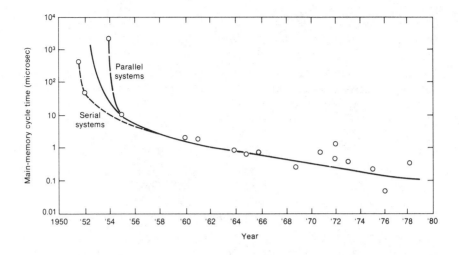

Figure 5-1 Main-memory cycle time versus year

basic principles — the fundamental trade-offs between speed, size, and cost (in terms of transducer or circuit count, not absolute), and some of the fundamental retrieval difficulties that arise in the process of storing and retrieving information in nonrandom storage systems [see also Matick, 77].

5-2. TYPES OF MEMORY SYSTEMS AND COST/PERFORMANCE GAPS

While there has often been much debate and speculation about what kind of storage is needed for practical computers, it should be understood that, with few exceptions, the fundamental requirements for computer applications of all types can be reduced simply to large, random-access, writable, high-speed. (both read and write) memory systems at very low cost. Small associative memories are useful in "paged" memory hierarchies.) While the size of main memory attached to computing systems has greatly increased in capacity, along with a substantial decrease in cost per bit, nevertheless the storage requirements for most systems still are so large as to make the use of only main-memory technology much too expensive. The appearance of a variety of hardware as well as software systems, storage allocation, data management, buffering, paging, and so on is simply a result of the fact that in most cases, the trade-offs between cost, speed, and size can be made more attractive by combining various hardware systems coupled with these special features. Thus, technology and systems requirements have together produced a variety of memory types. While the definitions of these various types of memories are somewhat arbitrary, there are five classes that are readily identifiable and frequently encountered in practice, namely:

1. Random access
2. Direct access
3. Sequential
4. Associative
5. Read only (postable and nonpostable)

Classes of Memory Systems

We shall describe each class and then proceed to give some rules of thumb for the access time and the cost of various systems relative to one another.

1. *Random-access memory* — a memory for which any location (word, bit, byte, record) of relatively small size has a unique, physically wired-in addressing mechanism and is retrieved in one memory cycle time interval. The time to retrieve any given location is made to be the same for all locations.
2. *Direct-access storage* — a storage system for which a specific location (word, record, and so on) is not physically wired in, and addressing is accomplished by a combination of direct access to reach a general vicinity plus sequential searching, counting, or waiting to find the final location. The access time depends on the physical location of the record at any given time; thus access time can vary considerably both from record to record, as well as to a given record when accessed at a different time. Since addressing is not wired in, the storage media must contain a certain amount of information to assist in the location of the desired data. This will be referred to as *stored addressing information* throughout this chapter.
3. *Sequential-access storage* — a memory for which the stored words or records do not have a unique address and are stored and retrieved entirely sequentially. Stored addressing information in the form of simple interrecord gaps is used to separate records and assist in retrieval. Access time varies with the record being accessed, as with direct access; however, sequential accessing may require searching of every record in the memory before the correct one is located.
4. *Associative (content-addressable) memory* — a random-access type of memory which, in addition to having a conventional wired-in addressing mechanism, also has wired-in logic that enables one to make a comparison of desired bit locations for a specified match, and to do this for all words simultaneously during one memory cycle time. Thus, the specific address of a desired word need not be known since a portion of its contents can be used to access the word. All words that match the specified bit locations are flagged and can then be addressed on subsequent memory cycles.
5. *Read-only memory (ROM)* — a memory that has permanently stored information programmed during the manufacturing process and can only be read and never destroyed. There are several variations of ROM.

Postable or programmable ROM is one for which the stored information need not be written in during the manufacturing process but can be written at any time, even while the system is in use, that is, can be posted at any time. However, once written, the media cannot be erased and rewritten. Another variation is a fast-read, slow-write memory for which writing is an order of magnitude slower than reading. In one such case, the writing is done much as in random-access memory but very slowly to permit use of low cost devices. Another version of slow-write memory is one with a changeable or replaceable storage medium, for example, magnets on a card, wires, or metal plates (capacitors) punched with holes. These are read-only memories that are programmable at any time but require considerable time (minutes to hours) to change.

Cost and Access-Time Comparisons

The primary reason for the large variety of memories is cost, and cost is related to the memory-access time. A short access time can only be obtained at a high cost and, conversely, inexpensive memories have slower access times. Approximate rules of thumb for cost and access-time comparisons of specific memory and storage are as follows (where B = bytes):

Cost or Price

$$\text{Cache } \cent/B = 10 \times \text{Main } \cent/B = 10^4 \times \text{Disk } \cent/B = 10^7 \times \text{Tape } \cent/B$$
$$\text{(Off line)} \quad (5\text{-}1)$$

$$\text{Gap} \approx 10^3 \qquad\qquad \approx 10^5 \times \text{Tape } \cent/B$$
$$\text{(Online)}$$

Access Time

$$\text{Cache } T_c = 10^{-1} \text{ Main } T_m = 10^{-6} \text{ Disk } T_d = 10^{-9} \text{ Tape } T_t$$

$$(5\text{-}2)$$

$$\text{Gap} \approx 10^5 \qquad\qquad \text{Gap} \approx 10^3$$

We see some large gaps between main memory and disks as well as disk and tapes. These large gaps in cost can only be brought about by large gaps in access time as indicated in Equation 5-2. The access time is sacrificed in order to achieve economy. This is an inherent characteristic that can only be understood by considering the physical system requirements for storing and retrieving information. This is covered in Section 5-3, where it is shown that addressing small pieces of information at high speed requires large numbers of transducers (decoders, drivers, sense amplifiers), and therefore is expensive. The cost can be lowered by sharing transducers, which necessitates a slower system. Thus, we shall be faced continually with the trade-offs between cost and speed which, along with size, provide a spectrum of memory systems to meet increasing storage requirements.

Storage-System Parameters

In any storage system, the most important parameters are the capacity of a given module, the access time to find any piece of stored information, the data rate at which the stored information can be read out (once found), the cycle time (how frequently the system can be accessed for new information), and the cost to implement all these functions.

The *capacity* is simply the maximum number of bits, bytes, or words one can assemble in one basic operating module which is totally self-contained; for example, 256K bytes of memory, 29M bytes on a disk pack.

Access time can vary depending on definition; the definition used here is different for random- and nonrandom-access storage. For random-access memory, the access time is the time span from the instant a request appears in an address register until the desired information appears in the output-buffer register or the proper location in memory where it can now be further processed. For nonrandon-access memory, the access time is the time span from the instant an instruction is decoded asking for nonrandom-access memory until the desired information is found but not read. Thus, access time is a different quantity for random- and nonrandom-access memory. In fact, it is the access time that distinguishes the two, as is evident by the definitions above. Access time is made constant on random-access memory, whereas on nonrandom storage the access time can and does vary substantially, depending on the location of information being sought and the current position of the storage system relative to that information.

Data rate is the rate, usually in bits per second, bytes per second, or words per second, at which data can be read out of a storage device. Data transfer time for reading or writing equals the product of the data rate and the size of the information being transferred. Data rate is usually associated with nonrandom-access memory where large pieces of information are stored and read serially. Since an entire word is read out of random-access memory in parallel, data rate has no significance for such memories. Data rate is a constant for a given system, but the data transfer time depends on the length of the data.

Cycle time is the rate at which a memory can be accessed, that is, the number of accesses per unit time, and is applicable primarily to random-access storage. For various reasons it does not necessarily equal the access time. If a random-access memory works in the destructive readout mode, the information must be regenerated before another access can be made. This will cause a wide disparity between access and cycle time. Even if non-destructive readout is used, there are quite often transients that must be allowed to die out. For example, drivers or sense amplifiers must recover from large transients that drive them into saturation; and ringing, which is caused by multiple pulse reflections on the array lines must be allowed to die out. Thus cycle time is often substantially larger than access time. Cycle time has little meaning on nonrandom serial storage; cycle time is essentially the access time plus data transfer time, both of which can vary widely on a given storage system as a function of time and of data being accessed.

5-3. FUNDAMENTAL SYSTEM REQUIREMENTS FOR STORING AND RETRIEVING INFORMATION

In order to be able to store information and subsequently find and retrieve it, a memory system must have the following four basic requirements:

1. Medium for storing energy
2. Energy sources for writing information, that is, write transducers on word and bit lines
3. Energy sources and sensors to read, that is, read and sense transducers
4. Information-addressing capability, that is, an address-selection mechanism for reading and writing

The fourth requirement implicitly includes some coincidence mechanisms somewhere within the memory to bring the necessary energy to the proper position on the medium for writing, and likewise a coincidence mechanism for associating the sensed information with the proper location during reading. In random-access memory, this coincidence is provided by the coincidence of electrical pulses within the storage cell, whereas in nonrandom-access storage it is commonly provided by the coincidence of an electrical signal with mechanical position. In many cases the write energy source serves as the read energy source as well, thus leaving only sense transducers for the third requirement. Nevertheless a read energy source is still a basic requirement.

The differences between all memory systems lie only in the manner by which the preceding four requirements are implemented and, more specifically, in the number of transducers that are required to achieve these necessary functions. Here a *transducer* denotes any type of device (for example, magnetic head, laser, transistor circuits) that generates the necessary energies for reading and writing, senses stored energy and generates a sense signal, or provides the decoding for address selection. We will now consider some of the similarities and differences between various memory systems based on the four requirements.

In all storage systems in use today (with the possible exception of holographic systems, which are mainly experimental) all storage is accomplished by means of storing some discrete quantity, such as magnetic moments, current, electric charge, or others; so the physical or mechanistic storage attributes of the media are not a distinguishing feature separating main memory from other storage. In fact, the same physical phenomenon, such as magnetism, can be and has been used for both. The magnetic phenomenon of magnetic recording systems is identical in principle, although different in detail, from that used in ferrite cores, flat film, and plated wire main memories. The fundamental difference between main memory and other storage lies in the second, third, and fourth requirement, namely in the writing, sensing, and addressing mechanisms, as shown in Figure 5-2.

In order to achieve a high-speed main memory system, it is necessary for each bit location to be electrically "wired" in order to receive (writing) and send (sensing) energy locally. The storage medium is stationary with all

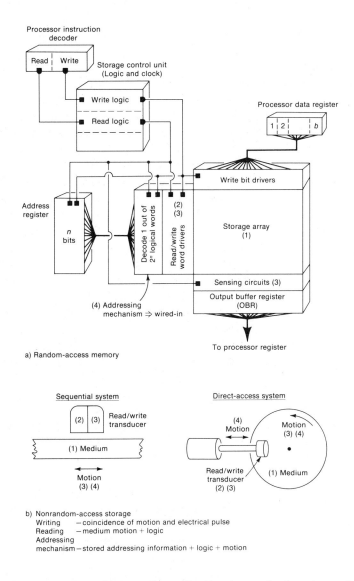

Figure 5-2 Differences in writing, reading, and addressing mechanisms for random- and nonrandom-access storage systems

writing and reading transducers hard-wired to the memory. Thus the read/ write transducers cannot be shared but rather are on constant alert to serve the bits designated in the hard-wired design. This is essential in order to provide high-speed reading and writing. Since these transducers are expensive, they constitute a substantial part of the memory cost. This is considered in detail in Section 5-5.

In contrast to this, the read/write transducers in nonrandom-access systems are generally shared over a large number of bits, thus greatly reducing the cost per bit. This is precisely what is done in disk, tape, and drum memories, where usually one read/write head assembly, sometimes having heads arranged in physical clusters, is used to reduce cost, and the storage medium is moved to provide access to large areas of storage. This results in substantial cost savings but also greatly increased access time. The degradation in access time for such storage is primarily a result of the mechanics involved in moving the medium (and the slider-head assembly in disk technology). If it were possible to design mechanical systems with time constants comparable to electronic systems, this access-time limitation could be reduced. This does not appear to be possible.

Just from these simple considerations of sharing transducers, it becomes apparent that mass storage will tend to be cheaper than main memory, indicating that multimedia storage systems are likely to be around for some time. Even if main memory were reduced to the cost of mass storage, there would still be problems in data organization that result from the way people use data. Suppose we have a large file such as an inventory part-number file—how do we organize this for best access? Since such files can and do change, we need a way to delete records, increase record size, and cross-correlate between various pieces of data in a file, which requires additional information to be stored along with the data. Since there is no way to determine such cross correlations and changes ahead of time, the physical, logical, and addressing means must allow for this, and must do so in a very general way. Thus it is becoming more evident that a spectrum of storage systems is a natural consequence of storage requirements, and this will become increasingly more evident.

5-4. FUNDAMENTAL REQUIREMENTS FOR A REVERSIBLE BINARY STORAGE MEDIUM

In order to construct a binary memory system of any type, it is first necessary to have a storage medium (the first requirement described in Section 5-3) to store energy in terms of some discrete physical quantity, such as magnetic moment or circulating current—that is, a symbolic representation of the two binary states of a bit of information. In order to accomplish this, a potential medium for binary storage must have at least:

1. Two stable (or semi-stable) energy states separated by a high-energy barrier (Figure 5-3)

2. Capability of switching between these two stable states an infinite number of times by the application of external energy
3. Capability for sensing the two energy states with an external energy source
4. Energy losses during the writing process for reliable storage [Swanson, 60; Landauer, 61, 62; Freiser and Marcus, 69]

The two energy states mentioned in item 1 do not necessarily have to be stable for an infinite time; in fact it is only necessary that they remain stable with time constants much larger than the time needed to "refresh" or rewrite the information. Many such storage systems have been built this way.

In order to implement this storage medium in a system, the additional requirements 2, 3, and 4 in Section 5-3 are necessary. These additional three requirements of the system can be fashioned around the media in numerous ways, and the different ways chosen represent another fundamental distinction between various memory systems.

In random-access memory, a considerable portion of the four system requirements is contained within the medium or basic storage cell itself, whereas in nonrandom-access memory, very little is contained within the medium or cell, and hence must be provided by other parts of the system. Thus in random-access storage the cell is rather complex, more difficult to fabricate, and more costly. This cost, added to the substantial number of "stand-by" transducers needed, results in an array that is high in cost but also fast and easily addressed. This complexity is duplicated many times within each cell and spread over a large array. While the array is more complex internally, from an external point of view it is quite simple, requiring very few external components for actual operation; for example, see a semiconductor memory module (as shown later in Figure 5-11). On the other hand, nonrandom-access memory cells are relatively simple and hence cheap, but the remainder of the system must be more complex. However, this complexity is not duplicated and the cost per bit can be reduced by having the additional complexity serve many inexpensive cells.

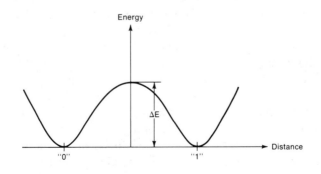

Figure 5-3   Bistable potential well for storing binary information

The device requirement for energy losses mentioned previously does not require losses in the quiescent or steady state since magnetic cores and tapes have no losses until the magnetization is reversed. However, for reliable writing of information, the storage medium must exhibit a certain fundamental amount of losses during the writing process and this represents a conflict between fundamental and practical constraints. Energy losses produce heat, which often entails serious cooling problems in memory design. Hence one strives for cells or media with as little heat loss as possible while realizing that heat loss can never be totally eliminated. The exact value for this fundamental limit has not been amenable to calculation from first principles, but it is known that losses in practical devices are still orders of magnitude larger than any fundamental limit [Keyes, 69, 72].

5-5. RANDOM-ACCESS MEMORY ORGANIZATION AND TRANSDUCER COUNT

While, technically speaking, random-access memory can refer to a number of specific memory types such as cache, read-only, and associative memory, we shall concentrate here primarily on main memory and more specifically on transistor memories. This section discusses primarily the 2-dimensional or 2D, $2\frac{1}{2}$-dimensional or $2\frac{1}{2}$D, and 3-dimensional or 3D organizations and implementations of random-access memory.

The designations 2D and 3D are derived from the number of functional terminals or degrees of freedom provided by the basic storage cell. The former is the most simple and the latter the most complex organization, with $2\frac{1}{2}$D falling in between. Random-access memory is organized into words with a given number of bits per word, b. During a read cycle, one entire word is fetched. Hence the reading process must select a word and sense each bit of that word. During writing, individual bits of a particular word must be selected to store the desired data. Hence the writing process requires simultaneous selection at the word and bit level. The various organizations simply reflect the physical interconnections between the storage cells in the array as well as between the array and the external circuitry, which are required to accomplish both reading and writing. The minimum functional array lines that must be provided to each storage cell are a word line, a bit line, and a sense line. However, only two of these are ever required at any one time, namely the word and bit line for writing, and the word and sense line for reading. Hence the bit and sense line may be a common conductor in the array but must be capable of performing two separate functions on the storage cell. It follows that this storage cell must then have a minimum of two independent functional terminals, as shown in Figure 5-4(a). This represents the minimum cell and array requirements as implemented in the 2D organization. In the more complex 3D organization, the minimum functional array lines which must be provided to each storage cell are two word lines (for coincident word selection), one bit line, and one sense line. Only three of these are ever required for any operation,

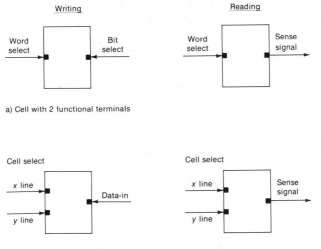

a) Cell with 2 functional terminals

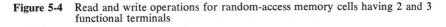

b) Cell with 3 functional terminals

Figure 5-4 Read and write operations for random-access memory cells having 2 and 3 functional terminals

namely two word lines and one bit line for writing, and two word lines and one sense line for reading, as shown in Figure 5-4(*b*). As before, the bit and sense line may be a common conductor, as is often the case. It follows that this storage cell must have a minimum of three independent functional terminals. A 2½D organization can make use of either the 2- or 3-terminal cell of Figure 5-4.

In the operation of any random-access memory system, the processor generates at least two basic pieces of information that are used by the memory subsystem to produce the required result. As shown in Figure 5-2, these two pieces of processor information are:

1. An address of n bits specifying the referenced word
2. An indication whether the operation is read or write

Once this information is provided, it is the job of the storage-system control unit to perform all the subsequently required gating and timing functions to decode the address and to read or write the specified word. The total number of separately distinguishable memory entities, E, possible is equal to the total possible number of combinations of the n address bits which is simply 2^n; hence

$$E = 2^n \tag{5-3}$$

Since E is usually given, the required number of address bits can be explicitly obtained by taking the $\log_2$ of both sides of the above equation to get

$$n = \log_2 E \tag{5-4}$$

In such a system, n must always be an integer (even or odd), since we can either have an address bit or not; so E must be an even number. In some cases, $E = W$, the number of total words in a memory; in other cases, $E = \sqrt{W}$ or other fractional part. In any case, these parts, which are really physical conductors of some sort, must be grouped in even numbers, and in fact in groups of 2^n to make efficient use of the address bits. In randomly-accessed memory systems, n is independent of the organization of the memory and E is thus equal to the total number of logical words that can appear in the output-buffer register. This is a fundamental relationship: The various memory organizations make use of these n bits in different ways, as we shall see. In some cases, n is divided into two equal groups of $n/2$ for 3D organization, or into (usually, not always) unequal groups for 2½D; it is not divided at all for 2D organization.

For writing, the sequence of operations performed by the control unit is as follows:

1. Gate the n bits from the address register into the decoder, to select one out of 2^n words.
2. Gate the data out of the processor data register to the bit drivers.
3. Gate the word and bit drivers to write the data. The word pulse in coincidence with a 1 bit pulse will write a 1 in that cell, whereas the word pulse in coincidence with a 0 bit pulse will write a 0. In some storage arrays, all cells along a word must first be set to 0 by a clear cycle and then only 1s are written. This type of operation is used in core arrays.

In some cases, 1 and 2 can be done simultaneously. In all cases, sufficient time must be allowed between sequential gating functions for the worst-case delays and electrical transient decays.

For reading, the sequence of operations performed by the control unit is as follows:

1. Gate the n bits from the address register into the decoder, to select one out of 2^n words.
2. Gate word read drivers to energize the selected word.
3. Strobe sense circuits to latch the data into the output-buffer register. (In some cases the output buffer may set on the sense signal without need for logic control by the control unit.)
4. Signal that data is available for use by the processor.

Sufficient time must be allowed between steps 2 and 4 for worst-case driver, array, and sensing delays. In addition, before a subsequent read or write cycle can be initiated, sufficient time must be allowed for all transient electrical signals, both in the array and circuits, to decay to acceptable levels. This often is a relatively long time, particularly after writing, where sense amplifiers are overdriven by noise or sense lines are raised to a high level and require a long recovery time. This is the fundamental problem that makes the access time different from the cycle time. Data can usually be completely read from the array and available in the output-buffer register but a new cycle cannot be initiated for a certain recovery-time period. Some typical values for a large core or transistor memory array are 300 ns read-access time, 500 ns read/write-cycle time.

The gating functions performed by the control unit are accomplished by means of clock pulses, which trigger the various circuits. The clock pulses are usually obtained from the basic processor clock. The processor and memory clocks are synchronized to one another to minimize logic complexity. The worst-case reading or writing delay is known to be a fixed number of processor clock periods, so a simple counter can be used by the processor to determine, after the initiation of a read cycle, for instance, exactly when the data is available for processing.

It should be recognized that, during the writing process, many storage cells receive a small excitation called a half-select or *disturb* signal which is insufficient to switch the cell. At cell locations where a half-select bit and a half-select word signal *coincide*, the two signals add to give a full-select excitation that switches the storage cell. This coincidence of signals occurs only at the desired cells. Ideally, all other cells that receive a half-select signal should remain in the previous state. However, in actual operation—since one cell may receive millions of such half-select disturb signals, the effects must not be accumulative; that is, the summation of all the small disturbs must not cause the device to switch. If it does, the device is disturb-sensitive and therefore not workable in a random-access memory.

The above discussions apply generally to all random-access memory organizations. Before discussing the various organizations, it is important to define the meaning of a memory word; in fact, it is necessary to define two types of words, namely, *physical word* and *logical word*. In 3D and 2D organization they are identical, but in 2½D, which is becoming more common, physical and logical words are quite different. A logical word is the total number of bits that are retrieved and delivered to the output-buffer register in one memory cycle or fetch. A physical word (in 2½D) consists of several logical words, but only one is delivered to the output register; that is, a physical word is the maximum number of bits energized during reading, but only a portion of these, the logical word, is fully switched or gated into the sense amplifiers and output register. Thus,

Physical word = total number of bits read out of storage cells during access

Logical word = total number of bits sensed and gated into output register

If one knows the size of the output register, the maximum size of the logical word is known. The physical word is the largest entity which must be addressed by the word-addressing mechanism.

The major reason for the appearance of various random-access memory organizations is the attempt to design an array with the highest speed, largest capacity, and lowest peripheral-circuit and array cost. We saw in Section 5-3 that this was the same motivating factor separating random- from nonrandom-access memory, and that it leads to the sharing of transducers in the latter, but with a sacrifice in access time. The various organizations of random-access memory can also reduce cost by sharing circuits, but here too it can only be done at a sacrifice in speed, as we shall now see.

We will discuss the various memory organizations in a very fundamental way that will be applicable to all types of cells and all technologies, e.g., cores, transistors, cryogenics, etc. For any given technology and at any given point in time, the organization used depends on many interacting factors. In early magnetic-core memories the need for large drive currents and the incompatibility of the arrays and peripheral circuits forced the designer in the direction of minimizing the number of drive circuits. This is achieved with a so-called 3D series organization, with large numbers of interconnections between physical arrays. The advent of integrated-circuit memory arrays required completely different trade-offs, resulting in a very different organization, namely, 2½D, and only occasionally 3D. We will discuss all of these organizations in detail. While these organizations are discussed in terms of selecting individual memory cells of an array, the same fundamentals apply, in general, when selecting arrays of chips, modules, cards, boards, or even complete memory modules.

2D Organization

The simplest memory organization, but the most expensive in peripheral-circuit count is the so-called 2-Dimensional (2D) or "word-organized" geometry of Figure 5-5. The physical and logical words are identical, so that an n-bit address must be decoded into $2^n = W$ distinct physical word lines. For modest-sized arrays this can become expensive, as shown later.

In 2D, no decoding is required on the bit lines since the processor data register in Figure 5-5 contains one bit for each bit of the memory word. A write operation copies the b bits from the data register into the memory cells selected by the word line. The data bits from the register either turn on or hold off the corresponding bit drivers. Likewise, no decoding is required on the sense lines since there is one sense amplifier for each bit in a physical word. A read operation causes all the b bits in any selected word line to be read out to the sense amplifier and from there to the output-buffer register. The number of bits in the address register is simply given by Equation 5-4, where E is now W. This type of operation is ideally suited to the 2-terminal cell of Figure 5-4(a).

The number of circuits that must be connected to a 2D array is easily deduced. Each word line must have one driver and each driver must be connected to one logic gate on the last stage of the decoder of Figure 5-5. Thus,

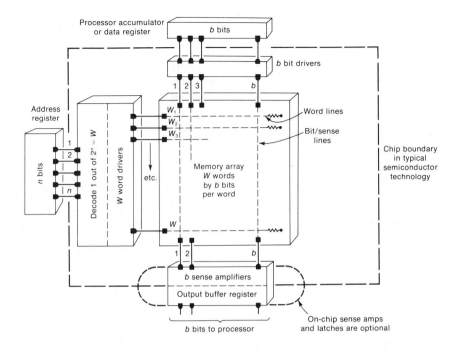

Figure 5-5   Schematic of 2D organized memory

a minimum of W drivers and W gates in the last stage of the decoder is required. Of course, more than W gates are required in the entire decoder. One driver is required for each bit line and one sense amp for each sense line; thus b bit drivers and b sense amps are required. These circuit requirements are summarized in Table 5-2.

It is apparent that, if an array as in Figure 5-5 consists of a large number of words (for example 8K) and relatively few bits per word (for example 32), then the physical structure is very long but narrow — that is, very long in the direction of bit/sense lines, but short in the direction of the word lines. This arrangement, while being most simple conceptually, is not only cumbersome in structure, but is extremely costly in terms of the number of circuits required for its operation. From Table 5-2, the above array of 8K words by 32 bits per word (i.e., 256K bits) would require 8K word drivers, 8K decode gates (last stage) but only 32 bit drivers and 32 sense amplifiers. The peripheral circuit count is over 16K which is equivalent to a modest-sized minicomputer. If all these circuits have about the same relative cost,* the peripheral circuit cost is proportional to 8K + 8K + 32 + 32. Obviously, this can be minimized by making the array more square, when possible, or 512 words by 512 bits in this case. Unfortunately, if the logical words are still 32 bits

---

*This is approximately true in many cases, but obviously varies with technology and type of cell used.

TABLE 5-2. TRANSDUCERS REQUIRED FOR VARIOUS RANDOM-ACCESS
MEMORY ORGANIZATIONS

Function	2D	2½D 2-terminal cell‡	2½D 3-terminal cell‡	3D (a)*	(b)**
Decoding Gates					
Word lines (last level)	W	$W_l/s = W_p$	$W_l/s = W_p$	$2b\sqrt{W_l}$	$2\sqrt{W_l}$
Bit lines	0	design dependent	design dependent		0
Read/Write Drivers					
Word lines	W	$W_l/s = W_p$	$W_l/s = W_p$	$2b\sqrt{W_l}$	$2\sqrt{W_l}$
Bit lines	b	b + sb switches	b + sb switches	b	b
Sense amps	b	b + sb switches	b	b	b

where
W_l = total number of logical words W_p = total number of physical words
b = bits per logical word s = segmentation (2½D) = W_l/W_p

‡ assuming one array or chip
*decoders on each chip (integrated circuits)
**decoders off-chip, series or parallel word lines (cores)

long, our physical words no longer equal our logical words so that a new organization is required. However, for smaller memories, where the array can be nearly square, 2D organization gives minimum wire length which can usually result in minimum delay.

One serious drawback with this type of organization is the difficulty of making effective use of error-correction circuitry. A typical memory system would consist of many arrays of the type described above. In semiconductor technology, these arrays would be chips with boundaries as shown by the dotted lines in Figure 5-5. For a chip having 8K words by 32 bits per word, a total chip failure would result in the loss of all 8K words and associated data. If the arrays could be organized in such a way that only one physical bit of any logical word was contained on any chip, a total single chip failure would result in the loss of only 1 bit in any logical word. Single-bit error-correction circuitry would then easily circumvent this with no degradation to the system. Such an array configuration *is* possible, but requires the 2½D organization described later.

The 2D organization has another limitation, namely, the need for a large number of I/O pin connections. For a logical word length of $b = 72$ bits, for instance, an integrated circuit chip organized as in Figure 5-5 would require at least 72 signal pins. This is more than the total number of all pins available on typical chips. However, even if 72 signal pins were available the designer still would tend toward one bit per chip for error correction.

2½D Organization

We saw in the above example of a 2D memory organization that it is desirable to make the number of logical words comparable to the number of bits per logical word, giving an approximately square array. However, in nearly all main memory systems, the number of logical words required greatly exceeds the number of bits per logical word. In addition, the number of logical bits per word is fixed by the processor architecture design and seldom exceeds 72 bits per logical word (including parity), whereas the number of logical words is seldom less than 1000; thus a factor of 10 is a bare minimum for W/b. One way to overcome this is to make a physical word contain more than one logical word; that is, to segment the 2D memory and piece it together to make a more nearly square structure. This produces what is commonly referred to as a 2½D memory organization [Russell, Whalen, and Leilich, 68]. Such an organization can use a memory cell with either 2 or 3 functional terminals as in Figure 5-4(a) and (b) respectively, giving two slightly different forms. The 2½D organization using three functional terminals is seldom used, while the 2-terminal 2½D organization is the most common in integrated circuit technology.

Let us start with a 2D array (which must use 2-terminal cells), as in Figure 5-5, with the number of words, W, much larger than the bits per word, b. This gives a long, thin array, which we will call a *segment*. Let us make the array more nearly square by placing a number of identical segments adjacent to each other and sharing the same physical word lines. Figure 5-6(a) shows such a scheme with the number of segments, or logical words per physical word of $s = 4$. Thus each physical word line has sb bits or s logical words. The processor data register only supplies b data bits, and the output buffer only accepts b bits; hence it is obvious that we must select one of the segments to drive with data pulses during writing, and likewise we must select one segment to sense and latch during reading. The reading and writing of the cells is identical to that of the 2D organization, but additional selection circuits at the data end of the bit line and at the sense end of the sense line ensure that only the desired cells receive data pulses or are gated into the sense amplifiers. In fact, once this selection has been completed, the selected segment looks and operates like a simple 2D array. There are fewer physical words than in 2D and hence fewer address bits required for decoding the word lines. The extra bits, n_2, in Figure 5-6 are used to decode the proper segment required for the desired logical word. The circuit count becomes more complex since, while there are still b bit drivers and b sense amplifiers, a substantial number of switches is required to gate the proper segment into the b drivers or sense amplifiers. In Table 5-2, an additional number of switches (equal to sb on each end) is specified and each of the switches may contain several transistors.

During reading in the above 2½D organization using 2-terminal cells, the read pulse must be supplied entirely by the word line with signals propagating on the bit/sense line. Because of this 2-terminal characteristic, all cells along a given physical-word line are sensed, and signals propagate on all sb sense lines. The selection circuitry decodes the proper sense lines for the correct logical word. Note, however, that if the cells are destructively read so that the stored information is lost, all sb cells along the physical word must be regenerated which requires much redundant circuitry, particularly when s

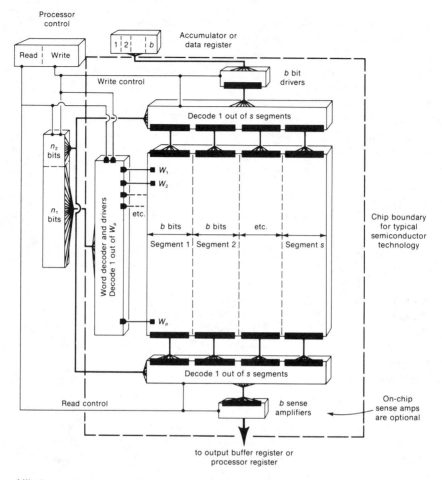

a) Word-organized segments of bit/sense lines

Figure 5-6(a)   Schematic of 2½ D organization using 2-terminal cells and word-organized segments of bit/sense lines

is large. Thus it is desirable, but not necessary, that 2-terminal cells for 2½ D organization possess nondestructive read-out characteristics.*

In Figure 5-6(a), the segments are shown with the bits of each segment adjacent to one another, that is, word-organized segments. It should be apparent that these bits of a given logical segment could be displaced from one another as in Figure 5-6(b), giving bit-organized segments. This latter organi-

---

*The transistor flip/flop cell of Figure 5-14, shown later in this chapter, possesses this capability and is often used in this type of organization. The one-device, dynamic FET cell of Figure 5-16, also used in this organization, can only be read destructively, which is a disadvantage. However, its small cell size results in a very substantial increase in density and decrease in power, which more than offsets the destructive-read disadvantage, so it is commonly used.

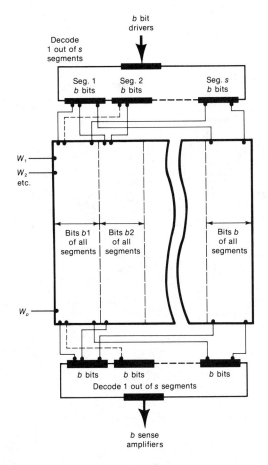

b) bit organized segments of bit/sense lines

Figure 5-6(b)   Schematic of 2½ D organization using 2-terminal cells and bit organized segments of bit/sense lines

zation has some advantages in terms of reliability and the effectiveness of error correction. For instance, spontaneous alpha particles in the one FET device cell of Figure 5-17 can erase several adjacent cells simultaneously [May and Woods, 1979; Yaney et al., 1979]. Physical separation of the bits insures that an alpha particle can erase only one bit of a logical word, thus permitting effective single-bit error correction.

The organization of Figure 5-6(b) can be carried one step further. Suppose the individual bits b1, b2, b3, and b4 of segment 1 and all other segments are *not* on the same chip but rather are on different chips. This gives the typical 1-bit-per-chip organization commonly used in semiconductor technology. A similar arrangement is also possible where 4 or 8 bits of a segment (logical word) are taken from one chip. Obviously other chips are needed to

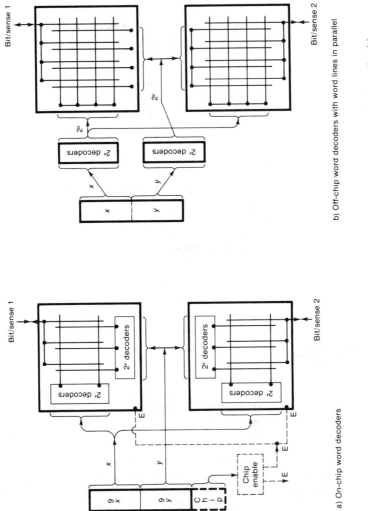

a) On-chip word decoders

b) Off-chip word decoders with word lines in parallel

Figure 5-7 3D, 1-bit-per-chip memory organization, showing 2 bits of a logical word, with bit/sense lines in parallel

form the logical word, and this organization is presented later in this section.

It is possible to circumvent the shortcomings of a 2-terminal destructive read-out cell in 2½D by using a 3-terminal destructive read-out cell. In this case, the writing process is identical to that described previously, but reading is slightly modified. The bit and sense lines are functionally separate so that a coincidence of a bit pulse with word pulse can be used during reading as well as during writing. This coincident reading is applied only to b cells during a read cycle, hence only b cells are switched destructively and only these must be regenerated, a substantial saving. Obviously, a nondestructively read cell is also workable in this organization.

Unfortunately 3-terminal cells require more area than 2-terminal cells, and the resulting decrease in density more than offsets any advantage of a 3-terminal cell in this organization. Hence it is seldom used in integrated circuit technology. However, the last significant vintage of ferrite-core memories did commonly use the 2½D, 3-terminal cell organization with series sense lines to eliminate selection circuitry on the sense lines. This organization was an important factor in achieving higher-speed core memories.

3D Organization

The most economical (in terms of transducer count) and slowest type of random-access memory is the 3D organization, which has long been used with ferrite-core arrays. This organization, which requires a 3-terminal cell, is one of the oldest and also one of the important factors that put magnetic cores in the forefront of main-memory technology. The economy in peripheral-circuit count results from the fact that since there is additional logic within each cell, many cells can be strung along a given line, requiring less peripheral selection circuitry. Unfortunately, this also tends to make the wire length and delays excessively long.

The basic principle in all cases relies on the use of two word lines, x and y, for coincident selection of appropriate bits for both reading and writing, as indicated in Figure 5-4 (b). Fundamentally, the coincidence of pulses on the two word lines provides an "enable" function on the selected cells. For writing, this enable function makes the cell sensitive to data on the bit line, and hence will switch the cell into the 1 or 0 state as specified by the bit line. For reading, this enable function either allows the selected cells to be interrogated by external sensing circuitry (transistor cells) or actually produces the sense signal within the cell, which is then propagated on the sense line (magnetic cores).

Figure 5-7 shows a typical 3D integrated-circuit memory organization with on-chip decoders in a 1-bit-per-chip organization. Each chip receives an x and y address for word decoding. A coincidence of pulses on the x and y lines selects one bit of the word on each chip. If the number of bits per chip exactly equals the number of logical words required in the memory, no additional decoding is required. There would be as many chips as there are bits in the logical word, with each chip supplying one bit. For instance, if we require 256K logical words with 72 bits per word, and if each chip contains 256K bits in a square array of 512 by 512, this memory can be achieved with 72 chips organized as in Figure 5-7(a). The total address of 18 bits would be broadcasted to each chip as 9 x and 9 y addresses, with each chip supplying one bit on every access. In such a case, the logical and physical words are identical. This would represent the pure form of 3D, where all selection of bits is obtained from the coincidence of the x and y word lines. In this example if the required memory capacity were larger, say 512K words, then (assuming the same chips) 144 chips plus additional decoding would be required. In particular, off-chip enable functions would be required (shown dotted in Figure 5-7(a)), which would select 72 of the 144 chips on any access. This would give a mixed organization, since the chips themselves are selected in a 2D organization while the bits on each chip are 3D selected.

Thus we see that for a pure 3D organization the physical word lines themselves are coincidentally selected, not just the bits; the physical and logical words, therefore, are equivalent. In order to minimize the peripheral-circuit count, the array is typically broken into a square of $\sqrt{W_l}$ by $\sqrt{W_l}$ words by b bits/word. The required number of address bits is still $\log_2 W_l$. The peripheral-circuit count is easily deduced from Figure 5-7. There are $2\sqrt{W_l}$ decoding gates on the word lines of each chip and an equal number of read/write drivers. Since there are b chips, there is a total of $2b\sqrt{W_l}$ decoding gates and an equal number of read/write drivers on the word lines. Since no selection is required on the bit/sense lines, there are b bit drivers and b sense amps. The values are summarized in Table 5-2 under column 3D(a). This organization provides a substantial saving in circuit count over a 2D organization. For instance, for $W_l = 256K$ words and $b = 72$ bits, a 2D organization requires 256K decoding gates and an equal number of word drivers, while a 3D as in Figure 5-7(a) requires only $2 \times 72 \times 512 = 72K$ decoding gates and an equal number of word drivers.

An important, fundamental point should be noted here, namely, that as the number of bits per chip and the capacity of main memory increases, the number of decoding and driving circuits becomes very large, and eventually would greatly exceed the number of circuits in the CPU itself (see Matick [77], p. 61 for detailed example).* One way to reduce the circuit count would be as follows. Rather than having word decoders and drivers on every chip, have them only on one chip and connect the x lines of all subsequent chips in series or parallel, as in Figure 5-7(b); do likewise with the y lines. This reduces the total circuit count by a factor of b, as indicated under column 3D(b) of Table 5-2 (a larger reduction is possible if a mixed 3D bit selection and 2D or 2½D chip selection is used). This slightly modified 3D interconnection scheme with series word lines was precisely that used in early 3D core

---

*Note that the individual peripheral circuits are considerably more complex than many memory cells.

memories. The difficulty with such a scheme today is that a large number of I/O pin interconnections would be required between the chips which is very difficult and unreliable. However, we can envision each "chip" of today as being an array "island" on a large wafer of tomorrow, with the interconnections being done photolithographically. As memory capacity and array density increase, such types of reconfiguration will become more attractive for reducing circuit count.

Transistor Memory Organization

Transistor memories have a distinct advantage over nearly all other technologies in that the peripheral circuits can be made as part of the same fabrication processes, and in many cases the decoding, driving, and sensing can be done using the identical device, with simple changes in the fabrication procedure. The major factors which have influenced semiconductor memory organizations are as follows:

1. High density and large number of bits per array or chip, but much less than the required memory capacity
2. Small physical size of arrays, i.e., typically 0.2-inch chips
3. Small number of I/O pins per chip
4. Compatibility between arrays and peripheral circuits, allowing latter to be placed on the array chip
5. Dominant failure mode typically a total "chip killer," causing loss of all bits on that chip

The first four factors influence the design toward a 2½D organization. The fifth factor influences the 2½D design toward a 1-bit-per-chip or a 1-bit-per-byte-per-chip layout, to allow error-correction/detection circuitry to be most effective.

Before proceeding with transistor memory organization, a very important fundamental should be emphasized. The notions of 2D, 2½D, and 3D organizations as they apply to arrays of memory cells also apply to arrays of chips, modules, cards, boards, or any level of organization; i.e., the "units" being selected need not be memory cells. Furthermore, the selection scheme may be different at different levels of the same system. A semiconductor chip organized as 3D selection of cells on the chips, may use a 2½D or 2D organization of an array of chips, as previously discussed with respect to Figure 5-7(a). The more common organization is a 2½D organization of cells on-chip and a 2D (but sometimes 2½D) organization of the array of chips to form the logical words.

The memory organization depends on the number of terminals on the storage cell. Both 2 and 3-terminal cells are possible with semiconductor technology. The advantage of a 3-terminal cell is that additional logic can be done at the cell itself, thus reducing the amount of logic selection necessary on the periphery of the array lines. However, this additional logic requires additional devices within the cell. This cell logic, in turn, typically requires more area, which pushes cells further apart, resulting in both longer delays and lower density. In addition, the extra cell logic is redundant and seldom used. In other words, the same logic is built into every cell and is used only when *that* cell is accessed. In a 2-terminal cell configuration this redundant logic is removed, and the equivalent selection logic is placed on the array lines where it is used for every access. Thus we are sharing the "transducers" and achieving 100% utilization rather than occasional usage, as occurs in a 3-terminal cell. As a result current memory systems seldom use 3-terminal cells or 3D organization. This organization was important in early core memories for reasons that are not relevant in integrated circuits. Thus we will consider only 2-terminal cells, and hence only 2D or 2½D organizations. (The 3D transistor organization has been briefly discussed under 3D Organization.)

When Number of Logical Words Equals Bits per Chip   Suppose we are designing a 256K-word by 8-bits-per-word memory and have available a technology capable of producing 256K bits per chip with whatever word, bit, and sense decoders we choose, all on-chip. Also there are available up to 8 I/O pins for data-in and 8 for data-out if we desire, in addition to address, control, and power pins for any organization we design. Obviously, 8 chips and 18 address bits are required. The question is, how do we organize the chips and memory, thereby specifying the on-chip circuitry. Let us try various organizations and see what advantages or disadvantages are incurred.

The most simple organization, conceptually, is a pure 2D scheme as in Figure 5-8. Each chip is identical in principle to the configuration of Figure 5-5 and consists of 32K words (logical equals physical) by 8 bits per word. Fifteen of the 18 address bits select one out of 32K words on each chip. Since only one of these 8 selected words can be the desired word, the remaining 3 bits provide the 1-out-of-8 chip-select function, as shown. No selection is required on the bit/sense lines, so these lines from all 8 chips can be dot ORed together (only sense lines shown). If these cells are destructively read-out, then 8 sense amps and regeneration drivers must be included on *each* chip. If the cells are read nondestructively, the sense amps can be off-chip, assuming that the circuit loading permits this.

This organization has two very serious disadvantages. First, each chip requires at least 32K decoder gates and 32K drivers. Counting each one as equivalent to a logic circuit, there are 64K circuits per chip and the equivalent of 512K gates total. This is larger than the circuit count in most large-scale computers, and hence is unreasonable. The second problem is that we cannot effectively use single-bit error correction and double-error detection. The most probable failure is, typically, a total chip failure. If this should occur, we lose all 8 bits from 32K words, and obviously single-bit correction is of no value. An even more serious problem is that multiple errors can be *incorrectly* interpreted as a single error by the correction circuitry and thus can be "corrected" to a totally false value. We can reorganize the memory to

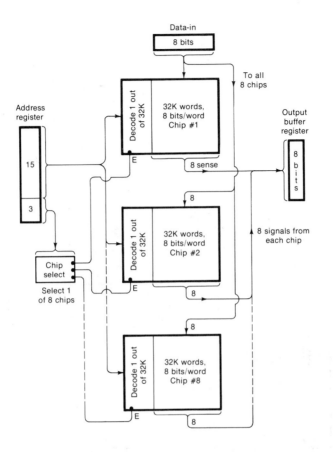

Figure 5-8 2D-organized transistor memory of 256K words by 8 bits/word, using 256K-bit chips

reduce both of these problems. First, we will reorganize Figure 5-8 to reduce the peripheral-circuit count, still accessing 8 bits per chip. Such an organization has some advantages. Then we will reorganize once again to allow effective error correction for chip failures.

The large number of circuits required in Figure 5-8 can obviously be reduced by using a 2½D memory organization, as shown in Figure 5-9. Each chip is identical in principle to that of Figure 5-6(a), and has 512 physical words, each containing 64 segments or logical words of 8 bits per segment. As previously, 3 of the address bits are required for chip-select and the remaining 15 go to each chip. However, it is now necessary to decode only 1 out of 512 word lines and 1 out of 64 bit/sense-line segments (i.e., 8 out of 512). There is a very large reduction in circuit count to roughly 1500 to 3000 circuits per chip,* an obvious advantage.

---

*Varies with definition of "switch" and the on-chip circuitry.

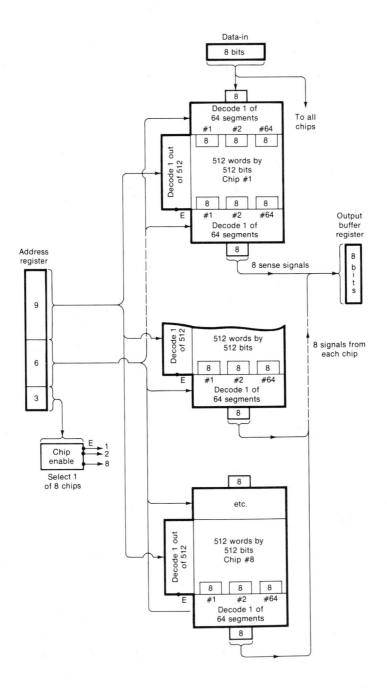

Figure 5-9 2½ D word-organized transistor memory of 256K words by 8 bits/word, using 256K-bit chips and a 2-terminal cell

However, this organization does nothing to allow single-bit error correction when a chip fails. This need not be serious in all cases. If no error correction is used, or if chip failures are not the predominant mode, then this organization could be used. It has the advantage that the sense lines for each chip can be dot ORed in some technologies, thereby reducing the circuit count. However, it requires more signal pins per chip which is often a disadvantage. Nevertheless, the trend is toward multiple-bit error correction and larger logical words, both of which make this scheme of accessing several bits per chip more attractive, and it will become more common.

It is possible to make single-bit error correction effective against chip failures by simply modifying the 2½D organization of Figure 5-9 to a 2½D, 1-bit-per-chip organization, as in Figure 5-10. In this case chip #1 supplies

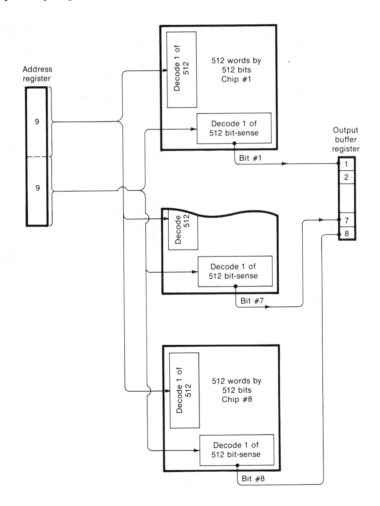

Figure 5-10   2½D bit-organized transistor memory of 256K words by 8 bits/word, using 256K-bit chips with 2-terminal cells and accessing 1 bit per chip

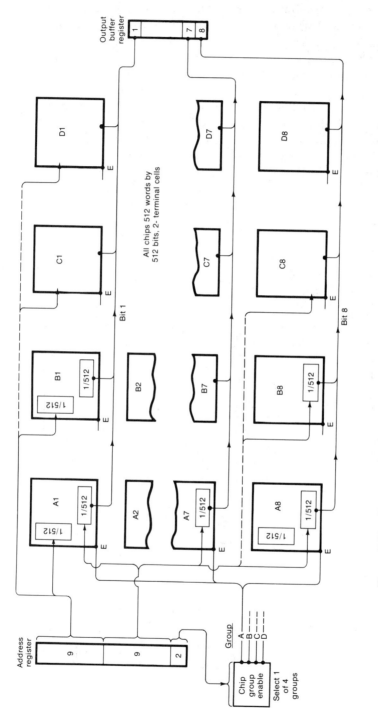

Figure 5-11 1M-word by 8-bits-per-word transistor memory, using 256K chips organized as 2½D on-chip with 2D direct selection of chips

bit position #1 of all 256K logical words, chip #2 supplies bit #2 etc. Rather than selecting 1 out of 64 segments, we now must select 1 out of 512 bit/sense lines on each chip, an obvious increase in decoding complexity. Every chip supplies one bit on every access, so no chip select is required. Note, the writing of data on the bit lines is completely analogous to reading, as was discussed in 2½D organization.

For the organization of Figure 5-10, if any chip fails and there are no other failures of any kind, single-bit error correction will make the failure unnoticeable to the user, although a service flag is usually set. If there are random single-bit failures on other chips, then a double error will occur when a word containing one of these bit failures is accessed. Correction circuitry is usually capable of *detecting all* double errors but not correcting them, so the memory comes "down." If there is more than one random-bit failure in any logical word simultaneous with one total-chip failure, this multiple-bit error can sometimes be misinterpreted as a single-bit error and be falsely corrected. The probability of this happening is usually very small, but finite.

When Number of Logical Words Exceeds Bits Per Chip   Suppose that we are given the same 256K-chips as used above, with the same freedom of chip design, but now wish to design a 1M-logical-word by 8-bits-per-logical-word memory. Further, assume that we wish to allow effective single-bit error correction for chip failures. The latter forces us to use a 1-bit-per-chip scheme similar to that of Figure 5-10. However, now we have 32 chips to organize and a 20-bit address. The most straightforward organization would be to duplicate the configuration of Figure 5-10 into 4 columns as in Figure 5-11. The 9 word and 9 bit/sense line addresses are broadcasted to all 32 chips. Since we want signals from only 8 chips, the two additional address bits are used to select 1 of 4 columns, i.e., 8 out of 32 chips. This could be done with an off-chip decoder that provides 4 enable signals directly to the 4 columns, as shown. This would be a 2D organization of the chips themselves (direct select), while the on-chip organization of bits is still 2½D.

An alternative method for selecting the chips would be to broadcast these 2 additional addresses to all chips and do the decoding on-chip. A coincidence of signals in an AND gate, for instance, would provide the enable signal. This would represent a 3D selection of the chips themselves. Both types of organization of chips have been used in practice, although in the latter case there is typically additional selection of chips at the card and board level, which makes the overall "chip" organization 2½D rather than pure 3D.

Memory Organization Using the One-FET-Device Cell   The random-access memory device of Figure 5-16 requires only one field-effect transistor (FET), one capacitor, one word line, and one bit/sense line as compared to the six FET devices (load resistors are FET devices), one word line, and two bit/sense lines required by the cell of Figure 5-14. Because of this reduced component count per cell, the one-FET device cell is capable of significantly larger

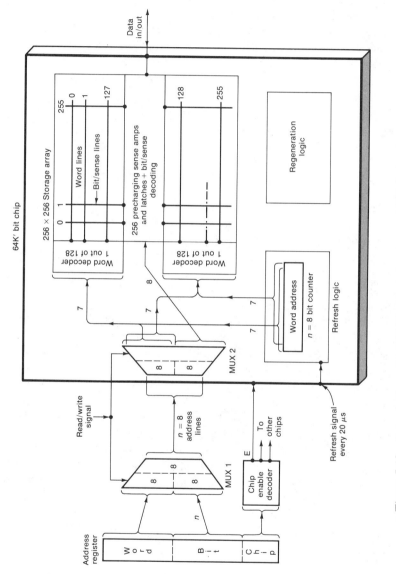

Figure 5-12 Organization of a 64K-bit chip, using the one-FET-device dynamic cell and multiplexed addressing

chip densities. Chips of 64K bits were introduced in 1978, and larger densities are possible. This type of cell has several drawbacks that affect the chip and memory organization. These are:

1. The cells are destructively read out, and hence must be rewritten after each read operation.
2. The stored charge leaks off the capacitor through the substrate, and hence must be regenerated every 2 to 5 ms, depending on temperature and specific technology.
3. The very small storage capacitor gives a very small sense signal due to the large bit/sense line capacitance, and hence precharging of the sense line is required before reading.
4. The cell has 2 functional terminals and hence can only be used in 2D or 2½D organizations.

The first and fourth points require every bit along any physical word line to be destructively sensed, whether 2 or 2½D organized. Hence we *must* have at least one sense amplifier and one data latch for each bit/sense line. Fortunately, this sense amplifier and latch can be used in a very simple manner to both rewrite and refresh. Refreshing is done for an entire physical word line, and consists of reading that word, followed by writing of the same word. The sense latch used for holding the read data also serves as the input register for writing. The third point requires the memory cycle to include precharging time, which lengthens the cycle time.

One possible organization for a 64K dynamic chip is shown in Figure 5-12. The storage array consists of 256 word lines by 256 bit/sense lines. Because a long bit/sense line will have larger capacitance, the sense amps are put in the middle of the bit/sense lines to increase the sense-signal amplitude. Since a balanced sensing scheme* is used, this presents no problem. The word lines and decoders are broken into two groups of 128 each. When a given physical word line is selected, all 256 bits are destructively sensed and the information latched into the 256 sense latches. If the read/write signal indicated a "write" operation, the desired input information is gated into the correct bit or bits in the sense latches, and the same word line is energized. This writes the correct information into the selected bits, and rewrites the previous information into the unselected bits. The actual number of bits selected typically varies from 1 to 9 depending on the organization. In any case it represents a 2½D organization, since a group of 1 to 9 sense amps (reading) or input latches (writing) is selected from a total of 256 bit/sense lines. A 2D organization would result if all 256 bits of each word formed the logical word. This is seldom used due to the chip-pin limitations and reliability problems.

---

*A simple flip/flop latch with some additional components for precharging serves as sense amplifier.

If a "read" operation is signalled, the process is similar to that above for a "write," except that after destructively sensing all 256 bits along a selected word, none of these are changed. Rather, the desired bits are nondestructively gated out through the I/O path, and the same word line is energized to restore the previous information. This regeneration for both reading and writing requires a small amount of control logic, as indicated by the "Regenerate Control" box of Figure 5-12.

Because of the inherent leakage of the stored charge, each bit must be "refreshed" every 2 to 5 ms. Since there *must* be 256 sense latches irrespective of whether 1 or more bits are sensed, refreshing can be done one complete physical word (256 bits) at a time. An entire physical word is simply read and then rewritten, with the sense amplifiers boosting any deteriorated signals back to full strength. If we assume a refresh cycle of 5 ms and a periodic refreshing scheme, then, since there are 256 word lines, one word must be refreshed every $5/256$ ms, or about 20 μs. This refreshing is controlled by a signal every 20 μs from the control unit that activates the refresh control logic box in Figure 5-12. A counter holds the address of the next word to be refreshed. The refresh signal causes the designated word to be refreshed and the counter to be incremented by 1. Thus in 5 ms all words and all bits will have been refreshed. This scheme is known as periodic or distributed refresh. A "burst" refresh scheme is also possible. In this case, all 256 words are refreshed sequentially in a burst mode, every 5 ms. Both schemes have advantages and disadvantages. If the memory has a cycle time of 1 μs, the periodic scheme cycle-steals or locks-out the processor access for every 1 out of 20 cycles. The burst scheme locks out the processor for 256 cycles every 5 ms. The latter scheme is desirable for cases where the processor accesses the memory for only short periods with long interludes, thus allowing burst refresh in between. In other cases this may be unworkable, thus demanding periodic refresh. A combination of the two schemes allows wider options but obviously complicates both the on-chip and off-chip logic.

It should be apparent that any or all of the additional control circuitry need not be on the chip. However, because of pin limitations most of it typically is on-chip. In fact, many commercial chips are so severely pin-limited, e.g., 18 to 24 pins total, that additional functions are required to handle the large address needed for high-density chips. The problem is easily illustrated. Assume an 18-pin package containing a 64K bit chip, as in Figure 5-12, requiring 16 address signals. If each is connected to a separate pin, there are only 2 left over for all other functions, including power, an impossible arrangement. However, both reading and writing require first a sensing cycle with a slow precharging operation of the bit/sense line *before* the word line is energized. Since the word-line access is a relatively faster operation, it can be initiated later with little or no penalty in access time. Thus the two separate operations can share the same address pins in a multiplexed scheme, as in Figure 5-12. First the bit/sense address is selected from the address register by the multiplexer, MUX 1. On-chip, MUX 2 gates the first access of any read/write cycle to the bit decoder. While the precharging is taking place,

MUX 1 selects the word address and MUX 2 directs this to the word decoders. Thus only 8 pins rather than 16 are needed for the address. Additional on-chip and off-chip logic is required, but is usually quite minimal. Obviously many variations of both the array organization and on-chip circuits are possible, but the principles are the same. Needless to say, most of these operations are transparent to the user. However, the "refresh" mode can impact the overall system performance, and hence is often important in the overall architecture.

Interleaving Architecture For a specified cycle time, any given technology can provide a self-contained memory module of only a limited size. Such modules are generally referred to as basic storage modules. For instance, a typical integrated-circuit module might consist of 4K to 256K words by 8 to 64 bits per word, with all circuitry self-contained. A larger memory capacity is obtained by piecing together many such modules with additional control logic. The access and cycle time of these modules are identical, but the operation of each is completely independent of all others. As a result, it is possible in some cases to achieve an apparent increase in the total system cycle time by staggering the initiation of fetches to each module. This is possible because the processor cycle time is faster than the memory-module cycle time. Suppose, for instance, that for each cycle time of a module, four processor cycles are completed. If four memory references are required, and if they are resident in four separate modules, then one module can be referenced on the first processor-clock period, a second module can be referenced on the second processor-clock period, and so on for the other two. Each module itself can only be referenced every four processor-clock periods, but in the above case the total system is now working at the processor-clock rate. If the memory references were all read cycles, a new word would appear every processor cycle time, as desired in an ideal memory. This technique is known as *interleaving*, and is used particularly in high-speed computers. In general computation, it is not possible to organize data such that subsequent references are always to a different module. Perfect interleaving is not possible in general. However, in paged virtual-memory systems interleaving can be quite useful, particularly in the cache-main memory hierarchy. The structure of the pages is known so successive words of a page are stored in separate modules of the main memory. When a page transfer to the faster cache is required, the words can be read out of main memory at a rate equal to the cycle time divided by the amount of interleaving. Thus for the four-way interleaving described previously, the page can be read out of main memory four times faster than it could be out of a single module, or noninterleaved system.

PROBLEMS

5-1.   Show that the number of bits needed in the address register for addressing main memory of a given size is identical whether it is organized as 2D, 2½D, or 3D.

5-2. Organize in block-diagram form all the essential features of a read-only memory, indicating the fundamental device requirements needed for operation and the potential circuit saving as in Table 5-2.

5-3. Show the general structure of a 32K-word by 64-bits-per-word transistor memory, using 64K-bit chips and organized as 2D, 2½D, and 3D. Indicate the number and types of circuits (driver, sense amps) for each organization.

5-4. Design a 64K-word by 32-bits/word, 3D-organized transistor memory in which there are no decoders nor any peripheral circuits on the chips. What are some of the advantages and disadvantages of such an organization?

5-6. RANDOM-ACCESS MEMORY DEVICES AND CELLS

Numerous technologies have been pursued as well as implemented in random-access memory, but only ferrite cores and transistor integrated circuits have had a large impact on computing systems. From the mid-1950s to the early 1970s, magnetic ferrite cores were the dominant technology for all main memory. Transistor integrated cells began to have a major impact in main memory in the early to mid-1970s, and by the late 1970s had made magnetic cores virtually obsolete. Hence we shall concentrate only on integrated circuit cells for random-access memory [see also Matick, 77; Scott, 70].

It was shown in Section 5-5 that the storage cell must have two or three independent functional terminals to be useful in a random-access array. Two-terminal cells can be used in the 2D or one form of 2½D organizations. Three-terminal cells can be used in the 3D or a second form of 2½D organizations. The number of terminals on the cell is a very important consideration in cell design since more terminals require a larger, more complex cell structure. This is particularly true in the newer, integrated-circuit type of memory cells. It is also true for ferrite cores, but to a lesser extent; more wires only require a larger core, the cell complexity remaining nearly constant.

While many circuit configurations exist for the *transistor integrated-circuit* storage cell, the basic bistable flip/flop was initially the most widely used. It is interesting to note that the internal storage used on some of the original computers (ENIAC at the University of Pennsylvania by Eckert and Mauchly) consisted of the same basic flip/flop circuit, but implemented in vacuum-tube technology. The high cost, large space, and large power dissipation of such devices precluded their being used for large memory arrays, and hence other technologies were developed (cores, drums, and so on). Now that large-scale integrated electronics has overcome the original problems, memory has completed a full cycle back to the original concept. We shall start with the basic flip/flop of Figure 5-13 which is essentially a one-terminal device, then add necessary components to make it a two-terminal device, as required for random-access memory. Additional complexity can then be added to provide a three-terminal device.

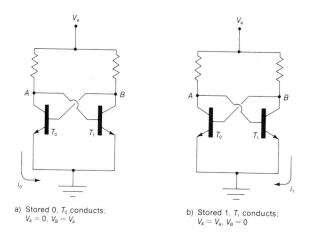

a) Stored 0, T_0 conducts;
$V_A = 0$, $V_B = V_a$

b) Stored 1, T_1 conducts;
$V_A = V_a$, $V_B = 0$

Figure 5-13   Basic transistor storage flip/flop

The operation of the basic flip/flop of Figure 5-13 is as follows:* The two transistors T_0 and T_1 form a normal flip-flop circuit, as shown in Part a. When T_0 is turned on, current flows through T_0 to ground, putting node point A at ground. This in turn puts the base of T_1 at ground potential, and thus holds T_1 off. If T_1 is off, node B must be at a voltage V_a, which is also at the base of T_0, holding it on. Thus, this would be a stable state with T_0 on and T_1 off, storing an arbitrarily labeled 0 (could just as well be called 1). To store the opposite state, that is, a 1, it is necessary to bring node B to 0 voltage and node A to V_a. This can easily be done with additional transistors tied to nodes A and B. This is exactly what is done in the common cell in use, and the manner in which this is done leads to many different cell designs. To understand this, note that the flip/flop has only two access points, A and B, both of which are functionally the same, that is to turn off one and turn on the other transistor. While there are two physical terminals A and B, only one can be controlled externally at a given time; hence it is in essence a one-terminal device as far as memory organization is concerned. For useful memory implementation, the minimal requirement is that points A and B must be coincidentally selected, each by two additional terminals. This requires at least one additional transistor for each node, and perhaps additional components. This accounts for the major differences in flip/flop-type cell design, namely, how points A and B are selected. If A and B are each selected for writing by coincidence of pulses on two terminals, as suggested above, then a device for 2D or 2½D organization results. For 3D organization, three terminals for selecting A and B must be provided, adding to cell complexity.

---

*In actual circuits, the voltage levels are different than stated here; but the basic principles remain the same, and are valid for both bipolar and field-effect transistors.

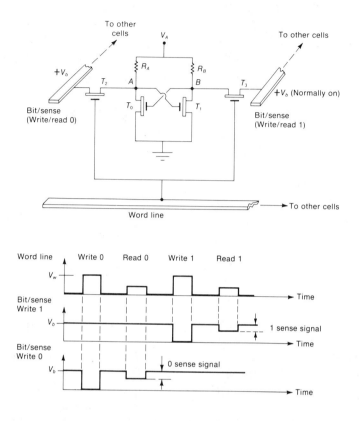

Figure 5-14   Two-terminal MOS transistor flip/flop storage cell (n-channel enhancement MOSFET)

A basic MOS storage cell with two terminals to select either node A or B is shown in Figure 5-14. A coincidence of pulses on a word line and either of the two bit/sense lines results in a coincident writing into the cell. The operation of this cell is as follows. Recall that to write a 0 or a 1, one node A or B must be brought to ground while the other node, B or A, must be floating or high. This is exactly what is done in Figure 5-14. To write a 0, regardless of the initial state of the cell, a positive voltage is applied to the word line in coincidence with a pulse to bring bit/sense line "write 0" to ground potential. The word pulse on the gate of T_2 turns it on and its source is at ground, so point A is brought to ground potential. If the cell was initially in the 0 state, point A would already be at ground, so nothing would happen. If the cell was initially in the 1 state, point A would initially have been at $+V_a$, with T_1 conducting. In this case A is brought to ground, causing T_1 to turn off and point B to increase to V_a, which causes T_0 to conduct and switches the cell to the 0 state. To write a 1, a word pulse is applied in coincidence with bringing bit/sense line "write 1" to ground, and the same sort of behavior results. For reading, a small word pulse is applied *without* a bit pulse, which causes both T_2 and T_3 to conduct slightly. Whichever node,

A or B, is at 0 volts will cause a small current to flow through its respective transistor, giving a small decrease in the normally "high" bit/sense line voltage. The sensing is nondestructive since the word-read pulse only strobes to see which state the cell is in. Note that for reading, the bit/sense lines are the "sense lines." Thus, while there is an inherent capability for coincident selection for writing into such a cell, there is no coincident selection capability for reading; that is, all cells along a pulsed word line are read, and hence this cell can only be used in 2D or $2\frac{1}{2}$D organization. This is a result of the fact that in essence, this cell is a two-input structure, that is, word and bit/sense. While there are actually three inputs, word, bit/sense 0, and bit/sense 1, the latter two serve only one function at a time, namely bit writing or bit sensing.

In order to make the cell of Figure 5-14 a 3-terminal cell, another "functional" selection terminal must be added that allows coincident selection of cells for reading in addition to writing. This can be easily accomplished by inserting another pair of transistors between the node points A and B and their respective bit/sense lines, such as those shown in Figure 5-15. We have, in essence, added another word line to the previous cell. These two lines, now labeled X and Y lines, require a coincidence of pulses before either writing or sensing can take place through the bit/sense lines. The operation of the cell is basically the same as previously. The three terminals of the cell are 1) X select, 2) Y select, and 3) bit/sense line pair. The digit (bit/sense) lines are isolated from nodes A and B by two transistors, and a direct connection

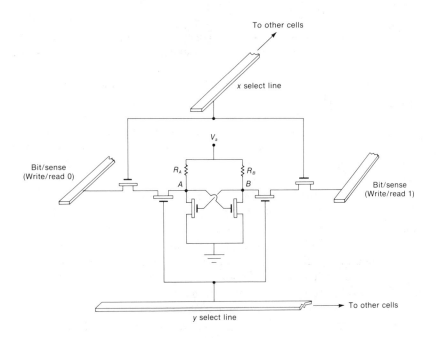

Figure 5-15   Three-terminal MOS transistor flip/flop storage cell

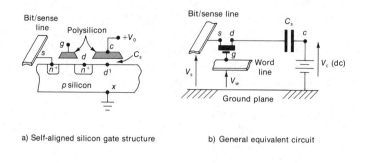

a) Self-aligned silicon gate structure   b) General equivalent circuit

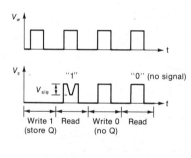

c) Pulsing sequence

Figure 5-16 One-device dynamic FET cell, shown in n-channel silicon-gate technology

is only made on a selected cell; the presence of a single, or half-select pulse on adjacent cells still leaves the digit lines isolated by at least one transistor, and hence this cell is undisturbed.

The same basic ideas above concerning random-access memory cells using MOS transistor flip/flops can be applied to bipolar transistor cells as well. In fact, the first commercial, mass-produced semiconductor memory cell used bipolar transistors in a 3-terminal cell configuration [Farber and Schlig, 72; Ayling and Moore, 71]. The primary difference between bipolar and MOS devices for memory is that the former are fast but the fabrication process is complex, requiring double diffusion and many steps that are expensive. MOS devices are much simpler to fabricate, but are slower than bipolar devices.

The six-device, two-terminal cell of Figure 5-14 can be greatly simplified by using a single FET device in conjunction with a capacitor in the so-called one-device, dynamic FET cell, as shown in Figure 5-16. Information is stored in terms of charge, Q (stored 1), or no charge (stored 0) on the plates of the capacitor C_s. The FET device merely provides the required minimum of two terminals for accessing the capacitor. The gate, g, of the FET serves as the word-line connection for both reading and writing. The FET source, s, serves as the bit-line terminal during writing, and as a sense terminal during reading. Obviously, such a structure can only be used in the 2 or 2½ D organization. All plates, c, of all storage capacitors, C_s, in an array are connected to a common dc voltage, V_c, as shown. If a voltage is applied to the gate, g, by means of the word line, the other plate, d or d', of C_s is essentially tied to the bit line via the FET channel, s-d. If the bit line is at ground potential, as shown in the first pulse sequence of Figure 5-16(c), then C_s charges up to the voltage V_c (stored $Q = 1$). If the bit line is maintained at $V_s = V_c$, as in the third pulse sequence of (c), then there is no voltage across C_s and no charge is stored. Reading is accomplished by just applying a word-line pulse with the bit line at V_s and sensing whether any charge (current) flows out of V_s to the cell. A current flows only if the cell had previously a stored charge, since V_s will attempt to discharge the cell, i.e., attempt to store a zero. Hence the reading is destructive and requires regeneration after each read. Another problem with the cell is that in the 0 or no-stored-charge state, point d' in Figure 5-16(a) is at a large protential very nearly equal to V_c. Thermally generated electrons within the silicon substrate are attracted to this large voltage and eventually would charge C_s to a finite charge state indistinguishable from a stored 1. Thus, each cell must be periodically refreshed (read and rewrite) before the degradation occurs. Fortunately this "leakage" time constant is typically milliseconds or larger, whereas the typical memory cycle time is a microsecond or smaller. Thus numerous memory references are possible before refreshing is necessary. Despite some of the inherent limitations, the substantial improvement in density and reduction in power has made this cell very attractive for main memory application. A further simplification of this storage cell is possible by eliminating the FET device. However, this excludes its use in a random-access array and permits only shift-register type operation.*

PROBLEM

5-5.   Show how 2-terminal cells with no inherent coincidence-selection capabilities can still be used in a random-access storage array.

5-7. DIGITAL MAGNETIC RECORDING PRINCIPLES

Digital magnetic recording is extremely attractive for data processing since the media (tapes and disks) can be removed, are unaffected by normal environmental changes, can be transported as a means of data file transfer, and can be reused many times with no processing or development steps necessary. Since magnetic recording is nonrandom-access, it does not require wired-in array hardware, so there is no cell or array configuration, and only the fundamental system and medium requirements of Sections 5-3 and 5-4 are necessary. The essential parts of a simplified, but nevertheless complete,

---

*For additional information on various types of semiconductor memory cells, see Hnatek [77] and Matick [77].

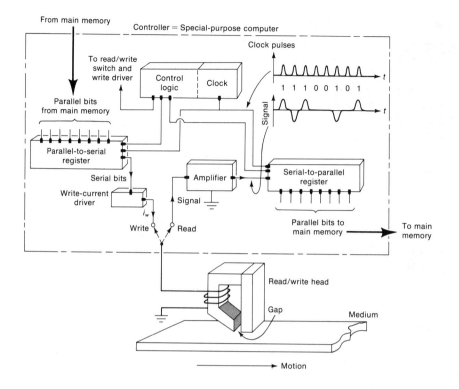

Figure 5-17 Essential features of simplified, complete magnetic recording system

magnetic recording system are shown in Figure 5-17, and consist of a controller (sometimes a large computer) to perform all the logic functions as well as write current generation and signal detection; serial/parallel conversion registers; a read/write head with an air gap to provide the magnetic field for writing and to sense the stored flux during reading; and finally the medium. The wired-in cells, array, and transducers of random-access memory have been replaced by one read/write transducer which is shared among all stored bits, and a controller, also shared.

The recording medium is very similar in principle to the ferrite material used in cores. The common material for all digital magnetic recording is Fe_2O_3 and has remained essentially unchanged for many years except for reductions in the particle size, smoother surfaces and thinner, more uniform coating, all necessary for higher density. The operation of the medium is nearly identical in principle to that of a ferrite core, that is, there are two stable states, $+B_r$ and $-B_r$, for storing binary bits* and the medium can be switched an infinite number of times by a field produced by the write head which exceeds the coercive force. The stored information is sensed by moving

---

*True in principle, but in practice the codes used do not allow a direct correspondence between the magnetization direction and stored bit.

the magnetic bits at constant velocity under the read gap to induce a time-changing flux and hence induce a sense voltage.

With respect to the system requirements, the energy source for writing is the "write" driver circuits within the controller and the write transducer, both of which are shared. The energy source for reading is the motor which drives the medium and converts the static field of a stored bit into a time-changing field.

The essence of magnetic recording consists of being able to write very small binary bits, place these bits as close together as possible, obtain an unambiguous read-back voltage from these bits, and convert this continuously varying voltage into discrete binary signals. We shall see that the write head is not a major factor in determining density since the writing is done by the trailing edge of the write field.

The minimum size of one stored bit is determined by the minimum transition length required within the medium to change from $+M_r$ to $-M_r$ without self-demagnetizing; the smaller the transition length, the larger will be the self-demagnetizing field. The minimum spacing at which adjacent bits can now be placed with respect to a given bit is governed mainly by the distortion of the sense signal when adjacent bits are too close, referred to as *bit crowding*. This results from the overlapping of the fringe field from adjacent bits when they are too close and this total, overlapped magnetic field is picked up in the read-head, giving a different induced signal compared to that produced by a single transition. Conversion of the analog read-back signal to digital form requires accurate clocking, which in turn requires clocking information to be built into the coded information, particularly at higher densities.

Neglecting clocking and analog-to-digital conversion problems for the moment, the signals obtained during a read cycle are just a continuous series of 1s and 0s. A precise means for identifying the exact beginning and end of the desired string of data is necessary, and furthermore, some means for identifying various parts within the data string is often desirable. Since the only available way to recognize particular pieces of stored information is through the sequence of pulse patterns, special sequences of patterns such as gaps, address markers, and numerous other coded patterns are inserted into the data. These can be recognized by the logic hardware built into the controller, which in all cases is a special-purpose computer attached to the storage unit. These special recorded patterns, along with other types of aids, are referred to as the *stored addressing information* and constitute at least a part of the addressing mechanism.

Coding schemes are chosen primarily to increase the linear bit density. The particular coding scheme used determines the frequency content of the write currents and read-back signals. Different codes place different requirements on the mode of operation and frequency response of various parts of the system such as clocking techniques, timing accuracy, head time-constant, medium response, and others. Each of these can influence the density in different ways but in the overall design the trade-offs are made in the direction of higher density. Special coding schemes are thus not fundamentally necessary, but are used for practical reasons.

Writing of the transitions (north or south) in the medium is done by the trailing edge of the fringe field produced by the write head. To see this, suppose we have a medium initially saturated throughout in the $+M_r$ direction, as in the bottom view (Part *c*) of Figure 5-18 (shown displaced for clarity), and we wish to write one transition. The medium is moving to the left, and at some time, t_0, we suddenly apply the write current i_{write} with polarity shown in the head (Part *a*). The H_x versus x curve in Part *d* shows the x or horizontal component of magnetic field created by the head on the medium. (Magnetic media are made to respond primarily to the x component of the applied field.)

Stopping the motion momentarily, we see that the field acting on the medium varies with distance, and any portion with the field equal to or greater than H_c (coercive force) will be nearly saturated at $-M_r$. However, for small values of H_x, less than H_c, the medium will respond with small changes in M; for instance, a field of H_1 in Part *d* can start reversing toward $-M_r$, but the medium cannot be fully reversed until a field of H_c is reached. Thus the transition (stored bit) extends approximately from x_1 to x_c. A similar transition exists on the right side of the gap, but if we now let the medium move to the left, the right hand transition never appears as a stored bit, since it is essentially held at a fixed position with respect to the head, or moves to the right within the medium. Thus, we are left with one permanent transition of distance x_1-x_c written by the trailing edge of the write head.

Read back signals can best be understood in terms of the reciprocity

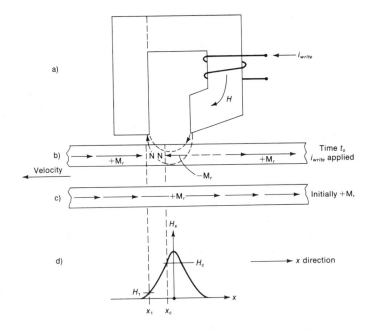

Figure 5-18   Writing process, showing writing by trailing edge of head

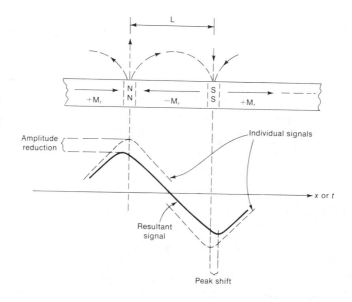

Figure 5-19 Bit crowding on read-back, showing amplitude reduction and peak shift

theorem of mutual inductance. This theorem states that, for any two coils in a linear medium, the mutual inductance from coil 1 to 2 is the same as that from coil 2 to 1. When applied to magnetic recording, the net result is that the time variation of the signal induced across the read head winding by a step-function magnetization transition (x_1–x_c very small) has a shape which is identical to the curve H_x versus x in Part d for the same position of the medium below the head gap. It is only necessary to replace x by vt, where v = velocity, for the translation of the x scale on H_x to the time scale on V_{sig} versus t. The H_x versus x curve with a multiplication factor is often referred to as the *sensitivity function*.

We saw above that the writing of a transition was done by only one small portion of the H_x versus x curve, whereas the sense signal is determined by the entire shape of H_x versus x; that is, the signal is spread out. It is this fact that gives rise to *bit crowding*, which makes the read-back process more detrimental in limiting density than the writing process. To understand bit crowding, suppose we have two step-function transitions of north and south poles separated by some distance L, as in Figure 5-19. When these transitions are far apart, their individual sense signals, shown by the dotted lines, appear at the read winding. However, as L becomes small, the signals begin to overlap and, in fact, subtract from each other,* giving both a reduction in peak amplitude and a time shift in the peak position, as shown. This represents, to a large extent, the actual situation in practice—the transitions can be written closer together than they can be read.

---

*Linear superposition is possible since the air gap makes the read head linear.

Clocking or strobing of the serial data as it comes from the head to convert it to digital characters is another fundamental problem. If perfect clock circuits with no drift and hence no accumulated error could be made, the clocking problem would disappear. But all circuits have tolerances and, as the bit density increases, the time between bits becomes comparable to the drift in clock cycle times. Since the drift can be different during reading compared to what it was during writing, serious detection errors could result. For high density, it is necessary to have some clocking information contained within the stored patterns. This is accomplished by the use of special codes as bit density increases. Clocking and its influence on the code, logic circuits, head design, and so on represents an area of important system design in practice (see Matick [77], p. 367, 397).

Density improvements in the past and future require the scaling of three major parameters to smaller dimensions and closer tolerances, namely the head air-gap, head-to-medium spacing, and medium thickness.

Locating previously stored data, as well as determining where to write new data, is much more complicated in magnetic recording systems than in random-access memory since there is no addressing capability within each bit cell.

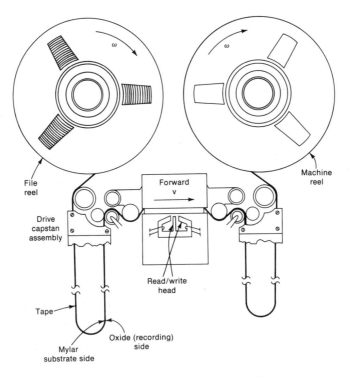

Figure 5-20 Schematic of sequential-access (tape) system

5-8. SEQUENTIAL-ACCESS STORAGE SYSTEMS

Flexible tape represents the primary sequential system, the most common one being ½-inch-wide mylar tape about 1 mil thick coated with about 0.5-mil-thick magnetic oxide. The tape, usually 2400 feet long, is contained on a reel about 10.5 inches in diameter. There are either 7 or 9 tracks written across the width of the tape, and hence either 7 or 9 read/write heads to store one complete character or byte at a time. Tape tracks, and hence bit cell widths, are in the range of 0.04 inches wide, but bit spacing along a track is much smaller. The latter is approximately the reciprocal of the linear density, or 1.25×10^{-3} inches for an 800-bits-per-inch system. The actual transition lengths (N or S regions in Figure 5-19) are generally about half this bit cell spacing. In many systems there are separate read and write gaps, as shown in Figure 5-20, in order to check the reliability of the recording by reading immediately after writing. The tape is mechanically moved back and forth in contact with the heads, all under the direction of a controller. The tape and heads both wear from abrasive contact and must eventually be replaced.

The important operational parameters are: tape speed, data rate, linear density, and rewind time. Some typical values are given in Table 5-3.

The stored addressing information in tapes is relatively simple, consisting of specially coded bits and tape marks in addition to interrecord gaps (IRG). The latter are blank spaces on tape that provide space for the tape to accelerate and decelerate between records, since reading and writing can only be done at constant velocity. The common gap sizes are 0.3, 0.6, and .75 inches for specifications shown in Table 5-4. Typically, a tape recorded at 800 bits per inch, storing records of 1K bytes each, using 8 tracks plus parity and a gap of 0.6 inches between each record can hold over 10^8 bits of data. Even though this represents a large capacity, the gap spaces consume nearly 50% of the tape surface, a rather extravagant amount. In order to increase efficiency, records are often combined into groups known as blocks, as shown in Figure 5-21. Since the system can only stop and start at an interrecord gap, the entire block is read into main memory for further processing during one read operation.

TABLE 5-3. TYPICAL PARAMETERS OF COMMON TAPE SYSTEMS

Tape Speed (inches/sec)	Data Rate (K bytes/sec)	Linear Density (bits/inch)	Rewind Time (sec)
18.75	15	800	minutes
37.5	30	800	minutes
75	120/60/41.5/15	1600/800/556/200	45-100
100	160/80	1600/800	72
112.5	180/90	1600/800	55-97
125	200/100	1600/800	55
200	320/160/111.2	1600/800/556	45-60
250	800	3200	45
200	1250	6250	45

TABLE 5-4. TAPE INTERRECORD GAPS (IRG)

Density (bits/inch)	IRG* (inches)
7 Tracks	
200	
556	0.75
800	
9 Tracks	
800	
1600	0.6
6250	0.3

*Standard accepted by most of the industry

5-9. DIRECT-ACCESS STORAGE SYSTEMS

There are two major types of direct-access systems, namely (a) movable-head (arm) disks and (b) fixed, one-head-per-track systems, the latter including both disks and drums, as shown in Figure 5-22. The former is more common since it is less expensive, as a result of a greater sharing of the read/write heads, and we shall concentrate mainly on this type. The recording head usually consists of one gap which is used for both reading and writing. This head is "flown" on an air cushion above the disk surface at separations in the

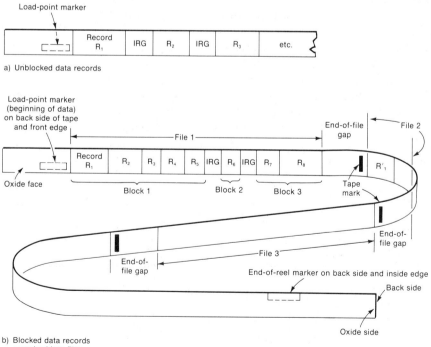

Figure 5-21   Data record formatting on tape

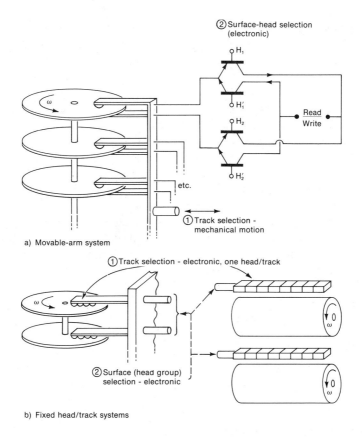

Figure 5-22   Schematic of direct-access systems

neighborhood of 50 to 100 microinches for different systems. A well controlled separation is vital to ensure reliable recording.

The medium consists of very thin coatings (about 100 microinches) of the
same magnetic material used on tapes but applied to polished aluminum disks.
Several disks are usually mounted on one shaft, all are rotated in unison, and
each surface is serviced by one head, as in Part *a* of Figure 5-22. The arms
and heads are moved mechanically along a radial line, and each fixed position
sweeps out a track on each surface, the entire group of heads sweeping out a
cylinder. A typical bit cell is 5×10^{-3} inches wide by $2000^{-1} = 0.5 \times 10^{-3}$
inches long for a 2000-bits-per-inch linear density. The transition length is
about half this size. Some typical disk parameters are:

Linear density:	1100 to 6000+ bits per inch
Track density:	100 to 200 tracks per inch
Rotation speed:	1200 to 3600 revolutions per minute
Arm movement:	50 ms between adjacent tracks
	100 ms across all tracks
Data rates:	0.5 to 10 million bits per second

The fundamental difference between various disk systems centers on the addressing mechanisms provided. In order to store and subsequently retrieve information there are six fundamental requirements for all systems. We must be able to:

1. Select a given track on a specific surface either by moving the heads in a movable-head system or by electronically selecting one head on a specific track in a fixed-head system.
2. Verify the position (track and surface); in a movable-head system the mechanical positioning can be in error and requires verification. In a fixed-head system, mechanical tolerance and other problems can result in misalignment or excessive head-medium spacing between a head and its associated tracks. (The user in principle does not have to verify positions each time but can take his chances; should an error occur, it is a fundamental requirement that position verification be possible to find the error. In addition, position verification can be used, in some cases, as an address for stored records.)
3. Have a well defined reference point for counting, clocking, and position reference for searching.
4. Record (write) data at various positions along a track.
5. Locate a previously stored record.
6. Determine when to start reading the located record and when to stop the data transfer to main memory.

All of these should be done efficiently, with as little wasted storage as possible. This is not a fundamental requirement but a practical one. In addition, there are numerous other requirements such as error detection and correction, identification of unusable tracks and alternates, and so on, that are important but arise because of practical problems. In principle, they can be eliminated with higher cost and special precautions. The preceding six requirements are more basic and cannot be eliminated even in principle, since they are an intimate part of the storage and retrieval problem. The manner in which these requirements are implemented not only varies substantially from one manufacturer to another, but also between various systems of a given manufacturer.

With respect to requirement 1, track selection, it has already been pointed out that both movable and fixed heads are used and, that the selection is either electronic or mechanical. With the exception of requirement 1, all the other requirements necessitate some form of stored addressing information. This can be essentially of two forms: One is very close or adjacent to the data it is associated with, the other is remote, such as on another track or surface. This latter might consist of index markers, clock and sector marks, or other information recorded on separate surfaces. It should be clear that they all serve the same function, namely, to help write and locate data.

Position verification (requirement 2) is handled in different ways, but in all cases it is adjacent to its associated data, since we may wish to read or write immediately after verification and hence should verify as close to the data as possible.

With respect to requirement 3, in order to write records with a known point of origin as well as have a point for future and continuing reference, all systems have some form of index marker to signify the start of the track. This is an arbitrary reference point, placed anywhere initially, and can be a physical mark (but electronically sensed) or stored bits on a separate surface. This is not as critical as position verification, and hence can be done with remotely stored addressing information.

With respect to requirements 4 and 5, writing and locating records at various positions along a track can be accomplished with either adjacent or remote addressing information, and both methods are used in practice.

For requirement 6, knowing when to start and stop reading requires some adjacent addressing information. The exact method for implementing these requirements dictates, in a very general way, the format of the records stored on direct-access storage. The format then chosen determines the storage utilization efficiency of the system, which in turn depends on the particular application, being good for some and less efficient for others.

All formats for stored records require the use of some adjacent addressing information, as shown in Part *a* of Figure 5-23. Some form of information must precede the data to separate the various pieces of data from one another and as an aid in addressing specific records. In the most simple formats, Part *b*, the stored addressing information is a gap, usually but not always of fixed length with some coded information that is interpreted by the controller. This

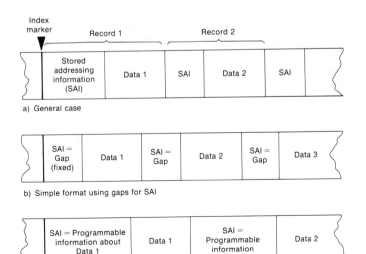

Figure 5-23 Fundamental track formats for direct-access storage systems

gap is usually not accessible to the programmer. The advantages of this system are that few bits are required for the addressing information and the overall electronics can be relatively simple. The disadvantage is mainly that this system is more suitable to well-organized data such as that found in scientific or engineering calculations. This is essentially the format in use, with slight modifications, on CDC 66XX and 76XX disk systems. It is not intended for use in a general environment, where highly variable data lengths are continually encountered.

For an environment that must accommodate wide variations in data organization, a more complex format such as that shown in Part *c* of Figure 5-23 is desirable. Here, the adjacent addressing information contains gaps, as in Part *b,* but more importantly it contains areas which are programmed information about the data and are valuable aids in locating records. In essence this is the format used in IBM System 360/370 disk systems, but with substantially more detail in the actual systems. The disadvantage of this format is the large amount of storage space consumed by the stored addressing information in many cases, and the additional complexity of the electronics and programming when the full capabilities are used.

The amount and complexity of the remote addressing information also determines the flexibility of the system and the cost. The addition of a separate disk for indexing, clocking, and sector addressing can greatly aid in implementing requirements 3, 4, and 5, but requires considerably more hardware and logic capability in the system.

Floppy disks are finding wide applications as very inexpensive, high-density, medium-speed peripherals. Floppy disks often consist of the identical, flexible medium as magnetic tape, but cut in the form of a disk 7½ inches in diameter, hence the name "floppy." Such disks, when spun, will straighten out. The read/write mechanism is usually identical to that described above, except that the head is in contact with the medium, as in tape. This causes wear, which is more significant than in ordinary disks, and requires frequent replacement of the disk and occasional replacement of the head, particularly when heavily used.

While some floppy-disk systems use only one track recorded as a spiral analogous to a phonographic recording, most use more sophisticated systems with movable heads and optical track-following servo. Many newer systems record on both sides, as illustrated in Figure 5-22(*a*). The major deviations from flying head disks are much smaller track density as well as data rate. The linear bit densities are quite comparable to that of tape. Typical parameters are 77 to 150 tracks per disk surface, 1600 to 6800 bits per inch, rotation from 90 to 3600 rpm.

5-10. ELECTRONIC SHIFT-REGISTER MEMORIES

Shift registers represent one of the oldest concepts for electronically storing and retrieving information in digital computers. The first experimental stored-program computer with address modification, the EDSAC, and the first commercial computer, the UNIVAC, both used ultrasonic mercury delay line type of shift registers for high-speed storage. The major appeal of shift-register storage is the relative simplicity and high density with low cost. The low cost is achieved by sharing the input and output transducers, as in magnetic recording on disks or tapes. In the latter, the stored information is shifted mechanically by moving the storage medium, while in electronic shift registers the medium remains stationary and the bits are moved within.

Most devices for shift-register applications can be organized either in a continuous loop, as in Part *a* of Figure 5-24, or a noncontinuous loop, as in Part *b*. In Part *a,* if no new information is entered, the data just continually circulates, similar to a disk. In Part *b,* the information is read out on the left end and must be reentered when circulating. The method chosen depends usually on the details and inherent properties of the chosen technology. Magnetic bubbles described below are readily implemented in a continuous loop, although a noncontiguous organization is quite possible. Charge-coupled devices, since they require periodic regeneration, require a noncontinuous loop. A large register may, in fact, have several segments. However, this detail is not a limiting factor in the application of the technology.

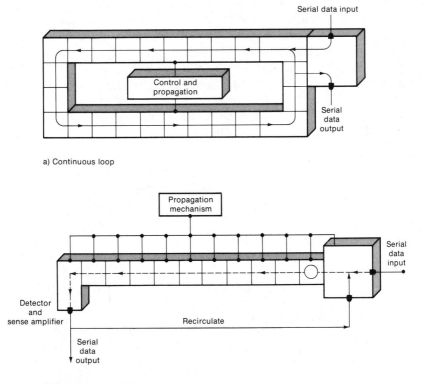

a) Continuous loop

b) Noncontinuous register

Figure 5-24 Schematic of shift-register type storage systems

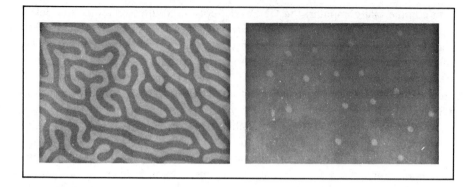

Figure 5-25   Microphotograph of magnetic bubbles as seen using faraday rotation

Magnetic-bubble-domain Storage

Magnetic bubbles represent one technology well suited to shift-register storage, with potential for high density at reasonable speeds. In order to understand the nature of a magnetic bubble, let us trace the series of events necessary for forming bubbles in an actual experimental case. Bubbles can only exist in thin platelets of suitable magnetic materials with large magnetic crystalline anisotropy and an easy axis of magnetization normal to the plane of the platelet. Such a material in its isolated condition consists of a serpentine pattern of domains, as in Figure 5-25, with equal areas of oppositely magnetized domains in the totally demagnetized case, so there is no net average remanence. If a bias field, H_b, is applied normal to the platelet, as shown in Figure 5-26, the domains with magnetization M in the direction of H_b will grow in size while those with M opposite to H_b will decrease in length,

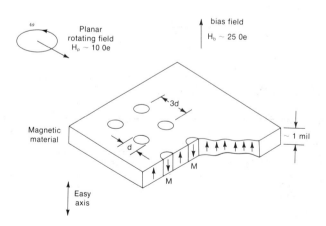

Figure 5-26   Schematic of bubble formation and magnetization pattern in suitable magnetic material

eventually reaching a nearly circular "bubble" shape. Thus a bubble is just a small region with one polarity of magnetization which is maintained within another larger region of opposite polarity of magnetization. A bias field of roughly 20 to 50 oersteds opposing the magnetization in the bubble domain is required for typical operation. The bubble diameter depends critically on the amplitude of the bias field, collapsing to zero if the field is too large, or reverting back to the serpentine pattern if too small.

The diameter and hence density of bubbles within the medium is dependent entirely upon the magnetic material parameters. This is very unlike other open-flux magnetic film devices in which the bit size and hence packing density is determined by the geometry in combination with the magnetic parameters. Thus bubble density can only be increased with better materials, assuming they can be found. A good rule of thumb for speed determination is that, irrespective of actual diameter, bubbles require roughly 100 ns per shift from one given location to an adjacent one, as described below.

For useful devices, we must be able to generate and annihilate bubbles when and where desired, shift them in some sort of storage register, and sense them, also when desired. Propagation or shifting of bubbles can be done in many ways, but one attractive way for shift-register storage makes use of magnetic permalloy overlays in the form of T and I bars. The generators and annihilators are also permalloy overlays but of a slightly different shape. These overlays are placed directly on the surface of the thin platelet as shown in Figure 5-27 and form a multistage shift register, one position for each T and I bar. The operation of the register is based on the fact that the bubbles have a given polarity of magnetic pole on the top surface, let us assume north poles, N, and the opposite pole polarity, south, on the bottom surface. If a magnetic field, H_p, is applied within the plane as shown, the permalloy overlays become magnetized with N and S poles. The dimensions of the T and I bars are chosen such that the long dimension is about three bubble diameters in length, whereas the width of the permalloy is smaller than a bubble diameter. The S poles induced along a long dimension on any permalloy bar attract the N poles of any nearby bubble whereas the N poles induced in the permalloy repel a bubble. The poles induced across the short dimension of any permalloy bar are too closely spaced to have any effect on the bubbles. Thus a bubble will reside, for instance, at the induced south poles on the leftmost I bar of Part *a*, Figure 5-27. Motion of this bubble from left to right is obtained by rotating the applied field, H_p, as shown. The rotating field induces successive S poles in successive T and I bars, with the induced S poles moving from left to right. Each 90-degree rotation of the applied planar field causes the induced south poles to move to the various position shown at times t_1, t_2, and so on. The north poles of the bubble follow these south poles and hence a shift register results. The arrangement shown represents a noncontiguous shift register, with a bubble generator, sensor, and annihilator.

These basic functions can be fabricated into many intricate shift register memories. Other functions, such as shifting between channels, address decoding, and even logic, can be performed with the same basic idea [Chang et al.,

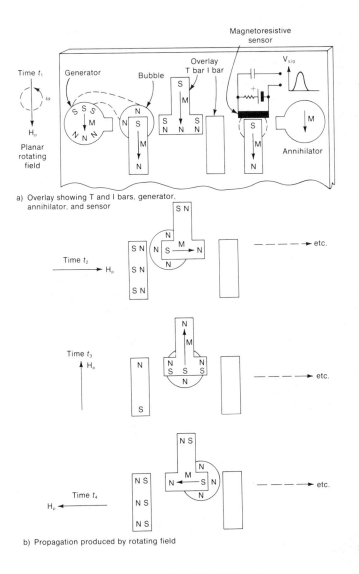

a) Overlay showing T and I bars, generator, annihilator, and sensor

b) Propagation produced by rotating field

Figure 5-27   Magnetic bubble shift register

71]. Thus all the memory functions of decoding, generation, switching, and sensing can be done with the same technology, and all these can be placed on the same chip to minimize interconnections. This is another distinct advantage of bubbles over other magnetic technologies.

Shift-register operation has been demonstrated in laboratory models at a shift rate of over 0.3 megabits per second and a density of greater than 1.55×10^5 bits/cm^2 (10^6 bits/in^2) [Bobeck, 70a]. Much faster operation at 3 megabits per second has been achieved using current loops [Bobeck, 70b] to drive the bubble rather than the slower T and I bar configuration.

Commercial bubble arrays of 100K bits using the T and I bar configuration became available in 1977. Such units, suited for mass storage in microprocessors, run at a maximum shift rate of 100K bits/sec. The bias field and driving coil are all self-contained in a unit 1.1 by 1 by 0.5 inches. The bubbles are of 5 micron diameter on a garnet chip approximately 0.2 inches square. Higher speeds and larger, more dense arrays will likely be forthcoming, and will compete with charge-coupled semiconductors for the shift-register type of electronic storage and as fixed-head disk file replacement.

Organization of Electronic Shift-register Storage

Let us consider one possible way to organize an electronic shift register, which would lend itself to large capacity with multiple-bit readout. We will assume that the chips contain 64K bits and that we wish to organize a 1M'-bit memory capable of reading out a 16-bit word with all 16 bits in parallel. It is desirable to have a small access time to adjacent 16-bit words, as well as a small average latency time to any random word. If we organize the chips as one register containing 64K bits, and use 16 such chips in parallel, we will have a 1M bit memory with fast access to adjacent (sequential) words, i.e., one shift, but the average access time is quite poor due to the long register length. The maximum access time would be 64K shifts, or 32K shifts average. If we shorten the register length, there will be more than 16 registers in parallel. We can still obtain a 16-bit read-out path by using the major/minor loop configuration of Figure 5-28. Suppose the chips are organized as 64 registers, each containing 1K bits. An additional I/O register is used on each chip, as shown, whose only purpose is to buffer the larger data path from the parallel data registers. All data registers shift in unison, so for any given position of these registers there are 64 bits available to each I/O register on each chip, i.e., 64 words for each register position. We may read these bits into the I/O register if we desire, or bypass them if this is not the desired position. If we do read these in, it is possible that the desired word is at the farthest position in the I/O register. Hence, we must shift all the I/O registers in unison to the last position. Note that we still have only one-shift access to any adjacent word, but the average access time has been reduced to $\frac{1}{2}(1K' + 64) = 544$ shifts, quite a reduction from the previous organization using 64K bits per register. Of course, this has been obtained only at the price of some additional complexity on the chip, as well as other control circuits. Needless to say, many other configurations are possible, giving different data widths and access times.

There are a number of important considerations that are dictated by the technology and application. For instance, in the most general application, we would like to be able to shift the major and minor loops independently. This would allow a sequential readout of 64 words from the I/O registers while a different position was being selected within the data register. Such an organization is not easily obtained with magnetic bubbles because shifting is done by a rotating magnetic field that covers the entire chip. Independently shifting

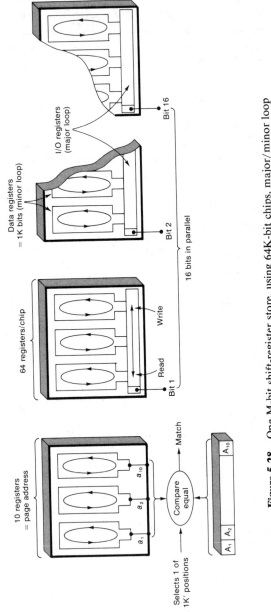

Figure 5-28   One-M-bit shift-register store, using 64K-bit chips, major/minor loop organization, and 16-bit parallel readout

I/O (major) and data (minor) registers is possible with charge coupled devices (CCDs) but requires separate clocking and control circuits, all of which take up chip space and hence cost more. However, many such schemes are available and provide a wide choice for the system architect.

For addressing such storage systems, there are a number of options. A simple way is to use a 10-bit semiconductor up/down counter, which always indicates the relative position of the data registers. Any given 10-bit address is compared with the address in the counter. If no match occurs, the system is shifted until a match does occur. Obviously an additional 6-bit counter and logic is needed to control the addressing of the I/O register, since the system of Figure 5-28 contains 64K words of 16 bits per word. Thus a 16-bit address is required to access these. The higher order 10 bits could be used to access the position of the data registers while the lower order bits access the I/O register. With magnetic bubbles, this addressing can be implemented as just described, or with bubble registers as illustrated in Figure 5-28. These addressing registers, which are the same length as the data registers and are shifted in unison, contain the address of each position. Each address is read and compared with the requested address as previously, until a match occurs.

PROBLEMS

5-6. For a single magnetic recording channel, determine the linear bit density and transport speed necessary to achieve a data rate of 10^7 bits per second.

5-7. For a magnetic tape reel of 2400 feet in length, recorded at 6400 bits per inch and containing a single file, determine the block size necessary to give an 80% recorded surface utilization.

5-8. Show how the T and I bar patterns of Figure 5-27 can be used to produce a continuously circulating bubble shift register.
Hint: Use a similar second channel adjacent to the first and connect the ends properly.

5-11. ERROR DETECTION AND CORRECTION

Stored information can be erroneous for various reasons: The intended information may have been stored incorrectly due to a permanent or intermittent fault in the storage cell or array, or noise in a writing circuit. Due to a similar failure mechanism, the information may have been stored correctly but read incorrectly, or the information may have been stored and read correctly, but the data as received at a destination (register) may be wrong due to a transmission error or an error in the receiver. Intermittent errors can and do occur due to noise on lines for many different reasons, such as when a heavy load is switched on or off the main power bus. While error-correction circuits can correct some of these, a simpler method is retransmission of the same stored information. However, this technique is not viable for permanent errors. Thus error-correcting codes are generally used as a means to circumvent permanent-type faults in the storage cells, arrays, or circuitry.

Very early magnetic-core memories generally employed only simple parity detection, and in some cases no error detection at all. The reason was that these memories were very reliable and relatively inexpensive to repair. The field-replaceable unit was an array plane typically containing 4K cores or less, and the associated circuitry was likewise of low-density cards and easily replaced. As core density increased in the late 1960s core planes became larger, containing 16K to 32K cores, while the total memory capacity increased dramatically. Even though the failure rates per bit improved or remained the same, the overall reliability decreased due to the increased capacity. Single-bit error correction was introduced at that time particularly on large memories used with large computing systems. The introduction of integrated circuits in the early 1970s increased bit density, memory capacity, and the cost of the replaceable unit, all contributing to a decrease in the overall reliability. While higher levels of integration generally reduce the failure rate per circuit or bit, the attendant increases in the total number of circuits or bits often offsets this improvement. Thus error detection and correction became important, especially as the overall system became larger.

We cover two kinds of error detection and correction in this section. The first type protects against random errors, and the second against bursts of errors. For random errors, the model assumed is:

> *Random-error assumption:* Each bit failure has a fixed probability of occurrence independent of other bit failures. The most likely errors in reading and writing words are those that affect single bits. The next most likely ones affect two bits, etc., with the probability decreasing as the number of errors in the word increases.

The random-error model holds for semiconductor memories and core memories when organized so that each bit in a word visits a distinct set of logic. A single fault in any logic group then affects a single bit per word, and does not induce more than one error in any one word.

The second type of error detection and correction protects against errors according to the following model:

> *Burst-error assumption:* When a failure occurs it is likely to affect a string of adjacent bits (or a region of physically adjacent bits). Outside the burst-error region, data are error-free. Within the region (that is, between the endpoints of the burst), there is equal probability of each bit being correct or incorrect. Short bursts are more likely than long bursts.

This model assumes that errors tend to occur in clusters, and it is intended to model errors on magnetic media such as tape and disks. A surface scratch or other imperfection on such media is usually large enough to encompass more than one bit, with the result that several bits in a region are affected. For this model a burst of length 3, with three bits in error, is much more likely than two single errors separated by a large physical distance. Consequently, the random-error model is a poor model of this situation, and codes that protect against random errors are less effective in protecting against bust errors than codes specifically designed for the burst-error model.

Following the introduction of certain general principles, we shall discuss the schemes for main memory first, then afterwards the cyclic redundancy code scheme.

General Principles

The essence of binary error-detection/correction is as follows: Given, a binary sequence of k information bits

$$I = I_1, I_2, \cdots, I_k \tag{5-5}$$

which can have 2^k possible combinations. Convert each of these sequences of bits into a new and larger sequence of bits given by

$$V = V_1, V_2, V_3, \cdots, V_n \tag{5-6}$$

where $n > k$, such that for any *allowable* errors in I, each new sequence V will be unique, and will correspond to only one possible correct binary sequence of I. The allowable errors are the errors we wish to detect or correct; i.e., for a single-random-error correction scheme, each V sequence will map to a unique correct I sequence only for single errors occurring in V. If two or more errors occur, the unique mapping may be true for certain sequences of errors, but definitely not for all.

While there are 2^n possible sequences for V, not all of these are usable in identifying an error; rather, only a subset of these 2^n sequences is used. This subset is known as a *code*, and the sequences, V, that make up this subset are known as *code words*. Each code word must have more bits than the original information sequence, I, i.e., $n > k$. Thus, an additional number of bits

$$m = n - k \tag{5-7}$$

is required, and these are known as the *redundancy,* or *check, bits.*

When an error occurs, it changes a code word into a different V sequence, or *n-tuple,* and that *n-tuple* may not be a code word. To correct an error, in essence, we look at the possible code words that may be the correct one. If there is some code word that is *the most probably correct* code word, we select it. If there is not a unique answer, we signal that an uncorrectable error has occurred. This decoding scheme of choosing the most probable code word is called *maximum-likelihood decoding,* and it is known to minimize the probability of making a mistake in the decoding process. For the random-error model, the code word that differs from the observed datum in the fewest bit positions is the most probable code word. For the burst-error model, the code word that differs from the observed datum in bit positions that correspond to the shortest burst is the most probable.

In the transformation of the possible information sequences, I, into the code words, V, the information bits could lose their original identity. In such a case, even if an error were *not* present we would have to process every received signal to recover the desired information. Since errors seldom occur, this would be wasteful as well as slow. We would rather, if possible, have the information bits be an explicit part of the code word, with the redundant check bits just catenated at the front or back end of the information, or interspersed. The latter is not only possible, but is used in all computer coding, and is known as a *systematic code.* The check bits are obtained as linear combinations of information bits, giving a *linear code.* Systematic linear codes are used both in main-memory (Hamming) and in tape-and-disk (cyclic redundancy) codes.

A simple example of a systematic linear code is that of even-parity error detection. Assume that there are 2 information bits and 1 parity check bit, so that $k = 2$ and $m = 1$, giving $n = k + m = 3$ bits, or an (n,k) code of $(3,2)$. Thus there are $2^3 = 8$ total possible bit sequences for V. However, since even parity is used, there must always be either no 1s or two 1s present, as determined by

$$C = I_1 \oplus I_2 \tag{5-8}$$

where C is the parity check bit and $\oplus$ means modulo 2 arithmetic. Modulo 2 arithmetic is the basis of all error-detection/correction schemes. The rules are simple, and are as follows:

$$0 \oplus 0 = 0 \qquad 0 \oplus 1 = 1$$
$$1 \oplus 0 = 1 \qquad 1 \oplus 1 = 0$$

Since there are only 2^2, or 4, possible information sequences in our parity example, there are only 4 possible code words, as illustrated in Table 5-5. Any single error in either the information or parity bit will result in an unacceptable code word. For instance, suppose the correct sequence is 011,

TABLE 5-5. Even-Parity Code

Information Sequence	Parity $C = I_1 \oplus I_2$	Code Word
0 0	0	0 0 0
0 1	1	0 1 1
1 0	1	1 0 1
1 1	0	1 1 0

but an error in either storing or recovering the data caused an error in the parity bit, giving 010. A parity-detection circuit detects odd parity and signals an error. If two errors occur such that the received sequence is 110 (error in first and last bit), no error is detected. Thus a single parity bit is capable of *detecting* any odd number of errors, but no correction is possible. For error correction, a more complex code is required.

To develop the techniques for encoding and decoding codes for protecting against random errors, we introduce the notion of Hamming distance:

> *Hamming distance:* The Hamming distance between two binary n-tuples is the number of bit positions in which they differ. For n-tuples x and y, the distance between x and y is denoted $D(x,y)$.

Now decoding codes for random errors can be viewed as picking the nearest code word to an observed datum. For example, consider a code with code words 00000, 01011, 10110, 11101. Let v' be the observed vector read from a memory location in which the actual vector stored was vector v. What is the most probable code word that was stored if the observed datum read from memory is 11000? Vector v' is, respectively, distance 2, 3, 3, and 2 from the code words, so that we conclude that an uncorrectable error has occurred. If the observed datum is 10000, then the distances are 1, 4, 2, and 3, so that we decode it as having been the vector 00000 originally. If the observed vector is 11011, it is respectively distance 4, 1, 3, and 2 away from the code words. Here we decode the vector as 01011.

For burst errors, an analogous situation holds. To decode, find the distance between v' and each code vector, c. Treat each difference as a binary vector that represents a burst error. The burst length is the span of bits from the first 1 in the difference vector to the last 1 in that vector. The most probable code vector, c, to pick as v is the code vector that differs from v' by the shortest burst. Thus, going back to the previous example, 11011 differs from the code words by bursts of length 5, 1, 4, and 2, so that we select the second code word as the original vector, v. When the observed word is 11000, the burst distances are 2, 5, 3, and 3, respectively, so that we pick the first word, 00000, as the most probable original vector.

Random-error Correcting Capability

With a model of how to correct and detect errors, we can now investigate the design of codes with good error-correcting properties. The notion of Hamming distance is a very powerful tool in this process. With this concept and a few other tools from linear algebra we can construct codes with guaranteed ability to correct single errors, and to detect double errors besides.

To determine the error-correcting capability of a code we have only to look at pairs of code words throughout the code and find out how close they are to each other. Should any particular pair be close, then a likely error would cause one code word to be confused with the other. From an intuitive point of view, therefore, a code should have all of its code vectors as far apart as possible from each other.

A key idea in the analysis of codes is that of minimum distance.

Minimum distance: The minimum distance, d, of a code, C, is the minimum Hamming distance between any two code words in the code.

In mathematical terms, the minimum distance, d, of a code is:

$$d = \min_{x,y \in C} D(x,y)$$

It is fairly simple to determine the error-correcting capability of a code in terms of its minimum distance. If a code is to detect e errors, and no correction is to be attempted, then we require

$$d \geq e + 1$$

for if e or fewer errors occur, no code word can be turned into a different code word by the error. The decoder should accept an observed vector as correct only if it is a code word, and signal a detected error if not.

· To correct t or fewer errors in any combination, we require that if t or fewer errors occur, the resulting observed vector will be closer to its original code word than to any other code word. For this to be the case, we require

$$d \geq 2t + 1$$

Figure 5-29 shows an argument that establishes this result. In the figure, x is the original code word, and after being corrupted by t errors, the observed word is z, a distance t from x. The decoder will decode z as x if it attempts to decode by seeking the most likely code word, provided that x is nearer to z than to any other code word. Vector y is some other code word. If y is further from z than x, then y is at least distance $2t + 1$ from x, and the code must have minimum distance at least $2t + 1$, since this holds for all pairs of code words x and y. For single-error correction, therefore, the minimum distance of a code must be at least 3.

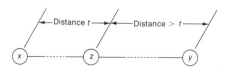

Figure 5-29   The nearest code vector to z is x, not y

Linear Hamming Codes The parity-check scheme described earlier can be used to create codes with minimum distance 3 in a rather simple and elegant way. With this minimum distance, a code can correct any single random error. Since the parity-check method is the basis of this method, let us reexamine how to construct codes with parity checks.

Consider the parity-check matrix, H, given below:

$$H = \begin{matrix} 1 & 0 & 0 & 1 & 1 & 0 & 1 \\ 0 & 1 & 0 & 0 & 1 & 1 & 1 \\ 0 & 0 & 1 & 1 & 1 & 1 & 0 \end{matrix}$$

H determines a code in the sense that a vector x of length 7 is in the code if it satisfies

$$H \cdot x^{\mathsf{T}} = 0$$

which is the same as saying that x satisfies the parity checks. What vectors are in the code determined by H? For our example, it is easy to check that $1\,0\,0\,1\,1\,0\,1$ is in the code, and so is $1\,1\,0\,1\,0\,1\,0$, but $1\,0\,0\,0\,0\,0\,0$ is not. It turns out that we can use H to create a systematic code with three information bits and four check digits. Note that H has the form

$$H = [I|A]$$

where I is a 3×3 identity matrix and A is a 3×4 binary matrix. Each row of H is a parity-check equation that indicates some subset of the positions of a code word. Each such subset must contain an even number of 1s.

The first row of H, for example, states that every code vector $c = (c_1, c_2, c_3, c_4, c_5, c_6, c_7)$ must satisfy

$$c_1 + c_4 + c_5 + c_7 = 0$$

with arithmetic done modulo 2. Since there are three parity checks, there are three check bits determined by H. Because of the structure of H, we can make the code it determines a systematic one if we let the last four positions be information positions and the first three be the check positions. Thus, if we know the value of c_4, c_5, c_6, and c_7 then the first equation determines c_1, the second c_2, and the third c_3. So to make a parity-check matrix, H, for a systematic code, we have only to use the reasoning here, as summarized below:

If H is an $(n - k) \times n$ parity-check matrix for a code C, and if the first $n - k$ rows and columns form an identity matrix, then the code determined by H is systematic if we choose the last k digits of the code as information digits and the first $n - k$ digits as check digits.

To summarize our findings thus far, we can generate a systematic code with a parity check matrix H, provided H has the structure described above.

If the code constructed this way happens to have minimum distance 3, then it will be able to correct any single random error. But how can we guarantee that the minimum distance of the code is 3 or greater? Hamming in 1950 found a clever way of answering this question. It depends on the linearity of the parity-check codes and on the notion of the weight of a vector. He showed that the minimum distance of a parity-check code is equal to the minimum number of 1s in a nonzero code vector, and with this result it is a short step to discover ways of building error-correcting codes.

To reconstruct Hamming's arguments, let us first define the weight of a vector.

> *Weight:* The weight of a vector, x, is the number of 1s in x. We denote the weight of x as $W(x)$.

The vector $(1\,0\,1\,0\,0)$ has weight 2 under this definition, and the vector $(0\,1\,1\,1\,0)$ has weight 3. The importance of this idea is that the distance between two vectors can be turned into a weight function. The key to the construction of single-error correcting codes lies in the relation

$$D(x,y) = D(x + y, 0)$$
$$= W(x + y)$$

In these equations, $x + y$ denotes the component by component EXCLUSIVE OR of the vectors x and y. If $x = (1\,1\,0\,0\,1\,0\,1)$ and $y = (1\,0\,1\,0\,0\,0\,1)$, then $x + y$ is the vector $(0\,1\,1\,0\,1\,0\,0)$. The sum of x and y under this definition has a 1 in each component in which x and y differ, so the distance between x and y is the weight of the sum vector $x + y$.

At this point the linearity of the parity-check codes comes into play. If x and y are code vectors, then so is $x + y$, because

$$H \cdot x^\mathsf{T} + H \cdot y^\mathsf{T} = H \cdot (x + y)^\mathsf{T}$$

Now the train of reasoning in the code construction process can be completed. The minimum distance between any two code words is equal to the weight of their sum, but the sum vector is itself a code word. Therefore, the minimum distance of a code is equal to the minimum weight of a nonzero code word. The problem of finding codes with minimum distance 3 is turned into the problem of finding codes whose code vectors are all weight 3 or more. This latter problem is considerably easier to tackle than the original problem of guaranteeing a minimum distance between any pair of words.

We now show how to construct a distance 3 code, and then how to decode code vectors with error-correction. Consider the matrix H:

$$H = \begin{matrix} 0 & 0 & 0 & 1 & 1 & 1 & 1 \\ 0 & 1 & 1 & 0 & 0 & 1 & 1 \\ 1 & 0 & 1 & 0 & 1 & 0 & 1 \end{matrix}$$

Note that the columns of this matrix are all of the nonzero binary vectors arranged in lexicographically increasing order. The code checked by this matrix is a (7,4) code with 16 code vectors, and the reader can verify by exhaustion that no code vector (except the all 0s vector) has weight less than 3. Although this matrix is not in the form for generating a systematic code that we discussed above, it can easily be put into such a form by rearranging the columns. In fact, columns 1, 2, and 4 can be moved to the left to form the 3×3 identity matrix we required earlier. As given here the matrix is the parity check for a systematic code whose check digits are in positions 1, 2, and 4.

We claim that every H matrix with a structure similar to the H matrix above is the check matrix for a single-error correcting code.

> *Single-error correction property:* A matrix H is a parity-check matrix for a single-error correcting code if and only if:
>
> 1. no column of H is all 0s, and
> 2. no two columns of H are identical.

To verify that the single-error correction property holds, observe just what conditions must hold for vectors of weight 1 and 2 to be in a code. For example, take $x = (1\,0\,0\,0\,0\,0\,0)$, and we find $H \cdot x^\mathsf{T} = (0\,0\,1)^\mathsf{T}$. Note that the 1 in the first position of x selects the first column of H when $H \cdot x^\mathsf{T}$ is computed, so that this result is equal to the first column of H. Using this same reasoning for the vector $y = (0\,1\,0\,0\,0\,0\,0)$ we find that $H \cdot y^\mathsf{T} = (0\,1\,0)^\mathsf{T}$, which is the second column of H. Thus, if x has a single 1, say in column i, then $H \cdot x^\mathsf{T}$ is equal to column i of H. Similarly, if z has weight 2, then $z = x + y$, where x and y are both of weight 1. Then

$$H \cdot z^\mathsf{T} = H \cdot x^\mathsf{T} + H \cdot y^\mathsf{T}$$

and $H \cdot z^\mathsf{T}$ is the sum of two columns of H. This sum is equal to the 0 vector if and only if $H \cdot x^\mathsf{T} = H \cdot y^\mathsf{T}$, which is true if and only if the two corresponding columns of H are identical. To prove that no vector in the code checked by H has weight 1 or 2, note that:

1. because no column of H is all 0s, no vector x of weight 1 satisfies $H \cdot x^\mathsf{T} = 0$, so the minimum weight is greater than 1; and
2. because no two columns of H are identical, no vector x of weight 2 satisfies $H \cdot x^\mathsf{T} = 0$, so the minimum weight is greater than 2.

Decoding Error-Correcting Codes The methods used to guarantee the minimum distance of an error-correcting code also show the way to construct practical decoders. As an example, consider the parity check matrix H:

$$H = \begin{matrix} 0 & 0 & 0 & 1 & 1 & 1 & 1 \\ 0 & 1 & 1 & 0 & 0 & 1 & 1 \\ 1 & 0 & 1 & 0 & 1 & 0 & 1 \end{matrix}$$

Every code vector x satisfies the equation

$$H \cdot x^\mathsf{T} = 0$$

Therefore, to determine if an observed vector v' is a code vector, simply calculate $H \cdot v'^\mathsf{T}$, and if the result is 0, v' is a code vector. Although we show the calculation $H \cdot v'^\mathsf{T}$ as a matrix calculation, it is nothing more than the calculation of the parity checks. Since all further actions of the decoder depend on $H \cdot v'^\mathsf{T}$, we give it a special name.

Syndrome: The syndrome of a vector, x, for a code checked by a parity matrix, H, is the column vector, $H \cdot x^\mathsf{T}$.

To decode an observed vector, v', and find its corresponding code vector, v, a decoder does the following:

1. Calculate the syndrome of v', and if it is 0, accept v' as the code word v.
2. If the syndrome is not 0, find the nearest code word v to v', and decode v' as v.

To find the nearest code word, we make use of the linearity of the code. All of the decoding information is contained in the syndrome. Suppose that the original vector is v, and it is corrupted by faults or noise to produce the observed vector, v'. Then we define the error vector, e, to be the difference vector that satisfies

$$v + e = v'$$

If somehow we can find e, then we can compute v by the relation

$$v = v' - e$$
$$v = v' + e \text{ (arithmetic modulo 2)}$$

where the second relation follows because, when arithmetic is done modulo 2, subtraction and addition are the same operation. From the linearity of the parity check codes, we find

$$H \cdot v'^\mathsf{T} = H \cdot v^\mathsf{T} + H \cdot e^\mathsf{T}$$
$$= 0 + H \cdot e^\mathsf{T}$$
$$= H \cdot e^\mathsf{T}$$

This relation says that the syndrome of the observed vector is equal to the syndrome of the error vector.

To make a practical decoder, one can simply tabulate the syndromes of all the error vectors that are correctable. After calculating the syndrome for a received vector, v', this syndrome is used to look up the error vector, e, in a special memory that holds the table of error-correction information. For the H matrix in our example, there are seven error vectors and syndromes, one for each single error. More generally, there is one error vector for each correctable error, and these could include all double errors, all triple errors, etc., for codes with sufficient error-correction capability. In the present example, the syndrome for an error in component i of a vector is column i of the H matrix, and this holds in general for error vectors with a single nonzero component.

In high-speed computers, the table look-up operation that maps syndromes into error vectors is relatively time-consuming, because it is itself a memory access. The extra access for error correction is rather undesirable when no error occurs, because it substantially increases the overall cycle time. A viable method for performing error correction is to compute only the syndrome during a memory access, and to report back the operand without waiting for an error correction. If an error does occur, this will be signalled by a nonzero syndrome. In case of error, the access is delayed for the error correction.

For the particular example we have used here, there is an even simpler method for performing error correction. We have constructed H so that column i of H is the binary representation of the number i. The syndrome of an error in component i is equal to column i, so that the syndrome itself tells where the error has been made. Hence, in our example, if the syndrome is the column vector $(1 \ 0 \ 0)^T$, then we know the error occurred in position 4. Although the H matrix in the example intersperses the information and the check bits, contrary to the structure we had assumed for systematic codes, the code is both systematic and easy to decode.

In computer systems that use these error-correction ideas, most implementations use either the table look-up scheme mentioned here or the special H matrix whose columns are the binary integers in ascending order. The H matrix is stored in the form of logic circuits which "calculate" the syndrome from the received vector. In few instances does error protection extend beyond single-error correction with double-error detection. However, multiple-error protection schemes have received some attention in special systems, and may become more widely used if changes in computer technology make such use attractive.

Codes for Burst Errors

Burst codes generally follow the same principles that have been identified for random-error codes, with a few differences in implementation and construction for special situations. Burst codes, like random-error codes, are linear codes, and are constructed from a parity-check matrix, H. The general idea in being able to detect and correct bursts is to be sure information is scattered thoroughly among the components of a code vector. Should some region of components of that code vector be lost, the information is not lost because it is contained elsewhere in the code vector.

Magnetic tape drives exhibit a classic application of burst codes. A typical drive has eight channels of information, with information appearing simultaneously on all eight channels at consecutive clock intervals. The burst mode nature of this type of device is such that a typical failure causes many consecutive bits to be lost in one channel. To overcome the burst error, the information is scattered across more than one channel. The most prevalent coding scheme for protection introduces a ninth channel that carries parity checks on the other eight channels, and additional checks in all nine channels appear at the end of blocks. This is basically a 2-dimensional scheme in which the block parity checks indicate which channel is in error, and the ninth channel parity check indicates at what point during a block transfer a channel error occurred.

Implementations of coding schemes of this type are based on a special class of linear codes known as *cyclic codes*. Although the specific details of the implementation of such codes are beyond the scope of the text, it is sufficient to indicate here that the error encoding and decoding schemes both depend on cyclic shift registers, which are fast and inexpensive devices in terms of present technology. The parity checks produced by cyclic shift registers for the cyclic coders are often called *cyclic redundancy checks* or CRCs. The interested reader is referred to Tang and Chien [69], Lin [70], and Peterson and Weldon [72]. Other sources of information on aspects of coding are found in Stone [73] and Swanson [75].

PROBLEMS

5-9. In problem 5-3 (see Section 5-5), suppose the dominant failure mode were bit-line failures. In order to provide reliability and error correction for such failures, would you reorganize your 2½D design?

5-10. In problem 5-9, suppose word-line failures were the dominant mode: What would you do to your system to provide reliability against such a failure?

5-11. Given a 256K-bit chip fabricated from the one-FET dynamic cell shown in Figure 5-16. It has been determined that alpha-particle radiation from the encapsulating material will occasionally occur, which will erase two adjacent bits of the chip (they are not permanently destroyed, but the information is lost). You are to organize a 128K-word by 8-bits-per-word, 2½D memory using these chips. Show the organization to allow single-bit error correction to be effective against alpha-particle soft-failures.

5-12. Prove that, for any Hamming code (distance 3), if a check digit over all code digits is added, the minimum distance is 4.

CHAPTER 6

Input/Output Processing

William G. Lane

In their "Preliminary Discussion of the Logical Design of an Electronic Computing Instrument," Burks, Goldstine, and von Neumann specified: ". . . there must exist devices, the input and output organ, whereby the human operator and the machine can communicate with each other." [Burks et al., 46]. They envisioned this communication in support of a one-man, one-machine environment, allowing for the possibility of simultaneous input/output (I/O) and computation, for storage of data in secondary memory (part of the I/O function), and for interactive operation between the user and his program.

But, since that time, the function of I/O processing has been greatly expanded and has become increasingly complex. Now, in contrast to the early days when each user was directly responsible, this function has been largely turned over to the computer. Multiprogramming and time-sharing systems allow multiple users to access both private and shared programs and data files simultaneously. Users compete for computer resources, sometimes by order of request and sometimes on a priority basis. Jobs are broken up, interleaved, and completed as time becomes available. And through it all, it is the I/O processor function that must arbitrate the momentary allocation of resources to a specific user, provide synchronization and control over the various devices involved and keep track of the actual data transfer so that the job may ultimately be "put back together," and so that the user can be assured that his or her program actually receives all inputs and transmits all outputs— each to or from the proper place and in the proper order.

6-1. THE INPUT/OUTPUT PROBLEM

Over the years, computer hardware designers have often tended to ignore the I/O function in the development of computer architectures. They cared little more than that the proper electrical connections were made, so long as the necessary timing signals were provided and the proper logic levels were observed. Software designers had to "make it work" and unfortunately, there was often little communication between the groups. Similarly, because it was the CPU that dominated system procurement, and since it was not good marketing strategy to "let the customer have control" and allow him to connect other manufacturer's peripheral equipment to the system, companies did not foster compatibility among I/O systems and devices. Customers were required to keep their systems pure and uncontaminated with "other equipment" so as not to void their maintenance agreements. Secrecy was both the rule and the practice until the middle 1960s, when two major events took place: First, a series of government rulings and court decisions required changes in industry practice and, second, a new computer manufacturer began marketing a small CPU complete with handbooks that told the purchaser how to build his own I/O interfaces.* This section outlines not only the interface problem but also the other factors that must be considered in the design of the total I/O subsystem. Each is amplified and discussed in detail in later sections.

Codes

Codes constitute the alphabet of a computer system, with separate bit patterns representing each specific letter, symbol, or number. They exist at three levels: internal to the CPU, in the interconnect link between the processor and its external devices, and within the external devices themselves. And, except for the American Standard Code for Information Interchange (ASCII), which has been established for character-set-sensitive input/output communication, there is little standardization. Depending on the specific use of the particular moment, specific codes in one area or level may vary in meaning from identical patterns in other areas or levels. Internally, the processor may be binary or decimal, word or character oriented (Bell and Newell [71] list twenty-five different internal word lengths (from 4 to 128 bits) for machines built through just 1970). Externally, the peripheral devices usually reflect the code of the external device, as shown in Table 6-1. In the communication links between, codes conform to the requirements of the devices and the central processor. Code translation may and can be required at each level of transition. (A complete listing of the ASCII code patterns and their specified use designations is given in Chapter 2.)

---

*Digital Equipment Corporation's PDP-8 minicomputer, first marketed in 1965, was widely accepted and used, both in stand-alone environments and as an auxiliary I/O processor for existing systems.

TABLE 6-1. COMMON CODES OF EXTERNAL DEVICES

Device	Codes*
Magnetic tape	Word binary, character, byte
Magnetic disk/drum	Word binary, character, byte
Punched paper tape	Word binary, character (5, 6, 7, 8)
Punched cards	Column binary (12), Hollerith, character
Printers	Character, byte
Plotters	Character, byte
Interactive terminals (keyboard, light pen, cursor, tablet, and so on)	Character, byte
Instrumentation, analog/digital converter	Signed binary word (10 to 15 bits), character, byte

*Unless otherwise noted, word binary is assumed to be the internal code length of the processor; character, 6 bits; byte, 8 bits. All others show the bit count variations in parentheses.

Operating Rates and Bandwidth

Every part in a computer system has two designated speeds: the maximum at which it can operate, and the actual level at which it is used. The first identifies its capacity for information transfer, or "bandwidth." It is fixed at design time and may not be changed by the user. The second is dictated by the application and is the driving force during system configuration.

Table 6-2 shows that actual operating rates vary widely, not only between different classes of devices but also between devices within the same class. These differences can be handled by providing for some form of speed compensation at the boundaries between system levels and by allowing several lower-speed devices to "share" a higher-speed connection to the CPU, providing care is taken to ensure that the collective bandwidths of the individual devices do not exceed the available bandwidth of the shared link.

Timing and Control

In normal operating environments, the central processor may be simultaneously communicating with one or more of its external devices (of the same or different types), but seldom with all and usually not in any predictable pattern. This, coupled with the speed-change requirement noted previously, requires the establishment of timing and control procedures to effect a proper connection and to provide "momentary interface synchronization" for the individual message pulses.

For communication initiated by the central processor, a simplified but typical sequence of events is:

1. The processor selects the desired external device and determines its operational status.
2. The processor signals the device to connect itself to the processor.
3. The processor requests the device to initiate the data transfer operation and to either receive or transmit the message elements.

4. For each element, the device signals the processor that it is ready to send or receive a new datum (this step is repeated until the entire message has been transmitted).
5. The processor detects the end of message and logically disconnects the device.

The reverse case, with transmissions initiated by devices, is similar except that the device must signal the processor to interrupt the program flow and alert the operating system that an external device needs attention (much like a doorbell rings or a telephone signals that someone outside wishes to communicate with those within). In both cases, action must be taken in a timely fashion to ensure that no signal is unintentionally disregarded and no data are lost, a distinct possibility that occurs when the CPU is simultaneously communicating with several high-speed, unbuffered devices.

TABLE 6-2. RANGE OF TYPICAL OPERATING SPEEDS

Device	Typical Device Rate	Character Equivalents per Second (Maximum Rate)
Physical systems measurements		
Individual	.01 to 50 samples per second	100
Multiplexed	up to 50,000 samples per second	100,000
Man	up to 5 actions per second	5
Communication modems	300 to 9,600 bits per second	1,200
Interactive terminals		
Teleprinters	10 to 120 characters per second*	120
CRT	10 to 960 characters per second	960
Vector graphics	5 to 480 vectors per second	960
Graphic Plotters		
Incremental	up to 1,000 increments per second	2,000
Vector	up to 200 vectors per second	400
Paper tape (5, 6, 7, 8 level)		
Readers	10 to 1,000 characters per second	1,000
Punches	10 to 150 characters per second	150
Cards (80 and 96 columns)		
Readers	100 to 2,000 cards per minute	3,200
Punches	100 to 250 cards per minute	400
Line printers (80 to 132 columns)		
Impact	100 to 3,000 lines per minute	6,600
Electrostatic	100 to 40,000 lines per minute	88,000
Magnetic tape (7, 9 track)	15K to 320K characters per second	320,000
Magnetic disk/drum	30K to 1.5M characters per second	1,500,000
CPU internal memory	.5M to 3.5M words per second	7,000,000
CPU internal bus	1M to 13M words per second	26,000,000

*Characters are assumed to be synonymous with bytes in indication of operating rates for device classes. Words, as noted, are assumed to be 16 bits (2 bytes).

Communication-link Structures

Internal data communication within a processor is, in general, word-parallel (or if not by words, then by equivalent blocks of 2, 4, or 8 parallel characters), where each bit requires a separate wire. The structure of the link between a processor and an external device, on the other hand, may be configured to allow transmission serial-by-bit, quasi-parallel (serial-by-character), or fully parallel (serial-by-word). It may be in one direction only (simplex), in either direction but only one way at a time (half-duplex) or in both directions simultaneously (full-duplex). The choice depends on the characteristics and the required speed of operation of the device, its proximity to the processor, and the projected cost of the link. Device control, selection, status, and timing synchronization must be transmitted over additional parallel circuits or they can be imbedded within the message pulse train itself. In parallel transmission, care must be taken to ensure that all lines in the parallel path exhibit the same electrical characteristics so that individual data and control bits are not delayed (skewed) with respect to each other. In serial transmission, a constant clock rate must be maintained over the duration of the message to avoid loss of synchronization. And finally, if telephone or other similar analog transmission facilities are to be used, additional devices, MODEMs (standing for MOdulator/DEModulator), must be used to convert the signal from digital to analog (and from analog to digital) format so that it may be impressed on (or removed from) the carrier.

Errors

Errors, particularly in I/O and other data-transfer operations, present major problems to computer systems [Gray, 72; Mills, 72]. Their detection, location, and correction depends, in part, on successful prediction and analysis of the probable manner and frequency of failure, not only in the thousands of components and circuits that make up the hardware, but also in the almost limitless combinations of instructions and codes that make up the program and data structures. To further complicate matters, errors may be intermittent or continuous in duration, single or multiple in occurrence, repeated or random in pattern, and internal or external in origin. The following list gives some of the sources of error and hopefully provides some insight into the magnitude of the detection problem:

1. Environment
    a) Dirt, moisture and pollutants in optical, magnetic, and mechanical storage media and devices
    b) Temperature and humidity
    c) Electromagnetic radiation, lightning, and so on
    d) Electrical power surges and transients
2. Component aging and misadjustment
    a) Circuit parameter drift

    b) Mechanical wear

    c) Skew

3. Previously undetected system "bugs"

    a) Unanticipated instruction sequences and code combinations

    b) Incorrect memory allocation and input/output buffer size

    c) Incompletely planned and tested combinations of system modules

4. User and operator mistakes

    a) Missequenced programs

    b) Incorrect operating and user procedures

    c) Unmounted or mismounted data storage media

The goal is to be able to locate and identify the malfunctioning component or procedure so that it may be replaced or corrected. In the meantime, the system should be able to recover from any errors that have occurred and, if possible, function on diminished power while the correction is in progress. All of this requires some form of redundancy, not only in hardware but also in the code or the data being transmitted (with increasing amounts being required as the complexity level of detection and automatic correction rises).* Redundancy can be in the form of additional checking bits in each character (parity), or at the end of the data record, through the reverse transmission of the received message (echo), retransmission of defective messages, and so on. Finally, to be complete, the error checking provisions must also include circuitry and routines for checking the checking provisions.

Communication Protocol

Communication protocol is any agreed-upon procedure for controlling data exchange between computers in a multicomputer network. It defines the grammar to allow the CPUs to converse with each other and specifies the:

1. Transmission mode (half or full duplex)
2. Message codes and formats
3. Error-checking redundancies and timeout constants
4. Error-recovery procedures

These are usually already established, unless one is creating a new network, and must be followed by each participant.

Standards

To avoid a complication similar to that at the tower of Babel, and to ensure compatibility between devices within a system as well as between systems in a network, several organizations have developed and published

---

*See treatment of error-detection/correction codes in Section 5-11.

"standards" that specify codes, functions, plug connections, record formats, operational procedures, languages, and so forth. Early ones were accepted as de facto, because most of the industry had already agreed or had been forced to comply in order to remain competitive. Lately, they have been developed by industry-wide committees and have been accepted by majority vote, sometimes only after years of discussion and modification. The list is lengthy and space does not allow identification of even their titles. For further information, the reader is referred to the X-series standards (Information Systems) in the American National Standards Institute (ANSI) index, to the Electronic Industries Association (EIA) index and to the index and the various publications of the Institute of Electrical and Electronic Engineers (IEEE), primarily *Computer* and *Spectrum*.

6-2. CPU-RESIDENT I/O PROCESSORS

Most present-day architectures provide, within the central processor, all the hardware and software features required for communication with the outside world. And, while they may vary from machine to machine in specific detail, all are functionally similar.

Conventional Architectures

Conventional third-generation single-processor computers have the organization shown in Figure 6-1. Except for the operator's control panel, all communication with external devices is through one or more of the following types of special I/O controllers known as channels:

1. *Selector.* The selector channel operates in a single mode, providing a momentarily exclusive path to a single high-speed, program-selected external device. The channel is totally dedicated to the selected device, and until released, may not be used for another I/O function, regardless of whether the device is actually transferring data or merely waiting to access the requested record.
2. *Character multiplexor.* This channel has two modes. One provides a momentarily exclusive path to a single medium-speed, program-selected device (burst mode); the other provides a time-shared, character-interleaved path for several low-speed devices (multiplex mode). In burst mode, the multiplexor acts like a medium-speed selector channel and, as such, must be totally dedicated to one device: In the multiplex mode, the channel serves several devices at the same time. Here, for example, the resultant character string from three devices with different rates and individual streams $A_1A_2A_3A_4\ldots$, $B_1B_2B_3B_4\ldots$, and $C_1C_2C_3C_4\ldots$ might be $A_1B_1C_1A_2C_2A_3B_2C_3A_4$ and so on.
3. *Block multiplexor.* This channel also has two modes. One provides a momentarily exclusive path to a single high-speed, program-selected device (selector mode); the other provides a time-shared, block-inter-

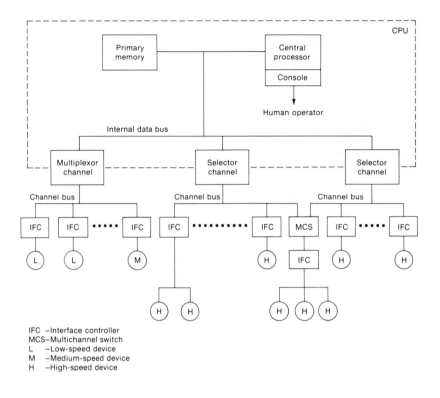

Figure 6-1 Conventional computer architecture

leaved path for several high-speed or buffered devices (multiplex mode). The multiplex mode allows the channel to be logically disconnected from the selected external devices during access wait times. Reconnection occurs after an interrupt signifying record ready for transfer. A study by IBM showed that the block multiplexor was able to deliver approximately three times the throughput at a third the response time of a conventional selector channel [Brown and Eibsen, 72].

All channels are bidirectional, and operate as either totally or partially independent, small, special-purpose processors, each with separate access to primary memory. Since transmission is often from mechanical devices, and hence is time-dependent, the channels are given priority and allowed to "steal" the necessary memory cycles to accomplish the transfer while the internal program waits. Channel programs may be resident within the channel hardware or may be stored in main memory. Interface controllers are required to connect each device electrically to its respective channel.

In systems with more peripheral devices than selector channels, alternate I/O paths can be provided, through use of program-selectable multichannel switches. Each switch connects one or more devices to several channels and permits the connection to be made to any available channel. This feature is not required with block multiplexors. Each of the three channel types is described in detail and diagrammed in the following text.

Selector Channel   The selector channel is a small limited-purpose processor that controls the transfer of single blocks of data between memory and selected external devices. Initialization requires location of the first word in primary memory, the length of the block to be transferred and the device identification. After initialization, the selector channel functionally provides:

1. The next memory location to be accessed in the I/O buffer (updated automatically with each datum transferred)
2. The number of words remaining to be transferred in the block (updated automatically with each datum transferred)
3. Assembly (or disassembly) of data elements to match the requirements of internal and external data-bus structures
4. Parity checking of or parity insertion into transferred data characters
5. Channel and device status reporting and interrupt generation
6. Data-pulse synchronization

Figure 6-2 shows the functional organization of a typical selector channel. The word assembly register (WAR) stores the contents of the word currently being transferred to (or received from) the external device. It operates in a character-shift mode. If the link between the channel and the device interface controller is halfword or fullword in width rather than one character, the shift pattern of the WAR is modified to correspond. The WAR is synchronized with the connected device's interface controller. As shown, it transmits or receives data from the devices in a single-character mode, while communicating with primary memory in a word mode (four characters at a time). The channel buffer register (CBR) contains the word currently being received from (or transferred to) main memory and operates in synchronization with the processor's internal clock. Transfer between the WAR and the CBR is parallel and asynchronous, thus providing the required speed change between the operating rates of the device and the processor. (Although channels could be constructed with only one data register for both word assembly and channel buffering, the next character might arrive before the present word has been transferred to memory and hence, the character would be lost.)

The current memory address is stored in the memory address register (MAR); the remaining block length, in the block count register (BCR). After word transfer between the channel and main memory, the MAR and BCR are respectively incremented and decremented by 1 to reflect the proper address and count.

A "transfer-complete" interrupt is generated when the block count becomes zero. Error interrupts are generated on detection of bad parity, on receipt of an error signal from the device interface controller, or if a character is lost on input. But, not all channel configurations are equipped with character-lost detector logic, and care must be taken to ensure that the aggregate

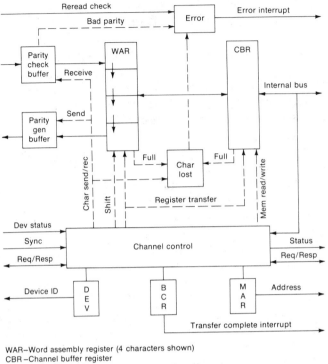

WAR–Word assembly register (4 characters shown)
CBR –Channel buffer register
DEV –Device ID register
BCR –Block count register
MAR–Memory address register

Figure 6-2 Selector-channel architecture

of all channel bandwidths does not exceed the effective bandwidth of main memory, so as to avoid character loss on input.

Character-multiplexor Channel The character-multiplexor channel, shown in Figure 6-3, can be viewed as a set of low-speed selector channels (subchannels). The connection to any one subchannel can be totally dedicated for a burst transfer or it can be passed cyclically to each subchannel in succession, only long enough to send or receive one character. In either mode, the channel controls the I/O operation in essentially the same manner as with a selector channel except that incrementing of memory addresses and decrementing of block counts are on a character rather than a word basis. Further, addresses and block counts for each subchannel are stored in fixed location lists in primary memory rather than in hardware registers in the channel.

In multiplex mode, the scan control polls the request flag flip/flop of each subchannel in succession. If the flag is set, a service request is issued and the subchannel mode flip/flop is interrogated to determine whether the requested operation is input or output. For output, the control sequence is:

1. Read, increment, and restore the character-location address from the memory address list.
2. Transfer the character from memory to the channel buffer.
3. Transfer the character to the subchannel character buffer; read and decrement the block count and test for zero.
4. Poll the next subchannel.

Input is similar except that the character must be transferred to the channel buffer at the same time the character address is read (Step 1) to enable its transfer to memory in Step 2. And, as with the selector channel, interrupts

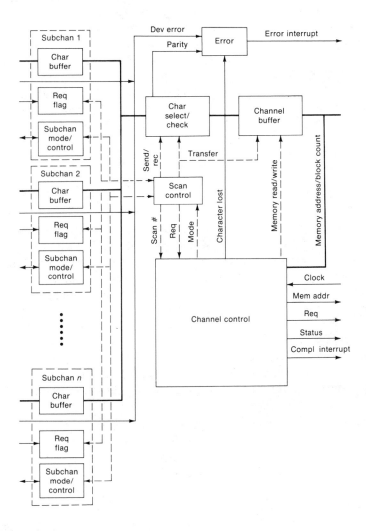

Figure 6-3 Character-multiplexor channel architecture

are generated on detected error and on block count equal to zero (transfer-complete).

In burst mode, the scan control is stopped at the selected channel and transfer proceeds in a manner similar to that in a selector channel.

Block-multiplexor Channel The block-multiplexor channel combines the desirable features of both the selector and character-multiplexor channels. As with the selector channel, the memory address and block count registers are implemented in channel-resident hardware, allowing incrementing and decrementing to take place simultaneously with data transfer. And, as with the character multiplexor, all subchannels can time-share the I/O path, except that the interleaving is by block rather than by character.

But, unlike the selector channel, the block multiplexor is able to disconnect and service other requests during the time that a selector channel must wait for a disk or other similar device to access the desired record. Reconnection is then made at the beginning of the addressed sector on an interrupt signal to the channel from the device interface controller. Provision must be made in the device-controller logic to reinterrupt the channel on the next revolution if the channel is busy when reconnect is requested.

Interrupt generation in the CPU is on detection of an error or on completion of block transfer.

Minicomputer Architectures

Minicomputers do not have independent channels in the conventional machine sense. Rather, each device interface controller connects directly into a universal I/O bus that can, under program selection, appear to each device either like a character (or word) multiplexor or like a conventional high-speed selector channel. Figure 6-4 shows this functional organization which allows I/O operations in two modes:

1. *Program-controlled I/O:* data transfer through the arithmetic accumulator, one character (or word) at a time
2. *Direct memory access* (DMA): data transfer directly to memory on a cycle-stealing basis without program intervention from the processor

Since DMA and program-controlled I/O are features that apply equally well to any bus position, any device may be controlled under either mode. Further, since DMA logic is duplicated in most minicomputers, all peripheral devices also have the equivalent of multichannel switches.

Program-controlled I/O The program-controlled I/O capability of the minicomputer is the most flexible, yet the most inefficient, of all the I/O procedures presently available. It depends on the availability of basic I/O instructions in the processor repertoire that will move data elements between

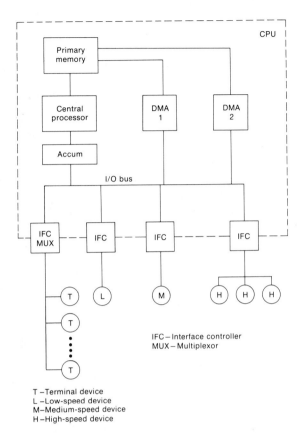

Figure 6-4 Minicomputer architecture

the arithmetic accumulator and an individual program-selected device on the I/O bus. This is done in much the same manner that the load/store instructions move data elements between the accumulator and a program-selected location in memory. But, since all I/O control is also the responsibility of the program, additional processor instructions must be provided to set and clear the various flag and control registers required by the handshaking sequence between the device and the processor.

Figure 6-5 shows the functional diagram of a typical program-controlled interface controller. (Most minicomputer manufacturers supply detailed peripheral and interfacing manuals that specify the design procedures to be followed in building custom interface controllers.) The buffer matches the processor's internal structure format on one side and the device's interface link on the other. Unused bits are dropped on output and filled with zeros on input. Code checking, word assembly, memory address incrementing, block count decrementing, and data element transfer must all be accomplished under a special I/O driver subroutine (unique to each type of device) using the arithmetic accumulator. Preemptive use of the arithmetic registers for I/O

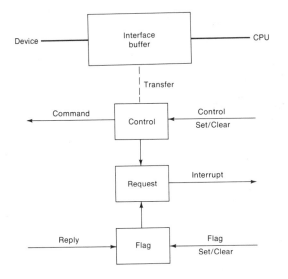

Figure 6-5 Program controlled I/O interface controller

operations also requires that the contents of the accumulator be saved before and restored after each character is transferred.

For output with a program-controlled interface, a typical sequence is:

1. Transfer the output word from memory to the accumulator (the memory address of the word is contained, either directly or indirectly, within the load accumulator instruction).

2. Transfer the word from the accumulator to the interface buffer (the device identification is contained within the move instruction as a bus address).

3. Issue a start-device command to the same bus address, specifying the operation as output.

4. Increment the memory address, decrement the block count and enter a "wait-loop" or return to the main program while the interface issues a start command to the device, transmits the character (or word), waits for a character-received reply, and generates a program interrupt.

5. Return to Step 1 or, if the block transfer is complete, issue a clear command to the interface to stop further device activity.

Input is similar except that the transfer is in reverse.

Since several instructions must be processed for each character transferred, the total bandwidth of this path is severely limited. Further, since character-lost detection is usually not included within the interface logic, the probability of invalid input occurring rises sharply as the I/O activity increases.

Direct Memory Access The DMA I/O control is an internal minicomputer hardware feature that connects the processor internal memory bus to the processor I/O bus in the same manner that a selector channel connects its interfaced devices to the internal data bus of a conventional machine. It includes separate memory address, block control, and device identification registers plus the necessary logic to steal memory cycles from the internal program and to control the transfer of data elements from the device interface through the I/O and internal data buses to memory. However, several differences exist between the DMA and a selector channel:

1. Since the DMA channels connect the internal data bus to a common I/O bus rather than to just a specific subset of external devices, any one device can be served by any DMA channel that is free at the moment (a capability that is equivalent to providing multichannel switches for each connected device).
2. Any DMA channel is capable of preempting consecutive memory cycles and of controlling transfer at full memory rate. The actual rate is dictated by the connected device.
3. Interrupts are generated only on block count zero (transfer complete) and not on error conditions since no error checking is provided within the DMA channel itself. Hardware error detection, if any, must be included in the device interface controller.

Communication Multiplexor and the RS232-C Interface

Communication between a keyboard terminal and a minicomputer can be through a serial interface controller (one per terminal) or, if a number of terminals are to be served, through a character multiplexor interface controller connected to the processor I/O bus. Functionally, this interface is the same as the character multiplexor shown in Figure 6-3 except that front-end circuitry must be added for each subchannel, as shown in Figure 6-6(*a*). The character assembly register (CAR) serves the same purpose as does the word assembly register (WAR) in a selector channel, except that here the conversion is between a serial bit stream and a parallel character format rather than between a serial character stream and a parallel word format. Figure 6-6(*b*) shows the asynchronous data format, which includes imbedded synchronization through a single start bit (0) and one or two stop bits (1) before and after the eight data bits which make up the character being transmitted. The opposite polarity of the start and stop bits assures that the beginning of each character is detectable, and provides a resynchronization point. Bit rates are selected either by hardware switch or by program control, depending on the specific connected device. External connections are per the RS232-C standard of the Electronic Industries Association [69], which specifies all voltage levels and use assignments for the standard 25-pin interface connector, and which applies to data communications in the 0 to 20,000 bits per second range, in both synchronous and asynchronous mode. It covers hardwired as well as telephone service (most communications multiplexors,

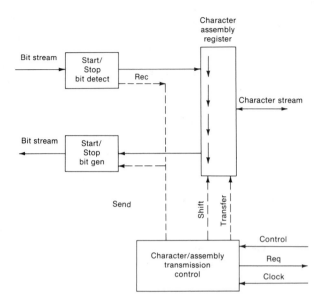

a) Bit serial interface controller

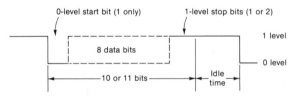

b) Asynchronous character format

Figure 6-6 Asynchronous character interface

terminals, modems and many other peripherals, such as line printers and plotters, are now designed and manufactured to be "plug compatible" with this specification).

Actual communication with the processor may be under program control or may be through the DMA channel, depending on the specific design. If program control is used, the multiplexor generates an interrupt for each character received or sent, and transfer to memory is software directed. In this case, the transferred word is packed to contain both the received character and the subchannel number to enable later reconstruction of the input information. With DMA, the multiplexor interrupts only on block count or on the receipt of a specific control character, such as carriage return, signifying end of line. And, as with the character multiplexor, memory addresses and block counts for each subchannel are contained in fixed location lists in memory.

Interrupt Structures

To avoid having to "lock up" the computer while it is waiting for a character or word to be actually transferred and received, and to have the capability of accessing several low-speed devices at the same time, it is necessary that the processor be provided with a multilevel interrupt structure that allows ready identification of any connected device needing service. Figure 6-7 shows a simplified schematic representation of a two-dimensional interrupt array. In practice, the line switches are latching circuits that are set (latched) by a signal from the device (unless previously inhibited by a device-interrupt mask command) and cleared under program control at the end of the interrupt service routine. Level switches, on the other hand, are latched on receipt of any interrupt on the level and are automatically reset when all those pending on that line are cleared.

Operation of the system, for a single interrupt, includes the following sequence:

1. An interrupt signal from the peripheral device latches the device-interrupt switch, which in turn latches the level switch, thereby creating a direct and unique signal path between the device and the processor.
2. The processor returns an interrupt acknowledge signal to the device over a parallel path controlled by the same switch array.
3. The device transmits its interrupt identifier to the processor over the I/O bus. The interrupt identifier may be the actual address of the interrupt service routine or it may be used as a pointer to a location in a table of service routine addresses.
4. The interrupt service routine stores the present contents of the program registers, services the device, restores the registers, clears the device latch switch, and returns control to the interrupted program in the manner detailed in Section 6-4.

Multiple interrupts are handled in the same way, in order of priority (by level and line distance from the processor), regardless of the sequence in which they are received. If each device is connected to only one level, the multilevel system is then essentially equivalent to a one-level system, in which the priority chains are concatenated into a single string, with the highest priority devices at the front and the lowest at the rear. Two facilities shown in Figure 6-7 give the multilevel priority system capabilities beyond those available in a single-level design. One is the ability to connect a single device to more than one level in the switch matrix, and to allow the program to select the proper priority according to the application at hand. The dotted box around the first switch location illustrates this capability and shows that this interrupt would be serviced on a "time-available" basis, after all level-one requests have been cleared. The second aspect is the group masking capability. Masking is provided for the total system, for a particular level or for an individual device by setting the interrupt-mask register to inhibit specific

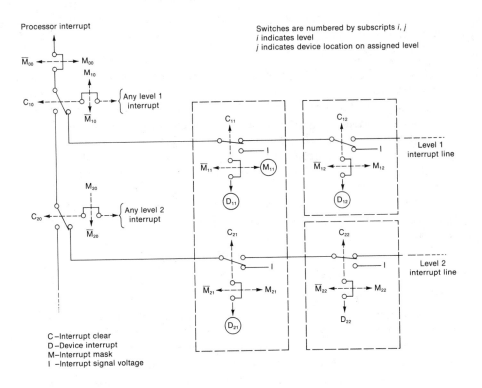

Processor interrupt

Switches are numbered by subscripts i, j
i indicates level
j indicates device location on assigned level

$\overline{M}_{00}$ M_{00}
         M_{10}

C_{10} {Any level 1 interrupt
         $\overline{M}_{10}$

C_{11} C_{12}

                                                      Level 1
                                                      interrupt line

$\overline{M}_{11}$ (M_{11}) $\overline{M}_{12}$ M_{12}

(D_{11}) (D_{12})

M_{20}
C_{20} {Any level 2 interrupt
         $\overline{M}_{20}$

C_{21} C_{22}

                                                      Level 2
                                                      interrupt line

$\overline{M}_{21}$ M_{21} $\overline{M}_{22}$ M_{22}

(D_{21}) D_{22}

C –Interrupt clear
D –Device interrupt
M –Interrupt mask
I –Interrupt signal voltage

Figure 6-7   Multilevel interrupt array
(Mask M_{11} and device interrupts D_{11}, D_{12}, and D_{21} shown actuated)

switches. This permits the processor to turn off all or portions of the entire interrupt system under program control. Specific programming considerations are discussed in Section 6-4.

I/O Bus Protocols

Information transfer on the I/O bus requires some control signals to prevent bus contention and to guarantee correct data transfer. While the details of the protocol for such transfers vary from system to system, there are some fundamental concepts that all follow. These are summarized here and illustrated with an example of their implementation in the Unibus for the DEC PDP/11 family.

The bus protocol serves two specific functions:

1. It provides a way to grant control of the bus to one requester when several requests for control occur simultaneously.
2. It provides control signals that synchronize the transactions on the bus, so that data are transmitted correctly in spite of varying propagation delays and device-response times.

These functions are normally performed on separate sets of signal lines on I/O buses, although some buses provide for multiplexing some of the control functions with data signals on a common set of lines.

Figure 6-8(*a*) shows a "daisy-chain" approach, one popular way of arbitrating multiple requests for a bus. All requests for the bus are ORed on the request line, where the presence of any request initiates a grant signal so that arbitration can occur. The grant signal is passed from module to module until it reaches the first requestor. It, in turn, stops the grant signal from continuing and indicates that it has control by activating BUS BUSY. Then when the requestor has completed its bus transaction, it removes the BUS BUSY signal and its request, allowing the arbitration cycle to begin again. (A more detailed description of the design of arbitration logic is given in Chapter 4 where it is applied to interrupt systems for minicomputers.)

Other methods of arbitration are also used, but the daisy-chain method is the most widely accepted because of its simplicity. Regardless of which method is used, the arbitration scheme must be designed to grant one and only one request at a time, even though a group of requests may be initiated

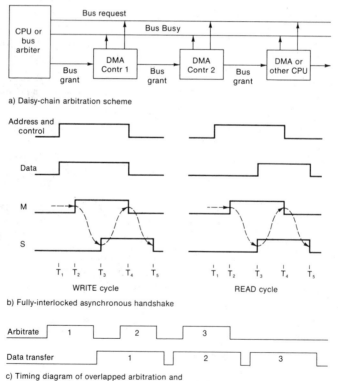

a) Daisy-chain arbitration scheme

b) Fully-interlocked asynchronous handshake

c) Timing diagram of overlapped arbitration and
   data cycles (numbers indicate corresponding cycles)

Figure 6-8 I/O bus protocol

simultaneously. And further, the granting of such a request must be independent of timing and propagation delays.

When a requester is granted control of the bus, it becomes the bus "master" and, as such, initiates the transfer across the bus to the selected bus "slave" and supplies the timing information to control the movement of the data. Figure 6.8(b) illustrates a widely used asynchronous handshake that removes timing dependencies. It is quite reliable because it is simple and because it interlocks all signals. Each signal is acknowledged with a response, making timing errors and data loss highly unlikely. The specific steps are:

1. Time T_1: The master places the command (READ/WRITE), the data (in a write operation only), and the address information on the bus. The address information is typically the device code for an I/O device or the memory address for memory.
2. Time T_2: The master raises the signal M to indicate that a bus cycle is starting and that other bus lines contain valid information. All slaves decode the address lines and the single selected slave initiates the activity specified by the command. For a READ operation, the slave proceeds to generate data for a response; for a WRITE operation, the slave accepts the data on the bus and proceeds to store it or operate on it.
3. Time T_3: At the completion of the slave activity, or at the earliest time possible, the slave indicates acceptance of the transaction by raising the signal S. The master receives the S signal and recognizes that the slave transaction has been completed. If the operation is a READ, the master accepts data from the bus and operates on it.
4. Time T_4: The master drops the M signal to indicate that the transaction is over.
5. Time T_5: The slave receives the dropped M signal, recognizes that the transaction is complete and terminates the cycle by dropping its S signal.
6. When the master receives the dropped S signal, it can initiate a new transaction or it can relinquish the bus to a new master.

Utilization of the complete procedure is recommended since it eliminates many problems that occur when only part of the interlocking is used. Deletion of step 6, for example, allows the master to proceed with a second transaction before waiting for S to drop, setting up the possibility that the master may interpret a high S value left over from the first transaction as a response to the second transaction.

A Bus Protocol Example: The Unibus

Digital Equipment Corporation has implemented the Unibus (universal bus) in the PDP-11 series minicomputers. It includes a wider structure than is needed for the data element itself (16 data bits plus 2 parity bits). Additional parallel lines indicate the element destination (device or memory

TABLE 6-3. PDP-11 UNIBUS SIGNALS

Name	Number of Lines	Function
Address	18	Identifies data element destination (memory location or device-bus address)
Data	16 plus 2 parity	Data element value
Type	2	Type of transfer (data in, data in pause, data out, and data out byte)
Control	8	Bus control, timing and status
Bus request	5	Priority interrupt request
Bus grant	5*	Bus grant (assign)

*All lines are bidirectional except the five bus grant lines, which are unidirectional.

address) as well as transmit the control and timing signals necessary to effect the transfer. As implemented, the Unibus is a ribbon cable, 120 conductors wide, with 56 signal lines bounded by and alternated between 64 ground wires. Signal functions include those listed in Table 6-3.

The five lines reserved for the Bus Request are used for requesting bus control by a master (DMA channel) at one priority level, and four levels for interrupt service by a slave. Each of these five request lines has a corresponding grant line organized as a daisy chain through the devices attached to the bus. The eight control lines include two handshake lines that perform the master (M) and slave (S) functions, as indicated in Figure 6-8(*b*). To achieve the highest possible performance, arbitration for the next data transfer on the bus is done concurrently while the present data transfer is active, so that no time is lost between data transfers waiting for an arbitration decision. The timing for arbitration and data transfer is shown in Figure 6-8(*c*) to make this time overlap clear.

A Proposed Standard: The S-100 Bus

During the mid-1970s, as minicomputers were becoming more and more widely accepted, another major technological breakthrough occurred. The semiconductor industry developed the capability to manufacture very large integrated circuits and to literally compress an entire CPU into a single chip while making orders-of-magnitude reductions in cost. But while these new microprocessors are very similar in structure to minicomputers, they presented the computer architects with a new set of problems. Low-cost CPU's cannot reasonably require high-cost I/O interfaces, and peripheral manufacturers cannot afford to develop separate interface controller designs for each different microprocessor. Hence, the industry has been more or less forced into developing a single interface standard to hold down costs. The result is a 100-line bus patterned after the PDP-11 Unibus design, which continues the master/slave concept and the parallel transmission of address, control, and data (16-bit word-serial). Morrow and Fullmer [78] published an annotated preliminary specifications of this standard, requesting "comment and suggested revision," in May 1978. Copies of the adopted version are available from the ANSI publications bureau.

An Existing Standard: The IEEE 488 Bus

An earlier standard, which was also influenced by the PDP-11 Unibus, was developed for a similar but different reason. A standard interface and communication protocol was needed for connecting electronic instrumentation and recording equipment to minicomputers in a process-control type environment. The RS232 bit-serial interface was too slow (20,000 bits/second maximum) and the PDP-11 Unibus was too expensive (here, because of the complexity involved, interface costs could exceed the costs of the peripheral). Since performance and cost are proportional to the link structure (performance, to the quantity of data transferred in one time period; cost, to the number of parallel wires and circuits), a trade-off was clearly required.

The designers selected a bus structure, called the IEEE 488, that would transmit asynchronous data in serial-by-byte, rather than serial-by-word, fashion, between a limited number of connected devices (up to 15), in a closely located configuration (20 meters maximum bus length), in a modified master/slave (talker/listener) mode. Signal circuits were reduced from 56 to 16 and cable wires were cut from 120 to 24. By 1979, several manufacturers had begun marketing LSI IEEE-488 bus-controller chips, which together with a few additional driver chips form a complete interface. The price range is in line with many lower-cost peripherals and the performance ratings are quite adequate for most applications, about 500K bytes/second (1M bytes/second maximum). Further information is available in two very good articles, one by Loughry [74] and one by Knoblock, Loughry, and Vissers [75]. Copies of the standard itself can be obtained from the IEEE.

PROBLEMS

6-1. Obtain channel architecture diagrams for any computer available to you.
   a) How do they compare to those described in Section 6-2?
   b) What features do they lack?
   c) What additional features do they have?

6-2. Analyze the interrupt structure of the computer available to you.
   a) How is the device priority determined?
   b) What masking is available?
   c) How is it invoked?
   d) How are multiple interrupts handled?

6-3. Obtain the structural diagram of a communications multiplexor. Determine the procedural steps necessary to input or output one record from each peripheral device attached, assuming all devices are active simultaneously.

6-3. SYSTEM-RESIDENT I/O PROCESSORS

The I/O problem, as outlined in Section 6-1, includes several functional requirements that are not treated by the conventional processor-resident I/O channel:

1. Code conversion where the external code does not match the internal (for example, ASCII to binary, BCD to binary, unpacked to packed decimal)
2. Error detection or correction where the error is only detectible over a span of characters or words
3. Format control where the I/O record must be assembled or disassembled before transmission or processing.

These, together with the channel initialization and some control operations, require additional program intervention and a dedication of processor resources that might be better spent on internal program processing.

Because of this drain, computers are considered to be *"I/O bound"* when I/O operations require a disproportionate share of the memory cycles available. One solution, often advanced by computer salesmen, is to change to higher-priced and faster peripherals. Another is to add a small front-end processor between the central processor and the peripheral devices, thus allowing the separation and dedication of tasks — I/O operations to the front-end processor and internal program processing to the central computer.

Disk-coupled Systems

Figure 6-9 shows the organization of a typical disk-coupled system. The front-end processor controls all the low-to-medium-speed input and output, buffers and assembles records from each device, checks for errors (requesting retransmission, if necessary), performs code conversions and line editing, and stores or retrieves programs and data structures on the shared disk. Control of the job flow through the system generally rests with the front-end processor. Its operating system manages the program queue and allocates the disk space for each program processed.

This organization is probably the easiest to implement, particularly where the two machines are built by different manufacturers. Neither must conform to the physical bus-timing and control restrictions of the other. Programs operate independently without cycle-stealing, and the only information that is required to be passed directly between the two machines consists of the program attributes (type, storage location, number of blocks). On input, this information is transmitted from the front-end processor when the program is ready for processing by the central processor. Conversely, when the central processor is finished, it notifies the front-end processor of the attributes of the output files that it has stored on the shared disk. Requests are honored by the shared-disk controller from either machine on a first-received basis if the disk is not busy, at the end of the block being transferred if the disk is

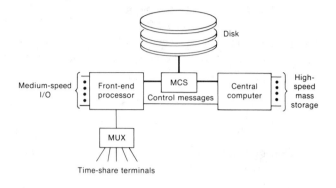

MCS - Multichannel switch

Figure 6-9 Disk coupled front-end processor

busy, or from the front-end processor only if a preemptive wait request has been issued to clear a rapidly filling input queue in front-end memory.

Direct-coupled Shared Memory Systems

The direct-coupled organization requires that both the front-end and central processors have essentially the same architecture and internal timing/control characteristics. In this configuration, primary memory replaces the disk as the shared coupling, but with information exchange interleaved on a word rather than a block basis.

Depending on the specific machine, connection may be any of the following:

1. DMA to DMA between separate computers where each channel is initialized by its respective processor and where each machine can access selected memory locations in the other
2. Through separate ports of primary memory where the front-end processor is given access priority in the case of simultaneous requests
3. Through a shared wide-band bus where the front-end processor is given bus-control priority in an asynchronous control environment or alternate cycles in the synchronous case.

The general advantages of the direct-coupled system over the shared-disk system is the ability to pass data and programs without the need for intermediate disk store. (Intermediate disk store may be required if queue lengths exceed available memory.) In the latter two connections, even the memory-to-memory move is eliminated.

Integrated Systems

The shared-disk and direct-coupled connections provide a way, after the architecture has been established, to configure a system that is essentially a dual processor. Some larger architecture, on the other hand, were initially designed as multiprocessors with integrated I/O processors. Typical of these are the CDC CYBER 170 series machines, which are based on the CDC 6000, shown in Figure 6-10. Ten peripheral processors are given access to central memory on a polled, time-slice basis. System control is resident in one of these, which, in turn, controls all task scheduling of the central machine as well as the nine other peripheral units. All are architecturally the same, all have access to any of the 12 I/O channels, and any can be assigned as master control. All models allow the addition of 10 more peripheral processors and 12 I/O channels.

The Hewlett-Packard 3000 system, shown in Figure 6-11, provides an example of an alternate design in the small-to-medium-sized systems area. On first look, it appears to be nothing more than a return to the conventional architecture of Figure 6-1, upgraded to include standard interfaces and external buses. But two major changes have been made:

1. Each bus-connect device controller has been provided with its own microprocessor.
2. A separate register set has been included for each subchannel in the I/O port (a DMA-like block multiplexor).

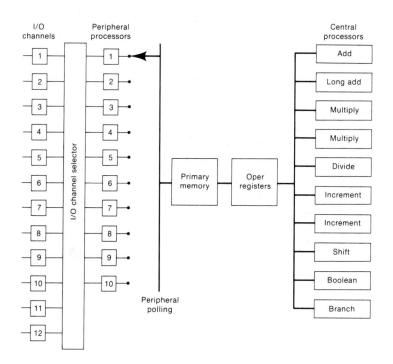

Figure 6-10 CDC 6000 Cyber 170 series structure

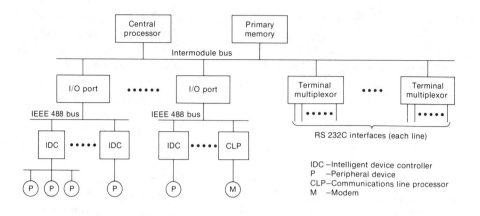

Figure 6-11   Hewlett-Packard 3000 series structure

Taken to the limit, these changes embody several significant conceptual design differences that allow distribution of the I/O function across all three system levels:

1. Peripheral dependent routines, such as I/O drivers and error detection/correction procedures, can be resident in the microprocessor contained in that device's controller rather than in the system's primary memory.
2. Message-length buffers in microprocessor memory can make each peripheral appear to the central processor as a buffered device and thus allow all communications to proceed at an electronic rather than mechanical rate.
3. A single standard protocol can be used for all communication between the CPU and its bus-connected peripheral devices, rather than having separate procedures for each.
4. I/O request stacking and control of message interleaving can be made a responsibility of the block multiplexor in the I/O port.
5. Device-to-device communications, such as disk to printer, can be accomplished using the external bus exclusively rather than requiring an I/O operation to and from primary memory.
6. Synchronous communications protocols controlling high-speed data exchanges from remote devices can be completely handled by the microprocessor in the communications controller without degrading the central processor operation.

PROBLEMS

6-4.   Analyze the peripheral devices attached to the computer that are available to you.

a) How is each device logically connected to the computer?
b) How is it physically connected?
c) What codes are utilized?
d) What transmission structure is required?
e) What hardware buffering is supplied?
f) What data rates are available?
g) What error-checking provisions are included at the peripheral?
h) What device control is allowed to the user?
i) Is it modifiable, and if so, how?

6-5. Review recent publications of the ACM and IEEE for papers on front-end processors. Analyze the functions assigned and the methods of communicating with the central processor.
a) What changes are indicated?
b) What additional architectural features are needed?
c) What additional software features?

6-4. PROGRAMMING CONSIDERATIONS

The architectural features described in the previous sections have been designed to facilitate the transfer of data elements between the central processor and its external devices. They accomplish the serial/parallel transformation, parity checking of individual characters, interleaved transfer of words to and from memory, modification of next memory address and remaining block counts, and the generation of program interrupts on hardware-detected errors and at the end of block transfer. These functions have been converted to hardware because their characteristics are stable and readily defined and because their implementation does not impair program flexibility.

User programs normally perform I/O through calls to I/O driver subroutines in the operating system. Drivers are normally reentrant, so that one routine can serve several devices, with the possibility that several can be active simultaneously. And they are also interruptable, so that a higher-priority device can be serviced without wait. The user specifies his required record length, its buffer location, and the device to be accessed. Additionally, he specifies other information such as record formatting requirements, file name, sector location, and character code. Everything else required to establish the program/hardware interface is the system architect's responsibility.

I/O Driver Linkage

Each I/O driver must provide for the return linkage to the main-line program by storing the return address and the contents of any status registers that would otherwise be lost by the routine. Normally these are stored in delicated memory locations unique to the routine and to the particular device, and are restored prior to return.

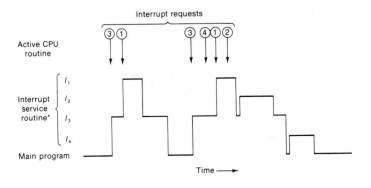

Figure 6-12 Interrupt receipt/service-time diagram

Interrupt Servicing

On recognition of a program interrupt, an immediate indirect jump is made to the subroutine address specified for the device. The return linkage is generated (other interrupts are inhibited during this phase to prevent loss of return address), and the interrupt is serviced. If a higher priority interrupt is received before the routine is finished, it is acknowledged and serviced, providing return linkage to the first interrupt routine. If the second interrupt is of the same or lower priorty, it is locked out until the first routine is finished and control is returned to the main-line program (other interrupts are also inhibited during the return jump, to allow proper restoration prior to servicing the next). The second interrupt is then serviced in the normal manner. Figure 6-12 shows an example for the case where several interrupts of different priorities have occurred over a short period. Note that each service routine follows the return linkage path generated at the time it was recognized, and that each interrupt is serviced in order of priority rather than by order of receipt.

Channel Initialization

Channel initialization requires that the device-identification code, the first memory-buffer address, and the block count be transferred, either to the channel itself or to specific list locations in memory, before a channel input/output operation can begin. Since it is possible that either the device or the channel might be busy, program provision must be made to allow for some form of interrupt to signal the processor (either after a set time lapse or when the device or channel status changes), so that a connect retry can be made. Provision must also be made to disconnect and reset the interface prior to routine exit.

Communication Subchannel Initialization

Initialization of a communication subchannel is similar to setting up of a conventional channel, as just described, except that the transmission rate of the device may also have to be selected. (A review of available terminals shows that 8 frequencies should be sufficient for most configurations: 110, 150, 300, 600, 1200, 2400, 4800 and 9600Hz.) If the connection is by telephone dial-up from an unknown device, it may be necessary to test several frequencies to determine the correct one. This can be done through a simultaneous multiple frequency sampling or through the repeated transmission of a known character until a proper match is made.

Format and Code Conversion

Format and code conversions are specified by the programmer and dictated by the characteristics of the device, the language being used, and the processor. This is accomplished in several steps, each of which requires a separate subroutine section. For input, these are:

1. Conversion of the external code to an internal code. If the external device has more than one possible code, such as in a card reader, then the I/O driver for that device has to be structured to deal with each one.
2. Separation of format-specified characters into separate strings representing single data elements. This may require deletion of delimiter characters such as decimal points, commas, slashes, or blanks, as well as the insertion of fill characters such as zeros or blanks.
3. Transformation of the adjacent characters of the string into a complete data word in the format required by the internal machine. Standards, for example, do not currently exist for the representation of floating-point words, and these may vary considerably in both length and form.
4. Transfer of the data word to its appropriate locations in memory.

Output is in reverse order, except that the record buffer must be initialized and the necessary device-control characters added.

Buffer Allocation

Each active device must be assigned one or more blocks of memory (buffers) to serve as intermediate storage for record assembly during input/output operations. The specific type and length depends on the characteristics of the external device, the application, the restrictions of the programming language, and the space available in primary memory. Figure 6-13 shows several possible structures:

1. Fixed-length linear buffers — generally used if the record lengths are easily predictable, as in card devices, line printers, and so on
2. Multiple (ping-pong) linear buffers — assigned to smooth the input/

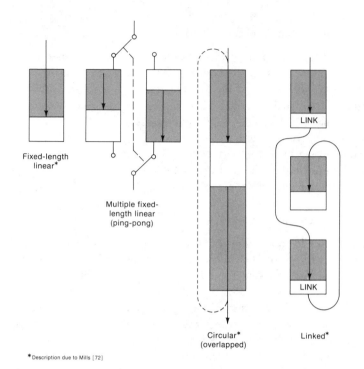

Fixed-length
linear*

Multiple fixed-
length linear
(ping-pong)

LINK

LINK

Circular*
(overlapped)

Linked*

*Description due to Mills [72]

Figure 6-13   I/O buffer structures

output flow and allow the device to be reading the next record while the program is processing the present one

3. Circular buffers — used where several records (of fixed or variable length) may be in the input queue before they are processed; common with keyboard terminals, where records may contain editing information affecting portions of the same or previous record (for example, backspace, delete previous line)

4. Linked buffers — used when record lengths within a sequence of transmissions are random and vary over a wide range

Error Detection and Recovery

Some form of error-detection capability is commonly provided in most system components of today. Depending on the level of intelligence contained, this may be more or less automatic and more or less comprehensive. It is the system designer's responsibility to determine both what error-detection capability is available (see the following list) and what is needed, and then to decide what actions must be taken to make the two match.

1. Most, but not all, CPUs and I/O devices generate and check character parity.

2. Some devices are equipped with reread stations and perform direct read-after-read or read-after-write comparisons; others have a second read station that checks only longitudinal even/odd parity or total bit counts.
3. Some devices allow communication in the "echo-plex" mode, where the character input at the keyboard is sent to the CPU and retransmitted from there to the device display.

But unfortunately, none of these features are universal, and each fails in some way: Character parity will not detect errors involving even numbers of bits, direct comparison during reread will not detect invalid record contents, and echo-plex, as described, requires human intervention.

It was necessary, therefore, to find a method that checks total records as well as individual characters and do it with a reliability as close to 100% as possible. One procedure that reduces the probability of undetected message errors to insignificant levels is known as the cyclic redundancy check (CRC), after the fact that all computation and checking can be accomplished with "cyclic" shift registers. In this method, the bits of a datum are treated as the coefficients of a polynomial, so that 1011, for example, represents $x^3 + x + 1$. This datum is encoded by multiplying it by a code polynomial; and, to keep all the resulting coefficients binary, the coefficients are computed modulo 2. Thus if the code polynomial is $x + 1$, then the coded form of 1011 is $(x^3 + x + 1) \cdot (x + 1)$ which is $x^4 + x^3 + x^2 + 1$, or 11101. The actual multiplication produces the term $2 \cdot x$; but, since coefficients are taken modulo 2, this term vanishes. To decode this coded form of the datum, simply divide the code word by $x + 1$, and the quotient is the answer. However, the division has to result in a zero remainder because the code word is a multiple of the code polynomial. If an error occurs, there is a very high probability that it will produce a polynomial that is not an even multiple of the code polynomial, and thus the error can be detected at the outcome of the division.

In actual practice, code polynomials are longer, usually degree-12 or -16. These develop 12- or 16-bit error codes, which must be appended to each message and which reduce the probability of having an undetected error to almost insignificant levels. For example, by using a degree-16 code polynomial, one can encode an 800-bit message in 816 bits. Assuming typical kinds of random errors, this message when decoded has a probability of undetected error less than 10^{-8}.

Once an error is detected, the action taken depends on the characteristics of the device, the type of error detected, the importance of the data, and the time available for analysis. In real-time control systems, for example, measurements are repeated each time period and, as a result, control programs are not generally susceptible to errors in individual readings so long as the specific data can be identified as *in*correct. The value or trend of the previous period is accepted until the next regular sampling occurs.

The error-handling procedures may attempt to correct the error based on the information at hand (if a sufficient number of check bits are available), or they may request a limited number of retries. The method used to retry the operation depends both on the device and the protocol of the link. For magnetic tape this requires a backspace and reread (or write); for magnetic disk, a reread on the next revolution; for cards, operator intervention and card reinsertion; and for remote communications, a retransmission not only of the record containing the error but also all of the records transmitted subsequent to it. This requires a handshaking between the transmitting and receiving devices, where the transmitter waits after each message for a positive or negative acknowledgment before sending another message. If the acknowledgment is positive, the next message is sent; if negative, the same message is repeated. This procedure is known as the stop-and-wait ARQ (automatic repeat request), and is detailed in papers by Burton and Sullivan [72] for communications networks and by Chien [73] for mass storage devices.

Record Structures

In contrast to the earlier design stages, where considerable flexibility exists, the software designer often finds that his choices must be restricted to a very limited set of possibilities. By this time, hardware devices have been selected, bandwidth capabilities have been fixed, and not much more remains than to determine the record lengths to be used in I/O operations. But this choice should not be made lightly, for it can have a considerable effect on the ultimate system performance. Several factors must be considered:

1. The physical capacity of the device and of the links involved (line length, card type, segment size, transmission rate, and so on)
2. The structural restrictions imposed by the programming language being used
3. The wait time required between separate records
4. The amount of memory that can be made available for assignment to I/O buffering
5. The probability of error occurrence during message transmission

The first three are self-explanatory. They are imposed by the physical properties of the system. The fourth is flexible, within limits, and in the case of telephone communications the fifth can sometimes be reduced by proper line/modem selection. But before any such selection is made, a criterion needs to be established. Burton and Sullivan [72] proposed that the primary objective be the maximizing of information throughput, and they provide an equation to accomplish this for data exchange in a telephone communications environment. The same equation applies to nontelephone communications as well.

$$T = \frac{n(1 - P(n))}{n + c \cdot v} \cdot v \qquad (6\text{-}1)$$

where T is the throughput rate in bits per second

n is the block length in bits

$P(n)$ is the probability that a block of n bits will contain an error

c is the time delay between the transmission of one block and the beginning of transmission of the next; it includes the line turn-around and signaling times of the communication links, the start/stop and access times of the devices, and so on

v is the transmission rate of the link or the device

$c \cdot v$ represents the number of bits that could have been sent during the wait period

A little explanation as well as caution is needed regarding several of the factors in this equation. $P(n)$, the probability of a record of length n containing an error, is not a constant. It is related to n, and generally increases as n increases. Error rates are stated in terms of their frequency of occurrence, assuming continuous transmission, and commonly vary from 10^{-4} to 10^{-12} depending on the type of link or device. Telephone lines, for example, are rated to produce no more than one error in 10^5 bits — unless the communication is over switched networks, in which case it is qualified with the additional limitation: no less than 80% of the time.

The record length chosen must be short enough not only to fit within the buffer space available but also to limit the retransmission or reaccessing of records. Burton and Sullivan suggest that n be chosen such that the factor $(1 - P(n))$ is never less than 0.95.

The product $c \cdot v$ is the wait-time bit length and, while it is fixed by physical properties of the system, its effect can be lessened by making n as large as possible with respect to it. The challenge is to choose the optimum record length and to minimize the effect of both $c \cdot v$ and $P(n)$.

Communications Driver Routines

Programming of communications driver routines now largely follows two accepted protocols:

1. Binary-synchronous communications (BSC): a character-oriented procedure that was introduced by IBM in 1966, and which is now more or less the de facto industry standard for medium-to-high-speed transmission over half-duplex telephone lines.
2. High-level data-link control (HDLC): a bit-oriented procedure that was more recently developed by the International Standards Organization (ISO) for high-speed digital and satellite transmission.

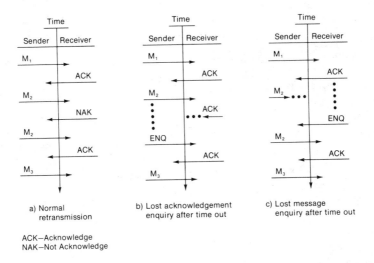

a) Normal
retransmission

b) Lost acknowledgement
enquiry after time out

c) Lost message
enquiry after time out

ACK—Acknowledge
NAK—Not Acknowledge

Figure 6-14 BSC short-block message sequence examples

Both allow the user to vary the message length and both employ multiple error-check procedures, including timeouts to prevent indefinite tie-ups while waiting for lost messages.

The BSC control embodies the ACK/NAK response concept and requires a line turnaround between messages (50 to 250 milliseconds, depending on the distance), as shown in Figure 6-14. Each message begins with two or more synchronizing characters (to establish a common clocking rate) and contains field elements that are each preceded by a special control character:

1. A header to identify the message
2. A text block containing the actual information or data
3. An error-check trailer

Figure 6-15 shows examples of two of the possible formats that might be used.

HDLC, on the other hand, provides for simultaneous two-way transmission and, as a result, eliminates much of the handshaking and intermessage waiting required by BSC. Line turnarounds are not required (unless the user elects to use the half-duplex mode), and message-receipt acknowledgments are imbedded in the message being sent rather than in a separate return transmission. Figure 6-16 shows how the following five elements are ordered in the six-field message frame:

1. A flag (bit code 01111110) to identify both the beginning and end of the message frame.

a) Short message—single text block

SYN–SYNC
SOH–Start of header
STX –Start of text
ETX –End of text
(start of trailer)

b) Long message—multiple text blocks

Figure 6-15 BSC message formats

2. A station address (8 bits) to identify the receiver.
3. A two-part control field (8 bits) to mark the sequence number of the frame being sent as well as the sequence number of the next frame needed back from the receiver.
4. A variable-length information field with no restrictions as to input bit pattern.
5. A CRC frame check word (16 bits).

Some explanation is in order. Because the protocol requires that a bit pattern of six 1s be interpreted as a flag, it is necessary to take precautions that prevent the transmission of a false flag. In the station address, combinations with six adjacent 1s are never assigned. In the control field, neither 4-bit frame number is ever allowed to exceed octal seven, and the record sequencing is adjusted to never allow the "message received" acknowledgment in the reverse transmission (indicated as one less than the number of the next frame requested) to lag by more than seven messages behind the frame currently being sent (the actual number by which it is allowed to lag will depend on the number of sending buffers available). The information and frame-check fields are even easier to handle. Here, all that is required is to have the sender insert a 0 after each sequence of five data-message 1s, and to set up the receiver to detect the difference between strings of five and of six 1s (the former requires the removal of a trailing 0; the latter must be interpreted as an end-of-frame flag).

Figure 6-16 HDLC frame format

PROBLEMS

6-6. Analyze the I/O buffer structures used by the operating system of the computer available to you.
  a) Are they appropriate or should they be changed?
  b) What would be the effect of doubling the memory allocated to each?
  c) How would the added resource be used?
  d) Would the structure change?

6-7. Analyze a circular buffer in which several records can be stored at one time. Assume transmission from a keyboard terminal. What provisions must be made to implement line editing such as tab, backspace, delete previous word, and delete previous line?

6-8. Analyze the I/O driver routines of any computer available to you.
  a) How is the return address generated and stored?
  b) During what portions of the routine are other interrupts masked?
  c) What register contents are saved and how are these protected in case this routine is interrupted by one of higher priority?

6-9. Analyze Equation 6-1. What modifications are necessary to allow for:
  a) Asynchronous communication at 11 bits per character?
  b) Error correction in event of a NAK reply?
  c) The noninformation content of the various header and trailer portions required in each record by the particular protocol?

6-10. Using a variation of Equation 6-1 and the characteristics of any system available to you:
  a) Compute the effective throughput rate for reading records from magnetic tape, assuming record lengths of 200, 400, 800, and 1600 bytes with no read errors and with a probability of a read error of 0.001 per record.
  b) What modification is required to allow for the additional time necessary to backspace the tape and reread a bad record?

6-5 BANDWIDTH UTILIZATION: A MEASURE OF EFFECTIVENESS

Because the I/O subsystem provides the interface between the CPU and the outside world as well as between the processor and secondary storage devices, the effectiveness of its operation can often be the determiner of the effectiveness of the entire system.

Efficiency Evaluation

In the noncomputer world, machines are rated by their work-output capacity and by their relative energy-conversion efficiency. Measurements of power, torque, and speed are independent of the devices attached and are, in most cases, relatively easy to make, since input and output are homogeneous. Efficiency is measured by the ratio

$$\eta = \frac{\text{work output}}{\text{work input}} = \frac{\text{work output}}{\text{work output} + \text{losses}} \qquad (6\text{-}2)$$

The second form of Equation 6-2 is the most important to the machine designer since, if he can identify the losses, he may be able to identify the areas of greatest opportunity for changes that will reduce the factors toward zero.

A somewhat similar situation exists with I/O processors. But work input and output, in this case, are by no means as easy to measure. The I/O subsystem must reconcile differences in speed, code, and word size; check for read, write, and transmission errors as well as for special control characters; control the operations of all channels, I/O buffers, and peripheral devices; and accomplish the format conversions specified by the user's program. The only homogeneous element is time. Here, therefore, work output becomes the time during which an actual data exchange is taking place; losses are the times that a resource is tied up and unavailable for other use, including the wait time to access the record plus the time necessary to accomplish all of the following:

1. Initialization and termination of a channel-block transfer
2. Program control of packing and unpacking characters in records
3. Code conversion and format editing
4. Error checking and recovery
5. Interrupt servicing, including operations to store and restore any pre-empted registers

Hence, while it may take many memory cycles to actually read or write a single element, the actual number of useful operations (the work output) is only one. Therefore it is possible to define a measure of I/O efficiency as

$$\eta_{I/O} = \frac{\text{number of data elements transferred}}{\text{total number of processor memory cycles required}} \qquad (6\text{-}3)$$

This equation provides the criterion for suggesting design-time trade-offs between and among all system levels.*

The equation just given, however, does little for the system implementor after the design is fixed. He must rely on other means to evaluate the effectiveness of his choices. One proven way is to analyze how each procedure utilizes the available bandwidth of the various affected elements. Recall that

---

*An expanded discussion and derivation of computer-efficiency equations is given by Lane [72].

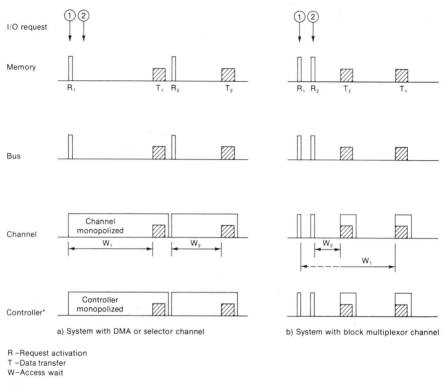

R –Request activation
T –Data transfer
W–Access wait

*Controllers with microprocessors would appear as shared devices

Figure 6-17   Bandwidth-utilization time diagrams

each device, communications link, channel, and CPU module has a maximum operating rate (bandwidth), and that the physical nature of their design allows some (such as buses and memories) to be time-shared by several programs or processes while requiring others (such as selector channels and peripheral controllers) to be momentarily assigned on an exclusive basis. Each system element must be individually examined for actual use to ensure that the information transfer rate required does not exceed either the remaining bandwidth available in shared devices or the total capacity of those that are monopolized by the process. Figure 6-17 shows typical time diagrams of bandwidth utilizations during a two-record transfer between primary and secondary memory where the disk records are in noncontiguous locations. In the first case, the architecture of the channel requires that it be continuously connected during the total time that is required to position the head and rotate the disk to the beginning of the record. The second case does not require monopolization of the channel during the wait period and, instead, allows the transfer of "closest" record first.

I/O Spooling: An Example of Bandwidth Utilization

In early batch machines, it soon became apparent that it would be impossible to match the I/O requirements of the job stream to the speed of the peripherals and, further, that it would be physically impossible or, at the very least, too costly to match the speed of the peripherals to the requirements of the programs. Many required "burst" mode reading of input data, followed by quiet computation, after which there was a period of continuous output. Something had to be done to smooth out the demands on the card reader and the line printer. In large installations, smaller off-line machines were used to continuously wind or "spool" (standing for System Peripheral Operation On-Line) the input program and data stream onto magnetic tape. Then, after each reel was sufficiently full, it was mounted on one of the larger machine's tape drives, where it could look like and be treated as a higher-speed "logical" card reader (the reverse procedure was used to spool output to tape for later off-line listing). As time went on the systems became more sophisticated, and the tape drives themselves began to be shared between the two machines, much in the same manner as "ping-pong" buffers are used today.

Modern systems have similar situations, except that the spooler files are maintained on disk rather than tape and the total environment has become more complex. Today, I/O may be batch or interactive in orientation, with multiple peripherals of similar or different types. In contrast to the old first-in-first-out (FIFO) procedure, where the spooler managed only two queues, one input and one output, with complete jobs in a simple, orderly sequence, the system must now have the capability to manage multiple queues per device, with "next job" selection based on priority level as well as time of receipt, and to hold specific output files for later alternate hard-copy listing after the user is satisfied with his soft-copy version.

And, finally, while spooled I/O is an accepted way to smooth the peripheral demand and more closely match the various capabilities of the different parts of the system, unless proper design procedures are followed, the costs can override the benefits. Figure 6-18 shows the spooled I/O path for both one- and two-processor systems. Because each I/O record is now handled three times rather than once (with all additional operations involving the disk), it is possible for the spooler to completely absorb most, if not all, of this unit's bandwidth. The only recourse is to block several logical records into a single physical record, so that the total number of disk accesses is reduced (and so that the associated access-wait time is distributed across several records rather than having the full amount be required by each). The specific number of records to be included in each block must be determined for each different system; but in all cases, the decision will be based on a trade-off between memory space available and the number of accesses that can be allocated to this function without exceeding the remaining bandwidth available on disk.

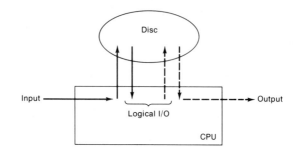

a) Single processor system

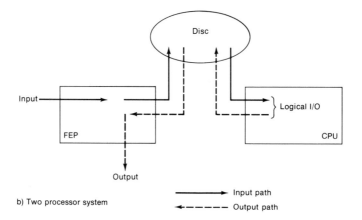

b) Two processor system

Input path ———————▶
Output path ◀— — — — —

Figure 6-18 I/O spooling paths

PROBLEMS

6-11. Analyze the achitecture shown in Figure 6-11.
   a) What I/O operations discussed in Section 6-5 are amenable to being distributed across the various system levels?
   b) How would each of these distributed functions affect the bandwidth utilizations in each system element?
   c) Where would bottlenecks likely appear and what precautions should be taken to prevent them?

6-12. Analyze the spooling-path diagram of Figure 6-18. Using timing characteristics and bandwidth capacities of any machine available to you, compute:
   a) The bandwidth needed to accomplish spooling operations, assuming that the input and output record-blocking factors allow only one logical record per physical record.

      b) The blocking factors needed to ensure that spooling operations would consume no more than 25% of the available channel bandwidth.

6-13. In some architectures, memory cycles are required by the channel for operations other than the actual transfer of data elements, such as modification of the next memory address and the remaining block counts if these are stored in fixed locations in primary memory. Compare the memory-bandwidth utilization requirements for this type of channel with those of the channel shown in Figure 6-2.

6-14. Compare the memory-bandwidth utilization requirements of programmed I/O to an I/O operation using DMA.

6-6. SUMMARY AND ADDITIONAL OPPORTUNITIES

The I/O system is usually designed to be "transparent to the user" and, as such, is often overlooked as an opportunity for architectural improvement. In actual fact, however, it can be one of the most time-consuming links in the chain between program input and result output. Several opportunities for architectural advances exist.

Microprogrammed I/O Control

Many of the current program operations listed in Section 6-4 are fully amenable to the microprogramming techniques discussed in Chapter 10. If these are converted to microroutines, many of the instruction accesses currently used should be able to be eliminated.

Transmission by Exception

Most input/output records contain filler characters (blanks or zeros) to complete a fixed-length format equal to the length of a disk sector, printed line, or punched card. Most languages and systems require the transmission of these characters with each record, even though they are unchanged for the duration of the particular format control. An additional bit identifying which characters are fixed and which are variable would allow all records after the first to be transferred in compact form, with the record containing only the variable information (each record would have to be preceded by a control character signifying whether it was a new or continued format).

Externally Clocked, Synchronous I/O

The interfaces between levels are complicated by the need for speed and word-length conversion. Multiple-track recording formats (parallel by word or by character) and clocking from the disk during data transfer would allow the disk to be matched to the internal memory rate and structure. Further, if the record is to be processed as a vector, it may be possible to eliminate the presently required intermediate unproductive transfer to memory by routing the data stream directly to the processor. (This variation changes the normally passive secondary memory, and allows it to act the same as active primary memory for selected applications.)

The Future

With the advent of reliable low-cost integrated circuitry, I/O channels are now becoming capable of many of the functions now distributed between the processor (and its programs), the channel, and the device controller. Microprogramming will make the channel even more adaptable and universal. Microprocessors will make device controllers capable of accepting different word structures and character codes, of detecting and correcting errors (including retransmission on either the same or alternate data paths), and possibly of accomplishing the entire formatting operation.

PART II

Advanced Topics

CHAPTER 7

Stack Computers

William M. McKeeman

7-1. INTRODUCTION AND NOTATION

A stack is a last-in, first-out data structure. In its simplest form it can be accessed by only two operations, PUSH and POP. A PUSH operation takes new data and pushes it onto the top of the stack, where it is saved. Subsequent PUSH operations bury the item deeper and deeper under each new data entry. A POP operation removes the most recently pushed data item from the stack, uncovering the item underneath.

The appellation "stack computer" designates a class of computers using one or more stacks. Stacks can be understood in isolation, and can be used independently of, and even in the absence of, other stacks. An actual implementation, however, has traditionally mixed a number of conceptually different stacks into one rather tightly-bound, interleaved structure. The easiest road to understanding is to describe each stack individually and then to show how they may be combined into more complex mixtures, if necessary. Each stack is described as a data structure, in terms of the data contained within it, and as a reflection of the programming language and machine language that drive it.

The use of stacks in computers is not a particularly recent event. Bauer [60] describes an evaluator using relays for a pushdown store, which was designed in 1950 and implemented in 1956. Randell and Russell [64], in a major contribution to the literature, give detailed diagrams and flowcharts for a very elaborate stack structure. Much of that structure is to be found in the KDF9 Computer [Randell and Russell, 64, appendix 3] and had a heavy influence on the Burroughs B6700. Wirth and Weber [66] also present an elegant stack architecture in an implementation of the programming language Euler. The

Burroughs B5000 was designed at the same time as the programming language ALGOL 60 appeared. It proved to be a reliable and versatile computer, partly due to its reliance on stack hardware. The Burroughs B5500, B5700, and B6700 carried this development further, perhaps even near the practical limit of complexity for such mechanisms. The Hewlett-Packard HP3000 (1972) has a somewhat less elaborate stack structure tailored more specifically to a demand for real-time response. The Burroughs B1700 appeared about the same time with a stack mechanism controlled by a writable microcode.

The Digital Equipment Corporation PDP-11, also of this period, has some rudimentary stack-construction and use facilities cleverly merged into a more conventional set of operations. Many of the ideas found in these computers were first expressed by Barton [61]. Wortman [72] has carried the ideas further in his doctoral thesis and also provided a basis for evaluating the relative merits of alternative mechanisms. The concept of multiple stacks arose during the collaboration of McKeeman and Wortman and the B1700 design group. Several others, notably Roger Packard and R. S. Barton, made contributions during this period. The concept of tagged data, an important adjunct to stack organization, is discussed by Wirth and Weber [66] and Illife [68]. Organick [73] gives a detailed treatment of the Burroughs B5700/B6700 series of computers. Doran [in Chu, 75] and the May 1977 issue of *Computer* magazine give excellent overviews of existing stack machines.

To avoid misunderstandings arising out of the various colloquial interpretations of the word "stack," we now offer some definitions which we will then use throughout this chapter. A datum of width n is visualized as a contiguous vector of n independent bits of information, thus it has any one of 2^n values. A datum is the basic unit for transactions between the various parts of the computer. The width of data is bounded from below by the number of values in the range of the data being represented, and from above by economic considerations of bus width, memory size, adder precision, and the like. The data pushed onto the stack comes from somewhere in the computer; the data popped goes somewhere. Each action involving PUSH and POP takes the form of an assignment. An assignment *to* a stack implies a PUSH onto the stack; an assignment *from* a stack implies a POP from the stack. Thus if X is some other place in the computer (for example, a register), and S is a stack, the assignments in Table 7-1 are the prototype for stack access.

TABLE 7-1. ASSIGNMENTS FOR PUSH AND POP

Action	Assignment
PUSH from register X onto stack S	$S := X$
POP from stack S into register X	$X := S$

Suppose X, Y, and Z are registers containing the integers 2, 3, and 4, respectively, and that S is an initially empty stack. Then the contents of the stack and the registers will be changed by assignments among them as depicted in the example in Figure 7-1.

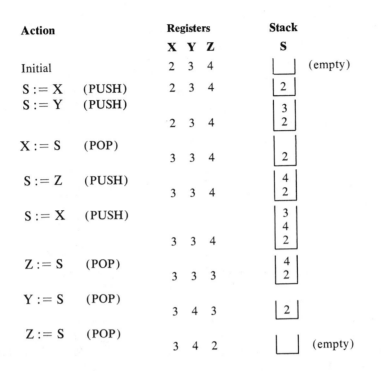

Figure 7-1   Sequence of stack assignments

When the stack is empty, a POP operation is pathological since there is no data to be removed. Also, stacks do not have infinite capacity. When a stack is full, a PUSH operation is pathological since there is no room for the new data item. These two conditions are called *stack underflow* and *stack over-flow* and the computer must be able to detect them and respond reasonably. Since there is no response that will preserve stack properties, computers usually react by interrupting the sequence of instruction execution much as when arithmetic overflow occurs in the adding circuitry.

There are some uses of stacks that require more elaborate access methods than just PUSH and POP. They will be described in following sections.

Since there are likely to be several stacks in one computer, we will normally use subscripted variables of the form S_i to denote stacks. To be more precise about the foregoing notation, whenever an S_i is used in a context where its value is needed, we imply that the value is "popped" off of the stack, leaving the next value in the stack exposed. Whenever an S_i is used in a context where its location is needed, we imply that a value is "pushed" onto the stack. For example,

$$S_i := 3$$

implies the value 3 is pushed onto the stack S_i;

$$S_i := S_i - S_i$$

implies the top two items are popped off S_i, subtracted, and then the result is pushed back onto S_i. As in APL [Iverson, 62], the assignments are read from *right to left,* so that the rightmost S_i in the example is the data item at the top of the stack before the assignment is executed and thus represents the subtrahend of the expression.

Certain other data structures are used in conjunction with stacks and therefore must be representable in the notation being described. In particular, main memory is a large array accessed via subscripts (absolute addresses). We would write

$$\text{MEMORY}[3] := S_i$$

to signify popping a value off S_i and placing it into location 3 of main memory. We will use other similar notations freely.

The reader must be constantly aware of the difference between the meaning given to the expressions involving stacks, just described, and that given to the expressions appearing in programming languages, which will also be used as examples throughout this chapter. In programming language expressions the sequence of evaluation of operators is normally left-to-right except as modified by operator hierarchy and parenthesization. Furthermore, the order of evaluation of operands is usually immaterial since their value is constant during the evaluation of the expression. The stacks, S_i, are, on the other hand, operands with side effects. The use of the value of an operand signals not only the use of the value but also the removal of that value from the stack. Here the order of evaluation of operands matters very much, and must be right-to-left, as stated previously.

7-2. STACKS

Simple stacks can be implemented in a variety of ways; more complex versions are generally restricted to being placed in main memory and being accessed through index registers. For example, if A, B, and C are index registers, and MEMORY is an array representing the main memory of the computer, we can define a stack as lying between A and C, with push-pop point B, as depicted in Figure 7-2.

The PUSH and POP of Table 7-1 can be defined as shown in Table 7-2. The advantage in expanding the detail of the stack mechanism in this way is that later some more elaborate access methods must be defined in terms of the given registers, and other registers must be added in a similar fashion for some even more complex stacks.

The disadvantage is in giving the reader an incorrect intuition about the sequentiality of the details of stack access. Note that much of the activity in the expanded PUSH and POP of Table 7-2 can be done simultaneously.

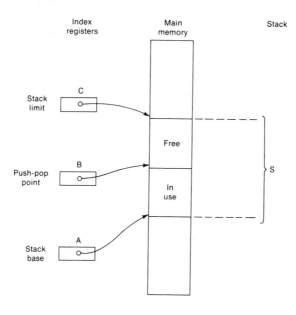

Index registers   Main memory   Stack

Stack limit   C

Free

Push-pop point   B

In use   S

Stack base   A

Figure 7-2   Stack in main memory

Designers have achieved substantial gains in efficiency by taking such opportunities for parallel processing into account.

Suppose, as another example, that we need a stack as depicted in Figure 7-3. The signals POP and PUSH are pulse controls that cause the corresponding actions to take place. Prior to pulsing PUSH, the datum must be on the bundle IN. The bundle TOP gives a continuous readout of the top of the stack except for a brief period after a PUSH or POP pulse. The outputs OFLO and UFLO signal the corresponding failures in the stack mechanism.

The main components in the stack will be some shift registers as illustrated in Figure 7-4. The input lines SHL and SHR are pulse controls that cause the corresponding actions to take place. The bit to be shifted in must be ready on the lines LI or RI respectively when the control pulse arrives. The lines LO and RO give continuous readout of the bits at the ends of the shift register. (LI signifies left-end input, LO signifies left-end output, etc.)

TABLE 7-2. THE ACTIONS PUSH AND POP DEFINED IN TERMS
OF A, B, C, AND MEMORY

Action	Definition
PUSH	IF B > = C THEN STACK__OVERFLOW
S := X	ELSE MEMORY[B] := X;
	B := B + 1;
POP	B := B − 1;
X := S	IF B < A THEN STACK__UNDERFLOW
	ELSE X := MEMORY[B];

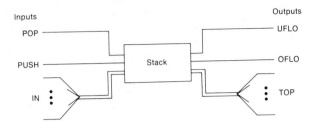

Figure 7-3 Simple stack mechanism

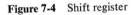

Figure 7-4 Shift register

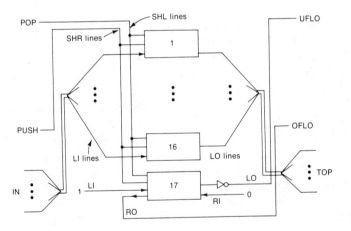

Figure 7-5 Simple stack built out of shift registers

For a stack of width 16, seventeen shift registers are combined as shown in Figure 7-5. The seventeenth register carries the underflow and overflow information. A logical 1 is gated into the left end with each PUSH, and a logical 0 is gated into the right end with each POP. Whenever a 0 propagates all the way from right to left, we have an overflow situation and similarly for a 1 from the left. The seventeenth register must be initialized to all 0s, for which no mechanism is displayed.

PROBLEMS

7-1. Specify, at some level of detail, another hardware implementation of a simple stack. How many different answers can you find for this exercise? Give a brief discussion of the effect each implementation has on the external characteristics of the stack, such as speed, overflow, underflow, and so on. (Refer to Figure 7-5.)

7-2. Using components available today, design a stack functionally identical to that in Figure 7-5. Provide for the initialization of the overflow/underflow register either in the hardware or as a sequence of external commands.

7-3. ARITHMETIC-EVALUATION STACKS S, S_i, S_r, S_a

The evaluation of arithmetic expressions is the most easily understood use of stacks. It is also perhaps the least consequential use of stacks, but does form a convenient starting point. Suppose we have an expression in programming notation:

$$2 + (3 - 1) - 4$$

It can be evaluated using a stack by the following sequence of actions:

1. Push 2 onto the stack.
2. Push 3 onto the stack.
3. Push 1 onto the stack.
4. *a*) Pop the two top data items off the stack (into some unnamed registers).
   b) Subtract the first to appear from the second.
   c) Push the result back onto the stack.
5. *a*) Pop the two top items off the stack.
   b) Add them.
   c) Push the result back onto the stack.
6. Push 4 onto the stack.
7. *a*) Pop the two top items off the stack.
   b) Subtract the first to appear from the second.
   c) Push the result back onto the stack.

This leaves the result, 0, as the only value on the stack.

The actions fall into two classes: placing operands on the stack and operating on the operands at the top of the stack. We can unambiguously indicate a sequence of such actions with a sequence of corresponding symbols. It is sufficient to denote PUSH actions with the value to be pushed and operations with the corresponding arithmetic operator. The sequence is called Reverse Polish (properly, operator-late, parenthesis-free notation of Łukasiewicz). The sequence of actions for the expression given previously is, for example, denoted by:

$$2\ 3\ 1\ -\ +\ 4\ -$$

Any expression can be translated into Reverse Polish. One can find a variety of translation algorithms in texts such as Randell and Russell [64].

Combining the Reverse Polish and the stack manipulation notation for the example above, we get Table 7-3.

TABLE 7-3. REVERSE POLISH AND STACK ACTIONS FOR THE EXPRESSION $2 + (3 - 1) - 4$

Reverse Polish Symbol	Stack Action*
2	$S := 2$
3	$S := 3$
1	$S := 1$
$-$	$S := S - S$
$+$	$S := S + S$
4	$S := 4$
$-$	$S := S - S$

*Refer to the last three paragraphs of Section 7-1.

Conventional computers accomplish arithmetic evaluation with registers instead of stacks. The instructions specify registers and memory locations which must contain the operands. As in the case of Reverse Polish, there are many published algorithms that translate expressions to conventional instruction sequences. They are, however, considerably more complicated than those for Reverse Polish code. In particular, the source operands in a register may not be needed as soon as calculated results are available, while the register housing these source operands may be needed for further calculations. As a result the translator must create a temporary variable for the value in the register. This value must be recovered when it is needed. The use of a stack eliminates the need for explicit temporary stores and the associated bookkeeping.

The size (or depth) of an arithmetic stack determines how complex an expression can be computed. So long as some provision is made for the infrequent occurrence of overflow, the size may be quite small (say depth 4, or perhaps 8).

The situation is more complicated when different types of data are mixed in the programming notation, for example, the integer 2 and the real number 2.0. The data may have different widths and the bit patterns different interpretations. There are many solutions, of which we shall examine three.

The first is to let the larger width determine the width of the stack and to inject explicit type-conversion instructions into the Reverse Polish. Such extension of the notation needs a new name; we shall call it Generalized Reverse Polish, or simply *Polish*. We must also have different operators for

TABLE 7-4. MIXED-TYPE ARITHMETIC EVALUATION

Polish	One-Stack Solution	Two-Stack Solution
2	$S := 2$	$S_i := 2$
r	$S := r(S)$	$S_r := r(S_i)$
3.0	$S := 3.0$	$S_r := 3.0$
1.6	$S := 1.6$	$S_r := 1.6$
$-_r$	$S := S -_r S$	$S_r := S_r -_r S_r$
$+_r$	$S := S +_r S$	$S_r := S_r +_r S_r$
1	$S := 1$	$S_i := 1$
r	$S := r(S)$	$S_r := r(S_i)$
$+_r$	$S := S +_r S$	$S_r := S_r +_r S_r$

the different types of data. We let "r" stand for conversion to type real, "$+_r$" stand for addition on type real, and so on. Then the expression

$$2 + (3.0 - 1.6) + 1$$

yields the Polish

$$2 \text{ r } 3.0 \ 1.6 \ -_r \ +_r \ 1 \text{ r } +_r$$

where everything is converted to type real before computation. The "One-Stack Solution" column of Table 7-4 lists the stack actions involved, and the corresponding sequence of values in the stack is shown in Figure 7-6.

A second approach is to provide a separate evaluation stack for each data type. In this case the type conversion operator "r" causes data to be popped off the integer stack, S_i, converted to real format, then pushed onto the real stack, S_r. The two different stacks may have different width and format, thus avoiding the necessity of coming up with a compromise for the single stack. In terms of the stack notation, the solutions are shown in the last column of Table 7-4.

The third solution is to use tagged data. Suppose that the data type is intrinsically recognizable (usually by the addition of some extra bits called *tag bits* as in Euler [Wirth and Weber, 66]). Then Polish can ignore the type differences by depending on the arithmetic algorithms of the hardware rec-

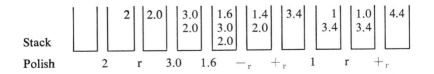

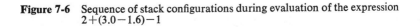

Figure 7-6 Sequence of stack configurations during evaluation of the expression $2+(3.0-1.6)-1$

ognizing what to do just before the actual operations take place. We write (r, 2.0) to denote a value 2.0 tagged as being in real format and (i, 2) to denote a value 2 tagged as being in integer format. Then the Polish

$$2 \quad 3.0 \quad 1.6 \quad - \quad + \quad 1 \quad +$$

results in the sequence of stack actions in Table 7-5.

TABLE 7-5. TAGGED-DATA SOLUTION
FOR MIXED-TYPE ARITHMETIC

Polish	Tagged-Data Solution
2	$S := (i, 2)$
3.0	$S := (r, 3.0)$
1.6	$S := (r, 1.6)$
$-$	$S := S - S$
$+$	$S := S + S$
1	$S := (i, 1)$
$+$	$S := S + S$

The values in the stack are illustrated in Figure 7-7. Note that while the first subtraction finds two operands of type real and thus simply performs a real addition, the following addition must first convert the integer 2 into real format before doing the addition.

Suppose that we have a purely combinatorial arithmetic unit, as shown in Figure 7-8. The two bundles X and Y are the input data and bundle C is a set of control lines $C_1, C_2, \ldots C_n$, one for each arithmetic operation the unit can perform. When one control line is up, and the data are on X and Y, the unit will, after a certain delay, provide the result, X C Y, on the bundle Z. A failure in the arithmetic algorithms (for example, integer overflow) is signaled on line E.

We want to combine the arithmetic unit in Figure 7-8 with the stack in Figure 7-3 to make a stack arithmetic processor, as shown in Figure 7-9. It is a sequential circuit, and we assume the availability of appropriately timed clock pulses on $CLOCK_1, CLOCK_2, \ldots$ The control line C_0 signifies a PUSH action from a datum ready on A. The other control lines C signal the operations corresponding to the arithmetic operations the arithmetic unit can carry

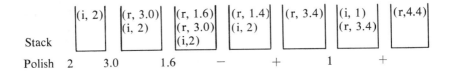

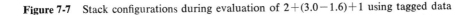

Figure 7-7   Stack configurations during evaluation of $2+(3.0-1.6)+1$ using tagged data

Inputs   Outputs

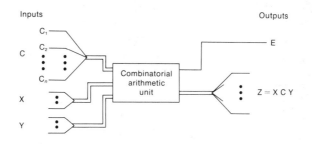

Figure 7-8   Arithmetic unit

out. B contains the contents of the top of the stack except during the period where the stack is being changed. The output lines E, UFLO, and OFLO signal the failures of the corresponding internal units.

We will require some registers of the form shown in Figure 7-10. The control line R is pulsed to cause the datum U to be read into the register. V is the current value of the register except for a short period after the line R is pulsed.

Figure 7-11 depicts a solution to the problem. The Push action is initiated on pulse $CLOCK_3$ in both the case where C_0 signals a PUSH and the case where two operands have been operated on and the result needs to be placed back into the stack. Pulses $CLOCK_1$ and $CLOCK_2$ trigger POP actions, the first to feed the data to the arithmetic unit and the second to discard the unneeded datum from the top of the stack to make room for the computed result. R_1 and R_2 are registers of a size consistent with the rest of the unit.

Variables can also appear in expressions. From the viewpoint of the arithmetic unit, a variable is identified with an area of main memory. How that

Inputs   Outputs

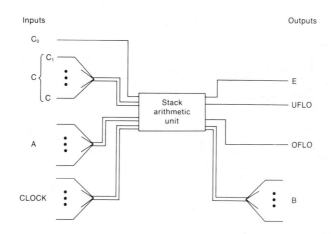

Figure 7-9   Stack-arithmetic unit

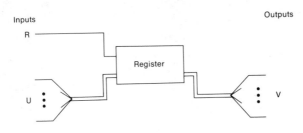

Figure 7-10   A register

identification is made, and how it is encoded, are deferred to the section on storage allocation. For the moment, we represent a variable by its name, with the understanding that the name ultimately is mapped into an absolute memory address. As a datum, an address is simply another type and may be stated in an address stack S_a. Each of the three previous solutions can be extended to handle assignment statements. For example, suppose we have the assignment

$$X := X + 3$$

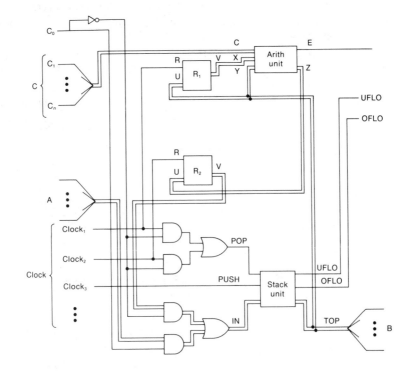

Figure 7-11   Stack arithmetic unit design

where X is of type real. We have to fetch a value from memory, convert 3 to real format, add them and replace the value in memory.

The transactions with memory depend upon how the values are encoded in memory itself. For purposes of discussion here, we assume that in memory the values have the same format they have in the evaluation stack. This implies that if we have a tagged-evaluation stack, S_a, we have tagged values in memory. The Polish and interpretation of the preceding assignment are given in Table 7-6.

TABLE 7-6. STACK ACTIONS TO EVALUATE
THE ASSIGNMENT $X := X + 3$

Polish	One-Stack Solution
X	$S := X$
X	$S := X$
M	$S := MEMORY[S]$
3	$S := 3$
r	$S := r(S)$
$+_r$	$S := S +_r S$
:=	$MEMORY[S] := S$

Polish	Three-Stack Solution
X	$S_a := X$
X	$S_a := X$
M	$S_r := MEMORY[S_a]$
3	$S_i := 3$
r	$S_r := r(S_i)$
$+_r$	$S_r := S_r +_r S_r$
:=	$MEMORY[S_a] := S_r$

Polish	Tagged-Data Solution
S	$S := (a, X)$
X	$S := (a, X)$
M	$S := MEMORY[S]$
3	$S := (i, 3)$
+	$S := S + S$
:=	$MEMORY[S] := S$

The data in the stacks S_a and S_i may happen to be identical in format. If so, they may be combined to simplify the three-stack solution in terms of hardware components. It is left to the reader to reformulate the stack notation description for this possibility.

Suppose we have a memory device as depicted in Figure 7-12. The bundles MA and MI must contain the memory address and memory datum respectively. When the control line W is pulsed, the contents of MI are placed in location MA. MO has the value of the contents of location MA except for a

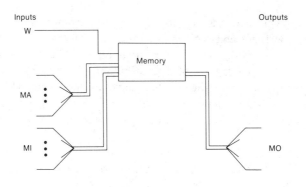

Figure 7-12 A memory

brief period after W is pulsed or MA is changed. The stack-arithmetic unit in Figure 7-9 and the memory unit in Figure 7-12 can be combined to provide for execution of the Polish in Table 7-6.

The arithmetic operations of the stack processor are relatively complex, requiring the relatively complex sequential implementation in Figure 7-11. They could be expanded into more primitive operations (for example, two POPs into different registers, a register-register arithmetic operation, and finally a PUSH of the result) which would expand the Polish form of the program but simplify the processor. In such an expansion, however, it is difficult for the computer designer to detect and take advantage of the inherent parallelism of the algorithms.

To understand the functioning of the stack in Figure 7-11, it is helpful to trace its functioning through a sequence of clock cycles. Suppose that $C_1 = 1$ and $C_0 = 0$, the conditions for a two-operand arithmetic operation. When $Clock_1$ arrives, two actions take place. Register R_1 accepts data from the top of the stack (U := TOP), and the POP line of the stack unit starts the process of removing the top value from the stack. The timing constraint to be checked is that R_1 has safely accepted its value and returned to a non-accepting state before the stack top has begun to change its value.

Between pulses $Clock_1$ and $Clock_2$, the arithmetic unit has inputs from R_1 and the top of the stack. Its output, Z, eventually becomes the arithmetic combination of its inputs as selected by operation C_1. The output is provided as input to register R_2.

When $Clock_2$ arrives, R_2 captures the output of the arithmetic unit. The POP line of the stack unit again begins the process of removing the top value from the stack. When everything has settled down, $Clock_3$ gates the output of R_2 back onto the stack top.

An alternative form for a stack to be used in arithmetic evaluation is shown in Figure 7-13. It has two output bundles, TOP_1 and TOP_2 (compare with Figure 7-3), which are, respectively, the top and the next-to-top items on the stack. In addition, the control line POP is replaced with a line PPP which has the effect of POP POP PUSH, discarding the two top items on the stack

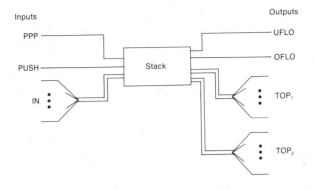

Figure 7-13   Stack for arithmetic evaluation

and replacing them with the datum on line IN. The arithmetic unit input can be directly attached to the two top levels.

Neither of the solutions above provides for unary operators (e.g., negate). The effect can be achieved either by modifying the stack structure or by use of arithmetic identities (e.g., $0 - X = -X$). The details are left as an exercise to the reader.

PROBLEMS

7-3.   Are any of the solutions in Tables 7-4 and 7-5 implemented by Figure 7-11? Discuss.

7-4.   Design a stack arithmetic processor similar to the one in Figure 7-11 using two stacks as in Table 7-4. Assume the availability of two arithmetic units, one for each type, and specify two stacks to be used with them.

7-5.   Along the lines of Figure 7-11, combine a memory unit and a stack arithmetic unit to process Polish with variables (i.e., manipulating addresses, doing loads and stores).

7-6.   Design a multiregister arithmetic processor that uses a stack for temporary results in arithmetic expressions. The action PUSH X_n and POP X_n are the transactions between the stack and register X_n. The action LOAD X_n, A puts the contents of memory cell A into register X_n. The action OP X_n, X_m replaces the contents of register X_n with the value X_n OP X_m. Compare your results with Figure 7-11. Under what circumstances would you recommend each design?

7-7.   Design, along the lines of Figure 7-5, an implementation of the stack in Figure 7-13.

7-8. Add a control line PP (i.e., Pop-Push) to Figure 7-13 to permit the implementation of unary operators, then redo Problem 7-7.

7-9. Design, along the lines of Figure 7-11, a stack arithmetic processor using the stack in Figure 7-13 instead of the one in Figure 7-3. How much gain in performance is there over the stack processor in Figure 7-11?

7-4. CONTROL STACK S_c

During execution of a program, the machine code resides in main memory and the control point is defined by the contents of a processor register called the program counter (denoted PC). During normal sequencing, PC is incremented by the current instruction width to establish a new control point for the next instruction. The main use of PC is to permit the processor to access memory for its instructions. PC also serves in special ways for the implementation of subroutines, loops, the consequences of conditional tests, and so on.

There are two control points important for subroutine entry and exit. PC must first be set to the entry point and execution of the subroutine allowed to proceed. At some point in time the subroutine is finished and PC must be reset to the value it had prior to the entry, allowing the calling routine to proceed. Suppose that Q is the entry point for a subroutine. The action

CALL Q

is used to get to the entry point, and the action

RETURN FROM Q

is used inside the subroutine to terminate its execution and return control to the point of call. All of this can be accomplished as shown in Table 7-7, using a stack called the control stack and denoted S_c. The value of PC is saved on S_c when a CALL is executed and the top of S_c is popped off and placed back in PC when a RETURN is executed. A stack can be used because CALL-RETURN pairs are nested in time.

The mechanism implied in Table 7-7 has a number of advantages. First,

TABLE 7-7. ALGORITHMS USING S_c FOR CALL AND RETURN

CALL Q	RETURN FROM Q
$S_c := PC$ $PC := Q$	$PC := S_c$

of course, is that the subroutines may call each other to any depth and in any order, even recursively. Also, no more storage is used than actually needed.

In a nonrecursive program, the maximum size of S_c can be computed prior to execution by, for example, a compiler. The control stack S_c is separate from, and independent of, other stacks. The importance of this comment is illustrated by the function subroutine, which uses the arithmetic stacks for its computations and the control stack for CALL and RETURN. The delicate sequencing of preparing the value to be returned, returning, and using the returned value is simplified by implementing the mechanisms in separate structures.

Table 7-7 was constructed on the assumption that the machine code for a program was fixed in memory during execution, and that the absolute address of the entry point could be recorded in the program code itself. It is, however, sometimes desirable to permit the code for a subroutine to be moved about in memory during execution (called dynamic relocation). The absolute addresses are kept in an execution-time table (called the program reference table, or PRT) and updated by the operating system that is doing the relocation. The machine code for the program then has only a record of the index of the entry point in that table. One must save in S_c two values: the index of the calling routine in the PRT and the control point in the calling routine *relative* to its entry. If P is the PRT index of the calling routine, and Q is the PRT index of the called routine, and T and U are registers in the processor, then the extended algorithm in Table 7-8 is sufficient.

TABLE 7-8. ALGORITHMS USING S_c FOR CALL AND RETURN WITH DYNAMICALLY RELOCATABLE CODE

CALL Q FROM P	RETURN FROM Q TO P
$S_c := (P, PC - PRT[P])$	$(T, U) := S_c$
$PC := PRT[Q]$	$PC := PRT[T] + U$

Other actions affecting PC, besides sequential instruction processing and subroutines, include loops and decisions. On conventional computers these actions are implemented through branches, conditional branches, and indexed branches. Sometimes the conventional solutions are carried over into stack computers. One can, instead, continue to elaborate on the constructs affecting S_c to achieve the same effects. The latter solutions are more in the spirit of the stack computer and are discussed below.

For example, there is a more powerful interpretation of the RETURN FROM construct than that implied by Table 7-8. Suppose that Q is a subroutine for a complicated algorithm and that Q has called various other subroutines to carry out the details. Deep into a sequence of such calls a condition is encountered that requires that the remainder of algorithm Q be abandoned. Then, in some other subroutine R, the construct

RETURN FROM Q

would be interpreted as a whole sequence of RETURN actions, eventually returning control to the point from which Q was called. Such a situation is sketched in Figure 7-14.

The appropriate multilevel return is combined with the dynamically relocatable solution in Figure 7-15. Note that it would be difficult to extend the solution in Table 7-7 in this way. As before, T and U are processor registers and Q is the index of the address of the entry of Q in the PRT.

A similar algorithm can be devised for the construct RETURN TO P. The interpretation for this construct depends on P having been called and not yet exited prior to the encounter of the RETURN TO P action. P has called some other subroutine which may have called others to an arbitrary depth. RETURN TO P has the effect of terminating all subroutines including the last one P called and returning control to P at the point where the last one would have normally returned.

In the discussion on arithmetic stacks, it was clear that single operators in Polish corresponded to single lines of the stack-manipulation notation. In the algorithms effecting S_c, however, conceptually monolithic operations CALL and RETURN have a more complicated appearance. It is proper to consider the alternatives for the Polish forms of CALL and RETURN, since complicated monolithic operations imply complicated monolithic hardware.

In the case of an arithmetic operation, it was possible to express the whole action as a sequence of simpler actions. The situation for CALL and RETURN is complicated by the fact that PC is being changed. In each algorithm in this section, the change of PC is the last thing done, which is a condition for being able to express the whole operation as a sequence of simpler operations.

```
P:  PROCEDURE OPTIONS (MAIN);
    S:  PROCEDURE(N);
            /*arbitrary algorithm;*/
        END S;
    R:  PROCEDURE(N);
            IF N < 0 THEN RETURN FROM Q;
            CALL S(5);
        END R;
    Q:  PROCEDURE(N);
            IF N < 3 THEN CALL R(N);
            CALL S(10);
        END Q;
        CALL Q(-1);
    END P;
```

Figure 7-14   PL/I program requiring a multilevel RETURN

$$T := nil$$
$$while \ T \neq Q \ do \ (T, U) := S_c$$
$$(T, U) := S_c$$
$$PC := PRT[T] + U$$

Figure 7-15 Algorithm for multilevel RETURN FROM Q initiated outside of Q

The most straightforward Polish form for CALL is a CALL operator followed in Polish by the absolute address of the entry (Table 7-7) or the index into the PRT (Table 7-8). Alternatively, the address could be pushed onto an arithmetic stack (say S_a), and the CALL operator would find it there.

One advantage of separating the access of the entry point address from the actual transfer of control is in allowing other ways of getting the address. The access to PRT (Table 7-8 and Figure 7-15) could in fact be done with whatever mechanism is used for subscripts in the arithmetic processor (see section 7-6). There are two other programming-language constructs that can also be implemented by subscripting into a table of entry points and then calling the selected subroutine.

The CASE statement of PASCAL [Wirth, 71] and ALGOL-W [Wirth and Hoare, 66] takes the form shown in Figure 7-16. It is interpreted to mean that the CASE expression is computed, and then the corresponding statement in the following block is selected and executed. It is equivalent to the SWITCH construct in earlier programming languages except that after execution of the selected statement, control is automatically returned to the point beyond the end of the block of statements.

If each statement_k is treated as a separate subroutine, the CASE statement can be implemented by tabulating the entry points for the m statements, then using n to index into that table and fetch the corresponding entry point to stack S_c, whereupon the solution to problem 7-13 can be used. A RETURN operator must, of course, be appended to each of the m subroutines to effect the RETURN action.

The IF-THEN-ELSE construct is in fact a subcase of the CASE statement where the only values of the selection expression are TRUE and FALSE (that

CASE n OF
      1: statement__1;
      2: statement__2;

         . . .

     m: statement__m;
END

Figure 7-16 PASCAL CASE statement selecting the nth out of m statements

$$PC := PRT[Q]$$

$$T := nil$$
$$\text{while } T \neq Q \text{ do } (T, U) := S_c$$
$$PC := PRT[Q]$$

Figure 7-17 REPEAT operation   **Figure 7-18** Multilevel REPEAT operation

is, 1 and 0). It can be implemented exactly as a CASE statement. The effect is to avoid altogether the familiar branching logic normally associated with the IF-THEN-ELSE and CASE constructs.

Loops can also be expressed in terms of manipulations of S_c. Suppose the body of a loop is also a subroutine. It is entered via a CALL. At some point in the loop (usually the bottom), it is discovered that the loop must be repeated. Then the algorithm in Figure 7-17 can be used. It corresponds to the algorithms for CALL and RETURN in Table 7-8. The body of the loop is identified by index Q into the PRT. All that is needed is to reset PC to the address of the entry point.

For the same reasons that a multilevel RETURN may be needed, a multilevel REPEAT may be needed. It is a combination of the RETURN TO action with the REPEAT action. The action

REPEAT Q

is interpreted as

RETURN TO Q AND REPEAT IT

Figure 7-18 gives an algorithm combining the result of problem 7-13 and Figure 7-17. The interpretation of the symbols is as before.

The multilevel RETURN and REPEAT operations are of indeterminate duration. Thus during their operation, they must inhibit the operation of the rest of the computer.

PROBLEMS

7-10. Register PC can be eliminated if the top of the stack S_c is itself the program counter. Using the notation

$$:= S_c$$

to denote that the top value of S_c is popped and discarded, redo Table 7-7.

7-11. Assuming that PC is held in a register of the form shown in Figure 7-10, and that S_c has the form shown in Figure 7-3, design an implementation of Table 7-7. The circuit should have two control lines CALL and RETURN and may use CLOCK lines such as those used in Figure 7-11. The value Q can be assumed to be available on an input bundle.

7-12. Suppose that a whole memory box like the one in Figure 7-12 is dedicated to the PRT. Combine the arithmetic unit (Figure 7-8), the memory, and a stack to redo problem 7-11 according to the algorithms in Table 7-8. The values P and Q can be assumed to be present on input bundles. (Where do they come from?).

7-13. Redo Figure 7-15 for a RETURN TO construct.

7-14. Recall the results of problem 7-10, and also the three-stack arithmetic processor in Table 7-6. If the entry address is pushed onto S_a, then the CALL takes the form of a stack-to-stack transfer identical in form to a type transfer. Redo Table 7-7 using this solution.

7-15. Suggest a way to combine the arithmetic stack and S_c. If a return address is saved on the arithmetic stack, then the value of a function would be returned in its place. Work out the details. Evaluate the idea.

7-16. The forms of S_c and PC are different in Table 7-8. Redo Table 7-8 along the lines of problem 7-10 by assuming that the PRT value and relative program counter can be combined prior to *every* instruction.

7-17. Extend the result in problem 7-12 to handle multi-level RETURN and REPEAT (Figures 7-15 and 7-18). You may assume the presence of a control line TICTOC which carries a sequence of suitably spaced pulses. An output, INHIBIT, must be up until the operation is complete.

7-18. Consider a looping construct in some programming language (for example, DO in FORTRAN or WHILE in ALGOL). Can it be implemented without any branching instructions beyond those in section 7-4? Is either a multilevel RETURN or REPEAT needed?

7-19. Suppose that integers and memory addresses both have the same format. Design a circuit that combines the algorithms for S_c in Table 7-7 and the arithmetic evaluation stack in Figure 7-9, using only one internal stack.

7-20. The combination in problem 7-19 does not work smoothly for languages with function subroutines, but does otherwise. Explain why this is the case.

7-21. Suppose that there is a single stack containing tagged data words, and that values of PC have a unique tag, c, (that is, CALL pushes a value of the form (c, P, PC − PRT[P]) into the stack). Design a circuit combining the stack in Figure 7-9 and the multilevel CALL, RETURN FROM, RETURN TO, and REPEAT operations (refer to Figures 7-15 and 7-18).

7-5. STORAGE FOR SIMPLE VARIABLES S_v, S_m

The concept of local variable arises from the combination of the programming language concepts of variable and subroutine. The local variables of a subroutine have the property that they can be accessed only from statements within the subroutine. They have undefined values when the subroutine is first entered and whatever values they have acquired during the execution of the subroutine may be lost when control is returned to the point of call.

All variables can be considered local variables if the program itself is a subroutine (called by some more global authority, such as an executive program).

When the definition of one subroutine is nested within the definition of another, the inner subroutine has access to the variables local to the containing subroutine but not vice versa. The scope of a variable (the set of places from which it may be accessed) is the body of the subroutine to which it is local and all subroutines defined within that subroutine. The PL/I program in Figure 7-19 illustrates the possibilities. The scope of the variable A is the whole program; the scope of variable B is the body of SUBROUTINE only.

As a consequence of local variables being undefined whenever the corresponding subroutine is not being executed, storage need not even be assigned to the local variables until the subroutine is called, and may be freed for other uses as soon as control has left the subroutine via a RETURN. This can be accomplished by using a stack, S_v, for the local variables. A PUSH on S_v corresponds to the allocation of storage for a local variable and a POP corresponds to deallocation. Generally speaking, one would expect several PUSH operations with each CALL action, corresponding to the several local variables in the called subroutine. As it happens, it is more convenient to associate the

```
PROGRAM:
  PROCEDURE OPTIONS(MAIN);
    DECLARE A FIXED;
  SUBROUTINE:
    PROCEDURE;
      DECLARE B FIXED;
      B = 2;
      A = B;
      RETURN;
    END SUBROUTINE;
    A = 1;
    /* AN ASSIGNMENT TO B HERE
        WOULD VIOLATE SCOPE RULES */
    CALL SUBROUTINE;
    RETURN;
  END PROGRAM;
```

Figure 7-19   Illustration of scope in PL/I

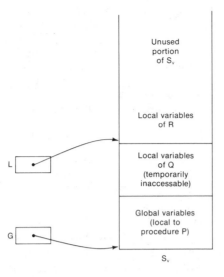

Figure 7-20 Implementation of S_v

PUSH actions with the local variables of the calling routine.

The local variables are not, however, accessed by PUSH and POP as in the case of the previous stacks. They are accessed at random at any time during the execution of their scope. Thus other access methods must be added to PUSH and POP. It is the need for other access methods, together with the fact that S_v may be rather large and thus best kept in main memory, that indicates a solution along the lines of Figure 7-2. The base registers can be used for more random access as well as for control of PUSH and POP.

Suppose that we are willing to settle for the ability to access only the most global variables (those in the main program subroutine, which contains all the other subroutine definitions) and the local variables of the subroutine currently being executed. The global variables are the first to be allocated in S_v and are thus at the bottom of it; the most local variables are the last to be allocated in S_v and are thus at the top of it. Such a solution is illustrated in Figure 7-20. The configuration of S_v corresponds to the situation when execution has just begun of the body of procedure R in Figure 7-14. The register G points to the base of the area containing the global variables and the register L points to the base of the area containing the most local variables (those of procedure R).

Six actions must be defined in terms of MEMORY and the registers G and L: scope entry, scope exit, and four kinds of variable access, where the data are presumed to be en route to some other stack in the computer (such as the arithmetic stack). They are given in Table 7-9. V(P) stands for the number of local variables in subroutine P. The data accesses are to the Kth variable in the corresponding scope. No mention is made of checking L for stack overflow or underflow, but it should be done.

TABLE 7-9. Six Accesses to S_v

Action	Algorithm
SCOPE_ENTRY out of P	$L := L + V(P)$
SCOPE_EXIT back into P	$L := L - V(P)$
PUSH the Kth global variable onto stack S	$S := MEMORY[G + K]$
POP a value from stack S into the Kth global variable	$MEMORY[G + K] := S$
PUSH the Kth local variable onto stack S	$S := MEMORY[L + K]$
POP a value from stack S into the Kth local variable	$MEMORY[L + K] := S$

The actions for SCOPE_ENTRY and SCOPE_EXIT are usually associated with the actions for CALL and RETURN. Note that the change to L can be thought of as protecting the local variables of the calling procedure by making them inaccessible. Dynamically, the sequence of events must be:

> SCOPE_ENTRY
> CALL
> . . .
> RETURN
> SCOPE_EXIT

Since the CALL operator must be in the code of the calling subroutine, so must SCOPE_ENTRY. RETURN is the last thing done in the body of the called subroutine, thus SCOPE_EXIT must also be in the code of the calling subroutine. That is convenient, since the value V(P) (Table 7-9) is more readily available to P, the calling routine. The combined operators (Tables 7-7 and 7-9), SCOPE_ENTRY, CALL, SCOPE_EXIT, in the calling subroutine, and RETURN in the called subroutine, are shown in Table 7-10.

A subroutine with no local variables needs a CALL without a SCOPE_ENTRY; a block in ALGOL or PL/I needs a SCOPE_ENTRY without a CALL. The implication is that the first action in Table 7-10 may, or may not, be a candidate for a single operator in Polish.

TABLE 7-10. Calling and Returning Algorithms

Action	Operator		Algorithm
Actions in the calling subroutine P to enter the scope of Q, call it, and exit the scope after return	Prior to executing Q	SCOPE_ENTRY	$L := L + V(P)$
		CALL	$S_c := PC$ $PC := Q$
	After executing Q	SCOPE_EXIT	$L := L - V(P)$
Action to return from Q to P		RETURN	$PC := S_c$

One further stack, S_m, the marker stack, can be of use. If the value of L is saved in S_m prior to changing L, then SCOPE_EXIT need only POP the needed value off S_m and back into L. The implication is that the number of locals $(V(P))$ is needed only at the time of call. This solution is analogous to the use of S_c for saving PC instead of tabulating all the potential return addresses ahead of time to be selected by the RETURN operator. As it happens, the contents of S_m are needed for the general case of nested addressing (as opposed to the global/local solution just discussed).

The actions for accessing variables (Table 7-9) must also be reflected in Polish. The Polish must carry the information of either global or local, and the offset K from the appropriate base register. Recall that the memory access in the Polish of Section 7-3 required that the address be on the stack. The same solution applies to S_v if the computations $G + K$ and $L + K$ are carried out by the arithmetic unit. That would imply a sequence of actions something like

$$S := G$$
$$S := K$$
$$S := S + S$$
$$S := MEMORY[S]$$

to access a simple variable. In an application where keeping the processor simple is paramount, it may be the proper solution. On the other hand, one can devise special hardware and a richer Polish so that the shorter sequence

$$S := G + K$$
$$S := MEMORY[S]$$

or even

$$S := MEMORY[G + K]$$

is used.

There are arbitrarily many ways of encoding the Polish. Some are better than others, depending upon which measure of efficiency one decides to apply. The following example is intended to tie together the preceding material in a reasonable way, making definite choices from the many possibilities. It is also intended to be a good choice under some circumstances, thus providing in addition a certain amount of intuitive guidance in choosing encodings.

Let us suppose that 8 bits is a convenient unit for encoding the Polish (due to memory structure or some other arbitrary external constraint). There is a stack S of width 16 combining the functions of S and S_c, as well as a stack S_v. One half of the 256 patterns will be reserved for the action $S := C$, where C is a constant in the range $0 \leq C < 128$. The remaining 128 patterns represent operations such as ADD and CALL. If we need more (unlikely), then one operation code can be set aside to signify that the next 8 bits are to be used.

TABLE 7-11. PARTIAL SET OF POLISH OPERATORS

Operator	Algorithm
LIT0, LIT1, . . . LIT127	Constant in the range 0 to 127 is placed on the stack
SHL7	$S := S * 128$
ADD	$S := S + S$
LOADG	$S := MEMORY[G + S]$
LOADL	$S := MEMORY[L + S]$
STOREL	$MEMORY[L + S] := S$
STOREG	$MEMORY[G + S] := S$
CALL	$PC, S := PRT[S], PC$
RETURN	$PC := S$
SCOPE_ENTRY	$L := L + S$
SCOPE_EXIT	$L := L - S$

The assignment of actual bit patterns is irrelevant; thus in the discussion we will use mnemonic names instead of the patterns. A partial table of operators is given in Table 7-11. It is assumed that PRT, S, and S_v are properly set up prior to initiating execution of a program and that each operator is a single instruction pointed to by PC. Figure 7-21 gives the machine code, using Table 7-11, for the program in Figure 7-19. Figure 7-22 shows an elaborate stack computer which uses separate stacks for S_c and S_m.

PROGRAM:	LIT0	address of A
	LIT1	constant 1
	STOREG	A = 1
	LIT1	number of locals in **PROGRAM**
	SCOPE_ENTRY	
	LIT0	address of **SUBROUTINE** in PRT
	CALL	
	LIT1	number of locals in **PROGRAM**
	SCOPE_EXIT	
	RETURN	to operating system
SUBROUTINE:	LIT0	address of B
	LIT2	constant 2
	STOREL	B = 2
	LIT0	address of A
	LIT0	address of B
	LOADL	value of B
	STOREG	A = B
	RETURN	to main program

Figure 7-21   Polish form of a PL/I program

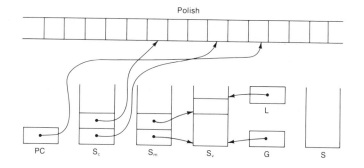

Figure 7-22   Elaborate stack computer

The global/local solution just described is less general than needed for ALGOL 60 and later languages that have adopted nested scope structures. The nesting of subroutine definitions mentioned at the start of this section may continue to arbitrary depth, permitting the innermost subroutine to access its own variables, those of the subroutine within which it is defined, and so on, out to the most global subroutine. The global/local solution can be used for such languages, but it fails to implement all the accessing implied by the nesting. There are, for a subroutine nested k levels into the program, k separate areas in S_v that should be accessible. One solution is to use k base registers in the place of the two bases G and L. This new set of base registers is called the display [Wirth and Hoare, 66], and is designated by the identifier D. The Kth register is denoted D[K].

When a subroutine defined at the Kth level of nesting is being executed, each of the containing subroutines has been called and has an area allocated on S_v. The most global is pointed to by D[0] and the local variables (nested in level K) are pointed to by D[K]. The intervening registers point to the locals defined on the corresponding level of nesting. D[0] thus takes the place of G and D[K] takes the place of L (see Figure 7-23).

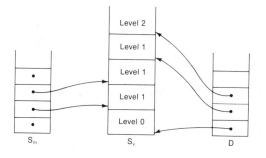

Figure 7-23   Local-variable stack addressed through the display

The values of D change only on scope entry and exit, so we may expand the SCOPE_ENTRY and SCOPE_EXIT operators to set them. Furthermore, assuming that we have used the stack S_m, all the values that must be in D are already somewhere in S_m.

There are two cases: either the programming language allows subroutines to be passed as parameters to other subroutines or it does not. If it does not, a subroutine can be called only if it is defined in one of the scopes that is accessible to the calling routine. The implication is that D is already correctly set except for the newly allocated local variables of the called routine. If the language does allow parametric subroutines, then the name of the subroutine can be passed to the body of a subroutine that is not accessible to the calling subroutine; thus all of D (except D[0]), might have to be changed. This can happen only in languages that have simultaneously nested scopes, recursion, and parametric subroutines. This case requires a solution of complexity that exceeds the benefits in most situations. It will not be further discussed here. The interested reader is referred to Randell and Russell [64].

The algorithms for scope entry and exit are shown in Table 7-12. The calling subroutine is P. The number of locals in P is V(P), P is nested K levels deep, the called subroutine is nested J levels deep (Note: $J \leq K + 1$). S_m now holds only the values of D that are saved, instead of all values of L. Referring again to Figure 7-23, note that some entries in S_m do not point to S_v (denoted by the missing arrows). The first entry into a level of scope causes a save of D[K] where it did not have a valid previous setting.

TABLE 7-12. SCOPE ENTRY AND EXIT USING D

Action	Algorithm
SCOPE_ENTRY	$S_m := D[J]$
	$D[J] := D[K] + V(P)$
SCOPE_EXIT	$D[J] := S_m$

PROBLEMS

7-22. One may design S_v so that the SCOPE_ENTRY and SCOPE_EXIT operations are executed in the called subroutine instead of in the caller. In this case one has the more direct view that SCOPE_ENTRY is allocating space for the variables of the called subroutine (as opposed to the previous view that SCOPE_ENTRY protects the variables of the calling subroutine). Redo Tables 7-9 and 7-10 for this case. What are the trade-offs?

7-23. S_c and S_v can be combined. SCOPE_ENTRY must allocate one extra cell for the saved program counter. Rewrite Table 7-10 for this possibility.

7-24. Table 7-9 cannot be easily combined with Figures 7-15 and 7-18. The problem is that the value V(P) for each subroutine that is exited must be available in one place. Propose a change to PRT that would facilitate the combination, and then work out the details.

7-25. Rework problem 7-24 using S_m.

7-26. Using the operators in Table 7-11 write Polish to compute each of:

$$2 + 2$$
$$2 + 127$$
$$2 + 128$$

2 + A where A is the 7th global variable

B + A where B is the 3rd local variable
and A is the 130th global variable

7-27. Give the Polish for Figure 7-14, extending Table 7-11 as necessary.

7-28. Redo Table 7-11 using separate stacks for S_c and S_m (refer to Figure 7-22).

7-29. Redo Table 7-11 using only one stack for all of S, S_c, S_v, and S_m.

7-30. Redo problem 7-29 to allow mutilevel RETURN and REPEAT. Recall problem 7-24.

7-31. Redo problems 7-28 through 7-30 using the scope entry and exit in Table 7-12. Where do the values J, K, and V(P) come from?

7-32. Present an argument that Table 7-12 correctly implements PL/I except for parametric procedures. Does it matter what the initial value of D is?

7-33. Find an example where calling a parametric subroutine is inconsistent with the algorithms in Table 7-12.

7-34. Discuss the problem of making the value V(P), the size of the local area of subroutine P, available to increment register L in the case of arrays dynamically allocated (ALGOL 60 or PL/I).

7-6. STORAGE FOR STRUCTURED VARIABLES

A structured variable is a collection of simple variables together with some predetermined method of data access. Arrays, strings, lists, records, tables, structures, queues, stacks, trees, sets, and ordered sets are types of structured variables that have appeared in programming languages. Some languages have, in addition, mechanisms for programmer definition of other types of structured variables.

The access of structured variables involves computations on addresses. While arbitrary computations could be envisioned, in practice they are almost entirely limited to indirection, addition, subtraction, and multiplication. Some types, such as arrays, are so commonly used that special hardware has been devised for their allocation and access.

The time that the size of a variable is known is an important consideration. In languages such as FORTRAN the size of all data structures is known and fixed at the time the program is compiled. In ALGOL 60 the size is fixed after SCOPE_ENTRY but before the first statement is executed in this scope. In PL/I the size of a string may vary dynamically within predetermined limits. In LISP the size of a list may vary dynamically with no predetermined limits.

The topic of data structures could fill a book [Stone, 72]. The best we can do here is to take some examples and indicate what mechanisms might be useful for their implementation. We will consider arrays first.

Suppose that the sizes of all arrays in a scope are known prior to the possible entry of another scope (not true of PL/I or ALGOL 60, since the array-bound computation may cause a SCOPE_ENTRY), and that the arrays are allocated in S_v. Then the needed increment $V(P)$ to the local-variable base register (L or D[K]) is known, and the allocation algorithms in Tables 7-9 and 7-12 can be used. Notice that by considering the SCOPE_ENTRY action as protecting the local variables of the calling subroutine we can wait longer to know how much storage needs allocation.

Even if not all the arrays are allocated when a new scope is entered, the algorithms mentioned can be used if no new allocations can take place prior to the SCOPE_EXIT leading back to the scope in question. It simply means that $V(P)$ must be determined anew prior to each SCOPE_ENTRY. This solution is adequate for ALGOL 60 and PL/I arrays with attribute AUTO-MATIC. It is not adequate for the PL/I ALLOCATE and FREE statements.

Even though arrays could be accessed directly by doing arithmetic on register L, there is advantage in allocating a single word for each array along with the other local variables in a scope. The word is called the *array descriptor* and contains the information needed to access the array. Such a situation is shown in Figure 7-24. There are four local variables, one of which has the value 3, and the others are arrays. The pointers in the array descriptors must be filled in when the array is allocated. In the normal case, size information is discovered immediately after scope entry by the initial code (or *prolog*) of the called subroutine.

Suppose that we have an indexing operation INX (which may just be an ADD in the simplest case), which combines the subscript value and the array descriptor to give a new descriptor pointing to the selected cell in an array. Then the Polish in Table 7-13 is an example of accessing arrays.

The array descriptor may contain more information than just the address in S_v. If the array data is tagged, the descriptor may contain the tag, so that the data type can be discovered without accessing the data itself. This is of critical importance if the address arithmetic for access depends on the type of the data, or if the data memory has no provisions for tags.

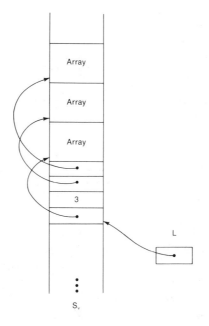

Figure 7-24 Arrays allocated in S_v accessed through pointers

The descriptor may also contain information allowing the access to be checked for array-bounds violations. If special hardware is dedicated to the checking task it can be done with no penalty in execution speed or code density. Since array overrun is a source of very troublesome programming errors, and since the inefficiency of bounds checking in conventional instruction sets is intolerable, the designer of bounds-checking hardware will find the cost/benefit ratio very good.

If the array descriptor contains the size of the array, then the indexing operation INX in Table 7-13 can be expanded into the algorithm in Table

TABLE 7-13. POLISH FOR THE ASSIGNMENT A[I] := 2

Polish	Action	Comment
I	S := I	Offset from L of the cell for I in S_v
LOADL	S := MEMORY[L + S]	Value of I
A	S := A	Offset from L of the cell containing the descriptor for A
LOADL	S := MEMORY[L + S]	Descriptor for A
INX	S := S INX S	Access operation given a new descriptor for the subscripted variable A[I]
2	S := 2	Value 2
STORE	MEMORY[S] := S	Store 2 in A[I] (Note that a new absolute store operation has been introduced.)

TABLE 7-14. ALGORITHM FOR SUBSCRIPTING: $S := S$ INX S

Action	Comment
$(T, U) := S$; $W := S$; if $W < 0$ or $W \geq T$ then ERROR; $S := W + U$;	T is the size; U is the address W is the value of the subscript Address of the subscripted variable

7-14. The descriptor is encoded as a pair (size, address), and the array is presumed to start with position 0. If the array does not start with position 0, the lower bound of the array must be subtracted from the subscript prior to the INX operation. Note that the checking and the address computation can proceed in parallel.

The stack S_v is not the only place where arrays can be allocated. They could have their own stack. In that case S_v might be tagged and the array stack untagged, since the array data all have the same tag, which can then be added once to the descriptor for the whole array.

Arrays might also be allocated in a free storage area (an ALGOL 68 heap). In this case the descriptors point out into the free area and the storage allocation actions imply the presence of a mechanism managing the free area. Again, there is no need for tags on the data in the free area, since the tag can reside in the descriptor. The data is dynamically relocatable, since only the descriptor contains the actual address. The free area solution is also capable of implementing the ALLOCATE and FREE statements of PL/I, which are asynchronous with the scope entry and exit actions of the Polish.

Allocating arrays in a free area has an additional advantage: storage need not be allocated until the data are actually accessed. Thus if information is added to the descriptor indicating whether the data have been accessed, the INX operation can include the call to the storage allocation actions. All of the above are implemented in the B5000 and its successors.

Although S_v is stack-like in nature, it is possible to allocate the storage for each local variable area or stack frame in a free area much as though they were arrays. The scope entry action, instead of incrementing the pointer into S_v, would use the address supplied by the storage allocation routine. The only information connecting the Polish and the variables is then the base register D (or G and L).

In some programming languages, it is possible to multiprogram several subroutines in a common environment. That is, several subroutines may execute asynchronously while accessing common data in S_v. The mechanisms in the previous sections can be used if the subroutines have their own private stacks S_c and S_m. In effect, the display D is used to bind the active subroutine to S_v. When execution is suspended in one subroutine so that another can resume, D is saved for the suspended subroutine and restored to the state it had when the resumed subroutine was last suspended. In effect the stack S_v becomes a tree, with a common area near the root, then branching out where the multiprogramming begins. This form of S_v is used in the B6700. Some further discussion can be found in Section 12-5, Memory Addressing and Virtual Memory.

PROBLEMS

7-35. Redo Table 7-14 to provide an operation INXLOAD with combines INX and LOAD. Is this likely to have a high payoff in performance? Discuss.

7-36. Pick data structure (list, stack, queue, record, structure) and design accessing operators for it. Does it make sense to include bounding information and checking? (Refer to Table 7-14.)

7-37. Assume that values in memory are tagged, integers with tag i, descriptors with tag d. Redo Table 7-14, checking to see that only descriptors are indexed, and only with integer values. What tag should be given to the result of the INX operation?

7-38. Redo Table 7-14 for descriptors of the form (*tag, presence, indexed, size, address*) where the *tag* is d, *presence* is a bit indicating whether or not the array is already in memory, *indexed* is a bit indicating whether the descriptor points to an array or an array element, *size* is the upper bound of the array if *indexed* is false and is the index value if *indexed* is true, *address* is the address of the array in memory if *presence* is true and the address of the array in the disk directory if *presence* is false (an address of 0 indicates the array has never been accessed at all, hence has no address at all).

7.39. Considering the solution to problem 7-38, what additional mechanisms must be supplied for scope entry and exit, LOAD and STORE, and the initialization of the descriptors in S_v? Redo Table 7-11 to reflect this change.

7-7. THE PARAMETER-PREPARATION STACK S_p

The preparation and passing of parameters to a subroutine is yet another function for which a stack is an appropriate mechanism. Parameters are, in effect, initialized local variables of the called subroutine. The values may be data types of the language or they may be pointers to variables that are local to other subroutines, most usually the calling subroutine.

While control is still in the calling subroutine, the parameter values must be computed in a stack S_p. The values in S_p must ultimately end up in the local variable stack, S_v, so the format of S_p should be the same as that of S_v. In particular, if S_v contains tagged data, then S_p must also. After the parameters are prepared, the new scope is entered, and stacked parameters are moved into the new area in S_v.

It is possible to have prepared some of the parameters to a subroutine and suddenly be forced to prepare a second set before the first set is used. The expression

$$\text{MAX (A, MIN (B, C, D), E)}$$

is an example. After the value of A is stacked, the parameters B, C, and D must be prepared for subroutine MIN. Finally, after the value of MIN is available and stacked on S_p, the value of E must be stacked and then MAX invoked.

The value of a function can also be considered a parameter; the direction of information flow is just different. The function subroutine may place its value on S_p, so that the calling routine may recover it there. When the returned value is arithmetic, the effect is to move the value from the arithmetic evaluation stack to S_p and back to the arithmetic evaluation stack.

The returned value may, however, be more complex. If the value returned is structured (for example, an array), more than one value must be moved, while it is sufficient to place in S_p only a descriptor of the information. The effect is to leave the values in place in S_v until after the RETURN, but prior to any ill effects of the SCOPE_EXIT. The values then are moved from the area of S_v about to be abandoned to the local (structured) variable that is its destination.

If the subroutine is multivalued, the values may be held in S_p to be used upon completion of RETURN and SCOPE_EXIT. For example, the function invocation

$$\text{A, B, C} = \text{F (X} + 1, \text{Y} - 1, \text{X} + \text{Y)}$$

where F is the (extended) PL/I procedure

```
F:  PROCEDURE (P1, P2, P3) RETURNS (FLOAT, FLOAT, FLOAT);
        RETURN (P1 + P2, P2 + P3, P3 + P1);
    END F;
```

requires a place to hold the value P1 + P2 while the remaining values are computed prior to return. Note also that if the computation of a later return value required a function call, the completed values are safe in S_p.

The necessary Polish operators are SAVE_PARAMETER, which places a computed value on S_p; USE_PARAMETER, which reverses the process; and INITIALIZE, which moves values from S_p into S_v. Algorithms for them are given in Table 7-15. S is an arithmetic evaluation stack, T is an intermediate register, L is the register pointing to the local-variable area in the newly called subroutine (perhaps one of the D registers). INITIALIZE needs the number of parameters; the value has been left on S. Note that if S_p were accessible directly, as is S_v, then INITIALIZE would not be necessary.

TABLE 7-15. OPERATORS USING THE PARAMETER-PREPARATION STACK

Operator	Algorithm
SAVE_PARAMETER (prior to CALL)	$S_p := S$
USE_PARAMETER (after RETURN)	$S := S_p$

INITIALIZE	$T := S;$
	 while $T > 0$ do
	 begin
	   $T := T - 1;$
	   $MEMORY[L + T] := S_p;$
	 end

PROBLEMS

7-40. Write code in Polish (Tables 7-13 and 7-15) for functions MAX and MIN, then write code for the expression MAX (A, MIN (B, C, D), E).

7-41. If S and S_p are combined, the Polish is simplified and the number of internal data transfers is reduced. It cannot be done, however, if we have multiple arithmetic evaluation stacks unless we have multiple S_p also. Discuss the trade-offs.

7-42. Pick a programming language and show whether or not, for a given program, an upper bound on the size of S_p can be computed.

7-8. COMBINING STACKS

We have described several stacks and their related computational tasks. It was mentioned in the introduction that stacks can be combined. Doing so reduces their number while complicating their use. The Burroughs B5000 and Hewlett-Packard HP3000 series computers each have a single stack. Even though combining stacks may not be a good idea, we feel it is important to discuss how to do it, both to understand some of the complexities of existing machines and to plan for the inherent difficulties when such a decision must be made.

A tempting combination is that of the arithmetic evaluation stack, S, and the local storage stack, S_v. Both have the same format for their entries. Suppose for the moment that everything is kept in memory. Then we can add a new register, T, to point to the next available cell on the stack, thus turning S_v, Figure 7-20, into the desired combination. The operations in Table 7-9 must then be elaborated to include the arithmetic operators and changed to reflect the new functions. SCOPE_ENTRY depends on the number of locals of the called procedure, making it necessary to put it in the called routine, rather than leave it a part of the calling sequence. (This is actually mostly a convenience, since the number of local variables to the called routine could be inserted by a sophisticated translator into the code for the calling routine. It usually is done as shown here, however). The details are given in Table 7-16. The design depends on the reasonable assumption that the arithmetic evaluation stack is empty just before either ENTER_SCOPE or EXIT_SCOPE is carried out.

Suppose now the computer designer decided to put the top M cells of the stack into fast registers, pushing into memory only when they are full. This is particularly advantageous with arithmetic operators such as ADD in Table 7-16, where three memory references are implied by the algorithm. Blake [77] presents some interesting data implying that $M = 4$ is sufficient. Now consider the PUSH instruction, however, where the actual source of the data is so near the top of the stack that, with this design, it would be in a register rather than in memory itself. This means that either the translator has to be sophisticated enough to access the register directly, or the memory access system has to be sophisticated enough to detect that the best value is not in memory at all but rather in one of the stack top registers. Here we find that the access mechanisms of the two different stack uses conflict, making the combination more difficult.

Suppose that we wish to combine S_p, the parameter stack, into the S-S_v combination. Since the purpose of S_p is to hold values produced in the caller to be used in the called routine, having those values in S violates the assumption upon which the previous solution is based. What must be done is to place the values of parameters in S_v as local variables *before* the SCOPE_ENTRY is executed, and to place the returned value(s) on the top of the stack after SCOPE_EXIT where they are ready for further computation. If we just leave the parameter values on the top of the stack and carry out the SCOPE_ ENTRY action in Table 7-16, the register L points *above* them. One could access them with negative offsets from L, as done in the B5000, or one can specially manipulate T and L to bring S_v into conformity with the configuration described in Section 7-7. Similar changes can be made in the other operations. The most difficult problem is the situation referred to in Section 7-7, where a partially prepared parameter list must be temporarily abandoned to enter the scope of a function used in the computation of a new parameter. What it means is that the spaces in S_v needed to hold parameters must be preallocated in such a way as to protect them without invalidating the SCOPE_ENTRY and SCOPE_EXIT algorithms.

TABLE 7-16. COMBINATION OF S_v AND S

Action	Algorithm
SCOPE_ENTRY out of P into Q	$L := T; T := T + V(Q);$
SCOPE_EXIT back out of Q into P	$T := L; L := L - V(Q);$
PUSH the kth global variable onto the arithmetic stack	$MEMORY[T] := MEMORY[G + K];$ $T := T + 1;$
POP global, PUSH and POP local are similar	
ADD the two top values of the stack	$MEMORY[T - 1] := MEMORY[T - 1]$ $+ MEMORY[T]; T := T - 1;$
Other infix operators are similar	

A straightforward solution is to use the marker stack, S_m. The SCOPE_ENTRY algorithm becomes $S_m := L$; $L := T$; $T := T + V(Q)$, and the SCOPE_EXIT becomes (for $L = T$, meaning that there is no function value to return) $L := S_m$; $T := T - V(Q)$. Parameters are addressed via negative offsets from L. If there is a function value, it must be moved from the old position of T to the new position of T, requiring yet another mechanism.

Continuing in this manner, one can fold in S_m, giving a S-S_v-S_p-S_m combination. The essential step is to leave a space in the local variables of each routine to save the old value of L (elegantly, $MEMORY[T] := L$; $L := T$; etc.). While it is a worthwhile exercise to work through the details, it is probably better to study a real machine, such as the B5000, B6700, or HP3000, or the algorithms in Randell and Russell [64], relating each action to the stack needs identified in this chapter. One can devise multistack architecture which behaves equivalently to single stack mechanism, and then study it for correctness, coding efficiency, generality and so on. One should note that the mechanism to handle recursive, nested, parametric procedures is provided in the B6700 and by Randell and Russell. Thus they are yet more general than any of the mechanisms suggested here. The multistack concept can be extended in this way if desired.

In summary, the tradition has been to have complex combined stack architectures. They are elegant, but frequently too tightly bound to be reasonably optimized, or to be adapted to other slightly different environments. They have also been too big a bite to swallow for designers from the multi-register tradition. Separate stacks, on the other hand, each justify themselves, and are increasingly feasible as the cost of processor logic decreases.

PROBLEMS

7-43. S_p can be combined with S_v. The parameters are eventually going to reside in the area in S_v directly above the present local variables, and can be placed there directly. The problem is that a function subroutine may be called during the computation of a latter parameter, causing a SCOPE_ENTRY action and therefore destroying the partially prepared parameter list in S_v. Rework Table 7-15 to combine S_p and S_v using whatever additional mechanisms you need.

7-44. S, S_p, S_v, and S_c can all be combined. To avoid unnecessary complications assume either only one kind of arithmetic (that is, integer) or a tagged stack, and rework Table 7-15.

7-45. Redo problem 7-44 and add the functions of S_m to the combined stack. What additional mechanisms do you have to use for multi-level RETURN?

7-46. Show that the combination of the algorithms in Tables 7-12 and 7-15 works for the scope rules of PL/I or ALGOL 60. Hint: Show that paired actions (for example, SCOPE_ENTRY and SCOPE_EXIT) always leave the addressing state invariant and that the display is always correct when CALL is executed.

7-9. EVALUATION CRITERIA

One traditional contest in evaluating computer designs is between stack computers and multiregister computers. The traditional measure is speed. More generally, we should ask, what are the costs and what are the benefits of a particular design? The answers differ with the viewpoint of the evaluator. The manufacturer, system programmer and practicing civil engineer have quite different values for the various characteristics of computers. As a result the efficiency of a design cannot be properly measured without taking into account programmer costs, the costs of unreliability, and so on. The difficulty in answering such a broadly stated evaluation question has often precluded the use of stack hardware.

Compilers, operating systems, and programs in ALGOL-like languages in general are both easier to write for, and run more reliably on, stack computers than on conventional computers. Stack computers are more complex and therefore more expensive to manufacture. And they usually do not run as fast as conventional computers for typical short pieces of program. The question is whether the improvements in the programming systems are worth the costs. The answer to this question changes with time. Hardware costs are decreasing and hardware speed is increasing. Programmers, however, seem to cost more. One can conclude then that the case for stack computers, whatever it was, is getting increasingly better. In some applications, such as intelligent computer terminals, the cost of the processor is negligible and its speed is such that it is idle most of the time.

One question that must be answered for any computer design, most especially those that depart from the established norm, is whether or not the needed programming systems can be implemented. The simplest approach is to collect a set of very simple programs, each of which uses either one programming primitive or, where there is interaction between primitives, two or more. Collectively they should span the programming language. Each program should then be rendered, by hand, into machine language. Assuming that the translation is successful, then one should estimate how difficult it is going to be for the compiler to do it and how efficient the result is going to be.

Having established the adequacy of a design in terms of its ability to support the primitives necessary to build the needed programming systems, one can begin to formulate some further questions which, if not decisive, are at least good indicators of the value of the design. The general model is that of resource occupancy. That is, for those items which are costly to have and to hold, how much time is necessary to accomplish some standard task? Speed is an unsophisticated measure of this kind: if using the CPU in fact preempts the whole computer, then one can evaluate the efficiency of use of the hardware by simply comparing the speed with which the CPU can accomplish a standard task. This traditional criterion fails in two ways. First, on computers where resources are shared (time-sharing or even file storage), CPU speed fails to expose some important details. Such concerns are obvious in some of the computer-center charging algorithms that are in common use, where memory residence, disk storage, tape mounts, and other resource uses are separately charged. Second, more global concerns, such as the time to write a program, including debugging, and the value of reliability in the final product, are not accounted for. For example, is 10% increase in speed worth 10% increase in the frequency of failures, with associated restarts?

Two interesting measures are storage efficiency and memory-reference efficiency [Fuller, et al., 77]. Storage efficiency refers to the compactness of the encoding of programs, with the idea that instruction sets that are efficient require fewer bits to encode programs than do inefficient instruction sets. Memory-reference efficiency refers to the amount of memory activity required to execute particular instruction sets. Efficient instruction sets result in fewer memory accesses than do inefficient ones. The general view is that stack instruction sets lead to better storage efficiency than do register instruction sets, but are likely to have poorer memory-reference efficiency than do register instruction sets. These views are largely based on specific instruction sets and not on the concepts themselves, and are biased by factors within the instruction sets quite orthogonal to the stack or register nature of the instruction set. In this section we attempt to indicate the reason for the existence of these views and try to isolate the true strengths and weaknesses of stack designs.

Let us first examine the issue of *storage efficiency,* and determine what factors govern the efficiency of instruction encoding. The general approach is to analyze the various fields in the instruction set, then choose codes that are near minimal for each field, based upon their frequency of occurrence in running programs. To be more precise, if there are N distinct instructions in the instruction set, and the ith instruction occurs f_i times in a standard program, and takes s_i bits to represent, the program instruction space is given by

$$\sum_{i=1}^{N} f_i s_i$$

The smaller this figure, the better the design from this viewpoint. One clearly wishes to minimize s_i for instructions with large f_i (or vice versa).

Stack machines are dramatically better than more conventional machines when measured by this criterion. It is not surprising to find a ratio of 1:3 or better between the Burroughs B5500 and IBM S/360 machines for a given program. Wortman [72] presents a careful analysis of this kind.

As an example of how far this concept can be carried, the Burroughs B6700 designers could have adopted (but did not) the instruction format in Figure 7-25, compressing the memory-accessing instructions into 8 bits.

Two bits are reserved for the operation code (Load value from memory, Load address, Load constant, and Other). One bit is reserved to signify whether the address represented by the LL-ON field is in the storage of the locally-executing routine (GL = 0) or is to be addressed via the display (GL = 1, see Figure 7-23). LL selects the display register, and ON is the offset above the selected display-register value. The boundary between the LL share of the field and the ON share of the field is decided by the level at

OP	GL	LL	ON

$\xleftarrow{\quad} 2 \xrightarrow{\quad} \ 1 \ \xleftarrow{\quad\quad\quad} 5 \xrightarrow{\quad\quad\quad}$

Figure 7-25   An 8-bit load from memory instruction

which the code is executing, since only entries in D below the present level of execution need be accessed. Table 7-17 gives the correspondence. Approximately 90% of all load instructions in the Burroughs operating system (for example) would fit within this coding scheme. The rest would need a rarely used (10%) but less tightly packed operation. For example, one of the "Other" codes (see above) might have been reserved for "long load" as depicted in Figure 7-26. The smallest width for the displacement ON would then be 11 bits, or 2048 accessible locals on any level. The comparison is with the 32-bit load instruction on the IBM S/360, a saving of nearly 4:1.

TABLE 7-17. ADDRESSING RANGES FOR THE 8-BIT LOAD INSTRUCTION

Level of Executing Code	Level Field Width (LL)	Displacement Field Width (ON)	Number of Accessible Non-local Names per Display Level (GL = 1)	Number of Accessible Local Names per Display Level (GL = 0)
0-1	0	5	32	32
2	1	4	16	32
3-4	2	3	8	32
5-8	3	2	4	32
9-16	4	1	2	32
17-32	5	0	1	32

Such savings are real and dramatic. They must, however, be kept in perspective relative to the overall evaluation problem. To digress from the main point of what savings are available and how much they contribute, we now wish to analyze the 8-bit load instruction from the viewpoint of the manufacturer (as was done at Burroughs during the B6700 design). Suppose the load instruction were cut from 16 bits to 8 bits, as noted above. Its frequency of occurrence is over 20% in most programs. Thus 10% of program space could be saved; that is, about 5% of program memory space, since data residence must be taken into account; that is, about 2% of main-frame cost; that is,

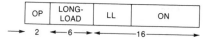

Figure 7-26   A 24-bit extended load from memory instruction

about 1% of manufacturing cost, taking into account peripherals and system software; that is, about ½ of 1% of computer time cost to the user who must pay for manufacturer profits, system maintenance, space to house the computer and machine operators; that is, about ¼ of 1% of the cost of computed results, taking into account the cost of program development, testing, debugging and data preparation. That is, not much of significance.

A more important effect can be seen when a needed program overflows the maximum memory available on the computer. Then programming costs shoot up as schemes for squeezing into memory are implemented. This problem showed up during the 1970s, with computers outgrowing their address spaces. More memory was demanded by the applications than the designers had provided for in their most generous designs. When the limit of addressibility was passed, the processors had to be modified to permit the additional memory to be accessed. Computers with 16-bit addresses in their instruction codes had to be changed. The changes were generally of the nature of program-controlled extension bits, a kind of auxiliary register, that was set each time a new bank of memory had to be accessed. In the worst case, the extension bits had to be set before every memory-referencing instruction, in case the new address happened to have crossed a boundary. At best it was a nuisance and inefficient; at worst it led to unreliable programs.

Stack machines, such as the Hewlett-Packard HP-3000, were much less affected, since the addresses were to be found only in the stack-addressing registers, not the program code. To extend memory required only larger registers and an extended way to set them, which was a function reserved to the operating system. Thus user programs were little affected.

The reason that stack designs do so well on memory-referencing instructions is that programmers rarely write individual subroutines that are so complex as to access hundreds or thousands of differently named variables. In any given subroutine, 32 names is generally more than adequate and does not constrain most programs. So the thirst for more addresses in register machines is not because the number of names per subroutine is growing. The major need for addresses stems from the register-machine practice of naming every variable, every subroutine, every array element, and every accessible entity by its memory address. There is no provision for reusing names, so that all names must be distinct. As programs and data grow larger, there is no recourse but to provide more addresses.

Stack machines provide for the reuse of names. That is, SIN can have a local variable accessible as MEMORY[L + 1], and EXP can refer to a totally different local variable in the same way. In both cases the program instructions access the variable by using the L register displaced by 1, and they rely on SCOPE ENTRY and SCOPE EXIT instructions to put the proper address in L.

While is is not mandatory to take advantage of first-in last-out allocation for subroutine calls, there is a price to pay in data storage when this is not done. Languages like ALGOL, PL/I, and PASCAL provide the facility to allocate and deallocate blocks of memory through the subroutine mechanism, which if disabled, would force the memory to be allocated as if all memory were active simultaneously; this could be many times larger than the greatest need for memory at any specific point in the program. These languages, when implemented on register machines, are virtually always implemented with stacks to hold local memory, parameters, and the like, with the stacks simulated by software. Hence, the subroutine entry and exit mechanism by itself justifies the use of stack instructions, and a growing number of machines have adopted stack instructions for this purpose, in spite of the use of register instructions for other purposes.

In looking at the other efficiency measure, *memory-reference efficiency,* the case for the stack machine is not as strong. Early implementation of stack machines relied on the use of a single stack for all purposes. This was a good idea at the time of their design, because of the high expense of additional stacks; but with hardware costs diminishing, a single-stack machine suffers severely from having an insufficient number of operands available inside the CPU. Frequently accessed variables quickly become buried in the stack after a few PUSHes, and eventually are pushed into main memory, where their access comes at greater cost. Hardware designers may build complex mechanisms to keep part of the stack in a fast local memory, and to retrieve items with smaller performance penalties; but they are forced into this design chore because of the inherent performance problems connected with the lack of high-speed data registers in a single-stack machine.

In some computations common subexpressions are quite frequent. That is, there is some value that is computed once and needed in more than one place within a short time. An example of such a value is the subscript in a two-or-more-dimensional array where a particular variable is being updated, or similar positions are being accessed in different arrays (e.g., A[expression] := A[expression] + 1). On register machines, such values can be safely tucked away in a processor register and used as often as necessary. (One should not, however, be misled that such optimizations come for free; the algorithms to keep track of such information are complex and costly to run.) On stack machines, one must either go to memory with the value and then recover it with an explicit STORE-LOAD pair, or do some tricks with the stack registers. More usually, one just recomputes the value on stack machines.

Sites [76] gives an elegant design which permits both the simplicity of a stack and the flexibility of registers for common subexpressions. The essence of the idea is to have one register behave like an arithmetic stack and the rest like ordinary registers. Stone [73] provided a hardware assist that allowed the program to be in Polish form but, through a pipelined hardware translator, caused the execution to be overlapped in a manner similar to that allowed by multiregister designs.

The material in this chapter is a somewhat unorthodox presentation of stack machines, because it isolates the several last-in-first-out processes going on concurrently during the execution of a stack-instruction sequence, and suggests that these each be implemented in a separate stack. Multiple stacks in a physical implementation do provide additional high-speed storage that is useful to improve performance, yet they require no additional bits in the instruction encoding, because the stack manipulated by any instruction is implicit in the action required for that instruction. Other ways of increasing the number of registers usable in a stack-instruction set will have additional positive effects on performance, so that stack instructions for high-speed computers should not be ruled out because of the performance penalties that may have existed due to stack instructions on early stack machines.

Other sources of performance penalties are the use of indirection to access local arrays (Figure 7-24), and the addition of an offset to the contents of a register to calculate every address. Register machines provide for high-speed storage in registers for addresses used frequently, to save additional memory references. Also, while indexed addresses are available, many instructions contain absolute addresses that access memory with no further addition or indexing necessary. In most stack machine implementations, indirect references through pointers in the stack have proved to be a source of performance degradation; but the requirement to calculate all addresses with an addition operation has eventually become a negligible factor as more hardware has been available in CPUs to speed up this operation or permit it to be done while something else is done.

In retrospect, the encoding efficiencies and performance deficiencies attributed to stack machines are undoubtedly anachronisms dating back to the first implementations of stack machines. Here we have identified the sources of these characteristics, and have provided a strong case for incorporating stack instructions for subroutine calls and local-variable allocation. The weaknesses in performance are undoubtedly due to the early work in trying to minimize the number of high-speed registers in a stack implementation, and might well be undone if the equal effort were devoted to maximizing the number of high-speed registers. At this writing there is very little evidence to compare the performance of a register machine to that of a stack machine with an equal number of registers, so the memory-reference efficiency of stack-instruction sets is still an open question.

PROBLEMS

7-47. Formalize the evaluation problem in terms of a cost/benefit difference. Be specific about the variables that must be known to make a decision. Use monetary units.

7-48. Assuming that one of your terms in problem 7-47 is memory residence for a program during its execution, outline a method for comparing the average memory residence demanded by a stack computer and a conventional computer. Both program and data must be considered.

7-49. Assume that the failure rate for two computers consists of two terms, one for hardware failures and one for software failures. Outline a method for comparing the failure rates of two different computers where you suspect that the additional hardware on one will cause more hardware failures but eliminate some software failures. Does the trade-off chosen depend on the cost of a failure to the user?

7-50. Taking reasonable estimates of cost for programmer salaries and computer rental, what is the trade-off in monthly rental, in a typical medium-scale computer shop, in eliminating all subscripting errors (an effect of the descriptor logic in Section 7-6)?

CHAPTER 8

Parallel Computers

Harold S. Stone

8-1. INTRODUCTION

Computation speed has increased by orders of magnitude over the past three decades of computing, with a major share of the increase in speed attributable to inherently faster electronic parts. The earliest electronic computers used vacuum tubes for logic functions and magnetic drums for central memory. Significant speed increases came when drums were replaced by magnetic cores, when vacuum tubes were replaced by transistors, and when both transistors and cores were replaced by integrated components. Today, we cannot obtain speed increases, as we have done in the past, by simply increasing the basic speed of the logic components; we must necessarily take other approaches to increase computational speed.

To understand why this is so, observe that many factors other than the switching speed of the logic determine the computational speed of a computer. Specifically, propagation delays have become significant in today's high speed computers, to the extent that signal-propagation time between widely separated modules well exceeds the delays due to device-switching time. Logic signals travel at the speed of light, or approximately 30 centimeters per nanosecond in a vacuum. For modules a meter apart, signal delays between the modules are 3 nanoseconds at least, and longer if the signal-transmission speed in the electrical conductor is slower than the speed of light in a vacuum. This signal-propagation time could largely be ignored in the 1960s, when logic delays were measured in the tens and hundreds of nanoseconds, but is significant as we enter the 1980s, when fast-logic delays are measured in hundreds of picoseconds. High-speed computers must be designed so that propagation delays are eliminated or not critical to the timing of the machine.

To the extent that past advances in integrated circuits have resulted in both higher speed and smaller dimensions, the advances have supported faster computation.

Future advances may not be so helpful as the past ones have been. Integrated-circuit manufacture is now approaching the practical limits of optical resolution, forcing a move to electron-beam machining techniques to achieve a further reduction in circuit dimensions. Meanwhile the cost of gates with existing technology has diminished to the point that it is economical to use 100 to 1000 times as many logic gates per computer today as was practical a decade ago. Obviously, with gates so inexpensive, the most appealing approach to high-speed computation is to put many processors together on a single problem, thereby attaining computation power through replication of logic, rather than relying solely on fast individual gates and small dimensions to reduce logic delay. The throughput of N identical computers is N times that of a single computer. The issue at hand is how to put the N computers together to operate on a single problem so as to achieve speed increases on the order of N in a practical and economically feasible way.

Before integrated circuits, it was conceivable to put together 2, 3, or 4 computers, but 100 or 1000 was wildly unrealistic. In the era of the microprocessor we now find a single microprocessor system, worth roughly $1000, having a power equivalent to processors of the late 1950s that sold for $1 million. If we are still willing to expend $1 million to solve important classes of problems, then one can reason that 1000 microprocessors might well be tied together in a useful way to exceed the capabilities of any conventional serial super-speed computer in the same price range. Where 1000 computers may be interconnected today, the future may find it practical to interconnect 10,000 computers. The fundamental questions lie not in whether or not N computers can be tied together, but rather in how to interconnect them and program them to obtain fast, reliable, and economical computation.

Parallelism in various forms had already appeared in computers produced during the 1960s, and has proved to be an effective approach. Nevertheless, at that time parallelism was limited by the cost of logic, so that computers were conventional serial processors, by and large, with moderate additional capability to support parallel operation. By the beginning of the 1970s several different types of truly parallel computers were under construction. By the end of the 1970s, most of these projects were in full operation, with second-generation successors in the making. While serial computers tend to share a common general structure, no two designs for parallel computers have been even remotely similar. Several competitive methods for organizing parallel computers have been proposed, with very little evidence on which to evaluate the merits of the different proposals. Only by the end of the 1970s, when a handful of different approaches had been tried, was there data being accumulated on which to make careful evaluations for future designs.

Flynn [66] helped initiate an organized study of high-speed computer architecture by showing that computer systems fall naturally into four classes. Within this classification system it is possible to make some nontrivial observations about the utility of a computer system and its relative cost-effectiveness for specific types of problems. Two of the classes represent divergent methods for organizing parallel computers that are the main subject matter of this chapter. One type of computer, the *array computer,* operates on vectors as basic units of information, and achieves parallelism through the parallelism of vector operations. Instruction execution in an array computer is similar to that in a conventional computer; in both types of computers, there is a single stream of instructions with loads, adds and branches. The array computer, however, manipulates many elements of a vector simultaneously, rather than just a single element at a time.

The alternative parallel architecture is the *multiprocessor.* This type of computer system consists of N processors plus interconnections for passing data and control information among the computers. Up to N different instruction streams can be active concurrently. The challenge is to put the N processors to work on different parts of a computation, so that the total computation is done at high speed by making efficient use of the processors available to it.

Yet another technique for achieving parallelism, called *pipelining,* has been used in supercomputers of the 1970s. It is sufficiently important as a general-purpose technique for improving performance to merit a chapter to itself, and appears in Chapter 9.

The present chapter is organized as follows. In the next section we describe the Flynn classes, then show crude models of the array processor and multi-processor, together with typical programs for which they are well suited. In later sections, the discussion focuses first on the array computer, then on the multiprocessor. We shall discover that the array computer is the less flexible and more specialized computer. It is extremely effective for computations that fit the constraints of a vector instruction set. But many problems do not have a rigid vector structure and do not adapt well to the array architecture. Future development in this area seeks to enlarge the class of computations that can be done efficiently on an array computer without compromising its effectiveness.

By comparison, the multiprocessor is much more flexible. But flexibility does not in itself guarantee high efficiency. There are still many open research problems concerning how to organize parallel computations on a multi-processor system so as to make the best use of N cooperating processors in the solution of a single problem. Here we investigate the problems of synchronizing the processors in a multiprocessor, of sharing data among processors, and of scheduling computations to utilize the computer-system resources efficiently.

8-2. CLASSES OF COMPUTER SYSTEMS

It is quite natural to classify parallel computers in terms of parallelism within the instruction stream and parallelism within the data stream. By *instruction stream* we mean, in this context, the sequence of operations that are executed in a processor. A serial computer is a computer with a single

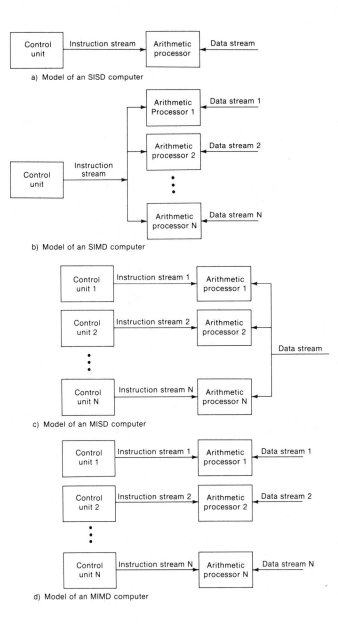

Figure 8-1 Computer models

instruction stream and a single data stream. At any given time during the execution of a program on a serial computer, there is at most one instruction in execution, and that instruction affects at most one datum. This is shown in Part *a* of Figure 8-1.

Flynn [66] observed that the methods for achieving parallel operation depended on replicating the instruction stream and the data stream. This gives rise naturally to four classes of computers. The *single-instruction single-data-stream* (SISD) computer is the serial computer mentioned above, and we shall denote this class of computer by the term *serial*. By replicating the data stream we create a processor of the type shown in Part *b* of Figure 8-1. This processor, known as the *single-instruction multiple-data-stream* (SIMD) computer, is a *vector* processor in the sense that each instruction operates on a data vector rather than a single operand. A vector processor can be constructed as an *array* processor, in which each vector element is treated by a different arithmetic processor, as described in the following section. But vector processors can be implemented in other ways as well, and pipelined implementations of such processors are treated in Chapter 9. The multiple data stream that feeds into a vector processor is the collection of individual data streams containing the elements of the vector operands. Each processor in Part *b* of Figure 8-1 has a complete arithmetic unit and local memory in the array-computer implementation of a vector computer, but each processor is not a full-fledged serial computer because it does not generate its own instruction stream. Not shown in Part *b* of Figure 8-1 are the necessary interconnections among processors to enable data to be shared among the processors. We shall describe these interconnections in Section 8-3.

Instead of parallelism in the data stream it is conceivable to have parallelism in the instruction stream. Part *c* of Figure 8-1 depicts a *multiple-instruction single-data-stream* (MISD) computer. In this case each operand is operated upon simultaneously by several instructions. This mode of operation is generally unrealistic for parallel computers, but there is at least one example of such a processor. Consider a punched-card processor that has the capability of operating on several data fields of a punched card simultaneously. The program for such a processor consists of subprograms of instructions for each data field, where each subprogram generates one instruction stream and the instruction streams are processed simultaneously. The single operand in this case is a punched card. While this admittedly is stretching the definition of a single datum, the example is useful because it illustrates the notion of an MISD computer.

The fourth class of computer combines parallelism in instruction and data streams. This is the *multiple-instruction multiple-data-stream* (MIMD) computer shown in Part *d* of Figure 8-1. This computer is composed of N processors, each of which is a complete computer, with the processors connected together to provide a means of cooperating during a computation. In this chapter we call such a computer system a *multiprocessor*. A multiprocessor with N independent processors then has N instruction streams and N data streams, one data stream per instruction stream.

Most serial computers manufactured today have data channels such as the direct-memory-access (DMA) channels described in Chapter 6. The channels themselves are very simple independent processors that operate on input/output data streams with a very small repertoire of instructions. Thus a computer system with one processor and one DMA channel fits the model of a multiprocessor. Although the processor and channel are not identical, there is no reason to insist that all of the processors of a multiprocessor be identical. The computations performed by a channel and by a central processor are vastly different, but because they are done in parallel, computation speed is greater than if all of the computation were done by a single processor. The challenge for the present is to design and use multiprocessors with not just 2 to 4 processors but with 100 or 1000 processors.

One of the early implementations of a multiprocessor with more than a few processors is the C.mmp at Carnegie-Mellon University, with 16 processors [Wulf and Bell, 73]; more recently came the Cm*, also at Carnegie-Mellon, with in excess of 30 processors and with capability to extend well beyond that amount, [Swan, Fuller, and Siewiorek, 77]. Many other examples were in use or in construction by the end of the 1970s, including a 16-processor communications message system for the ARPA computer network [Ornstein et al., 75; Heart et al., 73], and a multiprocessor in development at NASA Langley for the solution of partial differential equations [Jordan, 78].

Of the four classes of computers, the two of interest for parallel computation are the vector processor and the multiprocessor. These types of computers are vastly different in how they attain parallelism of operation. The vector processor is well suited to computations that can be broken up into a sequence of vector operations. If a computation has no specific vector structure or other natural iterative structure, then it is unlikely to be suitable for a vector processor, but it may be suitable for a multiprocessor. It need only have potential parallelism that can be exploited by independent instruction streams, which is quite possible even though the computation has no vector structure. Parallelism for a multiprocessor generally consists of breaking the computation into independent tasks that can be executed concurrently on independent computers. Then the results of the separate computations are combined.

The following example illustrates the relative characteristics of vector processors and multiprocessors. We have chosen an example that can be executed on both types of computers to strengthen the distinction between them.

The example is a matrix multiplication. We wish to compute $C = A \times B$, where A, B, and C are $N \times N$ matrices. To do the computation we use the well-known formula.

$$c_{i,j} = \sum_{k=0}^{N-1} a_{i,k} \times b_{k,j}$$

where A, B, and C have elements $a_{i,j}$, $b_{i,j}$, and $c_{i,j}$, respectively.

We show a program for the vector-processor computation in an ALGOL-like language. In this program we assume that there are N processors arranged as an array so that each processor can operate on one element of a vector. An entire row vector can be treated in a single operation. In the program the notation $(0 \leq k \leq N - 1)$ indicates that the operations are carried out for all indices k in the given interval simultaneously.

Matrix Multiplication Algorithm
(Vector Version)

for $i := 0$ **step** 1 **until** N $-$ 1 **do**
    begin comment initialize the sums to 0;
        $C[i, k] := 0, (0 \leq k \leq N - 1)$;
        for $j := 0$ **step** 1 **until** N $-$ 1 **do**
            begin comment add the next term to the sum;
                $C[i, k] := C[i, k] + A[i, j] \times B[j, k], (0 \leq k \leq N - 1)$;
        end of j loop;
    end of i loop;

In this algorithm, we compute all of the elements in the ith row simultaneously. Note that each element of the product matrix is a summation, and the summations are done serially rather than in parallel. However, because N summations are computed simultaneously, only N^2 vector multiplications are required for this algorithm as compared to the N^3 scalar multiplications required for the usual matrix multiplication.

The statement in the inner loop of this algorithm indicates that we must have the capability to multiply each element of the jth row of B by the constant $A[i,j]$, that is, we must be able to multiply a vector by a scalar. This suggests that it is highly desirable to be able to broadcast a single element (in this case $A[i,j]$) simultaneously to all processors to be used as an operand. Thus we see some need for communication among processors in a vector computer to enhance its capabilities. Interprocessor communication and data access are central problems in both the design and programming of vector computers. In the next section we investigate these problems more thoroughly.

To perform the same process on a multiprocessor, we must somehow parcel out the computation to the individual processors in the system. Conway [63] proposed an ingenious method for doing this by means of two primitive machine operations he calls FORK and JOIN. If NEXT is a label in a program, then when the instruction FORK (to) NEXT is executed, an independent computation is started at the label NEXT. In the meantime, the computation containing the FORK instruction continues execution at the instruction immediately following the FORK, so that a FORK splits one instruction stream into two streams that can be executed simultaneously on independent processors.

The JOIN instruction is something like the inverse of a FORK, because it brings instruction streams together. The statement JOIN N causes N independent instruction streams to merge into a single stream. In actual operation, the execution of instructions following a JOIN N instruction will not take place until the Nth independent process has executed the JOIN instruction.

With these two primitive operations understood, we examine the execution of a matrix multiplication algorithm on a multiprocessor.

Matrix Multiplication Algorithm
(Multiprocessor Version)

```
comment spawn N − 1 independent processes, each with
    a different value of k;
for k := 0 step 1 until N − 2 do
    FORK NEXT;
comment in the one process that reaches this point,
    set k to N − 1 in order to process the Nth element
    of a row;
k := N − 1;
NEXT: comment N different processes reach this point,
        each with a different value of k
for i := 0 step 1 until N − 1 do
    begin comment initialize each sum to 0;
        C[i,k] := 0;
        for j := 0 step 1 until N − 1 do
            begin comment add each successive term to the sum;
            C[i,k] := C[i,k] + A[i,j] × B[j,k];
            end of j loop;
    end of i loop;
JOIN N;
```

We have purposely written the multiprocessor program so that the actions performed by the independent processors are exactly analogous to the actions performed by the individual processors of the vector computer. There are important differences, however, that distinguish the two computations. Recall that the processors of a vector computer are synchronized, instruction for instruction, while a program is in execution. In contrast, the processes in the example for the multiprocessor need not be synchronized. In fact, they need not be identical instruction sequences, even though we have shown such an example for comparison purposes.

Another major attribute of multiprocessor computers is that they are insensitive to the number of processors that are available in a computer system. The reason for this stems from Conway's concept of how to assign processors automatically to computational tasks spawned by a FORK, and how to reassign each processor when the task it is executing dies at a JOIN. Conway suggests that the FORK NEXT instruction be executed as follows:

1. At the point of execution, some or all of the memory accessible to the executing process is identified as common to the spawned process. Pointers required to access this memory are created and allocated to the spawned process.
2. The task that executed the FORK instruction continues execution on the processor originally allocated to it.

3. If a processor is available, it is allocated to the spawned process. If no processor is available, the spawned process is queued and awaits execution.

When there are insufficient processors to do all N tasks simultaneously, one or more of the tasks are queued during the computation. How does a task become assigned to a processor and executed at a later time? This occurs when a JOIN instruction is executed. The interpretation of a JOIN is as follows:

1. For each JOIN instruction there is a unique counter which is initialized to 0. When the instruction JOIN N is executed, the counter is incremented and compared to N.
2. If the value of the counter is N, then this is the Nth task to pass the JOIN instruction. This task continues execution past the JOIN instruction on its assigned processor.
3. If the value of the counter is less than N, then more tasks must reach the JOIN instruction before proceeding beyond. The task now in execution is terminated. All resources private to it are returned to a resource pool. The processor assigned to the task is then reassigned to some other task that has been queued for service.

Since tasks are terminated at JOIN instructions, these instructions are natural points for the reallocation of processors to other tasks. Figure 8-2 shows a schematic diagram of the execution of the multiprocessor version of the matrix multiplication algorithm running on a four-processor machine when N = 10. Each task is identified with a value k. Note that tasks with $k = 0$, $k = 1$, and $k = 2$ are executed first because they are spawned first.

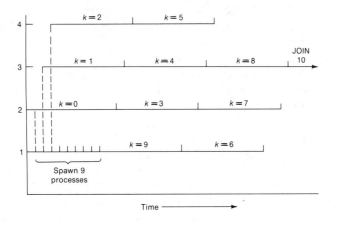

Figure 8-2 Timing diagram for a multiprocessor matrix multiplication

Tasks for $k = 3$ through 8 are queued. The task for $k = 9$ proceeds before these because it has a processor assigned to it during the spawning process, and this processor is not relinquished until the JOIN instruction is reached. The order of execution of the tasks for $k = 3$ to 8 is first-in, first-out in this example, but for more general problems any ordering consistent with precedence constraints is acceptable. We have not indicated how precedence constraints can be incorporated into a program for a multiprocessor, but we discuss this question further in a later section. In the meantime we mention that first-in, first-out scheduling of computational tasks is not necessarily the best, and we do not treat the scheduling question any further in this chapter. Nevertheless, the question of efficient scheduling is an important issue and looms as one of the outstanding problems that must be solved in a practical sense if multiprocessors with hundreds of processors are to be put into common use.

Note that problems of scheduling and of satisfying precedence constraints are absent in vector computers. Thus the increased flexibility of multi-processors comes at an increased cost in their programming and control. The cost-effectiveness and net throughput of multiprocessors, as compared to that of serial and vector computers, depends heavily on the effectiveness of the scheduling algorithm, on the overhead for scheduling, and also on how precedence constraints can be met without interfering with the parallelism attainable by the computer system. These problems are only beginning to be explored on prototype multiprocessors to date, and remain important problems for research in computer architecture.

8-3. ARRAY COMPUTERS

The previous section illustrates the classes of vector computers and multi-processors, but at a rather gross level of detail. In this section we examine the *array computer* in depth, noting that the array computer is a vector computer implemented as an array of arithmetic processors. Another way of implementing a vector computer is by means of pipeline design techniques, as described in Chapter 9. This section brings to light the most central question concerning the design of array computers, namely, to build in data access and communication facilities so that the array computer is useful for as large a variety of computations as possible. We investigate a number of capabilities to incorporate into array computers, but the reader should note carefully that the subject area is still evolving.

To evaluate the effectiveness of array computers, we look into techniques for performing typical computations with vector instructions. A number of surprising conclusions result from this evaluation. Perhaps most surprising is that an efficient algorithm for a serial computer may lead to a relatively inefficient algorithm for a vector computer. In fact, the best vector algorithm for a given problem may be adapted from an algorithm that is known to be inefficient for serial execution. Thus we cannot generally rely on knowledge of serial computation when we construct vector algorithms.

In the first part of this section we give a block diagram for a hypothetical array computer that greatly resembles the ILLIAC IV computer. A description of the use of the various features of the computer system appears in the second part. There we investigate fragments of instruction sequences that implement frequently used program constructs. We also investigate the data-communication requirements of vector programs to determine the most valuable interconnections to design into the computer system. In addition, we treat methods for storing data structures to take best advantage of the parallelism of the computer.

Toward the end of this section we look into general techniques for transforming a serial program into a vector program. Even though the techniques are said to be general, they apply only to a class of programs that exhibit a strongly iterative structure. We show how to apply these techniques to certain algorithms that appear to be sequential to obtain new vector algorithms with a good degree of parallelism. Unfortunately, these techniques do not work for all highly iterative programs, nor do there exist widely applicable techniques for casting programs into parallel form when they do not have an iterative structure.

Organization of an Array Computer

For this description we shall draw heavily upon the ILLIAC IV computer [Barnes et al., 68]. However, this discussion differs in many specific details from the ILLIAC IV, and we generally use a different and more descriptive terminology.

A block diagram of the array computer appears in Figure 8-3. Note the N independent processors and N independent memories, as we have described earlier. The memories are all connected to a high-speed data bus whose bandwidth is compatible with both the processor and input/output bandwidths. The maximum bandwidth is one word from each memory per memory cycle, which is N times the bandwidth of an individual memory. Note that there is a permutation network included here that permits information to be exchanged among the processors. The permutation network is shown as a processor-to-processor interconnection, but it may also be a memory-to-memory interconnection.

The control unit in this scheme is itself a computer, with its own high-speed registers, local memory, and arithmetic unit. The crucial difference between this processor and the others is that this processor can execute conditional branch instructions and can thereby determine the order in which instructions are executed. The arithmetic processors do not have this ability because the processors must always be in synchronization, and therefore cannot take different actions after a conditional branch instruction.

As in conventional machines, the instructions are stored in main memory together with data. The main memory in this system is the collective memory in the N processors. Hence, the instructions are fetched from the processors into an instruction buffer in the control processor. The communication path for this transfer is shown in the figure.

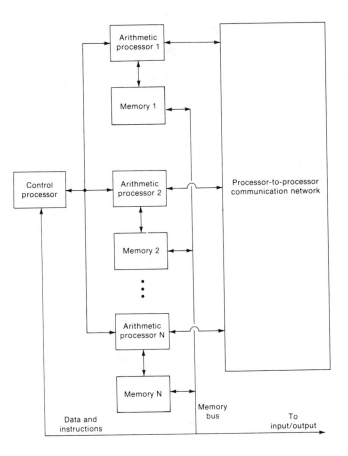

Figure 8-3   Block diagram of an array computer

The flow of instructions and data during execution is rather interesting in this type of computer. Each instruction is either a control instruction, in which case it is executed entirely within the control unit, or it is a vector instruction and is executed in the processor array. But the instruction stream is much like a conventional serial instruction stream, with each instruction executed in sequence. A primary function of the control processor is to examine each instruction as it is to be executed and to determine where the execution should take place. If the instruction is a control instruction, then it is executed in the control unit itself, otherwise it is broadcast to the processor array for execution there. In either case the instruction passes through the control processor, so that the control processor has the exclusive privilege to determine which instruction to execute next.

We shall shortly trace the execution of a fragment from a sequence of instructions to make these points clearer. Before doing so, we shall introduce just one more feature of the computer, and treat this in the example as well.

Our intuition tells us that index registers should be at least as important to have in this type of computer system as in a conventional system. We can place index registers either in the control processor or in the processing array and, in fact, they exist in both places in the ILLIAC IV. The index registers in the control processor have a global action on the processor array, because in this instance a single indexing operation affects all processors. During the execution of an instruction intended for the processor array, the operand address contained in the instruction can be modified by indexing in the control unit before it is passed to the processing array for final execution. This indexing action is completely analogous to indexing within a serial computer.

Indexing can also be done in the individual processor. The effect of indexing in the processor array is to force each processor to modify the broadcast operand address by an amount determined locally in each processor. The index offsets may all be the same or all different, or any arbitrary combination. We shall see later that this feature is invaluable for accessing rows and columns of an array with equal ease.

Vector-processor Instruction Sets

Having gone through a block diagram of the array processor, we are ready to examine the execution of a typical instruction sequence. For this example, let us return to the matrix multiplication example, and show the instruction sequence that implements the statement

for $j := 0$ **step** 1 **until** N $-$ 1 **do**
    begin
        $C[i,k] := C[i,k] + A[i,j] \times B[j,k]$, $(0 \leq k \leq N - 1)$;
    end

The matrices A, B, and C are stored as shown in Figure 8-4. In this example each operand address in the vector instructions is the address of a row vector of A, B, or C. Addresses of rows increase sequentially by unit amounts as shown in the figure.

Let us assume that each data processor in the array is a single-accumulator computer; we denote the accumulator in the kth processor as ACC[k]. The index registers in the control processor are denoted INDEX[i]. Then the vector instructions we need for this example are in Table 8-1.

The vector instructions are extensions of a scalar instruction set. When the A, B, or C appears by itself as operand address, we obtain the address of row 0 of the respective matrix. When the address appears in the form A[i] or B[j], the address is indexed by index register i or j, respectively, where the index register is understood to be an index register in the control processor. This is consistent with the conventions for assembly language for serial computers. The *vector store*, *add*, and *multiply* instructions are not shown in their indexed form, but we assume that they have indexed modes

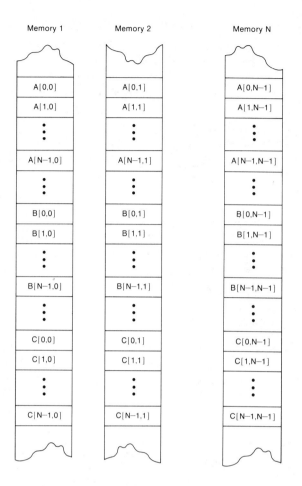

Figure 8-4 Storage format of matrices A, B, and C

similar to the *indexed vector-load* instruction. The *broadcast-scalar* instruction selects one of the N accumulators and broadcasts its contents to all other accumulators. To simplify the explanation, the operand of this instruction is an index register, but in actual implementation the operand might be an integer or an indexed integer.

There remains to exhibit the loop control and counting instructions that are executed in the control processor. These instructions are functionally identical to similar instructions found in any serial-computer repertoire. For this example we shall use the instructions in Table 8-2, but any equivalent repertoire may be substituted instead.

The instructions in Table 8-2 should require no additional explanation, except for the MEMORY[Y] notation in the action of the load-index instruction. Since there are N memories in the processor array and one more in the control processor, we should further specify which of the $N+1$ memories is

TABLE 8-1. VECTOR INSTRUCTIONS

Instruction	Example	Action
Vector load	LOAD A	$ACC[k] := A[0,k],$ $(0 \leq k \leq N - 1);$
Vector load (indexed)	LOAD A[i]	$ACC[k] := A[INDEX[i],k],$ $(0 \leq k \leq N - 1);$
Vector store	STO A	$A[0,k] := ACC[k],$ $(0 \leq k \leq N - 1);$
Vector add	ADD A	$ACC[k] := ACC[k] + A[0,k],$ $(0 \leq k \leq N - 1);$
Vector multiply	MUL A	$ACC[k] := ACC[k] \times A[0,k],$ $(0 \leq k \leq N - 1);$
Broadcast scalar	BCAST i	$ACC[k] := ACC[INDEX[i]],$ $(0 \leq k \leq N - 1);$

the intended reference of MEMORY[Y]. There are a number of standard ways to resolve the ambiguity in the encoding of the instruction, such as the use of special fields in the instruction, or of separate and distinguishable addresses for the different memories, or of address interpretation dependent upon processor state. For the purpose of this example, we do not need to resolve the ambiguity.

The encoding of the inner loop of the matrix multiplication example appears in Figure 8-5. Note that it is quite straightforward. We assume that index registers in the control processor have been allocated to hold the current values of j, as well as the value of N used to control and terminate the looping. The encoding is remarkably like the encoding for a serial computer, except that N operations occur while each arithmetic instruction is executed, instead of just one. The only visible difference here is the inclusion of the broadcast instruction BCAST to communicate the value of A[i,j] to all processors. This example is typical of many vector codes in that the inner loop of a serial computation (in this case, the loop on k) is replaced by vector operations.

The flow of information during the execution of the instructions in Figure 8-5 is again rather similar to instruction execution in serial computers. Because array computers are built to attain ultra-high speeds, the instruction

TABLE 8-2. INDEXING INSTRUCTIONS

Instruction	Example	Action
Enter index constant	ENXC i,1	$INDEX[i] := 1;$
Load index	LDNX i,Y	$INDEX[i] := MEMORY[Y];$
Increment index by constant	ICNX i,1	$INDEX[i] := INDEX[i] + 1;$
Compare index, branch if low	CPNX i,j,LABEL	**if** $INDEX[i] < INDEX[j]$ **then** **go to** LABEL;

LABEL	INSTRUCTION	OPERANDS	COMMENTS
1.		ENXC	j, 0	INDEX[j]: = 0
2.		LDNX	LIM, N	Place the value of N from memory into INDEX[LIM], the upper-limit register.
3.	JLOOP	LOAD	A[i]	ACC[k]: = A[i, k], $(0 \leq k \leq N - 1)$;
4.		BCAST	j	ACC[k]: = ACC[INDEX[j]], $(0 \leq k \leq N - 1)$; Each accumulator now contains the value of A[i, j].
5.		MUL	B[j]	ACC[k]: = ACC[k] × B[j, k], $(0 \leq k \leq N - 1)$; ACC[k] now contains A[i, j] × B[j, k].
6.		ADD	C[i]	ACC[k] now contains C[i, k] + A[i, j] × B[j, k].
7.		STO	C[i]	Update the value of the sum for C[i, k] in memory.
8.		ICNX	j, 1	INDEX[j]: = INDEX[j] + 1;
9.		CPNX	j, LIM, JLOOP	Branch to JLOOP and repeat until this loop is done N times.

Figure 8-5 Program for matrix multiplication on an SIMD computer

stream should be highly buffered in the control processor, and the memory bandwidth between the control processor and the processor array should be high enough to minimize the effect of instruction fetches on computation speed. As an example of these considerations, the ILLIAC IV fetches sixteen instructions at a time from the processor array into its instruction buffer. Moreover, instruction fetches are overlapped with operations that do not use main memory. These two design features, plus sufficient buffering in the control processor, guarantee that the ILLIAC IV rarely has to wait for an instruction fetch.

The facilities described thus far for the SIMD computer are sufficient for a very restricted class of computations. A few additional facilities greatly enlarge the class of problems that can be done efficiently. Perhaps the most important of these is the facility to mask computations to force some of the N processors into an idle state. We take this up presently. Later we discuss data communication and data structures.

Masking for Conditional Branching

Conditional branches are particularly vexing in an SIMD computer. Suppose, for example, a conditional branch instruction provides two alternatives, say, branch if the accumulator contains zero, otherwise no branch. What should happen if some but not all of the N accumulators contain zeros? The ideal solution is for the instruction stream to split into two streams, one for the zero accumulator case and one for the nonzero accumulator case. Unfortunately, the SIMD computer, as we have described it, cannot support two independent instruction streams simultaneously. Within the constraints imposed, the two cases must be done sequentially, as indicated in Figure 8-6. There is still parallelism, but the effective parallelism is roughly N/2 rather than N. We assume in Figure 8-6 that we can deactivate a selected subset of the processors, and execute an execution sequence in parallel on the subset that remains active. This way we can execute instructions for the zero-accumulator branch of the program on the processors with the zero accumulators. Then we execute the branch for the nonzero accumulators on the complementary set of processors. Figure 8-6 shows an example in which the two separate instruction streams merge into a single stream after their execution.

Note that in this example a serial computer does one branch for each datum, but never does both branches. The array computer, on the other hand, takes the time to execute both branches for each datum, although each processor is deactivated for one of the two alternatives.

Figure 8-6 Masking operations that simulate a conditional branch

To implement this type of masking facility, we use a one-bit register in each processor of the array. It is convenient to treat the N one-bit registers as a single N-bit register, which we call MASK. Then MASK[i] denotes the mask register of the ith processor. When MASK[i] contains a 1, processor i obeys the instruction broadcast by the control processor. When the mask bit is 0, processor i does nothing. In actual practice, it is both more economical and less likely to have an adverse affect on processor speed to disable only part of a processor when its mask bit is off. For example, memory storage operations and accumulator modification may be inhibited, but other portions of the processor, including portions not described here, may be left activated without changing the functional effect of the mask bit.

It is crucial that the mask bit of a processor be determined by data-dependent conditions. Moreover, it is often necessary to compute active subsets of processors through a series of set union, intersection, and complementation operations, which therefore require that mask settings be computable by logical operations on mask vectors. Here we follow the philosophy of the ILLIAC IV instruction repertoire. We assume that a vector of conditional tests with binary outcomes can be performed simultaneously in the N processors, and the resulting vector of bits is placed in a designated index register of the control processor. Thus, after a test is performed, the ith bit of the result indicates the outcome of the test in the ith processor.

To compute subsets of active processors, we include instructions for performing logical operations on the control processor's index registers, and we make provision for loading and storing the mask register from these index registers. It is also useful for some calculations to compute masks by using shift operations as well as logical operations. We simply assume that a full set of shift operations is included in the instruction repertoire without giving them explicitly.

A typical set of instructions for accomplishing the mask computations appears in Table 8-3, together with conditional-branch instructions for testing the outcome of a comparison operation. For subset computations there are three natural conditions to sense. Have none, any, or all of the processors satisfied the test? We show conditional-branch instructions for each of these possibilities. We also show instructions for extracting the first 1 bit of a bit vector, and the index of the first 1 bit of the vector. The ability to extract the first 1 bit is useful when a subset of processors responds to a conditional test, and we must then scan the responding processors sequentially, while performing some calculation in each one. We include the facility to compute the index of the first 1 bit, so that this index can be used in a broadcast instruction. Thus, a conditional test can be used to identify a subset of processors, after which the data from one of the selected subset can be broadcast to all processors.

A trivial example is given to illustrate the use of the mask registers and condition-setting instructions. For this example we look at a normalization

TABLE 8-3. CONDITION-SETTING, MASKING, AND BRANCHING INSTRUCTIONS

Instruction	Example	Action
Vector compare less	CLSS A,*i*	if ACC[*k*] < A[*k*] then INDEX[*i*], *k*th bit, is set to 1, otherwise reset to 0.
Vector compare equal	CEQL A,*i*	Similar to CLSS above.
Branch all	BRALL *i*,LOOP	Branch to LOOP if INDEX[*i*] has all 1 bits.
Branch any	BRANY *i*,LOOP	Branch to LOOP if INDEX[*i*] has any 1 bit.
Branch none	BRNON *i*,LOOP	Branch to LOOP if INDEX[*i*] has all 0 bits.
Logical AND of index	AND *i,j*	INDEX[*i*] := INDEX[*i*] AND INDEX[*j*];
Logical OR of index	OR *i,j*	Similar to AND above
Complement index	CMP *i*	INDEX[*i*] := NOT INDEX[*i*];
Load mask from index	LDMSK *i*	MASK := INDEX[*i*];
Store mask in index	STMSK *i*	INDEX[*i*] := MASK;
Set first 1 bit	FIRST *i*	If INDEX[*i*] has no 1 bits it is unchanged. Otherwise, all but the first 1 bit are reset.
Index of first 1 bit	NXFIR *i*	Replace the contents of INDEX[*i*] with bit index of its first 1 bit. Set INDEX[*i*] to all 1s if it originally contains no 1 bits.

operation. Suppose that A is an $N \times N$ matrix, and that we wish to normalize the rows of A by replacing $A[i,j]$ by $A[i,j] / A[0,j]$, provided that $A[0,j] \neq 0$. In an ALGOL-like notation this becomes:

> **for** $i := 0$ **step** 1 **until** $N - 1$ **do**
>   **if** $A[0,j] \neq 0$ **then** $A[i,j] := A[i,j] / A[0,j]$, $(0 \leq j \leq N - 1)$;

We actually perform the computation by computing the mask for $A[0,j] \neq 0$ before entering the loop, then we loop through the array without making any further tests. In the ALGOL-like notation, we can change the condition in parentheses from $(0 \leq j \leq N - 1)$, which indicates all processors are activated, to the condition $(M[j])$, which indicates that the only processors active are those corresponding to the 1 bits of the bit vector M. The statement now reads:

comment M is a vector of bits;
$M[k] := A[0,k] \neq 0, (0 \leq k \leq N - 1)$;
comment M now contains the result of the comparison;
for $i := 0$ **step** 1 **until** N $-$ 1 **do**
    begin comment normalize $A[i,j]$ only in
    the processors activated by M;
      $A[i,j] := A[i,j] / A[0,j], (M[j])$;
    end;

The implementation of this program fragment in machine instructions appears in Figure 8-7. The loop control instructions follow the now familiar form, as shown in Table 8-2. Note that the comparison is made and the mask register loaded prior to entry into the loop. We make use of a DIV instruction in the loop to do the division, and we note that it behaves similarly to the MUL and ADD instruction described in Table 8-1.

	LABEL	INSTRUCTION	OPERANDS	COMMENTS
1.		ENXC	$i, 0$	INDEX$[i]:= 0$;
2.		SUB	ACC	ACC$[k]:=$ ACC$[k]-$ ACC$[k]$, $(0 \leq k \leq N - 1)$; This clears all ACC registers.
3.		CEQL	A, M	if ACC$[k] = A[0,k]$ then set kth bit of INDEX[M], otherwise reset the kth bit. This creates the complement of the mask we require.
4.		CMP	M	INDEX[M] $:=$ NOT INDEX[M]; Complement the mask.
5.		LDMSK	M	Load the mask register.
6.		LDNX	LIM, N	Set the loop limit in INDEX[LIM]. INDEX $[i]$ has already been initialized to 0.
7.	ILOOP	LOAD	A[i]	ACC$[j] := A[i,j]$ if the jth mask bit is 1.
8.		DIV	A	ACC$[j] :=$ ACC$[j]/A[0,j]$ if the jth mask bit is 1.
9.		STO	A[i]	A$[i,j] :=$ ACC$[j]$ if the jth mask bit is 1.
10.		ICNX	$i, 1$	INDEX$[i] :=$ INDEX$[i] + 1$;
11.		CPNX	i,LIM,ILOOP	Branch to ILOOP and repeat until this loop is done N times.

Figure 8-7 Normalization program

The examples of the program fragments for an array computer suggest that programming such a computer is only slightly different from programming serial computers. There tend to be few conditional branches in vector programs, however, as we see from the present example. The masking operation here replaces one conditional branch, and the simultaneous computation on N items replaces an inner loop with its conditional branch at the end of the loop. Hence the array processor code in this case eliminates two conditional branches that would normally occur in serial computer code.

This completes the discussion of conditional control and branching in an array processor. The next parts of this section investigate interprocessor communications and data structures.

Interprocessor Communications

We have previously acknowledged that, in general, we shall permit data transfers to occur between processors in an array processor. Recall, from Figure 8-3, the network that interconnects the processors to support such exchanges. The question that we investigate in this section concerns the design of this interconnection network.

In order to maximize parallelism in an array processor, we must utilize as much of the available memory and processor bandwidths as is possible. To use the memory bandwidth, we must store data in such a way as to avoid memory-accessing conflicts. Two items that are accessed simultaneously must be placed in physically distinct memory modules, because a single module can access no more than one item at a time. Efficient utilization of memory bandwidth requires careful structuring of the data in its storage format. We discuss some approaches to the problem in the next part of this section.

With respect to the utilization of the processor bandwidth, we request that data, after being accessed from memory, be permuted if necessary to bring operand pairs together at available processors. As we shall see in the next part, data structuring for efficient memory access frequently causes data to be fetched in such a way that operand pairs are not properly aligned for parallel manipulation. To solve this problem we must install a permutation network in the processor. The nature of the permutation network is the subject of this part.

The permutation network that has the most flexibility is one in which every processor is directly connected to every other processor. Such a network is called a *complete interconnection* network. It is not difficult to show that in this network there are $N(N - 1)/2$ bidirectional links between N processors, where each link presumably has sufficient bandwidth to pass one operand per unit time. Note that the cost of a complete interconnection network increases proportionally to the square of N. This suggests that complete interconnection networks are not realistic for large N because the performance of an array computer increases linearly in N, at most. For sufficiently large N the cost of the complete interconnection network dominates the cost of the computer, and its cost could be so high as to nullify the gains from the parallelism. One

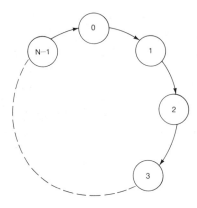

Figure 8-8   Cyclically connected collection of processors

argument in favor of the complete interconnection scheme is that logic costs can diminish to near zero, so that the cost of large networks may not be so high after all. Nevertheless, even with free hardware, it is worthwhile to use simple interconnections if they do not restrict the functional utility of the computer. With fewer interconnection paths, we can attain fewer gate delays in transmission paths, with an attendant increase in the basic cycle speed.

We should add that we can retain full interconnection flexibility, with logic growth proportional to $N \log_2 N$, if we permit the time to do a permutation to grow as $\log_2 N$ instead of being constant. Such schemes have been studied in the context of telephone-switching networks [Clos, 53; Benes, 65]. We choose rather to reduce the number and hence the flexibility of the interconnections, while maintaining as high a speed as possible.

We shall proceed here to exhibit interconnection patterns that are known to be good for a broad class of problems. In particular, we shall examine patterns that shift data cyclically among processors, and those that route the data by a permutation known as the perfect shuffle.

The *cyclic shift* interconnection pattern is shown in Figure 8-8. If we number the processors $0, 1, 2, \ldots, N - 1$, the processor i is directly connected to processors $i - 1$ and $i + 1$, where the addition is done modulo N. Note that for each i and j, processor i is connected to processor j, although not necessarily directly connected to processor j. Between the processors there are $i - j - 1 \bmod N$ processors through which data must flow while moving from processor i to processor j. A cyclic shift of data by an arbitrary amount can be done as a sequence of cyclic shifts by a unit amount.

The motivation for including the cyclic shift comes from the many parallel algorithms that contain assignment statements of the following type:

$$X[i] := (X[i - 1] + X[i + 1]) \div 2;$$

These statements usually occur in a context in which every element of the X vector has to be updated simultaneously, except for the first and last elements, which require special processing. Thus the vector operations require that the vector be aligned with itself shifted by a unit shift. Permutation interconnections of a unit cyclic shift in either direction are useful to perform this type of operation. To perform the special processing required for the first and last elements of the vector, we need the mask facilities mentioned previously. These do not detract from the general usefulness of the cyclic shift in this application.

This type of calculation shows up frequently in one-dimensional partial differential equations. Typically we have an iterative calculation in the sense that the vector updating process is done repeatedly until the result converges to a solution.

Computations in two and three dimensions entail generalizations of the basic iteration mentioned above. For example, a typical iteration might take the form

$$X[i, j] := (X[i + 1, j] + X[i - 1, j] + X[i, j - 1]$$
$$+ X[i, j + 1]) \div 4$$

The pattern for updating $X[i,j]$ is shown in Figure 8-9, and is often called the *four-point iteration*. In three dimensions the pattern has six points.

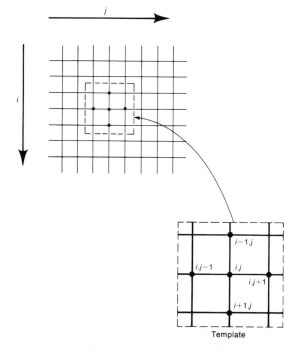

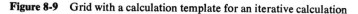

Figure 8-9 Grid with a calculation template for an iterative calculation

Although modern methods for solving partial differential equations have led to the development of iteration formulas with faster convergence properties than the ones given here, the formulas all have in common the characteristic of updating information at a grid point as a function of the values at nearby grid points. This observation led Slotnick to propose an array computer whose interconnection structure has the near-neighbor connections built in, as shown in Figure 8-10 (Slotnick, Borck, and McReynolds [62]).

The interconnection pattern that was actually built into the ILLIAC IV computer was greatly influenced by Slotnick's early research. The 64 processors are interconnected so that processor i is connected to processors $i - 1$, $i + 1$, $i - 8$ and $i + 8$ with addition taken modulo 64. When the processors are numbered as shown in Figure 8-10, we obtain the interior connections shown there plus others necessary to make cyclic shifts of unit distance or of distance 8.

Note that with these four cyclic shifts, any arbitrary cyclic shift can be constructed, and the number of shifts required is small compared to 64. In fact, every shift can be realized by a combination of no more than seven of the built-in cyclic shifts.

No other interconnection patterns are available in the ILLIAC IV. Thus, algorithms that require noncyclic data permutations are rather inefficient. While it is true that every permutation is realizable with the ILLIAC IV shifting and masking capability, some permutations may require as many as N mask-and-shift operations. Such permutations are effectively performed serially rather than in parallel, and thus are ill-suited to this type of interconnection pattern.

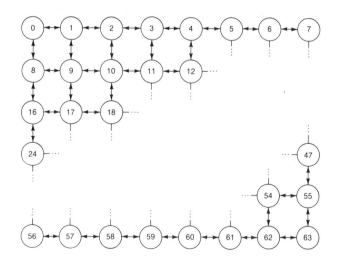

Figure 8-10 An 8 × 8 processor array designed for the four-point iteration

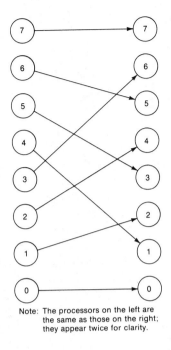

Note: The processors on the left are
the same as those on the right;
they appear twice for clarity.

Figure 8-11   The perfect-shuffle interconnection of eight processors

A more promising interconnection pattern is shown in Figure 8-11. It is called the *perfect shuffle*. The name is derived from the fact that the cards in a deck of playing cards undergo a perfect shuffle when the deck is divided into equal halves and the halves are combined into a single deck by interlacing the cards. Since bidirectional interconnections are normally not much more expensive than unidirectional interconnections we shall assume that the *inverse perfect shuffle* is available if the perfect shuffle is implemented. This is the permutation obtained by reversing the arrows in Figure 8-11. In many applications either will work as well; in some applications one of the two is favored over the other. For greatest flexibility, it appears to be advantageous to have both available.

There are a number of parallel algorithms that make effective use of the perfect shuffle or its inverse. The algorithms include algorithms for performing Fourier transforms, sorting, and matrix transposition. They are too specialized to include in full detail here, but we shall try to summarize the pertinent aspects. For a more complete discussion the reader is referred to Stone [71].

In the following discussion we shall assume that we have interconnections available for cyclic shifts of $+1$ and -1, and for the perfect shuffle and its inverse. The computations that we investigate have the general form shown here:

for $j := 1$ **step** 1 **until** $\log_2 N$ **do**
   begin
       Shuffle (Y);
       $Y[i] := F(Y[i + 1], Y[i]),$ (even i);
       $Y[i + 1] := G(Y[i + 1], Y[i]),$ (even i);
   end;

In this form, the vector Y is shuffled to align its components for parallel arithmetic. Then the functions F and G are applied to the even and odd elements, respectively. In general, the F and G functions depend both on i, the subscript of the arguments, and on j, the iteration number. Here we assume that F and G both operate on the old values of Y to produce the new values of Y, and that they act simultaneously.

A data-flow graph for this type of computation appears in Figure 8-12. Note that the data is stored initially in the N registers on the left of the figure. The data traverses a perfect-shuffle network, whereupon the F and G functions operate on pairs of data that occupy adjacent even-odd locations. The

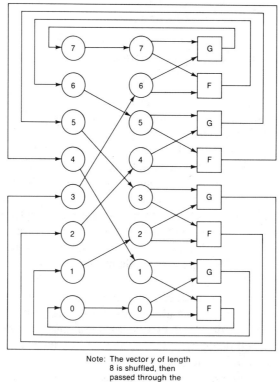

Note: The vector y of length
8 is shuffled, then
passed through the
F and G functions
and returned to place.

Figure 8-12 Data flow in parallel algorithm

results of the computation are returned to the registers on the left for another iteration. Figure 8-12 is intended to show the data flow, rather than the actual processor structure. We expect that an array computer will not have functional modules that evaluate F and G, but rather will compute these by means of stored programs, as we have illustrated previously. The data transfer between odd-even adjacent pairs is implementable with cyclical shifts of $+1$ and -1.

To give an intuitive feeling for the characteristics of the perfect shuffle, we show in Part *a* of Figure 8-13 how the influence of a datum stored initially in cell 0 is transmitted to other elements in the array after several iterations. After one iteration, the item originally in cell 4 has been combined with 0, and after two iterations those in 2 and 6 have been combined with 0 either directly or through interaction with 4. Finally, at the end of the third iteration, every element in the array has directly or indirectly been combined with the element originally in 0. But this property holds not only for the 0 cell, but for every cell in the array. More generally, for an array of size N, after $\log_2$ N perfect shuffles, every element has influenced every other element in the array. (This holds when N is a power of 2, but not for all N.) Part *b* of Figure 8-13 shows that after three shuffles in an array of size 8, the 0 element has been influenced by every other element in the array. Again this property holds not just for the 0 element but for every element. So the perfect shuffle network is something like an information-scattering network, in the sense that the interconnection pattern provides for complete communication among all processors in $\log_2$ N steps through the interconnection net.

To see how a network with good information-scattering properties is useful, consider the data-flow requirements of several important algorithms. For example, the Fourier transform of a set of N data points is such that each point in the transformed data depends on every input datum, and conversely, every input datum influences every transformed point. Any interconnection pattern used for a Fourier transform must provide for each input item to influence each item in the transformed data set. Thus it is easy to show that, with a pattern that provides for a cyclic shift of $+1$ and -1, on the order of N cyclic shifts at least are required to do a Fourier transform. But there is an algorithm due to Pease [68] that does the Fourier transform with the perfect-shuffle pattern in only $\log_2$ N iterations through a perfect-shuffle network. The algorithm is an adaptation of the fast Fourier transform, in which the F and G functions in Figure 8-12 do weighted sums of complex numbers. The fast Fourier transform algorithm requires on the order of N $\log_2$ N complex multiplications, which requires at least $\log_2$ N vector operations in an array computer that does N complex multiplications in parallel. Thus the perfect shuffle interconnection pattern provides a way to achieve the theoretical lower bound on computation time to within a constant factor. No other interconnection pattern can do better except to change the constant factor.

Another problem that has the need for a complete interchange of information is the problem of sorting N numbers. Sorting requires that each number be compared directly or indirectly with every other number. One expects that a perfect shuffle might be useful for such a purpose, and indeed this is the case. Batcher [68] discovered a very efficient parallel-sorting algorithm that was adapted to the array-processor configuration of Figure 8-12 by Stone [71]. The algorithm requires $(\log_2 N)^2$ passes through the processor, which is on the order of $\log_2 N$ more than one would expect. But no other interconnection pattern has been devised to date that eliminates the factor of

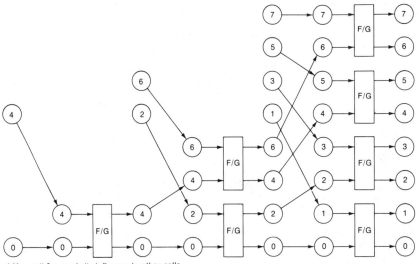

a) How cell 0 spreads its influence to other cells

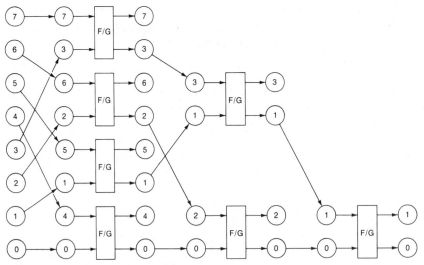

b) How other cells in the array influence cell 0

Figure 8-13

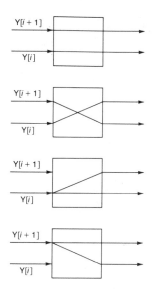

Figure 8-14 Possible cell states for cells in Lawrie's omega network

$\log_2$ N for the array processor, nor has it been shown that the factor of $\log_2$ N can be eliminated.

Lawrie [75] extended the capabilities of the perfect-shuffle type of connection pattern by considering what happens when each processor makes an individual decision on which F and G function to use. Lawrie's *omega network* is a perfect-shuffle network similar to Figure 8-12 that permits each processor to make one of four selections for data communication after each shuffle. They are shown in Figure 8-14, and are a straight-through connection, an interchange, copy $Y[i]$ to both outputs, and copy $Y[i + 1]$ to both outputs. Essentially, the F and G functions can be set independently to select either $Y[i]$ or $Y[i + 1]$. The motivation for this extension of the perfect-shuffle network is to provide a means for accessing rows and columns of a matrix and to access other data structures within matrices. This will become clearer later in this chapter where we discuss data-structure access. One capability of the omega network whose importance is immediately evident is the ability to perform arbitrary cyclic shifts of a vector of N elements in $\log_2$ N passes through the network. That is, for any values of s, $Y[i]$ can be moved to $Y[(s + i) \bmod N]$ in $\log_2$ N passes. Problem 8-4 (end of Section 8-3) shows how this can be done. Consequently, even though the omega network does not contain a cyclic shift within it, it can do arbitrary shifts very efficiently. Compare this to the ILLIAC IV connection pattern, which contains cyclic shifts of $\pm$ 1 and $\pm \sqrt{N}$. Such a pattern requires on the order of $\sqrt{N}$ passes to do an arbitrary shift, which is a function that grows faster than $\log_2$ N.

There is a large class of problems for which the inverse of a perfect shuffle appears to be attractive. This class is a special class of recurrence problems.

To show how the inverse of the perfect shuffle is used, we first illustrate the form of the recurrence equations, then show typical solutions for an array computer.

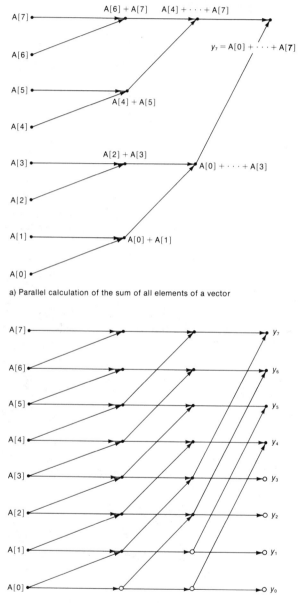

a) Parallel calculation of the sum of all elements of a vector

Note: Dark circles represent additions;
open circles represent null operations.

b) Parallel calculation of $y_i = y_{i-1} + A[i]$

Figure 8-15

First we show a simple example. To find the sum of the elements in a vector A, we typically use an iteration described by the following ALGOL-like statements:

$$SUM := 0;$$
for $i := 0$ **step** 1 **until** $N - 1$ **do**
$$SUM := SUM + A[i];$$

Now let y_i denote the value of sum after the ith iteration, and note that the iteration can be phrased mathematically in the form:

$$y_{-1} = 0$$
$$y_i = y_{i-1} + A[i];$$

This form of the algorithm is quite sequential, since we compute y_i before y_{i-1} for each i. It clearly requires time proportional to N to compute the value of y_N. But we know intuitively that we can compute y_N in only $\log_2$ N steps on a parallel computer with N processors, provided that we use a scheme like the one shown in Part a of Figure 8-15 for N = 8. Note that at the first step we sum even-odd adjacent pairs of elements, then we sum the sums of pairs at the second step, and finally sum the sums of four adjacent elements. Part b of Figure 8-15 shows a variation of this idea, in which we compute all values of y_i, $1 \le i \le 8$, simultaneously in $\log_2$ N steps. In this case, the nodes indicated by open circles do not form the sum of two operands, but merely pass through a single operand.

An array processor for computing the recurrence relations according to the scheme of Figure 8-15, Part b, is shown in Figure 8-16. It has the inverse perfect-shuffle interconnection between the nodes labeled "+" and those on the right, and it has a pattern that transmits the contents of Y[i] to Y[$i + 1$], which is cyclic shift by a unit amount. To perform the first stage of computation shown in Part b of Figure 8-15, each adder receives data from Y[i] and Y[$i - 1$] (except for the adder whose output is tied to line 0). We assume that each adder can be controlled by a local mask register, so that either Y[i] and Y[$i - 1$] will be added together (if the mask register contains the value 1), or the adder will merely pass through Y[i] (if the mask register contains the value 0). Thus the mask register permits some nodes to perform the operations of the circled nodes in Part b of Figure 8-15, while others perform the operation of the solid dot nodes. The general flow of the recursive-doubling algorithm in this type of array computer is:

initialize Y[i] to A[i], $(0 \le i \le N - 1)$;
for $j := 1$ **step** 1 **until** $\log_2$ N **do**
    begin Y[i] := Y[i] + Y[$i - 1$], (mask);
    inverse shuffle (Y);
    compute new mask;
end;

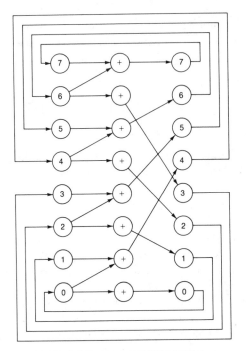

Note: The "+" can be any associative operator

Figure 8-16 An array computer ideally suited for recursive-doubling algorithms

In the first iteration, the sums computed are sums of adjacent elements of A. That is, $Y[i] = A[i] + A[i - 1]$. After the inverse shuffle, the items that are adjacent in Y are pairs of sums of elements of A, and, in fact, are $A[i] + A[i - 1]$ and $A[i - 2] + A[i - 3]$ in adjacent words, except in a few elements that represent special cases. Figure 8-17 shows the intermediate results in the computation and the intermediate values of the mask bits.

The reason this form of recurrence relation can be done in $\log_2 N$ steps is because addition is associative. That is, we can form the sum of N items by parenthesizing the N items arbitrarily into pairs without changing the result of the summation (provided that arithmetic is assumed to be done exactly). If the addition operation is replaced by any other associative operation, the same general form of the computation is still valid. Thus we can compute the product, the maximum, or the minimum of the elements of a vector in $\log_2 N$ steps because these operations involve associative operators. A list of the important cases appears in Table 8-4. Other forms, which do not have an associative operator, also appear in the table. Nevertheless, these forms can be placed in the same general framework as well. For example the linear recurrence $x_i = a_i x_{i-1} + b_i x_{i-2}$ can be changed into the form

Y	Mask	Sum	Inverse Shuffle	Mask	Sum	Inverse Shuffle	Mask	Sum	Inverse Shuffle
A[0] = $Y_{0,0}$	0	$Y_{0,0}$	$Y_{0,0}$	0	$Y_{0,0}$	$Y_{0,0}$	0	$Y_{0,0}$	$Y_{0,0} = y_0$
A[1] = $Y_{1,1}$	1	$Y_{0,1}$	$Y_{1,2}$	1	$Y_{0,2}$	$Y_{1,4}$	1	$Y_{0,4}$	$Y_{0,1} = y_1$
A[2] = $Y_{2,2}$	1	$Y_{1,2}$	$Y_{3,4}$	1	$Y_{1,4}$	$Y_{0,1}$	0	$Y_{0,1}$	$Y_{0,2} = y_2$
A[3] = $Y_{3,3}$	1	$Y_{2,3}$	$Y_{5,6}$	1	$Y_{3,6}$	$Y_{2,5}$	1	$Y_{0,5}$	$Y_{0,3} = y_3$
A[4] = $Y_{4,4}$	1	$Y_{3,4}$	$Y_{0,1}$	0	$Y_{0,1}$	$Y_{0,2}$	0	$Y_{0,2}$	$Y_{0,4} = y_4$
A[5] = $Y_{5,5}$	1	$Y_{4,5}$	$Y_{2,3}$	1	$Y_{0,3}$	$Y_{3,6}$	1	$Y_{0,6}$	$Y_{0,5} = y_5$
A[6] = $Y_{6,6}$	1	$Y_{5,6}$	$Y_{4,5}$	1	$Y_{2,5}$	$Y_{0,3}$	0	$Y_{0,3}$	$Y_{0,6} = y_6$
A[7] = $Y_{7,7}$	1	$Y_{6,7}$	$Y_{6,7}$	1	$Y_{4,7}$	$Y_{4,7}$	1	$Y_{0,7}$	$Y_{0,7} = y_7$

Figure 8-17 Intermediate values for recursive-doubling calculation of $y_i = y_{i-1} + A[i]$

($Y_{i,j}$ denotes $\sum_{k=i}^{k=j} A[k]$)

$$\begin{bmatrix} x_i \\ x_{i-1} \end{bmatrix} = \begin{bmatrix} a_i & b_i \\ 1 & 0 \end{bmatrix} \begin{bmatrix} x_{i-1} \\ x_{i-2} \end{bmatrix}$$

This is a vector-matrix equation which can be expressed as:

$$X_i = A_i \times X_{i-1}$$

where the vector $X_i = (x_i, x_{i-1})^t$, and A_i is the corresponding 2×2 matrix shown above. The latter form has a single operator, a matrix multiplication, which is associative. The latter form can be fitted directly into the form we require. This schema has been called *recursive doubling* by Stone [73] and by Kogge and Stone [73]. The interested reader should refer to these papers for further details.

At this point we have shown algorithms that use various permutations including cyclic shifts, the perfect shuffle, and the inverse perfect shuffle. These interconnections appear to be the most important ones, because they are well-suited to a variety of applications. At this writing these are only the interconnection schemes that have been implemented, either as described here or in an equivalent form. Processors that are dedicated to highly specialized algorithms should have interconnections designed for their algorithms. Such interconnections may depart radically from those described in this section.

Data Structures

Efficient use of array computers depends not only on the raw computational ability of the processor array, but on the ability to move data vectors from memory to the processors where computation is performed, and then return results to memory. Part of the data-movement facility is embedded in the interconnection patterns among the processors as indicated above. Still another part is embedded in the access mechanism to memory. By using

TABLE 8-4. FUNCTIONS SUITABLE FOR RECURSIVE DOUBLING

Function	Description
$X_i = X_{i-1} + a_i$	Sum the elements of a vector
$X_i = X_{i-1} \times a_i$	Multiply the elements of a vector
$X_i = \min(X_{i-1}, a_i)$	Find the minimum
$X_i = \max(X_{i-1}, a_i)$	Find the maximum
$X_i = a_i X_{i-1} + b_i$	First-order linear recurrence, inhomogeneous
$X_i = a_i X_{i-1} + b_i X_{i-2}$	Second-order linear recurrence
$X_i = a_i X_{i-1} + b_i X_{i-2} + \cdots$	Any-order linear recurrence homogeneous or inhomogeneous
$X_i = (a_i X_{i-1} + b_i)/(c_i X_{i-1} + d_i)$	First-order rational fraction recurrence
$X_i = a_i + b_i/X_{i-1}$	Special case of first-order rational fraction
$X_i = \sqrt{(X_{i-1})^2 + (a_i)^2}$	Vector norm

clever tricks in accessing memory it is possible to reduce some of the more intricate data-routing requirements to much simpler ones that can be carried out very efficiently.

The basic constraint that hampers peak utilization of memory is that each memory module can honor at most one request per memory cycle. In the most favorable circumstances, the N operands of a vector instruction lie in distinct memory modules, and thus can be fetched simultaneously. In the least favorable circumstances, the N operands all lie in a single memory module, and must be fetched sequentially. In the latter case, N memory cycles rather than a single cycle are required, and the efficiency of computation is quite low.

For one-dimensional computations, the vectors involved are normally stored so that vectors of length N have one element in each memory module. Longer vectors are stored analogously by distributing the elements cyclically among the memories.

Serious difficulties arise in two-dimensional problems. Typical of these are matrix computations in which rows and columns are both treated as vectors in intermediate calculations. Suppose, for example, that A is an $N \times N$ matrix to be processed on an N-processor array computer. Part a of Figure 8-18 shows A stored in a format known as *straight storage*. The figure shows a four-processor system, and the four memories are indicated as the four columns. Each memory is assumed to have its locations addressed starting at 0, and increasing as shown. Thus, there are N different words with address i, one in each of the memories, and this collection of N words forms the ith row of the system of N memories.

The figure shows rows of A stored in rows of memory, with rows aligned. In this case any row of A can be accessed in a single cycle, but N cycles are required to access a column because each column lies completely within one memory module.

Part b of Figure 8-18, on the other hand, shows a storage format known as *skewed storage,* in which successive rows of A are cyclically shifted by unit amounts. In this figure we see that each column of A is distributed across the memory modules. Hence, both the rows of A and the columns of A can be accessed in unit time. In row mode, instructions broadcast a row address, and that address is the actual address of an access. For column instructions, the vector of index registers private to each processor is preloaded with the index vector 0, 1, 2, . . . , N − 1. To access column i, this index vector is shifted cyclically until the 0 is aligned to memory i. Then the address of row 0 of the matrix is broadcast with an indication that indexing is required. The broadcast address is then modified locally at each processor, by adding the index element to it, and access is made at the indexed address. The figure shows the access of column 2. After both row and column access, the vector obtained is a cyclic shift of what normally is desired. The leading element of row or column i is in processor i, not in processor 0. A cyclic shift is often required to bring the data into position for further manipulation.

Skewed storage is a relatively inexpensive way to enhance the processing capability of an array processor. It does force cyclic shifting to be done as

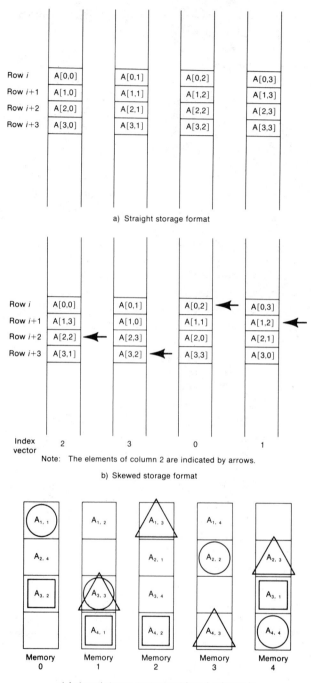

a) Straight storage format

Note: The elements of column 2 are indicated by arrows.

b) Skewed storage format

c) A skewed storage arrangement for a 4 × 4 array in five memory modules. Circles indicate a diagonal, triangles indicate a column, and squares indicate a square subarray.

Figure 8-18 Storage formats

part of the overhead to deskew skewed vectors, so skewed storage is not preferred if algorithms require access to rows only or to columns only. In either of these cases, the storage format used should be straight storage with either the rows or the columns stored across the memories. The skewed storage concept as described here is due to David Kuck in unpublished work that occurred during the early development of the ILLIAC IV.

Later work by Budnik and Kuck [71] showed how N + 1 memories can be connected to N computers to permit access to many different substructures within a matrix. An example of this idea is shown in Part *c* of Figure 8-18. Here there are five memories, but only four are accessed at any given time. Each row of a 4 × 4 matrix is stored across the memories, and each row is skewed by two elements with respect to the previous row. Obviously the elements of each row are simultaneously accessible since they lie in distinct memories and so are the elements of each column (elements in triangles). But this arrangement provides for access to diagonals (circled elements) and to square subarrays (squares) as well. Making use of this idea requires sophisticated and clever ways of removing the N desired items from the N + 1 items reported by the N + 1 memories, and then routing the items to the correct processors. The Burroughs Scientific Processor incorporates this type of storage mechanism in a system that has 17 memories and 16 processors.

At this point we turn attention to the use of the features described above in realistic program fragments. To give some intuition about the use of data structures in algorithms for array computers, we show various ways of solving simple examples.

The first example illustrates how to form row sums and column sums for two-dimensional arrays. In straight-storage format, the column sums of A, an N × N matrix, can be computed and stored in the vector SUM by means of the following program.

```
SUM[k] := 0,(0 ≤ k ≤ N − 1);
for i := 0 step 1 until N − 1 do
    begin
    comment the index is set to obtain the next element of each
        column by fetching the next row;
    SUM[k] := SUM[k] + A[i,k],(0 ≤ k ≤ N − 1);
    comment A[i,k] is added to the sum;
    end;
```

In this algorithm, the N sums are computed simultaneously as a collection of sums, but each individual sum is computed sequentially by marching down a column. Each memory fetch brings up a row of N items, and each item fetched is added to its respective column sums.

To form row sums, we might fetch one row at a time, then sum the elements in that row. To do this we shall use cyclic shifts, and use the notation SHIFT(A, $\pm i$) to indicate that element A is shifted to the processor whose index is greater or less by i, for $+i$ and $-i$, respectively. Since the shift is cyclic, the indices are taken modulo N, where N is the number of processors. The algorithm is then:

for $i := 0$ **step** 1 **until** N $-$ 1 **do**
    begin
        TEMP[k] := A[i,k],$(0 \leq k \leq$ N $-$ 1);
        for $j := 1$ **step** j **until** N $-$ 1 **do**
            begin
            comment compute the sum elements in row i of A by
                recursive doubling;
                TEMP[k] := TEMP[k] + SHIFT(TEMP[$k - j$],j),$(j \leq k \leq$ N $-$ 1)
            end j loop;
        SUM[i] := TEMP[N $-$ 1];
    end i loop;

The vector named TEMP is a vector consisting of one element in each processor. The inner loop shifts a copy of TEMP and adds it to itself, where the shift amount is initially 1, then becomes 2, 4, etc., following the scheme in Part a of Figure 8-15. This algorithm requires a time proportional to N $\log_2$ N rather than to N, which makes it much slower than the column-sum algorithm. A small trick yields a row-sum algorithm that almost matches the column-sum algorithm. The idea is to fetch diagonals and sum all rows simultaneously, to obtain a higher degree of parallelism. The fast row-sum algorithm is the following:

comment the A matrix is stored in a straight format with
    the kth column of A, A[0,k] through A[N $-$ 1,k], stored in the
    kth processor. LOCINDEX[k] is the local index register in processor k.
    SUM[k] collects the row sum of the kth row sequentially as it moves from
    processor to processor;

LOCINDEX[k] := k,$(0 \leq k \leq$ N $-$ 1);
comment LOCINDEX has been initialized to enable us to fetch
    diagonals;
SUM[k] := 0,$(0 \leq k \leq$ N $-$ 1);
for $i := 0$ **step** 1 **until** N $-$ 1 **do**
    begin
        SUM[k] := SUM[k] + A[LOCINDEX[k],k],$(0 \leq k \leq$ N $-$ 1);
        comment now shift the running sum to the next processor,
            and with it, shift the LOCINDEX register so that
            it continues to fetch an item indexed from the same
            row of A as it traverses the processors;
        SUM[k] := SHIFT(SUM[k],1),$(0 \leq k \leq$ N $-$ 1);
        LOCINDEX[k] := SHIFT(LOCINDEX[k],1),$(0 \leq k \leq$ N $-$ 1);
    end;
    comment the sum of the elements of row k is contained
    in SUM[k], and is found in the kth processor;

In this example, each fetch of a vector of elements from A brings up a diagonal of A. There are N distinct diagonal slices of A fetched in the inner loop, one for each iteration of the loop, and the N slices contain all of the elements of A. SUM[0] starts in processor 0 with the value of A[0,0] then moves to processor 1 when it obtains A[0,1]. At the last iteration it obtains A[0,N − 1], and then moves cyclically around to processor 0 at the termination of the algorithm. The value 0 for the corresponding element of LOCINDEX moves with SUM[0] as it traverses the processor array, thus guaranteeing that SUM[0] obtains elements of row 0 at each step. Note that SUM[1] starts with A[1,1] and successively obtains A[1,2], A[1,3], . . . , A[1,N − 1], and A[1,0]. The value 1 in LOCINDEX moves with SUM[1]. This algorithm requires a time proportional to N.

Through these examples we see the interplay of the data structures, the local index registers, and the interconnections. Some of the problems given at the end of this section explore these examples and others in which skewed storage is used as well.

Array Computers in Perspective

The discussion thus far illustrates the general characteristics of array processors, plus several techniques for increasing their effectiveness on particular problems. For a problem to be suitable for array computation it must have at least the following three characteristics:

1. The computation must be describable by vector instructions such that a majority of computation time is spent with many identical operations in action simultaneously on different data.
2. High-speed data routing between processors must be possible to do with the available processor interconnections.
3. Operands manipulated simultaneously must be capable of being fetched simultaneously from memory.

If any of these three conditions is not satisfied for a computation, then the computation may run essentially serially in an array processor. The class of computations that satisfy the points above is a special class of computations, and hence the array processor is not a general-purpose computer. The future challenge for array processors is to increase their flexibility while retaining their efficiency for vector computations. To this end, various extensions to the ideas presented in this section are currently being implemented and evaluated. One such approach is the coupling of 16 array processors, each with 64 processors, so that the arrays can act independently on different vector computations or gang together in various ways to act on large vector computations in a proposed follow-up to ILLIAC IV known as the Phoenix computer [Feierbach and Stevenson, 78]. This gives additional flexibility to the otherwise rigid requirements of an array computer.

Some application areas may never be treated by array computers because they are so ill-matched to the capabilities and constraints of array computers.

One such area is information retrieval. It is tempting to believe that an N-processor system can search a data base N times faster than a one-processor system, because N pieces of data can be inspected simultaneously. However, serial searching can be so efficient, due to techniques known as binary searching and hash-addressing, that the actual speed increase when an array computer is used for searching is more like $\log_2$ N. Karp and Miranker [68] observed this behavior for a typical search problem with realistic assumptions. Many search problems fit their assumptions, so their results hold for a broad class of search problems. For small N, a speed increase of $\log_2$ N is acceptable, but for large N it is intolerably low. This suggests that information retrieval and other applications involving file searching are better suited to serial computers or to computers with a low degree of parallelism. Of course, some search problems fail to satisfy the Karp and Miranker assumptions, and these may be quite reasonable to implement on parallel computers. A search for the nearest match in an unstructured data base has these qualities, and thus may be suited for parallel computers. Air traffic control is representative of an application involving this type of search, since a major problem of control is the identification of aircraft in close proximity to each other.

PROBLEMS

8-1.   Consider the perfect shuffle of $N = 2^m$ items where the items are indexed from 0 to $N - 1$. Let the integer i have the binary expansion $i_{m-1} \times 2^{m-1} + i_{m-2} \times 2^{m-2} + \ldots + i_0 \times 2^0$. Show that item i is moved by the shuffle to the position formerly occupied by item $i_{m-2} \times 2^{m-1} + i_{m-3} \times 2^{m-2} + \ldots + i_0 \times 2^1 + i_{m-1} \times 2^0$.

8-2.   Show that an 8×8 matrix can be transposed in three perfect shuffles when it is stored as a vector of length 64. Prove that m shuffles transpose a matrix of size $2^m \times 2^m$.

8-3.   Consider the reverse binary permutation, which is required for Fourier transforms. In this permutation, item $i = i_{m-1} \times 2^{m-1} + i_{m-2} \times 2^{m-2} + \ldots + i_0 \times 2^0$ is moved to position $i_{m-1} \times 2^0 + i_{m-2} \times 2^1 + \ldots + i_0 \times 2^{m-1}$. That is, the item originally in position i is moved to position i', where the binary representation of i' is simply the reverse of the binary representation of i. Suppose you can perform a cyclic shift of any amount in unit time. Show how to do the reverse binary permutation of N items, $N = 2^r$, in an N-processor computer with only $2r$ cyclic shifts of arbitrary amounts.

8-4.   We wish to show that an omega network can perform arbitrary cyclic shifts of a vector of length N, $N = 2^r$ for some r, in at most r steps through the network. Show by example how to obtain shifts of size 1, 2, and 3 in two steps for $N = 4$. When two elements are transmitted straight through an F-G cell in an omega network, we say the cell is in the 0 state, and if the elements are interchanged, we say the cell is in the 1 state. Consider states of the cells visited by the item initially in cell 0. Show that the states of the cells it visits are equal in value to the successive binary bits in the representation of the amount of the cyclic shift, and that this holds for all N that are powers of 2.

8-5. Show that an omega network can perform permutations of the form $p(i) = (t \cdot i) \bmod N$, where t is an odd positive integer less than n. Show by means of example for $t = 3, 5,$ and 7 for N = 16.

8-6. Find a formula for the setting of the cells in an omega network for any N that is a power of 2 to do an arbitrary cyclical shift of size s.

8-7. Construct a vector matrix multiplication algorithm, using the vector ALGOL-like notation, to do the computation $C = A \times B$ where A, B and C are each $N \times N$ matrices, and A is stored by rows and B by columns. Try to obtain an algorithm that requires on the order of N^2 steps for N processors.

8-8. Construct an algorithm to compute $C = A \times B$ as in 8-7, but this time let A and B be stored in skewed format. Again, try to construct an algorithm whose running time is on the order of N^2 steps for N processors.

8-4. MULTIPROCESSORS

In this section we look into the organization and control of multiprocessors, which fall into the MIMD class of computers within Flynn's taxonomy. The interesting problems for these machines are quite different from those of vector computers. Multiprocessors are suitable for a much larger class of computations than are array computers because multiprocessors are inherently more flexible. It is relatively straightforward to fit a computation to a multiprocessor computer, which is not the case for vector computations on array computers. However, to attain high-efficiency computation in a multiprocessor system, one has to solve problems of task synchronization and task scheduling. In some cases, improper synchronization or scheduling can lead to gross inefficiency, and in extreme situations of improper synchronization, computation may cease entirely. This is in sharp contrast to array computers. An array processor automatically synchronizes its processors because all processors obey the same single instruction stream. Moreover, there is no task scheduling problem since only one task at a time is performed on an array processor, rather than several different competing and conflicting tasks as in the case of the multiprocessor. Consequently the array processor's constraints eliminate the problems that surround the multiprocessor, though at the expense of flexibility.

In this section we look at the overall details of a multiprocessor system and investigate methods for performing computation on such a machine. We first focus on the structure of the system, both hardware and software, which is

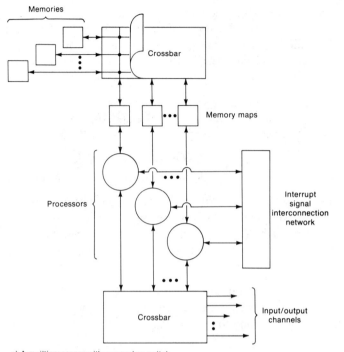

a) A multiprocessor with a crossbar switch
   arrangement to connect every processor to every
   memory module

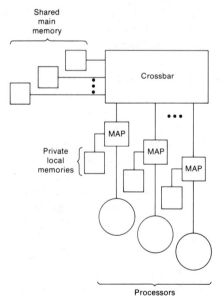

b) A multiprocessor with private local memories.
   The input/output system and processor intercommunication
   lines are not shown

Figure 8-19

necessary to support parallelism. Portions of the system not covered here are presumed to be similar to serial computers. The first part of this section illustrates hardware design methodologies for multiprocessor computers. Techniques for memory sharing are the focus of the second part. Next we investigate the problems of controlling parallel computation and look further into the FORK and JOIN instructions, as well as other synchronization operations. Finally we indicate how to structure computations so as to localize activity to particular regions of a multiprocessor, thus reducing interference among separate tasks.

Structure of Multiprocessors

The notion of connecting several processors together to create a powerful parallel processor appears to be primarily a problem in the hardware design. But this appearance is deceptive, because the implementation of such an idea requires a thorough consideration of hardware, operating systems, and ultimate applications in order to make an effective parallel computer. In this subsection we describe two different models for a multiprocessor: one a *tightly coupled* multiprocessor in which data can be communicated from one processor to any other processor at rates on the order of the bandwidth of memory, the other a *distributed* computer system in which communication delays between two processors depend on whether the processors are locally connected to each other or are connected through one or more layers of a routing network.

The first model of a multiprocessor computer is shown in Part a of Figure 8-19. There are N processors in this system, M memories, and P input/output channels. The interconnections among these modules as shown in the system are extensive. A switch connects every processor to every memory. The switch is shown as an N $\times$ M crossbar where each of the NM crosspoints is a potential connection. As usual, we assume that each memory can respond to a single request during one memory cycle, so that no memory services two processors simultaneously. However, one processor may transmit data simultaneously to two memories, if there is some reason to do so. A similar crossbar of size N $\times$ P connects the processors to the data channels and input/output buses.

Although we show only a single line from each memory and processor into the N $\times$ M crossbar, this line has sufficient bandwidth to transmit whole words of data instead of single bits. Thus one line in the figure may correspond to roughly 32 to 64 wires in a real implementation. Similarly the N $\times$ P crossbar has many wires per interconnection. These crossbars have a complexity that is enormous as N and M become large. For purposes of efficiency, we expect M to be at least as large as N, so that all N processors can gain access to the memories simultaneously Thus the number of crosspoints in the N $\times$ M switch grows as N^2; for sufficiently large N, the cost of the crossbar dominates the cost of the N processors and M memories.

This model of a computer system is similar to many early multiprocessor models that contain relatively few processors, usually only up to four. One very ambitious project of this type is the C.mmp multiprocessor at Carnegie-Mellon, with 16 processors [Wulf and Bell, 73]. Clearly, the crossbar is a potential problem as the number of processors grows, in that its cost grows faster than the additional processing power. Moreover, because of conflicts in access through the crossbar, useful computational power grows less than linearly with the number of processors in some situations. Hence the crossbar is not the ultimate answer for very large-scale multiprocessors.

One way to avoid some of the problems of the crossbar is illustrated in Part *b* of Figure 8-19. This system still retains a crossbar, but the major addition in this system is the use of a local memory in each processor. The objective here is to direct the majority of the memory accesses made by a processor to its own local memory rather than to main memory. This reduces traffic through the crossbar, and reduces conflicts and contention at that point. With less traffic going through the crossbar, the crossbar itself can be reduced in complexity and in size to bring its cost more in line with the costs of the remainder of the system. By being less tightly coupled than a pure crossbar, this system stands to gain performance.

While the notion of using a local memory is obviously a good one for the system shown in Part *b* of Figure 8-19, just how to implement such a memory is not immediately apparent. Under ideal circumstances, data that are being heavily accessed by a particular processor should migrate automatically to that processor's local memory without any specific requirement for a program to force this to happen. A less satisfactory solution is to have each processor make specific requests for data to be transferred to local memory when it is about to engage in a series of accesses on that data.

There are two severe problems with automatic data migration that have held back development of local memory with automatic migration. These are:

1. Each processor has direct access only to its own local memory and to main memory. If processor 1 attempts to access an item that is resident in processor 2's local memory, processor 1 will possibly obtain the wrong value of the item, since its access request will not be directed to processor 2's local memory.
2. Automatic migration appears to work well in a single-processor system, where there are no conflicting demands on data. This mode of operation is covered in somewhat more detail in Chapter 12 under the subject of cache memory. In a multiprocessor system, however, the problem is more complex, because two or more processors may each make heavy accesses on the same data. These data then cannot be placed in either local memory and must therefore be placed in a more remote shared memory. The result may be severe performance degradation.

Solving these two problems is a nontrivial difficulty for computer designers, and remains a challenge to date. One interesting approach to resolving the problems has been implemented in the S-1 computer now in development at Lawrence Livermore Laboratories. (The structure in Part *b* of Figure 8-19 is derived from the S-1 computer.) The idea is to control the type of access to memory through the use of special instructions, which by distinguishing between shared and nonshared variables force memory accesses to go to shared memory when necessary, and otherwise direct accesses to local memory whenever possible.

The LOAD instruction is therefore split into two different LOAD instructions — an ordinary LOAD and a LOAD SHARED-VARIABLE. The LOAD instruction directs its access first to local memory to determine if the datum is there, and if not, the datum is retrieved from main memory. A LOAD SHARED-VARIABLE instruction is forced to go to main memory without checking local memory. This guarantees that all processors have access to the current value of all shared variables.

Changing the value of a shared variable can be done in several ways. For STORE operations, one could use instructions similar to those used for LOAD operations, and have an ordinary STORE for nonshared variables while having a STORE SHARED-VARIABLE instruction for shared variables. A perfectly reasonable solution is avoid the distinction between shared and nonshared variables for STORE operations, and store all data both in main memory and in local memory whenever a STORE occurs. STORE instructions occur much less frequently than LOAD instructions, so that performance degradation due to directing all STOREs to main memory is not a major problem. Later in this chapter we shall investigate the use of shared variables as control variables called *semaphores*, which places very strict constraints on how they can be accessed.

The main conclusion we draw in comparing Parts *a* and *b* of Figure 8-19 is that the effect of the local memory is to permit higher performance. This is because data can move closer to the point of computation in Part *b* of this figure, where shorter delays and higher bandwidths are achievable than is possible if the data must reside in a more remote main memory accessible only through a crossbar network, where contention reduces the available bandwidth.

Since local memory is apparently a good idea, then why not exploit it even further? This has been followed up recently in several projects, one of which, the Cm* project at Carnegie-Mellon University, is depicted in Figure 8-20 [Swan, Fuller, and Siewiorek, 77]. Part *a* of this figure shows one *computer module*, the computational building block of the system. It consists of a processor, local memory, local I/O devices, and an interface to the rest of the network, known as a *local switch* (*Slocal* in Cm* terminology). A computer module presumably represents a system that can be fabricated on a single integrated circuit by the mid-1980s. As such it is a much higher-level basic component than are the gates and registers traditionally used as components in computer systems. The major unconventional characteristic of a computer module is the local switch. This device intercepts references from the processor to memory and I/O devices, and redirects these references either to the local memory and I/O for local operations or to the MAP bus if the accesses go to more remote computer modules. This system is called a *distributed* or *loosely-coupled* system.

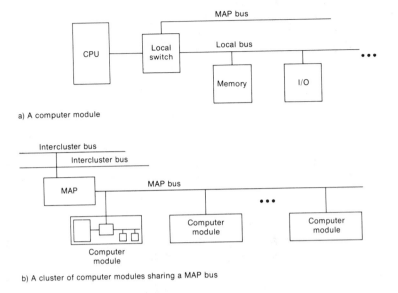

a) A computer module

b) A cluster of computer modules sharing a MAP bus

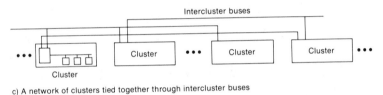

c) A network of clusters tied together through intercluster buses

Figure 8-20   The structure of the Cm* multiprocessor

Computer modules are connected together by two levels of buses, as indicated in Parts *b* and *c* of Figure 8-20. The lowest level of interconnection, shown in Part *b*, connects several modules together in a cluster that shares a single MAP bus. Clustering enhances the ability of processors to operate cooperatively on shared data since it brings together a pool of memory and processors, with very low overhead incurred on accesses from one local bus within the cluster to another in the same cluster. However the MAP bus is a bottleneck since at most one transaction at a time can use this bus. So contention for the bus increases, as the number of modules in a cluster increases, to such an extent that it does not increase performance to add computer modules to a cluster beyond a certain point. For the bandwidths and transaction frequencies in Cm*, Swan, Fuller, and Siewiorek [77] report that clusters in Cm* should be configured with between 1 and 14 modules per cluster, with the major consideration in limiting clusters to 14 modules being one of reliability. A cluster is sensitive to a failure that disables the MAP bus, since one failure on this bus disables the entire cluster.

To facilitate very large numbers of processors while limiting a cluster to 12 processors, Cm* has intercluster buses at the highest level of interconnection, as shown in Part *c* of Figure 8-20. The MAP detects memory references that cannot be honored on a local bus. These are redirected onto an intercluster bus to another MAP, which then places the memory reference onto its MAP bus. At this point the reference behaves much like an intercluster reference.

The two levels of interconnection of Cm* represents a dramatic departure from the one level of C.mmp. The C.mmp structure is such that each processor can access any item in memory in one memory cycle, in the absence of conflicting accesses caused by other processors. There is strong empirical evidence that most programs exhibit "local" behavior in the sense that memory references tend to be concentrated in particular regions at any given time, and the regions of activity change as the programs move from one phase to another. C.mmp provides more capability than programs actually use, and as a result its crossbar is a liability in terms of being a bottleneck, an expensive component, and a critical module whose failure causes total system failure. Cm* has a structure that takes advantage of local reference patterns. The idea is that as a program enters a phase in which it accesses particular parts of memory, these data will be placed in that processor's local memory. At that time, most memory references will be honored from local memory, thus reducing requests on the MAP bus and the intercluster buses to a negligible amount. If data are to be treated by several processors simultaneously, the data and processors are grouped into a single cluster if possible. This type of arrangement increases activity on the MAP bus, but the intercluster bus is still largely free of accesses. The intercluster bus of Cm* serves the same functional purpose of the crossbar of C.mmp in that it provides a way for each processor to access memory anywhere else in the system. But because most of the activity in Cm* is local in a computer module or concentrated in a cluster, the intercluster bus need not sustain a very high bandwidth, and is not a source of contention to the degree of the crossbar of C.mmp. Reliability of Cm* is potentially much greater than that of C.mmp, because Cm* can continue to operate in a degraded mode in the event of a failure of an intercluster bus or, in fact, of any bus in the system. Note that Part *c* of Figure 8-20 shows a Cm* structure with several intercluster buses, which gives even greater protection from bus failures than does a single bus.

This discussion of multiprocessors has centered on the structure of the systems, and has omitted a number of details of implementation specific to C.mmp and Cm*. The key idea brought out is that as processors increase in number, it is essential to structure the multiprocessor to take advantage of local reference patterns in some way.

Shared-memory Systems in Multiprocessors

In both C.mmp and Cm* there are modules called *memory maps* that direct memory references to specific regions. In this subsection we describe a general scheme for implementing memory maps and focus on their functional behavior. The purpose of a memory map is to translate an address produced by a processor into the address of a specific memory cell somewhere in the multiprocessor system. The memory maps shown for C.mmp direct processor references to specific memory modules. Cm* actually has two levels of maps. The local switch contains one such map that switches processor accesses either to the local bus or onto the MAP bus. The MAP performs a similar function at the next level. It receives access requests from the MAP bus, and redirects them to specific processors in the same cluster or onto an intercluster bus. While the different memory maps in these two systems differ in specific details, they all exhibit similar functional behavior when they operate on addresses.

The reason for including memory maps in a multiprocessor system is that programs should not, in general, reference specific physical locations in memory during execution, because this implies that the physical storage occupied by a program and by its data must be fixed during the execution of the program. In a parallel computation environment, the precise memory requirements for a group of programs in execution cannot be predicted ahead of time. In case we reach an impasse in execution, we must be able to remove items from physical memory or to move and compact items in physical memory in order to make room for new items. The memory map provides the necessary facilities for dealing with the memory problem, because the actual physical locations occupied by a program and data can be varied dynamically during program execution. Should data be moved, then the map function must be changed to reflect this change, so that the memory map can correctly translate program references to the data into true physical addresses.

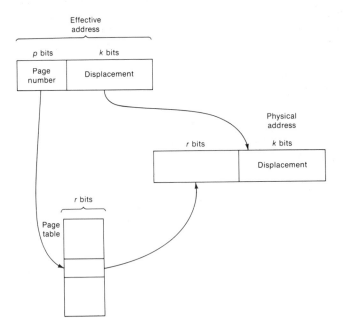

Figure 8-21 A typical paging scheme

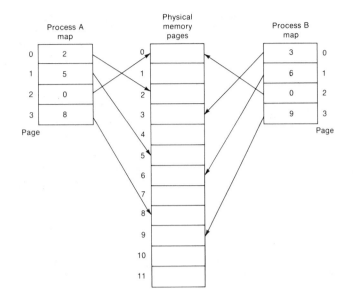

Figure 8-22 Example of paging used for memory sharing

The memory map also gives a convenient facility for permitting two or more programs to share data. The technique here is to set the map functions of two or more cooperating programs in such a way that references to the shared data are mapped into the same physical addresses of the data. References to private data are mapped into physical locations that are distinct for each program. Thus, programs can share specific data without sharing all data.

A reasonably straightforward implementation of memory mapping is the paging scheme illustrated in Figure 8-21. Here the addresses presented to the map are divided into two fields, one denoted *page number* and the other denoted *displacement within page*. The page number is used as the index of a page register whose contents replace the page number of the address. The resulting address is the physical address of the reference. Note that if the displacement field has k bits, then the displacement within page can vary from 0 to $2^k - 1$. Also, since the map function cannot alter displacement, items can be moved in memory only in contiguous blocks of size 2^k, which are called *pages*, and from which this mapping scheme takes its name. Figure 8-22 shows two processes sharing their page 2, while accessing distinct memory for other pages.

Consider how this scheme is implemented in the memory map of C.mmp. The processor produces an address of an item, which is translated by the map into a physical address. The crossbar breaks this address into two fields: One of them selects a specific cross-point, which in turn is connected to a particular memory module, and the other field indicates a physical word in the memory module. The first field then determines the routing through

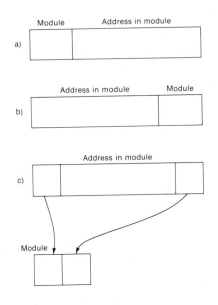

Figure 8-23 Module-selection schemes for decoding physical addresses

the crossbar, while the second field alone is transmitted over this route to the memory module.

The decoding function used by the crossbar has remarkable influence on the reliability, expandability, and efficiency of execution in a multiprocessor, so that it is worthwhile to explore this more carefully. Figure 8-23 shows three different decoding functions. The first function (Part *a*) extracts the leading *m* bits from a physical address and uses this as an index to select a particular memory module from a collection of 2^m modules. The remaining (lower-order) bits select an address within the module. This scheme is similar to the paging scheme, with contiguous storage addresses of size 2^r lying within one module. The second scheme (Part *b*) reverses the order of the two fields, so that the least significant *m* bits are used to select a memory module and the remaining (higher-order) *r* bits select an address within the module. Now addresses are interlaced among the memories so that a sequence of increasing physical addresses selects each of the memory modules in cyclical fashion in the order of increasing module index.

These two schemes represent extremes in the choice of decoding functions. The first scheme places contiguous addresses together, increasing the probability of memory-access conflict when two or more processors are sharing data within the memory. The second scheme tends to reduce storage conflicts, particularly accesses by several processors to shared data, because a data structure tends to be uniformly distributed among the modules. Sharing a single item, of course, produces conflicts if that item is accessed with great frequency, but this type of sharing is less usual than the sharing of moderate-size programs and data structures.

On the basis of the memory-conflict argument, the second of the two schemes appears to be preferable. However, this scheme is susceptible to reliability and expandability problems. Note that there must be 2^m modules present for this scheme to work, and a failure of any single module almost certainly causes total failure of the entire system. In the first system, the system can work with any number of modules from 1 to 2^r, provided that the decoding function identifies invalid address references, should a non-existent module index be generated. Also, if a module fails, the system can still function, though with less memory and degraded performance. The failed module is simply removed from the system and the system is restarted in such a way that the memory maps never produce physical addresses in the failed module.

Each of these schemes has been used in practice, and no single philosophy dominates. The third scheme (Part c of Figure 8-23) suggests a possible compromise. Here the module-index field is the concatenation of two fields, one from the least significant bits and one from the most significant bits. If the least significant field has size k, addresses are interlaced among groups of 2^k memory modules, which tends to reduce memory-access conflicts to a block of shared data. System expansion has to be done in blocks of 2^k modules, and a single failure disables an entire block of 2^k modules. If we use $k = 2$ or $k = 3$, then we obtain a reasonable compromise while the total number of memory modules in the system can be much larger than 2^k. The third decoding scheme or a variant of it appears to be the most attractive for systems with a large number of modules.

Besides the approaches exemplified by C.mmp and Cm* there are other approaches to multiprocessing, quite different from these, that are worthy of mention. Flynn, Podvin, and Shimizu [70] describe a system in which a pool of arithmetic and functional units is shared by several instruction streams, which is quite different from the notion of pooling and sharing memory as exemplified in C.mmp. Kuck, Muraoka, and Chen [72] propose a system more tightly coupled than C.mmp, in which tasks performed are individual arithmetic operations, as opposed to the much larger tasks performed within C.mmp and Cm*. The overhead to start up a new task on a processor is sufficiently great, for both C.mmp and Cm*, that it is not realistic to break tasks into such small operations as individual arithmetic operations. Kuck, Muraoka, and Chen [72] report that there are many opportunities for parallelism to be exploited when tasks are single arithmetic operations; but the work has yet to be advanced to the implementation stage, so as to establish that task-switching overhead can be done efficiently at this level.

Interprocessor Control

Two major questions have received the greatest attention in the literature and have influenced present approaches. The first question concerns what happens when two or more processors are in execution concurrently and must cooperate during the computation. Here the concern lies in synchronization of the processors so that the parallel computation can be carried out correctly. The second problem area concerns techniques for creating and terminating parallel execution paths within a program. We explore each of these and indicate how the problem can be solved using similar tools.

To illustrate an example of the first problem, we propose to perform a summation in parallel. The program is to form the sum of the elements of the vector $V[i]$, $1 \leq i \leq N$. To do this in parallel, the program forks into N branches, each of which performs the statement

$$SUM := SUM + V[i]$$

for i varying from 1 to N. Without synchronization and interlocking, the execution might occur as follows:

1. Processor 1 fetches the value of SUM from memory.
2. Processor 2 fetches the value of SUM from memory.
3. Processor 1 adds $V[i_1]$ to its private value of SUM and restores the new value of SUM in memory.
4. Processor 2 adds $V[i_2]$ to its private value of SUM, different now from the value in memory, and restores it in memory.

This sequence of instructions produces incorrect results, because the effect of adding $V[i_1]$ by processor 1 has been lost. The problem arises because processors 1 and 2 copy the value of SUM and operate on their private copies. For the program to be correct, a processor must be able to fetch and update the value of SUM without any intervening memory references to SUM.

The synchronization and interlocking can be done relatively easily, provided we implement certain instructions. Before describing the instructions and techniques for solving the problem, we find it convenient to define informally some terms that we have occasion to use. We shall call a sequence of instructions a *program*, which coincides with our usage on serial and array processors. By *process*, we mean an instance of a program that is in execution. In multiprocessors, one program may be in execution simultaneously on each of N processors, so that we call each one of these instances of execution a process. The system is assumed to be able to suspend a process and restart it, not necessarily on the processor on which it was suspended.

We propose to solve the problem at hand by using operations called WAIT and SIGNAL. Both of these operations supply a memory address as a parameter, and operate on the contents of that memory address. The operations must be indivisible in the sense that, once initiated, the item at the special address is fetched, modified, and returned to memory, and no other process may access the same memory cell until this operation is complete. The idea is to use WAIT and SIGNAL as shown below.

comment several processors may be executing statements before
    the WAIT and after SIGNAL;
WAIT (FLAG);

comment critical section. At most one processor reaches this
point at any time;
SUM := SUM + V[i];
SIGNAL (FLAG);

We call the statements between WAIT and its corresponding SIGNAL a
critical section. The variable FLAG controls access to the critical section.
The WAIT operation on FLAG permits a process to continue if and only if
no other process is in the critical section. When a process leaves the critical
section, it signals, which in turn permits exactly one of the waiting processes
to enter the critical section. In an ALGOL-like notation, the actions of WAIT
and SIGNAL are:

> **procedure** WAIT (FLAG);
>   **begin** FLAG := FLAG − 1;
>   **if** FLAG < 0 **then** suspend this process;
>   **end;**
> **procedure** SIGNAL (FLAG);
>   **begin** FLAG := FLAG + 1;
>   **if** FLAG ≤ 0 **then** awaken a program suspended by
>   this flag;
>   **end;**

We initialize FLAG to the value 1 at the beginning of the computation.
Except during execution of WAIT and SIGNAL, the value of FLAG is the
negative of the number of processes waiting to enter the critical section. Thus
if a process performs a WAIT and discovers the value of FLAG to be 0, it
can proceed. Likewise, if a process performs a SIGNAL and finds the value
of FLAG to be less than −1, at least one other process is waiting.

To obtain high-efficiency utilization of processors during a computation, it
is usual to remove a suspended process from a processor and permit another
process to proceed on the newly available processor. This suggests the need
for an operating system to control the changeover of processes, and to queue
suspended processes as well as ready-to-run processes when there are more
ready-to-run processes than processors available. This matter is pursued in
greater depth in Chapter 12, but we cover the pertinent details here.

First we assume that the actions of process suspension and process awakening invoke an operating system program. We also assume that variables used
as arguments of WAIT and SIGNAL have special attributes. For convenience,
we call a variable of this type a *semaphore*. Each semaphore has a queue
associated with it, and the entries in the queue refer to processes suspended
because of the value of that variable. The operating system suspends a process
by storing its state, and by enqueuing sufficient information to restart the
program.

When a process is suspended, its processor is available for other computation. The operating system selects a process from a queue of ready-to-run
processes, and restarts its computation.

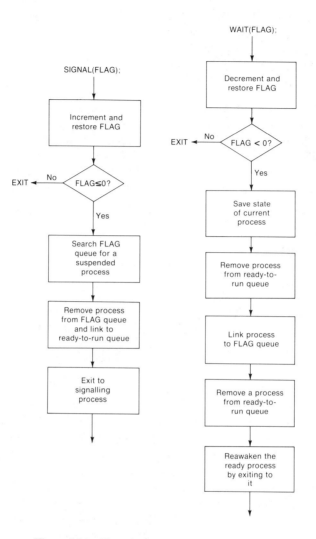

Figure 8-24 Flowcharts for SIGNAL and WAIT

During a SIGNAL operation, if a process needs to be restarted, the operating system selects one from the queue associated with the queue semaphore and places this on the ready-to-run queue. Figure 8-24 depicts the operating-system actions for execution of WAIT and SIGNAL.

This methodology permits a cooperation among several processes and provides for smooth switching of processors among the ready-to-run processes. The philosophy described here is principally due to Dijkstra [68].

The WAIT and SIGNAL operations can be used as general-purpose operations for synchronizing processes, not necessarily just to create critical sections. As an example of their use for synchronizing a pair of asynchronous processes, consider a program in which one process produces data to be consumed by another process. The producer and consumer are supposed to work independently, and asynchronously. We constrain the consumer to deal with items in the same order they are produced. Because the execution time of producer and consumer can vary arbitrarily, we assume that the producer places items in a queue, and that the consumer removes items from the queue. The problem is to suspend the producer when the queue is full and to suspend the consumer when the queue is empty.

A solution to this problem is illustrated graphically in Figure 8-25. The procedures for inserting into and deleting from a queue are named PUT and GET, respectively. The variable NOTFULL permits a WAIT to pass it if and only if fewer than *n* items are in the queue. Similarly, the variable NOTEMPTY permits a WAIT to pass it if and only if the queue has at least one item. This example is drawn from Wirth [69].

In actual implementation, WAIT and SIGNAL are usually implemented to interrupt with a call on the operating system when a process is to be suspended or awakened, because such an operation is more reasonable to implement as an operating-system function than as a machine operation. The crucial point in the implementation is that a variable must be fetched from storage, modified, and returned to storage without any other intervening access to that variable by another process. To perform this access we need special machine instructions, and special interlocks on the memories. Using

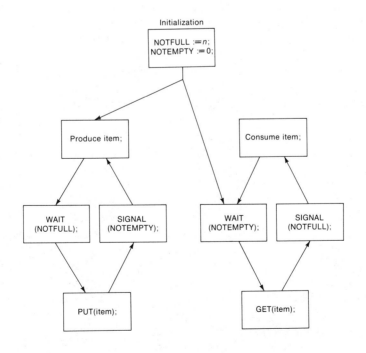

Figure 8-25 WAIT and SIGNAL operations for controlling a queue

the philosophy described here, an INCREMENT AND TRAP and DECRE-
MENT AND TRAP instruction are suitable for WAIT and SIGNAL, where
the trap conditions are given in the description of WAIT and SIGNAL.

One possible implementation of a WAIT is literally to wait by placing
the program in a loop that continuously tests the semaphore until a signal
is received. Although this appears to be terribly inefficient, it may actually be
the most efficient way to implement the WAIT in some instances. Consider
what happens if the overhead of a trap is very high, so that when a WAIT
occurs with a trap, a heavy penalty is incurred. Moreover, the process that
executed the WAIT is no longer active, so that when its SIGNAL occurs,
there is yet additional overhead incurred in restarting the process. Now suppose that two processes are closely interacting, perhaps with synchronization
every 100 microseconds, while the overhead of a trap may be on the order
of 1 millisecond. At least in this situation, the WAIT with continuous testing is far more efficient than a WAIT with a trap.

In the remainder of this section we investigate the FORK and JOIN operations and their implementations. These are similar to Conway's FORK and
JOIN as described in section 8-2, but are slightly modified to take advantage
of the Dijkstra synchronization operators.

Recall that a FORK initiates an independent process. The question at hand
is: How is this to be implemented? To answer the question, consider how
processes are initiated and how they are represented. The representation of
a process is the collection of all of the data required to initiate or continue
execution of the process. It includes among other things the state of all registers controlled by the process, the memory-map function of the process,
the links to the program instructions for executing the process, and the data
that specifies all access rights and resources owned by the process. A FORK
action creates a new process by creating a collection of data that represents
the new process. Then the new process is linked to the ready-to-run queue,
as if it had just been awakened.

If process A creates a new process, say process B, through the action of a
FORK, then B need not be an exact duplicate of A; and, in fact, at least the
program counter of B should differ from A's program counter. Note that the
ability to create an identical process with a different program counter is inherent in the notion of a FORK to a label in a program. Also of concern
are the other items in the representation of a process. In most implementations, process A can specify how to construct the representation of process
B in all of its detail. For access rights and privileges, process A can specify
that the new process has all of its rights or fewer, but not more. Similarly,
process A can limit the resources available to the new process. Finally process
A is recorded as the owner of process B, with the ability to terminate B under
program control.

Of specific concern is the problem of sharing information among processes.
In our examples we have instances in which one process for each value of i
is created, where $1 \leq i \leq N$. In actual implementation, the value of i for a
newly spawned process is placed in a specific machine register, and this regis-

ter is part of the stored state of the process prior to its first execution. When the process is awakened for the first time, the variable is loaded into a physical machine register, where it is available to the process. This is an example of information sharing in a limited sense, but no information can be communicated by this mechanism after forking creates a new process.

For more general sharing of information, the obvious method is to share memory by means of the mapping function. We set the map of a new process so that some pages in its memory are identical to certain physical memory locations of its creator process. This has already been shown in Figure 8-22. References to page 2 by both processes A and B are directed to the same page in memory, but the other pages of these processes are physically distinct. Note that the flags used by WAIT and SIGNAL operations must be in shared memory because they are normally accessed by two or more processes.

From this discussion of FORK, and from our earlier discussions of WAIT and SIGNAL, it is relatively straightforward to construct an implementation of the JOIN instruction. Following the implementation philosophy of WAIT and SIGNAL, we choose to implement JOIN with a single parameter, a semaphore. A typical example of the JOIN in a program is the following:

> FLAG := $-(N - 1)$;
> **comment** the semaphore FLAG is initialized to terminate $N - 1$
>   of the N processes that pass the JOIN statement;
> **for** $i := 1$ **step** 1 **until** $N - 1$ **do**
>   FORK to NEXT
>
>   . . .
>
> NEXT: **comment** N processes pass this point;
>   COMPUTEFUNCTION(i);
> JOIN (FLAG);

Only the last process to pass the JOIN statement continues past it. The first $N - 1$ processes terminate when they reach it. In an ALGOL-like notation, JOIN might be implemented as follows:

> **procedure** JOIN (FLAG);
> **begin**
>   FLAG := FLAG + 1;
>   **if** FLAG ≤ 0 **then** terminate process;
> **end;**

Note that this is quite similar to the SIGNAL operation. In fact, both can be implemented with the same instruction, INCREMENT AND TRAP, which interrupts if the memory cell is not greater than zero. Again we stress that the memory operations on FLAG must be noninterruptible.

At this point it should be clear that many other control operations can be implemented within the framework given here. The operations include control functions that operate on two or more semaphores, conditional execution of synchronization, and similar complex functions. The major issue in computer architecture is to support these operations at the hardware level with noninterruptible operations on semaphores, and operations for switching quickly from process to process.

This completes the discussion of synchronization and control in multiprocessors. There remain the problems of resource allocation and scheduling, which are treated in the next part of this section.

Resource Sharing and Scheduling

In this section we treat the problem of deadlock in multiprocessor computers. The issue here is not program correctness, but rather a problem that develops when resources are carelessly distributed among several different processes executing concurrently in a multiprocessor system. Deadlock is a problem that also occurs on conventional serial computers that support multiprogramming. This situation occurs when multiple processes are executing concurrently, regardless of whether the system is a single processor or several processors.

Of primary importance is the notion that processes operating in a computer system are sharing a pool of resources that includes processors, memories, input/output channels, and bulk storage. The pool must be allocated among the processes to honor all requests, and this must be done in a way compatible with the constraints on the system resources, so as to achieve high utilization of the resources. For example, requests for central memory at any given time may exceed the total amount of central memory in the system. Thus, one or more requests must be queued and granted at a later time. The allocation problem is to determine which requests to grant and which to enqueue, and to do so on an intelligent basis. One of the major points of this discussion is that some allocation strategies can lead to a situation known as *deadlock*, a situation in which part of the system shuts down in a permanent wait state that can be broken only by an external control. In many real situations, deadlock can be broken only by halting computation and reinitializing the machine.

To begin the discussion of deadlock, we present an example of system deadlock involving only processor and memory resources. We shall assume that processes request memory in large chunks, each chunk large enough to hold a number of pages sufficient to contain the bulk of memory references for a computation. A collection of pages with this property is often called a *working set*. After a process owns a working set of pages of central memory, it can be executed on a processor and can run for a relatively long time before needing access to other data. Occasionally, the process suspends itself while synchronizing with another process or with input/output operations. Thus, during the lifetime of a process that owns a working set of memory, it periodically owns a processor while executing and gives up ownership of a processor while suspended. This level of detail is sufficient for our discussion, but we note that, in systems with a hierarchy of memories, a process can own memory of several different types, and, contrary to our assumptions, can be swapped completely out of central memory.

Now to construct an example of a system deadlock, suppose that a process, process A, requires exclusive control of half of central memory for its first phase of execution, then requires exclusive control of a total of three-fourths of central memory for its second and final phase of execution. The process executes by requesting half of memory, and then proceeds through the first phase. When more memory is required, the process requests an additional one-fourth of memory, without returning control of the memory owned by it. The process enters its second phase and completes execution when the request for additional memory is granted. Note that the resources required by process A do not exceed the total resources of the system, and that the two requests made by process A are each permissible requests in themselves, although we shall shortly demonstrate that they may not be permissible in certain contexts.

Now let us assume that process B, an identical copy of process A, executes simultaneously, and asynchronously with process A. The following sequence of events might occur :

1. Process A requests and is granted exclusive control of half of memory.
2. Process B requests and is granted exclusive control of the remaining half of memory.
3. Process A requests an additional one-fourth of memory. Process A is suspended, pending the availability of memory. Memory owned by process A is assumed to be unavailable for use by process B.
4. Process B requests an additional one-fourth of memory, and it too is suspended pending available memory. As above, the memory owned by B is unavailable to other processes.

At this point, all of available memory is owned jointly by A and B. Process A cannot proceed until B terminates, and B cannot proceed until A terminates. An impasse exists, and the system is unable to do any useful computation.

The state of affairs that exists in this example is one in which a nonsatisfiable circular set of constraints exists. That is, A depends on B, but B in turn depends on A. This situation is called a *deadlock* or *deadly embrace* [Dijkstra, 68], and is a situation that has arisen frequently in systems that have not been designed specifically to avoid the problem. In this particular example, there are several possible methods to prevent deadlock. For example, we could force a suspended task to relinquish central memory by moving the task to back-up memory. However, instead of attempting to prevent each particular instance of the deadly embrace, we can formulate some global policy statements that can prevent the problem in general.

A careful analysis of deadlock shows that all of the following conditions must be satisfied:

1. A process must have exclusive control of some system resources.
2. A process continues to hold exclusive control of some resources while a request for more resources is pending. Moreover, the resources owned by the process cannot be removed from its ownership until the process specifically releases its control.
3. There exists a circular chain of ownership such that A_2 holds some resources required by A_1, A_3 holds resources required by A_2, and so on, with A_1 holding resources required by A_n.

Note that each of these conditions is present in the example. The resources in question can be central memory, as in the example, or processors, specific input/output devices, data channels, or even crosspoints in the crossbar switches. A simple way to prevent deadlock is to construct a system in which at least one of the conditions is never satisfied. For example, any of the following rules is a valid way to prevent deadlock:

1. A suspended process cannot retain control over a resource. It may be forced to relinquish control and request a renewal of ownership at a later time.
2. A process must place a single request for all resources it needs. It holds no resources until its request is granted, at which point it obtains everything required.
3. The resources are ordered as R_1, R_2, $\ldots$, R_n, and processes must request R_i before R_j if i is less than j. No circular constraint exists under this rule.

The point in giving the rules is to show that deadlock can be prevented with a global strategy. The example above indicates that deadlock can occur from a sequence of requests, each of which is reasonable in itself. Consequently, a strategy for deadlock prevention almost certainly cannot be a function of individual requests, but must necessarily be based upon the global context of requests. Thus, the problem of preventing deadlocks is traditionally treated by an operating system, which has global information, rather than by special hardware, which processes individual requests. The reader should consult the article by Coffman, Elphick, and Shoshani [71] for more complete information.

At this point we see that the process of granting requests for system resources is a hazardous one, for poor strategies can cause a disastrous deadlock in the midst of computation. But the question of good strategies for resource allocation goes beyond deadlock, for a system must be efficient as well as deadlock free. Efficiency can vary dramatically under different allocation strategies, even when the strategies under comparison are deadlock free.

In general, multiprocessor computer systems have all of the resource allocation problems of conventional serial computers, but processor scheduling and memory allocation tend to be the dominant problems. In the area of processor scheduling, fast optimum scheduling algorithms are available only for a few highly restricted cases, and the most realistic cases can be scheduled optimally only by algorithms that are basically enumerative. Lawler and Moore [69], for example, give efficient algorithms for several multiprocessor problems. Recent results in the study of complexity of algorithm indicates that processor scheduling and memory allocation problems may be so complex inherently that there is no hope of solving them with fast algorithms. The problem of performing optimum memory allocation and processor scheduling jointly appears to be even more difficult than doing these processes individually. In most cases, actual implementations of operating systems are often priority driven, in the sense that resource allocation and processor scheduling tends to favor processes with high priority. Priority-driven algorithms tend to be very fast, and in many situations produce allocations that are reasonable if not optimal. The algorithms do not solve the resource allocation problem, of course, because they are sensitive to the priorities assigned by the user. Thus the resource allocation problem is placed back in the hands of the user to solve through his assignment of relative priorities. Until good solutions to the resource allocation problem are known, priority-driven allocations appear to be as suitable as any other ad hoc allocation method.

Multiprocessors in Perspective

In closing this section, we note that the major problem areas for multiprocessors lie more in developing algorithms for multiprocessors than in building such systems. The major issue is that of partitioning a problem into many processes that can be executed in parallel on a multiprocessor. For just a few processors, partitioning is not a difficult problem, since many problems have sufficient inherent parallelism to keep a few processors active concurrently. When the number of processors climbs to 16 or 32, the problem becomes extremely difficult. Programs without a specifically iterative structure are seldom so complex that they have 16 to 32 distinct subprocesses. Programs with an iterative structure of this degree are likely to run more efficiently on array computers, where they can avoid the overhead incurred by synchronization and scheduling. When the number of processors climbs still further, say into the thousands and tens of thousands, multiprocessing algorithms for such systems at this writing appear to be hopelessly complex, unless the problems display a very strongly iterative or regular structure.

The development of multiprocessors lags several years behind the development of array computers. Powerful and inexpensive microprocessors make an ideal vehicle for constructing multiprocessors, so it is likely that interest will focus strongly in the multiprocessor area in the next several years. Ultimately, the high-speed computer that may emerge in the next decade is one that combines the efficiency of the array computer on iterative problems with the generality of the multiprocessor on unstructured problems.

PROBLEMS

8-9.   Consider the following method of sorting N items.

      Procedure QUICKSORT(LOW, HIGH, A);

      Array A[1:N], **integer** LOW, HIGH;

      begin integer PIVOTPOINT;

          comment QUICKSORT sorts the portion of A from
             A[LOW] to A[HIGH];

          call PARTITION(LOW, HIGH, A, PIVOTPOINT);

          comment PARTITION is a procedure that moves around
             the elements in A between A[LOW] and A[HIGH]
             so that for all I in the range LOW $\leq$ I $<$ PIVOTPOINT,
             A[I] $\leq$ A[PIVOTPOINT], and for all J in the
             range PIVOTPOINT $<$ J $\leq$ HIGH, A[PIVOTPOINT] $\leq$ A[J].
             PIVOTPOINT is an index selected by PARTITION
             and returned by PIVOTPOINT;

          if PIVOTPOINT $>$ LOW $+$ 1 **then** QUICKSORT(LOW,
             PIVOTPOINT $-$ 1, A);

          if PIVOTPOINT $<$ HIGH $-$ 1 **then**
             QUICKSORT(PIVOTPOINT $+$ 1, HIGH, A);
      end of QUICKSORT;

a) Give a brief explanation of QUICKSORT to indicate that you understand that it sorts A when called initially with the statement QUICKSORT(1,N,A);

b) Revise QUICKSORT to run on a multiprocessor by inserting FORK statements as necessary and corresponding JOIN statements. Indicate precisely what information has to be carried forth for each new branch of the fork from global data, and what information has to be handled in a private fashion for the fork.

c) Assume that the overhead of a FORK and of a JOIN is about the same as the time it takes to QUICKSORT an array of length 7 on a serial computer. Estimate the relative running times for a sort of 1023 items for a serial computer, and for multiprocessors with 2, 3, 4, 8, and 16 processors. (Assume that, by some miracle, PARTITION always manages to find a PIVOTPOINT exactly in the middle of the range.) The time for PIVOTPOINT is proportional to HIGH $-$ LOW.

d) Describe how to modify QUICKSORT so that it can interrogate via system calls to determine how many processors are in the total system and how many are idle, and then use this information to optimize its performance.

8-10. Formulate an algorithm for which two producers feed one consumer. Assume that the consumer need not consume items in the exact order they are produced, provided that subsets of items associated with each producer are consumed in order.

8-11. Prove that each of the three rules for avoiding deadlock is a correct rule.

8-12. The inner loop of a matrix computation uses the statement
for J := K **step** 1 **until** N **do**

$$A[I,J] := A[I,J] \times Q - A[K,J];$$

Assume that this statement is parceled out among the processors of a multiprocessor system so that each processor executes the statement for a different value of J. Assume also that the multiprocessor system has a central shared memory as indicated in Part *a* of Figure 8-19. When two different processors access the same memory module simultaneously, the module responds immediately to one processor, and the second processor has to wait one memory cycle, at which time it repeats its request.

a) Assume that the array is stored by rows across the memories, so that at ascending addresses are elements with index pairs, (1,1), (1,2), . . . , (1,N), (2,1), . . . , (2,N), . . . , (N,N), as ascending addresses cycle across the memories.

Diagram the cycle-by-cycle execution of the first five computation parcels under the assumption that all are initiated simultaneously, and that the number of memories is N.

b) Now assume that the array is stored so that each row of A lies in a distinct memory module. Repeat part (*a*).

c) Comment on the problem of data contention in this type of shared memory system, based on your observations.

CHAPTER 9

Overlap and Pipeline Processing

Tien Chi Chen

A computer system accepts a program as a job description, and mobilizes its own resources to produce the desired result. The designer's challenge is to exploit the freedom of internal processing to enhance performance and/or economy. Instead of doing one thing at a time, the machine can partition the work over a number of concurrently operating units.

This chapter discusses the principles of overlap and pipelining as general multiprocessing techniques honoring precedence requirements. Pipelining has a time synchronism reminiscent of vector parallel processing; the latter is also discussed in the broader context of synchro-parallelism.

A simple geometric theory shows that large performance degradation could result from small irregularities in a job. This can be alleviated through flexible routing and associative controls. The overlap and pipeline techniques are consistently applied to a high-performance general-purpose machine design, which incidentally shows the power of distributed control in a tagged architecture. The chapter concludes with a discussion of the architectural features of some thoroughly pipelined systems.

9-1. DIVISION OF LABOR AND ASSEMBLY LINES

Division of labor, a significant aspect of our civilization, is actually *multiprocessing*. A total job is partitioned into individual subjobs, to be parceled out to different working units. This way the handling of each subjob may not itself be done faster, but the *entire job* is completed much sooner.

Overlap and pipelining are essentially job-partition and management techniques that encompass possible precedence constraints.

The Partition of Workload

Arbitrary partition is usually impractical. Some jobs simply cannot be partitioned. The subjobs may not be identical in nature, and may contain obscure interdependencies which could even become intractable with excessive subdivision. Effective partition also hinges on the capabilities of the working units and the supervision and control mechanism available. These problems are interwoven in practice; analogs for all are found in computer architecture.

Often a job may be divisible in several mutually exclusive ways; the fact that it could be done one way does not imply that it must be so partitioned.

Example. The construction of three identical houses can be assigned either to three general construction teams, or to four specialist teams: a foundation working team, a frame and wall team, a roof team, and an interior trim team. The foundation team usually has to start working ahead of the others, because of the precedence requirement.

When a job is symmetrically partitioned into identical tasks, the working units can be identical in makeup and, further, the processing can be synchronized in time, greatly simplifying the control. This is a generalized form of vector parallel processing (see Chapter 8), but there may be no "instruction stream," nor any explicit control. We shall use the broader term *synchro-parallelism* to depict this phenomenon of identical units working in unison.

Example. A collection of 25 memory units is said to be linked in a synchro-parallel manner if each unit accepts a local address and delivers a corresponding memory word, for a combined output of 25 words per memory cycle.

Precedence Constraints

Subjobs often show interdependencies, restricting their concurrent execution. The most common among these is the *precedence constraint*, which demands that the subjobs must be processed in a certain prescribed order.

Precedence constraints may seem to preclude multiprocessing, as the total time cannot be shortened if the subjobs have to follow one another. Nevertheless, when there are enough similar tasks to do, concurrent handling is possible, one working unit on a *different subjob*. This way one increases the processing rate for the aggregate without necessarily reducing the overall time to complete any given job.

An Assembly Line

We can gain understanding from a production assembly line; an abbreviated account is given here.

In an automobile factory the job is the manufacture of many cars. Each car undergoes the following steps:

> Step 0 — installing the frame and power train
> Step 1 — bolting the body on the frame
> Step 2 — mounting the engine
> Step 3 — putting on seats and wheels

Clearly step 1 cannot start until step 0 has been completed. Details of the other steps also show precedence constraints.

An assembly line can be installed as a string of four processing stations. Station k handles step k exclusively, and is situated, say, to the right of station $k - 1$. The chassis of any car must pass through these four stations in sequence, to evolve into a complete car. The work required of each station is different; this specialization by itself already could enhance productivity.

The most significant gain, however, lies in that the four stations can be working on four different cars at the same time, each at a different state of completion.

Let us assume that each station takes exactly ten minutes to handle a car. At some time t_0,

> Station 0 may be building the chassis of car 1000
> Station 1 may be bolting on the body of car 999
> Station 2 may be mounting the engine of car 998
> Station 3 may be installing seats and wheels for car 997.

See Figure 9-1a.

Ten minutes later, cars 1001, 1000, 999, and 998 occupy stations 0, 1, 2, and 3 respectively, and car 997 rolls off the assembly line. See Figure 9-1(b). Thus a given chassis visits the stations in sequence; meanwhile any given

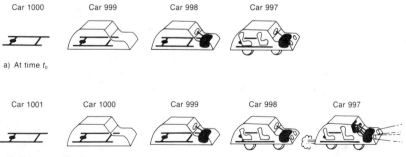

Car 1000   Car 999   Car 998   Car 997

a) At time t_0

Car 1001   Car 1000   Car 999   Car 998   Car 997

b) At time $t_0 + 10$ minutes

Figure 9-1 Automobile frame assembly

station is visited by cars one at a time, in increasing order of their numeric labels. We could say that a (potentially infinite) *vector* of car chassis is being shifted over a linear array of stations, at 10-minute intervals.

If the quadruple occupancy can be maintained, in the time required to manufacture one car, *four* cars will roll off the assembly line. The throughput of the assembly line therefore sees a fourfold increase through multiprocessing, despite the precedence constraint. The production rate is one car every 10 minutes, beginning with the fourth car.

The chassis, which contains most of the parts needed for processing, is transported from station to station, each time by moving over a short distance. There is no need to store things away, to be recalled later. The assembly line thus also implies economy of movement and storage. Precedence is not merely honored; it is actually exploited.

If the time spent on each station is variable, the average rate is harder to ascertain. Station 2 may be ready to start work on a new car, but if station 1 upstream is still working on it, station 2 is forced to become *idle*. Here the precedence requirement exacts its toll. Most automobile assembly lines have been designed to avoid idleness in work stations; one simple way is to equalize the processing times.

PROBLEMS

9-1. Find at least two reasons why it is usually easier to use division of labor to dig a bigger hole than a deeper one of the same enclosed volume.

9-2. Find three possible rules of precedence based on starting times and finishing times, that constrain the concurrent processing of subjobs A and B.

9-2. OVERLAP DESIGNS

Overlap is the phenomenon of concurrent processing, often towards some well-defined common goal. In a computer system, there can be overlap between the processor and the I/O unit (see Chapter 6); within the processor, there can be overlap between instruction preparation and execution. Overlaps at a finer level are also possible.

I/O Overlap

Overlapping of *I/O operations* with *processor operations* is natural and relatively straightforward. There is no precedence issue; the division of labor is that of "FORK to do I/O, proceed with CPU, then JOIN I/O and CPU."

The I/O unit first agrees with the CPU to start an I/O process; subsequently both the processor and the I/O unit proceed concurrently until the latter finishes. The processor is then alerted by an I/O completion signal. See Chapter 6 for more details.

I/O activity requires CPU resources, notably memory and data paths. In the original von Neumann design (1945-48), the path between memory and I/O units runs through the multiply-quotient register of the CPU, crippling the latter. The UNIVAC I (1951) has special input/output buffers, but data movement to and from memory still requires CPU service.

Fully overlapped I/O entailing the time-sharing of memory and asynchronous channels began with the IBM 709 (1958). As machines became more complex, the number and variety of concurrently operating I/O devices grew correspondingly. In the 1960s the cost of I/O equipment began to dominate the total hardware-system cost in large machines. I/O overlap and protocol have now become a major concern.

I/E Overlap

Overlap designs can honor precedence constraints within a computer's CPU; an example is the concurrent handling of *instruction preparation* (I, including instruction fetch, decode, effective-address generation, and operand fetch if any) and *execution* (E), with I setting up the stage for E in every instruction (See Figure 9-2).

We shall first discuss the precedence requirements in handling the instruction sequence in a program. While a machine should be designed so as to exercise internal freedom in order to gain economy, it also must produce results expected by the user at all detectable interfaces. The programmer's view is that, at any time, at most one instruction is being processed, and that within the instruction there is a precise processing order.

For the *j*th instruction, let I_j be the instruction preparation and E_j the subsequent execution, and $T(I_j)$, $T(E_j)$ the corresponding handling times. For all meaningful *j*, the following precedence rule is reasonable, since I_j paves the way for E_j:

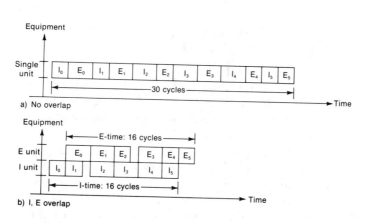

a) No overlap

b) I, E overlap

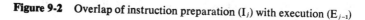

Figure 9-2   Overlap of instruction preparation (I_j) with execution (E_{j-1})

Rule 1. I_j precedes E_j.

Further, it is easy to avoid confusion by demanding

Rule 2. I_j precedes I_{j+1}; E_j precedes E_{j+1}.

Conventional wisdom suggests a third relationship, fully in tune with the user's view of one-at-a-time sequencing:

Rule 3. E_j precedes I_{j+1}.

This results in a simple, clean design. There is implied hardware economy: equipment can be shared between I and E units. In fact the two units can be combined.

A machine built to follow these three rules may be doing instruction processing, or execution, or neither, but never *both*. Rule 3 simply precludes the concurrent handling of I and E. The overall processing time for n instructions for this conventional processor is:

$$T = \sum_{1}^{n} [T(I_j) + T(E_j)] \tag{9-1}$$

All the above rules actually can be broken without altering the computed results. The most confining rule is Rule 3. The same results can be obtained via the more relaxed rule:

Rule 3'. E_j precedes I_{j+2} (as long as E_j does not alter I_{j+1}).

This permits E_j to be concurrent with I_{j+1} most of the time. Where there is no conflict between E_j and I_{j+1}, this machine has the shorter overall processing time:

$$T' = \sum_{0}^{n} \max [T(E_j), T(I_{j+1})] \tag{9-2}$$

with the convention $T(E_0) = T(I_{n+1}) = 0$.

If the I/E times are nearly equal, the overlapped processor tends to run twice as fast as a conventional design. If, on the other hand, either of the two kinds of processing dominates, the gain through overlap may not merit the extra effort.

The overlap design does not come for free. Equipment sharing now becomes difficult or impossible. Further, *interlocks* are needed, either to enforce the precedence rules or to detect and resolve occasional conflicts. The simplest interlock mechanisms are completion signals announcing the validation of all registers at the interfaces. A more powerful technique is to put validation tags on the interface registers; the contents of the latter are used only when the tags are on. These tags must be marked invalid between periods of validity. The tagging scheme allows decentralized overlapped processing down to an individual register or an individual operand, and is a powerful tool in high-performance machine design.

The Unoverlapped State

When a program interruption occurs, the execution of the current program is halted, possibly to be resumed later; meanwhile another program with higher priority (e.g., the monitor program) is activated. The halting often has to occur within a very short time interval.

The interrupting program, behaving like a new team of workers towards a different manufactured product, may need all the CPU resources excepting certain memory-like cells. A concise summary of the machine status of the interrupted program is needed for compact storage to facilitate subsequent program resumption.

With two or more instructions in various stages of execution, the actual physical state can be tedious, maybe impossible to capture.

The usual solution is to create, on demand, special *unoverlapped states* (also called logical states), corresponding to a snapshot of the physical state of an unoverlapped machine. This unoverlapped state is a valid, though uncommon, physical state. It usually refers to the moment when the machine is poised to start an instruction. Here the machine description is most concise, defined by the contents of the instruction counter and a few data registers. The subsequent work resumption is also straightforward. Furthermore, the unoverlapped state matches the user's view of machine computation.

Upon receiving a signal to produce an unoverlapped state, the machine selects a point in the program execution and creates the effect of an unoverlapped machine halting at this point. Every processor action leading to this point must be completed, and no advance processing beyond this point should appear to have been started. Very often, the point in time is so chosen that some units have to continue processing forward to reach it, while other units must invalidate the work in progress, to revert to an earlier physical state. The creation of the unoverlapped state thus amounts to a suspension of the overlap in the processor.

Upon resumption, the machine operates from the unoverlapped state, and may run inefficiently for a while until full overlap is restored. Thus each generation of the unoverlapped state entails a temporary loss of overlap efficiency.

Example. In a machine with I/E overlap, when a halt signal is received, the I-unit may have finished decoding instruction 2000, and the E-unit may be executing the arithmetic for instruction 1999. More often than not, the I-unit is altered to appear as if the decoding for 2000 has not been performed, and the instruction processing is said to halt exactly after instruction 1999 and before the start of 2000.

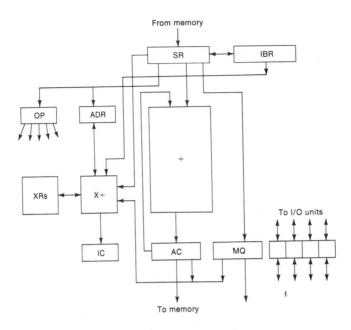

Figure 9-3   IBM 7094 computer schematic

An Overlapped Machine

Realistic constraints often cause deviations from the simple prescriptions of I/E overlap. As a true example we shall take the IBM 7094 machine (Figure 9-3). It is a late model in a long series of systematic machine developments, starting with the vacuum tube, fixed-point, unoverlapped 701, first shipped in 1953 [Rosen, 69].

The 7094 uses 36-bit words as units of information, for data as well as for instructions. The machine has a double-length (72-bit wide) memory; a memory fetch or store operation actually involves a pair of consecutively addressed words starting with the even-addressed word. The word accompanying the target word often can be exploited in the immediate future. In terms of "locality" (see Chapter 12), both the target word and the companion word tend to belong to the same working set. This is seen in double-precision arithmetic, which uses a word-pair as an operand. More important, the locality exists in instruction fetch, when an even-addressed instruction word is always fetched with the *next* instruction in sequence. As instructions are usually decoded in strict sequence, excepting the case of a (successful) branch, the co-fetched instruction word is usually immediately needed. When a branch occurs, the target should preferably be an even-addressed location; an odd-addressed target tends to be less rewarding.

Storing is done by fetching the word-pair, replacing the intended word, then storing back the entire pair.

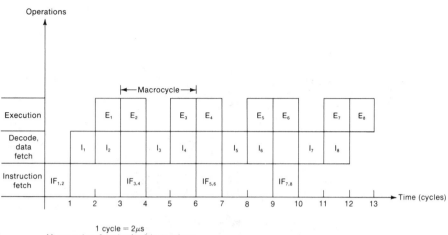

Operations

1 cycle = 2μs
Macrocycle = 3 cycles for 2 instructions

Figure 9-4 I/E overlap in the 7094 for repeated adds

Instruction fetch in the 7094 is a special I-operation, independent of the other I-operations. Figure 9-4 shows a typical processing pattern using three rows, representing I-fetch, other I-operations including data fetch, and execution. The program executes a sequence of fixed-point add instructions. Here each instruction requires a duration of at least 2 cycles, but the average cost for one instruction is 1.5 cycles because of overlap. A cycle here, incidentally, is 2.0 microseconds, equalling a memory-cycle time.

The processing bottleneck in Figure 9-4 is actually memory access. As the I-time includes a data fetch (DF), the memory unit is busy at every cycle; true gaps in processing occur only in executions. The 7094 II, a follow-up machine, separates memory words into even-addressed and odd-addressed banks ("interleave by 2") and can achieve a rate of one instruction per cycle for the same problem. The cycle is still matched with memory-cycle time, both improved to 1.4 microseconds. See Figure 9-5.

Multiple processor overlap designs potentially can increase machine performance by several-fold, but the complex interlock control can be self-defeating. Pipelining (Section 9-3) is an extreme form of multiple overlap, in which the timing interlock is replaced by synchronized time clock pulses.

PROBLEM

9-3. In I/E overlapped machines, an instruction which stores the accumulator contents into the next instruction address can create problems. Specify an interlock mechanism to do the work *correctly* though not necessarily efficiently, and explain it using the design represented by Figures 9-3 and 9-4.

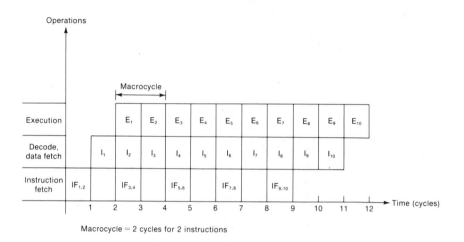

Macrocycle = 2 cycles for 2 instructions

Figure 9-5 Improved I/E overlap for repeated adds

9-3. PIPELINING AS A DESIGN PRINCIPLE

Pipelining is a processing technique aiming for a steady throughput. The processing power is decentralized, and is distributed more or less uniformly over the processing path. The number of datapaths is relatively small, and the data movement is systematic, at least in simple pipelines.

Consider a number of processing stations, called *pipeline stages* or *segments,* each capable of doing a unit of its own work in a fixed cycle time. By stringing many stages together, one can observe precedence constraints and still reach a total work rate equal to the sum of the work rate of each of the stages. This is the principle of pipelining.

The pipeline is closely related to the industrial assembly line described in Section 9-1. As in the assembly line, precedence is automatically honored; also, it takes time to fill the pipeline before full efficiency is reached, and also to drain a pipeline totally.

Steady-State Behavior of a Simple Pipeline

A simple pipeline is a time-synchronized assembly line with neither side-branches nor feedback. Consider a collection of M special-purpose microprocessing stages $(S_0, S_1, \ldots, S_{M-1})$: The jth member can accept a_j bits of input, and do local work w_j within the time interval t_j (see Figure 9-6). At the end of the interval it produces b_j bits of output, and is ready to accept new inputs. Then one can string these M units together, one after the other, for the purpose of doing work Σw_j. It is noted that the term "work" is used loosely; it is not necessarily the same term used in physics.

With the data-width matching conditions,

$$b_j = a_{j+1} \qquad \text{for all } j \qquad (9\text{-}3)$$

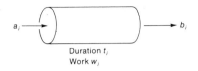

Figure 9-6   Microprocessing stage (S_j)

and the time-matching conditions

$$t_j = \tau = \text{constant} \qquad \text{for all } j \qquad (9\text{-}4)$$

a simple, M-stage pipeline (Figure 9-7) results. This pipeline has a processing duration of $M\tau$, but at every cycle it can receive one set of inputs, generate one set of outputs, and perform an amount of work equalling $\Sigma\, w_j$.

Starting this pipeline at time t_0, and supplying a_0 bits at every cycle, a steady state is reached at time $(t_0 + M\tau)$; subsequently a new set of b_{M-1} bits emerges at every cycle. See Figure 9-8.

After the pipeline is filled, and before it is drained, every stage is busy, with the jth stage doing work w_j. The steady-state work rate is there $\Sigma\, w_j$ per cycle.

The global input at time $(t_0 + k\tau)$ is a task T_k, which moves through the pipeline at a steady rate. When the task emerges at time $(t_0 + (k + M)\tau)$, the total number of subtasks done on T_k is the union of all subtasks, and the work done on T_k is $\Sigma\, w_j$, exactly equal to the pipeline work done per cycle.

While the duration of processing increases with the number (M) of pipeline stages, the steady-state throughput, measured by the work done per cycle, also increases correspondingly.

A simple observation is that the joining of two pipelines with equal cycle times is again a pipeline, with a steady-state throughput equalling the *sum* of the two original steady-state throughputs.

In terms of the rate of task handling, the pipeline at the steady-state finishes one task per cycle, insensitive to the size of the task, and independent of the number of stages required or the distance covered. Though the example is for

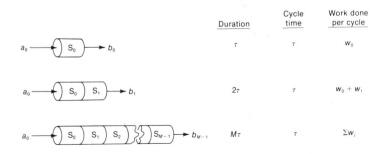

Figure 9-7   Simple pipelines

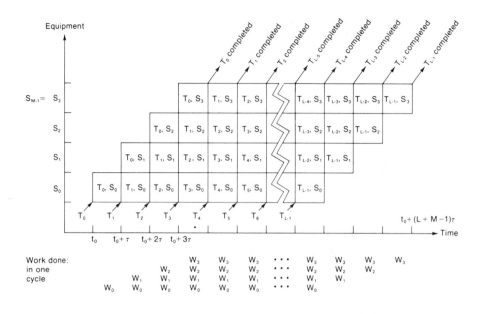

Figure 9-8 Flow of tasks $\{T_k\}$ through a simple pipeline

unary (one input operand) processing, the extension to multiple operands is straightforward. For two operand inputs, for example, each stage has inputs a and a', and output b from the preceding stage has to match one of these.

We consider here only the case of pipeline stages with equal time intervals. Unequal intervals create bottlenecks and congestions; for an analysis see Ramamoorthy and Li [77].

Sequencing in Floating-Point Addition

We shall now study an algorithm, and consider its possible pipeline designs. Consider the execution of a normalized floating-point addition between two binary floating-point numbers $M = a \times 2^p$ and $N = b \times 2^q$ with a, $b < 1$. The operations are required to follow the equation

$$a \times 2^p + b \times 2^q = (a \times 2^{p-r} + b \times 2^{q-r}) \times 2^r$$
$$= c \times 2^r = d \times 2^s \qquad (9\text{-}5)$$

where $r = \max\ (p,q)$ and $1 > d \geq 0.5$. When c is 0, special handling is needed.

Multiplication and division of the fractions by powers of the radix (2 here) are done simply by shifting.

The detailed steps in doing the floating-point addition are as follows (see Figure 9-9):

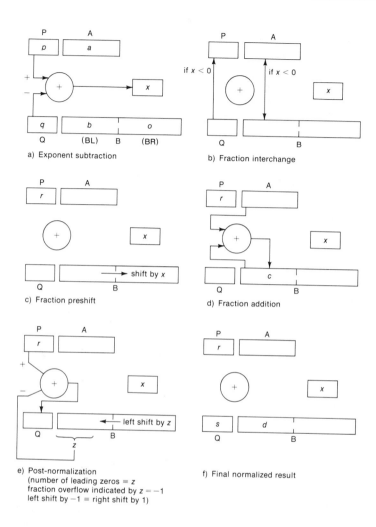

Figure 9-9 Steps in normalized floating-point addition in a conventional machine (exception handling not shown)

a. Exponent subtraction: Put a,p,b,q in registers A,P,BL,Q respectively*. Compute $x = p - q$. BR is cleared to 0.

b. Fraction interchange: If $x < 0$, the contents of A and BL are interchanged, Q replaces P, and $-x$ replaces x. No action need be taken otherwise.

c. Fraction preshift: $B \times 2^{-x}$ replaces B; this is done by a binary shift. B must be a double-length register to contain the result.

d. Fraction addition: $A + B$ replaces B.

*We shall use A,P,B,Q to mean the *contents* of registers A,P,B,Q respectively in what follows. BL and BR stand for the left and right halves of B.

e. Postnormalization: One of four possible actions is taken:
   1) If $|B| > 1$, $B \times 2^{-1}$ replaces B, and $P + 1$ replaces P.
   2) If $1 > |B| \geq 0.5$, no special action need be performed.
   3) If $0.5 > |B| > 0$, first find $z =$ the left-zeros count (the number of leading zero bits after the binary point) of B. Then $B \times 2^z$ replaces B, also $P - z$ replaces P.
   4) If B is zero, the number is an "order-of-magnitude zero." The commonest treatment is to replace the entire word by the bit pattern representing a "true zero."
f. Exponent exception treatment: Normally, B after proper truncation is identified with the final fraction d in Equation 9-5 and P is identified with the final exponent s. If there is exponent overflow or underflow, special treatment is needed. Usually exponent underflow causes the replacement of the entire result by true zero, and exponent overflow leads to a program interruption.

Designs for the Floating-Point Adder

The conventional unoverlapped design allows only one execution at a time in the floating-add unit. The exponent subtraction and the fraction addition use the same adder; likewise all shifting is assigned to the same hardware, as shown in Figure 9-9.

On the other hand, each step outlined in the previous subsection can be implemented by a separate unit. Then all six units can be overlapped in execution; at any time, each unit is handling a different execution.

To do this, it is necessary to provide a separate exponent adder distinct from the fraction adder, also a separate preshifter distinct from the postshifter. Further, each stage must own a private set of registers to contain the operands, and mechanisms are required to move operands from stage to stage. The inflated register requirements had been a heavy burden for overlap and pipeline designs until recently, when the cost of registers has dwindled into insignificance.

Figure 9-10 contains a sketch for a pipelined floating-point adder. The exponent subtraction, fraction interchange, and preshift are done in the same stage (Stage 0), fraction add is done in Stage 1, and postnormalization and automatic corrections of formats in Stage 2. While each stage may not take exactly equal time originally, the longest duration defines the pipeline cycle. The "early finisher" stages must hold the results until the time pulse arrives. A mechanism to facilitate this waiting process is called a *latch*. It holds an operand indefinitely, releasing its contents only when triggered (in the pipeline case, by a time signal).

Limitations to Pipeline Performance

The speed of light in a vacuum, $c = 3 \times 10^{10}$ centimeters per second, is accepted to be the upper limit to signal propagation speed. It is often said to pose a limit to computing performance, but this is not strictly true. The

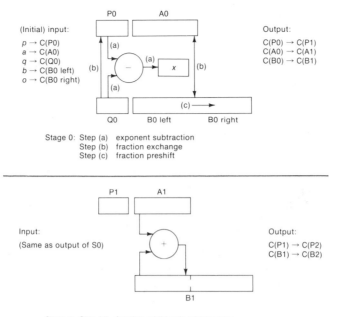

(Initial) input:

$p \rightarrow C(P0)$
$a \rightarrow C(A0)$
$q \rightarrow C(Q0)$
$b \rightarrow C(B0$ left$)$
$o \rightarrow C(B0$ right$)$

Output:

$C(P0) \rightarrow C(P1)$
$C(A0) \rightarrow C(A1)$
$C(B0) \rightarrow C(B1)$

Stage 0: Step (a) exponent subtraction
Step (b) fraction exchange
Step (c) fraction preshift

Input:

(Same as output of S0)

Output:

$C(P1) \rightarrow C(P2)$
$C(B1) \rightarrow C(B2)$

Stage 1: Step (d) fraction addition in wider adder

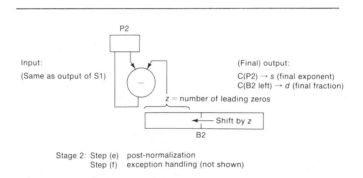

Input:

(Same as output of S1)

(Final) output:

$C(P2) \rightarrow s$ (final exponent)
$C(B2$ left$) \rightarrow d$ (final fraction)

z = number of leading zeros

Shift by z

Stage 2: Step (e) post-normalization
Step (f) exception handling (not shown)

Figure 9-10 Pipelined floating-point adder

quantity c bounds the duration of any process which must move signals over distances. This limits monoprocessing, but not pipeline processing to first order.

When the monoprocessing task is subdivided into M pipeline stages of equal length, to process a large number of identical tasks, each task is done in one Mth the monoprocessing time. As long as one is free to choose M, the speed of light poses no obstacle to steady-state pipeline performance.

There is, however, a limit also to the subdividing process. For example, a stage probably will be much longer than a hydrogen atom radius. Arbitrary time subdivisions also imply arbitrarily small uncertainty in time. According to the time-energy uncertainty principle in quantum theory, this means an arbitrarily large uncertainty in energy required. Proper handling then would require an arbitrarily large energy reservoir.

PROBLEM

9-4. Devise a 6-stage pipeline for the floating-add problem, not necessarily following the subdivisions given in the text. Under what conditions is this design meaningful?

9-4. THE PIPELINE STAGE

In every stage of a pipeline, the input is accepted at the start of a cycle. Within the cycle it is transformed into the output, which often becomes the input of another stage at the beginning of the next cycle. A latch is usually installed at the end of the stage, for release of results triggered by time signals.

There are stages of much simpler construction; see Section 9-5 on shift-registers. Also, there are stages with much more complex interfaces, especially when the pipeline has no simple linear structure. The designer must balance between economy, computing power, and cycle time, for the best compromise.

Pipeline Operands

A pipeline stage usually handles fixed-length operands, though the length could differ from one stage to the next. The operand often represents a single number, but more commonly it carries *tags* along with it. See Figure 9-11(*a*).

A tag adds greatly to the flexibility of processing. It behaves like a micro-code specific both to the operand and to the stage monitoring it.

While there could be many tags of various types, the commonest are among the simplest. The best example is the *validity bit*. Another is the *source*

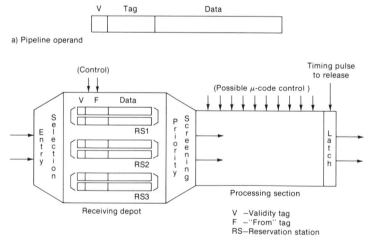

a) Pipeline operand

b) A pipeline stage

V —Validity tag
F —"From" tag
RS—Reservation station

Figure 9-11   Pipeline operand and stage

or "*from*" tag identifying the immediate source of the data. It is just a portable backward pointer. A twin of the source tag is the (next) *destination* tag, a portable forward pointer.

Output Format

In some pipeline systems, nondelivery of valid output is permitted in principle, yet *something* must be delivered every cycle. The stage can simply produce an arbitrary result, tagged clearly as invalid. Such a nonsubstantial result is often called a "bubble."

In a nontrivial pipeline the stage output may be routed to a number of places. Rather than generating a number of identical results, and marking the destination of each, the more usual practice is to stamp every output with the name of the unit, and let the potential receivers decide whether to use it. Only one output need be produced. Potential receivers will receive exact copies through a fan-out circuit.

A stage may generate several distinct outputs every cycle, each for a different purpose; especially is this true in a pipeline network (see Section 9-5). There the operands move along different paths, and there is no confusion.

Input Screening

The input situation is more complex, due not so much to the need for multiple inputs as to the possible contention for real-time service.

True multiple inputs occur for a simple add operation, which takes two arithmetic operands. Input data could also be accompanied by coded control in the form of tags or extra operands. The handling of multiple operands is no harder than that of the single operand in either case, except that waiting may be required if arrivals are not simultaneous.

Often an input is the OR of two or more sets of potential inputs; the inconsequential inputs must then be zeros.

The validity tag can play a significant role. A 1 (say) can be used to mean "meaningful data has arrived" in a buffer register, thus qualifying the accompanying input data to enter the processing portion of the stage. Afterwards the validity tag in the buffer register is reset to 0 (invalid), showing that the register content has outlived its usefulness.

If two or more sets of potential inputs vie for the same input channel, one must select no more than one set, and buffer the rest for a later turn. A front-end endowed with such selection and buffering facilities can evolve into a *receiving depot* (see Part *b* of Figure 9-11) to do some or all of the following:

1. Admit those (copies of) qualified operands with proper source tags matching the known requirements.
2. Provide storage for them while they await their turn. The set of operands needed for the same processing inside the stage are housed in the same cluster of registers called a *reservation station*.

3. Further screen the qualified operands, subject to coprocessing and priority restrictions, so that no more than one operand set is sent into the
processing portion of the stage.

The receiving depots may have so much work to do that they are pipeline
stages in their own right. They are programmed by a scheduler, possibly in
real time, via the setting of the source tags needed for input matching.

The output is usually made to carry the reservation station name, for
proper identification. Except possibly for timing, a reservation station fulfills
all requirements of a *virtual stage*. For an example of its use see the subsection on internal forwarding in Section 9-8.

Internal Processing

The processing within a stage is relatively uncomplicated as it presents
no routing problem. To synchronize with other stages, the work must be
finished within a cycle. The processing could be strictly conventional, or could
be a NO OPERATION when the stage is simply a register, serving as a
noncompute delay.

Conditional NO OPERATION also occurs upon detection of "invalid"
operands. This selective neglect is the data-centered counterpart to the disabling of PEs (processing elements) in PE-centered vector processing. In
pipelines, however, an alternative routing strategy can conceivably obviate the
dispatching of unneeded operands.

The simplest type of nontrivial processing is *unary*, involving only one
operand; examples are sign change, reciprocal generation, bit reversal, recoding, associative search, checkbit generation, and number conversions.

More commonly, the processing involves two operands in conventional
arithmetic. Three operands are needed in three-input adders, with or without
carry-save; in the latter case, the pipeline output would be a number pair.

The nature of processing within the stage can be defined and altered by
microcodes. Then the stage must have the required decoding ability. Some
stages may also contain a rudimentary memory, for microcodes and constants. An entire microcomputer could conceivably serve as a pipeline stage,
but extreme flexibility is obtained only at the expense of long cycles and/or
extra hardware.

The transition from a conventional device, doing one thing at a time,
to a pipeline, producing an output at every cycle, usually requires the systematic insertion of latch circuits to preclude mutual interference. These
latches mark the stage boundaries of a pipeline, holding the output from a
given pipeline stage for synchronized release by a time-pulse trigger. The
processing duration could increase due to latching. Hallin and Flynn [72]
have shown, however, that for arithmetic functions using combinational circuits a latch devised by J. Earle entails no additional delays if the cycle time
is equal to 4 or more logical delays.

For additional information on the engineering aspects, see Cotten [65]
and Loomis [66].

9-5. PIPELINE LINKAGES AND CONTROL

We now consider more general pipeline organizations. In so doing, a number of important arithmetic designs can be put in perspective, and more powerful interconnected systems can be studied.

Linkage Patterns

A simple pipeline is a finite string of pipeline stages, linked in such a way that stage j delivers its output exclusively to stage $j + 1$. It is easy to use, easy to analyze, and very useful. Realistic situations often call for more complex linkages, or even their dynamic switching. Their effective control also increases in complexity.

One of the most important linkages to be added is *feedback* or *recursion*, such that an output from a stage becomes the input to some previously used stage. A simple form of recursion is accumulation; its usefulness cannot be denied. Complicated recursion patterns, however, may cause endless looping within the pipeline, through scheduling oversight or system failure.

The general pipeline stages could still be considered to have been arranged in a straight-line fashion. But the complex linkage patterns may make such a view unrewarding.

A pipeline stage can have lateral inputs and outputs. Very often the lateral operands differ from the forward operands in number, length, cycle time, and purpose. Figure 9-12 shows a pipeline digit-adder [Hallin and Flynn, 72] in which the wave fronts of lateral input operand pairs evolve into wave fronts of sum digits.

Here the pipeline inputs are the carries from the previous stage, the outputs are carries for the next stage. The lateral inputs are the operand digits, and the lateral outputs are the sum digits. At time $t_0 + k\tau$, stage j produces sum digit d_j for the $(k - j - 1)$th addition. In the steady state, a complete sum is obtained at every cycle, yet the sum digits appear one at a time for any particular sum; the pipeline produces one digit from each of the addition tasks.

Pipeline Networks

A system of N simple pipelines, each of M stages, can be linked through systematic lateral input and outputs, to become a two-dimensional pipeline network. Then the jth stages of all pipelines can be linked into a vertical pipeline of N stages. This way data flows along both orthogonal directions, and the total work done per cycle in the steady state equals the summation over the work done in the two-dimensional array of stages. It is both interesting and instructive that such a rectangular network can be viewed either as N crosslinked horizontal pipelines in synchro-parallelism, or alternatively as M crosslinked vertical pipelines in synchro-parallelism.

A pipelined multiplier, generating one product per cycle, can be cast into a two-dimensional network (see Figure 9-13). This multiplier handles $[(abcd)_k$

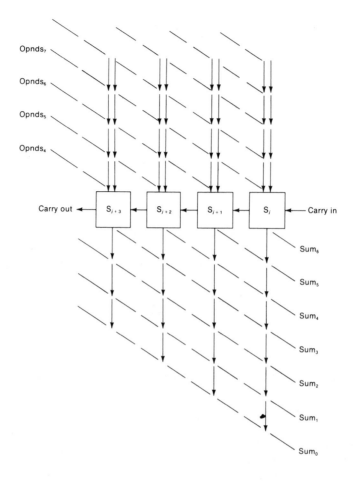

Figure 9-12   Pipelined adder based on digit adder stages

$\times (efgh)_k$] at time $t_0 + (k + 5)\tau$. Each diagonal line represents a different multiply; the kth multiply is being done by inputting $(ag)_k$, $(cf)_k$. Each vertical path is a pipeline, as is every horizontal path. The pipelined version of the Wallace tree multiplier, which shortens the total duration as well, is best viewed in three dimensions.

Shift-Register Memories as Primitive Pipelines

Magnetic bubble memories and charge-coupled devices (CCD) are shift-register memories in which data are pulsed along one-dimensional tracks. These are primitive pipelines, where the pipeline stage is just a memory cell. CCD cells can hold analog data, and are important in image processing. Bubble cells are strictly binary.

A question is, whether nontrivial processing can take place in such primitive pipelines. The answer, surprisingly, is in the affirmative, especially for the

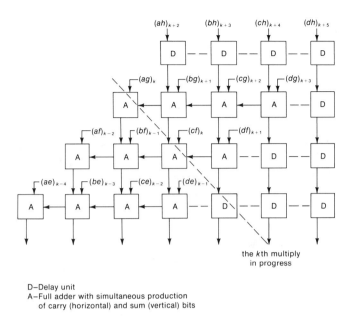

D—Delay unit
A—Full adder with simultaneous production
   of carry (horizontal) and sum (vertical) bits

Figure 9-13 Four-bit pipelined multiplier

magnetic bubbles. Interestingly, the processing actually takes place *between* the pipeline stages.

Pipelined Magnetic-Bubble Logic

Magnetic bubbles (see also Section 5-10) are tiny, identical cylindrical magnets perpendicular to the surfaces of a magnetic garnet film. These magnets are made of the same materials as the film, representing only magnetic discontinuities localized in position. A magnetic bubble may move along a track formed by a permalloy pattern on the film; the pattern gives the appearance of moving magnetic poles of attraction under the influence of a periodic magnetic field. Memory cells are defined along the track, each cell corresponding to the span of the movement of one bubble over one field cycle. A bubble thus moves at the rate of one cell position per cycle.

At any time, a cell may or may not contain a bubble, and is said to contain a binary 1 or 0 respectively. As the bubbles move, the "voids" appear to move in synchronism; this way one defines a shifting piece of binary data. Identical in movement, the bubbles and voids have different effect on electrical resistance of conductors near by. Bubble data thus can be read and can be translated into electrical signals.

Hardware Boolean logic deals with the effect of a set of binary input on signals along an output track. It can be implemented by selectively *steering* a bubble or a void through the output track. The bubbles themselves, through mutual repulsion, supply their own steering power.

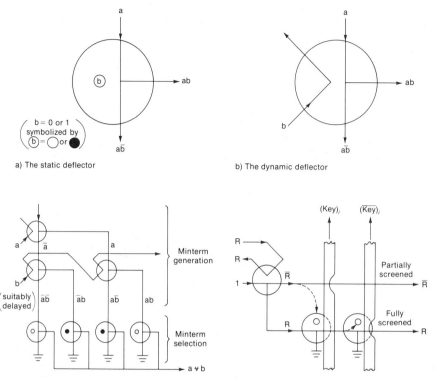

a) The static deflector

b) The dynamic deflector

c) A repersonalizable, pipelined boolean logic array

d) An associative search scheme

Figure 9-14　Magnetic-bubble logic

Figure 9-14(a) shows a *static deflector,* which performs the same function, with the control stream replaced by a rewritable control bit, which could be a void or a tightly held true bubble. The Boolean functions achieved are the same as in the dynamic case.

Figure 9-14(b) shows a 2-input, 3-output device known as a *dynamic deflector.* A southbound bubble-information stream (A) is steered at the point of nearest approach by the control stream (B) on the left. A 1 moves to the right if and only if both of the bits involved had been bubbles (i.e., 1s). A 1 is issued along the downward track if and only if there is a bubble from A but no bubble from B. These results represent the Boolean connectives AB and A$\overline{\text{B}}$, respectively. The logic is thoroughly pipelined; at every cycle a new output emerges, and a new set of input can be introduced. The control stream, not being destroyed, could be reused elsewhere.

A systematic arrangement using these two devices exclusively is shown in Figure 9-14(c). The set of dynamic deflectors resolves the n inputs into 2^n minterms, and the set of 2^n static deflectors selects the desired subset. Multiple fan-outs and fan-ins are automatically avoided in the time-staggered pipelined design, to be ORed together. The net result is a repersonalizable, pipelined Boolean logic array.

The steering of bubble data, being a control function, is an important form of generalized logic. Using selective steering, bubbles can also do associative search, text editing, storage management, and sorting.

Figure 9-14(d) shows an associative search mechanism. The bubble data are first recoded in a two-cell-per-bit form. The key values are sent as electrical signals, also in true and complement form, to react with the complement and true forms respectively of the bubble information. Any match here means a mismatch with the true key, and a bubble is automatically dislodged to become a deflector control bit, deflecting subsequent bits of the "true" stream. The record which passes through in its entirety is a qualified record. For details see the review by Chen and Chang [78].

Pipeline Scheduling

The pipeline scheduling problem, studied by Davidson and coworkers [75] is the economical fitting of tasks of known fixed structure to the pipeline, given a job which has been partitioned into a number of tasks, each using some or all of the stages of a pipeline, assuming that the linkages and protocols exist for the interstage routing.

In innerloops of large scientific programs, often all tasks are identical in their use of pipeline stages. The scheduling there is straightforward, especially if each stage is used exactly once, as in the case of the simple pipeline. The problem becomes nontrivial when the tasks are not identical, or when they use some stages more than once.

Let the pipeline stages be labelled S_0, S_1, S_2, ..., S_{M-1}, and the successive input times be $t_k = t_0 + k\tau$. Imagine the processing of a single task by the pipeline. One can construct a space-time diagram in which slot (j,k) is occupied (marked by X) if the task needs stage S_j during cycle k. Such a diagram is a *reservation table** for the processing of the task. An example is given in Figure 9-15(a). Note that the stages can have multiple input and output, and that a pipeline stage of a two-cycle duration can be represented by two consecutive occupancies. Typically, the table is sparse. The challenge for the scheduler (who could. be a programmer, a compiler, or an interpreter) is to bring in other tasks to fill the vacancies.

Within each stage, two occupied slots (j,k) and (j,m) are said to be separated by the distance $|m - k|$, measured in cycles. These distances turn out to be more important than the absolute positions being occupied.

The task can be characterized succinctly by a compact vector, called the *collision vector*. First pool all distances from all the stages together into a list, with replicated values eliminated. Let the largest distance found in the

---

*The reservation table used by Davidson et al. happens to have the stage subscripts increasing *downwards*. Our choice is compatible with the graphic representation in Figure 9-8.

list be n (cycles). The collision vector is defined as $C = C_n, C_{n-1}, \ldots, C_2, C_1$, where

$$
\begin{aligned}
C_j &= 1 \quad \text{if distance } j \text{ is in the list} \qquad\qquad (9\text{-}6) \\
&= 0 \quad \text{otherwise.}
\end{aligned}
$$

Note that the subscript increases towards the left; this allows C to be treated as an integer.

The collision vector may be null, namely, without any elements. It is customary to replace this null vector by the one-element vector 0.

Scheduling of Identical Tasks

The introduction of a task into the pipeline is called an *initiation*. Two tasks are said to collide when they meet in the same space-time slot; such an event is usually to be avoided. Pipeline scheduling aims to optimize the number of collision-free initiations for the tasks given. In general, when the reservation table has k entries along some row, the best scheduling can realize, on the average, no more than one collision-free initiation in k cycles. Actual scheduling usually falls short of this limit.

The collision vector allows the construction and maintenance of a dynamic *reservation status* vector, which gives all available options in scheduling, based on the nature of the tasks and the previous history of initiations. The simplest, yet also the most important, scheduling is for identical tasks; Davidson's treatment is given below.

1. The system is characterized by a status vector $D = D_n, \ldots, D_2, D_1$, contained in a register. Initially, the pipeline is empty, and D has all zeros.
2. D is right-shifted by one, with 0 entering D_n. If the bit which has dropped off the register is a 0, collision-free initiation is possible as an option. If the option is exercised, the new D is further replaced by (new D) $\vee$ C.
3. End of scheduling cycle. Loop back to 2 as often as needed.

Davidson *et al.* examine the "drop-off" bit before the shifts; the extra time gained is important when scheduling in real time, to synchronize with actual pipeline processing.

An intuitively appealing strategy is to initiate a task whenever possible. This is not always optimum, but is known to be so if C has at most one nonzero bit. This *greedy strategy*, applied from the beginning, is shown below for the reservation table in Figure 9-15(a).

0. START	00000000	
1. Shift	00000000/0	Initiation allowed and taken.
After OR	10110001	
2. Shift	01011000/1	No initiation.

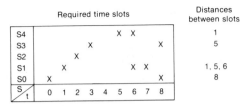

a) The reservation table

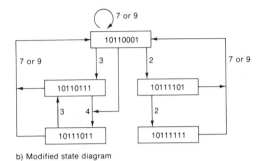

b) Modified state diagram

Figure 9-15   Scheduling of identical tasks

3. Shift	00101100/0	Initiation allowed and taken.	
After OR	10111101		
4. Shift	01011110/1	No initiation.	
5. Shift	00101111/0	Initiation allowed and taken.	
After OR	10111111		
6. Shift	01011111/1	No initiation.	
7. Shift	00101111/1	No initiation.	
8. Shift	00010111/1	No initiation.	
9. Shift	00001011/1	No initiation.	
10. Shift	00000101/1	No initiation.	
11. Shift	00000010/1	No initiation.	
12. Shift	00000001/0	Initiation allowed and taken.	
After OR	10110001	Same as end of Step 1. Go to 2.	

The result here shows 3 initiations in $2 + 2 + 7 = 11$ cycles, for an average performance of 0.27 initiations per cycle. The efficiency is 27%.

The modified state diagram, Figure 9-15(b), shows the status-register values after every possible initiation. The optimum strategy "ping-pongs" between D = 10110111 and 10111011, with two initiations every 7 cycles, achieving an efficiency of 28.57%. This happens also to be a greedy strategy, but requires passing through 4 intermediate cycles.

The scheduling theory has been found valuable in the generation of algorithms for special pipeline machines such as the IBM 3838 [Kogge, 77b].

It is deterministic, applicable to tasks with flow patterns known in advance. It has been used to schedule dissimilar tasks. The insertion of "noncompute delays" for identical tasks can increase all distances, to the maximum value n. The greedy strategy there is then optimal.

The *optimal scheduling* of general pipeline tasks remains an unsolved problem. There are strong hints that the general problem may belong to the *NP-complete* class, and may take an astronomical amount of time to solve. Certain simple scheduling problems, however, do have optimal solutions, and for complex ones one may be content with good strategies supported by heuristics. See Ramamoorthy and Li [77] for an extensive discussion.

Microcode Control

Both the stage definition and routing can be subject to control by micro-code; the latter, if changing from operand to operand, may appear as tags or input operands.

More commonly, the microcode control is imposed systematically on the pipeline from a separate control unit, often in real time, cycle by cycle. Another possibility is to embed the microcode within the pipeline stages.

External microcodes are the basis for algorithm-oriented pipeline processors such as the IBM 3838. The microcodes tend to be horizontal in nature, for maximum simultaneous control. Kogge [77a] distinguishes between two types of microcode. The microcode which defines the behavior of the pipeline for one cycle is termed *time-stationary*, in the sense that each microinstruction represents a snapshot of pipeline behavior. The alternative form of microcode follows the flow of data, and is called *data-stationary*. The data-stationary code has been found more flexible to program, less space-consuming, and easier to optimize. On time-stationary machines, the use of the data-stationary scheme calls for the installation of extra buffers, but a microassembler can go a long way to achieve the desirable effect.

We note in passing that all tags behave like data-stationary microinstructions, though most have limited scope, usually covering only one or two stages before being replaced by new ones.

PROBLEMS

9-5. Devise a bubble logic scheme that will generate the Boolean function $(A\overline{B})\overline{(C\overline{D})}$.

9-6. Find two dissimilar tasks, represented by different reservation tables yet possessing the same collision vector, $C = 10110$. Apply the greedy strategy, and obtain the resultant efficiency. Can the two tasks be intermixed by the identical-task scheduling algorithm?

9-6. ANALYSIS OF TIGHT-COUPLING

Synchro-parallelism is based on symmetric job partitioning into identical tasks. Pipelining, on the other hand, exploits unsymmetric job partitioning with fixed precedence. Both pipelining and synchro-parallelism typify multi-processing by tight-coupling, in that all units operate in unison. We now discuss them together.

The Job in Equipment-Time Diagram

The handling of a computer job requires committing equipment over intervals of time. We can thus represent a job by enclosed areas in a space-time diagram; the space here refers to equipment arranged in some prescribed way. The processing of the job is represented by covering the profile by using actual equipment within some time interval. With skillful arrangement, the profiles of a single job often can appear as one continuous area; this will be assumed for our discussion here. We are concerned with the case where each piece of equipment is a (possibly dissimilar) processor, with similar cost characteristics. The number of processors used is sometimes called the *multiplicity*.

The *size* of a job is measured by its "area" in the equipment-time diagram. The trading of equipment for time is possible as long as the area remains unchanged. The *performance* of the system is measured by its throughput, expressed as the number of effective processors needed to complete the job. It equals the ratio

$$P = \frac{\text{job area}}{\text{time interval spanned by the job}} \qquad (9\text{-}7)$$

This is often much lower than the peak performance represented by the multiplicity.

The Elusive Cost

Performance is clearly important in multiprocessing systems; so is the performance per unit cost. Yet it is very difficult to make general statements about the cost. For a microelectronics manufacturer,

$$\text{the cost to produce } m \text{ items} = A + mB \qquad (9\text{-}8)$$

roughly. The development cost, A, is often several orders of magnitude greater than the manufacturing cost, B. To recoup A, the manufacturer offers volume discounts, and the price of two items is not twice that for one item. The buyer may be a manufacturer for a higher-level product, with a different cost equation and another pricing policy. In any case, doubling the number of processors does not necessarily mean doubling the cost.

The Model Job and a Measure of Repetition

The job may have inherent repetitions; within a time interval many processes may be identical in form, though different in operands used, and thus could take advantage of synchro-parallelism. This is typified by the operations in the innerloops of a program. The number of such identical processes

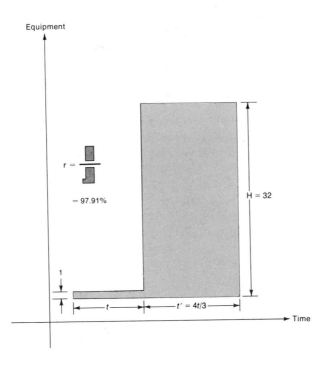

Figure 9-16 Space-time diagram of a model job profile

gives the inherent height*(H) of the job within the time interval. As an example, in the addition of two 32-element vectors to produce a third vector, the inherent height is 32.

The model job profile in Figure 9-16 retains salient features of actual jobs, yet allows detailed analysis. It involves only two contiguous rectangular areas (panels). These areas have inherent heights 1 and H, with corresponding time durations t and t′.

We define a *repetition ratio* for multiprocessing by

$$r = \frac{\text{area of the tall panel}}{\text{area of job profile}} \qquad (9\text{-}9)$$

Here the short panels have unit height, and we have

$$r = \frac{Ht'}{t + Ht'} \qquad (9\text{-}10)$$

Synchro-Parallel Processing

The job in Figure 9-16 can be handled by a synchro-parallel processor of multiplicity N. It behaves like a steadily moving plow of height N, sweeping

*The number of processors required.

over the job profile to achieve complete coverage. In one sweep, the part of the profile with a narrow height is covered completely (though perhaps wastefully), and the extra processors have to be disabled. Those parts taller than N need n sweeps, each time starting at a different height,

$$n = \left\lceil \frac{H}{N} \right\rceil \geq 1 \qquad (9\text{-}11)$$

(namely, $n = H/N$ if N divides H exactly, else it is equal to the smallest integer larger than H/N). Note that

$$\frac{H}{n} \leq N \qquad (9\text{-}12)$$

Figure 9-17 shows the case with $H = 32$, $N = 20$, hence $n = 2$.

Processing is most efficient when the job height is a multiple of N, with all processors gainfully employed. Otherwise there is underuse of equipment. There is an additional cost to disable the unused processors. Resweeping also requires bookkeeping actions (such as branching back to the top of a loop in vector computations). Both the bookkeeping cost and the cost to disable a subset are ignored here.

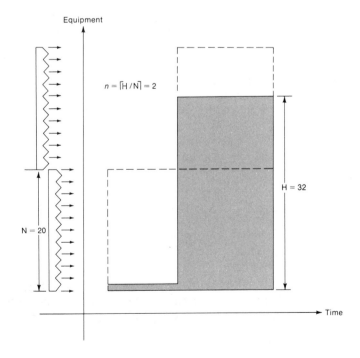

Figure 9-17 Sweeping by parallel processor to cover the job profile

The expected performance, P, defined as the number of effective processors, is seen in Figure 9-17 to be

$$P = \frac{(t + Ht')}{(t + nt')}$$

$$= \frac{1}{\left(1 - r + \dfrac{nr}{H}\right)} \qquad (9\text{-}13)$$

It is important to note that, regardless of the number of processors employed, P can never exceed the limit $1/(1 - r)$ imposed by the job.

The General Case

A realistic job can be represented as a number of contiguous panels of heights $\{H_k\}$ and duration $\{t_k\}$ respectively. H_k can even be zero, signifying throughputless interlocks. Let n_k be the number of sweeps to cover the kth panel,

$$n_k = \left\lceil \frac{H_k}{N} \right\rceil, \qquad \text{if } H_k \neq 0$$

$$= 1 \text{ otherwise} \qquad (9\text{-}14)$$

Then one readily obtains the local performance $\{P_k\}$

$$P_k = H_k/n_k \qquad (9\text{-}15)$$

and the global performance is just a weighted sum over the P_ks:

$$P = \frac{\sum H_k t_k}{\sum n_k t_k}$$

$$= \frac{\sum P_k n_k t_k}{\sum n_k t_k} \qquad (9\text{-}16)$$

Pipeline Performance

Figure 9-8 shows a simple pipeline with L tasks flowing through M stages. The pipeline could be viewed as plowing through the job profile formed by the collection of tasks, using the same theory as above.

The multiplicity here is called M rather than N; it matches the job height at all times. The total duration is $M + L - 1$ cycles. The jagged contours may seem to call for the use of the general formula, Equation 9-16. A simple trick, however, gives the job area directly. By moving the first $M - 1$ columns over to fit the last columns, a rectangle of M rows and L columns is formed; its area is ML. In the altered picture, the pipeline sweeps over the rectangular area *as well as* the noncompute delay of $M - 1$ cycles.

Using the result above we obtain the performance for a simple pipeline:

$$P_p = \frac{\text{job area}}{\text{time consumed}}$$

$$= \frac{LM}{L + M - 1} \tag{9-17}$$

This quantity corresponds to an effective synchro-parallel processor with

$$N_{eff} = M \tag{9-18}$$

sweeping horizontally over a model job characterized by

$$H_{eff} = M \tag{9-19}$$

$$r_{eff} = 1 - \frac{1}{L} \tag{9-20}$$

Thus the pipeline is subject to the same kinds of performance bounds as in synchro-parallelism.

If the job is not a rectangular panel, but carries an overhead like the model job in Figure 9-17, the problem becomes harder to analyze. This overhead may have a height of $h \leq M$, over a duration t. Then the job area is $ht + LM$, and the time spent is $t + L + M - 1$. We have, immediately

$$P_p = \frac{ht + LM}{t + L + M - 1} \tag{9-21}$$

The overhead can seriously degrade performance when t is comparable to $L + M$.

Vector Processing

We shall now study the interrelation between synchro-parallelism and pipelining within the context of vector computation, where the unit of processing is actually a vector or a higher-dimensional array, within which every element is treated the same way. Important examples occur in algorithms for solving partial differential equations and in matrix computations.

A conventional "scalar" machine fragmentizes the computation by dealing with one vector element at a time, often using loops and adding to the bookkeeping cost. It is much more straightforward to use synchro-parallelism or pipelining.

We shall study vector computation of the type

$$\mathbf{U} := \mathbf{V1} \times \mathbf{V2} + \mathbf{V3}$$

for vectors $\mathbf{U}$, $\mathbf{V1}$, $\mathbf{V2}$, and $\mathbf{V3}$, all of length H. The innerloop for a scalar machine involves the sequence

$$L_j, M_j, A_j, S_j$$

for j running from 0 to $H - 1$, with L_j, M_j, A_j and S_j representing the jth load, multiply, add, and store, respectively. The four instructions define a task of $M = 4$ steps; each is assumed to take equal time to simplify discussions.

In a synchro-parallel machine the entire vector could be handled as a unit of computation (see Figure 9-18). All the tasks together form a fully repetitious job profile with height H. However, when N general processors are engaged, each given the work equivalent to one traversal of the inner loop, there still could be underusage of hardware due to the N, H mismatch.

The same job can be handled using a pipeline with $M = 4$ stages, consisting of a loader L, a multiplier M, an adder A, and a storer S. While each processor in the synchro-parallel system handles an entire task for a data stream, each pipeline stage handles one step of the task for all tasks, one at a time, at the rate of one task per cycle.

The pipeline in Figure 9-8 is viewed as stationary, with the task flowing through it. Alternatively, one could also view the job profile as stationary and move a pipeline through it. This allows a more explicit contrast with synchro-parallelism. The simple pipeline is seen as a slanted jagged edge

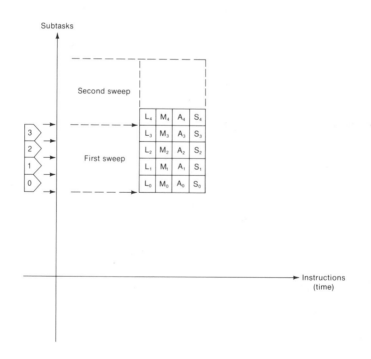

Figure 9-18   Synchro-parallel handling of vector job

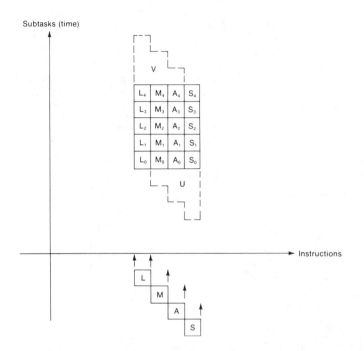

Figure 9-19   Pipeline handling of vector job

which moves from south to north, orthogonal to the synchro-parallel processor movement, and which achieves complete coverage by sweeping over a jagged parallelogram. See Figure 9-19.

The above shows that vector processing can exploit synchro-parallel multiprocessors or pipelined processors. The term "vector processors" is often used to denote either.

The VAMP Study

A good way to increase the utilization in a synchro-parallel machine is to entrust the collective arithmetic requirements of the latter to a sophisticated pipeline design. Such a scheme was advocated by Senzig and Smith [65] in the VAMP (Vector Arithmetic Multi-Processor) design.

They observed that in vector parallel machines, the cost of arithmetic units can be reduced by sharing a small number of powerful pipelined arithmetic units among the N processors. In their design all memories are also collected into one large interleaved unit, and are served by a memory bus; see Figure 9-20.

The processors are only "virtual," each represented by a few registers. An N-bit (screening) register specifies the active subset of virtual processors; another N-bit (condition) register summarizes the condition of a previous test. A vector accumulator register contains the cumulative sum or product of the contents of the individual accumulators. The interface to the interleaved memory is a memory data register.

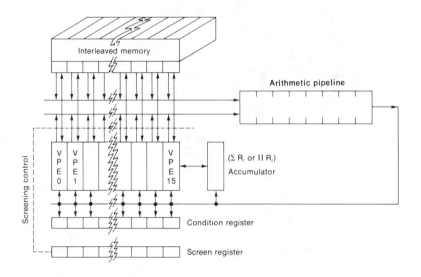

Figure 9-20 VAMP

A typical vector arithmetic operation involves accumulators of successive (enabled) virtual processors, paired with successive elements of the memory data register. The operand pairs enter the arithmetic pipeline, a pair at a time and the results are returned to the accumulators. Each pipeline unit delivers one output per cycle. As the processors are served in succession, there is no true simultaneity of action; but simultaneity may never be needed. The successive use of the processors and memory boxes implies that control and broadcast commands can also be delivered with fixed time-lags, by time-sharing a small set of buses, to replace the costlier fan-out in vector designs. The separation of the memory from the processors also allows easier data sharing.

The condition-register contents can be loaded into a screening register to disable a selective subset of the virtual processors. The disabled virtual processors need not affect the arithmetic resources. This is in sharp contrast to the synchro-parallel design, in which an unused processor withdraws its share of processing power from the system.

This form of processing, with parallel (virtual) processors handling the same operations in succession at a fixed time-lag can be called *time-lagged parallelism*. It has the twin virtues of relieving traffic congestion and of synchronizing with a pipelined interface. A comparison with vector parallelism is summarized in Table 9-1.

Senzig and Smith were also the first to suggest using the primitives of APL as part of the machine language. Their study went a long way to clarify the interrelations between pipelining and synchro-parallelism, and has had a lasting impact on subsequent pipeline designs. Flynn et al. [70], for example, incorporate this form of pipeline operation in their multiprocessor design.

TABLE 9-1. CONTRAST BETWEEN SIMD AND VAMP

	Synchro-Parallel	VAMP
Memory	Distributed, one unit per PE	Centralized but interleaved
Arithmetic unit	Distributed, one unit per PE	Centralized, powerful pipeline
PE	Memory + arithmetic unit + registers	Registers
Arithmetic time duration	Local arithmetic time	Proportional to the number of enabled PEs
Simultaneity	Exact	Systematic time lag
Masking action	Disables PE, performance withdrawn	Fewer entries into pipeline, arithmetic performance retained

PROBLEMS

9-7. Using a synchro-parallel multiprocessor to process a model job with $H = N = 32$,

    a) For what value of r is $P = N/2$?

    b) What can this analysis show for the general case with N, H unequal?

9-8. In a simple pipeline, what is the minimum L to make P_p equal to $M/2$?

9-7. PERFORMANCE ENHANCEMENT FOR TIGHT-COUPLING

The tightly-coupled multiprocessors have many similar characteristics, and complement each other in many ways. Their common inflexibility can be overcome through the addition of associative control, supported by freedom of data movement and permutations.

Mutual Reinforcement

Far from being opposing extremes, synchro-parallelism and pipelining actually complement each other. The regular two-dimensional pipeline network (see Figure 9-13), for example, is based on the linking of a number of linear pipelines, pulsed in synchronism. The VAMP design shows that synchro-parallelism can be imitated by time-lagged parallelism using pipelining.

Synchro-parallelism can even augment simple pipelines when there is a need for a short cycle even though some procedures have indivisible long cycle times, A set of K units, each taking K cycles to complete its work, can be connected in parallel to deliver one result per cycle. One needs only to install fast switches in front and behind, to select the parallel resources in cyclic order to synchronize with the pipeline pulses. (The matching of fast circuitry with interleaved, slower memories, creates an interesting problem to be addressed in the subsection, "Example: Memory Interleaving.")

Common Complications

In terms of instructions executed in conventional machines, completely repetitive jobs seldom occur. As shown above, a small admixture of serial computing can have a disproportionately adverse effect on the overall performance of synchro-parallel mechanisms. Pipelines show the same kind of sensitivity to job inhomogeneity, *even* for jobs which are handled by sychro-parallel machines with 100% efficiency.

The cause of underusage of equipment lies in the rigidity of the tight-coupling, and the cure lies in adding flexibility.

In the ILLIAC IV computer, basically a synchro-parallel machine, a separate overlapped control unit is used for bookkeeping functions, exposing the synchro-parallel multiprocessor only to the tall portions of the jobs. Operational only in 1977, this feature has doubled the speed in executing highly parallel problems [Bailey, 77].

In vector parallel processing, data-dependent conditional operations link some operands to the control mechanism, precluding smooth synchro-parallelism. A test on operand signs, for example, potentially subdivides the vector collection of processors into two distinct classes for separate treatment.

Even if most operands react identically, one lone exception suffices to disable $N - 1$ other processing units. Skillful programming, indeed, is needed to encourage effective homogeneous treatment.

There is, further, an intercommunication problem; if processor j needs to send information to processor k, it does not follow that processor $j + q$ needs to send to $k + q$, for all q. But arbitrary intercommunication-flow patterns are hard to enforce without loss of efficiency.

These difficulties have their counterparts in pipeline processing, adding to control cost while decreasing average efficiency. Tasks are permitted to enter a pipeline only if all anticipated exceptional occurrences are known to be resolvable automatically inside. Temporary input blockage may be created to avoid unresolvable difficulties. For example, the task T_k may create a condition upon being processed by stage S_j, and this condition may affect the processing of T_{k+1}. The pipeline feeder control may have to keep T_{k+1} outside the pipeline until the condition becomes known; by then the stages S_0 through S_j will be idle.

To avoid frequent pipeline drain, the stages can be made more flexible, or the pipeline can be redefined to handle complex happenings. A way to give different treatment to differently signed operands is to use tags for detailed control (for selective neglect, as an example).

Self-Optimization

Though minor irregularities in one job profile lead to excessive unused capacity, other jobs can be summoned to take up the slack; this is *multi-programming*. One can subdivide a given task into locally independent subtasks, arranging their execution to fit the internal processing patterns so as to enhance the average performance. For repetitive computations, such tailoring can be scheduled by careful hand-honing, assisted by Davidson's scheduling scheme. For a discussion see Kogge [77b]. The job can also be entrusted to a compiler, though less effectively.

A high-performance system, however, can mobilize its own internal resources to exploit dynamic task independence rather than task regularity. While the control problem is harder, the technique is essentially generalized table management by associated control. The hardware requirement consists of memories to buffer waiting tasks and coded signals, and mechanisms for selection and switching; in other words, associative memory with supporting logic.

This is an example of *self-optimization* by the machine in real time. Like all self-optimization processes, the resultant processing is hard to anticipate in detail, yet the time-averaged performance becomes predictably better. This gross performance enhancement at the price of loss of detailed knowledge is clearly acceptable for jobs where real-time details are not a major concern.

Example: Memory Interleaving

A good example of self-optimization is found in the handling of the memory-interleaving problem. A pipelined memory-access system, confronted with imperfect time quantization, can employ synchro-parallelism using, say, K memory units, each taking K processor cycles to deliver a word. To avoid undue extra cost, no actual memory replication is used; only the addresses are interleaved, so that all addresses equaling j modulo K refer to memory box j. This way the input stream of addresses now behaves like an admixture of K different streams; nevertheless, consecutive addresses refer to different boxes, and the one-output-per-cycle maximum rate can be honored for well-chosen address-request sequences. The performance gain of the interleaved system is measured by

$$g = \frac{\text{throughput of the interleaved system}}{\text{throughput of the single-box memory}} \qquad (9\text{-}22)$$

The lower limit of the performance gain is 1; this occurs in delivering, in strict sequence, a column of elements of a $(K \times K)$ matrix, stored by row. The maximum gain, K, is reachable in the delivery of a row of elements in the same matrix.

It can be shown that for random requests the average throughput in a first-come, first-served system is not proportional to K. A 100-fold-interleaved system gives only a 12.21-fold average throughput.

The performance gain roughly equals $K^{0.56}$ [Hellerman, 73]. Knuth and Rao [75] have found that it exactly equals Knuth's Q function. Actually, a better approximation is $(\pi K/2)^{1/2} - 0.28$, with an error of less than one percent for all $K \geq 2$.

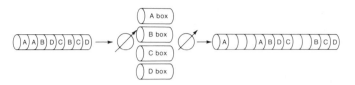

a) Memory interleaving based on first-come, first-served discipline. Note bubbles in output pipeline.

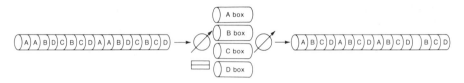

b) Buffer memory associated with the switching. The output pipeline is nearly full but delivery is out of sequence.

Figure 9-21   Memory interleaving

In actual computations, the performance due to interleaving should be somewhat better than the average, because the instruction fetches are inclined to be sequential. It suffices to say, in any case, that the delivery delay is uncertain, and the overall performance is not proportional to the interleave count K.

The difficulty can be overcome by buffering the input queue, honoring only those requests which refer to boxes currently available. Figure 9-21 shows the dramatic improvement with only two buffer registers. The system, with the queue-selection mechanism, optimizes its own throughput. This is an example of the insertion of noncompute delays in a pipeline; this insertion is data-driven in real time, not easily scheduled externally.

Typically, the ordering of the delivery sequence does not mirror the input sequence, and detailed prediction of system happenings becomes difficult. The gross output pattern, on the other hand, now tends to exhibit a good local statistical distribution.

The original ordering can be restored using a set of buffer registers, causing extra delays. Whether restored or not, the delivered words must carry identification tags to permit recognition despite the out-of-sequence delivery. The simplest tag is a source tag naming the memory box.

PROBLEM

9-9.   Using 32 random integers as input, find the effect of buffering on a fourfold-interleaved memory using (a) no buffers, (b) a one-register buffer, and (c) a two-register buffer. Does one need four buffer registers?

9-8. CONTROL MECHANISMS IN HIGH-PERFORMANCE MACHINE DESIGNS

We shall now discuss use of overlap, pipelining and other multiprocessing techniques in a large general-purpose computer. This computer executes conventional instructions, but not necessarily in the specified order, and certainly not one at a time. Nevertheless, it attempts to provide results identical with those from unoverlapped computers. Indeed, the machine will appear as unoverlapped during all normal interruptions, as if out-of-sequence processing has not occurred.

The compatibility with other machines extends the performance spectrum of a line of machines without imposing a relearning burden on the user. Nevertheless, an understanding of the internal organization could often allow more efficient-running programs.

While trying to be "user transparent," the system often pays heavily in the control cost. The major issue turns out not to be raw arithmetic power, but rather the interlocks and tagging disciplines to honor the precedence specified by the user program, despite the completely reshuffled processing. For a theoretical discussion see Keller [75].

Examples of high performance machines are the CDC 6600 and 7600, the IBM System/360 Model 91 and System/370 Model 195, the Amdahl 470 V/6, and the CRAY-1.

Instruction Processing

To lend concreteness to the discussions, we shall assume a computer CPU with the dataflow indicated in the diagram in Figure 9-22, using the notation defined in Table 9-2. We further assume only four kinds of CPU instructions, all of equal length:

1. Arithmetic (including load, $+$, $-$, $\times$, $\div$, shifts)—the result goes to AC and sets pertinent bits in the condition register CR.
2. Index arithmetic—the result goes to an index register and sets CR.
3. Store from the accumulator.
4. Conditional branch based on a 1-bit condition: branch if and only if the bit is 1.

This machine, though capable of meaningful processing, does make use of simplifying assumptions, and is adequate only for a discussion of the performance-enhancement principles. It corresponds to no known machine.

A schematic for instruction processing is given in Figure 9-23. It is simpler to consider the updating of the instruction counter as following the decoding of an instruction, rather than as occurring at the beginning of the next.

To ensure precedence sequencing, the decoding should be in the program-specified order. After initial decoding, the instructions are subdivided into

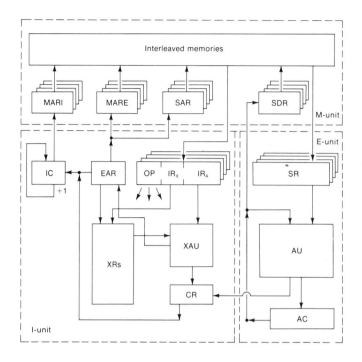

Figure 9-22   Hypothetical overlapped processor

semi-independent streams of tasks and assigned to the proper units. The M-unit performs all memory activities, while the E-unit handles arithmetic and logic; the index arithmetic and branching are done largely within the I-unit.

Within the E-unit, the tasks specified by the instructions are executed in the program-directed order; the same is roughly true in the I-unit. The M-unit need not follow any processing sequence for fetch operations; a special precaution, however, needs to be exercised for stores, as will be shown in "Store-Fetch Interlock" later in this section.

Memory-Accessing Mechanisms

For economy, the bulk of the random-access memory is in low-cost semi-conductor technology, with submicrosecond access times, reasonably fast but no match for the expected CPU processing rate. To deliver the proper band-width, the large memory is interleaved, and buffered against the "square-root catastrophe"; there perhaps should be a cache to reduce the effective access time. It is therefore desirable to have several each of MARI, MARE, SAR, SDR, IR and SR, also powerful associative-selection mechanisms. This way the memory and the memory bus are effectively decoupled from the CPU.

The decoding action is relatively fast; independent indexing is done in a district index-arithmetic unit, separate from the standard arithmetic unit. The

TABLE 9-2. NOTATION USED IN FIGURES 9-22 AND 9-23

Notation	Meaning
AC	Accumulator
AC_s	Sign field of AC
AU	Arithmetic unit
CR	Condition register
EAR	Effective address register
EAR_s	Sign field of EAR
IC	Instruction counter
INDEX [IR_x]	Index register selected by IR_x
IR	Instruction register(s)
IR_A	Address field of IR
IR_x	Index field of IR
MARE	Memory address register(s) for E-unit
MARI	Memory address register(s) for I-unit
MEMORY [MARE]	Data word fetched from memory based on MARE
MEMORY [MARI]	Instruction word fetched from memory based on MARI
OP	Operation code field of IR
SAR	Store address register(s)
SDR	Storage data register(s)
SR	Storage (output) register(s)
XAU	Index arithmetic unit
XR	Index register

instruction buffer should be large enough to contain an innerloop of modest size.

Arithmetic

The high-performance machine usually has several units for arithmetic; the CDC 6600, for example, has 10. These units, with well-defined input, processing, and output, are easily pipelined. A 48-bit Wallace-tree multiplier, for example, can be handled by a 5-segment pipeline to generate one product per cycle of 4 logical delays [Hallin and Flynn, 72]. The mechanism uses one cycle to preencode the multiplier operand, one cycle to halve the number of addends to 24, then three cycles to compress the number of addends from 24 to 3, and finally, four more cycles for a 3-input long addition.

An entire floating-point execution can be pipelined also. Many simple instructions, such as fixed-point addition and logic instructions, can be executed in one cycle; they can be considered pipelined.

While arithmetic pipelines are easy to design, usage frequency may not justify their construction. The IBM System/360 Model 91, or its successor the System/370 Model 195, has a pipelined 2-cycle floating adder, but a

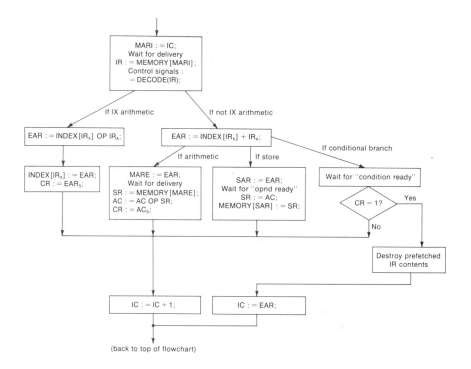

Figure 9-23 Instruction-handling schematic

nonpipelined 3-cycle multiplier; the CDC 7600 has a 5-cycle multiplier pipelined every 2 cycles, mainly to replace the pair of nonpipelined multipliers in
its predecessor, the 6600 computer. Divisions occur less frequently than
multiplications, and are seldom pipelined. Often a reciprocal estimator is
used, which, in conjunction with a multiplier, can give the effect of division.

It will be seen later (see "Internal Forwarding") that out-of-sequence
executions can occur in the arithmetic unit even with a single accumulator.
The machine always tries to give correct results despite the out-of-sequence
operations. At any time several chains of computations may be handled.

A characteristic of a pipeline is that the pulsed delivery is independent of
the number of stages. The insertion of a checking stage does improve reliability without affecting steady-state throughput.

The Gap of Ignorance and Unoverlapped States

While overlap and pipelining increases the overall throughput, the total
processing duration for an instruction may actually increase. The time lag
between the initial instruction fetch and the final execution completion may
be several times the average time interval between instruction completions.
This lag constitutes a *gap of ignorance* (see Figure 9-24), within which the
CPU is unable to divine the instruction outcome.

Fortunately, in most parts of instruction handling the outcome of previous instructions need not be known. The arithmetic instructions, for example, can usually be dispatched as fast as the decoder and the memory can allow, with little chance of conflict.

However, a conditional branch based on arithmetic outcome cannot be decided without having finished the arithmetic. A premature use of the condition register, before the true outcome becomes available, can be disastrous.

A safe tactic is to wait for arithmetic completion before proceeding with the branching action. This takes nearly the full gap time, and the branch, if successful, may mean a costly instruction fetch.

The IBM System-360 Model 91 fills this gap partly by prefetching the branch target instruction and some subsequent instructions, holding them in abeyance until the arithmetic outcome is known. Then, after one of the two alternatives is selected, the other is ignored. A similar effect is seen if the branch target is within the instruction buffer.

The high-performance machines may also make an educated guess on the test outcome, and favor one of the two alternatives. When the instruction buffer is large enough to contain a loop, the guess should favor the continuation of looping.

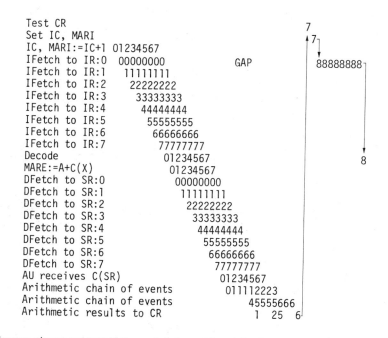

The diagram shows separately 8-way-interleaved I and E memories, and two overlapped arithmetic-execution sequences of the form: load, multiply, add, store, load, multiply, add, branch on adder outcome. The gap size here is 14 cycles; it has an effect of a 24-cycle delay if the branch target is fetched only after examining the true CR contents.

Figure 9-24   The gap of ignorance

While waiting for arithmetic completion, little can be done with the subsequent instructions, and the conditional branch instruction physically realizes an overlapped machine state in which the arithmetic execution has been completed, but no specific branching action has yet been taken. This state does not refer to an instruction boundary, and differs somewhat from the one used in program interruption (section 9-2, "Unoverlapped State"). All the same, the high overlap in the system is replaced temporarily by monoprocessing, while the hardware capability is underutilized.

Unoverlapped states in a highly overlapped processor are much harder to generate than in the case of simple I/E overlap. Not only are there more unfinished instructions to consider, there is greater chance for some of the operations to have altered the machine irrevocably, and these operations can no longer be invalidated. To run all unfinished instructions to completion may appear to be a safe strategy, but this sometimes takes too long to be worthwhile, or may change the machine irrevocably in such a way as to defeat the original purpose of the interruption. This "imprecise interrupt" problem occurs in many high-performance machines.

The resumption of overlapped processing means the re-creation of a gap of ignorance, during which the overlap power of the machine is underused. In general we can conclude that the frequent creation of unoverlapped states is detrimental to the performance of highly overlapped mechanisms.

Store-Fetch Interlock

Some of the more important precedence-preserving operation features in high-performance machines are delineated below. It should not be too surprising that there is extensive distributed processing via the use of tags.

Consider the instruction sequence below:

$$AC := AC + MEMORY [1024];$$
$$MEMORY [1000] := AC;$$
$$AC := AC - MEMORY [1000];$$

Since the arithmetic execution is the last subtask within the instruction handling, the second instruction is decoded within the gap of ignorance created by the first. The STORE instruction must not be performed until the proper data resides in the accumulator.

Meanwhile the machine can try to execute the third instruction, which is a conventional fetch-type instruction. Data fetches are normally done in the middle part of the instruction processing, and thus may still be within the same gap of ignorance as the second instruction. In other words, the third instruction could fetch something from location 1000, even before the storing of the correct data. Such a premature fetch would give a wrong answer in the accumulator (the right answer, incidentally, is 0).

To guarantee the correctness of the outcome, the following constraint must be honored:

Do not read from (or write into) a location until all pending writes (reads) have been made.

A feasible scheme to handle the interlock follows:

1. On encountering a store instruction, put the store address in an available storage-address register (SAR), and mark it valid. The store instruction is treated as a pseudo-arithmetic instruction and follows the arithmetic execution sequence to ensure the proper handling of the accumulator operand.
2. On encountering a fetch-type instruction, the fetch address is treated as a pending fetch address.
3. All pending fetch addresses are compared against the contents of all valid SARs. The fetches can proceed normally only if there exists no match. The matched fetch addresses remain pending.
4. When the accumulator has valid contents to be stored, its contents are copied into a store-data register (SDR) corresponding to the valid SAR; this frees the arithmetic unit to proceed freely.
5. The true store action occurs between SAR, SDR, and memory. Afterwards, the pertinent SAR and SDR are marked invalid; this frees the pending fetches with addresses matching the SAR.

The pending-address scheme is required not only for data fetches through MARE, but also for instruction fetches and index loads through MARI. Further, the prefetched contents of the instruction buffer may be invalidated by an inopportune store. Fortunately, with the advent of indexing, the need for instruction modification (hence storing into I buffers) has largely disappeared. With a sufficient number of intervening instructions, the precedence is automatically honored. For a systematic discussion of interlocks see Ramamoorthy and Li [77].

The above mechanism guarantees correctness in execution; we now show how performance can be enhanced also.

Internal Forwarding

The completion of the fetch instruction using the rules in the previous section requires the sequence:

1. Wait for the proper information to arrive at the SDR.
2. Store into memory: MEMORY [1000] := SDR.
3. Fetch from memory: SR := MEMORY [1000].

Rather than paying for two, possibly slow, memory operations, we note that the correct information resides in SDR, and step 3 can be short-circuited by a fast register-to-register transfer known as store-fetch forwarding:

$$3'. \text{ SR} := \text{SDR}$$

as practiced in the IBM STRETCH computer in 1961.

More generally, in Figure 9-25(a), the sequence

$$Q := P; R := Q \quad \text{symbolized by the directed arc (PQR)}$$

is replaced by $Q := P; R := P$ symbolized by the arcs (PQ, PR)

thus

$$(\text{PQR}) \text{ is equivalent to PQ, PR}$$

This is known as *store-fetch forwarding*. Another one, also featured in the STRETCH, is *fetch-fetch forwarding*, which uses the fetch mechanism of one instruction to short-circuit a subsequent fetch for the same operand. The data needed can come from SR directly, saving a memory access. In Figure 9-25(b), fetch-fetch forwarding is seen as essentially the reverse of store-fetch forwarding:

$$(\text{QP, QR}) \quad \text{is equivalent to QPR}$$

The economy derives from the fact that any path involving memory (Q here) is time consuming, and is to be avoided when possible.

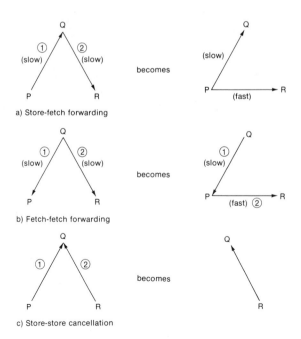

a) Store-fetch forwarding

b) Fetch-fetch forwarding

c) Store-store cancellation

Figure 9-25   Internal forwarding

The instruction sequence

$$Q := P; \quad \text{then } Q := R$$

can be replaced by $Q := R$ alone; the second instruction proves the redundancy of the first, as seen in Figure 9-25(c). This is an instance of *store-store cancellation* symbolized by the statement

$$(\text{PQ then RQ}) \text{ is equivalent to RQ}$$

The high-speed cache in a memory hierarchy is actually a systematic generalization of the internal forwarding principle. The entire cache is a large buffer in front of the main memory. All paths from the memory to the CPU are short-circuited whenever the cache is known to contain the required data. See Chapter 5 for details.

Internal Forwarding in the Model 91

An interesting example of internal forwarding occurs in the IBM System/360 Model 91 computer [Chen, 64; Tomasulo, 67]. This case also illustrates the power of tag processing. Consider the Gaussian elimination sequence in ALGOL:

> **for** $J := K$ **step** 1 **until** N **do**
> $A[I,J] := A[I,J] \times Q - A[K,J];$

The innerloop is compiled into something like

$$R0 := A[I,J];$$
$$R0 := R0 \times Q;$$
$$R0 := R0 - A[K,J];$$
$$A[I,J] := R0;$$

where R0 is register 0.

This can be represented by the linear graph in Figure 9-26, where the multiplier and the adder are represented by points A and M.

The fetch, store, multiply, and add operations, as well as all intermediate paths, could be pipelined for one output per cycle. But the sequence of identical tasks, represented by the program loop, makes three passes through the noncompute delay R0, making it the bottleneck. Consequently the best pipeline processing rate is one task in three cycles.

In the Model 91 the arithmetic units are served by reservation stations which are internally addressable. Internal forwarding is routinely practiced to eliminate unneeded noncompute delays, by manipulating the "from" tags as back-pointers in list processing.

The forwarding assignments make use of store-store cancellation

$$(\text{AR, then BR}) \text{ is equivalent to BR}$$

and the easily proved statement

ARBR is equivalent to ABR

even when A, B are arithmetic rather than storage facilities. The actual tag processing is a real-time insertion of node B into a referral chain AR.

Forwarding occurs whenever a register cannot deliver a needed operand, but is known to be waiting for it. The cancellations occur at the interfaces between instructions (see Figure 9-26), and the routing of the operands makes use of a common data bus [Tomasulo, 67]. The mechanism reduces the demand on user-addressable registers, so that just one suffices to handle several chains of computations concurrently.

For the innerloop above, Model 91 ends up handling a macro-instruction.

$$
\begin{array}{l}
R0 := A\,[I,J]; \\
R0 := R0 \times Q \\
R0 := R0 - A\,[K,J] \\
\hline
A\,[I,J] := R0 \\
\hline
A\,[I,J] := A\,[I,J] \times Q - A\,[K,J]
\end{array}
$$

not unlike the original ALGOL statement (see Figure 9-27). This shows a dilemma in high-performance machine design. Starting from conventional machine instructions and using complex hardware, the clever mechanism merely succeeds in reinstating an uncompiled state of the program. It appears that special machines, using special new machine languages, might do the users' job more directly, and at lower cost. This problem is addressed in Section 9-9.

In the arithmetic execution above the issue is not so much the computing power of the pipelined units, but the manner of sequencing through them,

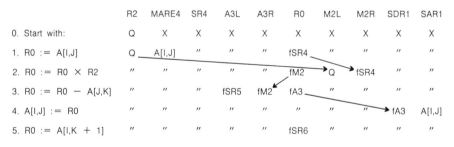

	R2	MARE4	SR4	A3L	A3R	R0	M2L	M2R	SDR1	SAR1
0. Start with:	Q	X	X	X	X	X	X	X	X	X
1. R0 := A[I,J]	Q	A[I,J]	"	"	"	fSR4	"	"	"	"
2. R0 := R0 × R2	"	"	"	"	"	fM2	Q	fSR4	"	"
3. R0 := R0 − A[J,K]	"	"	"	fSR5	fM2	fA3	"	"	"	"
4. A[I,J] := R0	"	"	"	"	"	"	"	"	fA3	A[I,J]
5. R0 := A[I,K + 1]	"	"	"	"	"	fSR6	"	"	"	"

SR5, SR6 not shown.
M2: the second multiplier reservation station
A3: the third adder reservation station
X means don't care; f means "forward from."

Figure 9-26 Tag processing in internal forwarding

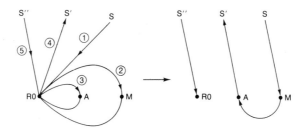

Figure 9-27   Internal forwarding in Model 91

for correctness and speed. Internal forwarding demonstrates the possible power of real-time self-scheduling. The exploratory *dataflow-machine designs* take the arithmetic units for granted, but concentrate on their systematic control. In these designs, instructions are made to flow through the arithmetic hardware as soon as operands and signals needed for their correct execution become available. In principle, at least, optimal processing is automatically achieved. For details see Dennis and Misunas [75], also Dennis and Weng [77].

9-9. SPECIAL PIPELINE SYSTEMS

We shall discuss a few actual designs of special pipeline machines for vector processing, in which the conventional mores of a general-purpose machine can largely be ignored.

After a decade of development, testing, and user experience, these machines have justified themselves by their high average performance, though their peak performance remains elusive in practice. Not surprisingly, the best pipeline algorithms differ markedly from the best monoprocessing algorithms. Nor are they the same as the best synchro-parallelism counterparts; though pipeline linkages allow more flexible control, pipeline drain still poses a unique challenge. Different pipeline machines also call for special treatment, as the presence or absence of a single feature often means a great deal [Voight, 77]. An important question is how to transmit the user's knowledge of job regularity to the machine [Gary, 77]. Often the effective use of these machines requires detailed hand optimizing, though compilers and "vectorizers" have been used with good results.

The CRAY-1 Vector Unit

The CRAY-1 computer is a highly overlapped machine in the tradition of the CDC 6600 and CDC 7600. Housed in a unique cylindrical package to minimize intercomponent distances and to permit efficient cooling, it features an extremely fast machine cycle (12.5 ns) and a large (up to 1 million 64-bit

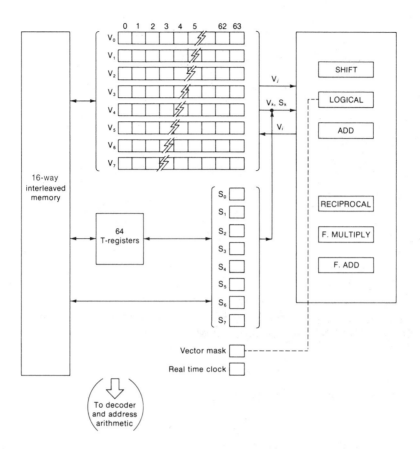

Figure 9-28   CRAY-1 vector unit

words), fast (50ns cycle) memory, 16-way interleaved. For conventional scalar problems, an instruction takes 1 to 14 machine cycles, at a CPU performance of 5.4 to 80 million instructions per second.

CRAY-1 has, further, a vector arithmetic unit (see Figure 9-28), which is able to execute 140 floating-point instructions per microsecond for well-formulated vector computation.

The unit has 8 V *(vector) registers,* each with 64 words. A vector operand is a number of elements from the same vector register, counting from the first element, up to a programmable limit of 64. Instructions are available to load into the vector registers, also to store from the vector registers blocks of up to 64 words, at specified address increments between memory operations. Because of interleaving, the maximum rate of one word per cycle is achieved as long as the increment is not a multiple of 8; otherwise the rate can lower to 4 cycles per word.

Vector-arithmetic instructions use a 3-address format, and are executed at the rate of one operation per cycle, after an overhead cost of 8 cycles. One of the operands can be a scalar; it is expanded into vector form by replication.

Usually computations involving 3-element vectors already are handled faster using the vector facility than as scalars.

The result of compare operations generates a bit mask in the vector mask (VM) register, which however is not intended to compress vectors into more condensed form, but rather to combine two vectors, selectively, into one vector of the same length. An entire vector can also be shifted as a giant bit-vector.

In vector arithmetic there are pipelined floating units for logic, add/ subtract, multiply, and reciprocation ($1/x$). The latter develops a half-length result (31 fraction bits), which can be the basis of a Newtonian iteration to yield a 47-bit quotient fraction in two more vector instructions. A chaining feature, based on internal forwarding, allows the linking of vector instructions to form vector macroinstructions, still at the maximum rate of one output per cycle. Using chaining, useful floating-point innerloops can be executed at the rate of one operation in 0.57 cycles, or 140 million instructions per second.

Being an overlap machine, the CRAY-1 gives imprecise interrupts, which may mean waiting the entire length of a vector instruction. For an account see Baskett and Keller [77] and Sites [78].

An Array Processor

The IBM 3838 array processor [IBM Corporation, 77] is a highspeed attachment to a general-purpose host computer in the IBM System/370 series through an I/O channel; see Figure 9-29.

It contains 5 functional units capable of completely overlapped operations: a channel interface with a 1.5 to 3.0-million-bytes-per-second transfer rate; a bulk storage of 256K, 512K or 1024K bytes with a cycle time of 800 ns, to be shared by up to seven 3838 users, 8-way interleaved for an effective speed of 40 million bytes per second; a data transfer controller for the control of routing of data between the functional units; a control processor with a 16,384-word writable control storage; and last but not least, an arithmetic processor with a 16K-byte control storage which can be doubled, a 16K-byte working storage, a sine/cosine generator for fast Fourier transforms, a reciprocal estimator, a multiplier, and two adders.

The last three arithmetic units are built as 4-stage pipelines with a cycle time of 100 ns. The system thus can perform one multiply and two adds per cycle.

The 5 functional units operate completely asynchronously, and their optimal use requires careful sifting of details. To minimize the programming burden, user instructions actually trigger premicrocoded *algorithms,* including standard vector-matrix operations, and very complex arithmetic packages. One algorithmic instruction, for example, performs the forward fast Fourier transform in complex floating-point arithmetic.

The Control Data STAR-100

The STAR-100 machine has a basic pipeline cycle time of 40 ns. Floating-point additions and multiplications of short operations (32-bit) can be

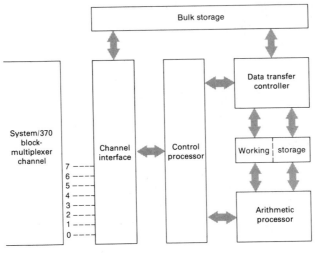

a) Overview

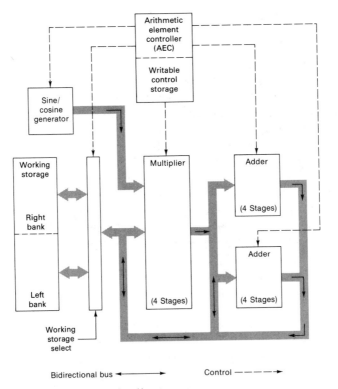

b) Arithmetic processor and working storage

Figure 9-29   The IBM 3838 array processor

handled at a rate of 100 million instructions per second, with up to four operations done simultaneously per cycle. For long (64-bit) operands the maximum rates are 50 million adds and 25 million multiplies per second.

The STAR memory has a cycle time of 1280ns, is interleaved by 32, and can deliver 512 bits every 40ns. The 512 bits are subdivided into four streams, each of 128 bits: two for the operands, one for the result, and the last for input/output requests and control-vector references. Memory buffers are used to even out address conflicts of the interleaved memory.

The 64-bit floating add is implemented in four pipeline stages (exponent compare, fraction shift, fraction add, then renormalize and transmission). Like the ILLIAC IV, the same unit can handle two short adds in parallel instead of one long add, and the two adder units then behave like four short adder units.

A 32-bit multiply employs a Wallace tree terminating in an add operation using half of an adder. A 64-bit multiply is done using standard double-precision arithmetic involving four short multiplies.

The machine has two nonidentical sets of arithmetic units (see Figure 9-30). One of these units also handles the divide and square-root functions. A multipurpose unit handles sparse vector, bit-string, and character string operations.

The STAR instruction design is similar to the VAMP, and makes use of APL primitives.

The development history of STAR had not been without pains for the developer and the user. See Lincoln [77] and Hendrickson [77]. The rather large overhead for each vector instruction (68 or more cycles) has required very long vectors to reach a high performance level.

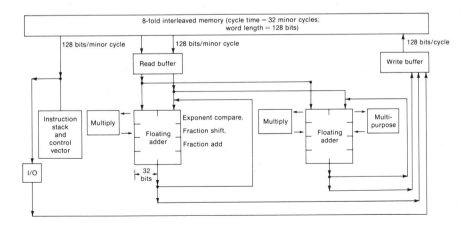

Figure 9-30 The CDC STAR-100

The Texas Instruments ASC

The ASC (Advanced Scientific Computer) is a general-purpose pipeline machine with particular accommodations for modularity; see Figure 9-31 [Watson, 72].

The memory control unit (MCU) is asynchronous in design, so as to be able to attach to any memory or processing units. The overall memory rate is 640 million 32-bit words per second. The central memory has a 160ns cycle time, and delivers eight informational words as a unit, with a Hamming error-correction code for each of the eight words. Interleaving is by eight units. A backup semiconductor storage with 1 microsecond cycle time is available. A paging technique with a protection scheme is employed.

The central processor employs both scalar and vector instructions, allowing 16-, 32-, and 64-bit operands. The processor can have up to four pipeline arithmetic units and each can deliver a result every 60ns. The vector instructions feature automatic three-dimensional indexing. Each pipeline unit has a memory buffer unit to even out the memory deliveries, and can reuse the outcome of a previous execution. The pipeline has eight stages, with bypasses to behave as one of a number of arithmetic-function generators (see Figure 9-32), in either fixed- or floating-point format. A pipeline drain accompanies function redefinition to ensure correctness of results.

The peripheral processor consists of eight virtual processors, which are eight skeleton processors that share a common processing, control, and data-storage resource.

Historical Note

The word "pipeline" and a sister term "streaming" probably originated within the IBM STRETCH project (1954-62), which developed both the highly overlapped STRETCH and the radically different 7950 Stream Pro-

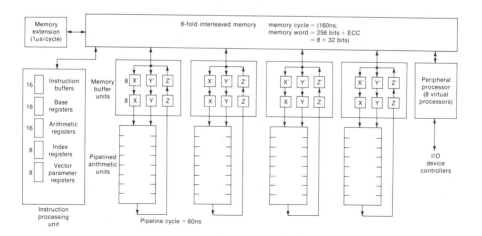

Figure 9-31 The Texas Instruments ASC

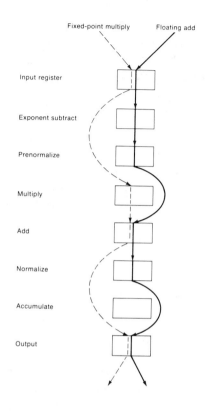

Figure 9-32 ASC arithmetic pipeline

cessor [Campbell et al., 62]. The latter is probably the first comprehensive pipelined machine. The computation is handled by two automatic input data streams, P and Q, and an automatic return stream, R. Each stream has its own buffer, is indexed separately, and can perform array indexing. The operations include byte processing, high-speed table lookup, inflight monitoring, and responses (adjustments) to unusual stimuli.

9-10. SUMMARY AND CONCLUSIONS

Overlap and pipelining are important multiprocessing tools for improving system performance, especially when the task subdivisions show distinct precedence linkages. The duration of a task no longer presents an obstacle for performance if there are enough tasks to exploit the decentralized computing power.

In overlap processing, the machine exercises internal processing freedom to gain performance, as long as it produces the correct outcome of computation at all user interfaces. The "correctness" is usually defined in terms of standard machine-instruction sequences, which can become confining. In striving for ever higher performance, interfacial protocol grows in complexity.

Pipelining unifies the protocols by time pulses, and aims at the elegance of orderly information flow. Thus it belongs to the category of tightly-coupled multiprocessing, like synchro-parallelism.

Both are in tune with the requirements of modern LSI microelectronics. Synchro-parallelism provides circuit systematicity, and pipelining reduces interconnections via orderliness in the time domain. Indeed, the two techniques complement each other. They are important components of high-performance machines. They merge in pipeline networks, again in the VAMP design. Both are extremely effective in handling vector computations on their own, and are similarly deficient in overcoming job inhomogeneity.

As LSI technology advances, associative control will become inexpensive, and self-optimization should add flexibility to tight coupling. On the other hand, systematic structures akin to cellular logic and dataflow machines may also become economical enough to merit serious study.

NOTATION

N	Multiplicity of synchro-parallel mechanism
M	Multiplicity of pipeline stages
H	Height of job profile
L	Number of tasks
r	Repetition ratio
n	Number of sweeps; also length of collision vector
w_j	Amount of work at the jth stage
τ	Pipeline cycle
P	Performance of synchro-parallel mechanism
P_p	Performance of pipeline
I	Instruction preparation
I_j	Instruction preparation for instruction j
E	Execution
E_j	Execution for instruction j
S_j	The jth pipeline stage
t_j	The jth time cycle
T_k	The kth task
T_{kj}	The jth step in handling T_k
C	The collision vector. $C = (C_n, \ldots, C_1)$
SAR(s)	Storage address register(s)
SDR(s)	Storage data register(s)
SR(s)	Storage register
MARE(s)	Memory address register(s) for E-fetch
MARI(s)	Memory address register(s) for I-fetch
IR(s)	Instruction register(s)

PROBLEMS

9-10. Consider the I/E overlap processing of 100 instructions, $j = 4k + m = 1, 2, \ldots, 100$. Compute the overlap ratio and comment on the result in each of the following cases:

a) $T(I_j) = T(E_j) = 1$

b) $T(I_j) = 0.5; T(E_J) = 1$

c) $T(I_j) = T(E_j) = 0.5, 0.75, 1.25, 1.5$ for $m = 0, 1, 2, 3$ respectively.

d) $T(I_j)$ is the same as in (c); $T(E_j) = 0.75, 1.25, 1.5, 0.5$ for $m = 0, 1, 2, 3$ respectively.

e) $T(E_j)$ is the same as in (c); $T(I_j) = 0.75, 1.25, 1.5, 0.5$, for $m = 0, 1, 2, 3$ respectively.

9-11. In processing a multi-panel job using a synchro-parallel multiprocessor of multiplicity N, the sweeping in effect subdivides the panels into two classes, the "tall" panels with height no less than N, and the "short" panels with heights strictly less than N. Analogous to Equation 9-10 we define

$$r = \frac{\text{combined areas of the tall panels}}{\text{total area of job}}$$

If h is the height of the tallest of the short panels, show that the global performance is bounded by

$$P < \frac{h}{1 - r}$$

9-12. The performance of tightly-coupled systems can be analyzed in terms of a performance function $F(r,x)$, defined by

$$F(r,x) = \frac{1}{1 - r + r/x}$$

For $x \geq 1 \geq r \geq 0$, this function is never less than 1, and it grows with increasing r, or x, or both.

a) Prove that, for the synchro-parallel processing of a model job (Figure 9-16), the performance is

$$P = F\left(r, \frac{H}{n}\right)$$

and show that P cannot exceed N, H, $F(r,H)$, $F(r,N)$, and $1/(1 - r)$. Can **P** *reach* any of these bounds? Under what conditions?

b) Prove that in the simple pipeline case (Figure 9-8), the performance is

$$P_p = F\left(1 - \frac{1}{L}, M\right)$$

9-13. For a future job calling for the performance of 20 conventional processors, compare the two strategies:

a) Buying a multiprocessor. Each processor has a peak performance of 2 conventional processors, and has a purchase price of $10,000.00.

b) Developing and building a special type of multiprocessor. Each processor has a peak performance equalling 10 conventional processors. The cost follows Equation 9-8 with A = $1 million, B = $10. For what demand (in terms of conventional processors) are the two strategies equal in merit? Assume for this problem the peak performance of the multiprocessors is always realized. Ignore differences in installation overhead, programming cost, and delivery delays.

9-14. One of the fastest and most accurate methods to sum 2^{k+1} normalized floating-point numbers together is to group the operands in pairs, do the individual adds, then repeat by regrouping, until only one operand remains. [See Linz, 70; Gregory, 72.] Comment on the result if the adds are done using synchro-parallelism with

a) $N = 2^k$.
b) $N = 2^{k-1}$.
c) $N = 2$.
d) Use, instead, a simple 4-stage pipeline, each stage is capable of a full floating-point addition.
e) Same as (c), except that each stage handles only a fourth of an addition, but is four times as fast. Sketch a special extra mechanism to yield a single sum.
f) Same as (d), but the designer is free to define the linkage among the stages. What is an optimum configuration for $k = 3$?

9-15. Given two pipelines, both with M stages. What is the performance of the joined pipeline for L jobs, relative to that of only one pipeline? Relative to that of 2L jobs flowing through one pipeline? Examine the situations for L = M/10, L = M, and L = 10M.

9-16. Assume a VAMP multiplier duration of four cycles, pipelined at one cycle per multiply. The raw processing rate of eight of these is equivalent to 64 fully engaged, nonpipelined multipliers, each consuming eight cycles.

a) How many actual multiplies would be needed to serve 64 virtual processors, if all of them need to start and finish within the same eight-cycle interval? Ignore the time needed for operand pickup from and return to the virtual processors.

b) Comment on possible changes in the design assumption in (a) to reduce hardware cost.

9-17. A three-stage floating-point adder pipeline normally cannot generate a total, even with recursion. This problem can be handled using a one-cycle noncompute delay under a one-bit microcode control, as shown in Figure 9-33. The true adder output appears along b if K = 0, else

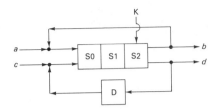

Figure 9-33 Microcontrol of delayed recursion

it appears along d. The path not receiving the true adder output carries a floating-point 0.

a) Starting with all stages full, and with zeros entering a and c, what is the control-bit sequence to obtain the total? Give a cycle-by-cycle account of the contents of the stages.

b) What is the fastest way to sum ten numbers together, starting with an empty pipeline?

9-18. The kth stage in the fixed-point cumulative multiply pipeline (Figure 9-34) can be microcontrolled by a bit B_k, such that, for the cycle in which the code is received by the stage,

$B_k = 1$ means proceed with normal processing;

$\quad = 0$ means NO OPERATION, the stage serving as a noncompute delay. For the task

$$\Sigma \, a_j, \text{ then } \Sigma \, a_k b_k$$

a) Show a feasible microcode sequence. Is there unwanted global output?

b) What would the microcode sequence be if the control bit B_k is delayed exactly by k cycles?

c) If the microcode is carried by a_k as a four-bit tag, bit k to be read by stage k, how would you design the tags?

Compare the three schemes on the basis of convenience in use, coding space, and hardware complexity.

9-19. Devise an internal forwarding scheme for the same instructions given in the Model 91 example, using "destination" tags rather than "from" tags. Comment on the relative merits of the forward and the backward pointer schemes.

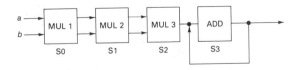

Figure 9-34 A cumulative multiply pipeline under microcode control

CHAPTER 10

Interpretation, Microprogramming, and the Control of a Computer

Michael J. Flynn

10-1. INTRODUCTION

Many readers are familiar with the concept of an interpretive program. This is simply a set of routines that directly process or operate on a source program—statement by statement—rather than first translating it into some intermediate form. The *instruction* set of a computer is also a "source language," and programs written in this language are *interpreted*—instruction by instruction—in the process that is commonly known as *execution*. In Section 10-2 of this chapter we review the familiar notion of instruction covered earlier in Chapters 3 and 4.

The routines that interpret instruction execution represent the internal *computer control* and can be implemented in a number of different ways. One approach is to write an interpretive subroutine for each of the machine instructions. These subroutines are stored in a special control storage and consist of control descriptors called *microinstructions*. This chapter is basically concerned with the viewpoint that control of the computer rests in *primitive operations* that are sequenced in subroutine fashion in order to interpret an instruction (*microprogramming*).

In Section 10-3 we deal with the nature of these primitive operations. Just as with higher-level operations, primitive operations have two aspects—operational and sequential. For its *operational* part the primitive operation must connect the appropriate source unit to its corresponding destination. It also must ensure that no unwanted information transfers take place. This operation takes place in a primitive time quantum called the computer's *cycle time*. Section 10-3 describes methods of connecting functional units to one another, and various types and forms of cycles. Thus, Section 10-3 is devoted to *what* has to be controlled. The actual primitive itself, the micro-instruction, can take on a number of different forms. These give rise to different microinstruction forms—the *how* of instruction control. In Section 10-4 we discuss microprogramming, using subroutines of these microinstruction to interpret conventional machine instructions. Microprogramming is not a new concept; it dates back almost thirty years. Just as notions of control in languages have changed radically over this time, so too has the notion of microprogramming. Most important is the understanding that this technique can be generalized so that one particular machine is able to interpret more than one instruction set. This process is called *emulation*.

Of course, technology itself has influenced the development of control techniques. Most notable is the availability of fast read/write-control storage. The fact that this storage can be easily altered demonstrates its more general use as a new level of storage hierarchy. This not only influences computer architecture—the way the computer is organized, as discussed in Section 10-5 —but also substantially changes our notions of fixed instruction sets and points to the development of special interpretive languages (each of which would cater to a specific higher level language), as discussed in Section 10-6.

10-2. INTERPRETATION OF CONVENTIONAL INSTRUCTIONS

The machine instruction provides the basic specification for all control action. As mentioned in Chapters 3 and 4, a machine instruction usually takes two source operands and produces a single result. An operand may not correspond exactly to a physical word in storage. It may, in fact, refer to multiple words. For our purposes we can assume that a typical reference operand is a single physical word. The instruction, then, has five logical functions:

1. Specify the address (location in storage) of the first source operand
2. Specify the address of the second source operand
3. Specify the address of the result of the operation
4. Specify the operation to be performed on the two source operands
5. Specify the address of the next instruction in the sequence

Thus a general instruction appears as:

Operation	Source address 1	Source address 2	Result address	Next instruction address

These specifications may or may not be made explicitly. The location of many of these addresses can be implied (by use of an accumulator, assuming instruction locations lie "inline," and so on), saving space in the instruction at the

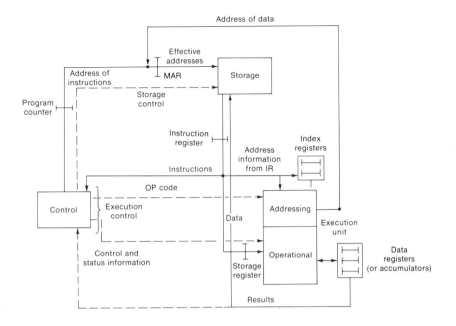

Figure 10-1   Flow of information in a computer

expense of additional instructions in the sequence required to bypass or reini-
tialize the implication.

In order to get a better understanding of the execution unit and the control
mechanism, consider the functional units that make up the processor: control unit, execution unit, and storage. As shown in Figure 10-1, the execution
unit may be further broken down into two basic pieces—addressing and
operational. The storage module is a conventional memory with data retrieval
by address. All system elements are activated by the control unit acting on
registers in the processor. The registers are distinct from storage and the
execution unit. Thus, the operation of any functional system element involves
transfer of information from one or two registers through the execution unit
and the return of a result to another register (perhaps one of the source
registers). Typical operations are illustrated in the example in Section 10-4.

An instruction is executed in four basic phases, as shown in Figure 10-2.
After the instruction has been transmitted to the instruction register (IR) from
storage (first phase), the operation part of the instruction drives the control
unit through a sequence of control steps. The initial control steps calculate a
source address (second phase) and fetch the source datum into the storage
register (third phase). Following that, a sequence of steps is performed with
two registers as sources and another register as a result (fourth phase). These
control signals are, in part, determined by the operation itself. Certain test

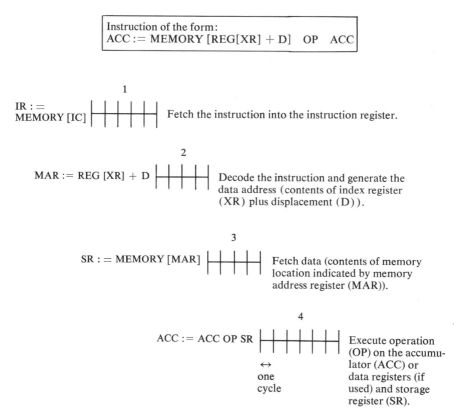

Instruction of the form:
ACC := MEMORY [REG[XR] + D]   OP   ACC

1

IR :=
MEMORY [IC]   Fetch the instruction into the instruction register.

2

MAR := REG [XR] + D   Decode the instruction and generate the
data address (contents of index register
(XR) plus displacement (D)).

3

SR : = MEMORY [MAR]   Fetch data (contents of memory
location indicated by memory
address register (MAR)).

4

ACC := ACC OP SR   Execute operation
(OP) on the accumu-
↔   lator (ACC) or
one   data registers (if
cycle   used) and storage
register (SR).

Figure 10-2   Sequencing through a simple instruction

signals are examined continually by the control unit to determine the next control command.

The operation in the execution (fourth) phase might be an ADD, for example. In order to accomplish this, however, a number of suboperations is necessary, as shown in Figure 10-3. First, the sign of each of the source data has to be inspected. If a complement of the operation is required, it may involve the injection of an additional 1 into the least significant data position (as in two's complement arithmetic). Finally, after the ADD there is a potential recomplementation (again, depending upon the representation) and an inspection for overflow.

10-3. BASIC CONCEPTS IN CONTROL

Before discussing techniques of control, consider what is being controlled. Information is processed within a functional unit by a specific configuration of logic gates (combinatorial logic) in a single time unit, or by a sequence of steps through such logical configurations (sequential logic). The communication may be transmitted and transformed in one time unit by the data paths of the system. A sequence of transmissions from register to register requires multiple cycles. This section investigates the general requirements for controlling the data paths of the system as well as various kinds and forms of internal cycles that the designer may use.

Data Paths and Control Points

A machine, exclusive of control, consists largely of registers and combinatorial execution logic (adders, shifters, and so on). Each register position in the system can be gated to one of a number of other registers during one cycle. The interregister connections, together with the registers and resources,

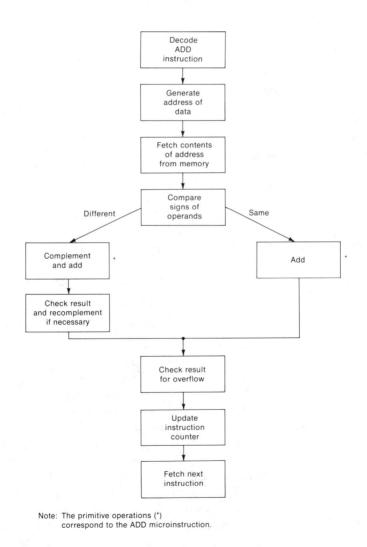

Note: The primitive operations (*)
correspond to the ADD microinstruction.

Figure 10-3 ADD machine instruction, with sign and magnitude data representation

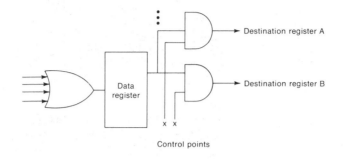

Figure 10-4 Gating logic

are referred to as the "data paths" of the system. The output of each register activates AND gates that are directed to each of the destinations reachable from the source register in one cycle (see Figure 10-4).

Larger processors generally have direct connection to specific destination registers, as shown in Figure 10-4. Smaller systems frequently use a bus to reduce the number of direct paths and their control. A bus-oriented system has a common communication path for several registers. Both entry to the bus and exit from the bus into a destination register must be gated by control lines. The extra control is justified by the lower cost associated with the reduction in paths.

There are two types of data paths, as shown in Figure 10-5:

1. Those paths that connect the source register to a destination register (perhaps itself) without any intervening transformational logic
2. Those paths connected from a source register into an execution unit and then directed to a destination register

Figure 10-5 shows the data paths for the ith bit of a storage register, an adder, and an accumulator. In this example, the accumulator register is added to a word from memory which has been placed in the storage register; the sum is returned to the accumulator. This occurs during the execute phase shown in Figure 10-3. A simple ADD instruction may have a three-cycle execute. One cycle is used for inspection of the signs of each of the operands before the addition, the second cycle is used for the addition, and the third cycle is used for sign and overflow inspection. During the second cycle the information in bit i of the storage register is gated to bit i of the adder, activated by an appropriate control signal, labeled *SR-to-adder*. This allows the information from bit i of the accumulator and bit i of the storage register to activate the two inputs to the ith position of the adder. This together with the carry from bit $i - 1$ position determines the sum, which is gated through OR into the accumulator. The accumulator does not actually change its value upon receiving this signal, but at the end of the cycle a sample pulse is used to set this

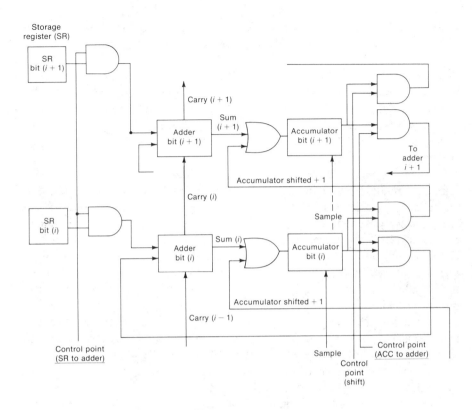

Figure 10-5 Two types of data paths

new information into the accumulator. At the same time, new information can be entered into the storage register. If the instruction, instead of being an ADD instruction, were a SHIFT instruction, we would use a path from each bit of the accumulator to its neighbor. Notice that operations involving the adder require a substantial number of logic decisions before the final value can be determined and set into the accumulator, while the SHIFT operation involves only two decisions.

In general, if the execution unit (for example, the adder in the preceding example) has internal storage, it may be treated as a multiple-cycle operation. If it does not, then the time required to direct information from a register through the execution unit and back to a register defines the register cycle time. Combinatorial logic has no memory by itself; all information is lost at the end of one cycle, unless it is stored in a register.

Control points are the hardware locations at which the output of the processor-instruction decoder activates specific registers and operation units. Control points basically govern intracycle register-to-register communications. For each register in the processor there is a fixed number of other registers to which data may be transmitted in one cycle. For each such possibility, a separate AND circuit is placed on the output of each bit of the source register, with the entry into the destination register being collected from all possible sources by an OR circuit.

For example, consider a 32-bit computer with eight registers. Assume that each register can communicate with three other registers in one cycle. The number of control points required for register communication is therefore $3 \times 8 \times 32$ or 768. In addition, assume the machine has three execution units, each of whose 32-bit outputs can be gated to one of four registers. This accounts for an additional $3 \times 4 \times 32$ or 384 control points. There are additional control points for the selection of a particular function within a designated module. This might account for 100 more control points. Thus, there are a total of somewhat over 1200 control points that must be established each cycle by the output of the instruction decoder. Fortunately, in most computer design situations, many of these control points are not independent. For example, bit 7 of a certain register is not separately gated to another register, but rather the entire contents of the register is gated to its destination register. Since only one line is required to control these multiple control points, the total number of outputs required can be significantly reduced. These outputs are then referred to as independent control points. For the hypothetical system described, there might be anywhere from 50 to 200 independent control points, depending upon the variety of instructions.

The operation code specifies the operation to be performed; by itself it is insufficient to specify multiple control steps for the execution of an instruction; some additional counting mechanism is also required. If the control implementation is to be done with hardware implementation—using a combinatorial network—then a counter is used to sequence through the control steps to transmit signals to control points. This counter identifies the particular step of the instruction that is executed at any moment. The combination of the sequence count and the operation is the input to the network, which then describes the exact state of each control point at each cycle of every instruction (see Figure 10-6).

Cycle Time

The cycle time of a computer is the time required to change the information in a set of registers. This is also sometimes referred to as a *state-transition* time. The internal cycle time may not be of constant value; there are typically three different ways of clocking a processor:

1. *Synchronous fixed* — In this scheme all operations are composed of one or more clock cycles, with the fundamental time quantum being fixed by the design. Such systems are also referred to as clocked, since usually a master oscillator (or clock) is used to distribute and define these cycles.
2. *Synchronous variable* — This is a slight variation of the former scheme, in which certain long operations are allowed to take multiple cycles without causing a register state transition. In such systems there may

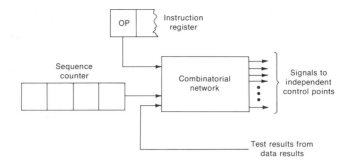

Figure 10-6 Hardware control

be several different cycle lengths. For example, a register-to-register transfer of information might represent one basic cycle, while a transfer from a register to an adder with return to a register requires perhaps two or three basic cycles. The fundamental difference between these two schemes is that the synchronous fixed scheme stores information into registers at the end of every cycle time, while the synchronous variable scheme sets information into registers after a number of cycles depending upon the type of operation being performed.

3. *Asynchronous operation* — In a completely asynchronous machine there is no clock or external mechanism that determines a state transition. Rather the logic of the system is arranged in stages. When the output value of one stage has been stabilized, the input at the stage can admit a new pair of operands.

Asynchronous operation is advantageous when the variation in cycle time is significant, since a synchronous scheme must always wait for the worst possible delay in the definition of the time quantum required. On the other hand, when logic delays are predictable, synchronous techniques have an advantage, since several additional stages of logic are required in the asynchronous scheme to signal completion of an operation. In actual practice, most systems are basically synchronous (either fixed or variable), with some asynchronous operations used for particular functions of the machine, such as in accessing main memory.

The cycle itself is composed of two components: 1) the time necessary to decode the control information and set up the control points, and 2) the time necessary to transmit and transform the data (the data state transition). In simple machines the cycle is the sum of the control decoding time and the data state transition time. In second generation computers with hard-wired control logic, control time was approximately 35 percent of the entire cycle and the data state transition was the remaining 65 percent of the cycle (see Figure 10-7). With the use of microprogram store for the implementation of the control function in third generation computers, the control time increased and overlapping of the two became more prevalent.

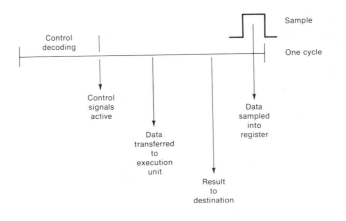

Figure 10-7 Action within a cycle

10-4. MICROPROGRAMMING

Control of a processor involves the specification at each cycle of all of the control points of the system. In this section we review the concept of microprogramming and the evolution of that concept over the past several years. We then look at specific types of microinstructions: methods of specifying the various kinds and types of control mechanisms which may be required. (This is really a generalization of the discussions of control in Chapters 3 and 4.) Finally we give a detailed example of a simple processor to see how all of these control aspects are realized via a microprogram and microinstructions.

Concept of Microprogramming

Microprogramming refers to the use of storage to implement the control unit. In the simplest cases, the operation code in the machine instruction is used as a (partial) address to the first microinstruction. This microinstruction contains the required control-point values as well as the address of the following microinstruction in the sequence for operation interpretation. Alternatively, the microinstructions can be placed inline, and the address field is eliminated. Microprogramming, like many other words in a computer system vocabulary, has come to take on a variety of meanings in different applications situations. In fact, it has evolved in several stages since it was first used thirty years ago by M. V. Wilkes [51]. Many different interpretations of the word stem from a variety of equivalent implications that are derived from basically the same principles.

Originally microprogramming meant the systematic and orderly control of the functional modules of a computer system. We must distinguish between microinstructions and instructions: functions performed by a microinstruction can usually be implemented by combinatorial logic. Equivalently, we may view the machine instruction as causing a main memory state change, while the microinstruction causes a register state change. Since the exact nature of main memory and registers is not always well defined (a register referred to by instructions may actually be locations in main memory, and vice versa), reliance on this distinction for a microinstruction can lead to confusion. For example, an operation, from a physical point of view, is the primitive logic that performs an absolute binary addition. It does not include such associated functions as sign detection, complementation, check for overflow, and so on. Inclusion of these features into the ADD operation is a sequence of steps (microinstructions) that together make up a machine-language instruction.

Other notions of microprogramming are possible. Many of these notions rest on one of the properties or applications of microprogrammed systems that are possible with a storage implementation of the control function of an instruction and are not possible with direct Boolean implementation. One such application is emulation. Informally, emulaton is the interpretation of a machine language (machine-instruction set). Since a nonmicroprogrammed computer can only emulate the machine code for its own Boolean equations, it is limited to the emulation of the single language for which it is designed [Rosin, 69]. In a microprogrammed system, since the control function is implemented via storage, if the storage is changed with a different set of sequences, the control unit of the system can be used to emulate more than one machine language, although not necessarily with equivalent efficiency.

Evolution of Microprogramming

Microprogramming has evolved through three distinct phases. The earliest phase involved the use of microprogramming for engineering convenience. The control storage contains simple descriptions of the gating patterns of each of the control points for each cycle. Ease of engineering change and design were important considerations. For these early microprogram implementations, diode matrix technology was well suited. Microprogrammed implementation of control during this era is perhaps best illustrated by Wilkes's ideas, as shown in Figure 10-8. Wilkes viewed the microprogrammed control store as consisting of two diode matrices. The first matrix determines the control information for the data paths, while the second matrix determines, at least in part, the next microinstruction to be selected to continue the interpretation of the given instruction. The choice of the next microinstruction is influenced by a selected datum, for example the sign bit of an accumulator. If the sign is negative, one microinstruction might be called; if the sign is positive another might be invoked. This is required so that proper complementation rules can be used for addition and subtraction.

The decoding tree shown in Figure 10-8 has the function of transforming a pattern of n bits into a unique selection of 1 out of 2^n possible outputs. Thus, for example, a 4-bit binary input into a decoder tree has four input variables. These define sixteen possible configurations, from 0000 to 1111. The output of the tree has sixteen lines or possible events. Each output line corresponds to one and only one of the input configurations, and is activated when that input configuration is present. When an output line is activated, it

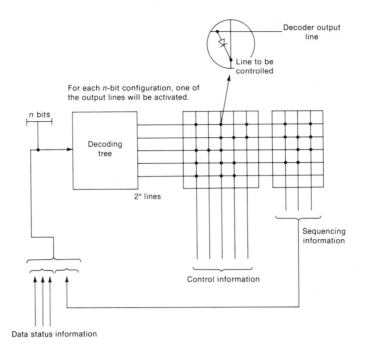

Figure 10-8 Wilkes's microprogrammed control storage

also activates all lines out of the matrix that are connected to it via diodes. The diode action allows current to pass from the drive or input line into the output line. Of course, if no diode connects an input line to an output line, no current is transmitted and that line remains in a zero state. These diode arrays give a simple and regular implementation to the control function. However, speed could be a problem. In early implementations no speed problems developed since main memory was quite slow, about 10 micro-seconds cycle time, and the diode matrix had an access time of under .5 microsecond. The ratio of control access time to main memory access time is an important one. When there is a large number of internal cycles in each memory cycle, the microprogramming task is relatively simple and straightforward. One register-to-register transformation is performed per internal cycle, and performance is essentially limited by the main memory cycle. As the main memory access time decreases, however, microprogram-ming techniques must become correspondingly more sophisticated. If there are only one or two internal machine cycles for each main memory cycle, it is necessary to have multiple data transfers in each machine cycle. That is, the microinstruction must simultaneously control a number of resources internal to the system. This gives rise to a type of internal parallelism within the processor.

During the decade of the fifties the relatively slow main memory technology made implementation of the microstorage array rather easy. A variety of technologies were used for control storage, but diode storage was probably the most widely used. During the latter 1950s, with the introduction of magnetic core memories, the ratio of access time between main memory and the control storage dropped rather sharply, making it difficult to execute the required number of microinstructions for a machine instruction in a reasonable amount of time. This became especially important in light of the development of fast transistorized logic circuits for the wired implementation of the control function.

The second generation of microprogrammed systems is distinguished by its small number of internal machine cycles per main memory cycle. By the early 1960s main memory speed had dropped to under 1 microsecond; yet the technology for control store had not noticeably improved—the best access for read-only store varied between 200 and 400 nanoseconds. In addition, read-only storage technologies tended to be exotic. The technology was not common with any other part of the machine and was not always reliable. However, by this time the arguments for using microprogramming went well beyond the reasons cited by Wilkes. In 1964, with the announcement of the IBM System/360, an important application for microprogramming had been added—*emulation* of multiple machines on a single host system [Tucker, 65 and 67]. It made the customer's transition from an old to a new system much more palatable, in that the customer could, with one system, support his old software as well as develop new applications with new programming languages and facilities.

The third generation of microprogramming dates from about 1970, with the advent of fast read/write control store. With the development of bipolar monolithic technology, one has a storage medium with the same access time as combinatorial-logic gating delays, since they are made out of the same material. The writable capability of control store represents an important transition, since now the control store becomes a true member of the memory hierarchy. In Section 10-5, we examine the impact of third-generation micro-programming on computer architecture. Similar technological improvements have produced fast, high-density read-only memory for traditional control-storage application. Several of these technologies have erasable or programmable facilities, allowing the designer flexibility in modifying control programs.

Microinstructions

The microinstruction is, by definition, the control mechanism that causes each data-register change. The flexibility in this interaction allows a variety of possible microinstructions. Terms such as horizontal and vertical formats, nanoinstruction, and packed or unpacked microinstructions have been used, sometimes ambiguously, to describe certain differences.

If, within the control of a single functional unit, the microinstruction contains a separate description of each independent control point in the resource (for example, the true description of the control gating), that activaton is said to be an *unpacked* or *exploded form* of the microinstruction (see Part *a* of Figure 10-9). This form is most expensive in terms of space but provides the ultimate flexiblity, in that any combination of control-point values may be

a) Single-resource control (unpacked)

Control-point values	Next address

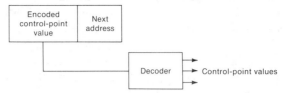

b) Single-resource control (packed)

Encoded control-point value	Next address

Decoder → Control-point values

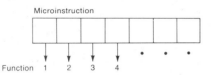

c) Multiple-functional-unit control

Microinstruction

Function   1   2   3   4   • • •

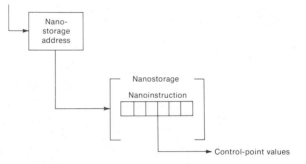

d) Two levels of interpretation

Microinstruction contains:

Nano-storage address

Nanostorage

Nanoinstruction

→ Control-point values

Figure 10-9   Some concepts used in microinstruction formats

specified at any time. As an alternate to this unpacked form, a specific number of combinations of control-point values may be chosen. These combinations, then, may be coded into a few bits and, through use of a decoder, may be regenerated when the microinstruction is executed (see Part *b* of Figure 10-9). This is called a *packed form,* and it saves space at the expense of flexibility. Occasionally the distinction between packed and unpacked forms of microinstructions is expressed by referring to them as *vertical* and *horizontal* microinstructions, respectively.

As previously mentioned, the functional units of the system may be partitioned into a number of independent units that can be used simultaneously. If this partitioning is done, then the microinstruction that activates these functions simultaneously contains a separate information field for each function. Thus in Part *c* of Figure 10-9, a functional unit might be an adder, a shifter, a unit for loading and/or storing information into a register, or a test and branch unit. Notice that these can be operated simultaneously, as long as they do not make conflicting use of a datum. The distinction between the control of a single function through the use of control points, whether by packed or unpacked microinstructions, and the multiple-functional-unit control illustrated in Part *c* of Figure 10-9 is worth noting. Of course, the control for an adder still requires a set of control points, whether or not a microinstruction specifies the adder action only or the action of multiple units. This simultaneous use of resources gives rise to a type of internal parallelism that is explicit—visible to the microprogrammer—yet within the single instruction stream. This is unlike the type of internal parallelism of certain highly pipelined machines such as the CDC 6600 and IBM 360 Model 91, whose parallelism is also transparent to the programmer, as described in Chapter 9. In any event, this use of the microinstruction for identification of possible simultaneous use of resources has also been referred to as a *horizontal microinstruction*. The alternative is to use a universal single resource. Its corresponding control mechanism is sometimes referred to as a *vertical microinstruction*.

Some computers use a level of control which interprets a microinstruction, sometimes referred to as a nanolevel. In this mode a packed microinstruction, usually with only one or two fields, is used as the basic control mechanism. However, instead of driving the resources directly, it indirectly refers to the resources through another interpretative level, the *nanoinstruction*. The nanoinstruction is usually a horizontal instruction that contains the exploded form of the control description. This technique is used on machines such as the Nanodata Corporation QM1. Part *d* of Figure 10-9 illustrates this concept in which the *microinstructions* represent a sequence of addresses and each address points to a nanoinstruction. A nanoinstruction may be horizontal, with multiple resource specifications. The purpose of this technique is to reduce the size of the storage needed to represent the microprogram.

Simple Microprogrammed Machine

In this section we illustrate the use of a read-only memory to control a simple digital machine. This fictitious machine was organized by Rosin [69] to exemplify the use of microprogramming for implementing the control function of a computer. Rosin proposed an emulator but left the "control" details unspecified. The proposed machine used a single accumulator with 4096 words of main memory and a maximum of 16 operations. All operations are of the form: ACC := ACC OP MEMORY [ADDRESS].

The machine has the following memories and registers:

SR:	storage register	MM:	main memory
MAR:	memory address register	CM:	control (read-only) memory
AC:	accumulator	MIC:	microinstruction counter
IC:	instruction counter	MIR:	microinstruction register
IR:	instruction register	REG:	added output register

In addition, the following transformational resources are provided:

> Adder (with no storage resources)
> Increment unit
> Clear unit

The block diagram of the machine is given in Figure 10-10. The machine has thirteen independent control points. Each point controls a particular line. The lines that have to be controlled are:

0 — AC → SR	7 — IR_{0-11} → MAR
1 — SR → ADD → REG	8 — IC → MAR
2 — AC → ADD → REG	9 — INC IC
3 — REG → AC	10 — MM READ
4 — SR → AC	11 — MM WRITE
5 — SR → IR	12 — CLEAR AC
6 — IR_{0-11} → IC	

When control point 0 is activated, the following transformation takes place: SR := AC. Following this, the contents of AC are gated onto the AC-SR data path and read into SR at the end of the cycle. When control point 1 is activated, the contents of SR are gated through the left port of the adder at the beginning of the cycle. If control point 2 is simultaneously activated, the following transformation is completed at the end of the cycle: REG := SR + AC. If control point 2 is not activated then the contents of SR are gated through the adder and transferred to REG at the end of the cycle. Activation of control point 9 causes the following transformation to take place: IC := IC + 1. Activation of control point 10 causes SR := MEMORY [MAR] after one main memory cycle, and activation of control point 11 causes the transformation MEMORY [MAR] := SR. Activation of control point 12 has the following effect: AC := 0.

The control part has a read-only memory of 16 bits × 1K words. Each machine instruction is interpreted by a routine residing in control memory. When an instruction I is fetched in IR, contents of IR_{12-15} are transferred to MIC_{0-3}. This causes the contents of one of the locations 0 through 15 to be placed in MIR. A jump is then executed to a particular location in control memory where the routine that will interpret I resides. The words in control memory can have two possible formats.

Format 1:

In format 1, bits 0 to 12 indicate the control points to be activated. Bit $i = 1$ specifies that control point i is to be activated. Whenever a word with format 1 is brought into the MIR, the specified control points are activated during that microcycle.

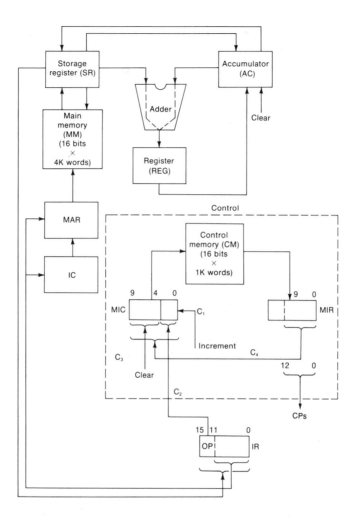

Figure 10-10 Block diagram of a simple digital machine

Format 2:

15	14	13	12	11	10	9			0
0							(address)		

Format 2 indicates how MIC is to be modified, and is used for branching.

Control memory is accessed whenever a change in the contents of MIC takes place. Let us assume there are two bits, *a* and *b*, which are set depending on the contents of AC: *a* equals 1 if and only if AC is zero, and *b* equals 1 if and only if AC is negative. Let B_i denote the *i*th bit of MIR. Then T = $(B_{15}, B_{14}, B_{13}, B_{11}, B_{10}, a, b)$ denotes a particular value of the seven bits. Four control lines, C_1, C_2, C_3, and C_4, are used to change MIC. A cycle starts with a decode of the seven bits (see Figure 10-11).

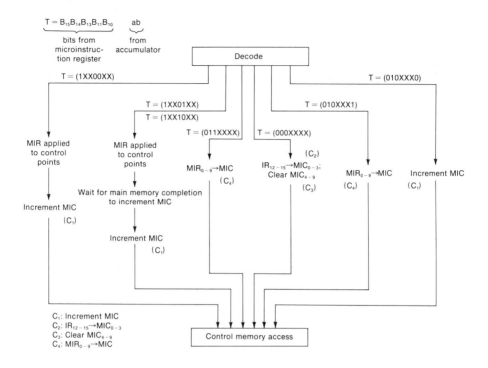

Figure 10-11   Bit decoding

The $T = 1XX00XX$ path indicates the usual case of a microinstruction of format 1 type whose ICP's are to be applied immediately and whose completion will occur in one cycle. The $T = 1XX01XX$ or $1XX10XX$ paths, on the other hand, are the main memory and the read and write cases—these will not complete in one cycle. Here, the MIC is not incremented until a main memory completion signal is received.

Bit 15 selects between formats 1 and 2. Bits 14 and 13 are used only in the format 2 case—they distinguish between three types of branching situation: $B_{15}\ B_{14}\ B_{13} = 011$ is used for an unconditional transfer (i.e., the low ten bits of the current microinstruction are entered into the microinstruction counter); 000 indicates an unconditional transfer initiated from the OP code field of the instruction register. These four bits are used to enter a table in the first 16 words of control storage. Each entry in the table is a transfer to the corresponding microprogrammed routine. Finally, the 010 case indicates a conditional transfer—if the b bit (from the accumulator) is 0 (i.e., accumulator positive), normal MIC incrementing is performed; if $b = 1$ (accumulator negative), the transfer takes place. The a bit is tested by $B_{15}\ B_{14}\ B_{13} = 001$. This is not used in any of the examples indicated; however, transfer on zero functions and more extensive detailing of the machine would use this feature.

We can now define a microcycle as the time taken for the first path: decode, MIR applied to control points, increment MIC, control memory

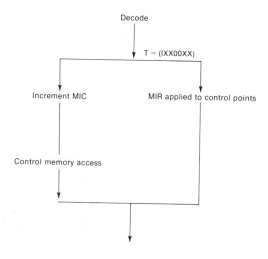

Figure 10-12   Control cycle with parallel execution

access. In fact, the cycle time can be reduced considerably by doing two operations in parallel as shown in Figure 10-12.

Care must be taken to ensure that MIR is undisturbed by the access until application of signals to the control points is complete. The microcycle then becomes the time required to decode, increment MIC, then access control memory. The decoding is done by a combinatorial network described in Figure 10-11, and the required control lines, C_1, C_2, C_3, and C_4, are activated. The control memory thus operates in a completely synchronous manner except when a read or write to main memory is in progress. In this case, control memory is not accessed until a signal is given to C_1 by the main memory indicating that it has completed its cycle.

Figure 10-13 gives the contents of control store for IFETCH (instruction fetch), ADD, and STORE ZERO. This figure also gives the routines for interpreting the following machine instructions: IFETCH (0000), ADD (0001), CLA (0010), STORE AC (0011), TRA (0100), TRA IF ACNEG (0101), and STORE ZERO (0110). CLA denotes "clear and add" and TRA denotes "transfer." Figure 10-14 gives timing diagrams for IFETCH, ADD, and STORE ZERO.

For simplicity's sake, this example ignores input/output control and certain aspects of sign control for arithmetic routines.

10-5. MICROPROGRAMMING AND COMPUTER ARCHITECTURE

As mentioned earlier, the replacement of read-only storage for implementing control with read/write storage can substantially impact not only the way control is implemented but also the overall architecture—the instruction set—

LOC	CONTROL STORE 15	14	13	12	11	10	9	8	7	6	5	4	3	2	1	0	COMMENTS
0 0 0 0 0 0	0	1	1	X	X	X	0	0	0	0	0	1	0	0	0	0	Jump to microroutine for interpreting IFETCH
0 0 0 0 0 1	0	1	1	X	X	X	0	0	0	0	0	1	0	1	0	0	Jump to microroutine for interpreting ADD
0 0 0 0 1 0	0	1	1	X	X	X	0	0	0	0	0	1	1	0	0	1	Jump to microroutine for interpreting CLA
0 0 0 0 1 1	0	1	1	X	X	X	0	0	0	0	0	1	1	1	0	1	Jump to microroutine for interpreting STORE AC
0 0 0 1 0 0	0	1	1	X	X	X	0	0	0	0	1	0	0	0	0	0	Jump to microroutine for interpreting TRA
0 0 0 1 0 1	0	1	1	X	X	X	0	0	0	0	1	0	0	0	1	0	Jump to microroutine for interpreting TRA IF AC NEG
0 0 0 1 1 0	0	1	1	X	X	X	0	0	0	0	1	0	0	1	0	0	Jump to microroutine for interpreting STORE ZERO
0 0 0 1 1 1	0	1	1														
	0	1	1														
	0	1	1														
.	0	1	1														
.	0	1	1														
.	0	1	1														
	0	1	1														
	0	1	1														
	0	1	1														
0 0 1 1 1 1	0	1	1														
																	IFETCH
0 1 0 0 0 0	1	X	X	0	0	0	0	1	0	0	0	0	0	0	0	0	START IFETCH, (control line 9), IC→MAR
0 1 0 0 0 1	1	X	X	0	0	1	1	0	0	0	0	0	0	0	0	0	MM READ (MIC not incremented till read complete); INC IC
0 1 0 0 1 0	1	X	X	0	0	0	0	0	0	0	1	0	0	0	0	0	SR→IR
0 1 0 0 1 1	0	0	0	X	X	X	X	X	X	X	X	X	X	X	X	X	$IR_{12-15} \rightarrow MIC_{0-3}$
																	ADD
0 1 0 1 0 0	1	X	X	0	0	0	0	0	1	0	0	0	0	0	0	0	START ADD, $IR_{0-11} \rightarrow$ MAR
0 1 0 1 0 1	1	X	X	0	0	1	0	0	0	0	0	0	0	0	0	0	MM READ (MIC not incremented till read complete)
0 1 0 1 1 0	1	X	X	0	0	0	0	0	0	0	0	0	0	1	1	0	SR→ADD→REG; AC→ADD→REG
0 1 0 1 1 1	1	X	X	0	0	0	0	0	0	0	0	0	1	0	0	0	REG→AC
0 1 1 0 0 0	0	1	1	0	0	0	0	0	0	0	0	1	0	0	0	0	GO TO IFETCH

Figure 10-13 (Part 1 of 2) Map of microstorage for control of Rosin's machine

CONTROL STORE

LOC	15	14	13	12	11	10	9	8	7	6	5	4	3	2	1	0	COMMENTS
																	CLA
0 1 1 1 0 0	1	X	X	0	0	0	0	0	1	0	0	0	0	0	0	0	START CLA, IR$_{0-11}$→MAR
0 1 1 1 0 0	1	X	X	0	0	1	0	0	0	1	0	0	0	0	0	0	MM READ
0 1 1 1 1 0	1	X	X	0	1	0	0	0	0	0	0	1	0	0	0	0	SR→AC
0 1 1 1 1 0	0	1	1	X	X	X	0	0	0	0	0	1	1	0	0	0	GO TO IFETCH
																	STORE AC
0 1 1 1 0 1	1	X	X	0	0	0	0	0	1	0	0	0	0	0	0	1	START STORE AC, IR$_{0-11}$→MAR; AC→SR
0 1 1 1 1 0	1	X	X	0	1	0	0	0	0	0	0	1	0	0	0	0	MM WRITE (MIC not incremented till write complete)
0 1 1 1 1 1	0	1	1	X	X	X	0	0	0	0	0	1	1	0	0	0	GO TO IFETCH
																	TRA
1 0 0 0 0 0	1	X	X	0	0	0	0	0	1	0	0	0	0	0	0	0	START TRA, IR$_{0-11}$→IC
1 0 0 0 0 0	0	1	1	X	X	X	0	0	0	0	1	0	1	0	0	0	GO TO IFETCH
																	TRA IF ACNEG
1 0 0 0 1 0	0	1	0	X	X	X	0	0	0	0	1	0	0	0	0	0	START TRA IF ACNEG, IF ACNEG,
1 0 0 0 1 0	0	1	1	X	X	X	0	0	0	0	0	1	0	0	0	0	GO TO TRA
1 0 0 0 1 0	0	1	1	X	X	X	0	0	0	0	1	0	1	0	0	0	GO TO IFETCH
																	STORE ZERO
1 0 0 0 0 1	1	X	X	0	0	0	0	0	0	1	0	0	0	1	0	0	START STORE ZERO, AC→ADD→REG
1 0 0 0 0 1	1	X	X	1	0	0	0	0	0	0	0	0	0	0	0	0	CLEAR AC
1 0 0 0 1 1	1	X	X	0	0	0	0	0	1	0	0	0	1	0	0	1	IR$_{0-11}$→MAR; AC→SR
1 0 0 1 1 0	1	X	X	0	1	0	0	0	0	0	0	1	0	0	0	0	MM WRITE; REG→AC
1 0 0 1 0 0	0	1	1	X	X	X	0	0	0	0	0	0	1	0	0	0	GO TO IFETCH

Figure 10-13 (Part 2 of 2) Map of microstorage for control of Rosin's machine

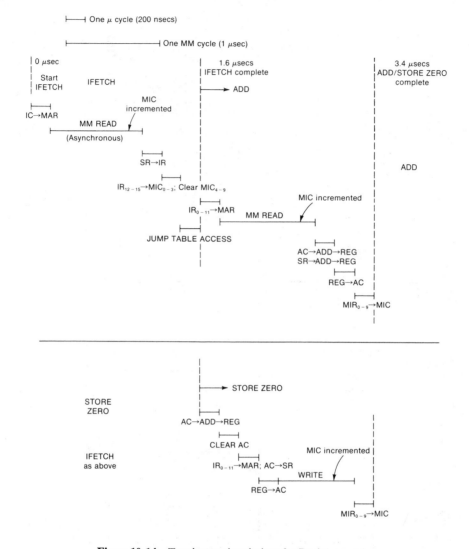

Figure 10-14 Two instruction timings for Rosin's machine

of a particular computer. In this section we investigate the impact of read/write control storage on computer organization. We then look at some aspects of modern microprogrammable computers, as well as an example of how third-generation microprogramming impacts computer design.

Read/Write Microstorage and Its Impact

The availability of read/write storage can be expected to play an important role in the evolution of machine organizations. Traditional second- and third-generation machines have been organized about two artifacts:

1. The importance of the machine language as a ready interface with the human
2. The quite long access time to main memory for data and instructions, compared to the time required to move data from a register

The machine-language programmer of today does not program in assembly code for convenience, but for efficiency; that is, in order to control the physical resources of the system in an optimal way. Ease of use is not as important a consideration in the development of a machine language as efficiency. This, coupled with improved memory, implies a significant change in computer organization: an increase in parallel or concurrent use of resources. Since hardware is inexpensive, units are made independent in the hope that their concurrent operation will produce more efficient programs.

How can the control of the resources of the system be made visible to the programmer? First let us review the evolution of the machine language as we know it and compare it with microprogrammed systems.

An essential feature of a microprogrammed system is the availability of a fast storage medium. "Fast" in this sense implies that the memory-access time is approximately the same as the cycle time of the processor. Another important attribute of modern microprogrammed systems is that this fast storage is writable from main memory. This defines the concept of "dynamic microprogramming." Consider the timing chart for a conventional (nonmicroprogrammed) machine instruction as shown in Figure 10-2. Due to slow access of instruction and data, a substantial amount of instruction-execution time is spent in overhead operations. Contrast this with the situation shown in Figure 10-15, which illustrates the execution of an instruction on a microprogrammed computer.

In Figure 10-15 there is an implicit assumption of homogeneity of memory, that is, that data and operands are all located in the same fast storage as the instructions. The latter assumption is valid when the control storage is writable.

The preceding implies another significant difference in conventional machines and microprogrammed machines, namely, the power of the operation to be performed by the instruction. In the conventional machine, given the substantial accessing overhead, it is important to design each instruction to do as much as possible in computing a result. To do otherwise would necessarily involve a number of additional accessing overheads; thus we have the

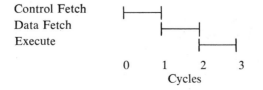

Figure 10-15 Microinstruction execution

evolution of the rich and powerful instruction sets of the second- and third-generation machines. With dynamically microprogrammed systems, the basic operations will tend to remain (as in simpler microprogrammed processors) primitive.

In the traditional system, since the overload penalties are so significant, there is little real advantage in keeping the functional units of the system simultaneously busy or active. Use of such parallelism may result in 17 or 18 cycles required to perform an instruction rather than 20—hardly worth the effort. A much different situation arises with the advent of dynamic micro-programming. Consider a system partitioned into functional units such as adder, storage, address-calculation unit, and so on. If the microinstruction can be designed in such a fashion that during a single execution one can control the flow of data internal to each one of these units, as well as com-municate between them (see Figure 10-16), significant performance advan-tages can be derived. Of course these advantages come at the expense of a wider microinstruction. Microinstruction size can be reduced by the residual control technique: filtering the relatively static control information out of the microinstruction into a register that is set up by a microinstruction.

In any event computer architecture cannot help but be influenced strongly by the availability of fast memory, the use of primitive (one-cycle) operations, and explicit parallelism to simultaneously control the resources of the system. The third-generation microprogrammed systems can achieve a performance

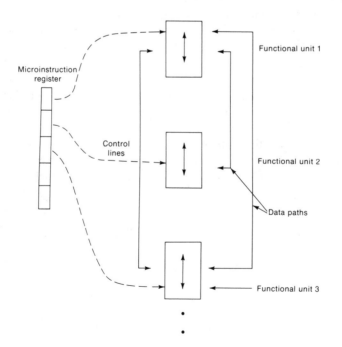

Figure 10-16 Simultaneous resource management

speed-up in direct proportion to the reduced access time of microstorage memory over main memory. Thus, a factor of up to an order-of-magnitude performance improvement is potentially available, since the main memory accessing time represents such a considerable portion of instruction execution.

Some Microprogrammable Machines

A number of interesting characteristics serve to distinguish and characterize modern microprogrammable systems:

1. The "soft" computer architecture—as represented by the Nanodata QM1 and the Burroughs B1700 especially, and the Burroughs D Machine (B-700) to a lesser degree. These systems take advantage of the fast read/write control-store capability by providing a number of processor features to allow easy emulation across a variety of image or target machines, and hence are called "soft" architectures. These processor features usually include:

    a) Extensive field handling and selection facilities
    b) High-speed shifting abilities
    c) Extensive bit testing
    d) Flexible specification of data paths (residual control)

2. Storage of data in the read/write control storage—the direct execution of data operands from the high-speed control store allows the possibility of high performance, since the access time to the data is shortened by having the data present in this high-speed storage media. The control store acts as a type of explicit cache. This technique is used in the sample organization presented at the end of this section.

3. The alterability of the control store in certain systems—the control store may be altered, but usually only from an external peripheral device, thus restricting the introduction of new interpretive routines.

4. The characteristics of the micro/nanoinstructions—the QM1 and the D Machine have a two-level control structure, with unpacked nanoinstructions and packed microinstructions.

5. Even for hosts dedicated to particular image machines, extensive use of read/write control storage allows such applications as:

    a) Microdiagnostics: hardware diagnostic programs, using microprogrammed test sequences.
    b) Operating-systems accelerators: frequently used operating-systems functions, contained as special routines in control storage.

    For these and other applications, recent product announcement shows a trend to significantly larger control-store sizes.

6. Probably the most pervasive recent use of microprogramming is in the area of I/O device control. Small LSI-oriented, microprogrammable hosts are increasingly being used as device controllers for large disk or similar electromechanical storage complexes.

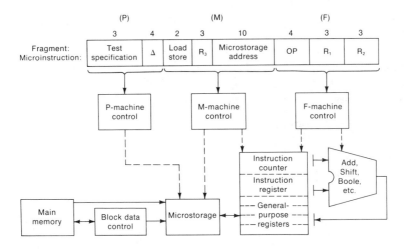

Figure 10-17 Computer architecture diagram

Sample Computer Architecture Using Read/Write Control Storage

Consider the organization outlined in Figure 10-17 [Cook and Flynn, 70; Neuhauser, 73]. This is a simple two-level control structure with a packed field microinstruction. There is no nanocontrol level; however, there are multiple functional units to be controlled.

Let the general-purpose registers contain the instruction register and instruction counter. Assume that the instruction width is the same as the data-word width (perhaps 32 bits). A typical host instruction is partitioned into three fragments, each of which is essentially a primitive instruction (see Figure 10-17):

1. A register-to-register operation (OP)—the contents of R_1 and the contents of R_2 are used as arguments and the result is placed in R_1.

$$REG [R_1] := REG [R_1] \quad OP \quad REG [R_2]$$

This can be thought of as the functional part of the instruction (F-part).
2. A load or store from microstorage into the general-purpose registers— immediate values can be contained in the address field in this instruction fragment.

$$MEMORY := REG [R_3]$$
$$or$$
$$REG [R_2] := MEMORY$$
$$or$$
Other operation
specified by OP

This is the memory-management (M-part) of the instruction.

3. The branch instruction—this includes specification of a test mask and an offset value (Δ) relative to the location counter ($*$), and defines the procedural (P-part) of the instruction.

$$\text{REG } [0] := \text{REG } [0] \pm \Delta$$

or

$$\text{REG } [0] := \text{REG } [0] + 1$$
on condition

The net effect is to control the operation of three finite-state machines simultaneously. Actually it will not always be possible to have concurrent operations, for two reasons: Inconsistent use of the registers by two of the fragments could cause a conflict. Also, it may not be possible to write code that uses all three fields in many instances. In any event, the foregoing instruction resembles a familiar microinstruction. It executes in essentially one machine cycle—perhaps 200 nanoseconds using ordinary circuitry. Depending upon the arrangement of microstorage, conflicts between the load/store fragment and the next instruction-fetch mechanism could double the instruction-execution time.

For transfer of input data to and from main memory, an alternate instruction format is used. This instruction format is block oriented, and asynchronously moves blocks of data between microstorage and main storage. Thus main memory is in many ways treated as an input/output device. Notice that this treatment of control store, except for its explicit nature, is very similar to cache-based memory systems already in use.

The reader is encouraged to complete the details of this organization (problems 10-12 through 10-17) and compare it with Rosin's machine, described in Section 10-4.

10-6. INTERPRETATION

Interpretation, Emulation, and Directly Executable Languages

An *interpreter* is a program that executes each statement in a source program as it is produced. It also selects the statements of the source program in a sequence determined by the execution, and presents the results of the executed program as final output [Iverson and Brooks, 65].

In general, then, the interpreter has two parts: (1) the set of routines that corresponds to the set of operations in the source-program language and (2) a control routine that sequences source statements and selects operations for decoding. The arguments for each operational routine should be defined or be readily computable at the time control is passed to the routine. An interpretive program is a one-pass program that does not require any further scanning of the source text before its execution can be begun.

The notion of emulation and interpretation are equivalent. However, by common usage, the interpreter usually is thought of as a program residing in main storage while the emulator is thought of as a program residing in micro-storage. This, of course, is an arbitrary distinction; therefore we use these terms synonymously.

A *directly executable language* (DEL) is a source language for an inter-preter. It is difficult to formalize the DEL notion since it is actually a property of, or a restriction to, a language, which provides for the efficient execution of interpretive or emulator programs. Notice that many familiar languages do not have the DEL property. Languages not directly executable include sym-bolic assembly code, relocatable binary code, and assembly programs with macros, since either the arguments or the operations are not completely defined as they are first encountered. On the other hand, one could conceive of a rather high-level language suitable as a DEL; that is, a directly execut-able language that resembles our familiar higher-level languages, but which obeys the argument-definition and operator-decoding restrictions and provides for orderly sequencing of source statements.

Emulation of Conventional Machine Languages

In the past, emulation has mainly involved the interpretation of machine language with the use of microprogramming techniques for instruction inter-pretation [Rosin, 69]. It is relatively easy for a single physical system to interpret more than one machine language. The physical machine, as defined by its microinstructions and their actions, is called the *host machine*. Machine languages emulated by sets of microprogrammed routines are called *image machines* or *target machines*. It is possible to write an emulator for one image machine in terms of another image machine language; thus one can conceive of layers of emulators. However, more common usage of the term emulator implies that the interpretive set of programs is written in the microlanguage of the host processor.

Probably the most widely known use of emulation is the IBM System/360. Most of the models of System/360 and System/370 are microprogrammed [Tucker, 67] (with the notable exceptions of the Models 91 and 195). Each model of the System/360 and System/370 series is quite a distinct machine, with widely differing performance characteristics, data paths, size, and price. However, each has the common machine language of the System/360. In all of the microprogrammed models of the System/360, the interpretation of the machine language is done by an emulator that resides in microstorage. This emulator consists of a series of routines, and each routine represents a particular System/360 instruction.

The emulation of a machine other than a 360 is not so straightforward [Tucker, 65]. Consider a Model 65 that emulates a 7090. The "emulation" of a 7090 on a Model 65 is more accurately described as a simulation of the 7090 using a combination of techniques including 360 instructions, special instructions, and 7090-type instructions. The hybrid approach to emulation reduces the size of microstorage needed to provide emulation for the 360 and the 7090. In the Model 65, each 7090 instruction is interpreted by an emulation subroutine contained in main memory, as shown in Figure 10-18. This subroutine uses special instructions as well as conventional System/360 instructions. One of the special instructions is the DIL (do interpretive loop), which is a microprogrammed routine that does a fetch and interpretation of the next 7090 instruction. In addition to the DIL instruction, a number of other subroutines are added to the microstorage to assist in emulating specific 7090 instructions. The configuration of main storage during emulation is shown in Figure 10-18; the emulation of three 7090 instructions is shown in Figure 10-19 [Tucker, 65].

A Theory of Ideal Interpretive Machines

The notion of a DEL is closely related to the notion of an "ideal" machine for some specified higher-level language (HLL) environment. Consider the problem of traditional machines: trying to identify and factor out the architectural instructions in programs from the functional instructions (i.e., those specifically indicated in the HLL source). For example, the existence of load

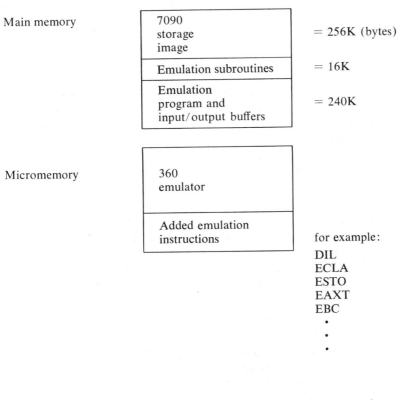

Main memory

7090 storage image	= 256K (bytes)
Emulation subroutines	= 16K
Emulation program and input/output buffers	= 240K

Micromemory

| 360 emulator |
| Added emulation instructions | for example: DIL ECLA ESTO EAXT EBC ⋮ |

Figure 10-18 Configuration of main memory and micromemory in a System/360 Model 65 emulating an IBM 7090

7090 Instruction	360 Emulation Routine	
AXT Address to index true	EAXT	Microroutine that does AXT
	DIL	Microroutine that does fetch and interpretation of next instruction
AXC Address to index complemented	LCR	360 instruction that complements the address
	EAXT	Microroutine
	DIL	Microroutine
TMI Transfer on minus	ESTO	Microroutine that puts the value into a work area of the 360 (the simulated accumulator)
	TM	360 instruction, test under mask (to obtain the sign bit)
	EBC	Microroutine that does a 7090 branch if the test is satisfied

Figure 10-19 Emulation of IBM 7090 instructions

or store accumulator instructions in a program representation is largely architectural, since they specify a movement among the storage resources of a system rather than a movement required in the original source program. To analyze this it is useful to define three types of instructions (Flynn [74]):

1. *M-type instructions,* or memory overhead instructions. These instructions move data within the storage hierarchy.
2. *P-instructions,* or procedural instructions, modify instruction sequencing (e.g., BRANCH).
3. *F-instructions,* or functional instructions, which actually transform a datum (e.g., ADD).

Instructions that simply move data in a partitioned memory space, or unconditional branches that alter ordinary sequencing implications, are "overhead" instructions. In most HLL representations it is unlikely that one would find a corresponding instruction. Thus, M- and P-type instructions are more likely to be nonfunctional, while F-type are more likely to represent operations actually specified in the higher-level language representation. (Compare the partitioning of the microinstruction example in Section 10-5.)

The above partitioning may seem somewhat naive; its validity could only be claimed for technical object code. In a SORT program a MOVE might be an F-type instruction. However, separating an architectural artifact from a program function is easier when one has both the source-program representation (HLL) and the object-code representation.

It is interesting to define three ratios:

1. *M-ratio*—ratio of M-instructions to F-instructions
2. *P-ratio*—ratio of P-instructions to F-instructions
3. *NF-ratio* (nonfunctional ratio)—ratio of the sum of M- and P-instructions to F-instructions.

Some early data on these ratios are tabulated in Table 10-1 for the IBM 7090, the System 360, and the PDP-10. In this simple view, the "ideal" machine would have a zero entry for all ratios. The listed machines require between 2.6 and 5.5 nonfunctional instructions for each functional instruction, implying that the size of the program could be reduced by this factor.

TABLE 10-1. INSTRUCTION RATIOS

	"Ideal"	IBM 7090	IBM 360	PDP-10 [Lunde, 75]
M-ratio	0.0	2.0	2.9	1.5
P-ratio	0.0	0.8	2.5	1.1
NF-ratio	0.0	2.8	5.5	2.6

Ideal Representations Given a source HLL program representation, how exactly should one define—in space and time measures—the inefficiencies of the object code caused by the introduction of needless overhead instructions? Of course, one could simply compare, bit by bit and instruction by instruction, several different object-code representations of the same program. However, a more informative approach is to define an ideal interpretation of the program in meaningful architectural terms. Then one can specify the efficiency measure of a particular machine representation with respect to that source program—simply by comparing the ideal to the achieved program size and interpretation time. While it all seems simple enough, specifying an ideal machine is a formidable problem in itself. Every machine designer has at least an inkling that his own design is very close to being ideal. Some premises seem clear enough:

1. The measure should be technology independent, i.e., we are interested in comparing the ideas behind the machine representation, not whether or not one machine has access to a more modern integrated-circuit collection.
2. We assume that the source program is a good representation for the original algorithm. While it is clear that this is frequently not the case, there is very little that a machine designer can do except interpret, as best he can, the program as specified in the given HLL.
3. There are several general measures of program representation possible. However we shall concentrate on only two: space to represent the object program and time to interpret that representation. This excludes compiler considerations; it is implicitly assumed that the compiler problem can be handled simply as another problem. Given a compiler written in any HLL, we can measure the space required for its

representation and the time required for the interpretation of that representation.

4. We make the uniform-occurrence assumption: that all artifacts of the HLL program representations are used with equal probability. This is, of course, not true; but it seems unnecessary to require *a priori* frequency-distribution data of the source program. The idealized measure proposed below could be easily extended to include a Huffman-type encoding of the representation.

With these assumptions in mind, let us define the *canonic interpretive form* (CIF) of a program. This form has space measured in number of bits of program size, and time measured in number of instructions interpreted and in number of memory references to a target name space. The rules for the measures of CIF for a program are as follows:

1. *The 1:1 property*—For each nonassignment operation in a higher-level language (HLL) statement, one instruction unit is allowed in the CIF.

2. Instruction-unit size—
   a) Each instruction unit consists of a single operation container, OP, of size $\log_2$[number of HLL operations in a scope (or program environment)] bits. (For familiar higher-level languages, scope corresponds to "subroutine" or "function".)
   b) A single operand container is allowed for each unique HLL statement variable.
   c) The size of this operand container is: $\log_2$[number of HLL variables in a scope] bits.

3. *Memory references*—
   a) Each HLL procedural statement creates a single procedural instruction unit. Each such procedural instruction causes one reference.
   b) Each computed variable name causes one reference.
   c) Each scope entry causes one reference (read).
   d) Each scope exit causes one reference (write).

We are assuming that the source program to which this measure is applied is in optimal form. The generation of the CIF is relatively straightforward. For each nonassignment operation in a source statement in the original HLL representation there is one instruction in the CIF. For the moment one might think that a traditional three-address format would accomplish this. However, rule 2 requires that only unique variables be identified explicitly. The statement $X + X \rightarrow X$ has only one unique variable; thus by rules 1 and 2 this statement should be represented by a single instruction unit consisting of a single operation and single operand specification.

An Example Consider the following subroutine body of a FORTRAN program:

1. I := X * Y + Z * Z
2. B := A[I] * B
3. IF [B] 10,20,30

where variables I, B, X, Y, Z are integers whose initial values are in memory and whose final values are to be stored in memory for later program use (declared common). It is assumed that the labels 10, 20 and 30 are nontrivial statements in the same subroutine, and that this routine uses no new variables and operations other than those cited in the three statements.

In order to find the ideal program representation, first compute the required container or field sizes for operands, operations, and labels:

Unique operands: 1, X, Y, Z, B, A, and an element of the array A[I] which we call A_i (this is a single element or operand). Thus:

$$\text{operand identifier size} = \lceil \log_2 7 \rceil = 3 \text{ bits}$$

Unique operations: *, +, array element computation which we will designate @, IF.

$$\text{operation identifier size} = \lceil \log_2 4 \rceil = 2 \text{ bits}$$

Unique labels: 10, 20, and 30

$$\text{label identifier size} = \lceil \log_2 3 \rceil = 2 \text{ bits}$$

Thus our canonic-form program would be:

		Instruction	
Statement 1	2 3 : `*` `Z`	1	−5 bits
	2 3 3 : `*` `X` `Y`	2	−8 bits
	2 3 : `+` `I`	3	−5 bits
Statement 2	2 3 3 : `@` `A` `I`	4	−8 bits
	2 3 : `*` `B`	5	−5 bits
Statement 3	2 2 2 2 : `IF` `10` `20` `30`	6	−8 bits

Totals: 6 instructions; −39 bits

Notice that the * operation in instruction 1 requires a different transformation than the same operation in instruction 2 and both use implicit storage to hold their results for use in instruction 3. Thus it is impossible to achieve such conciseness; however, we can approach this by introducing a powerful class of formats; which we will discuss later.

In statement 2 (instruction 4) the identifier A_i was not used, since once the value was determined it could be implicitly stored and is not effected by later use. In an IF statement, one assumes that the previous result is the predicate (as in this case); otherwise the computation of the predicate would involve an additional instruction. Thus IF (P + Q) 10,20,30 would require:

$$+ \; P \; Q$$
$$\text{IF } 10,20,30$$

The number of required memory references can be computed as:

    1 for instruction run up to IF
    1 for IF instruction destination
    1 for scope entry
    1 for scope exit
    1 for reference to a computed name, A[I]

Total $\overline{5}$

Below is a listing produced by IBM System 370 optimizing compiler (FORTRAN IV level H opt = 2).

L	11	Load Base → R11
L	9	
L	8 Z	Z → R8
L	7 X	X → R7
M	6 Y	(X * Y → R6, R7 pair)
LR	5 8	Z → R5
MR	4 , 8	(Z * Z → R4, R5 pair)
LR	10 , 5	copy Z * Z resulting into R10
AR	10 , 7	compute I → R10
LR	3 , 10	I → R3
SLL	3 , 2	
L	5 , B	
M	4 , A	indexed by I (R3); A[I] * B → R4,5
ST	5 , B	store result in B
LTR	5 , 5	set condition code
BC	8 , 20	
BC	3 , 30	
	(10 is default)	

The above increased program size is a result of the split name space and restricted formats. The DEC 20 does somewhat better. We present summary statistics in Table 10-2.

TABLE 10-2. COMPARISON FOR THE EXAMPLE

	System 370	DEC 20	CIF
Number of instructions	17	10	6
M-type	9	4	0
P-type	2	2	1
F-type	5	4*	5
Program size (in bits)	448	360	39
Memory references	28	20	5

*The indexing in a MOVE instruction is functional with respect to CIF, as it computes A[I].

In the next section we will examine one approach to a theory of DEL synthesis aimed at approaching the CIF—namely, to create an almost "ideal" HLL architecture.

General Principles of Directly Executable Languages

The problem of developing efficient directly executable languages is similar to the problem of developing an efficient language of any type, be it higher-level or machine language. For example, the design of such languages depends upon assumed user behavior and the physical characteristics of the base machine. A directly executable language should be developed with reference to particular higher-level languages that will be translated and particular base machines that will be used to interpret programs of that language. Some general statements concerning the nature of efficient DELS can be made.

An efficient DEL should be a reasonably good output medium for compilers. It should require a relatively small amount of space for DEL program representation. Also, the time required for transformation of a higher-level source language fragment into an equivalent DEL fragment should be minimal. Since the compiler has many functions that are dependent upon the source program rather than the object DEL, we must consider such functions separately; for example, functions such as source-program scanning and global optimization are source-language dependent, while code generation is DEL dependent. DEL aspects include the following:

1. The DEL should facilitate efficient code generation by being in close correspondence to the source. It is also desirable that the DEL be a transparent representation, i.e., designed so that the source could be easily reconstructed.
2. The DEL should avoid needlessly restricting critical physical resources that must be allocated by the compiler. In a 360 language, for example, there is a fixed identification of the number of general-purpose registers (16). This is so in spite of the fact that on some machines there are physically no such registers (they are, in fact, part of the physical memory) and in other implementations there are many more than 16 registers (buffers and cache memory). This particular DEL, then, interferes with the compiler's responsibility to assign variables to storage space.
3. Where possible the DEL should allow for the generation of code that

is independent of the structure of the data on which it operates. That is, it should be possible to execute a DEL routine against several different types of input-data organizations simply by redefining the data structure, without recompiling the entire program.

The rapid interpretation of the DEL program representation is of considerable importance. Here a number of conditions must be satisfied:

1. The number of microinstructions required to decode and to implement a given DEL operation should be minimized.
2. The number of microinstructions required to pass parameters into an interpretive routine must be minimized.
3. The average width of a DEL statement must be minimized; this is accomplished through variable-length instructions and literal specification.

Notice the contrast between the DEL and the microinstruction language. The microinstruction is designed to make physical resources available (or visible) for potential control. Hopefully this may be done with concurrency and independence of operation. The rapid execution of all fragments of the microinstruction is of prime importance, together with efficient coding and representation of each of the resources identified.

The DEL has a much more general function. It must be a good output medium from the compiler, as well as a good interpretive medium. Thus different source languages will have different DELs. The DEL must be changeable to suit a variety of source-language environments. On the other hand, the DEL will be more valuable if it can serve as an input medium for more than one interpretative emulation. Thus, it should allow identification of required logical resources in a flexible, hierarchical manner. That is, it should allow for a variety of interpretations based upon the actual physical resources which are available in a particular host machine. It is the responsibility of the interpreter to provide for this. Existing machine languages are deficient in many respects. They limit compiler specification of the storage space. The interpreters for these languages are static, as are the languages themselves. The full interpreter for the entire language must be available regardless of the characteristics of the source language. No new interpretive routines can be easily introduced into the machine-language repertoire.

Developments in Directly Executable Languages

DELs can be generated for implementing specific compilers or as output from specific higher-level language compilers for interpretation and execution (see Figure 10-20). Thus we can have a compiler DEL (CDEL) as well as an execution DEL (EDEL); either of these DELs might be trivial in a particular implementation. That is, either the compiler may be written completely in microinstructions or the compiler produces microinstructions as its output.

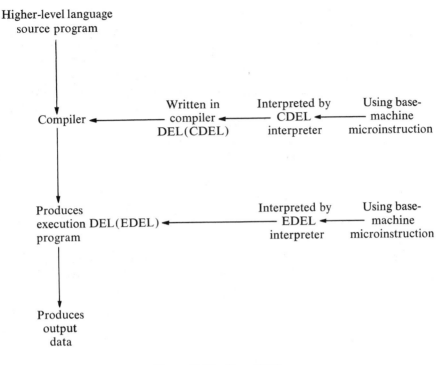

Figure 10-20 Use of DELs

For a DEL to have value it must represent an efficiency savings in space or time (or both) during the compilation or execution of the program.

The most notable early work in the area of DELs was that of Weber [67], who experimented with the high-level source language EULER, a subset of ALGOL, and used an IBM System/360 Model 30 as the base machine. Weber chose to implement the EULER compiler completely in Model 30 microinstructions. This compiler produced a string-like execution DEL that resembles EULER. The Model 30 itself had a 50-bit microinstruction arranged in packed, multiple fields. Approximately 2000 microwords were used for the System/360 interpretation in the Model 30. Weber reported that in his experimental system the EULER compiler used 500 microinstructions (that is, 500 microwords). The string-language execution interpreter used 2500 microwords. He reported a performance improvement in the execution of the compiled programs of up to a factor of 10, depending upon the nature of the source program.

The Burroughs Corporation at Paoli, Pennsylvania has developed the TRANSLANG, a translator language that is an assembler for interpreter macroprograms, in conjunction with the development of their D Machine. Reigel et al., in their paper [72] on the D Machine (the "interpreter"), cite the need for specific interpretive languages or execution DELs which correspond to the various higher level languages. He indicates that an ALGOL execution DEL might resemble machine code for the Burroughs B5500, while a COBOL execution DEL might resemble the B3500-type machine code.

The Burroughs B1700 reduces Reigel's speculations to practice. The B1700 uses a series of interpretive S languages—one each for FORTRAN, RPG, COBOL, and BASIC. These S languages operate under control of a master control program; in addition, there is a more general system-description language, SDL, which has its own interpreter. Since the B1700 makes active use of the read/write control store, only the interpreter required by the user program is present in the control store at execution time.

While not concerned with microprogramming per se, there have been two other notable attempts at "high-level language machines." Both were hard-wired and tailored to specific languages. The earlier was a study by Bashkow et al. [67], in which they proposed a FORTRAN machine; their study projects an order-of-magnitude performance improvement in execution time over traditional instruction sets. Rice and Smith [71], on the other hand, developed a new language called SYMBOL, and a hard-wired implementation of this machine has been constructed and is under study. The nondynamic nature of these hard-wired implementations seems to be a serious limitation to their general acceptance.

10-7. SUMMARY

Various methods have been used in the past to implement the control of a computer. Control, in this sense, is synonymous with interpreting an instruction through a sequence of steps that take specified source data and produce a proper result and then transfer control to the next instruction in an orderly manner. One of the most interesting implementations of internal computer control is the use of storage. Special storage media have been developed over the years to allow control of the computer resources on a step-by-step basis. This step or state transition within the computer is controlled by a *microinstruction*. The ensemble of microinstructions that interpret a machine instruction is called a *microprogram* for that particular instruction.

As the storage media which contains the microprogram became increasingly more sophisticated, microprogramming assumed additional functions. In particular, the possibility of the *host machine* being able to interpret a number of different machine languages was introduced. This process is called *emulation*. Emulation in a general sense is synonymous with interpretation.

With the advent of fast read/write microstorage, new developments both in architecture and in machine languages become possible. The traditional role of the microinstruction remains the same: to make visible the physical resources of the computer. However, it is no longer necessary to remain with fixed and restricted machine languages. In the larger sense, the term microprogramming is really inadequate. What we really mean is interpretative programming. The source language for the interpreter is a *directly executable language*. The object language is the microinstruction. The novelty in all this is that the DELs may be flexible, changeable, and extensible.

Machines that support the implementation of variable DELs have been termed *soft* computer architectures. In emulation of specific image machines, these architectures may not give as good performance as comparable machines designed specifically for that instruction set. However, their performance should be reasonable and their other advantages noteworthy. In particular these advantages include:

1. The ability to emulate a wide variety of image machines
2. The ability to support intermediate interpretive-language levels—directly executable languages which may be expanded or changed dynamically
3. The ability to get significant performance improvements on specific problems where that application is programmed completely at the microinstruction level.

Reference Comments

The introduction to interpretation in Chapter 10 follows the Iverson and Brooks [65] treatment. The sample computer described is a variation of a 16-bit machine discussed in considerable detail in Cook and Flynn [70]. The sample 32-bit machine described at the end of Section 10-5 is actually a version of a system at Stanford University [Neuhauser, 73]. Certain sections, definitions, and discussions contained in this chapter have been abstracted from earlier works of the author, especially articles on microprogramming and emulation [Ralston, 74; Flynn and Rosin, 71]. The treatment of emulation is strongly influenced by Hoevel [73], Tucker [67 and 65], and Weber [67]. The papers of Tucker and Weber are frequently cited and well known in the field. They merit reading by any serious student of the area. For general references the reader is recommended to Wilkes's original paper on microprogramming [51] and Rosin's survey and exposition [69]. The simple microprogramming machine used in this chapter comes from Rosin. For a detailed treatment of microprogrammed machine structure, see Husson [72]. Further bibliographic material can be found in Wilkes [69], Jones et al. [72 and 73], and Davies [72]. Jones is quite comprehensive, while Davies is an especially useful guide to key papers in the field. The DEL treatment was developed jointly with L. Hoevel, and is more fully discussed in Hoevel [77, 78] and Flynn [77].

PROBLEMS

10-1. Refer to Figure 10-2 of this chapter. Assume that a simple processor has a memory with a 5-cycle access time and a 5-cycle regeneration time. Draw a sequencing diagram and a flowchart for:
  a) A STORE instruction (that is, MEMORY [REG [XR] + D] : = ACC)
  b) A conditional branch instruction
10-2. Refer to Figure 10-7. Show how control overlap might operate between sequential cycles.

Problem 10-3 through 10-9 refer to Rosin's Machine (see Section 10-4, "Simple Microprogrammed Machine").

10-3. Write the Boolean equations for the decode of microinstruction Format 2.

10-4. Show the intracycle operations required for nonoverlapped operations. Repeat for the overlapped case.

10-5. Write the microprogram for multiplying the accumulator by a memory operand. (Note: Define additional ICP's.)

10-6. Write the microprogram for a shift instruction whose format specifies a right or left shift of the accumulator by an amount specfied in the instruction (up to 16). (Note: Define additional ICP's.)

10-7. Show a memory map for microstorage for problem 10-6.

10-8. Show a timing diagram for problem 10-6.

10-9. How would you revise Rosin's machine to allow for a read/write-control storage?

10-10. It is desired to emulate the action of the serial decimal adder using Rosin's machine as a host. Discuss how this implementation might be accomplished.

10-11. How does emulation differ from simulation? Discuss this in the context of the IBM Model 65 emulating the IBM 7090.

The following problems refer to the sample architecture at the end of Section 10-5.

10-12. Specify a typical set of operations (see Chapter 4, Section 4-3, for hints).

10-13. Specify the required load and store operations.

10-14. Specify a typical set of test specifications.

10-15. Write an emulator for the ADD instruction of Rosin's machine.

10-16. Draw a timing diagram for problem 10-15 and compare with the example in Figure 10-14, assuming the same cycle times.

10-17. Discuss the nature of the cycle time in Rosin's machine as compared with the sample machine.

Acknowledgments

I am especially indebted to my colleagues Dr. Lee Hoevel and Dr. T. Agerwala for their helpful suggestions and assistance with certain sections of this chapter.

CHAPTER 11

Performance Evaluation

Samuel H. Fuller

11-1. INTRODUCTION

Computer systems have evolved into a wide variety of structures, some of which are complex systems that often include more than one central processor; many input/output channels or processors; and 30, 60, or more drum and disk storage units. Even as late as the early 1960s, almost 20 years after the stored-program computer was originally developed, technology, programming systems, and user demand had not pushed computer systems beyond simple, one-job-at-a-time processing. Engineers and systems programmers received a rude awakening when multiprogramming systems were introduced, with the third generation of computer systems (circa 1964), and did not perform up to expectations. Many current computer systems are as complex as such other artificial systems as high-performance aircraft or modern skyscrapers. The discouraging fact is not the complexity of computer systems but that computer engineers do not have the range of tools to evaluate performance that aeronautical or civil engineers do.

Since performance evaluation in its current state of development is as much an art or skill as it is a science, this chapter has two purposes: first, to present those aspects of performance evaluation that are well understood and to develop the associated mathematics; and second, to discuss the additional concepts that underlie pragmatic efforts to evaluate complex computer systems. However, the best way to learn the pragmatic aspects of performance evaluation, as with any skill, is to apply the basic concepts to real problems. For this reason, several of the problems at the end of this chapter outline small performance monitors that have relatively simple implementations. The effort spent developing one of these monitors, using it in the context of a measurement experiment to collect data, and finally critically analyzing the resultant data is probably the most effective way to learn the rudiments of performance evaluation.

The need for performance evaluation does not come from a single source. Therefore, a set of measures or analysis techniques adequate for one performance evaluation study may well be inadequate for another study. In the following discussion, we partition the need for performance evaluation into three primary areas: *design*, *purchase*, and *optimization* studies. While this division is somewhat arbitrary, it does provide a useful vehicle to discuss the various needs for evaluation.

Performance evaluation needs to play a strong, continuing role in the design and development of new computer systems. Engineers and systems programmers should use projections of performance to guide the development of their system; designs based solely on the elegance of the system architecture or the processor's instruction set are at best academic exercises. In this realm of performance evaluation we include not only the evaluation of new central processor designs, but also the evaluation of other hardware components (for example, secondary storage units, input/output processors, etc.) as well as software systems (for example, schedulers, memory-management systems, and compilers).

The second area of performance evaluation concerns the decision to purchase or lease a unit of hardware or software, or a complete computer system. This differs from performance evaluation for design in at least two important respects: configurations of the systems in question are usually operational and available for inspection and testing, and the options open to the purchaser are limited to several announced product lines rather than the complex space of alternatives open to the designer of a new product. For these reasons, performance evaluation for a purchasing decision can rely more on measurement and detailed (but costly) models than can performance evaluation for design.

The third area of performance evaluation is concerned with the optimization of a specific computer system. Typical questions in this area include: how many disk drives do we need and how should they be distributed over the available input/output channels; how much of the operating system should reside in primary memory and what modules should reside on the drum? These questions begin to multiply when we consider multiprocessor systems and must decide which processors should control which input/output devices. The nature of performance evaluation for optimization is fundamentally different from the two other areas of performance evaluation. It most often involves incremental, and often reversible, changes. There is the opportunity for continual monitoring of a system's performance to detect trends or shifts in user demands. As inefficiencies in the system are discovered, new scheduling or memory-management policies can be tried as well as reconfigurations of the hardware.

Before proceeding to discuss the elements of performance evaluation, let us first put the problem in proper perspective. When we use a computer system, the central processor is usually the most visible component of the system.

However, when we must consider the performance of a computer system, the central processor is only one of many components, albeit an important one, in the system. Moreover, the hardware is only a portion of the total cost of running a computation facility. A survey of 1974 budgets for data processing centers helps to put these comments in clearer focus [McLaughlin, 74]. The survey included 194 centers. An average of 39 percent of the total data processing budget was allocated for hardware. The remaining money was spent on salaries (47 percent) and miscellaneous costs (14 percent) such as supplies, consulting, training, and so on. Of the money spent for hardware, typically less than half was spent for the central processor and main memory; the majority of the hardware budget was spent on such peripherals as drums, disks, card readers, and line printers. These figures should indicate that maximum utilization of the central processor does not necessarily minimize the cost of running a computing system. A useful cost/performance analysis of any computer system must include some measure of the productivity of the programmer.

Following this introduction, we present the fundamental concepts of performance evaluation in Section 11-2. We begin with the classic measures and parameters that are used to characterize computer systems. The shortcomings of these simple measures are discussed, but there is real value in measures that quickly enable anyone to grasp the scope of the computer system's capabilities. Careful application of these simple measures can be useful. Next, a range of stochastic, or queueing, models is developed. These analytical models are excellent tools when there is a need to explore a wide range of possible alternatives or to understand the functional dependence of the system's performance on the controllable parameters of the system. Simulation models are discussed in Section 11-4, and emphasis is placed on the construction and verification of these models. Finally, the basic techniques for evaluating the performance of an operational system are presented.

Section 11-6 covers fundamental measurement techniques. Although measurement techniques per se are of limited interest, analytical and simulation models require measurements to guide in the selection of realistic assumptions. Moreover, studies of operational systems require a set of measurement tools in order to monitor the results of the tests.

11-2. MEASURES AND PARAMETERS OF PERFORMANCE

No single measure of performance can give a truly accurate measure of a computer system's performance, just as no single parameter can characterize the performance of an aircraft or the utility of a skyscraper. Different measures are needed to characterize a computer used in the numerical solution of a set of simultaneous linear equations and a computer used in an airline reservation system. Moreover, even when we are considering a single application on a particular computer system, it is misleading to use a single parameter of performance. The following discussion considers this problem in detail.

Memory Bandwidth and Add Times

In an effort to characterize a computer system's performance, a natural tendency is to enumerate a small number of the parameters of the system. For example, the *cycle time of main memory* or the *time to execute an add instruction* have traditionally been used to indicate the power of a computer system. These parameters, however, can be misleading. A PDP 11/05 has a memory-cycle time of 0.9 microseconds and an IBM 370/155 has a cycle time of 2.1 microseconds, yet by any rational measure of computational power the IBM 370/155 ranks above the PDP-11/05. Similarly, the Varian 620f has an add time of 1.5 microseconds and the Burroughs 5500 has an add time of 3 microseconds, and again the Burroughs machine is a more powerful computer than is the Varian machine. The fact that we neglect such parameters as word length, the number of ways the memory is interleaved, and the structure of the input/output system resulted in the misleading comparisons. As we include more parameters in our comparison we get a better idea of the actual performance of a particular system. A list of current computers, along with a set of their major parameters, is provided on a periodic basis by the publication DataPRO [79].

Although memory-cycle times and add times are poor measures of performance, it is sometimes necessary to determine a small but reasonable set of performance measures based solely on parameters of the hardware structure. It is interesting to approach this problem, as have Bell and Newell [71], by asking what is the single most accurate measure or parameter of computer performance, the second most meaningful, and so on. This exercise is of limited utility, but there are times when a quick gauge of a computer system's capabilities is needed and the only information available is its hardware parameters. The notion of *instructions per second,* called MIPS (millions of instructions per second), has often been proposed as an indicator of a computer system's performance. It captures the gains realized by many of the more advanced techniques of processor design, for example, cache memories, pipelining, and interleaved memory units. However, MIPS is inappropriate for vector machines such as the CDC STAR or the Texas Instrument ASC, since a single instruction often results in many operand fetches and stores. The same phenomenon is seen in computers designed to interpret high-level languages: again the ratio of instruction fetches to operand fetches is low. (In fact, how low this ratio is provides a good measure of how effectively a machine embodies the concepts of high-level language emulation.) To correct this deficiency with the MIPS measure, MOPS (millions of operands per second) is sometimes used. As measures of performance, MIPS and MOPS share the same serious deficiency with the cycle time of memory—they neglect word length. As a result, the millions of bits per second (*memory bandwidth*) that are processed by the central processor is generally more appropriate. If we must choose a single, simple parameter of performance, memory bandwidth is a good choice.

Candidates for the second and third most critical measures of a computer system's performance are the *size of main memory* and the *size of secondary memory* in bits, respectively. It is questionable how productive it is to extend this enumeration any further. However, it should be pointed out that all three measures suggested do not explicitly take into account the word length. For example, when we are processing relatively small integers, 16-bit words may be sufficient to hold all numbers of interest. Hence machines with 32 bits per word, while having twice the memory bandwidth and twice as large a main memory as a machine with 16 bits per word, may perform at essentially the same rate for some applications.

MIPS, MOPS, and memory bandwidth are actually upper bounds on performance rather than first-order estimates when these measures are derived strictly from hardware characteristics of the machines. For example, the IBM 360/91 is capable of initiating a new instruction every 60 nanoseconds and hence has a potential instruction-execution rate of 16.7 MIPS. However, measurements of the IBM 360/91 indicate it rarely exceeds 3 or 4 MIPS. The discrepancy results from instruction sequences that branch in such ways that the 360/91 central processor cannot fetch the instructions fast enough to keep the instruction decoder saturated. Similarly, multiprocessor systems have memory bandwidths higher than the "effective" bandwidths measured in operations. Here the difference arises from the processors not cooperating perfectly and, as several processors attempt to access the same memory bank, queueing results and performance degrades. The correction of these measures from maximum (and often unattainable) rates to effective, or average, rates takes us into the evaluation of operational computer systems. We reserve the rest of this discussion for Section 11-5, where we consider the evaluation of operational computer systems.

Fundamental Measures

In the remainder of this section we consider more complex, and hopefully more accurate, representations of performance than we have just seen in our discussion of hardware parameters. As we go beyond the basic parameters of a computer system in an effort to find more meaningful measures of performance, we face a bewildering array of possible measures. Although it is neither possible nor practical to give a definitive list of all the appropriate measures for computer systems, it is useful to note that measures fall into the two fundamental classes, *response time* and *throughput* measures. Response time measures, sometimes also called *waiting time* or *turnaround time*, are measured in seconds and describe the length of time from a request for service until the request is completed. For example, many time-sharing systems attempt to minimize the response time seen by the user to a request from his terminal. In this case, the response time is defined as the time from the carriage return until the user receives a response. The response time, or access time, of a disk is often an important parameter of a computer system. This is the time from when the central processor requests a record from the disk until it receives an interrupt saying that the record has been transformed into primary memory. In batch-processing systems the response time is more often called turnaround time and is the interval of time from submission of the job until the job is completed and the result printed on the line printer, stored on tape, or saved on some other storage medium.

Throughput measures attempt to gauge how well the capacity of the system is being used rather than how responsive the system is to the demands of the user. The classic measure of throughput is the number of jobs per day processed. This is often refined by partitioning the jobs into classes and measuring the throughput for each class. A measure closely related to throughput is *utilization*, that is, the fraction of time a specified component is busy. Utilization is an even more direct indicator of how much of the capacity of the system is being used. Utilization studies have sometimes centered on the central processor, but a meaningful analysis of the effective utilization of the system must consider all the components of the computer system.

11-3. STOCHASTIC MODELS

When our need to describe the performance of a computer system, or a series of computer systems, exceeds the simple parameters of the hardware structure discussed in the previous section, we must address the underlying stochastic nature of operating computer systems. Requests for service arriving at processors within the computer system often can only be modeled as a random process. The amount of computation required by a process (task) at a central processor or input/output processor is commonly modeled as a random variable because of the data-dependent branching in the program and the variety of tasks processors are called upon to service. The area of mathematics often called *queueing theory* encompasses the set of analytical models that most adequately describe computer systems. Over a dozen books exist on the theory of queues and over a thousand papers have been written that analyze queueing structures. On the other hand, a discouragingly large fraction of practical queueing systems continue to elude exact analysis. Some people find these two observations a pessimistic commentary on work in queueing theory; however, the situation in queueing theory is consistent with most other areas of applied mathematics: real systems are very complex mechanisms, and tractable mathematical models must often be simplified approximations to the real systems.

Because of the limitations of queueing theory, simulation techniques (discussed in the next section) must be used in conjunction with queueing models. Simulation models can accurately model more complex structures than can queueing models. Queueing models find their main utility when qualitative and approximate quantitative answers are needed. They describe the performance of a queueing structure as a function of a number of parameters, for example, the number of central processors, speed of secondary storage, or number of on-line terminals. To get the same information through simulation often takes many hours of computation, and even then the performance of the computer system over a wide range of configurations and job mixes is still not as clear as when an analytical solution is available. As stated in the introduction of this chapter, both queueing and simulation models play an essential role in the performance evaluation of computer systems.

It would be impractical to cover all of the significant results in queueing theory here. This section analyzes several queueing models that are fundamental, have application to the analysis of computer systems, and form the basis for many of the more advanced models. Every queueing structure includes the following four characteristics:

1. *Arrival process* — A mechanism that generates requests to be serviced by the processor. The delivery of card decks to a computing system is an example of an arrival process. An important statistic of the arrival process is the modeling of the interarrival times. The models discussed in this section assume that the interarrival times are random variables drawn from an *arrival-time* probability-distribution function.
2. *Service mechanism* — The primary demand of a task after it arrives is that it be serviced by one or more of the processors in the system. Like interarrival times, service times are modeled as random variables with a *service-time* probability-distribution function.
3. *Queueing discipline* — When requests for service arrive at a processor faster than they can be serviced, a line, or queue, forms and a policy is needed to determine the order in which outstanding requests will be processed.
4. *Routing* — When there is more than one processor in the queueing system, the manner in which requests circulate among the queues must be specified.

In the models that follow we make a number of different assumptions concerning these four characteristics in order to develop models that cover a wide range of computer structures.

Interarrival-Time and Service-Time Distributions

Poisson Arrival Process   The arrival process that is simplest to treat mathematically is the Poisson (completely random) arrival process. X-rays striking a Geiger counter, automobiles entering an intersection, and incoming calls to a telephone exchange are all examples of processes that have been successfully modeled as Poisson processes. In computer systems, the arrival of individuals at a card reader, the failure of circuits in a central processor, and requests from terminals in a time-sharing system are processes that are essentially Poisson in nature. The property common to all these examples is that the events are generated from a very large population and each member in the population is acting independently. The arrival at a past or future instant does

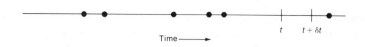

Figure 11-1   Arrival epochs for a Poisson process

not affect the arrival, or non-arrival, at the present instant. This lack of de-pendence on the past (and future) is commonly called the *Markovian,* or *memoryless,* property. As we will see in a moment, the independence of arrivals is responsible for the simplicity of the analysis of the Poisson arrival process.

To describe a Poisson process we begin by letting λ be the average arrival rate of the Poisson process. Figure 11-1 is a time line with marks at several *epochs,* or points in time, to denote arrivals. The fundamental assumption that an arrival is independent of all other arrivals can be stated with the following two postulates:

1. The probability of an arrival between epochs t and $t + \delta t$ is $\lambda\delta t + o(\delta t)$, where $o(\delta t)$ denotes a quantity of smaller order of magnitude than δt.*
2. The probability of more than one arrival between epochs t and $t + \delta t$ is $o(\delta t)$.

From these postulates it is possible to derive an expression for $P_n(t)$, the probability of n arrivals during an interval of duration t.

First consider $P_0(t + \delta t)$, the probability that there are no arrivals during time $t + \delta t$. The postulates indicate that the number of arrivals in disjoint intervals are independent events, and hence:

$$P_0(t + \delta t) = P_0(t) P_0(\delta t)$$
$$= P_0(t) \{1 - [\lambda\delta t + o(\delta t)]\}. \qquad (11\text{-}1)$$

Since $o(\delta t)$ simply indicates a quantity whose order of magnitude is less than δt, multiplying $o(\delta t)$ by any coefficient independent of δt is still $o(\delta t)$. Hence Equation 11-1 reduces to:

$$P_0(t + \delta t) = P_0(t) [1 - \lambda\delta t] + o(\delta t)$$

and dividing by δt we obtain:

$$\frac{P_0(t + \delta t) - P_0(t)}{\delta t} = -\lambda P_0(t) + \frac{o(\delta t)}{\delta t}$$

*More precisely, $\lim\limits_{\delta t \to 0} o(\delta t)/\delta t = 0$.

Now taking the limit as $\delta t \to 0$ we are left with the simple first-order ordinary differential equation:

$$\frac{d}{dt} P_0 (t) = - \lambda_0 P_0 (t) \tag{11-2}$$

From the boundary condition that $P_0 (0) = 1$ we find:

$$P_0 (t) = e^{-\lambda t} \tag{11-3}$$

We follow a similar development to find $P_n (t)$ for $n > 0$. Now, however, there are two nonnegligible ways to get n arrivals in the interval $t + \delta t$: either n arrivals during interval t and none during interval δt, or $n - 1$ arrivals during interval t and a single arrival during interval δt. Recall that the probability of more than one arrival during δt is $o(\delta t)$. The general restatement of Equation 11-1 is:

$$
\begin{aligned}
P_n (t + \delta t) &= P_n (t) P_0 (\delta t) + P_{n-1} (t) P_1 (\delta t) + o(\delta t) \\
&= P_n (t) [1 - \lambda \delta t] + P_{n-1} (t) \lambda \delta t + o(\delta t)
\end{aligned} \tag{11-4}
$$

$$\frac{P_n(t + \delta t) - P_n(t)}{\delta t} = - \lambda P_n (t) + \lambda P_{n-1} (t) + \frac{o(\delta t)}{(\delta t)}$$

Again, taking the limit as $\delta t \to 0$:

$$\frac{d}{dt} P_n (t) = - \lambda P_n (t) + \lambda P_{n-1} (t), n > 0 \tag{11-5}$$

For $n = 1$ the preceding differential equation reduces to

$$\frac{d}{dt} P_1 (t) = - \lambda P_1 (t) + \lambda e^{-\lambda t}$$

Since $P_1 (0) = 0$ we find:

$$P_1 (t) = \lambda t e^{-\lambda t}$$

Similarly, we can solve Equation 11-5 for $n = 2, 3, \ldots$ and in general we have:

$$P_n (t) = \frac{(\lambda t)^n}{n!} e^{-\lambda t} \tag{11-6}$$

Figure 11-2 shows the Poisson probability function for $\lambda = \frac{1}{2}, 1, 4,$ and 10. Both the mean and standard deviation of the Poisson function are λt.

Exponential Service-Time Distribution   In the preceding discussion on the Poisson arrival process, we stated that the fact that it enjoys the memoryless, or Markovian, property is very important for our later work. The same statement

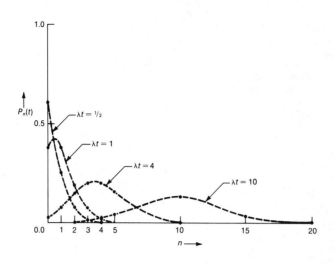

Figure 11-2 The Poisson probability density function

applies to service-time distributions; the exponential distribution is the only distribution to enjoy the Markovian property. Let μ be the average rate of service completions at a processor. We now make an assumption similar to the central assumption used in the development of the Poisson arrival process: let the probability of the completion of service between epochs t and $t + \delta t$ be $\mu \delta t + o(\delta t)$. The exponential distribution directly follows from this single postulate.

Let $S(t)$ be the probability that service is not completed by time t. Then

$$
\begin{aligned}
S(t + \delta t) &= S(t)\, S(\delta t) \\
&= S(t)\, \{1 - [\mu \delta t + o(\delta t)]\} \\
&= S(t)\, [1 - \mu \delta t] + o(\delta t)
\end{aligned}
$$

$$
\frac{S(t + \delta t) - S(t)}{\delta t} = -\mu S(t) + \frac{o(\delta t)}{\delta t}
$$

Taking the limit as $\delta(t) \to 0$ we obtain:

$$
\frac{d}{dt}\, S(t) = -\mu S(t)
$$

Using the boundary condition that $S(0) = 1$, we find:

$$
S(t) = e^{-\mu t}, \ t \ge 0 \tag{11-7}
$$

$S(t)$ is commonly known as the *survivor function*; the more commonly used *distribution function* $F(t)$ is just $1 - S(t)$, so:

$$
F(t) = 1 - e^{-\mu t} \tag{11-8}
$$

and the *density function,* $f(t)$, is

$$f(t) = \frac{d}{dt} F(t)$$
$$= \mu e^{-\mu t}, t > 0 \qquad (11\text{-}9)$$

In other words, $f(t)$ is the probability that service is completed between t and $t + \delta t$.

The similarity between the Poisson arrival process and the exponential service-time distribution is seen when we recognize that the interarrival times of a Poisson process are exponentially distributed with parameter λ.

$$Pr \{\text{interarrival time} \leq t\} = 1 - P_0(t)$$
$$= 1 - e^{-\lambda t}$$

Simple Queueing Structure: A Single Processor with Exponential Interarrival and Service Times

The first queueing structure we analyze is simple: Poisson arrival process, exponential service time, and a single, simple processor. This queueing structure is often denoted as the $M/M/1$ case.* Figure 11-3 is a schematic representation of this case. The fact that the model is simple does not imply it is of little use. On the contrary, the model is often a good initial approximation to a number of computer structures.

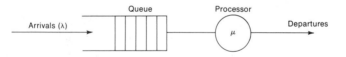

Figure 11-3 $M/M/1$ queueing structure

For example, consider a data concentrator, or preprocessor, for a computation center. The data concentrator supports the remote terminals communicating with the computation center. The function of the data concentrator is to buffer the messages from the terminals in its local memory, perform some initial preprocessing of the message, and then either pass the message on to the central computer for further processing or respond directly to the terminal

---

*This notation follows from a general scheme in the queueing literature that has the basic form $A/B/n$ where A identifies the arrival process: M for a Markovian, or Poisson, process, G for a general distribution, and D for constant interarrival times; B identifies the service-time distribution and uses the same abbreviations as the arrival process; and n represents the number of processors serving the queue.

if the request is relatively trivial. A number of important questions must be answered when designing such a data concentrator:

1. How much time can be spent preprocessing each message? The answer to this question will have a direct impact on the power of the processor that is required as well as the extent of preprocessing attempted.
2. How much memory must be included in the concentrator to ensure that the message buffers overflow infrequently?
3. What is the average response time seen by terminals to trivial requests handled by the data concentrator? What is the variance of the response times?
4. What fraction of time will the data concentrator be free to either handle low-priority input/output devices or run maintenance routines?

We assume that the arrival of messages forms a Poisson process with an average arrival rate of λ messages per second. In addition, we model the processing time per message as an exponentially distributed random variable. For the moment let us assume a first-in, first-out (FIFO) queue discipline. (Later in this section we take a more detailed look at alternative scheduling disciplines.)

To begin the analysis of our simple queueing structure we return to the elementary considerations used in the development of the Poisson process and the exponential service-time distribution. Let $p_n(t)$ denote the probability of the system being in state E_n at epoch t, that is, having n messages in service or waiting for service. First consider $p_0(t + \delta t)$, the probability of the data concentrator being idle (in state E_0) at epoch $t + \delta t$. There are two significant ways for the processor to be idle at epoch $t + \delta t$: either to be in state E_0 at epoch t and have no new messages arrive during the interval δt, or to be in state E_1, have the single message complete its processing, and have no new messages arrive during the interval δt. The chance of more than a single arrival or departure is of order $o(\delta t)$. We can express these observations in the equation:

$$p_0(t + \delta t) = (1 - \lambda\delta t)\,p_0(t) + (1 - \lambda\delta t)\,\mu\delta t p_1(t) + o(\delta t)$$

$$= (1 - \lambda\delta t)\,p_0(t) + \mu\delta t p_1(t) + o(\delta t)$$

We can also write similar equations for $p_n(t + \delta t)$ where $n > 0$. However, it is now also possible to get to state E_n at epoch $t + \delta t$ by being in state E_{n-1} at epoch t and having an arrival during the interval δt. Hence we see:

$$p_n(t + \delta t) = (1 - \mu\delta t)\,\lambda\delta t p_{n-1}(t) + (1 - \mu\delta t)(1 - \lambda\delta t)\,p_n(t)$$
$$+ (1 - \lambda\delta t)\,\mu\delta t p_{n+1}(t) + o(\delta t)$$

$$= \lambda\delta t p_{n-1}(t) + [1 - \lambda\delta t - \mu\delta t]\,p_n(t) + \mu\delta(t)p_{n+1}(t) + o(\delta t), n = 1, 2, \ldots$$

By collecting terms and taking the limit as $\delta t \to 0$ we are left with the following set of simultaneous, ordinary differential equations:

$$\frac{d}{dt}\,p_0(t) = -\lambda p_0\,(t) + \mu p_1\,(t) \tag{11-10a}$$

$$\frac{d}{dt}\,p_n(t) = \lambda p_{n-1}\,(t) - (\lambda + \mu)\,p_n\,(t) + \mu p_{n+1}\,(t), \quad n = 1, 2, \ldots \tag{11-10b}$$

If we supply sufficient boundary conditions, the preceding set of differential equations can be solved to give the complete, time-dependent performance of the queue [Cox and Smith, 61, Chapter 3]. Such time-dependent information can be very important if bursts of arrivals, or other severe congestion, are probable and we wish to find the expected length of time needed to alleviate the congestion.

We are often more interested in the long-term, or steady-state, behavior of the system than we are in any initial transient behavior. We can find the steady-state solution by setting $d/dt\,(p_n\,(t)) = 0$ for $n = 0, 1, 2, \ldots$ When we do this we are left with the simple recurrence relations:

$$\lambda p_0 = \mu p_1 \tag{11-11a}$$

and

$$(\lambda + \mu)\,p_n = \lambda p_{n-1} + \mu p_{n+1}, \quad n = 1, 2, \ldots \tag{11-11b}$$

These recurrence relations are called the *balance equation, steady-state equation,* or *equilibrium equations* of the queueing structure. Note that we have replaced $p_n(t)$ by p_n in Equation 11-11, since p_n is the equilibrium probability of being in state E_n, independent of any particular epoch t in time. From Equation 11-11a we find

$$p_1 = \frac{\lambda}{\mu}p_0$$

or if we define ρ to be the ratio λ/μ:

$$p_1 = \rho p_0 \tag{11-12}$$

and from Equation 11-11b we get:

$$\mu p_2 = (\lambda + \mu)\,p_1 - \lambda p_0$$

$$p_2 = \rho^2 p_0$$

Continuing to use Equation 11-11b we see in general:

$$p_n = \rho^n p_0 \tag{11-13}$$

In order to explicitly solve for p_n in terms of λ and μ, the parameters of the model, we will need to use the normalizing equation:

$$\sum_{0 \leq i < \infty} p_i = 1 \tag{11-14}$$

In other words, the equilibrium probabilities relate to disjoint events that span the space of all possibilities and hence must sum to unity.

$$\sum_{0 \le i < \infty} p_i = \sum_{0 \le i < \infty} \rho^i p_0$$

$$= p_0 \sum_{0 \le i < \infty} \rho^i$$

$$= \frac{p_0}{1 - \rho}, \rho < 1 \qquad (11\text{-}15)$$

Now from Equations 11-14 and 11-15 we get:

$$p_0 = 1 - \rho$$

and in general

$$p_n = \rho^n (1 - \rho), n = 0, 1, 2, \ldots \qquad (11\text{-}16)$$

Note that Equation 11-15 is undefined for $\rho = 1$. In fact, the preceding analysis of the steady-state behavior of the $M/M/1$ queueing system is only meaningful for $\rho < 1$. Recall that $\rho = \lambda/\mu$ and, unless $\lambda < \mu$, requests are arriving at a faster rate than they can be serviced. In other words, for $\rho \ge 1$ no steady-state solution exists, because the arrival process has saturated the processor and the queue is growing without bound. ρ plays a prominent role in queueing theory and is commonly referred to as the *traffic intensity* of the queueing system.

Now let us return to the example of the data concentrator and apply the results of our analysis to answer the questions about its performance.

Equation 11-16 directly answers some of our original questions. Since p_0 indicates that the processor has no outstanding messages to process, we find the data concentrator free $(1 - \rho)$ of the time. The observation that the processor is *not* idle with probability ρ is a general fact that transcends the simple $M/M/1$ case: in *any* single-processor queueing structure, the utilization of the processor is equal to the ratio of the arrival rate to the service rate.

Equation 11-16 also provides some guidelines on the amount of memory required to buffer memory. Suppose the data concentrator has sufficient local memory to hold k messages. Then our model indicates that the probability we need more than k buffers is:

$$Pr \text{ \{more than } k \text{ buffers required\}} = \sum_{k < n < \infty} p_n$$

$$= \sum_{k+1 \le n < \infty} \rho^n (1 - \rho)$$

$$= \rho^{k+1} (1 - \rho) \sum_{0 \le n' < \infty} \rho^{n'}$$

$$= \rho^{k+1} \qquad (11\text{-}17)$$

We may also be interested in the average queue length, $\bar{Q}$,

$$\bar{Q} = \sum_{0 \leq n < \infty} n p_n$$

$$= (1 - \rho) \sum_{1 \leq n < \infty} n \rho^n$$

$$= \rho (1 - \rho) \sum_{1 \leq n < \infty} n \rho^{n-1}$$

$$= \rho (1 - \rho) \sum_{1 \leq n < \infty} \frac{d}{d\rho} (\rho^n)$$

$$= \rho (1 - \rho) \frac{d}{d\rho} \left\{ \sum_{1 \leq n \leq \infty} \rho^n \right\}$$

$$= \rho (1 - \rho) \frac{d}{d\rho} \left\{ \frac{\rho}{1 - \rho} \right\}$$

$$= \frac{\rho}{1 - \rho} \qquad (11\text{-}18)$$

In order to find $\bar{W}$, the average waiting time (or response time) of a message at the data concentrator, we make use of one of the most important identities in the theory of queues: $\bar{Q} = \lambda \bar{W}$. See Conway, Maxwell, and Miller [67] or Jewell [67] for proof of this fundamental result. Hence the expected waiting time of a message at the data concentrator is simply:

$$\bar{W} = \lambda^{-1} \frac{\rho}{1 - \rho}$$

$$= \frac{1}{\mu - \lambda} \qquad (11\text{-}19)$$

The effect that the processing time per message has on the performance of the concentrator should now be clear. Strictly speaking, as long as $\mu \geq \lambda$, or equivalently $\rho < 1$, the system performs properly. Figure 11-4 shows the waiting time, queue size, processor utilization, and buffer memory overflow as a function of ρ.

The expected waiting time for the $M/M/1$ case, Equation 11-19, is a special instance of the more general formula for the $M/G/1$ case:

$$\bar{W} = \lambda^{-1} \left\{ \rho + \frac{\rho^2 (1 + C^2)}{2 (1 - \rho)} \right\} \qquad (11\text{-}20)$$

where C is the coefficient of variation of service time, that is, the ratio of the standard deviation of service time to the expected service time. ($C = 1$ for an exponential distribution.) Equation 11-20 is called the *Pollaczek-Khinchine formula*.

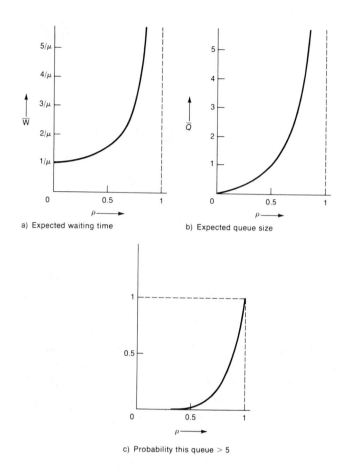

a) Expected waiting time

b) Expected queue size

c) Probability this queue > 5

Figure 11-4   Performance of the M/M/1 queueing structure

In the remainder of this section we develop extensions of the simple $M/M/1$ queueing structure that are often of practical interest. First we consider a few generalizations of the single-processor and service-time assumptions. Later we consider some simple queueing networks that provide better models of computer systems than does the Poisson arrival assumption. Finally, we study some variations of the third major aspect of a queueing structure: the scheduling discipline.

Multiprocessors and Service-Time Distributions That Are a Function of Queue Length

We now consider the generalization of the $M/M/1$ model to an $M/M/n$ model for the analysis of multiprocessor systems. Although there has been interest in multiprocessor systems for many years, the advent of the very low-cost minicomputer has resulted in the relatively recent application of multiprocessor systems to practical problems. An example of this is the development of multiprocessor message processors for the ARPA network and the construction of a multiprocessor at Carnegie-Mellon University that has (up to) 16 miniprocessors. For more information, see the discussion of multi-processors in Chapter 8.

Suppose we decide to investigate the possibility of using several processors to perform message processing. The decision to consider a multiprocessor system can stem from more than performance considerations. Stringent reliability considerations often dictate a multiprocessor design. In some cases the requirement for a highly modular system results in a multiprocessor design so that each installation of the system can tailor the processing power to its local requirements.

There are several ways to organize a multiprocessor version of the data concentrator. For example, each processor could have its own private queue, with each message being routed to one of the processor queues upon arrival. The messages could be assigned to the processors simply on a cyclic basis, that is, the ith message goes to processor i modulo n, where n is the number of processors in the system. A queueing structure with a higher performance is shown in Figure 11-5, where there is only a single queue, and whenever a processor finishes serving a message it goes to the queue for another message.

In this model we maintain the assumptions of our first example: a Poisson arrival process, an exponential service-time distribution for processing each message, and a FIFO scheduling discipline.

First, consider a two-, or dual-, processor system. The equilibrium equation relating p_0 and p_1 is identical to the single-process case, Equation 11-11a, because even though we have two processors, we assume only one processor can be used to service a single message. But now consider the next equilibrium equation:

$$(\lambda + \mu)\, p_1 = \lambda p_0 + 2\mu p_2 \tag{11-21}$$

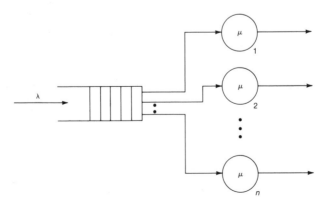

Figure 11-5 The $M/M/n$ queueing structure: a simple model of a multiprocessor

This equation is different from the corresponding equation for the single processor case. The difference is the coefficient of 2 before the last μ; and this equation indicates that when there is more than one outstanding request both processors can service a message, and that the probability of a service completion from one of the processors is $2\mu\delta t$. The following recurrence relation describes the remaining equilibrium equations:

$$(\lambda + 2\mu)\, p_n = \lambda p_{n-1} + 2\mu p_{n+1}, \quad n = 2, 3, \ldots \tag{11-22}$$

Solving this set of equilibrium equations in a manner analogous to the single processor case, we find:

$$p_0 = \frac{1 - \rho'}{1 + \rho'} \tag{11-23a}$$

$$p_n = 2(\rho')^n \, \frac{1 - \rho'}{1 + \rho'}, \, n = 1, 2, \ldots$$

$$\text{where } \rho' = \frac{\lambda}{2\mu} \tag{11-23b}$$

We now generalize this two-processor case to the k-processor case. Let:

$$\rho' = \frac{\lambda}{k\mu}$$

and

$$S = 1 + k\rho' + \frac{(k\rho')^2}{2!} + \ldots + \frac{(k\rho')^{k-1}}{(k - 1)!} + \frac{(k\rho')^k}{k!\,(1 - \rho')}$$

Then we find:

$$p_i = \frac{(k\rho')^i}{i!\, S}, \, i = 0, 1, \ldots, k - 1 \tag{11-24}$$

$$p_i = \frac{k^k(\rho')^i}{k!\, S}, \, i = k, k + 1, \ldots \tag{11-25}$$

Figure 11-6 compares a number of multiprocessor configurations in which the total processing power is held constant. In other words, $k\mu = 1.0$ for all configurations, and hence the eight processors in the $k = 8$ case are each one eighth the power of the single processor in the $k = 1$ case. The first graph shows the expected waiting time as a function of p' for one, two, three, five, and eight processors. The second figure shows the probability of the queue exceeding four messages in each case.

An example of a queueing structure with queue-dependent service-time is the model of the shortest-latency-time-first (SLTF) file drum shown in

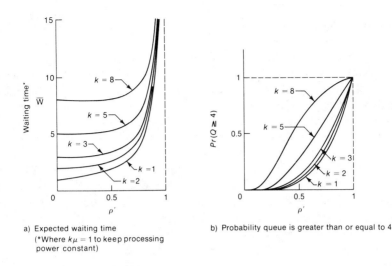

a) Expected waiting time
(*Where $k\mu = 1$ to keep processing power constant)

b) Probability queue is greater than or equal to 4

Figure 11-6   Performance of M/M/k queueing structures where $k = 1, 2, 3, 5, 8$

Figure 11-7. The drum rotates at a constant angular velocity, with period τ, and the read/write heads are fixed. Blocks of information, often called records, or files, are read or written onto the surface of the drum as the appropriate portion of the drum passes under the read/write heads. Once a decision has been made to process a particular record, the time spent waiting for the record to come under the read/write heads is called *rotational latency* or just *latency*. With a drum-storage unit organized as a file drum we do not

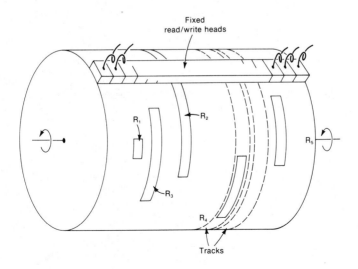

Figure 11-7   File drum

constrain the records to be of any particular length nor do we impose restrictions on the starting position of records. For convenience, let our unit of length be the circumference of the drum.

As indicated by its name, the SLTF file drum uses the shortest-latency-time-first scheduling discipline. At all times, an SLTF policy schedules the record that will come under the read/write heads first as the next record to be transmitted. For example, in Figure 11-7, assuming the drum is not transmitting record 2, an SLTF policy will schedule record 5 as the next record to be processed.

The measurement of an operational computer system [Fuller and Baskett, 75] has shown that the starting addresses of successive input/output requests can be realistically modeled as independent random variables uniformly distributed around the circumference of the drum, and that the length of the records can be approximated by exponentially distributed random variables with a mean of one third of the drum's circumference.

Although more complex models of the SLTF file drum have been analyzed [Abate and Dubner, 69; Fuller and Baskett, 75], a simplification that results in a surprisingly good approximation is to model the service-time and the immediately preceding latency interval with the following queue-size-dependent service rate:

$$\frac{1}{\mu_n} = \frac{\tau}{n+1} + \frac{1}{\mu} = \frac{\mu\tau + n + 1}{\mu(n+1)} \tag{11-26}$$

where μ^{-1} is the mean record-transmission time and n is the number of outstanding requests. It follows in a straightforward manner that the equilibrium equation for the drum model are:

$$\lambda p_0 = \mu_1 p_1, \tag{11-27a}$$

$$(\lambda + \mu_n) p_n = \lambda p_{n-1} + \mu_{n+1} p_{n+1}, \quad n = 1, 2, \ldots \tag{11-27b}$$

The preceding set of recurrence relations can be solved directly with forward substitution and yields:

$$p_1 = \frac{\lambda}{\mu_1} p_0$$

$$p_2 = \frac{\lambda^2}{\mu_1\mu_2} p_0$$

and in general:

$$p_n = \frac{\rho^n}{\mu\tau + 1} \binom{\mu\tau + n + 1}{n + 1} p_0, \quad n = 0, 1, \ldots \tag{11-28}$$

where $\rho = \lambda\mu$ and $\binom{m}{n}$ is the binominal coefficient $m!/n!\,(m - n)!$.

As before, the sequence $\{p_n\}$ must sum to unity, that is:

$$\sum_{0 \le n < \infty} \frac{\rho^n}{\mu_T + 1} \binom{\mu_T + n + 1}{n + 1} p_0 = 1$$

and hence

$$p_0^{-1} = \frac{1}{\mu_T + 1} \sum_{0 \le n < \infty} \binom{\mu_T + n + 1}{n + 1} \rho^n \qquad (11\text{-}29)$$

With the aid of the binomial theorem the preceding relation reduces to

$$p_0 = \frac{\rho (\mu_T + 1)(1 - \rho)^{\mu_T + 1}}{1 - (1 - \rho)^{\mu_T + 1}} \qquad (11\text{-}30)$$

Using Equations 11-28 and 11-30 we see that for this model of a SLTF file drum we are able to get explicit expressions for p_n, the probability of being in state E_n. Now to find the average waiting time we use Little's formula ($\overline{Q} = \lambda \overline{W}$), where $\overline{Q}$ is the average queue length given by:

$$\overline{Q} = \sum_{0 \le n < \infty} n p_n$$

$$= \frac{\rho (\mu_T + 1)}{(1 - \rho)(1 - (1 - \rho)^{\mu_T + 1})} - 1 \qquad (11\text{-}31)$$

Finite Population Queueing Systems

We now turn our attention to modifications of the Poisson arrival assumption that has been common to our earlier models. In the queueing structure of Figure 11-8 we do not have an arrival process at all, but a closed network consisting of a single central processor and a finite number of "sources." In this model, assume that all the source servers have exponential service-time distributions. Note that there is no queueing for the source servers; a source server has an exponential holding time, and then requests service from the central server. After possibly queueing for, and then receiving, service at the central processor, control is returned to the source server and it begins another holding time.

The queueing structure of Figure 11-8 is a classic queueing model and is termed the *machine repairman,* or simply the *finite-source,* model. It is called the machine repairman model because it is often explained as a model of a set of machines in a job shop that occasionally fail. Upon failure they require maintenance from a repairman, and the machines may need to queue for repair if another machine breaks down before the repairman can fix the first machine. In this context, λ is the failure rate of an operating machine and μ is the repair rate of the repairman.

The importance of the finite-source model for the analysis of computer systems becomes clear when we consider a time-shared or remote-job-entry

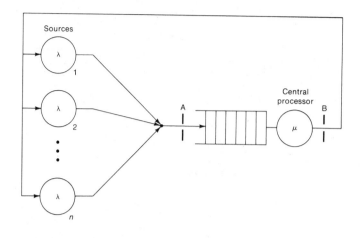

Figure 11-8 Finite-source queueing structure

system. The sources now correspond to users at terminals, and the central server, or repairman, corresponds to the central processor. To begin with, let us assume FIFO queueing at the central processor (in the next subsection we investigate more effective scheduling disciplines).

As in our previous examples, we can write down a set of equilibrium equations. Now, however, it is the arrival rate that is a function of the queue size, rather than the service-time. Specifically, if n sources are processing results at epoch t, the probability of an arrival during the interval between t and $t + \delta t$ is $n\lambda\delta t$. As before, the chance of more than one arrival during δt is $o(\delta t)$. The equilibrium equations are:

$$n\lambda p_0 = \mu p_1 \qquad (11\text{-}32a)$$

$$[(n - i)\lambda + \mu]\, p_i = (n - i + 1)\,\lambda p_{i-1} + \mu p_{i+1} \quad i = 1, 2, \ldots, n - 1$$
$$(11\text{-}32b)$$

$$\mu p_n = \lambda p_{n-1} \qquad (11\text{-}32c)$$

Solving the preceding set of equations we get:

$$p_i = \frac{n!}{(n - i)!}\rho^i p_0$$

Using the normalizing equation, that is, $p_0 + p_1 + \ldots + p_n$ must sum to unity, we find:

$$p_0 = \left\{ \sum_{0 \leq i \leq n} \frac{n!}{(n - i)!}\,\rho^i \right\}^{-1} \qquad (11\text{-}33)$$

An important application of the finite-source model is the modeling of time-sharing systems. An important characteristic of interactive time-sharing systems is the response time of the central processor as seen by a user. The response time is the waiting time (W) of a request at the central processor.

Let us solve for $\overline{W}$, the average response time seen by the user of a time-sharing system. An observation that significantly simplifies our analyses is that the arrival rate of requests to the central processor (point A in Figure 11-8) must be equal to the departure rate (point B in Figure 11-8). Each user, or source, has an average "think" time of λ^{-1}, sees an average response time of $\overline{W}$, and hence is in the thinking state the following fraction of time:

$$\frac{\lambda^{-1}}{\lambda^{-1} + \overline{W}}$$

There are n users and each generates requests at a rate of λ requests per second when in the thinking state. Therefore, the central processor sees a total arrival rate at point A of:

$$n\lambda \, \frac{\lambda^{-1}}{\lambda^{-1} + \overline{W}}$$

or more simply:

$$\frac{n\lambda}{1 + \lambda\overline{W}} \tag{11-34}$$

There is a departure rate of μ from the central processor as long as at least one user has an outstanding request. Hence we have an average departure rate of:

$$\mu\,(1 - p_0) \tag{11-35}$$

Equating Equation 11-34 to Equation 11-35 and solving for $\overline{W}$ we obtain:

$$\overline{W} = \frac{n}{\mu\,(1 - p_0)} - \frac{1}{\lambda} \tag{11-36}$$

In Figure 11-9 $\overline{W}$ is plotted as a function of n, the number of users. It can be shown (see Problem 11-7) that as n grows $\overline{W}$ approaches the asymptotic expression

$$\frac{1}{\mu}\left\{ n - \frac{1}{\rho} \right\} \tag{11-37}$$

where $\rho = \lambda/\mu$.

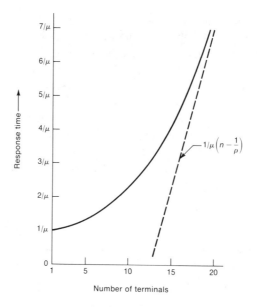

Figure 11-9 Response time for a JOSS-like system using FIFO scheduling in the central processor

These results were first discussed by Scherr [67], who found that this simple model predicted remarkably well the measured performance of MIT's CTSS time-sharing systems. Measurements of the JOSS system [Bryan, 67] add credibility to this model, because user think times were shown to be exponentially distributed (with a mean of 30 seconds).

Now consider the system in Figure 11-10, where both servers have queues. In particular Figure 11-10 is a model of a central-processor/SLTF file-drum system, where the service time of the processor is assumed to be exponential and the model of the drum is the same as developed previously. A fixed number of tasks, denoted here as m, circulate in the system, alternately requesting service at the processor and the drum. Typically, the behavior of real multi-programmed systems is more complex than this, but this model does allow us to study the feedback effects inherent in such systems. Since drums are often used as secondary storage device, this processor/drum model captures the major points of congestion, and hence the queueing behavior of many actual multiprogramming systems. The balance equations for this model are:

$$\lambda p_0 = \mu_1\, p_1 \tag{11-38a}$$

$$(\lambda + \mu_n)\, p_n = \lambda p_{n-1} + \mu_{n+1}\, p_{n+1}, \quad 1 \le n < m \tag{11-38b}$$

$$\mu_m\, p_m = \lambda p_{m-1} \tag{11-38c}$$

The solution to these equilibrium equations follows our previous work.

We see:

$$p_n = \left(\prod_{i=1}^{n} \rho_i \right) p_0, \; 1 \leq n \leq m \qquad (11\text{-}39)$$

$$p_0 = \left\{ \sum_{i=0}^{m} \prod_{j=0}^{i} \rho_j \right\}^{-1} \qquad (11\text{-}40)$$

where $\rho_n = \lambda / \mu_n$.

These expressions for the equilibrium probabilities are used to plot the expected response times of the drum and the utilization of the processor for various degrees of multiprogramming, as shown in Figures 11-11 and 11-12.

Scheduling Disciplines

We now consider the third aspect of a queueing system: the scheduling discipline. In our previous discussions we have assumed a first-in, first-out (FIFO) policy. In fact, our previous results apply to more than just the FIFO case. The *expected* waiting time and *expected* queue length are independent of the particular queueing discipline used, provided the policy is not based on the service-time requirements of the requests. Therefore, expressions for $\overline{W}$ and $\overline{Q}$ that we have already derived apply to such service-time-independent scheduling disciplines as last-in, first-out (LIFO) and random, as well as FIFO.

Although FIFO, LIFO, and random policies share the same expression for expected waiting time and queue size, they differ in the other statistical measures of their performance. For example, the second moment, $E[W^2]$, of the waiting time for the three disciplines is:

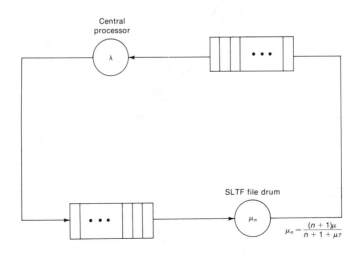

Figure 11-10   Cyclic queue model of processor/drum system

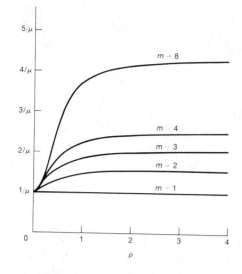

Figure 11-11 Expected waiting time at drum
$$\mu\tau = \tfrac{1}{3}$$

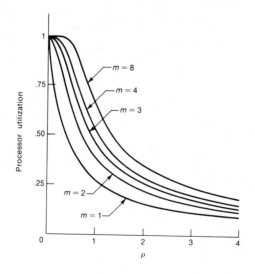

Figure 11-12 Expected processor utilization with SLTF drum
$\rho = \frac{\lambda}{\mu}; \tau = 1; \mu = \tfrac{1}{3}\tau$
$m =$ degree of multiprogramming

$$E_{\text{FIFO}}[W^2] = \frac{\rho(1 + \rho)}{(1 - \rho)^2} \qquad (11\text{-}41a)$$

$$E_{\text{LIFO}}[W^2] = \frac{1}{1 - \rho} E_{\text{FIFO}}[W^2] \qquad (11\text{-}41b)$$

$$E_{\text{Random}}[W^2] = \frac{1}{(1 - \rho/2)} E_{\text{FIFO}}[W^2] \qquad (11\text{-}41c)$$

These simple expressions can be used to find the variance, or *central* second moment, from the formula:

$$\text{Var}[W] = E[W^2] - (W)^2$$

In systems operating under deadlines or attempting to minimize the frustration level of users, it is important to minimize the variance as well as the mean of the waiting time. An example of a scheduling policy that is not independent of service-time requirements is the shortest-remaining-processing-time (SRPT) policy for drums. It is a straightforward exercise in order statistics to show that $\overline{W}$ for the simple $M/M/1$ queueing structure using SRPT is:

$$\overline{W}(t) = \frac{\rho/\mu}{1 - \rho[1 - e^{-\mu t}(1 + \mu t)]^2} \qquad (11\text{-}42)$$

Note that the expected waiting time under SRPT is less than the waiting time for FIFO and the other service-time-independent policies. It is a general result of scheduling theory that SRPT is the scheduling policy that minimizes the expected waiting time (and from Little's formula, the expected queue size).

Unfortunately, in most computer systems we cannot use SRPT discipline because we do not have a priori knowledge of the service-time requirements of outstanding requests. Many of the priority schemes used in computer systems attempt to approximate an SRPT discipline. For example, in the simplest case we might try to partition requests arriving at the processor into two classes: compute-bound and input/output-bound. We expect the compute-bound tasks to require a substantially longer service time than input/output-bound tasks, which ask for only a small amount of processor time before requiring further service at a disk, terminal, printer, or other device. Now if we give input/output-bound tasks priority over compute-bound tasks, we might expect, from analogy with the SRPT case, that we reduce the waiting time at the processor. We can generalize this two-level priority example to an n-level priority scheme if we have sufficient information about the tasks to classify the jobs into the n classes.

To understand the effect of an n-level priority-scheduling discipline, let us return to the simple $M/M/1$ queueing structure: a Poisson arrival process, exponential service-time, and a single server. Now, however, let arrivals have a priority associated with them. Arrivals with priority i form a Poisson arrival sequence with arrival rate λ_i and have an exponential service-time distribution with parameter μ_i, $1 \le i \le n$. In the following analysis we derive the primary performance parameters of the system.

First we make the observation that it is sufficient to analyze only a two-priority system. In any priority system with preemption, the highest priority level, call it level 1, behaves as if it were the only class of requests queueing for service. In other words, Equations 11-18 and 11-19 express $\overline{Q}_1$ and $\overline{W}_1$, respectively, if we simply replace λ by λ_1 and μ by μ_1.

For a priority level greater than 1 (denoted here as i), we treat an arrival in one of three ways, based on the priority level (k) of the request. If the arrival has a lower priority than the priority level of interest $(k > i)$ then it can be ignored for the same reason given when $i = 1$. The remaining arrivals are partitioned into either *low* priority requests $(k = i)$ or *high* priority requests $(k < i)$. In the set of equilibrium equations that follow, let $p_{j,k}$ denote the equilibrium probability of being in a state with j high-priority requests and k low-priority requests. The equilibrium equation can be stated as:

$$\{\lambda_H + \lambda_L + \mu_H \zeta(j) + \mu_L \zeta(k)[1 - \zeta(j)]\} p_{j,k}$$
$$= \lambda_H p_{j-1,k} + \lambda_L p_{j,k-1} + \mu_H p_{j+1,k} + \mu_L [1 - \zeta(j)] p_{j,k+1} \quad (11\text{-}43)$$

where $j = 0, 1, 2, \ldots$; $k = 0, 1, 2, \ldots$; $\zeta(m)$ is the unit step function that is unity if $m > 0$ and zero otherwise; and any $p_{j,k}$ with a negative subscript is zero. The solution of this set of simultaneous equations defined by Equation 11-43 can be solved in a direct manner to obtain:

$$\overline{Q}_L = \sum_{0 \le j < \infty} \sum_{0 \le k < \infty} k p_{j,k} = \frac{\rho_L}{1 - \rho_L - \rho_H} \left[1 + \frac{\mu_L \rho_H}{\mu_H (1 - \rho_H)} \right] \quad (11\text{-}44)$$

Little's formula can be used to find $\overline{W}$.

A class of scheduling disciplines generally termed *feedback scheduling disciplines* have been found to be very useful in many time-sharing and multiprogramming systems. The purpose of using feedback disciplines is to give better service to short requests than is possible with simple service-time-independent disciplines like FIFO and LIFO. SRPT gives the quickest service to the short requests, but as we have said before, in most computing systems, we do not know the service-time requirements of the requests queued for service.

The simplest feedback-scheduling discipline is the *round-robin* (RR) discipline, illustrated in Figure 11-13. In RR scheduling, arriving requests enter a FIFO queue to await service. When the request begins service at the processor, it is allowed to continue for a maximum quantum of time, denoted as q. If the request completes service within the quantum it simply leaves the system. However, if service is not complete by the end of the quantum, the request is preempted from the processor and put back on the end of the queue.

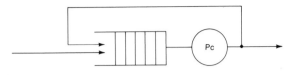

Figure 11-13   Round-robin (RR) model

Service is resumed only after the request again reaches the front of the FIFO queue. This sequence is continued until the request finally completes service. The analysis of the general RR queueing model is beyond the scope of this text, but Figure 11-14 indicates its practical value.

If we let $q \to 0$ in an RR system, we get what is called *processor sharing*. The main value of the processor-sharing model is that it results in some surprisingly simple results that aid in our understanding of feedback scheduling schemes. Specifically, the expected waiting time for a processor-shared RR system is:

$$\overline{W}(t) = \frac{t}{1 - \rho} \qquad (11\text{-}45)$$

where t interval of service required a task.

Now note that our original $M/M/1$ FIFO model can be considered the limiting case of the RR scheme when $q \to \infty$, so that Equations 11-19 and

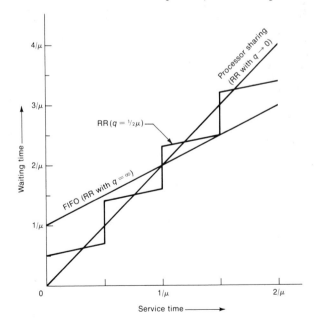

Figure 11-14   Expected waiting time for RR

11-45 bound the range of performance attainable with **RR** scheduling disciplines.

Discrete-Time Markov Chains

In the preceding queueing models of this section we have started with a set of difference equations and through a limiting process derived a set of differential equations that in turn lead to the equilibrium equations we have found so useful. Many interesting problems can be studied by using the difference equations directly, and here we consider two such examples to illustrate this method.

Analysis of a Processor's Stack   A number of central processors are designed around the concept of a stack rather than a simple accumulator or set of general-purpose registers. (Chapter 7 has a detailed discussion of such processors.) Probably the best known of the stack machines is the Burroughs B5500 and its successors. The stack in the B5500 is essentially a last-in, first-out queue, or push-down stack, and the primary operations of the processor include pushing operands onto the stack; popping operands from the stack; performing unary operations on the operand at the top of the stack (for example, complement, branch if operand zero, and so on); and binary operations between the two top elements of the stack, leaving the result on top of the stack.

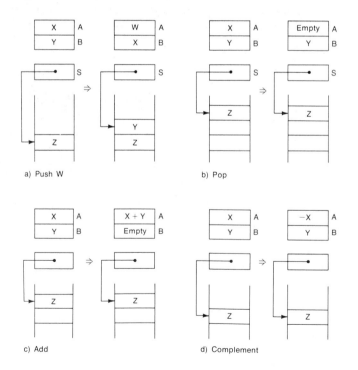

Figure 11-15   Operation of the B5500 stack

In order to increase the efficiency of a stack processor, the top few elements of the stack are kept in high-speed registers in the processor, while the remainder of the stack is kept in main storage. A stack pointer in the processor identifies the beginning of the stack that resides in main storage. Figure 11-15 shows the effect of push, pop, complement, and add on a processor with the two top elements of the stack implemented as high-speed registers. Note that when an operand is popped from the stack and when the two operands of the binary operation are replaced by the single result, an operand from main memory is not brought into memory to keep the stack registers in the processor full. In general, the best scheme is to only push or pop operands into the portion of the stack in main memory when absolutely necessary and to use flags associated with the high-speed registers to indicate which registers contain an operand. An important option in the design of a stack processor concerns how much of the stack should be implemented in high-speed registers. The following analysis should help answer this question.

We begin by partitioning the instructions of the stack processor into the classes listed in Table 11-1. The parameter associated with each class represents the frequency of occurrence of instructions in that class.

TABLE 11-1. INSTRUCTION CLASSES FOR A STACK PROCESSOR

Instruction Type	Frequency of Occurrence
Push	α
Pop	β
Unary operator	γ
Binary operator	δ
Other	ϵ

Now let E_n be defined as the state in which n of the high-speed registers contain operands and $P_n(i)$ be the probability that the processor is in E_n immediately after the completion of instruction i. We can now write the set of difference equations that describe the time variations in the contents of the stack.

$$P_0(i + 1) = (\epsilon + \beta)P_0(i) + \beta\, P_1(i)$$
$$P_1(i + 1) = (\alpha + \gamma)P_0(i) + (\gamma + \epsilon)P_1(i) + (\beta + \delta)P_2(i)$$
$$P_k(i + 1) = \alpha\, P_{k-1}(i) + (\gamma + \epsilon)P_k(i) + (\beta + \delta)P_{k+1}(i)$$

.

.

.

$$P_N(i + 1) = \alpha\, P_{N-1}(i) + (\alpha + \gamma + \epsilon)P_N(i) \qquad (11\text{-}46)$$

Now, in equilibrium, $P_k(i + 1) = P_k(i)$ for $k = 0,1,\ldots,N$. Let p_k denote the equilibrium probability of being in state E_k. Now the preceding time-dependent equations reduce to:

$$p_k = [\alpha + \Delta_{0,k}\,\gamma]p_{k-1} + [\epsilon + a\Delta_{N,k} + \beta\Delta_{0,k} + \gamma(1 - \Delta_{0,k})]p_k$$
$$+ [\beta + (1 - \Delta_{0,k}\,\delta)]p_{k+1} \quad k = 0, 1, \ldots, N \qquad (11\text{-}47)$$

where $\Delta_{i,j}$ is the Kronecker delta function that is unity if the two parameters are equal and zero otherwise.

The preceding set of simultaneous equations can be solved when we use the additional normalizing equation:

$$\sum_{0 \le k \le N} p_i = 1$$

More important than the probability of being in each of the states is the expected number of accesses to the part of the stack in main memory that are required per instruction.

$$\text{E[accesses/instruction]} = (\underline{\gamma} + 2\underline{\delta})p_0 + \underline{\delta}p_1 + \underline{\alpha}p_N \qquad (11\text{-}48)$$

Multiprocessor Model   Discrete-time Markov-chain models can be used to model queueing structures for which we want to approximate service times as constant rather than exponentially distributed. For example, consider the dual-processor system of Figure 11-16. In this model we assume the service times of each of the memory modules to be constant and for, simplicity, we assume that all the modules are synchronized. As in the stack processor, we now have epochs that recur at regular instants in time. If we further assume that the processors are fast enough to issue new requests immediately after receiving their current request, we can model the multiprocessor by the queueing structure of Figure 11-17. Let the probability that each processor requests a word from any memory module be ¼, and assume that successive requests to memory are independent events.

In the dual processor system $p_{i,j,k,l}$ denotes the equilibrium probability that there are i requests outstanding to memory module 1, j to memory module 2, k to memory module 3, and l to memory module 4. Since there are two processors:

$$i + j + k + l = 2$$

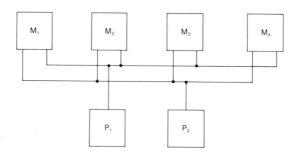

Figure 11-16   Physical structure of multiprocessor

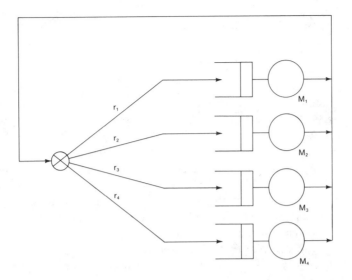

Figure 11-17   Queueing structure of multiprocessor

This constraint limits the number of states in the model to 10. The four states $(2, 0, 0, 0)$, $(0, 2, 0, 0)$, $(0, 0, 2, 0)$, and $(0, 0, 0, 2)$ represent the situation where both processors attempt to access the same memory module. In these cases only one request is satisfied and the other is queued and served during the following memory cycle. Because the two processors are identical and the four memory modules are also identical, we see from symmetry:

$$p_{2000} = p_{0200} = p_{0020} = p_{0002}$$

and

$$p_{1,1,0,0} = p_{1010} = p_{1001} = p_{0110} = p_{0101} = p_{0011}$$

Therefore the two equilibrium equations for p_{2000} and p_{1100} can be simplified as follows:

$$p_{2000} = \frac{1}{4} p_{2000} + \frac{1}{16} (p_{1100} + p_{1010} + p_{1001} + p_{0110} + p_{0101} + p_{0011})$$

$$= \frac{1}{4} p_{2000} + \frac{3}{8} p_{1100}$$

$$p_{1100} = \frac{1}{4} (p_{2000} + p_{0200}) + \frac{1}{8} (p_{1100} + p_{1010} + p_{1001} + p_{0110} + p_{0101} + p_{0011})$$

$$= \frac{1}{2} p_{2000} + \frac{3}{4} p_{1100}$$

Now, using the additional constraint that the equilibrium probabilities must sum to unity, we obtain

$$p_{2000} = \frac{1}{16}$$

$$p_{1100} = \frac{1}{8}$$

From the equilibrium probabilities we see that the average memory bandwidth is $\frac{7}{4}$ accesses per memory cycle (as opposed to the maximum memory bandwidth of 2).

This completes our introduction to analytical models of computer systems. There are many more queueing models that have application to computer systems, and in Section 11-7 we give a guide to these more advanced techniques and models. Many of the assumptions we have made here are quite restrictive, and there is the question of whether they can be considered approximations to the behavior of real computer systems. In fact, a number of studies cited in this section have addressed this criticism of queueing models, and they show that queueing models, when appropriately applied, can be good approximations to the actual behavior of computer systems. On the other hand, there are numerous instances when a more detailed analysis of system behavior is needed than can be provided with queueing models, and other instances when the system to be analyzed simply does not lend itself to being approximated by known analytical methods. In these cases simulation techniques, which are discussed in the next section, are the most appropriate tools available to the analyst.

11-4. SIMULATION MODELS

We now turn our attention to another modeling technique: *discrete-event simulation*. While simulation models can be built to analyze arbitrarily complex structures, the price we must pay is time. For example, to reproduce the results of Figures 11-11 and 11-12 with a simulation model required approximately eight minutes of central processor time. (The model was written in ALGOL and run on a PDP-10.) If a model is simple enough to be analyzed with queueing models, it is certainly advantageous to use the latter.

Let's backtrack for a moment to see exactly what type of simulation is appropriate for the study of computer systems. Simulation techniques are used to study phenomena ranging from the flight dynamics of supersonic aircraft to theories of cognitive processes. The type of simulation discussed here, and the type that is most appropriate for the modeling of computer systems, is discrete-event simulation. Figure 11-18 is a flowchart of the basic structure of such a simulation. A central feature is the fact that it is event driven. In other words, time is not a continuous variable nor is it incremented by uniform intervals in the model (as it might be in weather simulation or the simulation of the flight of a supersonic aircraft), but it is always advanced to the time of the next event. The execution of an event is simply the updating of the state of the simulation to reflect the occurrence of the event. After the

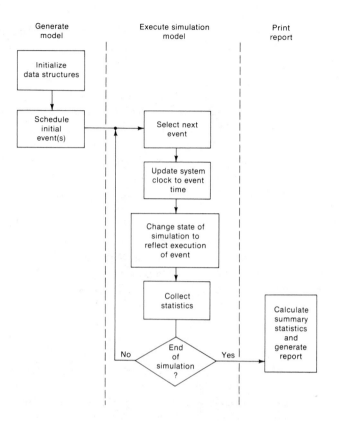

| Generate model | Execute simulation model | Print report |

Figure 11-18 Basic structure of a simulation program

event is processed the simulation clock is updated to the next event and the process is repeated. In many cases the lengths of intervals in the simulation— for example, interarrival times of jobs, length of processing time required by jobs, number of disk accesses, and so on—are modeled as random variables, hence the term *Monte Carlo simulation.*

The other discrete-event simulators that are appropriate for the modeling of computer systems are *trace-driven simulators.* In this case the trace-driven simulator is driven by a stream of measured event times. For example, rather than assume the arrival of jobs to a computer system to be a Poisson process with mean arrival rate λ, we record the actual interarrival times of jobs at an operational computer system and use this trace of event times to drive the simulation model. We do not consider trace-driven simulators any further here, but for more details see Cheng [69] and Sherman et al. [72].

Random-Number Generation

The generation of a stream of random variates is central to any Monte Carlo simulation. This section discusses the major aspects of generating a sequence of random numbers on a digital computer. The pedagogically appealing methods of flipping coins, shuffling cards, or spinning roulette wheels are too slow to be seriously considered, but analog units that use as their underlining random process the "shot," or thermal noise, of an electron tube were used in early attempts to generate a sequence of random numbers. However, although relatively fast, the process produced by these analog devices shares a deficiency with coin tossing: it is nonreproducible. If we wish to run a set of simulations comparing different implementations of some policy, it is advantageous to subject them to the same random-number stream. Another reason for using reproducible generators is that debugging simulation programs is much easier when random-number sequences can be repeated. The RAND Corporation addressed this reproducibility issue when they published their widely used table of one million random digits [RAND, 55]. These tables are available on magnetic tape and have been used to produce random sequences for a number of applications.

It is a bit cumbersome to read streams of random digits from magnetic tape. Early in the development of computers, attention turned to searching for an algorithmic method of generating a stream of random numbers. This technique was first suggested by von Neumann in 1946, when he proposed the *middle-squares* method of generating a random sequence. In the middle-squares method the next random digit in the sequence is generated by squaring the current random digit and using the middle digits of the product as the next random number. Although von Neumann's middle-squares method does not generate a very random sequence [Knuth, 69], another simple recurrence does; it is the *linear congruential generator*. The general form of a linear congruential generator is:

$$x_{i+1} = (ax_i + b) \text{ modulo } m \tag{11-49}$$

It has become common to call a linear congruential generator with $b = 0$ a *multiplicative congruential generator* and one with $b \neq 0$ a *mixed congruential generator*. Although the general form of congruential generators is simple, care must be taken in the choice of a, b, and m to avoid the use of a poor generator. A famous example concerned the multiplicative generator:

$$x_{i+1} = (262147 \, x_i) \text{ modulo } 2^{35} \tag{11-50}$$

This generator was widely used on early IBM machines [Greenberger, 65], and has the attractive property that 262147 is $2^{18} + 3$ and hence the multiplication can be implemented as one shift and three adds. The deficiency of Equation 11-50 becomes apparent when we express a random digit in the sequence as a function of the two previous digits rather than simply the immediately preceding digit.

$$x_{i+2} = (6x_{i+1} - 9x_i) \text{ modulo } 2^{35}$$

If we plot x_{i+2} as a function of x_i and x_{i+1} we see the points fall onto one of a small number of planes. Any simulation that uses Equation 11-50 to generate "random" points in three-dimensional space, for example, is likely to yield very misleading results.

With this example serving as a cautionary note, let us consider how to construct a good random-number generator. There exists a rich literature on the subject of random-number generators, and linear congruential generators in particular, but Knuth [69] has done an excellent job of summarizing what is known about these generators. He has suggested that the following six rules be used when constructing a linear congruential random-number generator:

1. x_0, the starting random digit (sometimes called the *seed*), may be chosen arbitrarily. The last random digit of a previous simulation or the time of day are common choices for the value of x_0.
2. The number m should be large and is usually chosen to make the modulo operation trivial (for example, 2^{31} or 2^{35}).
3. If m is a power of 2, let a modulo $8 = 5$. If m is a power of 10, let a modulo $200 = 21$.
4. $\sqrt{m} < a < m - \sqrt{m}$ and $m/100 < a$.
5. Let b be an odd number (and not a multiple of 5 if m is a power of 10) such that:

$$b \cong \frac{3 - \sqrt{3}}{6} m$$

6. The least significant digits of x_i are less random than the most significant digits. Therefore, to generate a sequence of random integers from the range $0, 1, \ldots, k - 1$, multiply x_i by k and then truncate, rather than use x_i modulo k.

After selecting a specific random-number generator, it is important to verify that the generator is producing reasonably random sequences. There are a number of statistical tests, for example, the chi-squared test and the Kolmogorov-Smirnov test, as well as a number of empirical tests, to validate the randomness of the generated sequence. The reader is encouraged to apply a number of these tests before blindly accepting a new random-number generator. Knuth [69] and Fishman [73] give good introductions to the problem of verifying random-number generators. The most common word lengths for computers are 32 and 36 bits, and random number generators that meet the above six rules, as well as a reasonable battery of statistical and empirical tests, are:

$$x_{i+1} = (314159269 \, x_i + 453806245) \text{ modulo } 2^{31}$$

$$x_{i+1} = (3141592653 \, x_i + 2718281829) \text{ modulo } 2^{35}$$

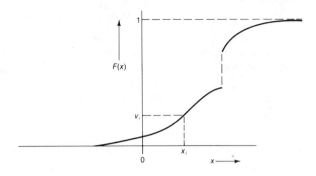

Figure 11-19   Generation of nonuniform random numbers

The final point that we make here is how to generate a random variate from an arbitrary distribution. Suppose we must draw random variates from some arbitrary cumulative distribution function $F(x)$. We know that $F(x)$ is a monotonically nondecreasing function that rises from 0 to 1. Suppose we use a random-number generator to obtain a random variate, call it v, uniformly distributed over the interval $[0, 1)$. Now find x_i

$$x_i = F^{-1}(v_i)$$

where $F^{-1}(v_i)$ is the inverse of $F(x)$ and is a mapping from the unit interval $[0, 1)$ into the domain of x (see Figure 11-19). It is easy to show that the sequence $\{x_i\}$ is a sequence of numbers randomly distributed with distribution function $F(x)$. An important example is the generation of exponentially distributed random variables. If $\{v_i\}$ is a sequence of uniformly distributed random variables, then we can generate $\{e_i\}$, a sequence of exponentially distributed random variables with distribution function:

$$F(x) = 1 - e^{-\lambda x}$$

with the relation:

$$e_i = -\lambda^{-1} \ln v_i$$

Another important distribution is the normal distribution (with mean 0 and standard deviation 1):

$$F(x) = \frac{1}{\sqrt{2\pi}} \int_{-\infty}^{x} e^{-u^2/2} \, du$$

Since $F(x)$ involves an integral, the preceding technique is not easily applied. However, from the Central Limit Theorem we know that the sum of N independent and identically distributed random variates with mean μ and variance

σ^2 is also a random variate that approaches the normal distribution for large N with mean $N\mu$ and variance $N\sigma^2$. Therefore we can approximate a normally distributed random variate with mean μ and variance σ^2 from N uniformly distributed random variates:

$$y = \sigma \left(\frac{12}{N}\right)^{1/2} \left(\sum_{1 \le i \le N} v_i - \frac{N}{2}\right) + \mu$$

To eliminate the square root computation, 12 has been a popular choice for N.

An Example: A Simple Multiprogramming System

Now that we have seen the general structure of a discrete-system simulation, as outlined in Figure 11-18, and know how to generate a sequence of random numbers to drive the simulation, we are now able to consider a specific example: the simple multiprogramming system illustrated in Figure 11-20. The simulation of this system illustrates the central points of most simulation models. The computer system consists of two units: the central processor and a paging drum. The system allows at most M jobs to enter the processing loop simultaneously; if jobs arrive for service at the computer system and there are already M jobs being processed by the system, the arriving jobs enter a FIFO queue. Once a job is in the multiprogramming mix, it alternately requests a burst of processor time and then requires a page to be accessed (read or written) from the paging drum. A job continues to receive service alternately from the central processor and the drum until it has received a predetermined amount of central processor time. Upon receiving the total amount of processor time it leaves the computer system, triggering another job to enter the multiprogramming mix if the job queue is not empty.

The following assumptions are needed to provide a complete specification of the simulation model:

1. The arriving jobs form a Poisson process with mean arrival rate λ.
2. The maximum degree of multiprogramming is M.
3. The total computation time required by a job is a random variable with

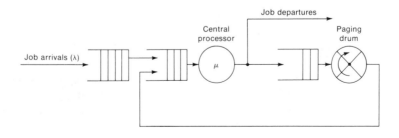

Figure 11-20 Simple multiprogramming system

mean η, variance σ^2, and having a log normal distribution.

4. The computation time required by a job between input/output requests is an exponentially distributed variable with mean μ.

5. The paging drum contains K sectors and rotates with a constant angular velocity with period T. When a job accesses a page from the drum it directs its request for a page to any one of the K sectors with equal probability.

6. All the queueing in the model is FIFO.

Central to the simulation model are the primary data structures that define its "state," or current status. Figure 11-21 shows the data structures for our multiprogramming system model. There are several scalar variables: the *clock* that indicates the current epoch in time being simulated; the *seed* that is the last pseudorandom variate generated and is the basis for generating the next random variate; *CPU busy* and *drum busy* are Boolean variables that are true if the processor and drum, respectively, are busy processing a job.

The large array in Figure 11-21 describes the state of the jobs in the simulation. The entries in each row specify:

Arrival: The time the job arrived at the computer system for service.

CPU time: The total amount of processor time required to complete servicing the job.

Event time: The time the event associated with the job is scheduled to occur. Some jobs will not have an event time if they are queued waiting to begin service on a processor.

Event type: For those jobs that have an event pending, this field specifies the type of the event. The six event types are (1) arrival of a new job, (2) termination of a processor interval to request an input/output operation, (3) termination of a processor interval because the job is done, (4) the current record being read or written from the paging drum is in position to begin its transfer, (5) the paging drum has completed its current transfer, and (6) the simulation is completed.

The *link* field of each job is used to link it into one of the five lists of the simulation. The *event queue* is a list of events, linked in order of pending execution. The head of the list is pointed to by the event queue, and the first element in the queue is the next event processed. The *job queue, processor (CPU) queue,* and *drum queue* are the three queues shown in Figure 11-20. All are FIFO and have pointers to their head as well as their tail to facilitate the addition and deletion, respectively, from these queues. The *free queue* is simply a list of unused job descriptions. Jobs are taken from this queue when they are scheduled to arrive at the computer system and are added to the free queue upon departure from the system. For simplicity, this queue

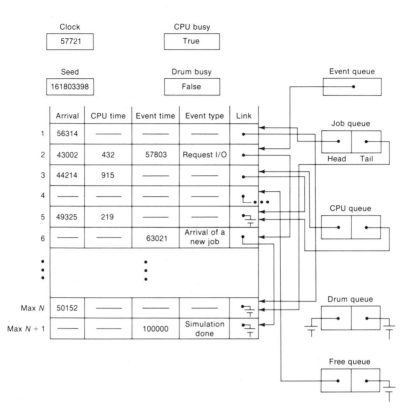

Figure 11-21 Major variables and data structures of simulation model

is implemented here as a stack, or last-in, first-out queue.

The flowchart of Figure 11-22 is an expanded version of Figure 11-18. Note that for each of the five events shown, the simulation updates the state of the model, schedules a future event or queues a request when the unit is busy, and collects summary statistics.

After considering the simulation model of this section it can be seen that there are a number of procedures and concepts that are common to any simulation. A number of languages have been developed in recognition of this fact and the simulation languages that have gained the widest acceptance include GPSS, SIMSCRIPT, and SIMULA. While it is beyond the scope of this chapter to go into these languages in any detail, we should recognize that they all are designed to accomplish the following things:

1. Generate random variates
2. Create, modify, and generally describe processes (jobs) that move through the simulation
3. Delimit and sequence the phases of a process
4. Facilitate the queueing of processes
5. Collect, generate, and display summary statistics

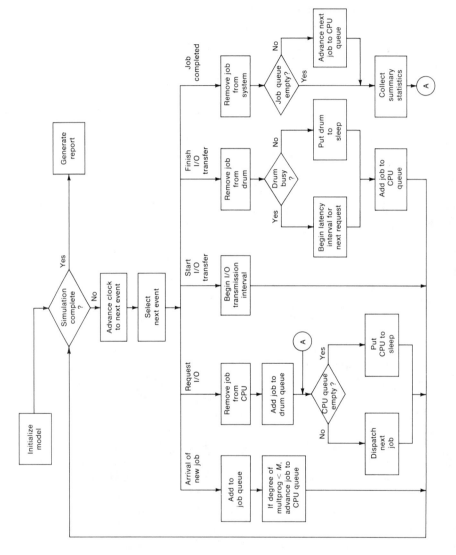

Figure 11-22 Flowchart of multiprogramming model

Estimation of the Variance of Simulation Results

A difficult problem concerning any simulation is the determination of the variance of the summary statistics. In any well-designed simulation, the precision of the results improves as the simulation is run longer; this phenomenon is called *stochastic convergence*. The problem with stochastic convergence is that it is slow. In order to double the precision of a simulation, we must quadruple the number of events simulated. This section discusses the number of input/output requests that must be simulated in order to achieve a specified precision in the summary statistics.

The simulation's estimate of the mean of a random variable, call it $\overline{X}$, is:

$$\overline{X} = \frac{1}{n} \sum_{1 \le i \le n} X_i \tag{11-51}$$

where n is the number of times an event is simulated, and X_i is the value of the ith occurrence of the event. A few examples of events of interest in this simulation are: job waiting time, input/output waiting time, central-processor-busy intervals, and input/output-busy intervals.

Let σ^2 be the variance of X and $\sigma_{\overline{x}}^2$ be the variance of the sample mean $\overline{X}$. Suppose the X_is are independent, identically distributed (iid) random variables; successive processor-busy intervals, or input/output-busy intervals are good examples of iid random variables. The Central Limit Theorem guarantees that the sample mean is normally distributed for large n, and from the linearity properties of the expectation operation [Parzen, 60, p. 206] it follows that:

$$\sigma_{\overline{x}}^2 = \frac{\sigma^2}{n} \tag{11-52}$$

Hence the standard deviation of $\overline{X}$, which we will use as a convenient measure of precision, is:

$$\sigma_{\overline{x}} = \frac{\sigma}{\sqrt{n}} \tag{11-53}$$

This expresses a fundamental property of Monte Carlo simulation: the accuracy of the simulation's summary statistics is proportional to $1/\sqrt{n}$. While this simple analysis is sufficient for the estimation of busy intervals and processor utilization, it is not adequate to estimate the precision of the sample mean of events that are correlated; input/output waiting time is an important instance of a random event that is likely to be correlated with a neighboring event. In other words, if request i experiences an unusually long wait time, it is very likely request $i + 1$ will also have a long wait time, since it was probably queued behind request i for most of i's waiting time. A simple analysis, however, can still be of value even in this more complex case. The variance of the sum of a set of identically distributed random variables is:

$$\sigma_{\overline{X}}^2 = \frac{\sigma^2}{n} + \frac{2\sigma^2}{n} \sum_{k=1}^{n} \left(1 - \frac{k}{n}\right) \rho\left(k\right) \tag{11-54}$$

where $\rho(k)$ is the autocorrelation coefficient and:

$$\rho\left(k\right) = \frac{1}{\sigma^2\left(n - k\right)} \sum_{1 \leq i \leq n-k} \left(X_i - \overline{X}\right)\left(X_{i+k} - \overline{X}\right) \tag{11-55}$$

Simulators described in this chapter are capable of executing 10^4 to 10^5 events in a reasonable amount of time, and the autocorrelation coefficient for waiting times is usually insignificant for lags greater than 100. Therefore, Equation 11-55 can be approximated by:

$$\sigma_{\overline{X}}^2 = \frac{\sigma^2}{n} \left[1 + 2 \sum_{1 \leq k \leq 100} \rho\left(k\right)\right] \tag{11-56}$$

This expression for $\sigma_{\overline{X}}^2$ can be used in place of Equation 11-52 to estimate the precision of the simulation results. Another practical technique for estimating the precision of the sample mean of correlated events is discussed by Fishman [67]. He suggests a spectral analysis of the time series of successive events to determine the equivalent number of independent events, and then uses Equation 11-52 to estimate the precision of the sample mean.

11-5. EVALUATION OF OPERATIONAL COMPUTER SYSTEMS

We now consider the evaluation of actual computer systems, not models of computer systems. The analytical and simulation methods we have just discussed are valuable tools to the analyst; however, it should also be recognized that the limitations of present analytical techniques and the expense of detailed simulations require that these modeling techniques be augmented with the evaluation of an actual system processing program. Moreover, it is often useful to compare the results of analytical or simulation models with the performance of the real system in order to test the validity of the assumptions underlying the mathematical models.

We begin this section with the old but still valuable technique of determining the instruction mix of a processor. An instruction mix simply enumerates the relative frequency of the use of each instruction in a processor's instruction set. After our discussion of instruction mixes, we move on to consider kernels, benchmarks, and synthetic jobs. These techniques provide a more complete measure of a computer system's performance and are widely used in the evaluation of machines for purchase and as aids in configuration and optimization studies.

Instruction Mixes

Instruction mixes address the need to get a more accurate measure of a central processor's performance than is given by the add time. Instruction mixes are also an important indicator of the way a specific architecture is used and can be a valuable guide to engineers concerned with implementing a particular processor architecture. Table 11-2 lists five instruction mixes. Care must be exercised when we attempt to extrapolate general conclusions from these mixes. A particular instruction mix is often the result of a hopefully representative, but nonetheless restricted, set of programs. Probably the most striking observation from Table 11-2 is the small percentage of the time spent doing arithmetic operations and the large percentage of time spent doing loads, stores, and branching. These instruction mixes further highlight the weakness of using the add time (or worse, the multiply or divide time) as a measure of the performance of the processor. The frequency of branch instructions, roughly a third, explains why pipelined instruction-execution units are so difficult to design. It is very hard to predict what instructions will be executed very far into the future.

With the instruction mix, and the timing for each instruction, we can estimate the MIPS rate for a processor. As already indicated, however, it is difficult to account for such advanced processor features as caches, pipelining, and interleaved memory in the MIPS calculation. The performance of these processors is dependent on the order in which instructions are executed and not just on instruction frequencies.

The main value of the instruction mix seems to be in processor design. The efficient implementation of any architecture can be significantly aided by knowledge of the instruction mix. Particularly when designing a processor via microprogramming, the instruction mix gives a good indication which instructions need to be implemented as efficiently as possible and which instructions can be implemented so as to conserve the size of the microprocessor's control store. Mixes are also useful for high-performance machines such as the IBM 360/91, the CDC 6600, and their descendants. These processors contain several independent arithmetic units, and instruction mixes indicate the traffic these units must handle.

Kernels, Benchmarks, and Synthetic Jobs

Since we generally lack models of program behavior more sophisticated than instruction mixes, when we need more information than instruction mixes can provide we turn to actual programs, or fragments of programs, and run these on the computer (or simulator if we are designing a new computer). The techniques discussed here are the set of tools, in order of increasing generality, available for determining the performance of an operational computer system.

Kernels A kernel is a fragment of a program that includes the most frequently executed portion, or "inner loop"; it is the nucleus of the program.

TABLE 11-2. INSTRUCTION MIXES

Instruction Type	IBM 704/650 [Gibson, 70]	IBM 704/650 [Arbuckle, 69]	[Lunde, 74]	PDP-10 Scientific Mix [Knight, 66]	PDP-10 [Knight, 66] Commercial Mix	CDC 3600 [Foster et al., 71]
Data Transmission						
Load, Store, and Move	31.2	28.5	42.4			30.0
Data Manipulation						
Fixed						
Add/Subtract	6.1		12.4	10.0	25.0	1.2
Multiply	0.6		1.1	6.0	1.0	0.1
Divide	0.2		0.5	2.0		0.1
Floating						
Add/Subtract	6.9	9.5	4.9	10.0		0.5
Multiply	3.8	5.6	2.6			0.5
Divide	1.5	2.0	1.1			0.2
Other (for example, shift, logical operations)						2.7
Indexing	6.0	22.5	4.9			13.4
Program Control						
Compares	3.8					1.2
Branches	16.6	13.2	28.2			38.3
Other		18.7	1.9	72.0	74.0	11.9

Examples of typical kernels include the inversion of a matrix, calculation of a Social Security tax, or editing and formatting a page of text for a line printer.

We may use kernels to overcome some of the shortcomings of instruction mixes in evaluating the instruction set of a processor. For example, processors such as the Burroughs B6700 have a sophisticated stack mechanism that significantly simplifies the programming of procedure calls, coroutine linkage, and so on. Simply examining the instruction mix of the B6700 gives us no measure of the gains in performance with this mechanism. (Many features of the instruction set, such as the B6700 stack, were implemented to ease the programming of the machine, not primarily to increase performance. However, it is important to know the performance of a processor's architecture, as well as its "elegance.") Another good example is the PDP-11. This minicomputer has a substantially richer set of addressing modes than most other minicomputers, and the value of these addressing modes cannot be measured by simply comparing the instruction-execution rate to several other minicomputers. The PDP-11 may well need to use fewer instructions than other minicomputers to execute an algorithm.

In addition to the power of the instruction, kernels can also provide an effective measure of many of the more advanced implementation concepts found in many processors, for example, cache memories, pipelined instruction-execution schemes, and multiple arithmetic units. The effectiveness of all these concepts is dependent on the details of the sequence of instructions executed, such as the size of the inner-loop calculations, the relative positions of branch instructions, and the memory-reference pattern used to access operands. All of these details of program execution are reflected in the kernel's performance.

Although kernels offer a significant improvement over instruction mixes, they have a number of limitations. First, and most significantly, they measure the performance of the processor/main memory and do not evaluate the input/output structure at all. If the performance of the entire computer system is needed, other methods must be used. While it is relatively easy to measure the instruction mix over a wide range of programs and apply the mix to processors with similar architectures, kernels often must be specifically coded for the machine under evaluation, and consequently it is usually not feasible to collect more than five to ten kernels for a given study. The question then arises as to how to choose the small set of kernel programs that constitute a representative mix for the machine. To some extent this can be answered by comparing the instruction mix generated by the kernels with the instruction mix of the operational computer (if an operational version of the computer exists).

Benchmarks To provide a measure of the performance of the entire computer system, rather than just the central processor and main memory, we must extend the concept of a kernel to include input/output operations. Specifically, a benchmark is a complete program, which is considered to be representative of a class of programs, and which includes input/output operations. Examples of benchmarks include polytape sort programs, chess-playing programs, and program compilation.

There are a few other important differences between kernels and benchmarks than simply the inclusion of input/output operations in benchmarks. Note that the performance of a benchmark may be significantly affected by the configuration of the computer system in addition to the speed of the processor. It is no longer sufficient to say that we have run our benchmark on a CDC 6600; we now need to include the amount of main storage available, which may well affect the number of overlays required or page faults sustained, as well as the configuration of the input/output devices. This is certainly useful when one must decide between two or more specific systems, but often is troublesome when one is interested in comparing two computer organizations, independent of a specific installation configuration.

To more accurately estimate the performance of a computer system executing an actual job stream, it is necessary to measure a mix of benchmarks on the system rather than running one benchmark at a time. The overhead incurred by the operating system in managing the multiprogramming of the mix is a good estimate of the overhead that will actually be incurred. The need to run a mix of benchmarks can also apply to the evaluation of the processor. For example, the effectiveness of a cache is in part dependent on how often a running program goes through a transient phase where performance is poor while the cache is loaded.

Benchmarks share a number of disadvantages with kernels. It is often costly to collect a set of benchmarks, and after they are collected we face the problem of evaluating how representative they are of the real workload.

It is a common practice to program benchmarks in a higher-level language such as FORTRAN, ALGOL, or PL/I. This not only eases the task of generating the benchmarks, it makes them somewhat machine independent, so that one set can suffice for the evaluation of a number of systems with different architectures. It also provides a measure of the effectiveness of the language translators provided on the machines in question.

Synthetic Jobs A synthetic job, as the name implies, is an artificial program that exercises all the components of the computer system in a manner representative of an actual job mix. Synthetic jobs are highly parameterized to allow them to simulate a wide range of program performance. They do not refine the evaluation of computer system performance provided by a benchmark; they exist only to ease the construction of benchmark-like jobs.

A number of articles [Hamilton and Kernighan, 73; Sreenivasan and Kleinman, 74] describe techniques for measuring an operational system's average number of disk accesses, processor demands, and storage requirements per job. These measurements are then used to construct a representative set of synthetic jobs.

The actual algorithm performed, as well as the information read and written from secondary storage units, is often trivial. For example, the kernel cf the synthetic job is commonly nothing more than a sum of integers. The important point is that all phases of the synthetic job be parameterized and cyclic, so that arbitrary ratios of compute to input/output operations can be generated.

There is little reason to write synthetic jobs in anything but a high-level language. Buchholz [69] has written a synthetic job that is less than 100 PL/I statements but is able to mimic a wide range of benchmarks.

Before leaving this section let us return to our earlier statement in Section 11-2 which said that if we have to use a single measure to characterize computer performance, the maximum memory bandwidth is the leading candidate. If we now allow ourselves to consider measures besides direct parameters of the hardware, the performance of a set of benchmarks, or an abstraction to a set of synthetic jobs, is probably a more accurate single measure than is the maximum memory bandwidth.

11-6. MEASUREMENT

We conclude this chapter on performance evaluation with a discussion of measurement techniques. The analytical and simulation methods we have already discussed are of little utility if their initial assumptions do not model reality. For example, Figure 11-23 is the cumulative distribution function of the duration of compute-time intervals between input/output operations [Pinkerton, 69]. Highly skewed distributions such as this have been measured on a variety of computer systems; models which assume that the compute-time intervals are drawn from a normal distribution, particularly when the mean is greater than the standard deviation, are immediately suspect. On the other hand, blind measurement, without a model or hypothesis to guide the measurement experiment, is also of little use. It is easy to collect many tape reels of largely meaningless data if measurements are not guided by some model of system behavior.

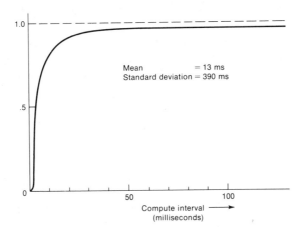

Mean   = 13 ms
Standard deviation = 390 ms

Compute interval ⟶
(milliseconds)

Figure 11-23   Cumulative distribution of compute time between input/output requests

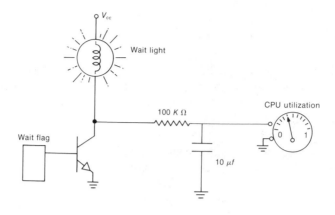

Figure 11-24 Wait meter

The simplest measurement tools are often the processor console and maintenance panels. For example, most processors include a wait light on the console. This light indicates the state of the wait flag in the processor state. When the wait flag is set, the processor is idle. (Older processors simply went into a tight one- or two-instruction loop whenever there was nothing to do, but this degrades performance if other processors or input/output channels are trying to access memory and must wait for the "idle" processor to fetch its instructions.) Simply watching this wait light can give a crude approximation of the utilization of the processor. A common refinement is to attach the simple circuit shown in Figure 11-24 to the wait light. It is an averaging circuit that measures the voltage across the wait light with a voltmeter. Another simple but sometimes useful technique is to watch the maintenance panel, or read/write arms of the drum or disk storage units. If one disk appears to be experiencing considerably heavier traffic than another disk, reallocation of files between the two devices may improve system throughput. While these observations of system performance are fun and easy to perform (everyone enjoys a short walk around the machine room occasionally), they are no substitute for more thorough and precise measurements. Display lights on the console and other panels are generally indicators of utilization, and there are many other measures that are of interest. The next section outlines the range of performance monitors that are of practical interest.

Types of Performance Monitors

Performance monitors for computer systems are available in many forms, often designed to measure very different parameters of the operational system. In order to provide some context in which to discuss the array of monitors that have been developed, the following distinctions between performance monitors are enumerated.

1. *Hardware versus software monitors* — This is the most obvious distinction between performance monitors. Hardware monitors are implemented as freestanding hardware units capable of sensing bits and words of the computer system's state. Software monitors are a collection of system routines capable of interrogating software structures such as queues, control locks, and so on. The hardware/software boundary has begun to blur as processors include features, often in microcode, to enhance the measurement process and hardware monitors are connected as peripherals to the host (measured) machine.

2. *Event-driven versus sampling techniques* — This distinction refers to the monitor's basic data-collection techniques. In event-driven systems the monitor is notified every time a significant event is triggered. Sampling systems use an interval timer to wake up the monitor periodically and, when awake, the monitor looks at important lists and variables to determine the state of the system. Sampling techniques have the advantage for software monitors that the overhead can be made arbitrarily small by selecting a sufficiently large sampling interval.

3. *Tracing versus summary data* — Tracing monitors generate and save a record of information for every significant event or sample. Summary monitors typically only maintain running averages.

4. *Real-time processing versus post-processing* — Some monitors simply display their results at a terminal or via a set of meters for use by the operator or users of the system. Other real-time monitors attempt to use performance information collected to dynamically adjust a set of system parameters, for example, the HASP execution-task monitor [Strauss, 73]. Post-processing monitors are more common; they spool their data onto tape for later analysis by programs that are not under any serious deadline constraints.

5. *User versus system information* — There is often a significant difference in the implementation of monitors designed to evaluate user programs and those designed to evaluate the global performance of the computer system. The monitor for the user program can often call upon many standard system routines for assistance. Measurement hooks can be inserted at compile time, the runtime environment of the program can be modified to collect information, or the user program can be run interpretively. Although these techniques are not usually available to system monitors, the use of virtual machines [Goldberg, 73] may prove to be of considerable assistance.

In this section on measurement techniques, we use the event-driven/sampling dimension to organize our discussion. However, we will point out further differences along the other dimensions as the opportunity arises.

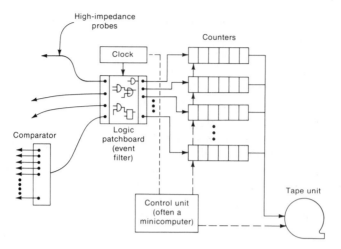

Figure 11-25 Conventional hardware monitor

Event-Driven Techniques

There exists a range of event-driven measurement techniques. Let us begin with the typical hardware monitor shown in Figure 11-25. The figure shows the major components of the monitor.

The heart of the monitor is the bank of 8 to 32 counters. In some of the early monitors the most significant bits of the counters were electromechanical, but now they are entirely electronic. Each counter consists of an 8–12 digit BCD counter. A BCD counter makes less efficient use of the bits in the counter, but this does allow the counter to be more easily read visually.

The counters are driven by lines from a logic patchboard that consists of an assorted collection of gates, latches, and decoders. The inputs to the patchboard are probes that monitor the signals of interest in the computer system. Generally the probes are designed, much like an oscilloscope probe, to impose a minimal electrical load on the monitored signal so that they can be freely moved around the system without fear of disturbing the hardware. Part a of Figure 11-26 shows a simplified patchboard and how it might be wired to count the number of disk arm movements on disks A, B, and C. It is useful to consider the logic patchboard as an event "collector" and "filter." In other words, it takes a collection of primitive signals from the host machine and manipulates and interprets them in such a way that meaningful signals are sent to the counters.

The purpose of the clock in the hardware monitor is to enable the counters to measure the duration of intervals, as well as simply the number of intervals. Note that in Part b of Figure 11-26 the circuit of Part a has been modified to measure the utilization of the input/output channel. Actually counter 1 is accumulating the total number of clock ticks generated, so that the ratio of counter 1 to counter 0 will give the utilization of the input/output channel.

Latches, or flip-flops, are included on the patchboard to allow the measurement of sequences of events. For example, you may suspect inefficiencies in the disk arm-movement algorithm and want to know the fraction of disk transmissions that are preceded by arm movement. Another item found on most patchboards is a 3-to-8 or 4-to-16 decoder. These are useful when information must be unpacked from fields in instructions or operands.

Another important component shown in the block diagram of the hardware monitor is the comparator. This unit connects to a bus, usually the address bus, and compares the contents of the bus to an internal register. The result of the comparison is then fed to the patchboard for use in defining events for the counters. A pair of comparators is often used to bracket an interval of memory. This allows the monitor to discriminate between the utilization of different software systems. Finally, the monitor must have some storage facility such as a magnetic tape to periodically dump the contents of the counters.

The hardware monitor that has just been described might well be termed a "first-generation" monitor. A number of these monitors are offered commercially, but this basic organization was first used in 1962 by IBM's Basic

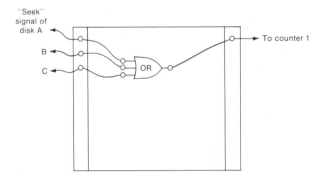

a) Count number of arm movements on
   disks A, B and C

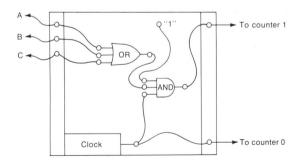

b) Count duration of arm-movement intervals

Figure 11-26 Logic patchboard

Counting Unit, which was designed to measure the performance of IBM 7090 systems.

First-generation hardware monitors were summary monitors and could only provide average measures—for example, drum transmissions per second or utilization of the central processor. A number of more recent monitors include the ability to generate histograms. For example, one may be interested in the distribution of transmission times to an input/output device, not just the average transmission time. Histograms can be generated by first timing the transmission interval, as before, and on termination of the transmission using the contents of the counter as an index into a table in a buffer storage. Every time an entry in the table is accessed the index is incremented.

In order to provide this histogram-generation capability, and other more advanced features, second-generation hardware monitors often include a minicomputer as the primary control element. Now a range of peripherals can be supported: disk, tape, display scope, and others, and a modest amount of preprocessing of the data collected by the hardware monitor can be done before it is stored on disk or tape. The minicomputer can also indicate the progress of a measurement experiment via a teletype or display terminal, so that the analyst can verify that he has not made some gross error in configuring the measurement session.

So far we have presented the hardware monitor as a device that passively observes the host machine. While there are cases where this situation is adequate, and even desirable, the more common situation is to allow the hardware monitor to interrupt the host processor or otherwise feed information back to the host machine (possibly via storing information in the main memory of the host computer, for use by the processor in memory management or scheduling decisions). Another important advantage of linking the hardware monitor to the host machine is that the host machine can now control the measurement experiment. The ability to use the hardware monitor as an extension of software monitoring routines can substantially increase the utility of the hardware montor [Fuller, Swan, and Wulf, 73].

Much of the capability that has just been described for the hardware monitor can also be provided in a suitably designed software monitor. Input/output devices such as drums, disks, tape units, and terminals usually operate at a rate several orders of magnitude slower than the instruction rate of the processor. It is not uncommon for a processor to operate at 10^6 instructions per second, while a disk has an arm seek time of from 10 to 100 milliseconds and a data transmission time of from 1 to 50 milliseconds. Hence, with very little overhead, instructions can be inserted into the disk-control routines to count the number of seeks per second, utilization of the disk input/output channel, and many other summary statistics commonly associated with a hardware monitor. Moreover, a software monitor can measure such things as the queue length to the disk, and the time from the instant the program requests a record from the disk and enters the disk queue until its request is granted. In other words, many times we are interested in the status of software structure, such as the disk queue, and software monitor is the most direct way to measure it. Due to the difference in the basic speeds of the processor and the disk, we should be able to effectively monitor it without putting an appreciable load on the processor. If the overhead for measurement does become objectionable, however, we can turn to the sampling techniques that are discussed later. Another very important measure of system performance is memory utilization, and in many computer systems the only effective way to monitor the utilization of this valuable resource is through a software monitor.

The question may now arise, why ever use a hardware monitor? Portability and high bandwidth are the outstanding features of a hardware monitor. Regardless of the operating system—and every installation has a different version of the operating system, even if they share the same basic system—a hardware monitor can relatively quickly measure many of the basic parameters of system performance. The other feature of a hardware monitor is its high data rate from the measurement probes and into the counters. (The data rate from the counters to tape is not substantially different from the data rate available to software monitors from main storage to tape drives.) Particularly in studies where we are evaluating the performance of hardware components of the system, these high data rates may be necessary. For example, measuring the amount of conflict for memory occurring when both input/output processors and the central processor are attempting to access the same memory module can only be done with a hardware monitor.

TABLE 11-3. COMMONLY TRACED EVENTS

Event	Record Content
Input/output interrupt	Device signaling interrupt, type of interrupt (for example done, error, and so on), time of day
Request input/output service	Name of process requesting service, type of request, device requested, time of day
Start input/output device	(Essentially the same information as for request input/output service)
Dispatch process on processor	Name of process, time of day
Trap to supervisor from user program	Name of process, service requested of supervisor, time of day

In addition to the collection of summary statistics, event-driven monitors are also capable of collecting event traces. Many operating systems include an event-tracing facility to aid in debugging. Table 11-3 lists the most commonly traced information. This information can be used in the diagnosis of a system's failure. The operating system usually includes a moderate-sized buffer to hold the most recent events. When the table is full the tracing process simply overwrites the previous information. If such a trace facility exists in the operating system, to get a tracing monitor we need only divert the trace information onto a tape instead of letting it be overwritten in the memory-resident table.

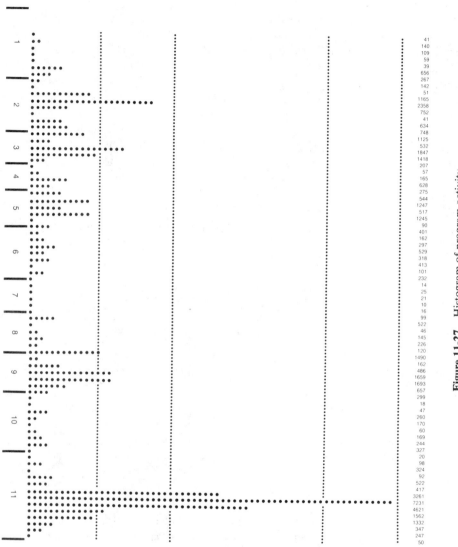

Figure 11-27 Histogram of program activity

A trace facility has a number of important uses in the performance evaluation of computers. It can be used as the input to the trace-driven simulation discussed in Section 11-4, or it may be used to measure the service-time distribution of the various processors in the system, for use in developing one of the queueing models of Section 11-3.

Another type of event-tracing monitor is needed in studies of memory hierarchies; it deals with the sequence of accesses to main memory by the central processor rather than the coarser events of the trace facility just discussed. The alternative implementations in this case are to interpret the instruction-execution process or alter the microcode to capture all references to memory [Saal and Shustek, 72]. Needless to say, this is a time-consuming process; often a 50 to 200 times degradation in processing power is suffered when instruction execution must be emulated.

Sampling Techniques

There are many instances in the measurement of computer systems where we can get an accurate measure of performance without counting every event. For example, if we are interested in the utilization of an input/output channel, we can test whether or not the channel is busy several times a second for several minutes and we will get as accurate an estimate of channel utilization as if we trapped every start and stop of the channel and integrated the results over the measurement interval.

A common example of a sampling monitor is illustrated in Figure 11-27. The figure is a histogram of a user program activity. To generate this histogram the sampling monitor periodically interrupted the processor and examined the contents of the program counter. If the program counter was within the program's region, the content of the program counter was used to index into an array, the selected element in the array was incremented, and after the measurement interval was completed the array was used to generate the histogram. From this histogram, if the efficiency of the program must be improved, segment 11 should be closely studied for possible recoding, but segments 1, 7, and 10 are of little consequence.

The histogram in Figure 11-27 has an interesting shortcoming. Examination of the source listing shows that segment 11 is a subroutine called from segments 2, 5, and 7, but the histogram offers no information as to which calling site initiated the most invocations of the subroutine. A useful modification to the sampling monitor would be to allow it to examine the run-time environment of the program and credit a particular sample to the calling site as well as to the subroutine itself.

The edited output of a sampling monitor designed to collect system information is shown in Figure 11-28. The first part of the output itemizes the sampling rates for the various measurements. The minimum sampling interval for this run is 0.5 seconds, which was used to measure input/output channel and device utilization; the maximum sampling interval is 2.5 seconds, used in the measurement of main memory and software-module utilization. A few

```
MACHINE ACTIVITY AT A GLANCE - MONITORING COMPLETED
                       DATE:   71.306
                      ENDED:   12.29.41
              TIME MONITORED:   3.00 MINUTES


                      PARAMETERS
           CYCLE RANGE
              MAIN MEMORY       5
              SOFTWARE MODULES  5
              QUEUES            2
              I/O DEVICES       1
              CHANNELS          1
           CYCLE TIME       0.50 SECONDS

                       ACTIVITY
           CPU UTILIZATION                              61.10%
           ANY I/O SELECTOR CHANNEL BUSY               87.32%
           I/O ACTIVITY INDEX                81,729
           I/O INTERRUPTS                    19,262         6,421 PER MINUTE
           DEVICES USED                          41
           TOTAL SUPERVISOR CALLS (SVC'S)    99,193        33,064 PER MINUTE
               EXECUTE I/O CHANNEL PROGRAMS  39,283        13,094 PER MINUTE
               OPENING OF FILES                  81            27 PER MINUTE


                  POSSIBLE BOTTLENECKS
           128K REGION AVAILABLE                       79.71%
           AVERAGE CORE WASTED                           132K
           TAPE CONTROL UNIT WAITING                   12.97%
           DISK CONTROL UNIT WAITING                     .58%


                    PROGRAMS USED
           PROCESSORS
                      FORTRANG        2
                      FORTRANH        2
                      LINKEDIT        2
                      MAIN            1
                      SORT            2
                      UTILITY         6
           STEPS INITIATED           17
```

Figure 11-28   Summary statistics of a system monitor

of the measurements shown in Figure 11-28 are event-driven measures. For example, the input/output-interrupt rate and SVC rate are derived from event-triggered routines, and in fact it would be very difficult to estimate these rates with a sampling technique. The statistics shown in Figure 11-28 were collected with very little overhead—on the order of 2 percent. Therefore, while these statistics may not include all one needs to know about the system's performance, it costs so little that it can be used on a continuing basis to monitor performance.

11-7. GUIDE TO FURTHER READING

Although there has always been a desire to build higher-performance computer systems since the first days of computing, the need for sophisticated performance analysis did not become critical until the third generation of computer systems was introduced in the early 1960s, as we mentioned in the introduction to this chapter. Calingaert [67] wrote one of the earliest papers to outline and discuss the main issues in the area of performance evaluation. More recently, Johnson [70] has given an interesting overview of the area, and attempts to focus on some of the inadequacies in our current methods. The articles by Lucas [71] and Lynch [72] also provides an introductory discussion of performance evaluation.

The method of difference-differential equations used to study the stochastic models in this chapter has many applications, and can be generalized to many situations beyond those discussed in this chapter. See Morse [58] for further discussions of this technique. Although beyond the scope of this chapter, more powerful techniques exist for the analysis of queueing structures. These other techniques, which employ generating functions and Laplace-Stieltjes transforms, are introduced in a number of texts such as Kleinrock [75]; Cox and Smith [61]. Several texts now exist that treat queueing theory strictly in the context of modeling computer systems [Coffman and Denning, 73; Kleinrock, 75].

The literature on the analysis of priority disciplines is extensive, but Conway, Maxwell, and Miller [67] provide a good general introduction to the topic, and McKinney [69] as well as Coffman and Kleinrock [68] survey the more specialized area of feedback scheduling policies. See Fuller and Baskett [75] for a discussion of queueing models of drums and disks.

An area of queueing theory that has important applications in the modeling of computer systems is the analysis of networks of queues. These more general models are capable of capturing many of the important properties of large computing systems that have many processors and input/output devices. Jackson [63] and Gordon and Newell [67] wrote the important original papers in this area, and Conway, Maxwell, and Miller [67] and Kleinrock [75] provide a clear introduction to the subject. Buzen [73] has written an article that applies the main results of queueing networks to several common types of computer systems.

The theory of discrete-time simulation is covered in a number of introductory texts [Fishman, 73; Gordon, 69; Naylor et al., 66]. The problem of verifying the results of simulation experiments is still a topic of active research, and the reader is directed to a number of articles for further discussion [Fishman, 67; Crane and Iglehart, 74]. While it is possible to write simulations in general-purpose programming languages, several languages have been specifically developed for simulation. SIMULA is an ALGOL-based language designed for simulation, and an article by Dahl and Nygaard [66] describes SIMULA's central features. Nielson [67] and MacDougall [70] describe specific simulations of computer systems that provide good examples of simulations of computer systems.

The evaluation of operational computer systems and measurement techniques are relatively pragmatic topics that have not received much attention in the literature. References on benchmarks and synthetic jobs were given in Section 11-5 [Buchholz, 69; Hamilton and Kernighan, 73; Sreenivasan and Kleinman, 74]. A number of articles outline the structure of specific hardware monitors [Estrin et al., 67; Aschenbrenner et al., 71] and software monitors [Cantrell and Ellison, 68]. Drummond [73] gives a detailed discussion of standard practices in the evaluation and measurement of computer systems.

PROBLEMS

11-1. Suppose there are two independent Poisson processes with parameters λ_1 and λ_2. Consider the "compound" process that is defined to have an arrival when either of the two Poisson processes has an arrival. Find the probability function for this compound process that is analogous to Equations 11-6 and 11-3 for the simple Poisson process.

11-2. A processor with an exponential service-time distribution is modified as shown:

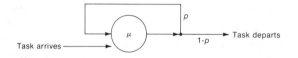

Upon every completion of service at the processor, a task is immediately routed back to the processor for another interval of service with probability p. This choice of being recycled occurs after every service, so that a single task may receive 1, 2, 3, . . . service times. Find the service-time distribution of the modified processor with feedback.

11-3. Verify Equation 11-44, the expression for the expected queue size of a model with an n-level priority queueing discipline.

11-4. Consider the following $M/M/1$ model of an IBM 360/50 computer system:

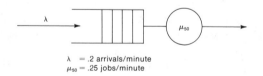

$\lambda = .2$ arrivals/minute
$\mu_{50} = .25$ jobs/minute

a) Find the average waiting time of a job (that is, the time from arrival of the job in the queue until service is complete and the job leaves the system), the average queue size, and the utilization of the 360/50.

b) The preceding IBM 360/50 system is easily saturated, and in order to reduce the waiting time an IBM 370/155 was purchased and added to the system. In other words:

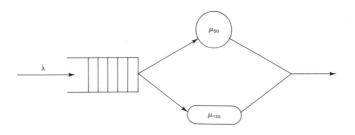

In this configuration assume that once a job begins on either the 360/50 or 370/155 it runs to completion on that machine. The IBM 370/155 is much faster than the IBM 360/50, and in fact assume that the 370/155 is α times faster than the 360/50. Derive an expression for the waiting time (from job arrival to completion), queue size, utilization of the 360/50 and utilization of 370/155.

c) Suppose we want to minimize the average waiting time (from job arrival to completion); at what point (that is, for what α and λ) will it be better to just pull the plug on the 360/50 and run all the jobs on the 370/155? (In reality, the IBM 370/155 is from 3.5 to 4.0 times as fast as an IBM 360/50.)

11-5. Show that the departure process of an $M/M/1$ queueing system is a Poisson process.

11-6. Consider the following $M/M/1$ queuing system with a queue limited to N positions:

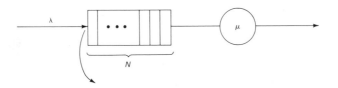

a) Find the equilibrium probability that an arriving request is rejected because the queue is full, and the probability that the processor is idle.

b) Given that a request has been accepted into the queue, find its average waiting time.

11-7. [Kleinrock, 69]. Show that for n sufficiently large, Equation 11-37 becomes a good approximation to Equation 11-36, the average response time of a time-sharing system with n users. (Hint: Use the original definition of p_0 as given in Equation 11-33 and use the fact that $\rho n \gg 1$ for large n.)

11-8. A number of terminals now on the market each contain an 8-bit microcomputer. One major advantage of these terminals is that they do not need to interrupt the central processor after every keystroke; they can buffer a line of input and interrupt the central processor only on a carriage return, break character, other control character, or if the buffer in the microcomputer is full. An important question with regard to these terminals is, How does the rate of interrupts to the central processor vary as a function of the microcomputer's buffer size? Let us model this problem as a Markov chain where an epoch is defined at each keystroke, and E_i is the state in which i characters of the buffer are full. Suppose:

$$Pr \{\text{standard alphanumeric character}\} = .90$$
$$Pr \{\text{backspace (that is, rubout)}\} \qquad = .07$$
$$Pr \{\text{control character}\} \qquad\qquad = .03$$

a) Find an expression for the expected number of keystrokes per interrupt as a function of N, the number of characters in the microcomputer's buffer.

b) Assume that the amount of time the central processor needs to service an interrupt is:

$$300 + 15c \text{ microseconds}$$

where c is the number of characters being transmitted from the terminal to the central processor. Plot the number of terminals needed to saturate the central processor as a function of the buffer size. Assume five keystrokes per second per terminal.

11-9. Design a mixed, linear congruential random-number generator for a 16-bit-per-word minicomputer. Assume that the minicomputer uses a standard two's complement number representation, and hence let $m = 2^{15}$. Point out the advantages, deficiencies, and possible remedies for the generator you specified.

11-10. Write a simulation of the simple $M/M/1$ queueing structure presented in Section 11-3. Instrument your simulation to estimate the mean and variance of the waiting time.

a) Plot the mean and variance of the waiting time as a function of the number of arrivals simulated. Compare these curves with expressions derived from the analytical model.

b) Estimate the autocorrelation of the sequence of successive waiting times as suggested in Equation 11-56. Add bars to the plot for part a that extend $\pm \sigma_{\bar{x}}$ from the estimate of the average waiting time. How many requests must be simulated until you are "confident" that the estimate of the waiting time is accurate to two significant (decimal) digits?

11-11. In a general-purpose programming language such as Pascal or Fortran write the simulation model of the multiprogramming system described in Section 11-14. Structure your program so that separate procedures are used to generate the random variates, select the next event for execution, and queue and dequeue events at the service centers. How useful will these procedures be in simulations of other types of computer exercise?

11-12. In many computer systems the data collected for accounting purposes is also useful for performance-evaluation studies. In this exercise we use accounting data to validate the Markovian assumption of the queueing models discussed in Section 11-3. Write a program that will scan several days (or weeks) of accounting data and construct histograms of interarrival times and service-time requirements for the tasks run on the system.

   a) Compare these histograms to exponential density functions that have the same mean as the histograms. How do the histograms compare to the density functions?

   b) What is the coefficient of variation (C) of the service time? Use the Pollaczek-Khinchine formula (Equation 11-20) to estimate the turnaround time, that is, $\overline{W}$, of tasks. How does this compare with the observed turnaround time? Why?

11-13. The common way to collect an instruction mix for a particular type of processor is to first write an interpreter for the processor's instruction set. Then measurement procedures are added to the interpreter to tabulate the frequency of instructions executed. This technique has a number of disadvantages: the interpreter can be time-consuming to write and debug and, since the interpreted programs run anywhere from 20 to 200 times slower than programs run directly on the actual processor, the interaction of input/output transfers and program execution time is severely distorted. An alternate approach is to write a sampling monitor that periodically interrupts the central processor, finds the instruction the processor was going to execute next, increments the appropriate entries in the instruction-mix table, and continues this sampling process until a sufficient number of instructions have been measured. Build a sampling monitor to tabulate an instruction mix for the processor of a locally available system. Use the validation techniques given in the last part of Section 11-4 to estimate the precision of the instruction mix collected. Compare your results to the instruction mixes in Table 11-2.

11-14. Implement a very low-overhead, summary, software monitor to measure the utilization of the central processor(s), input/output channels or processors, and the major input/output devices. Use either a sampling or a trace-driven technique, whichever is most convenient to implement on your local system. Plot the utilization of the processors and devices as a function of time. Use both a small grain, say a report every one to five minutes, and a large grain, one every half hour to hour. Look for idle devices, saturated or bottleneck units, and how utilization of the units varies as a function of the time of day. It is a rare computer system that does not display some anomalous behavior that when corrected results in a nontrivial improvement in system performance.

CHAPTER 12

Operating Systems and Computer Architecture

Richard L. Sites

12-1. INTRODUCTION

Hardware design philosophies and design details can drastically affect the ease of building an operating system for a computer, and the efficiency of the resulting hardware/software combination. This chapter treats the architectural features of a computer that strongly interact with an operating system.

An operating system is fundamentally responsible for resource management [Madnick and Donovan, 74]. An operating system may simply be input/output driver programs (say, for a microprocessor), or it can be progressively more complex until it becomes a complete multiprocessing time-sharing executive (see Figure 12-1). The resources involved usually include processor time for one or more processors, main-memory space, I/O channels and devices, and secondary-memory (file) space. The two main themes of resource management are controlled *sharing* of resources and enforced *separation* of resources. A shared resource may be a large data base, as in an airline reservation system, or it may be CPU time, as in a large time-sharing system. Separation of resources usually involves data, and is implemented through memory-protection hardware, file password-checking software, and other mechanisms.

Sections 12-2 and 12-3 discuss the concepts of controlled sharing and enforced separation in more detail; in doing so, they expose some issues that are treated as distinct topics in the remaining sections. These two sections assume that the reader has read about interprocessor control in Section 8-4, earlier in this book. Section 12-4 discusses the specific architectural issue of context swapping, that is, the saving and reloading of all the registers, protection status, and clocks for a software process. Memory designs and their relationship to memory allocation and memory protection (in particular,

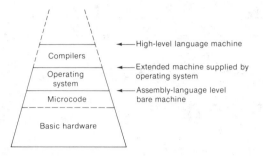

Figure 12-1 An operating system provides an *extended machine* with additional services (such as easy-to-use I/O with automatic error recovery) that the base machine does not provide. The rest of the software for the computer uses this extended machine.

architectural issues associated with cache memories and virtual memories) are discussed in Section 12-5. Section 12-6 discusses the additional complications introduced by having multiple processors instead of just a single one. The term "processor" is generalized to include *any* asynchronous device that has independent access to memory, such as a DMA channel. Virtual machines are presented in Section 12-7 as a logical extension of the previous considerations in the chapter. This last section represents the full complexity of all the architectural features mentioned, while returning to our framework of controlled sharing and enforced separation.

12-2. CONTROLLED SHARING

A computer system with an operating system is often used to perform multiple tasks, where these tasks either run concurrently on multiple processors in the system, or one task at a time runs on a single processor, with provision for running another task when the first one must wait for some event, such as the completion of an I/O transfer. The concept of controlled sharing deals with an orderly sharing of resources among these multiple tasks. In this chapter, the words "process" and "task" are used as synonyms, but the latter is preferred, in order to avoid confusion between the words "process," "processor," "processes," and "processors."

Some systems are designed so that a single processor is dedicated to a single task, and that processor does nothing else useful while waiting for an event. Even in such simple systems, though, issues of controlled sharing can arise whenever many such dedicated processors are connected together, since the usual reason for interconnection is to share some common data. Another system is one designed for a single (human) user, a single CPU, and a single user task. Even in this case, the desire to overlap computing and I/O can result in a structure with at least two different types of tasks—one for the user and one for each active peripheral device. For the rest of this chapter, we shall assume that the operating system, and hence the underlying hardware architecture, must support multiple asynchronous tasks even if only in a restricted way. In the next few sections, we shall discuss systems with only a single processor, then in Section 12-6 we shall introduce the additional complexity of having multiple processors.

From the architectural point of view, the two most important resources to be shared are the CPU itself and data in main memory. These two kinds of sharing are the primary focus of this section. At the end of the section, brief mention is made of sharing data in secondary storage and sharing I/O devices, neither of which introduces new architectural concepts.

Sharing the Processor

To support multiple tasks on a single processor, one resource that must be shared is the CPU itself. This sharing can be implemented by having the operating system maintain a *ready list* of tasks that are available to run when they receive control of the processor. Other tasks in the system not available to run are those waiting for some event to occur. A *dispatcher* subroutine within the operating system selects one of the tasks on the ready list, initializes the hardware registers, then passes control to that task. When a running task, A, must wait for some event (such as an I/O interrupt, or the completion of another task), it is removed from the ready list and the dispatcher selects some other task, C, to run. This is called a *task switch*. When the event for which A is waiting later occurs, A is placed back on the ready list, and may be given control immediately or it may wait its turn. The selection of A or some other task to run is made by a *scheduling algorithm* within the dispatcher (see Figure 12-2). This algorithm may be a simple round-robin scheme (cyclical execution of the tasks in the ready list), or it may involve a

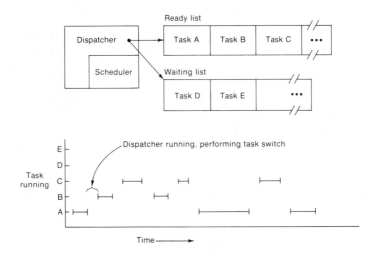

Figure 12-2   Sharing a single CPU among many tasks

complicated priority ordering of the ready list. In general, some unrelated task, B, may be running when the event for which A is waiting occurs, and the scheduling algorithm might choose to preempt B, by suspending B and initiating A. Thus, a general user task such as B may be interrupted between *any* two instructions (or within an instruction on some machines), and other tasks run for a while before B's execution is continued. This creates profound problems in sharing data between B and other tasks.

To support such CPU sharing, the architecture must provide some way to trigger task switches, and some way to save and restore hardware registers containing data associated with a single task. Hardware context switching (saving and restoring registers) is discussed in detail in Section 12-4, while the triggering mechanisms are discussed here. A full task switch is usually an operating-system-assisted action, involving the ready list and the dispatcher described above. The architecture need only provide some way to pass control to the dispatcher, either because of an external event or because a running task needs to relinquish control.

An external event triggers a task switch by causing an interrupt, which in turn causes a hardware context swap. In essence, the interrupt passes control directly to the dispatcher, which then perhaps makes ready a waiting task and chooses which task to run next. The dispatcher subroutine does not run as a task in the normal sense, but instead runs with all of the machine's resources available and passes control to a chosen task, along with a subset of these resources. Enforcing the use of only that subset is discussed in Section 12-3.

A running task could trigger a task switch by branching to or calling the dispatcher using normal instructions (as was typical in the early 1960s), or it can use the same interrupt and context-switching mechanism needed for external events. The latter is preferred, so that the dispatcher can run in an environment with more (or different) privileges (such as access to the ready queue) than the running task. Thus, an architecture should provide an explicit "trigger task-switch" instruction for a running task to use to wait for an external event or to ask for a service from some other task. It is useful for this instruction to provide at least one field that is passed as a parameter across the context switch. This parameter can be used to tell the dispatcher the reason for relinquishing control. For example, the IBM System/360 Supervisor Call (SVC) instruction [IBM, 70] is used to switch context to the operating system, passing an 8-bit field from the instruction as a parameter specifying which of a possible 256 supervisor services (open a file, get more memory, etc.) is needed.

Early CDC 6600 computers have no such task-switch instruction, making it very difficult for a program to request operating-system services. The problem is rectified in later models of that machine, which may optionally include a Central Processor Exchange Jump instruction for this purpose [Thornton,70].

For reasonable sharing of the CPU, however, it is often necessary to provide a specific external-event generator—a clock. Under many circumstances, an operating system will want to *time-slice* the CPU, that is, allow one task to run for some maximum amount of time, then force a task switch to some other task. If tasks are unreliable, then one may get into an infinite loop and never relinquish control. In this case, an external interrupt from a clock is the only way to continue sharing of the CPU. We return to this subject under Resource Hogging in Section 12-3.

For sharing of the CPU, an architecture need only provide an explicit trigger task-switch instruction, an external signal mechanism that also triggers a task switch, and a clock that can generate such a signal. For sharing main-memory data, an architecture must provide an interlocking instruction, as discussed below.

Sharing Main-Memory Data

Recall the example of SUM := SUM + V[i] from Section 8-4. Without any interlocking, execution of this statement by two different tasks on a single CPU may occur in the following order (see Figure 12-3):

1. Task B fetches the value of SUM from memory.
2. An event happens, and the dispatcher passes control to task A.
3. Task A fetches the value of SUM from memory, adds its V[i] to SUM and stores this new value of SUM back in memory.
4. Task A completes, and the dispatcher eventually returns control to task B.
5. Task B adds its V[i] to the *old* value of SUM that it originally fetched, then stores the new erroneous value of SUM in memory.

This *update error* can (and will!) occur in *any* context that involves uncontrolled sharing of data if an update cannot be done as a single uninterrupted

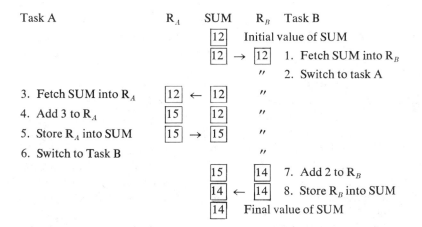

Figure 12-3   Update error: the final result should be 17

action. Manifestations of this error include selling an airplane seat to two different people, giving both callers a busy signal when they simultaneously reach the same telephone, and losing a character typed in the middle of execution of a test-for-new-keystroke subroutine.

In order to avoid update errors, the underlying hardware architecture for any operating system must include at least one instruction for interlocking so that *any* multiple-instruction update sequence can appear to be a single indivisible action. The essential features of an interlocking instruction include all the following:

1. It must test or read some condition.
2. It must change that condition.
3. The test-change sequence must be a single, indivisible operation at the lowest hardware level.

Any such instruction can be used to implement the WAIT and SIGNAL primitives of Chapter 8, and these primitives in turn can be used systematically to avoid update errors. An early instruction of this form is the IBM 360 Test and Set (TS) instruction, which tests a single bit in memory, then sets that bit to one. If such a semaphore bit is initialized to zero, then the first task to do a TS on that bit finds that it is zero, and sets it to one. Any subsequent task that does a TS on the same bit finds it already one (i.e., locked) and leaves it one. The TS instruction was not in the IBM 360 instruction set when the machine was announced in April, 1964, but it was added soon afterward when the operating-system implementors discovered it is logically necessary. Similar instructions on other machines include Swap Register with Memory and Add One to Memory (see Problem 12-1). In addition to allowing no interrupts during their execution, these instructions must guarantee no other accesses to the subject memory location by other processors, channels, or I/O devices, during their execution. This in turn has a serious consequence in the design of the memory-interface bus in a computer: there essentially must be a hardware control-wire that signals to the memory that a processor is doing an uninterruptable read-modify-write memory cycle, and that no other device is allowed access until the entire cycle is complete.

Given hardware support for some kind of interlocking instruction, is any particular style of instruction easier to use than another style? To answer this question, we will look at a specific shared-resource problem, that of adding and deleting elements from a queue shared between two tasks A and B. This is an interesting problem in its own right, but the shared queue is also the high-level data structure for controlled sharing of data that is found in most operating systems. If we can build efficient and rigorously correct ENQUEUE and DEQUEUE primitives, then we are in a good position to build a complicated but reliable operating system. The Concurrent Pascal system [Brinch Hansen, 71], and the Bell Labs UNIX system [Ritchie and Thompson, 74] are two examples of queue-driven operating systems.

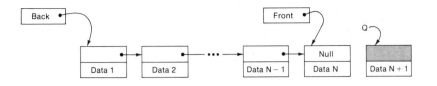

Figure 12-4   A shared queue, implemented as a singly-linked list. Q points to a
new element to be added to the queue.

Our queue is built as a single-linked list, with anchor pointers for the first
and last elements, as shown in Figure 12-4. We wish to build ENQUEUE
and DEQUEUE primitives that add or delete an element, respectively, and
which never create update errors. We will look at four solutions, each using
a different interlocking mechanism: user-task control of interrupts, operating-
system control of interrupts, user-task Test and Set, and user-task Compare
and Swap. The solutions are in approximate historical order, and each has
advantages over its predecessor. (See Problem 12-5 for a fifth method.)

Enqueue Method 1 (late 1950s)   For a single-processor system, one solution
prevents any possibility of task switches in the middle of an update by using
the sequence:

1. Turn off all interrupts.
2. Do the necessary pointer manipulation.
3. Turn on interrupts.

This solution was used on early, unprotected operating systems in which any
user program had the ability to turn the hardware interrupt system on and
off. As we shall discuss in the next section, direct user control over the interrupt system is undesirable and unacceptable because, once given control, a
user can either erroneously or maliciously cripple the activities of other user
or input/output tasks. The solution above does not work with multiple processors, as we shall see in Section 12-6.

Enqueue Method 2 (early 1960s)   A second solution is to have any task that
must do an ENQUEUE or DEQUEUE call an operating-system service
routine to do the pointer manipulation. The call can be a task switch that
changes from a user task to a system task. The system task turns off the
interrupts, performs the pointer manipulation for the queue, turns on the
interrupts, then returns to the calling task. The essence of this second solution
is that by asking an operating system routine to do the interrupt masking and
queue manipulation, we need not compromise the protection mechanisms of
the machine. This solution is used in the original IBM 360 operating system.
We pay a price, however, for asking the operating system to do our work for
us: on most machines, the overhead of switching to another task and back is

orders of magnitude longer than the execution time of the two or three instructions actually needed to update the queue. Thus, heavy use of the supervisor-assisted ENQUEUE/DEQUEUE is inefficient.

Enqueue Method 3 (mid 1960s)   A third solution is to leave the interrupts on (allowing the possibility that a task switch will occur), but to use a Test and Set style of instruction to provide a "queue being updated" semaphore. For ENQUEUEing the element pointed to by Q in Figure 12-4, the sequence is:

1. Test and Set semaphore associated with this queue.
2. If locked, branch back to 1. (Busy waiting loop.) (After getting past 2, the semaphore is locked and this task "owns" the queue.)
3. LINK(Q) := null
4. P := FRONT
5. FRONT := Q
6. LINK(P) := Q
7. Set semaphore to zero (unlocked).

This solution is logically correct, but has a performance flaw. Suppose task A executes steps 1 and 2, gaining ownership of the queue, gets part way through the next four instructions, then an interrupt occurs and the scheduler ends up choosing task B to run next. If task B then tries to add an element to the same queue, the task will enter a "busy waiting" loop doing steps 1 and 2 over and over. This is a classical *deadlock* (see Section 8-4), in which task A holds some resource (the semaphore), and task B holds another (the CPU), and each task is waiting for the other to release its resource. The only way out of this loop is eventually to generate another interrupt that has the effect of dispatching task A again, so it can unlock the semaphore. On many systems, there is no way to guarantee that task A will ever run again if task B is in a busy wait loop. Other systems can force, say, a round-robin change in tasks on the ready list every 1/10 of a second (controlled by a real-time clock interrupt), but this really relies on a global scheduling mechanism to get "unstuck" from what should be a simple and exact local problem. In addition, this solution will not work if task B could be a privileged operating system routine that *must* complete before allowing any more task switches.

The problem with solution three is that while task B is executing its busy wait loop on the single CPU, task A cannot possibly be making any progress toward releasing the shared resource. We would prefer to find a mechanism that guarantees some progress (and hence avoids deadlock), and that does not involve the overhead of calling an operating-system service routine. One such mechanism, described next, was introduced in the IBM 370 computer series [IBM, 70].

Enqueue Method 4 (early 1970s)   Our fourth solution uses an instruction called Compare and Swap (CS). Formally, the instruction

CS OLD,NEW,ADDR

sets in motion the following sequence of actions:

1. Compares the contents of register OLD to the contents of memory location ADDR.
2. If the values are equal, the contents of register NEW are stored at ADDR. (This is the normal case, with the CS equivalent to Store NEW,ADDR.)
3. If unequal, then the current value at ADDR is loaded into OLD.
4. In both cases, a condition code is set so that a subsequent conditional branch can find out what happened.

The crucial part of this instruction is that no interrupts or other-device memory accesses are allowed between the comparison and the store. The CS instruction has the three essential properties of an interlocking instruction, but it is carefully designed to be much more useful than a Test and Set instruction.

To understand the somewhat strange definition of this instruction, let us look at how it can be used to build our ENQUEUE/DEQUEUE primitives. For ENQUEUE, the (in-line, user-mode) code sequence is:

1. LINK(Q) := NULL
2. P := FRONT
3. CS P,Q,FRONT   (usually, FRONT := Q)
4. If FRONT was not equal to P, branch back to step 3.
5. LINK(P) := Q

This sequence is exactly the same as steps 3 to 6 in solution three, except that the assignment FRONT := Q in that sequence has been replaced by the CS-branch pair, and we have no semaphore at all. So long as there is not an interrupt between instructions 2 and 3, the values of P and FRONT will be equal at the CS instruction, so it will store Q into FRONT, just as solution three did. If, however, a task switch occurs exactly after instruction 2 and the new task adds an element to the queue before control returns to instruction 3, then the comparison in the CS will fail, as indicated in Figure 12-5 with Task B interfering with Task A. In this case of actual (as opposed to potential) interference from another task, the CS instruction loads the *new* value of FRONT into P, and the branch retries the store. So long as a second interfering task switch does not occur between the branch and the second execution of the CS, this retry finds FRONT and P equal, does the store of Q, and continues. If there is heavy interference from other tasks, this construct may loop more than once, but each time some other task is *guaranteed* to be making progress adding its own elements to the queue (otherwise, FRONT wouldn't change).

The idea behind the CS instruction can be described more generally by the following algorithm. In the algorithm, X is a shared variable in memory, X' is a private copy of that variable used by the processor in some fashion (in this case as an argument to function F) to compute a new value for X,

Task A   Task B   Data structure

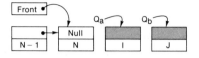

1. Link(Q$_a$) :=null
2. P$_a$:= Front

         1. Link(Q$_b$) :=null
         2. P$_b$:= Front

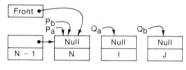

         3. CS P$_b$,Q$_b$,Front   (Front=P$_b$, so stores Q$_b$ into Front)

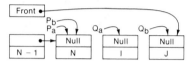

3. CS P$_a$,Q$_a$,Front   (Front≠P$_a$, so loads P$_a$ from Front)

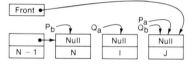

4. Branch ≠ to 3.   (Branches)
3. CS P$_a$,Q$_a$,Front   (Front=P$_a$, so stores Q$_a$ into Front)

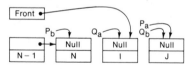

4. Branch ≠ to 3.   (Falls through)
5. Link(P$_a$) :=Q$_a$

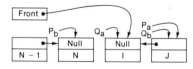

         4. Branch ≠ to 3.   (Falls through)
         5. Link (P$_b$) :=Q$_b$

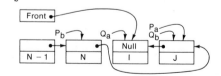

Figure 12-5   Two tasks doing interleaved ENQUEUEs using CS instruction. Q$_A$ and Q$_B$ point to new elements to be added by tasks A and B. Task A starts to add its element I, then gets interrupted by task B, which partially adds its element J. Task A then completes adding I by linking it to J, and task B finally completes linking J to the original queue. Note that during the intermediate manipulations, the queue itself appears unchanged. This is proper, and simply reflects the fact that the ENQUEUEs have not yet finished.

NEWX, which is passed to the other tasks. The crucial point comes when the processor is ready to restore the new value in memory. At this point, the processor checks to see if the old value has changed, and if not NEWX replaces X. If so, the value just fetched as X starts the whole process again. The algorithm is:

$X' := X;$	This copies X from memory to a processor register X'.
LOOP: NEWX $:= F(X');$	
begin	Indivisible section.
TEST $:= (X' = X);$	TEST stores the Boolean result of the comparison.
if TEST *then* X $:=$ NEWX *else* $X' := X;$	Actually, a second memory fetch of X is not required. The copy of X just tested replaces X' if TEST is false.
end;	The indivisible section is the Compare and Swap.
if NOT TEST *then goto* LOOP;	

In the example on queueing, the function F is the function that recomputes the queue pointers for an insert. Clearly, the CS instruction is more general and more useful than just queue inserts, and it can in fact be used for any synchronization process, provided that the process requires indivisible access to exactly one variable. If two or more variables are required, then the programmer has to create a critical section that contains the access to these variables. If a CS for two variables were a necessity, then such could be added, probably with difficulty, to an instruction repertoire. (The IBM 370 Compare Double and Swap instruction allows a pair of *adjacent* variables.)

The CS instruction by itself may not resolve difficulties in synchronizing tasks. It is essential to prevent endless loops by assuring that at least one task using the CS instruction makes progress in its activity. If none do, then all tasks may loop endlessly.

To show some of the versatility of the CS instruction on an example related to the ENQUEUE, consider the opposite process of DEQUEUE. As in ENQUEUE, note that at least one task makes progress when interactions occur in inspecting shared variables. For DEQUEUE, the code sequence is:

1. P := BACK	
2. If P $\neq$ null then	Set up data-structure change.
3. Q := LINK(P)	
4. CS P,Q,BACK	Make progress, or some other task did.
5. If BACK was not equal to P, branch back to step 2.	Try all over again if some other task did.
6. Else the queue is empty.	(See the Problems.)

In this sequence, it is critical that we do not perform the BACK := LINK(BACK) operation in step 4 until we are sure that BACK is not null. An update error would occur if task A fetched the (nonnull) value of BACK, then task B gained control, fetched the same BACK, deleted one element (leaving BACK null), and returned control to task A. At this point, task A must not proceed blindly to delete the same element. The CS instruction checks to see if this happened, and if so, the branch goes back not to step 4, but all the way to step 2 to redo the test. (Remember that CS itself does the reload of P, so we don't have to repeat step 1.) A simpler instruction, such as the Swap Word with Memory found on the Burroughs B6700 [Organick, 73] or the Digital Equipment Corporation PDP-10, does not allow us properly to test BACK then change it. This issue is further explored in Problems 12-2 to 12-4, along with more discussion of empty queues.

In summary, the Compare and Swap interlocking instruction allows us to build efficient ENQUEUE/DEQUEUE primitives without resorting to manipulation of the interrupt hardware, without the overhead of a supervisor call, and without the possibility of deadlock. In contrast to solutions one and three, which use paired primitives to effect the interlocking (interrupts off/interrupts on and lock/unlock), the CS instruction does not have the potential problem of failing to execute the second half of the pair, through some program error. In common with the other solutions, the CS requires that the locked quantity or measure of progress be concentrated into a single data item in shared memory. The CS interlocking mechanism is used only if some interference *actually* occurs. Thus, we pay no heavy penalty to guard against *potential* but perhaps quite rare interference. Reliable and efficient queue primitives can then be used to build a more complicated operating system.

Sharing Secondary-Memory Data

In addition to sharing data in main memory, it is also possible to share a file of data in secondary memory, or to share an I/O device. The interlocking principles for files are the same as for main memory, but the strategies are different because access to an interlock word in the file itself can take a long time. A common solution to the update-error problem in files is to allow only one task at a time to have *write* access to the file. This software solution completely avoids the possibility that two different tasks could write words in the same file. If the shared file represents so much data that locking the entire file is unreasonable, then locks on individual records can be implemented. These locks may be in main memory or in the records themselves but, in both cases, no new architectural features are needed, since the ultimate software-enforced locking can be done via the instructions discussed above.

Sharing I/O Devices

If an I/O device is shared between two data channels, there must be some locking associated with the *channel switch* in the device, so that an entire sequence of commands (i.e., seek, read, check) can be completed by one channel without interference by the other channel. Typically, channel commands such as "test and lock device X" and "unlock device X" are supplied in the channel architecture. If channel B wants to use a device which is locked by channel A, then the driver program for channel B can either wait for an interrupt on channel A to signal that it might be fruitful to try again, or (if channel B is connected to another CPU that will not see any channel A interrupts) it can simply try again every 100 milliseconds or so. Further discussion of this multiple-processor situation is deferred until Section 12-6.

PROBLEMS

12-1. Implement the WAIT and SIGNAL primitives of Chapter 8 using:
   a) The Test and Set instruction, which tests a single bit in memory, then sets that bit to a one. A subsequent conditional branch can be based on the old value of the bit.
   b) The Swap Word with Memory instruction, which interchanges a word in memory with a word in a register. A subsequent instruction can test the old value in the register.
   c) The Add One to Memory instruction, which increments the value in a memory location. A subsequent conditional branch can be based on a zero result value.
   d) The Compare and Swap instruction described in this chapter.

   All of the above instructions prevent update errors by allowing no other memory accesses between reading the old value and writing the new value in memory.

12-2. Modify the CS ENQUEUE code of this section so that adding an element to a completely empty list also sets BACK to point to the new element. The same logic that stores into BACK can also be used to SIGNAL some task waiting for the queue to become nonempty.

12-3. a) Give an example of two tasks doing interleaved ENQUEUE and DEQUEUE on the same *nonempty* queue, using the CS sequences given in this section.
   b) Give an example of two tasks doing interleaved ENQUEUE and DEQUEUE on the same *empty* queue, using the CS sequences given in this section. Are there any problems?
   c) Modify the ENQUEUE and DEQUEUE, using the CS sequence given in this section, to keep a single dummy entry always on the queue. This will prevent FRONT from ever becoming NULL.

12-4. Build a DEQUEUE function using the Swap Register With Memory instruction, such that there can be no update error, even with two interleaved DEQUEUEs on a single one-element queue.

12-5. The *munch register* was introduced by Steele [75] as a way of coordinating two list-manipulation tasks potentially working on the same list. Each task has a munch register, with the following properties: (1) If task A attempts to load the nonnull value X into its munch register and X is equal to the *other* task's munch register, task A waits until the other munch register is no longer matching; (2) whenever X is not equal to the other munch register, it is loaded into task A's munch register. To use munch registers for interlocking, each task (by software convention) loads its munch register with the address of a word that it is going to modify, modifies it, then loads its munch register with a special null value (say zero). If one task is trying to modify a word that the other task is currently modifying, the first task will wait until the other one clears its munch register.

a) Suppose that two tasks are sharing a data area of 50,000 words. If each word has a separate one-bit semaphore associated with it, how many bits of interlock information are needed? How many data items could a single task have locked at once?

b) With the same 50,000 shared words, if each task has a munch register, how many bits of interlock information are needed? How many data items could a single task have locked at once?

c) Extend the definition of munch register to include N tasks all sharing the same data.

d) If the shared data in *a* above were stored on disk and represented 50,000 airplane seats, and the tasks represented N different sales agents, which of the three interlocking mechanisms below would you prefer, and why? What are the disadvantages of the other two methods?

(1) A single semaphore for the entire file of airplane seats.

(2) A semaphore for each individual seat (50,000).

(3) A munch register for each sales agent (N).

12-6. A computer could have an instruction that adds an element to a linked list and one that removes an element from a linked list. The latter instruction would in some way provide a condition-code setting, a jump, or a skip to indicate that the initial list is empty.

a) What are some of the advantages of having two instructions *instead* of a Test and Set or a Compare and Swap interlocking instruction?

b) What are some of the disadvantages? (Hint: describe some desirable operation which could be done easily with TS or CS instructions, but which cannot be done with direct ENQUEUE/DEQUEUE instructions.)

12-3. ENFORCED SEPARATION

Complementary to controlling the sharing of resources, an operating system must also control the separation of resources, so that the one task cannot interfere with the operation of another task except through mutually agreed-upon shared data. Tasks can interfere with each other in obvious ways by reading and writing information, but they can also interfere in subtle ways, such as (1) one task (or group of tasks) using such a large proportion of the processor time that some other task is never able to run, or (2) one task writing such a large file that the entire file-system storage is filled up and the system is crippled. It is the responsibility of the operating system, usually in conjunction with some hardware help, to enforce the separation of resources used by various tasks.

Main-Memory Protection

A starting place for enforcing this separation between tasks is to have a *memory protection* mechanism that restricts a given task to using only an allotted portion of the main memory. Such a mechanism checks each fetch and store performed by the task, and verifies that the access requested is actually allowed. Among the possible ways of achieving memory protection, we mention four in this chapter:

1. Bounds registers
2. Memory key
3. Mapping-table keys
4. Distinct address spaces

Bounds Registers   A simple bounds register specifies a lower and an upper bound on the addresses allowed (Figure 12-6). All fetches and stores within this range are performed, and any other reference forces an error trap. If task A is run with the bounds register set to the pair (1000,2999) and task B is run with the pair (3000,6500), then the two tasks cannot interfere with each other's main memory data, so long as neither task can change the bounds register.

In a system that is designed merely to avoid problems due to unintentional errors, it may be acceptable to allow any task to modify the bounds register, but to trust that such changes will be done carefully. Normally, however, an operating system must also prevent malicious attempts to access another task's data. In this case, it is necessary that the machine have some form of different privileges for different tasks, with a normal user task not privileged either to change the bounds register or to increase its set of privileges. Initially, we adopt the hardware mechanism of *system-mode* vs. *user-mode* bit in some control register. In system mode, all instructions can be executed

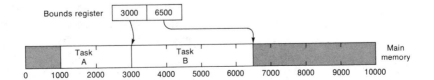

Figure 12-6   Separation of main memory. Task A's instructions and data are in locations 1000-2999, while task B's instructions and data are in locations 3000-6500. The *bounds register* values shown only allow access to locations 3000-6500. Access to any address outside this range results in an error trap.

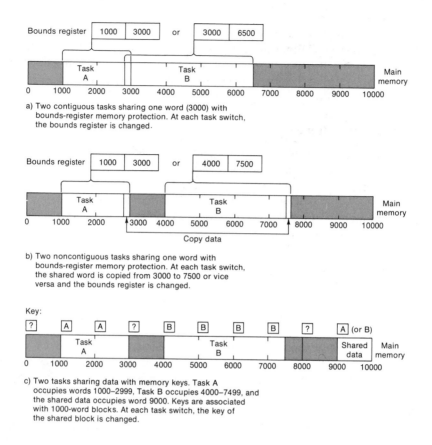

Figure 12-7

and all hardware registers that specify privileges (including the system-/user-mode bit) can be modified. In user mode, instructions that exceed the current privileges or change those privileges are *trapped* (i.e., generate an interrupt). Portions of the operating system, including the interrupt handlers and the dispatcher, run in system mode. We assume that this system-/user-mode mechanism is part of the machine's architecture, and return to discussing memory protection.

The bounds-register mechanism assumes that all the main memory needed by a single task can be allocated in one contiguous area. This assumption interacts with the overall memory-management design of the operating system, and may not be easy to achieve. For example, it is difficult for two tasks to share exactly one semaphore word using bounds registers, since that word must be the highest accessible word for one task and the lowest for the other (see Part *a* of Figure 12-7). It is impossible for three tasks to have all combinations of shared words using only bounds registers and no movement of data each time task switches are done. On machines with bounds registers, shared data is usually moved into the allowed address range of each task just before it is dispatched, as shown in Part *b* of Figure 12-7.

To alleviate this problem partially, some machines have 2, 3, or 4 bounds registers, but the essentially restrictive nature of data sharing is not changed. Multiple bounds registers often allow the instructions for a task to be physically separate from the data, and may also allow the data to be in 2 or 3 noncontiguous areas. Multiple bounds registers usually do not allow the sharing of common instruction sequences (subroutines) between different tasks. In particular, direct calls from a user task to a (common) operating-system service routine are not usually allowed, simply because the user task is not able to address instructions outside of its one area. A complete context-switch instruction, as in Section 12-2, must be used to access any shared code.

Memory Keys A second memory-protection mechanism is to associate an *access key* with each memory location. This can be done with one bit per word, as in the Burroughs B5500, or with one key for every block of 256–1024 words, as is more commonly done. The key may separately specify read, write, or execute protection, and may also specify a user name or task number. The IBM 360 has one key for every 2048 bytes (512 words) of memory, and each key specifies read protect, write protect, and a four-bit task number. The task number in the key must match the task number in a hardware-status register, except that key zero in the status register matches all memory keys. Substantial portions of the IBM 360 operating system run with key zero, so those routines have unrestricted access to all of memory. Keys allow a given task to access noncontiguous areas of main memory, but sharing of data is still difficult. First, sharing can only be done for entire 2048-byte blocks, not just single words; and second, it is necessary to go through the awkward process of changing the keys on shared blocks at every task switch, so that when task A is running, the memory key of a shared block matches A, and when task B is running, the same memory key matches B, as shown in Part *c* of Figure 12-7. Changing keys is a bit faster, however, than the data movement needed with bounds registers.

Mapping-Table Keys A third approach to memory protection associates the access keys with each task instead of with the physical memory. For each task, there is a table (or set of tables) specifying the access status of each block of memory that a task can possibly address (see Figure 12-8). With separate tables, switching between tasks A and B only involves changing an access-table pointer register, and does not involve changing physical memory keys for shared blocks. These access tables are usually built as extra bits within the page tables for mapping virtual memory (treated in Section 12-5 below).

Distinct Address Spaces The above discussion implicitly assumes that different tasks are all run in the same *address space,* so they can all generate the same set of memory addresses. A fourth way to enforce memory protection is to have each task run in its own unique address space, so that the addresses it

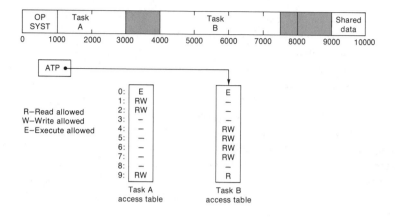

Figure 12-8 Memory protection via access tables associated with each task. At each task switch, the access table pointer (ATP) is changed.

can possibly generate are never the same as the addresses generated by another task. This is done in the IBM 370, which has a full *virtual address* of 40 bits—16 bits of task number and 24 bits of byte address within that task's address space. Because the unique task number is part of the virtual address, no two tasks can generate the same virtual addresses, and hence each has a distinct address space. As discussed in Section 12-5, these 40-bit virtual addresses are mapped to 24-bit *real addresses,* and this mapping may have task A's address 3000 and task B's address 7000 both refer to the same real location, thus implementing sharing of memory blocks directly as a part of the address mapping.

Intertask Communication

The concepts of sharing and separation conflict in a fundamental way. Consider separation based on distinct address spaces and the problem of asking a service routine to read 200 words of data from a disk, and to place that data in a buffer in the requesting task's address space. For the purposes of enforced separation, it is desirable for the service routine to run in its *own* address space, not that of the requesting task. This is to prevent the requesting task either from interfering with the channel commands of the service routine, as mentioned below, or from gaining access to more than the allowed amount of data (and to prevent the service routine from doing the same to the requesting task's data outside of the designated 200-word area). For instance, the service routine might read a 1000-word disk block in order to supply the 200 words requested. In order to enforce separation of data, the requesting task must not be allowed to access the other 800 words of that block.

If the service routine runs in its own address space, however, it has no way to move the requested data from its address space to that of the requesting task. Worse yet, it may not even have a way to access the request *parameters* from the calling task, since these parameters necessarily start out in the requesting task's address space (Figure 12-9). This problem of passing parameters and results between tasks is inherent in any system that simultaneously tries to enforce separation of task resources and to allow one task to perform a service for another task.

An apparent solution to this dilemma is to have a service routine (or machine instruction) that moves data from one address space to another. Unfortunately, without some control over, or error checking of, the address-space names passed as parameters to this routine, it would be possible for any task to request moves into or out of any other task's address space, thus circumventing the separation mechanisms. Such a move routine is in fact necessary, so task or address-space names become a commodity that must be protected by the operating system. In the example above of reading 200 words from disk, the operating-system link between the requesting task and the service routine must copy the parameters into the service routine's address space. One parameter might be a read-only object that represents a window (i.e., address and length) into the requesting task's 200-word buffer. To do the final data transfer into this buffer, the uncorrupted window parameter can be passed to the intertask move routine or instruction, which then moves the data across address spaces into this well-controlled window.

Operating-system/hardware-architecture design must enforce strict separation of resources yet simultaneously be efficient for intertask sharing, so that the time required for intertask data movement is not excessively high. The memory-protection architecture must be designed with this constraint in mind.

Secondary-Memory Protection

In addition to memory-protection mechanisms for main store, there must be memory-protection mechanisms for the file system. For the same reason that a user task must not be allowed to change its memory-bounds register, a user task must not be allowed to perform I/O operations on arbitrary files. This could be done via a bounds scheme similar to that for main memory, listing the device numbers and tracks, records, etc. on each device that a particular task is allowed to access. But, as a practical matter, full I/O with interrupts and error recovery is so complicated that user-mode programs are usually prohibited from doing any I/O at all. Instead, a user task calls an operating-system service routine to perform an I/O request. This happens

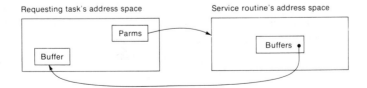

Requesting task's address space   Service routine's address space

Parms   Buffers

Buffer

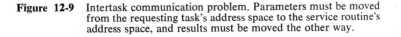

Figure 12-9 Intertask communication problem. Parameters must be moved from the requesting task's address space to the service routine's address space, and results must be moved the other way.

much less frequently than accesses to main memory, so file protection can be supplied efficiently enough as part of these service routines, with no additional architectural considerations.

There is however, one architecture-related software consideration: If the machine's architecture is such that I/O operations are controlled by channel commands in main memory, it is important that a user task have no access to these commands while they are being used. Otherwise, a task could request an allowed READ, wait for the service routine to do its error checking, then modify the associated channel commands to specify an entirely different operation. For well over five years, this was a protection flaw in an early IBM 360 operating system, OS/360.

Protection Context

In general, the protection status of a task is reflected in various hardware registers containing keys, bounds, user-mode bits, task numbers, etc. These registers are part of the environment of the task, and must be changed when switching from one task to another, just as the program-accessible registers must be changed. The instruction counter, programmer-accessible registers, protection status, and other hardware registers and mode bits associated with a task are collectively referred to as the *hardware state* of the machine. On older machines and on modern microprocessors, the state might be less than 100 bits, but in large, fast machines with many registers, the state can reach thousands of bits.

In addition to the hardware state, there usually are many software-supported words of information associated with each task. These words contain data such as the accounting time charged to that task, the address of a routine to handle fixed-point overflow interrupts, images of control cards for that task, and status of I/O operations. These words of *software state* information (see Figure 12-12, page 616) must also be changed when switching tasks. Architectural issues associated with changing these states are discussed in Section 12-4.

A generalization of protection registers and user-mode bits is the concept of *capabilities* [Dennis and van Horn, 66; Fabry, 74]. Briefly, a capability-based system is one in which each task runs in an environment that specifies *all* the privileges or capabilities allowed for the task. Some tasks may have the capability to perform specific I/O operations, while other tasks do not; some tasks may have access to many *objects,* while others may have access to only a few. In general, capabilities are dealt with on a more abstract level than the raw memory bits of the machine, hence access protection is defined for an object, which may be a single word or a very complex data structure or an I/O device, instead of for a block of (say) 512 words of physical memory.

When implemented in their full generality, capability-based systems can incur substantial performance penalties at every access. Sometimes, a capability-based design is cut back and simplified, and some hardware support is defined for the most frequent operations. Such a process happened in the

MULTICS system developed at MIT and Bell Labs [Corbato and Vyssotosky, 65; Corbato et al., 72; Organick, 72]. The original design defined a set of 32 concentric access *rings,* or levels in a protection hierarchy. The innermost rings were used by the operating system, and outer rings were intended for user programs. Any given ring has fewer privileges than those inside it, and more privileges than those outside it. After the development of rings, operating-system designers found that a strict nesting of privileges is too restrictive. The ring system, while clever and elegant, may well be displaced by protection techniques that allow for more general handling of privileges.

The original MULTICS system was implemented on a General Electric GE-645 computer that had almost no hardware support for quickly changing context from one ring to another. Thus, whenever a user program had to call upon an operating-system service routine in an inner ring (or one module of the operating system had to call upon a more privileged module), it was necessary to go through a rather slow and awkward *gatekeeper* program [Daley and Dennis, 68] that checked that the call, parameters, and data areas involved were all legitimate. Current versions of MULTICS run on a successor machine, the Honeywell 6180, which includes hardware support for frequent linkages between rings [Schroeder and Saltzer, 72]. In the evolution of the current system, the number of rings supported was dropped from 32 to 8.

Resource Hogging

If one task (or group of tasks) completely dominates the use of some resource, then another task may never be allowed to run. The first task is definitely interfering with the operation of the other task. In order to prevent hogging of memory or file space, tasks are usually given upper bounds on how much they can request, or requests are forced to be done incrementally, and at some point an incremental request is denied because available space is almost used up.

Preventing hogging of processor resources requires some hardware help. First, if a machine supporting multiple tasks has a nonprivileged HALT instruction that any task can execute, then hogging can occur simply by executing a HALT. Second, if a task can loop indefinitely at a time when no I/O transfers are occurring, then it is possible that no interrupt will ever occur to trigger a task switch. In this case, some kind of clock is needed as a source of periodic interrupts, so that *time-slicing* between tasks can be forced, as mentioned in Section 12-2. Of course, the scheduling algorithm must be arranged so that it does not just give control back to the infinite-loop task when such a clock interrupt occurs.

If a machine can only take interrupts *between* instructions, then resource hogging can occur if there is some way to start an instruction that never terminates. This can happen on a machine with multilevel indirect addressing (i.e., the address in the instruction is not the data address, but is used to fetch a new, indirect, data address from memory, and each such indirect address can specify another one), if the indirect addresses form a circular chain of addresses. The IBM 7030 (Stretch) had a one-millisecond *timeout* on instruction-execution time specifically to prevent locking up the machine this way. The IBM 7094, which was used for running the early CTSS timesharing system at MIT [Corbato et al., 62], has an EXECUTE instruction that points to another instruction to be executed. This could itself be an EXECUTE, and an infinite chain of EXECUTE instructions on that computer cannot be interrupted, even by the operator's STOP button. Anyone (including this author) could lock up the entire system at will.

PROBLEMS

12-7. Assume that task A wants to pass a three-word parameter list to task B, and that the memory-protection mechanism allows access to 512-word blocks on 512-word boundaries. (The mechanism could be physical-memory keys, page-table entries, or some other scheme.) The supervisor-assisted linkage from task A to task B gives B read-only access to the necessary memory block(s).

    a) If the parameter list is entirely contained in one block, how many unnecessary words is B allowed to access?

    b) If the parameter list happens to straddle a block boundary, how many unnecessary words is B allowed to access?

    c) What information might be in these excess words, such that it would be damaging if task B sent a copy of these words to a third party?

    d) If the supervisor does not know how many words are in the parameter list, how many blocks of memory must it give B access to?

    e) Propose an efficient memory-protection mechanism which permits a three-word parameter list to be passed to another task without allowing *any* access to surrounding words. (Patent it.)

12-8. *a)* What is the timeout interval for a computer to which you have access? Where did you find out? Can you experimentally verify it?

    b) What is the execution time of this machine's slowest instruction (typically Divide or multiword Move)? Would the timeout interval have to be changed if this instruction were extended to operate on double-length data, and hence ran slower by a factor of 2 to 4?

12-4. INTERRUPTS AND CONTEXT SWITCHING

Context swaps are the focus of control for sharing a processor. The word "context" means both the hardware state and the software state. Operating-system design is quite sensitive to the time required for a context swap: a factor-of-3 change in this time across different machines may force much different operating-system structures for those machines. Conversely, a particular operating-system design may dictate additional hardware support for fast context swaps, as we mentioned about MULTICS in the previous section.

At least two different cases of context swaps arise. One case occurs when a (user) task is interrupted briefly for an operating-system task to service an interrupt, but then control returns to the original user task. Another case occurs when one task is interrupted and control is passed to an entirely different task. In this second case a full context swap must be done, while in the first case it may be sufficient to save only a small part of the hardware state and none of the software state; this is usually faster than a full swap.

In a real-time system that is exchanging data with some external device, there are absolute constraints upon the time allowed for the computer to respond to a single data item or interrupt. In such an environment, a very fast partial context swap is desirable. This is one motivation for machine designs such as the Digital Equipment Corporation PDP-11 and the IBM 360 (see Figure 12-10), in which only one or two words are saved during the hardware response to an interrupt. The real-time interrupt routine that is given control by such an interrupt typically saves a few more words of registers, executes a handful of useful instructions, restores those few registers,

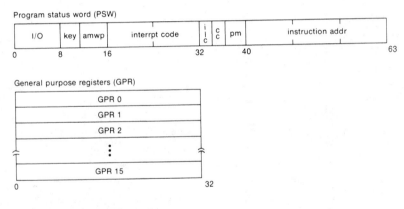

Program status word (PSW)

General purpose registers (GPR)

Floating-point registers (FPR)

I/O —Interrupt masks for channels 0-7
key—Memory protection key
a   —ASCII/EBCDIC mode
m —Machine check interrupt mask
w —Wait state (equivalent to interruptable halt)
p —System/user (programmer) mode
ilc —Instruction length code (2, 4, or 6 bytes)
cc —Condition code
pm—Program mask (masks integer overflow, decimal overflow,
          floating-point overflow, zero divide)

Figure 12-10 IBM 360 complete hardware state (IBM 370 PSW is different). Total state is 832 bits, but only the 64-bit PSW is saved by the interrupt hardware.

then exits back to the originally executing task. In this situation, the time to save the entire hardware state could completely swamp the time actually taken to execute the handful of useful instructions.

Another way to accomplish fast context swaps is to have multiple register sets; the Xerox Sigma-7 computer, for example, has four sets of general-purpose registers. Instead of saving and restoring the registers in main memory, as must be done on the superficially similar IBM 360, the interrupt hardware simply switches to an entirely different set of general registers. This system is not very flexible, since each register set must be dedicated to exactly one use in order to gain the intended speed advantage, but in some real-time systems with only one or two interrupt processes, it is a quite efficient solution. In such systems, one set of registers is usually used by the operating system, one set is shared (via the normal save/restore in main memory) among all the user tasks, and the other sets are dedicated to interrupt routines for specific real-time devices.

The ultimate solution for swapping contexts is to avoid swapping them at all. Carrying the Sigma-7 approach to an extreme suggests that instead of dedicating a set of general registers to an operating system or to an I/O program, we could dedicate an entire processor. This entails only a few more registers and control logic, and in the era of microprocessors, an entire self-contained processor is readily at hand to dedicate as the designer sees fit. This is precisely the philosophy exemplified in Chapter 6 for the HP-3000 series machines. The I/O is serviced by dedicated microprocessors with direct access to memory. These microprocessors maintain their own context, never swapping the context with user programs, and thus greatly reduce the problem of context swapping. This example strongly suggests that problems like context swapping and others mentioned later in this chapter can be treated by innovative use of hardware that was in the past ruled out because of high expense.

If an operating system is designed to support frequent full-task switches instead of real-time interrupts, then the *minimum* context-swap time becomes much less important than the *total* context-swap time. In this situation, it is useful for the interrupt hardware to save all (or nearly all) of the hardware state, since any unsaved portion will have to be saved anyway by software instructions in order to complete a full context swap. The CDC 6600 exchange-package mechanism [Thornton, 70] shown in Figure 12-11 is an example of this full saving. As it turns out, saving 16 words of context on the CDC 6600 is not much slower than saving one word. Storing one word takes 1000 nsec, but because the interleaved memory system can start a new store to a different memory bank every 100 nsec and there are at least 10 different banks, storing 16 words takes only 2500 nsec.

We can see a trade-off here between having a large context and having a fast interrupt response or a fast task-switch time. Recall that the context includes both the hardware state and the software state (Figure 12-12). A large hardware state may be desirable in order to have programs use many fast registers. An extreme example of this is the Cray-1 computer with 72 24-bit registers, 584 64-bit registers, and a few others, for a total hardware

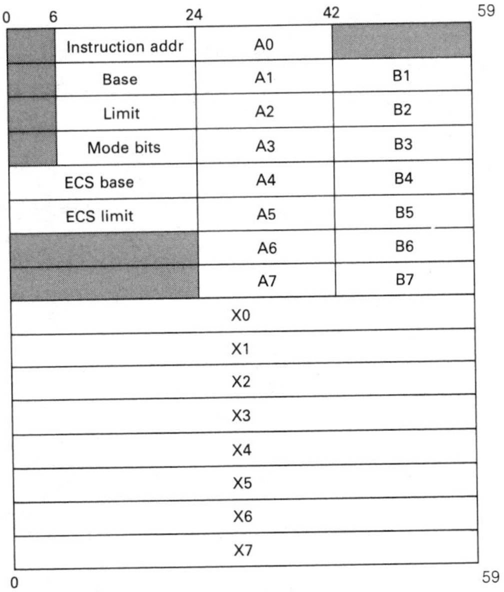

Base — Memory protection base register
Limit — Memory protection limit register
ECS — Extended core storage (secondary memory with
its own base-limit pair)
A0-A7 — Address registers
B0-B7 — Index registers (B0 is always zero)
X0-X7 — Data registers

Figure 12-11 CDC 6600 complete hardware state (exchange package). Total state is 960 bits, and all bits are saved by the interrupt hardware.

state of over 39,000 bits. This is definitely a machine on which full context swaps take a noticeable amount of time (close to 1300 instruction issue times).

A large software state is usually not desired, but it can simply "grow" during the development of an operating system, without anyone noticing the way its increasing size affects the task-switch. Occasionally, a few words that should be saved as part of the hardware state are instead relegated to the software state, but such oversights are usually more of a nuisance than a critical time problem. The problem is much different if the overlooked hardware bits are not accessible at all.

It can be a disastrous design flaw if some crucial bit of information is left out of the machine state stored by the interrupt hardware. For example, if a machine has variable-length instructions but the length of the current instruction is not saved when interrupted, then this makes it logically impossible to back up to the beginning of an interrupted instruction. In a similar way, the CDC 6600 saves no information about block transfers (to Extended Core Storage) that might be in progress at the time of an interrupt. So such transfers must be restarted at the beginning instead of where they left off, a process

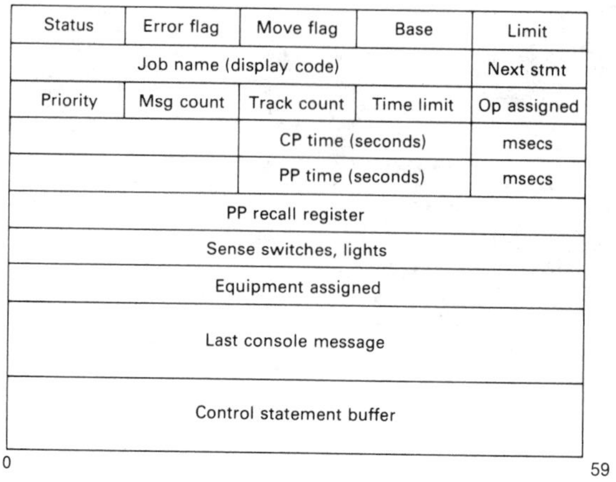

Status	Error flag	Move flag	Base	Limit
Job name (display code)				Next stmt
Priority	Msg count	Track count	Time limit	Op assigned
		CP time (seconds)		msecs
		PP time (seconds)		msecs
PP recall register				
Sense switches, lights				
Equipment assigned				
Last console message				
Control statement buffer				

0   59

Base — Memory protection base address
Limit — Memory protection limit address
CP — Central processor
PP — Peripheral processor

Figure 12-12 Software state for an early CDC 6600 operating system

that can waste as much as a millisecond moving information that has already been moved. An example of avoiding this instruction-progress flaw is found in the HP-3000, which sometimes packs two instructions per word. The status information stored on interrupt includes a specific bit which says "first half of two-instruction word executed."

On many machines, the real-time clock value is not saved on interrupt, so accounting for task time usually involves corrections to approximate the time between the interrupt and the software instruction that saves the clock. A "Swap Clock" instruction, that saves the old value and simultaneously loads a new value, without ever missing a clock tick, can help to keep the timing exact. Another solution, found on the Cray-1, is to increment a clock synchronously with instruction fetching, so any time corrections can be calculated exactly (incidentally, the execution time of a short sequence of instructions can be measured exactly).

Overall, the facilities provided for swapping the entire context of a task, including the software state and all the normally overlooked bits of the hardware state, are probably the most important single part of a machine's architecture when viewed from the point of view of an operating-system designer. The memory-mapping architectures discussed in the next section are a close second.

We have indicated earlier that one way to deal with context swapping is to dedicate processors to specific contexts so that swapping is unnecessary. In the long term, this may prove to be the most viable approach, but for the present it should be viewed as a potentially attractive approach that must be evaluated against the other approaches described here.

PROBLEMS

12-9. *a*) Describe the *complete* hardware state of some machine not described in this chapter. How many bits are there in this state? How many bits are saved by the interrupt hardware?

b) What are the popular applications for this machine, and how might this popularity be influenced by the context-switching hardware?

12-5. MEMORY ADDRESSING AND VIRTUAL MEMORY

An operating system must dynamically manage the allocation of main memory. This management motivates and directly interacts with architectural features that map or relocate memory addresses. In a more fundamental way, dynamic memory management interacts with the way in which a machine architecture specifies the basic operations of addressing data and addressing instructions. The provision of index registers, stack pointers, relative branches, and other basic design features in an addressing architecture directly determines the access styles which are convenient on a particular machine, and these in turn strongly mold the dynamic memory-allocation services provided by an operating system.

Requests for more main memory (and inversely, requests to free a no-longer-needed area) occur in all but the simplest computer systems. Requests may be triggered by the need to load a new subroutine from disk, by the need to allocate a data array or extend a data stack, or by the need to add more elements to a linked-list structure. Since an operating system has the responsibility for resource management in general, and main-memory management in particular, some operating-system module must respond to these requests. In our assumed environment of multiple tasks, the operating system must further respond to competing and conflicting requests. In this section, we discuss memory-addressing designs by building up layers of complexity, starting from the point of view of an operating-system service routine that handles a single task's request for more contiguous main memory.

The discussion is divided (somewhat arbitrarily) into two topics, Memory-Addressing Designs and Virtual-Memory Mapping. The first topic deals with architectural issues in the generation of an *effective address,* while the second topic deals with mapping an effective address into a physical address of the specified datum or instruction.

In this chapter, "effective address" means the final logical address of a datum or instruction, after all programmer-specified relative addressing, indexing, and indirect addressing operations have been performed, but before any automatic logical-to-physical address mapping is done. Recall from Section 12-3 that a *virtual* (or logical) address is the fully-qualified address of an item from the machine-language programmer's point of view, while a *real* (or physical) address is the actual place in a memory hierarchy that the item is really stored.

Memory-Addressing Designs

If task A requests more contiguous main memory from the operating system, it may not be possible to satisfy this request without moving the instructions and data associated with task B, which happens to occupy the memory next to task A. On simple machines, this movement of B is not possible because (1) the instructions and data contain absolute memory addresses that are no longer valid if moved and (2), even more difficult to correct for, registers may contain absolute addresses that are completely indistinguishable from integers. One possibility is to swap out all of task B's instructions and data to secondary storage, run task A in the larger space thus made available, then later (when A has completed, or has shrunk its memory requirement) swap B back into *exactly* the same locations. While this is a possibility, and is actually done in some operating systems, it can hardly be called a "solution," since a request from task A has a very definite and detrimental effect on task B. Worse than being swapped out, task B may find that it never gets swapped in again, even if there is enough total free memory space for it, because the exact locations it must run in are never all free at once.

Base-Limit Relocation   One solution to this problem of moving B but still being able to execute it is to introduce a *base-limit* register pair, as found on the CDC 6600. The base specifies a constant to be added to all memory addresses generated by the running task, and the limit specifies a maximum allowable address. This base-limit register pair is exactly the bounds register described in Section 12-3, except that it now performs the additional function of *relocation* of all main-memory addresses, by adding the base to them. Task B running in locations 3000 through 6500 generates addresses assuming that it is running in locations 0 through 3500, and the base-limit values of [3000, 6500] result in both the checking and the relocation of all task B addresses. If a request for more memory from task A moves B to locations 4000 through 7500, none of the task B data, instructions, or registers are modified, and task B still generates addresses in the range 0 through 3500. After being moved, task B has a base-limit pair (supplied by the operating system) of [4000,7500].

Relocatable Instructions   Adding a layer of complexity, we could have an architectural philosophy that allows dynamic instruction relocation, but still uses absolute addresses in the data. To do this, all branch instructions specify *self-relative* addresses instead of absolute, so that an instruction at address 3700 branching to 3500 would specify a relative (to itself) offset of -200, instead of an absolute address of 3500; alternatively, a *base-relative* address of 500 could be specified (assuming a base of 3000, as shown in Figure 12-13). With relative branches, a block of instructions for a single subroutine can be placed *anywhere* in memory and it will execute properly. This offers the operating system great flexibility in allocating space for instructions.

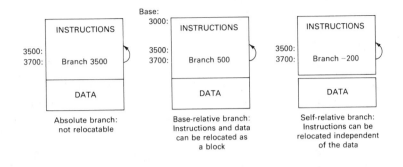

Figure 12-13 Three styles of branch addressing

Linkage between subroutines can be accomplished either so that an entire *package* of many linked subroutines may be relocated anywhere in memory, or so that individual subroutines may be moved with respect to each other. A single package may be built using absolute, base-relative, or self-relative call instructions, just like the branches above. But a monolithic package may become large and unwieldy. The alternative requires an indirect-address table (Figure 12-14) and cooperation between the hardware and the operating system. The hardware subroutine-call instruction specifies the relative address of an indirect-table entry, and this entry in turn specifies the (absolute) address of the actual subroutine. The operating system keeps the indirect tables up to date as it moves various subroutines around in main memory. The indirect table thus allows an individual subroutine to be moved, instead of forcing

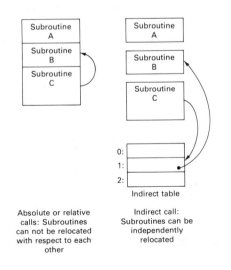

Figure 12-14 Two styles of subroutine-call addressing

all the code in a linked package to be moved. Relative branches and indirect tables may slow down a computer (because of the extra additions and memory fetches involved), but they allow a flexibility in storage allocation that may more than compensate for the extra time or hardware needed.

Relocatable Data Making instructions relocatable solves only half of the problem. We would like to make the data relocatable also. A simple, non-architectural way to do this is to introduce a software design rule that no absolute addresses can appear in the data (as done in the IBM 370 PL/1 Checkout compiler); but in most machines such a rule cannot be applied to the contents of registers. If a block of data can be repositioned in memory by an operating system at arbitrary times, and the registers can contain either addresses or integers at these times, then it is impossible to update the registers properly to reflect the move. (The PL/I Checkout compiler moves data blocks only at times when the registers contain no absolute addresses.)

If we can partition the registers so that absolute addresses appear in specified registers and data in others, then it *is* possible to make the links in all data structures relocatable. In this case, all data-structure pointers could be made *self-relative,* that is, specify an offset from their own location, and absolute addresses calculated from these pointers are kept only in certain registers. (Analogously, the absolute address computed from a relative branch is kept in a specified register, the instruction counter.) Corresponding to base-limit relocation, we can establish the definition that all data-structure pointers are *offsets* from the base of a data area, and then keep the absolute base address in a special machine register. Such a base-address register is found in the HP3000, which has all data in a stack in main memory, and all data addresses are offsets from the stack base (or a few other specific stack pointers). The UNIVAC 1108, GE-645, and other machines have one base-limit pair for instructions, and a second pair for data. On these machines, the base registers cannot be changed by the user program, but only by the operating system. The original IBM 360 design attempted to provide up to 15 base registers for many disjoint code and data areas, but a fatal flaw of allowing arbitrary user-program access to these registers prevented realization of the hoped-for dynamic relocation. An additional paging mechanism was eventually implemented in the later IBM 370 series.

Descriptors The single data base-register approach has the same flaw that we found in having a single code-base register—the data area is one monolithic package and must either be moved in its entirety or not moved at all. We would like the additional flexibility of scattering noncontiguous data areas anywhere in main memory and moving each area without necessarily moving any other area. Taking our cue from the indirect table for subroutine calls, we can add one more layer of complexity and use a *descriptor-based* addressing system.

The B5000 and its successors has such a system, in which data areas such as arrays are pointed to by special descriptor words [Organick, 73; also Section 7-6]. Access to an array element on the B6700 involves an indirect

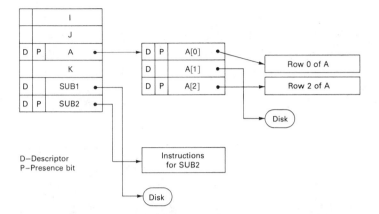

Figure 12-15   Data and instruction areas partitioned into 7 segments. The segments associated with SUB1 and row A[1] are currently swapped out to disk (presence bit is off).

reference through the descriptor, in exactly the same way that a subroutine call on that machine involves an indirect reference through a descriptor. In both cases, the descriptor contains the absolute address and the length of the code or data area. Compared to base-limit registers (above) and page faults (below), descriptors are much more effective in catching subscript range and other address-calculation errors. Descriptors are specially marked, so that user programs cannot normally modify them, and so that the operating system can find all descriptors pointing to a data or program area, and update the address contained in them when that area *(segment)* is moved.

A trivial extension of the descriptors described so far allows us to move a segment out of main memory completely. In addition to an absolute address and length, B6700 descriptors contain a *presence bit* that specifies whether the target segment is in main memory or swapped out to disk. If it is swapped out, the address field gives a disk block address. Figure 12-15 shows an example of a 2-dimensional array and some subroutines partitioned into segments.

So far, we have described quite a powerful and flexible nonpaged segmentation system. References to array elements or to subroutines are mapped via indirection through the descriptors, but references to scalars or to branch addresses within a subroutine do not invoke this indirection. To specify an effective address, the address field in an instruction may be base-relative or self-relative (implying an addition operation) or may point to an entry in an indirect table (implying an extra memory fetch). Another layer of complexity allows us to cope with very large segments by mapping *every* effective address to a physical memory location.

Virtual-Memory Mapping

It is important to keep the normal segment size much smaller than the total available memory size. As Knuth has observed [Knuth, 68, Section 2.5,

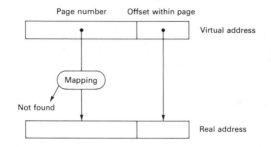

Figure 12-16   General virtual-memory address mapping

p. 447], dynamic memory-allocation schemes fall apart if they frequently must deal with allocation requests that are larger than about 1/10 of the total available memory (because too much time is spent moving large segments around, or too much space is wasted between segments). The early HP-3000 COBOL compiler had this problem: the compiler used a single 24K-word data segment on a machine with 32K words of main memory. Other tasks on the machine were swapped out for noticeable amounts of time during a COBOL compilation.

It may not be possible to keep all the code and data segments small enough in practical situations such as large compilations on small machines. An architectural solution to this problem is to break each segment into smaller pieces, called *pages,* and to allocate memory in terms of these smaller pieces. In such a paging scheme, determining the physical location of a word referenced involves not only the indirection required by segment descriptors (if any), but also involves further indirection to map an address within a segment into the current location of the corresponding page.

This mapping is conceptually just the simple lookup implied by Figure 12-16: the high-order bits of the virtual address are mapped into the high-order bits of a real memory address, while the low-order bits of the address remain unchanged. Such a mapping allows a large area, such as the COBOL compiler's data segment above, to be addressed as contiguous virtual addresses, while the actual data reside in various noncontiguous real-memory areas, not all of which are necessarily in main memory at once.

Any system in which *all* effective virtual addresses are further mapped into real addresses is called a *virtual-memory* system, with the word "virtual" meaning that the illusion of a single real memory is supplied. The purpose of having a virtual-memory system is to allow a much greater flexibility in the physical placement of a particular datum within a possibly multilevel *memory hierarchy.* A multilevel memory hierarchy is an ordered collection of physical memory systems, each one typically larger and slower (and hence cheaper per bit) than the preceding one. In addition to allowing easy solutions to our original problem of relocating data and instructions in memory, a virtual-memory system also allows the illusion of a large, fast memory to be provided at lower hardware cost.

While a virtual-memory system is conceptually a simple mapping of virtual addresses to real ones, it in fact introduces a wealth of architectural subtleties. We will first discuss the gross architectural features needed for address mapping, then discuss the subtle side effects that may be represented only indirectly in the final architecture of the computer.

Virtual-to-Real Address Mapping

Addresses to be mapped in a virtual memory system are usually divided into a nonmapped field and a mapped field. The size of the nonmapped field defines the granularity of the mapping, ranging from single words (bytes, bits, or whatever the storage unit is) to groups of 1024 words or more. A single such group of words in the virtual-address space is called a *page*, and a single such group of words in the real-address space is called a *page frame*. Thus, if the nonmapped field is the six low-order bits of an address, virtual pages of 64 words are mapped to real page frames of 64 words. There may be more pages than page frames, in which case a big virtual-address space is being mapped into a smaller real-address space. Such a mapping could allow a large program to run (albeit slowly) on a small machine, as we shall see in detail below. Conversely, there may be more page frames than pages, in which case a small virtual-address space is being mapped into a larger real-address space. Such a mapping could allow many tasks with, say, 16-bit virtual addresses to be run on a machine with, say, 18-bit real addresses. This is in fact a quite common technique for extending architectures (such as the PDP-11) that originally allowed too few address bits.

In a multilevel memory hierarchy, virtual addresses are mapped into either a real address in the fastest (highest) level of the memory hierarchy, or into a *page fault* or "not in the highest level" signal. This signal is used to initiate a search for the required data in lower levels of the memory hierarchy, perhaps followed by movement of the actual data to a higher level. It is this possibility of a page fault on *any* access to memory that so severely complicates virtual memory designs, both because a page fault may occur *within* an instruction (instead of between two), and because typically the operating system tries to run another task while the required data is fetched from the lower memory level.

Three different address-mapping techniques are common:

1. One-level table
2. Two-level table
3. N-way associative table

The first two allow any page to be mapped to any page frame, while the last restricts a particular page to be mapped to one of N specific page frames.

One-Level Table   A one-level address-mapping table consists of a single *page table* containing one entry for each possible page. The entry contains the corresponding page frame number or a "not there" indication. The IBM

Series/1 computer [IBM, 78] has such a mapping table. The virtual byte-addresses are 16 bits, the page size is 2K (2048) bytes, and the real addresses are 24 bits. The 2K page size implies 11 nonmapped bits, so the mapping is from 5 high-order bits of virtual address to 13 high-order bits of real address. This requires a single table with 32 entries of at least 13 bits each. (As mentioned in Section 12-3, a common memory-protection scheme is to include a few bits of read/write/execute-access privileges in each page-table entry. Often, one other bit is used to indicate "this entry is invalid—generate a page fault.")

A one-level page table is not very efficient if the virtual-address space is large. For example, if the Series/1 had 32-bit virtual addresses, instead of 16, the page table would be not 32, but 2,097,152 entries! This would be impossible if the main memory were only 128K bytes. As a rule of thumb, no page table should be bigger than about one page in size; so assuming 2-byte entries, no Series/1-like page table should exceed 1024 entries.

Two-Level Table A two-level address-mapping table has the obvious structure shown in Figure 12-17: high-order virtual-address bits are used to select an entry in a *segment table,* each entry of which points to a corresponding page table. Middle address bits are used to select an entry from the page table, and that entry specifies the real page-frame address. Our 32-bit virtual address above could be partitioned into a 10-bit segment field, a 10-bit page field, and a 12-bit unmapped field. The segment table is then 1024 entries long, each of the 1024 possible page tables contains 1024 entries, and each page is 4096 bytes long. The segment table is permanently held in one page frame of main memory, while the individual page tables can either be in main memory or "swapped out" to the next lower level in the memory

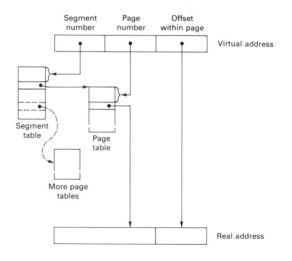

Figure 12-17 Two-level mapping table

hierarchy, typically a disk or drum. In turn, the actual pages of data/instructions can either be in main memory or on disk.

A two-level table does not save any total space (in fact, it costs us exactly the additional space for the segment level), but it does allow only a *portion* of the entire mapping table to be in main memory at once. This is a great advantage if the usage of the virtual address space is not very dense, i.e., if not all (of say 2^{32}) possible virtual addresses are actually used, but only clusters of a few thousand (or hundred thousand) addresses are used over a brief time period (perhaps a few seconds).

The names of the two levels of tables are deliberately suggestive: if the virtual addresses to be mapped actually consist of [segment number, word within that segment] pairs (as we might find when large data areas or groups of instructions are treated as distinct segments), then the segment number can be used in the first level of mapping and the high-order bits of the word number can be used in the second level. Such a use of segment numbers tends to cluster virtual addresses quite nicely—over a brief time period, only a handful of different segments are normally accessed, so only virtual addresses within these segments need to be mapped. Page tables and actual pages for other segments need not be in main memory, and not all pages of the active segments need be in main memory. Thus, a segmentation scheme like the one described for the B6700 can coexist easily with a paging scheme, although the two mechanisms are otherwise distinct.

More than two levels of mapping could be used, but few virtual addresses are big enough to require this. Also, each level of mapping initially implies an extra main-memory fetch (assuming tables with more than about 64 entries are kept in memory, not hardware registers), so more levels means slower access.

Finally, we note that there are many variations of this basic scheme in use. For example, the DEC VAX-11/780 uses no page-number field, but instead treats the address produced by the segment table as a virtual address, which goes through the same mapping process. In any case, the purpose of the two levels is to provide a way to retain only some of the mapping tables in main memory.

N-Way Associative Table   An N-way associative mapping table (also called *set associative*) trades flexibility of page placement for smaller table size and potentially faster access. Instead of reserving a page-table entry for each possible page in the virtual address space, an entry is reserved only for each page *frame* in the real address space. If the virtual-address space has 2,097,152 pages and the real address space has 8192 page frames, this is quite a savings in table space. Each page-frame entry contains the page number, if any, of the page currently mapped to that frame. To answer the question, Where is page K? would normally require searching *all* the page frames for a matching value K. To reduce this search, an N-way associative mapping restricts each page to be in only specific N page frames. For example, 4-way associative mapping restricts each page to be mapped to one of only four specific page frames; only these four need be searched for a matching page number. For small values of N, such searches can be done in parallel by special comparison hardware.

Because of the placement restriction of N-way associative mapping, a program could use many pages that happen to be all mapped to the same set of page frames. Those frames could be heavily used, while the rest of main memory could be only lightly used. This is an unacceptable performance burden if there are more than N pages involved and if the time it takes to access a page at the next lower level of the memory hierarchy is quite high. Because of this, N-way associative mappings are not usually found in main-memory paging schemes, where the next level of memory is typically a disk with access time 1000 to 10,000 times longer than that of main memory. Instead, N-way associative mappings are often used in *cache memory* designs (see Figure 12-18, below), where the second level of the memory hierarchy is typically a main memory with an access time only 4 to 10 times slower than the cache. Cache memories are discussed in more detail below.

Architectural Issues

So far, we have only introduced the subject of address mapping, and have not yet discussed the architectural issues implied by having such a mapping. The rest of this section discusses the following points:

- Choice of page size
- Speedup memories
- Transparency of speedup memories
- Page-fault interrupts
- The interaction of I/O with memory mapping

To set the stage, we assume a three-level memory hierarchy consisting of (1) an 8K cache memory with an access time of 100 nsec., (2) a 256K main memory with an access time of 1 μsec., and (3) a 16M secondary memory (disk) with an access time of 30 msec. A datum not found in the cache (cache miss) is sought in main memory, and a datum not found in main memory (page fault) is found on the disk. When a cache miss occurs, the processor simply waits for the datum to arrive from main memory; when a page fault occurs, the operating system tries to run another task while accessing the disk as a normal I/O device. This last assumption is based on the idea that 30 msec. is enough time to do at least two task switches and still do some useful work in the alternate task(s).

Page Size   The size of a single page corresponds to the nonmapped portion of an address. A small page size of one word is most flexible, but it implies mapping tables that are potentially just as big as the data. On the other hand, a page size as large as 1/10 of physical main memory creates the same dynamic-memory allocation problems that originally motivated our entrance into the world of virtual memory. Thus, the choice of a page size is a compromise, with the important factors being:

1. Size of the mapping tables
2. Frequency of checking for crossing page boundaries
3. Next lower memory-level access time and transfer-rate characteristics
4. Overhead in operating system to manage page swaps

The second factor relates to architectures that have multiword data items (such as instructions, double-precision numbers, or character strings). In such cases, the processor must check for page boundaries within a single data object (unless N-word items are always *aligned* on N-word boundaries, and the pages are also aligned on N-word boundaries, as in Problem 12-13). The third and fourth items capture the idea that it is not worthwhile to transfer 8-word pages to a disk, but 2-word "pages" may be appropriate for transferring between main memory and a cache.

Speedup Memories   The mappings described above imply a substantial mapping overhead for *each* access to memory. We need to take advantage of the fact that the addresses referenced by a program tend to cluster, at least over brief periods of time. A *speedup memory* is such a mechanism: recently-accessed data is copied into the speedup memory, and subsequent accesses look first in the speedup memory. Let us see how this idea can be used to short-circuit a two-level address mapping.

An access to a single data item normally requires *three* memory accesses in a two-level address mapping—one for a segment-table entry, one for a page-table entry, and one for the data item. Consider now a speedup memory containing the [virtual page, real page frame] pairs for four recent accesses. To map a new access request for page K, we first look at the four speedup-memory locations. If any one of them contains page number K, then the corresponding page frame number K' is immediately available, as shown in Figure 12-18, and we do not have to access main memory for segment- and page-table entries. In this application, a speedup memory is often called an *associative memory* (AM) or a *translation lookaside buffer* (TLB). So long as the search in the speedup memory is fast, and the *hit ratio* of successful matches to total tries is high, then the entire scheme can make virtual memory address translation take very little time.

The GE-645 has an 8-word associative memory in which all eight words can be searched simultaneously in a small fraction of the time required for a main-memory access. Whenever a miss occurs and some page number K is not found in the AM, the least recently used entry is replaced by an entry for K. The IBM 370/168 has a translation lookaside buffer of 128 entries. The search uses a 2-way associative mapping of page number K into two possible TLB entries. If one of these contains K, then the corresponding K' is used immediately. If neither entry matches, the least recently used of those

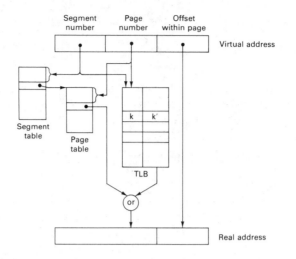

Figure 12-18 Two-level mapping table with Translation Lookaside Buffer (TLB)

two entries is replaced by a new entry for K. The usual hit ratio for both machines is over 90%.

Not only can a speedup memory be used to hold copies of mapping-table entries, it can be used for holding copies of main-memory data and instructions. In this application, a speedup memory is often called a *cache memory*. Whenever a word is accessed in memory, its address is sent to the cache memory. If a match is found, the cache-memory data is used without need to wait for the main memory. Cache memories are usually designed with very small page sizes of 2 to 32 storage units (bytes, words). The page is often termed a *line*, and is usually exactly the size of a physical main-memory storage item times the interleaving factor, i.e., the maximum amount of data that can be obtained in one storage cycle of all main-memory banks. Thus, the IBM 370/168 has physical main memory organized as 4 interleaved banks each 8 bytes wide, and the cache line is 32 bytes. The Cray-1 has 16 interleaved memory banks each 1 word wide, and its instruction cache has lines of 16 words. The address-match lookup in a cache-memory system must be done quickly, so a cache is often organized as 2-, 4-, or 8-way associative, with parallel comparison hardware for each associative group, as shown in Figure 12-19. Problem 12-12 explores the issue of virtual *vs.* real addresses sent to a cache.

Speedup memories do not start out being a part of the architecture visible to a computer programmer—they simply allow an implementation to deliver results more quickly than might be expected. This *architectural transparency* is quite desirable, but it turns out that the fact that caches and lookaside buffers contain *copies* of data can make them noticeable in a quite ugly way if the original data are changed and the speedup memory continues to supply old data. Let us look at a few of these problems.

Transparency of Speedup Memories If an architecture allows multiple seg-ment-tables, with a hardware register pointing to the beginning of the cur-rent segment table, then we have multiple distinct address spaces (as in Section 12-3), and a simple change of the segment table pointer when switch-ing tasks serves to change address spaces completely, except for one non-transparent problem.

As soon as the operating system switches to a new address space, all the lookaside entries in any associative mapping registers are invalid. The hard-ware design must make sure that no old mapping entry is used in the new address space, otherwise the newly-started task B might erroneously access physical words containing data from the just-interrupted task A, thus creating a hole in the protection mechanisms (and extremely mysterious happenings for task A).

A design principle involved in creating lookaside registers, caches, instruc-tion-prefetch buffers, etc. is that:

If a datum is copied and the copy is to match the original at all times, then all changes to the original must cause the copy to be immediately updated or invalidated.

Lookaside registers contain a copy of parts of page tables. Whenever a single page-table entry is changed (perhaps because that page was just swapped in from secondary storage), the lookaside registers must reflect that change, and whenever the entire set of page tables is changed (by a task

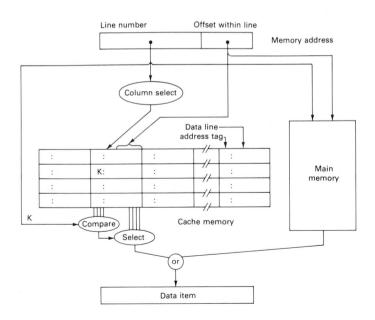

Figure 12-19   Data fetch using 4-way associative cache memory

switch), the lookaside registers must reflect that entire change. One way to keep the lookaside registers properly updated is to have an instruction that sets *all* lookaside entries to "invalid." Such an instruction is used in the original GE-645 for MULTICS; but the programming group soon observed that there is a significant speed penalty in invalidating all the registers—the next memory references go through the slow indirect-table lookup until the lookaside registers are reloaded with useful entries [Schroeder, 71]. If the reason for invalidating the entire set of lookaside registers is the changing of a single page-table entry, then the reload time may be too expensive a price to pay. In this case, a more refined "invalidate single entry" instruction is needed, so that a copy of the specific changed page-table entry can be invalidated without destroying the rest of the useful lookaside entries.

As lookasides grew larger in the early 1970's, from 8–16 entries to 128–256 entries, a second invalidation phenomenon became apparent. Tasks started with a completely invalid lookaside can be interrupted again just about the time they fill the lookaside with useful entries, so tasks may always be paying the reload cost. This has been observed on some IBM 370 operating systems that interrupt a user to handle an unrelated I/O interrupt, then immediately return to the interrupted task. Upon return, the reinitiated task runs slowly for hundreds of instructions, only perhaps to be interrupted again. Worse than the time penalty for the user task is the time penalty for the I/O service task, which *always* runs with a useless lookaside memory, because the service routine is only a few hundred instructions long, and never has an opportunity to reload the lookaside memory completely. (Exactly the same phenomenon occurs at exactly the same times in the cache memory for those systems.)

A solution is implemented in the IBM 370/168 and later machines [IBM 76]. The lookaside registers on these machines have the usual virtual-address, real-address, protection, and invalid-entry fields, but they also have a "task-id" field. This field is a short encoding of the task number or segment table pointer value. This allows the lookaside to contain mapping entries for more than one task (address space), but only those entries matching the currently running task are used. So a task such as an I/O service routine may be restarted with some of its mapping entries already in the lookaside registers, left over from the last time that task ran. Also, switching to a new task no longer requires all lookaside registers to be invalidated as part of the context switch. Instead, most registers simply will not match the new "task id," and will slowly get replaced as table entries are needed by the new task. (To remove some of the cache-reload conflicts, the cache on the 370-168 mod III is *split:* part is always used for operating system tasks, and the rest for user tasks.)

The net result of (possibly) having a set of lookaside registers is that the basic machine architecture must include one or two rather subtle invalidation instructions or mechanisms, and the operating system for that machine must use the instructions or trigger the implied mechanisms at the proper times.

This is by no means impossible to implement in the architecture of a computer, but it is a little more complicated than it would appear at first glance. Certainly, an inadequate set of invalidation instructions creates a performance problem for the operating system, and the fact that logically transparent mechanisms have substantial effects on performance makes the programmer's job harder, not easier.

Note that the collection of lookaside registers is part of a program's context registers, so that solutions for fast context swapping should ideally include these registers as part of the state swapped when a context change occurs. For practical reasons this is not done. If context swapping is eliminated by using dedicated processors for operating system and I/O functions, then the problem treated here goes away. Unfortunately, this is replaced by the entirely different problem of keeping the data in each set of lookaside registers consistent with the other sets of lookaside registers when changes occur. We have more to say about this later.

Page-Fault Interrupts   In addition to supplying a mechanism for quickly mapping a virtual address to a real address, it is necessary for a hardware/operating-system combination to provide a mechanism for handling *page faults,* i.e., for handling a reference to a word that is not currently in main memory. It is impossible to design good virtual memory hardware without thinking carefully about the exact design of the page-fault handler. In fact, it is best to write and analyze (see Chapter 11) the *complete* page-fault handler before finalizing the corresponding hardware design.

A typical page-fault handler is given control by the normal interrupt mechanism when a page-table entry specifies "this page is not in main memory." The first job for the page-fault handler is to determine which page was referenced, and then determine where it is, if anywhere. (If a segment is being lengthened, there may be no previous copy of the page.) So a requirement of the virtual-memory hardware is that there be some way to determine what page was actually referenced. On machines with *progressive indexing* (incrementing or decrementing an index register when it is used, also called *autoincrement*), or with multilevel indirect addressing, it can be difficult or impossible for a software routine to reconstruct the effective address. In such cases, the hardware state saved on interrupt must include indications of the instruction progress and the effective address involved. The early PDP-11 computers have this problem: after a normal interrupt, there is no state information saved about whether the first or second address field is being decoded, and whether the autoincrement/decrement registers have already been updated or are about to be. Later models that support virtual memory have the required mechanisms for finding the effective address and leaving the index registers in a well-defined state. The IBM 370 Load Real Address (LRA) instruction solves the problem of which page was referenced by providing the address of the segment- or page-table entry for the missing page.

A page fault typically violates an assumption made about the interrupts on a machine—a page fault can happen in the *middle* of an instruction, while other interrupts are usually constrained to happen *between* instructions. At the point of interrupt, the fault handler must determine how far the instruction has progressed, and what must be done to restart the instruction. Many instructions can be restarted simply by backing up the instruction counter (recall Section 12-4) and reexecuting the instruction from the beginning, but other instructions may have already made irrevocable changes to the registers or memory. These latter instructions *must* be restarted in the middle, and the saved state must include enough information to do this properly.

The IBM 370 Move Characters (MVC) instruction is an example of an instruction that can be prechecked for page faults. The MVC instruction moves up to 256 characters from a source field in memory to a destination field in memory. Since the IBM 370 page size is 2048 or 4096 characters, neither field can span more than two pages. Implementations of the MVC instruction can therefore precheck for page faults by accessing the first and last bytes of each field. If these four accesses create no page faults, then the operation proceeds; otherwise nothing has been moved, the page fault occurs, and the MVC can be restarted from the beginning.

On the other hand, the IBM 370 Move Characters Long (MVCL) instruction can move up to 2^{24} (16M) bytes, and operands can span far too many pages to precheck (or even have in main memory all at once). So implementations of MVCL must be able to be interrupted at every page boundary, and the saved state must include the residual source and destination addresses and lengths, to restart the instruction wherever it left off. It is most convenient if the restart information does not expand the state of the machine. Partly because of this state consideration, the MVCL instruction is defined to have its address and length arguments in the normal IBM 370 general registers, and these values are defined to be updated (changed) upon normal completion of the instruction. At the time of a page fault, these registers are set to reflect the partial completion of the move, so these modified values can be used to restart the instruction where it left off.

After a page fault is taken, enough state is saved to restart properly, and the effective address is identified, then the actual page desired must usually be brought into main memory from secondary memory. If all page frames in main memory are currently in use, then the page handler must decide upon a page to swap out first. In order to make a reasonable decision, it is useful for the page handler to have access to some usage information for the various pages in main memory. This can be as elaborate as the "time between references" clocks maintained for each page in the Ferranti, Ltd. ATLAS [Kilburn, 62] or a complete least-recently-used list as in the Control Data Corporation STAR-100 [CDC, 75], or it can be as simple as a "referenced" bit set for each page frame whenever the frame is referenced and reset periodically. In selecting a page to be swapped out, there is also some advantage in knowing whether a page has been changed since the time it was last brought in. If unchanged, the page need not be copied back out to secondary storage. Both "referenced" and "changed" information are easily maintained by hardware, and are difficult to maintain otherwise.

Another factor in the decision of which page to swap out is the fact that it is harmful to swap out a page that is going to be used immediately by the restarted instruction. Since the instruction itself may span pages, and each of two operands might also, it is easy to see that six or more pages may be required in main memory simultaneously just to execute a single instruction. The page-fault handler must be provided with enough information to determine the addresses of all these pages, so that it can make available the pages for at least one instruction to complete (or make progress, in the case of MVCL and similar instructions with operands potentially spanning more pages than there are in the real main memory) when it returns to the interrupted task.

In all cases, the address-mapping tables are part of the state of a task, and any task switch must include switching the tables. If the mapping tables are referenced indirectly via a single hardware register, then this part of the context switch can be quite fast. However, if the mapping tables must be in a large number of specific registers or specific memory locations, then context switching can be quite slow. Context switching time must be balanced against the time required by indirect memory-cycles.

Virtual Memory and I/O   A final architectural consideration in a virtual-memory system is how to map memory addresses used by I/O channels: Should channels use virtual or real addresses? If a channel uses virtual addresses, then it can transfer data directly into a task's virtual-address space, but only if the channel is provided with a consistent set of mapping tables for that address space. These must be independent of the tables used by the processor, since the processor normally executes other tasks concurrently with I/O transfers. A possible problem for channels using virtual addresses is that the address translation is too slow to keep up with a high data-rate device.

On the other hand, a channel that uses real addresses must contend with the problem of a user-task request with a buffer area that crosses a page boundary, and where the two real page frames involved are not contiguous. Either the channel must be able to transmit a single record using a list of noncontiguous data areas in memory, or the operating system must provide a contiguous real-memory buffer and then copy the data between that buffer and the user task's buffer. The operating system must also guarantee that all pages used by a channel are actually in main memory—so channel accesses never generate page faults. This can result in a large number of page frames being *locked down* (forced by software convention to stay in main memory) for many milliseconds until an I/O operation completes.

The interaction between I/O channels and cache memories is treated as a multiprocessing problem in Section 12-6.

The design of any memory system that maps addresses can become quite complex and subtle, but with some serious cooperation between computer architects and operating-system designers, the cost and efficiency goals of both can be realized.

PROBLEMS

12-10. Many machines allow no indirect addressing, or exactly one level of indirection. Others, however, allow arbitrarily long chains of indirect addresses. Assume a multiple-level indirection machine with 16 page frames of 1024 words each and a user address space of 64 pages.
  a) Describe an indirect chain of 17 elements that *always* generates a page fault no matter which 16 pages happen to be in physical main memory.
  b) What hardware is needed so that an instruction referencing such an indirect chain could actually finish executing? What cooperation is needed from the page-fault handler? What information must the hardware supply to the page-fault handler to *guarantee* that the instruction will progress toward completion?
  c) Suppose that an indirect link in a chain of indirect addresses can optionally specify incrementing the link after it is used (auto-increment). What additional hardware, if any, must you add to the answer for part *b?*
  d) Is it desirable for a virtual-memory machine to have multiple levels of indirect addressing? Why?
  e) How does the problem of indirect chains relate to the problem of implementing the MVCL instruction described in Section 12-5?

12-11. At the beginning of this section, we assumed a paging system with a 30-msec. access-time disk. Consider the effect of replacing this with a 3-msec. access-time drum.
  a) If the operating system takes 2 msec. to do a task switch, is it still desirable to switch tasks on a page fault? Explain your answer. If no, what would you do instead? How sensitive is your answer to small changes in any of the above numbers?
  b) *Page thrashing* is a situation in which almost all of a computer's time is spent switching tasks because of frequent page faults, with almost no time spent doing useful work. Explain how an operating system designed for a disk as above might page thrash when run using a drum. Explain how an operating system designed on the assumption of a 200-μsec. task-switch time might page thrash when the actual task-switch time turns out to be 10 times longer.

Most early time-sharing operating systems went through periods of dismal performance when originally optimistic design assumptions turned out to be false. The first versions of IBM's TSS/67 and HP's MPE-3000 were actually withdrawn from the market for over a year and redesigned. The lesson here is to do a substantive evaluation and modeling of design assumptions (see Chapter 11) before spending years writing an operating system.

12-12. Consider a computer system with both virtual memory and a cache. The general association between an effective address and the data at that address involves both a virtual-to-real address mapping and an address-to-data cache lookup.

a) If the virtual address is sent to the cache, the virtual-to-real address mapping (for a possible main-memory access) can be done *in parallel* with the cache lookup. If two different virtual addresses can be mapped to the *same* real address, describe how this system can produce erroneous results. How would you prevent this?

b) If the real address is sent to the cache, it is still possible to overlap the address translation and part of the cache lookup. The Amdahl 470/V6 address translation always leaves the low-order 11 address bits (page offset) unchanged. The cache is N-way associative. If some of these 11 bits are used to select one of 64 cache columns, which of the following cache steps can be overlapped with the virtual-address translation of the high-order bits?
   (1) Column select.
   (2) Read N cache-address tags in selected column.
   (3) Compare N address tags to real address.
   (4) Select one of N data lines.

c) In the system described in part b, which steps can be overlapped if some of the *mapped* address bits are used to select the column?

d) In the above system, assume that the virtual address translation is done via a two-level table lookup with TLB, as in Figure 12-18. Address translation via the TLB takes 1 clock cycle, cache fetch takes 2 clock cycles, main-memory fetch takes 5 clock cycles, and there is no time overlap between address translation and cache access for data. Address-table entries not found in the TLB may be found either in the cache or main memory, so there are five different ways for the translation to proceed (TLB, segment-table entry S in cache with page-table entry P in cache, S in cache with P in main memory, etc.) Similarly, there are two ways for data read to proceed (cache or main memory). The fastest possible read of a data item takes 3 clock cycles, 1 for TLB translation, and 2 for cache data. Assuming a TLB hit ratio of 0.90, and a cache hit ratio of 0.80, enumerate all 10 possible read patterns, the time taken for each, and the probability of each occurring. What is the average read time of this system?

12-13. The IBM 370 MVCL instruction must check for its operands crossing page boundaries, as explained in this section. The IBM 370/168 implementation of this instruction moves data in groups of eight bytes, aligned on 8-byte address boundaries. Since the page size (either 2048 or 4096 bytes) is a multiple of 8, no single group can cross a page boundary. The IBM 370/168 checks for page boundaries between each group, and in doing so, it makes the MVCL instruction slower than an equivalent software loop using the bounded-length MVC instruction (the IBM 360 software loop that was the motivation for including MVCL in the IBM 370 architecture). Suggest an alternative implementation of MVCL (other than the trivial substitution of some larger number for "8" above) which does not check for page boundaries as frequently, but which still page-faults at the proper time(s).

12-14. Consider a memory hierarchy consisting of a main memory with 1 μsec. access time, and a secondary memory built of charge-coupled devices (CCDs) with an average access time of 300 μsec.

a) If a data item is not found in the main memory, under what circumstances should the processor simply wait the 300 μsec., and under what circumstances is it better to page-fault to the operating system?

b) In each case above, should the CCD memory be connected directly to the processor-memory bus, or should it be treated as a true I/O device? Why?

12-15. The original IBM 360 architecture requires memory operands in memory-to-register instructions to be *boundary aligned,* i.e., an eight-byte long real has to start at an address that is a multiple of 8. All such operands are 2, 4, or 8 bytes long. Starting with the IBM 360/85 and continuing in the IBM 370 series, this alignment restriction was removed. Later, paging was introduced in the IBM 370 series, with page sizes of 2048 or 4096 bytes (on 2K or 4K boundaries). Discuss how nonaligned operands and page-fault checking interact to slow down *all* memory-to-register instructions on these later machines.

12-6. MULTIPLE PROCESSORS

Having multiple processors in a computer system introduces additional complications over systems with multiple tasks running on a single processor. In this section, the term "processor" is taken in a very general sense to include *any* asynchronous device that has independent access to memory. In a multiple-processor configuration, any data shared among processors may change value at any time whatsoever. This obviously complicates software interlocking. It also complicates the hardware implementation because there must be logic to arbitrate between truly simultaneous requests.

In a configuration with two processors and a shared memory, disabling the interrupt system on the first processor no longer guarantees *per se* that adding an item to a common queue is not corrupted by the concurrent addition of another item, since another task can now be running on the second processor. Thus, in a multiple-processor environment, the first two interlocking solutions given in Section 12-2 simply do not work correctly. Solutions using Test And Set or Compare And Swap instructions work, so long as the critical read-modify-write sequence of these instructions cannot be interlaced with accesses to the same location by other processors. This in turn implies a special kind of memory-bus protocol, or a carefully designed multiple-port memory.

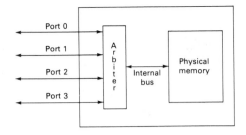

Figure 12-20   A four-port memory system, with four distinct external busses

In a system with a single shared memory bus, as shown in Figure 4-9, it is necessary for one of the bus-control lines to mean, "Some device has control of this bus, and no other device may access memory until this signal goes away." A processor executing an interlock instruction must assert this signal continuously during both the read and write portions of the instruction, thus preventing an update error due to access by another process. (Any error in removing this signal creates a resource-hogging problem.)

Alternately, a shared-memory system may be built with multiple ports instead of a shared bus (see Figure 12-20). In a four-part memory system, there are four distinct memory buses, each with its own set of address, data, and control lines. One of the control lines has the meaning "I want to do a memory access now." Part of the memory system watches all four such lines, and whenever exactly one line is asserted, this *arbiter* connects the corresponding address and data lines to the single bus inside the memory system. If requests from two different ports overlap, the arbiter is responsible for choosing between simultaneous requests and for delaying the second request until the first completes. Each requester (processor) must be able to tolerate these delays. Details on how this is done appear in Chapter 6.

There is a fundamental problem in trying to build arbiters out of physical components. If two external, asynchronous requests arrive at precisely the same time, any physical arbiter may hesitate in a *metastable state* (between binary 1 and 0) trying to decide which request arrived first [Chaney et al., 72]. Although this hesitation may often be shorter than a microsecond, *there is no upper bound* on the duration of the metastable state in real components. If the arbitration or other synchronization system is built assuming that some decision will be made after a *fixed* amount of time (i.e., by the time the next clock pulse comes along), and the probability of nearly simultaneous events is high, then the system can be noticeably unreliable. In truly asynchronous systems, the arbitration problem can be minimized or eliminated through detecting the metastable state and not triggering (starting) the subsequent series of clock pulses until the metastable resolves itself, if ever. This is slightly different from delaying or ignoring an existing series of clock pulses during the metastable state, since gating a running clock pulse only introduces another arbitration problem.

A shared memory can be used by two CPUs, but it can also be used by other kinds of generalized processors. One such application is the refreshing of dynamic memories, which require that every location (or row of locations) be accessed periodically, every few milliseconds. One way to perform refreshing is to interrupt the normal processing periodically and branch to a small loop which reads every memory row once, then return to the interrupted program. This method has the disadvantage that all useful processing is locked out while hundreds of refresh memory cycles occur. This may be unacceptable in real-time systems or during an I/O transfer. Another method is to build a shared-memory system in which one of the "processors" is simply a refresh access generator consisting of an address counter and a slow clock. This processor requests a single memory access every 30–100 microseconds, such that the total memory is refreshed every few milliseconds. Thus, the refresh cycles are distributed in time, so that no processor is locked out for more than a few memory cycles at a time, and this occasional lockout is handled by standard arbitration logic.

An I/O channel is a separate processor in the sense of this section—it accesses a shared memory concurrently with accesses by a CPU. This causes the usual problem that data being read or written by the I/O channel may change at arbitrary times, interfering with CPU use of the same data. This particular problem rarely occurs in practice, because an operating system is designed to withhold access to data while they are actively being transmitted to an I/O device (i.e., semaphores are not kept in I/O buffers). There is, however, a related problem that must be solved for machines with cache memories.

If a CPU writes a block of data into a main-memory I/O buffer, then starts an I/O channel copying that data to an external device, the data are transferred reliably with a standard memory. However, if the main memory has an associated cache memory, then the data stored by the CPU may still be in the cache, but not yet in main memory, when the channel (or other processor) is started. If the channel accesses only main memory and not the cache, then the wrong data will be transferred.

As usual, there are various solutions to this problem. The channels in the Amdahl 470 series [Amdahl, 76] go directly to the cache, and from there to main memory as needed. In this arrangement, the existence of a cache memory is completely transparent to the channel. However, the existence of the channel is not transparent to the cache: there is the potential problem of the channel generating so many memory requests that the cache is overloaded, either in terms of spending almost every available memory cycle servicing the I/O channel(s), or in terms of allocating almost all the space in the cache to I/O data instead of CPU data. (It turns out that the Amdahl 470/V6 is well balanced; the fairly low 10-megabyte maximum aggregate channel rate represents only about 4% of the available cache cycles.)

The cache memories in the IBM 370 series always do a *write-through* when writing into the cache. This means that any data stored by the CPU goes both to the cache and to the main memory. The I/O channels thus always access the proper data when transferring *from* main memory to an external device. However, if an I/O channel transfers *into* main memory, it is possible that the CPU will read old data from the cache. Write-through helps output writes, but not input reads. The operating system can always keep the data straight by flushing the cache before and after each I/O transfer, but this requires an explicit "cache invalidate" instruction and the attendant performance penalty, analogous to the use of lookaside registers in Section 12-5.

Alternately, during input the channel can write data into the main memory and send a series of "I modified the data at this address" messages to the cache. The cache mechanism responds to these "shoulder-tapping" messages by selectively invalidating or reloading any copies of those words that it happens to contain.

In general, a computer system with multiple processors can have a single cache accessed by all processors, or each processor can have its own private cache along with some way to maintain proper control over copies of data in the other caches. With a single cache, the design constraint is to make the cache fast enough to handle the increased load of multiple processors. With multiple private caches, hardware designers could ignore the coordination problem and make the operating system(s) force cache invalidations when necessary, or the hardware designers can provide shoulder-tapping between the various processors. In the shoulder-tapping scheme, every store into the cache for one processor does a store-through to the shared main memory and transmits a message to all the other caches, telling them the address of the datum just modified. These messages essentially say, "If you have a copy of this word, mark it invalid, so it must be refetched from the shared main memory." The shoulder-tapping traffic rate can be quite high—in a system with four processors and four caches, each cache must be able to handle one data access from its own processor and three shoulder taps from the others during every memory cycle. Unless shoulder taps are implemented to be faster than a regular cache access, it is cheaper to build a single shared cache.

A similar problem occurs with memory-mapping tables—processor 1 may change an entry in a page table while processor 2 is using that table, and in fact has a copy of the changed entry in a lookaside register. There must be some way for processor 1 to signal processor 2 that such a change has occurred. Sometimes this requires a "signal other processor" instruction, which the operating system executes at the appropriate times.

We have again seen an example of our general design principle:

If a datum is copied and the copy is to match the original at all times, then all changes to the original must cause the copy to be immediately updated or invalidated.

Multiple processor systems present another level of sharing and separation complexity over single processors. The computer architect must have a clear understanding of the additional problems in order to present the operating-system writer with an acceptable foundation.

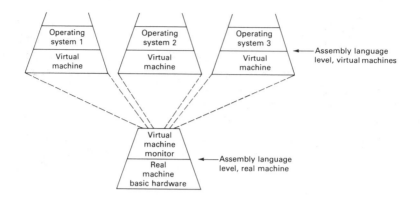

Figure 12-21 Three virtual machines simulated on one real machine
(compare with Figure 12-1)

12-7. VIRTUAL MACHINES

The sharing and separation aspects of virtual memories and multiple
processors can be extended one step further to the concept of entire *virtual
machines* [Parmelee et al., 72; Goldberg, 73], in which each user is presented
with the illusion of a complete raw machine, as shown in Figure 12-21. By
a combination of software and hardware, many virtual machines can be
simulated on a single real machine (or even on a multiprocessor configuration). The software to accomplish this is called a Virtual-Machine Monitor
(VMM). The protection advantages of separate address spaces are extended
one level further, so that each user appears to have his own machine, on
which even a simple unprotected operating system can be run without any
possibility of interfering with other users. If the virtual machine presented
matches the real machine in exacting detail, it is even possible to debug
new versions of the virtual-machine monitor itself on a virtual machine instead
of a real one. This can be a great benefit in the secure development of those
parts of an operating system that interface directly with the raw machine, and
thus run completely unprotected. Virtual machines can also be used to test
software on many different virtual-hardware configurations, without need to
acquire the corresponding physical hardware.

In essence, a virtual-machine monitor works by *interpreting* each user's
program, mapping each virtual-machine memory address to a real-machine
address, mapping each virtual-machine register to a real-machine copy (perhaps in main memory), mapping each virtual-machine I/O device to a
(portion of) a real-machine I/O device, and simulating each instruction so that
its effects are reflected in the copies of the memory and hardware state for
the appropriate virtual machine. We will call this process "*virtualizing* a real
machine." For example, each of three users might believe that he is running
on a machine with its memory-bounds register set to $<2000,3999>$, while

in fact the three users' sets of information are stored in real locations $<1000,2999>$, $<3000,4999>$, and $<5000,6999>$. The virtual-machine monitor simply loads the real machine's bounds register with the proper pair before initiating a user's program, and that user does not know the difference.

For this scheme to work properly, each user-program read of the (virtual) bounds register must trap to the VMM, which supplies $<2000,3999>$ instead. Similarly, each user-program write of the bounds register must trap to the VMM, which keeps a private copy of the bounds-register value that each user thinks he has. A user's change to his virtual bounds register will in general trigger the VMM's changing the real bounds register the next time that user is initiated. An architecture that is missing some of these crucial traps cannot support virtual machines.

In order to simulate virtual machines efficiently, it is necessary in practice that most user-program instructions execute directly on the real machine, with no intervention from the VMM. Only when the user program executes a certain class of *privileged* or *sensitive* instructions (detailed below) need the VMM gain control. To as large an extent as possible, the real machine's hardware is used to perform the above mappings from virtual resources to real ones, since they otherwise entail a severe performance overhead. For example, any address-translation mechanism available on the real machine is used to map virtual-machine addresses (including virtual-machine virtual addresses) to real-machine addresses. The page-table manipulation required for this is straightforward, but the part of the virtual-machine monitor that handles page-fault interrupts must distinguish between those that must be handled directly (the same user program running on a real machine would not have encountered that page fault) and those that must be passed back to a virtual machine in the form of a page fault on the simulated configuration.

By far the largest performance overhead in providing virtual machines comes from the need to execute operating-system programs in user mode, thus causing a trap whenever a privileged operation is executed or a memory-protected storage area is accessed. If the raw hardware architecture requires a long sequence of such instructions in order to perform some common function, such as an I/O transfer, then the trapping overhead may be excessive. To alleviate part of this overhead, a few models of the IBM 370 series include "VM accelerator" microcode to execute some common privileged instructions directly in user mode without trapping at all.

Another performance problem occurs if the architecture requires real-time, nonbuffered responses to bits or words involved in I/O. For example, some common I/O sequences in the IBM 370 involve the CPU's changing a chain of channel commands as the channel executes the chain. Obviously, this cannot be simulated properly if the real I/O channel is given a *copy* of the channel-command chain (with real-device addresses and main-memory addresses) and the virtual-machine program that modifies the chain operates on the *original* chain (with virtual-device and memory addresses). To "solve" this particular problem, the dynamically-modified channel programs generated within IBM's standard operating systems are specifically simulated so that they work properly, and other such channel programs are not guaranteed to work as specified on a real IBM 370.

A second real-time example is found on the PDP-11, which performs I/O by setting and reading special bits in the uppermost 4K words of the machine's address space. In order to allow a virtual-machine monitor to map from virtual I/O devices to real ones, user programs must be prevented from using the uppermost 4K of the address space on the real machine. This can be prevented either through address mapping or through memory protection, but in either case, it requires a trap to the VMM whenever a memory location within the upper 4K is referenced. Since I/O sequences in general involve real-time changes to some of the bits in this address region (such as a "busy" bit set or reset by an external device), trapping to the monitor can result in unacceptably slow CPU response, resulting in turn in lost data characters or missed disk revolutions. The architectural problems of virtualizing a PDP-11 are in fact quite varied, ranging from the problem mentioned in Section 12-5 about saving the machine state of half-done instructions when page faults occur, to the problem of needing memory protection at the word or bit level instead of the page level for the uppermost 4K word addresses [Bell and Strecker, 76].

In order for a machine architecture to be virtualizable, it must not allow one user to be able to interfere with the state of another user task, and any such attempts must cause a trap to the VMM. We assume that the architecture has a *system mode* vs. *user mode* distinction, as in Section 12-3, and that privileged instructions are those that are illegal (trap) in user mode. Then an architecture with a nonprivileged HALT instruction cannot be virtualized, since any virtual program that executes a HALT stops the entire real machine, not just one user's virtual machine. In a similar way, an architecture that simply treats privileged instructions executed in user mode as NOPs (such as the Cray-1 for some instructions) cannot be successfully virtualized, since control will not be passed to the VMM to simulate that privileged instruction.

If all privileged instructions trap to the VMM, and the right instructions are privileged, then an architecture can be successfully virtualized [Popek and Goldberg, 74]. Briefly, all the *sensitive* instructions in an architecture must also be privileged, where a sensitive instruction is one that (1) affects the processor mode (system or user), or (2) changes the amount of protected resources available, or one whose behaviour is (3) dependent on its location in real memory, or (4) dependent on the current processor mode. Some existing machines have sensitive instructions that are not privileged, so these machines can never be virtualized. For example, the PDP-10 "return to user mode" instruction (JRST 1) does not trap when executed in user mode. So the VMM does not have a chance to change the *simulated* mode, and hence may simulate a later privileged instruction that should have been refused. The interested reader is referred to the Popek and Goldberg paper for more details.

If the underlying architecture can in fact be virtualized, then presenting users with a complete and exact virtual machine can be the basis for a particularly secure mode of operation, and an effective tool for developing operating systems.

PROBLEMS

12-16. In simulating a virtual machine with a real-time clock, what clock value should be supplied, the real-machine time-of-day (wall clock), or the virtual time-of-day (which does not increment when other virtual machines are running)? Suggest other areas in which a virtual machine cannot match a real machine in exact detail.

12-17. If a real machine has a hardware-state bit (perhaps overflow-interrupt mask) that can be set by a nonprivileged instruction, but cannot be read at all (and is not saved by the context switch hardware), can such a machine be virtualized? Can it if the bit is set only by privileged instructions? Explain your answers.

12-18. If an I/O error is detected in a virtual machine system, can the error be passed back to one of the virtual machines, or must it be handled only by the VMM? If the error is passed back to a virtual machine, and the operating system running on that machine tries to perform an error-recovery sequence for disk device type A, when this virtual device is actually being mapped to a real device of type B, what must the VMM do in order for the error-recovery procedure to be successful?

Bibliography

Abate, J., and Dubner, H. 1969. Optimizing the performance of a drum-like storage. *IEEE Trans. on Comp.* C-18:992–97.

Allison, D. R. 1977. A design philosophy for microcomputer architectures. *IEEE Computer,* February 1977, pp. 35–41.

Allmark, R. H., and Lucking, J. R. 1962. Design of an arithmetic unit incorporating a nesting store. *Proc. IFIP,* pp. 694–98. Reprinted in Bell and Newell (1971).

Almasi, G. S.; Keefe, G. E.; Lin, Y.; and Thompson, D. A. 1970. A magnetoresistive detector for bubble domains. Presented at 16th Annual Conference on Magnetism and Magnetic Materials, November 1970, at Miami Beach, Fla.

Amdahl Corporation. 1976. *Amdahl 470 V/6 machine reference manual.* Form number MRM 100-1.

Amelio, G. F.; Tompsett, M. F.; and Smith, G. E. 1970. Experimental verification of the charge coupled device concept. *Bell Sys. Tech. J.* 49:593–600.

Arbuckle, R. A. 1966. Computer analysis and thruput evaluation. *Computers and Automation,* January 1966, pp. 12–15.

Aschenbrenner, R. A.; Amiot, L.; and Natarajan, N. K. 1971. The neurotron monitor system. *AFIPS Conf. Proc., 1971 FJCC* 39:31–37. Montvale, N. J.: AFIPS Press.

Avizienis, A. 1964. Binary-compatible signed-digit arithmetic. *AFIPS Conf. Proc., 1964 FJCC* 26:663–72. Baltimore: Spartan Books.

Ayling, J., and Moore, R. D. 1971. Main monolithic memory. *IEEE J. of Solid-State Circuits* SC-6:276–79.

Bailey, F. R. 1977. Computational aerodynamics—ILLIAC IV and beyond. *COMPCON 77 Digest of Papers,* IEEE Computer Society International Conference, February 1977, San Francisco, pp. 8–11.

Barnes, G. H. et al. 1968. The ILLIAC IV computer. *IEEE Trans. on Comp.* C-17:746–57.

Barton, R. 1961. A new approach to the functional design of a digital computer. *AFIPS Conf. Proc., 1961 Western Joint Computer Conference* 19:393.

Bashkow, T. R. et al. 1967. System design of a FORTRAN machine. *IEEE Trans. on Comp.* EC-16:485–99.

Baskett, F., and Keller, T. W. 1977. An evaluation of the CRAY-1 computer. In *High Speed Computer and Algorithm Organization,* edited by D. J. Kuck et al., pp. 71–84. New York: Academic Press.

Bass, C. 1976. Microprocessor architecture vs. high-level language execution. *1976 Wescon Professional Program,* Session 28/0, September 1976, Los Angeles, Calif.

Batcher, K. E. 1968. Sorting networks and their applications. *AFIPS Conf. Proc., 1968 SJCC* 32:307–14. Washington, D.C.: Thompson Books.

Bauer, F. L. 1960. The formula-controlled logical computer "Stanislaus." *Mathematical Tables and Other Aids to Computation* 14:64–67.

Beausoleil, W. F.; Brown, D. T.; and Phelps, B. E. 1972. Magnetic bubble memory organization. *IBM J. of Res. and Dev.* 16:587–91.

Belady, L. A. 1966. A study of replacement algorithms for a virtual-storage computer. *IBM Sys. J.* 5:78–101.

Bell, C. G., and Newell, A. 1971. *Computer structures: readings and examples.* New York: McGraw-Hill.

Bell, C. G., and Strecker, W. D. 1976. Computer structures: what have we learned from the PDP-11? *Proc., 3rd Annual Symposium on Computer Architecture,* 1976, pp. 1–14.

Benes, V. E. 1965. *Mathematical theory of connecting networks and telephone traffic.* New York: Academic Press.

Berkeley, E. C., and Bobrow, D. G., eds. 1964. *The programming language LISP: its operation and applications.* Cambridge, Mass.: Information International, Inc.

Blake, R. P. 1977. Exploring a stack architecture. *Computer,* May 1977, pp. 30–39.

Bobeck, A. H. 1970*a.* The magnetic bubble. *Bell Lab. Record,* June/July 1970, p. 163.

———. 1970*b.* A second look at magnetic bubbles. *IEEE Trans. on Magnetics* MAG-6:445–46.

Bobeck, A., and Scovil, H. 1971. Magnetic bubbles. *Scientific American,* June 1971, pp. 78–90.

Bobeck, A. H. et al. 1969. Application of orthoferrites to domain-wall devices. *IEEE Trans. on Magnetics* MAG-5:544–53.

Bobeck, A. H. et al. 1970. Uniaxial magnetic garnets for domain wall "bubble" devices. *Applied Physics Letters* 17:131–34.

Bossen, D. C.; Chang, L. C.; and Chen, C. L. 1978. Measurement and generation of error correcting codes for package failures. *IEEE Trans. on Comp.,* C-27:201–4.

Bowers, D. M. 1973. An analysis of computer terminals. *The Office,* October 1973, pp. 89–124.

Boyle, W. S., and Smith, G. E. 1970. Charge coupled semiconductor devices. *Bell Sys. Tech. J.* 49:587–93.

Bremer, J. 1970. A survey of mainframe semiconductor memories. *Computer Design,* May 1970, pp. 63–73.

Brinch Hansen, P. 1971. Short term scheduling in multiprogramming systems. *Third ACM Symposium on Operating Systems Principles,* 1971, Stanford University, Stanford, Calif., pp. 101–5.

Broadbent, K. D., and McClung, F. J. 1960. A thin magnetic-film shift register. *1960 International Solid-State Circuits Conference, Digest of Technical Papers,* February 1960, pp. 24–25.

Brown, D. T.; Eibsen, R. L.; and Thorn, C. A. 1972. Channel and direct access device architecture. *IBM Sys. J.* 11:186–99.

Brown, D. T., and Sellers, F. F. 1970. Error correction for IBM 800 bit per inch magnetic tape. *IBM J. of Res. and Dev.* 14:384–89.

Brown, J. L. et al. 1964. IBM System/360 engineering. *AFIPS Conf. Proc., 1964 FJCC* 26: 205–32. Baltimore: Spartan Books.

Bryan, G. E. 1967. JOSS: 20,000 hours at a console—a statistical summary. *AFIPS Conf. Proc., 1967 FJCC* 31:769–77. Montvale, N.J.: AFIPS Press.

Buchholz, W. 1962. *Planning a computer system.* New York: McGraw-Hill, 1962.
———. 1969. A synthetic job for measuring system performance. *IBM Sys. J.* 8:309–18.

Buchholz, W. 1969. A synthetic job for measuring system performance. *IBM Sys. J.* 8:309–18.

Budnick, P., and Kuck, D. J. 1971. The organization and use of parallel memories. *IEEE Trans. on Comp.* C-20:1566–69.

Burks, A. W.; Goldstine, H. H.; and von Neumann, J. 1946. Preliminary discussion of the logical design of an electronic computing instrument. *U.S. Army Ordnance Department Report,* 1946. Reprinted in Bell and Newell (1971), pp. 92–119.

Burton, H. O., and Sullivan, D. D. 1972. Errors and error control. *Proc. of the IEEE* 60:1293–1301.

Buzen, J. P. 1973. Computational algorithms for closed queueing networks with exponential servers. *Communications of the ACM* 16:527–31.

Calingaert, P. 1967. System performance evaluation: survey and appraisal. *Communications of the ACM* 10:12–18.

Campbell, S. G.; Herwitz, P. S.; and Pomerene, J. H. 1962. A nonarithmetical system extension. In *Planning a computer system: Project STRETCH,* edited by W. Buchholz, pp. 254–71. New York: McGraw-Hill.

Cantrell, H. N., and Ellison, A. L. 1968. Multiprogramming system performance measurement and analysis. *AFIPS Conf. Proc., 1968 SJCC* 32:213–21. Washington, D.C.: Thompson Books.

Chaney, T. S.; Ornstein, S. M.; and Littlefield, W. M. 1972. Beware the synchronizer. *COMPCON 72 Digest of Papers, 6th annual IEEE Computer Society International Conference,* September 1972, San Francisco, pp. 317–19.

Chang, H.; Fox, J.; Lu, D.; and Rosier, L. L. 1971. A self-contained magnetic bubble domain memory chip. Presented at the Solid-State Circuits Conference, February 1971, at Philadelphia, Pa.

Chen, T. C. 1964. The overlap design of the IBM System/360 Model 92 central processing unit. *AFIPS Conf. Proc., 1964 FJCC* 26 (part II): 73–80. Washington, D.C.: Spartan Books.

———. 1971. Parallelism, pipelining, and computer efficiency. *Computer Design,* January 1971, pp. 69–74.

Chen, T. C., and Chang, H. 1978. Magnetic bubble memory and logic. In *Advances in Computers,* vol. 17, pp. 223–82. New York: Academic Press.

Cheng, P. S. 1969. Trace-driven system modeling. *IBM Sys. J.* 8:280–89.

Chien, R. T. 1973. Memory error control: beyond parity. *IEEE Spectrum,* July 1973, pp. 18–23.

Christopherson, W. 1961. Matrix switch and drive system for a low-cost magnetic-core memory. *IRE Trans. on Elec. Comp.* EC-10:238–46.

Chu, Y. 1962. *Digital computer design fundamentals.* New York: McGraw-Hill.

————. 1975. *High-level language computer architecture*. New York: Academic Press.

Clare, C. R. 1973. *Designing logic systems using state machines*. New York: McGraw-Hill.

Clos, C. 1953. A study of non-blocking switching networks. *Bell Sys. Tech. J.* 32:406–24.

Coffman, E. G., and Denning, P. J. 1973. *Operating systems theory*. pp. 209–18. Englewood Cliffs, N.J.: Prentice-Hall.

Coffman, E. G., Jr.; Elphick, M. J.; and Shoshani, A. 1971. System deadlocks. *Computing Surveys* 3:67–78.

Coffman, E. G., and Kleinrock, L. 1968. Feedback queueing models for time-shared systems. *J. of the ACM* 15:549–76.

Collins, D. R. et al. 1974. Electrical characteristics of 500-bit $Al - Al_2 O_3 - Al$ CCD shift registers. *Proc. of the IEEE* 62:282–84.

Computer Design 1970. Faster, simpler magnetic memory developed. May 1970, p. 26.

Conti, C. 1969. Concepts for buffer storage. *IEEE Comp. Group News*, March 1969, pp. 9–13.

Control Data Corporation. 1975. *STAR-100 computer hardware reference manual*. Form number 60256000-09.

Conway, M. E. 1963. A multiprocessor system design. *AFIPS Conf. Proc., 1963 FJCC* 24:139–46. Baltimore: Spartan Books.

Conway, R. W.; Maxwell, W. L.; and Miller, L. W. 1967. *Theory of scheduling*. Reading, Mass.: Addison-Wesley.

Cook, R. W., and Flynn, M. J. 1970. System design of a dynamic microprocessor. *IEEE Trans. on Comp.* C-19:213–22.

Coonen, J., et al. 1979. A proposed standard for binary floating-point arithmetic. ACM SIGNUM newsletter, Special Issue, October 1979, pp. 4–12.

Corbato, F. J., et al. 1962. An experimental time-sharing system. *AFIPS Conf. Proc., 1962 SJCC* 21:335–44.

Corbato, F. J.; Clinger, C. T.; and Saltzer, J. H. 1972. MULTICS—the first seven years. *AFIPS Conf. Proc., 1972 SJCC* 40:571–84.

Corbato, F. J., and Vyssotsky, V. A. 1965. Introduction and overview of the MULTICS system. *AFIPS Conf. Proc., 1965 FJCC* 27:185–96.

Cotten, L. W. 1965. Circuit implementation of high-speed pipeline systems. *AFIPS Conf. Proc., 1965 FJCC* 27 (part I): 489–504. Washington, D.C.: Spartan Books.

Cox, D. R., and Smith, W. L. 1961. *Queues*. London: Methuen and Co. Ltd. and New York: Wiley.

Crane, M. A., and Iglehart, D. L. 1974. Simulating stable stochastic systems. *J. of the ACM* 21:103–23.

Cyre, W. R., and Lipovski, G. J. 1972. On generating multipliers for a cellular fast Fourier transform processor. *IEEE Trans. on Comp.* C-21:83–87.

Dahl, O., and Nygaard, K. 1966. SIMULA—an ALGOL-based simulation language. *Communications of the ACM* 9:671–78.

Daley, R. C., and Dennis, J. B. 1968. Virtual memory, processes, sharing in MULTICS. *Communications of the ACM* 11:306.

DataPRO Research Corp., Delran, N.J. 1979.

Davidson, E. S.; Shar, L. E.; Thomas, A. T.; and Patel, J. H. 1975. Effective control for pipelined computers. *COMPCON 75 Digest of Papers,* IEEE Computer Society International Conference, February 1975, San Francisco, pp. 181–84.

Davies, P. M. 1972. Readings in microprogramming. *IBM Sys. J.* 11:16–40.

Denning, P. 1970. Virtual memory. *Computing Surveys* 2:153–89.

Dennis, J. B., and Misunas, D. P. 1975. A preliminary architecture for a basic dataflow processor. *Proc., 2nd Annual Symposium on Computer Architecture,* 1975, Houston, Texas, pp. 126–32.

Dennis, J. B., and Van Horn, E. C. 1966. Programming semantics for multiprogrammed computations. *Communications of the ACM* 3:143–55.

Dennis, J. B., and Weng, K. K.-S. 1977. Application of dataflow computation to the weather problem. In *High Speed Computer and Algorithm Organization,* edited by D. J. Kuck et al., pp. 143–57. New York: Academic Press.

Digital Equipment Corporation. 1973. *PDP-11 peripherals handbook.* Maynard, Mass.

Dijkstra, E. W. 1968. Cooperating sequential processes. In *Programming Languages,* edited by F. Genuys, pp. 43–112. New York: Academic Press.

Drummond, M. E. 1973. *Evaluation and measurement techniques for digital computer systems.* Englewood Cliffs, N.J.: Prentice-Hall.

Electronics Industries Association. 1969. RS-232-C standard interface between data terminal equipment and data communications equipment employing serial binary data interchange. Electronics Industries Association, August 1969.

Estrin, G.; Hopkins, D.; Coggan, B.; and Crocker, S. D. 1967. Snuper computer— a computer in instrumentation automation. *AFIPS Conf. Proc., 1967 SJCC* 30:645–56. Washington, D.C.: Thompson Books.

Fabry, R. S. 1974. Capability-based addressing. *Communications of the ACM* 17:403–11.

Faggin, F. 1978. How VLSI impacts computer architecture. *IEEE Spectrum, May* 1978, pp. 28–31.

Farber, A. S., and Schlig, E. S. 1972. A novel high-performance bipolar monolithic memory cell. *IEEE J. of Solid-State Circuits* SC-7:297–98.

Farina, M. V. 1968. *Programming in Basic, the time-sharing language.* Englewood Cliffs, N.J.: Prentice-Hall.

Feierbach, G., and Stevenson, D. K. 1978. The Phoenix array processing system. *Phoenix Project Memo. 7,* NASA Ames Research Center, November 1978, Mountain View, Calif.

Fishman, G. S. 1967. Problems in the statistical analysis of simulation experiments: the comparison of means and the length of sample records. *Communications of the ACM* 10:94–99.

———. 1973. *Concepts and methods in discrete event digital simulation.* New York: Wiley.

Flynn, M. J. 1966. Very high-speed computing systems. *Proc. of the IEEE* 54:1901–9.

Flynn, M. J. 1974. Trends and problems in computer organization. *Proc. of the 1974 IFIPs Congress,* pp. 3–10.

Flynn, M. J. 1977. The interpretive interface: resources and program representation in computer organization. In *High Speed Computer and Algorithm Organization,* edited by D. J. Kuck et al., New York: Academic Press. pp. 41–69.

Flynn, M. J.; Podvin, A.; and Shimizu, K. 1970. A multiple instruction stream with shared resources. In *Parallel Processor Systems, Technologies, and Applications*, edited by L. C. Hobbs, pp. 251–86. Washington, D.C.: Spartan Books.

Flynn, M. J., and Rosin, R. F. 1971. Microprogramming: an introduction and a viewpoint. *IEEE Trans. on Comp.* C-20:727–31.

Foster, C. C. 1970. *Computer architecture.* New York: Van Nostrand Reinhold.

Foster, C. C.; Gonter, R. H.; and Riseman, E. M. 1971. Measures of op-code utilization. *IEEE Trans. on Comp.* C-20:582–84.

Freiser, M., and Marcus, P. 1969. A survey of some physical limitations on computer elements. *IEEE Trans. on Magnetics* MAG-5:82–90.

Fuller, S. H., and Baskett, F. 1975. An analysis of drum storage units. *J. of the ACM* 22:83–105.

Fuller, S. H.; Swan, R. J.; and Wulf, W. A. 1973. The instrumentation of C. mmp, a multi-(mini)processor. *COMPCON 73 Digest of Papers*, 7th Annual IEEE Computer Society International Conference, March 1973, San Francisco. pp. 173–76.

Fuller, S. H., et al. 1977. Evaluation of computer architectures via test programs. *AFIPS Conf. Proc., 1977 NCC* 46:161–73. Montvale, N.J.: AFIPS Press.

Gary, J. M. 1977. Analysis of applications programs and software requirements for high speed computers. In *High Speed Computer and Algorithm Organization*, edited by D. J. Kuck et al., pp. 329–54. New York: Academic Press.

Gear, C. W. 1969. *Computer organization and programming.* New York: McGraw-Hill.

Gelberger, P. P., and Salama, C. A. T. 1972. A uniphase charge-coupled device. *Proc. of the IEEE* 60:721–22.

Gibson, J. C. 1970. The Gibson mix. TR 00.2043. Systems Development Div., IBM Corp., Poughkeepsie, N.Y., June 18, 1970.

Gilligan, T. J. 1966. $2\frac{1}{2}$ D high speed memory systems—past, present, and future. *IEEE Trans. on Elec. Comp.* EC-15:475–85.

Goldberg, R. P. 1973. Architecture of virtual machines. *AFIPS Conf. Proc., 1973 National Computer Conference* 42:309–18. Montvale, N.J.: AFIPS Press.

Gordon, G. 1969. *System simulation.* Englewood Cliffs, N.J.: Prentice-Hall.

Gordon, W. J., and Newell, G. F. 1967. Closed queueing systems with exponential servers. *Operations Research* 15:254–65.

Gray, J. P. 1972. Line control procedures. *Proc. of the IEEE* 60:1301–12.

Greenberger, M. 1965. Method in randomness. *Communications of the ACM* 8:177–79.

Gregory, J. 1972. A comparison of floating point summation methods. *Communications of the ACM* 15:838.

Hallin, T. G., and Flynn, M. J. 1972. Pipelining of arithmetic functions. *IEEE Trans. on Comp.* C-21:880–86.

Hamilton, P. A., and Kernighan, B. W. 1973. Synthetically generated performance test loads for operating systems. *1st Annual SIGME Symposium on Measurement and Evaluation*, February 1973, Palo Alto, Calif., pp. 121–26.

Hamming, R. W. 1950. Error detecting and error correcting codes. *Bell Sys. Tech. J.* 29:147–60.

Hauck, E. A., and Dent, B. A. 1968. Burroughs' B6500/B7500 stack mechanism. *AFIPS Conf. Proc., 1968 SJCC* 32:245–51. Washington, D.C.: Thompson Books.

Heart, F. E.; Ornstein, S. M.; Crowther, W. R.; and Barker, W. B. 1973. A new minicomputer/multiprocessor for the ARPA network. *AFIPS Conf. Proc., 1973 NCC* 42:529–37.

Hellerman, H. 1973. *Digital computer system principles.* 2nd ed. p. 245. New York: McGraw-Hill.

Hendrickson, C. P. 1977. When you wish upon a star. *COMPCON 77 Digest of Papers*, IEEE Computer Society International Conference, February 1977, San Francisco, pp. 4–7.

Higashi, P. 1966. A thin-film rod memory for the NCR 315 RMC computer. *IEEE Trans. on Elec. Comp.* EC-15:459–67.

Hintz, R. G., and Tate, D. P. 1972. Control Data STAR-100 processor design. *COMPCON 72 Digest of Papers*, 6th Annual IEEE Computer Society International Conference, September 1972, San Francisco, pp. 1–4.

Hoagland, A. 1963. *Digital magnetic recording.* New York: Wiley.

———. 1972. Mass storage—past, present, and future. *AFIPS Conf. Proc., 1972 FJCC* 41 (part II):985–91. Montvale, N.J.: AFIPS Press.

Hodges, D. A. 1968. Large-capacity semiconductor memory. *Proc. of the IEEE* 56:1148–62.

Hoevel, L. 1973. Ideal directly executed languages: an analytic argument for emulation. Computer Research Report #29. Electrical Engineering Dept., The Johns Hopkins University, Baltimore, Md., December 1973.

Hoevel, L. W. 1978. Directly executed languages. Ph.D. thesis in Electrical Engineering Department, The Johns Hopkins University, Baltimore, Maryland.

Hoevel, L. W., and Flynn, M. J. 1977. The structure of directly executed languages: a new theory of interpretive system design. DSL Technical Report #130, Stanford University, March 1977.

Hratek, E. R. 1977. *A user's handbook of semiconductor memories.* New York: Wiley.

Hsiao, M. Y. 1970. A class of optimal minimum odd-weight-column SEC-DEC codes. *IBM J. of Res. and Dev.* 14:395–401.

Husson, S. S. 1970. *Microprogramming: principles and practices.* Englewood Cliffs, N.J.: Prentice-Hall.

Hwang, K. 1979. Computer arithmetic: principles, architecture, and design. New York: Wiley.

IBM Corporation. 1970. *IBM System/370 principles of operation.* Form number GA22-7000.

IBM Corporation. 1976. *IBM System/370 model 168 functional characteristics.* Form number GA22-7010-4.

IBM Corporation. 1977. IBM 3838 array processor functional characteristics. GA24-3639-1, file number S370-08.

IBM Corporation. 1978. *Series/1 digest.* Form number G360-0061-1.

IEEE Trans. on Comp. 1971 and 1973. Special issues on fault tolerant computing. Vols. C-20 and C-22.

Iliffe, J. 1968. *Basic machine principles.* New York: American Elsevier.

Iverson, K. 1962. *A programming language.* New York: Wiley.

Iverson, K., and Brooks, F. P. 1965. *Automatic data processing.* Ch. 8, Sect. 2. New York: Wiley.

Jackson, J. R. 1963. Jobshop-like queueing systems. *Management Science*, October 1963, pp. 131–42.

Jewell, W. S. 1967. A simple proof of: $L = \lambda W$. *Operations Research* 15:1109–16.

Johnson, J. B. 1971. The contour model of block structured processes. *SIGPLAN Notices* 6:52–82.

Johnson, R. R. 1970. Needed: a measure for measure. *Datamation*, December 15, 1970, pp. 22–30.

Jones, L. H. et al. 1972. An annotated bibliography on microprogramming: late 1969–early 1972. *SIGMICRO Newsletter (ACM)*, July 1972, pp. 39–55.

Jones, L. H., and Carvin, K. 1973. An annotated bibliography on microprogramming II: early 1972–early 1973. *SIGMICRO Newsletter (ACM)*, July 1973, pp. 7–18.

Jones, R., and Bittmann, E. 1967. The B8500-microsecond thin-film memory. *AFIPS Conf. Proc., 1967 FJCC* 31:347–52. Montvale, N.J.: AFIPS Press.

Jordan, H. F. 1978. A special purpose architecture for finite element analysis. *ICASE*, NASA Langley Research Center, Report No. 78-9, March 29, 1978.

Joslin, E. O. 1965. Application benchmarks: the key to meaningful computer evaluation. *ACM Proc. of the 20th National Conf.*, August 1965, Cleveland, Ohio, pp. 27–37.

Kahan, W. 1965. Further remarks on reducing truncation errors. *Communications of the ACM* 8:40.

Karp, R. M., and Miranker, W. L. 1968. Parallel minimax search for a maximum. *J. of Combinatorial Theory* 4:19–35.

Katzan, H., Jr. 1973. *Computer data security.* Sect. 2.5, Virtual Storage. New York: Van Nostrand Reinhold.

Keller, R. M. 1975. Look-ahead processors. *Computing Surveys* 7:177–95.

Keyes, R. 1969. Physical problems and limits in computer logic. *IEEE Spectrum*, May 1969, pp. 36–45.

———. 1972. Physical problems of small structures in electronics. *Proc. of the IEEE* 60:1055–61.

Kilburn, T.; Edwards, D. B. G.; Lanigan, M. J.; and Sumner, F. H. 1962. One-level storage system. *IRE Transactions on Electronic Computers* EC-11, 2:223–35. Reprinted in Bell and Newell (1971), pp. 276–90.

Kleinrock, L. 1969. Certain analytic results for time-shared processors. *Proc. of the 1969 IFIP Congress*, pp. 838–45.

———. 1975. *Queueing systems: theory and applications.* New York: Wiley.

Klingman, E. E. 1977. *Microcomputer system design.* Englewood Cliffs, N.J.: Prentice-Hall.

Knight, K. E. 1966. Changes in computer performance. *Datamation*, September 1966, pp. 40–54.

Knoblock, D. E.; Loughry, D. C.; and Vissers, C. A. 1975. Insight into interfacing. *IEEE Spectrum*, May 1975, pp. 50–57.

Knuth, D. E. 1968. *The art of computer programming, vol. 1: fundamental algorithms.* Reading, Mass.: Addison-Wesley.

———. 1969. *The art of computer programming, vol. 2: seminumerical algorithms.* Reading, Mass.: Addison-Wesley.

———. 1971. An empirical study of FORTRAN programs. *Software: Practice and Experience* 1:105–33.

Knuth, D. E., and Rao, G. S. 1975. Activity in an interleaved memory. *IEEE Trans. on Comp.* C-24:943–44.

Kogge, P. 1977*a*. The microprogramming of pipelined processors. *Proc., 4th Annual Symposium on Computer Architecture*, March 1977, pp. 63–69.

————. 1977*b*. Algorithm development for pipelined processors. *Proc., 1977 International Conference on Parallel Processing*, p. 217.

Kogge, P. M., and Stone, H. S. 1973. A parallel algorithm for the efficient solution of a general class of recurrence equations. *IEEE Trans. on Comp.* C-22:786–93.

Kosonocky, W. F., and Carnes, J. E. 1971. Charge-coupled digital circuits. *IEEE J. of Solid-State Circuits* SC-6:314–22.

Krambeck, R. H.; Walden, R. H.; and Pickar, K. A. 1971. Implanted barrier two-phase CCD. Presented at the IEEE International Electron Device Meeting, October 1971, Washington, D.C.

Kuck, D. J. 1977. A survey of parallel machine organization and programming. *Computing Surveys* 9:29–60.

Kuck, D. J.; Muraoka, Y.; and Chen, S. C. 1972. On the number of operations simultaneously executable in FORTRAN-like programs and their resulting speedup. *IEEE Trans. on Comp.* C-21:1293–1310.

Landauer, R. 1961. Irreversibility and heat generation in the computing process. *IBM J. of Res. and Dev.* 5:183–91.

————. 1962. Fluctuations in bistable tunnel diode circuits. *J. of Applied Physics* 33:2209–16.

Lane, W. G. 1972. Pipeline array processing, an efficient architectural alternative. Ph.D. dissertation, University of California, Davis.

Lawler, E. L., and Moore, J. M. 1969. A functional equation and its application to resource allocation and sequencing problems. *Management Science*, September 1969, pp. 77–84.

Lawrie, D. H. 1973. Memory-processor connection networks. Report No. UIUCDCS-R-73-557. Dept. of Computer Science, University of Illinois, Urbana, February 1973.

————. 1975. Access and alignment of data in an array processor, IEEE Trans. on Comp. C-24:1145–55.

Lin, S. 1970. An introduction to error-correcting codes. Englewood Cliffs, N.J.: Prentice-Hall.

Lin, Y. S., and Mattson, R. L. 1972. Cost-performance evaluation of memory hierarchies. *IEEE Trans. on Magnetics* MAG-8:390–92.

Lincoln, N. R. 1977. Supercomputer development—the pleasure and the pain. *COMPCON 77 Digest of Papers*, IEEE Computer Society International Conference, February 1977, San Francisco, pp. 21–25.

Linz, P. 1970. Accurate floating-point summation. *Communications of the ACM* 13:361–62.

Little, J. D. C. 1961. A proof for the queueing formula: $L = \lambda W$. *Operations Research* 9:383–87.

Loomis, H. H., Jr. 1966. The maximum rate accumulator. *IEEE Trans. on Elec. Comp.* EC-15:628–39.

Loughry, D. C. 1974. What makes a good interface? *IEEE Spectrum*, May 1974, pp. 52–57.

Lucas, H. C. 1971. Performance evaluation and monitoring. *Computing Surveys* 3:79–91.

Łukasiewicz, J. 1951. *Aristotle's syllogistic: from the standpoint of modern formal logic.* Oxford: Oxford University Press.

Lunde, A. 1974. Evaluation of instruction set processor architecture by program tracing. Dept. of Computer Science Technical Report, Carnegie-Mellon University, Pittsburgh, Pa., July 1974.

Lunde, A. 1975. More data on the O/W ratios. *Computer Architecture News* 4:9–13.

Lynch, W. C. 1972. Operating system performance. *Communications of the ACM* 15:579–85.

MacDougall, M. H. 1970. Computer system simulation: an introduction. *Computing Surveys* 2:191–209.

McKeeman, W. M. 1967. Language directed computer design. AFIPS Conf. Proc. *1967 FJCC* 31:413–17.

McKinney, J. M. 1969. A survey of analytical time-sharing models. *Computing Surveys* 1:105–16.

McLaughlin, R. A. 1974. A survey of 1974 DP budgets. *Datamation*, February 1974, pp. 52–56.

MacSorley, O. L. 1961. High-speed arithmetic in binary computers. *Proc. of the IRE* 49:67–91.

Madnick, S. E., and Donovan, J. J. 1974. *Operating systems.* New York: McGraw-Hill.

Massey, J. L., and Garcia, O. N. 1972. Error-correcting codes in computer arithmetic. In *Advances in Information Systems Science, vol. 4*, edited by J. T. Tou, pp. 273–326. New York: Plenum Press.

Mathias, J., and Fedde, G. 1969. Plated-wire technology: a critical review. *IEEE Trans. on Magnetics* MAG-5:728–51.

Matick, R. E. 1972. Review of current proposed technologies for mass storage systems. *Proc. of the IEEE* 60:266–89.

―――. 1977. Computer storage systems and technology. New York: Wiley.

Mattson, R. et al. 1970. Evaluation techniques for storage hierarchies. *IBM Sys. J.* 9:78–117.

May, T., and Woods, M. 1979. Alpha-particle-induced soft errors in dynamic memories. *IEEE Trans. on Elec. Devices* ED-26:2–9.

Meade, R. 1971. Design approaches for cache memory control. *Computer Design*, January 1971, pp. 87–93.

Mills, D. L. 1972. Communication software. *Proc. of the IEEE* 60:1333–41.

Moore, G. E. 1976. Microprocessors and integrated electronic technology. *Proc. of the IEEE* 64:837–41.

Morris, R. 1968. Scatter storage techniques. *Communications of the ACM* 11:38–44.

Morrison, P., and Morrison, E., eds. 1961. *Charles Babbage and his calculating engines: selected writings.* New York: Dover Publications.

Morrow, G., and Fullmer, H. 1978. Proposed standard for the S-100 bus. *IEEE Computer*, May 1978, pp. 84–89.

Morse, P. M. 1958. *Queues, inventories, and maintenance.* New York: Wiley.

Mrazek, D., and Morris, M. 1973. How to design with programmable logic arrays. Application Note AN-89. National Semiconductor Corp., August 1973.

Murphy, B. T. 1964. Cost-size optima of monolithic integrated circuits. *Proc. of the IEEE* 52:1537–45.

Murphy, J., and Wade, R. M. 1970. The IBM 360/195. *Datamation*, April 1970, pp. 72–79.

Naylor, T. H. et al. 1966. *Computer simulation techniques.* New York: Wiley.

Neuhauser, C. 1973. An emulation oriented, dynamic microprogrammable processor. Computer Research Report #28. Electrical Engineering Dept., The Johns Hopkins University, Baltimore, Md., November 1973.

Nielsen, N. R. 1967. The simulation of time sharing systems. *Communications of the ACM* 10:397–412.

Organick, E. I. 1972. *The MULTICS system: an examination of its structure.* Cambridge, Mass.: MIT Press.

———. 1973. *Computer system organization: the B5700/B6700 series.* New York: Academic Press.

Ornstein, S. M.; Crowther, W. R.; Kraley, M. F.; Bressler, R. D.; Michel, A.; and Heart, F. E. 1975. Pluribus—a reliable multiprocessor. *AFIPS Conf. Proc., 1975 NCC* 44:551–59.

Osborne, A. 1976. *8080 programming for logic design.* Berkeley: Osborne.

Osborne, A. 1977. *6800 programming for logic design.* Berkeley: Osborne.

Osborne, A. et al. 1978. *Z-80 programming for logic design.* Berkeley: Osborne.

Parasuraman, B. 1976. High-performance microprocessor architectures. *Proc. of the IEEE* 64:851–59.

Parhami, B. 1973. Associative memories and processors: an overview and selected bibliography. *Proc. of the IEEE* 61:722–30.

Parmelee, R. P.; Peterson, T. I.; Sullivan, C. C.; and Hatfield, D. S. 1972. Virtual storage and virtual machine concepts. *IBM Sys. J.* 11:99–130.

Parzen, E. 1960. *Modern probability theory and its applications.* New York: Wiley.

Patel, A., and Hong, S. J. 1974. Optimal rectangular code for high density magnetic tapes. *IBM J. of Res. and Dev.* 18:579–88.

Pear, C. B., ed. 1967. *Magnetic recording in science and industry.* New York: Reinhold Publishing.

Pease, M. C. 1968. An adaptation of the fast Fourier transform for parallel processing. *J. of the ACM* 15:252–64.

Peatman, J. B. 1977. *Microcomputer-based design.* New York: McGraw-Hill.

Peterson, W. W., and Weldon, E. J., Jr. 1972. Error-correcting codes. Cambridge, Mass.: MIT Press.

Peuto, B. L., and Shustek, L. J. 1977. Current issues in the architecture of microprocessors. *IEEE Computer,* February 1977, pp. 20–25.

Pinkerton, T. B. 1969. Performance monitoring in a time-sharing system. *Communications of the ACM* 12:608–10.

Pohm, A., and Zingg, R. 1968. Magnetic film memory systems. *IEEE Trans. on Magnetics* MAG-4:146–52.

Popek, G. J., and Goldberg, R. P. 1974. Formal requirements for virtualizable third generation architectures. *Communications of the ACM* 17:412–21.

Pugh, E. 1971. Storage hierarchies: gaps, cliffs, and trends. *IEEE Trans. on Magnetics* MAG-7:810.

Radoy, C. H., and Lipovski, G. J. 1974. Switched multiple instruction, multiple data stream processing. *Proc., 2nd Annual Symposium on Computer Architecture* (IEEE Pub. 75CH0916-7 C), pp. 183–87.

Raffel, J. et al. 1961. Magnetic film memory design. *Proc. of the IEEE* 49:155.

Ralston, A., ed. 1974. *Auerbach computer encyclopedia.* Philadelphia: Auerbach.

Ramamoorthy, C. V., and Li, H. F. 1977. Pipeline architecture. *Computing Surveys* 9:61–102.

RAND Corporation. 1955. *A million random digits with 100,000 normal deviates.* Glencoe, Ill.: The Free Press.

Randell, B., and Russell, L. 1964. *ALGOL 60 implementation.* New York: Academic Press.

Reigel, E. W.; Faber, U.; and Fisher, D. A. 1972. The interpreter—a microprogrammable building block system. *AFIPS Conf. Proc., 1972 SJCC* 40:705–23. Montvale, N.J.: AFIPS Press.

Reyling, G. 1974. PLAs enhance digital processor speed and cut component count. *Electronics*, August 8, 1974, pp. 109–14.

Rice, R., and Smith, W. R. 1971. SYMBOL—a major departure from classic software dominated von Neumann computing systems. *AFIPS Conf. Proc., 1971* SJCC 38:575–87. Montvale, N.J.: AFIPS Press.

Ritchie, D. M., and Thompson, K. 1974. The UNIX time-sharing system. *Communications of the ACM* 17:365–75.

Rosen, S. 1969. Electronic computers: a historical survey. *Computing Surveys* 1:7–36.

Rosin, R. F. 1969. Contemporary concepts of microprogramming and emulation. *Computing Surveys* 1:197–212.

Rothmuller, K. 1979. Comparing microprocessors architecture. *Mini-Macro Systems,* 00:000–000.

Rothmuller, K. 1976. Task partitioning in programmable logic systems. *IEEE Computer,* January 1976, pp. 19–24.

Rubenstein, H.; McCormack, T. L.; and Fuller, H. W. 1961. The application of domain wall motion to storage devices. *1961 International Solid-State Circuits Conference, Digest of Technical Papers*, February 1961, pp. 64–65.

Ruggiero, J. F., and Coryell, D. A. 1969. An auxiliary processing system for array calculations. *IBM Sys. J.* 8:118–35.

Rusch, R. B. 1969. *Computers: their history and how they work.* New York: Simon & Schuster.

Russell, L.; Whalen, R.; and Leilich, H. 1968. Ferrite memory systems. *IEEE Trans. on Magnetics* MAG-4:134–45.

Saal, H. J., and Shustek, L. J. 1972. Microprogramming implementation of computer measurement techniques. SLAC-PUB-1072. Stanford University, Stanford, Calif., July 1972.

Scherr, A. L. 1967. *An analysis of time-shared computer systems.* Cambridge, Mass.: MIT Press.

Schmid, H., and Busch, D. S. 1968. An electronic digital slide rule. *The Electronic Engineer*, July 1968, pp. 54–64.

Schroeder, M. D. 1971. Performance of the GE-645 associative memory while MULTICS is in operation. *ACM Workshop on System Performance Evaluation,* pp. 245–277.

Schroeder, M. D., and Saltzer, J. H. 1972. A hardware architecture for implementing protection rings. *Communications of the ACM* 15:3.

Scott, N. 1970. *Electronic computer technology.* Ch. 10. New York: McGraw-Hill.

Senzig, D. N., and Smith, R. V. 1965. Computer organization for array processing. *AFIPS Conf. Proc., 1965 FJCC* 27 (part I):117–28. Washington, D.C.: Spartan Books.

Sherman, S.; Baskett, F.; and Browne, J. C. 1972. Trace-driven modeling and analysis of CPU scheduling in a multiprogramming system. *Communications of the ACM* 15:1063–69.

Shima, M. 1978. Two versions of 16-bit chip span microprocessor, minicomputer needs. *Electronics,* December 21, 1978, pp. 81–88.

Siewiorek, D.; Bell, C. G.; and Newell, A. 1980. *Principles of computer structures.* New York: McGraw-Hill.

Sites, R. L. 1978. An analysis of the Cray-1 computer. *Proc., 5th Annual Symposium on Computer Architecture,* 1978, Palo Alto, Calif., pp. 101–6.

———. 1978*b.* A combined register-stack architecture. *SIGARCH News* Vol. 6, No. 8. p. 19 (April 1978).

Slotnik, D. L.; Borck, W. C.; and McReynolds, R. C. 1962. The SOLOMON computer. *AFIPS Conf. Proc.,* 1962 FJCC 22:97–107, Washington, D.C.: Spartan Books.

Spain, R. J. 1966. Domain tip propagation logic. *IEEE Trans. on Magnetics* MAG-2:347–51.

Sreenivasan, K., and Kleinman, A. J. 1974. On the construction of a representative synthetic workload. *Communications of the ACM* 17:127–33.

Steele, G. L. 1975. Multiprocessing compactifying garbage collection. *Communications of the ACM* 18:495–508.

Stone, H. S. 1970. A pipeline push-down stack computer. In *Parallel Processor Systems, Technologies and Applications,* edited by L. C. Hobbs et al., pp. 235–49. New York: Spartan.

———. 1971. Parallel processing with the perfect shuffle. *IEEE Trans. on Comp.* C-20:153–61.

———. 1972. *Introduction to computer organization and data structures.* New York: McGraw-Hill.

———. 1973*a.* An efficient parallel algorithm for the solution of a tridiagonal linear system of equations. *J. of the ACM* 20:27–38.

———. 1973*b.* Discrete mathematical structures and their application. Chicago: SRA.

Strauss, J. C. 1973. An analytic model of the HASP task monitor. *1st Annual SIGME Symposium on Measurement and Evaluation,* February 1973, Palo Alto, Calif., pp. 22–28.

Sutherland, I. E. 1963. Sketchpad: a man-machine graphical communication system. *AFIPS Conf. Proc., 1963 SJCC* 23:329–46. Baltimore: Spartan Books.

Sutherland, I. E., and Mead, C. A. 1977. Microelectronics and computer science. *Scientific American* 237:210–28.

Swan, R. J.; Fuller, S. H.; and Siewiorek, D. P. 1977. Cm*: a modular multimicroprocessor. *AFIPS Conf. Proc., 1977 NCC* 46:637–44.

Swanson, J. A. 1960. Physical vs. logical coupling in memory systems. *IBM J. of Res. and Dev.* 4:305.

Swanson, R. 1975. Understanding cyclic redundancy codes. *Computer Design,* November 1975. p. 93–99.

Tang, D. T., and Chien, R. T. 1969. Coding for error control. *IBM Sys. J.* 8:48–86.

Texas Instruments, Inc. 1972. ASC, a description of the Advanced Scientific Computer System. Publication M1001P. Texas Instruments, Inc., April 1972.

———. Undated. Texas Instruments TMS 1802 NC one-chip calculator circuit. Bulletin CB-143. Texas Instruments, Inc.

Thiele, A. A. 1969. The theory of cylindrical magnetic domains. *Bell Sys. Tech. J.* 48:3287–335.

———. 1970. Theory of the static stability of cylindrical domains in uniaxial platelets. *J. of Applied Physics* 41:1139–45.

Thornton, J. E. 1970. *Design of a computer: the Control Data 6600.* Glenview, Illinois: Scott Foresman.

Tomasulo, R. M. 1967. An efficient algorithm for exploiting multiple arithmetic units. *IBM J. of Res. and Dev.* 11:25–33.

Tompsett, M. F.; Amelio, G. F.; and Smith, G. E. 1970. Charge coupled 8-bit shift register. *Applied Physics Letters* 17:111–15.

Tucker, S. G. 1965. Emulation of large systems. *Communications of the ACM* 8:753–61.

———. 1967. Microprogram control for System/360. *IBM Sys. J.* 6:222–41.

Turck, J. A. V. 1972. *Origin of modern calculating machines.* Reprint of 1921 edition. New York: Arno Press.

Vadasz, L.; Chua, H.; and Grove, A. 1971. Semiconductor random-access memories. *IEEE Spectrum*, May 1971, pp. 40–48.

Voight, R. C. 1977. The influence of vector computer architecture on numerical algorithms. In *High Speed Computer and Algorithm Organization,* edited by D. J. Kuck et al., pp. 229–44. New York: Academic Press.

Wakerly, J. F. 1977. Microprocessor input/output architecture. *IEEE Computer,* February 1977, pp. 26–33.

Watson, W. J. 1972. The TI ASC—a highly modular and flexible super computer architecture. *AFIPS Conf. Proc., 1972 FJCC* 41 (part I):221–28. Montvale, N.J.: AFIPS Press.

Weber, H. 1967. A microprogrammed implementation of EULER on IBM System/360 Model 30. *Communications of the ACM* 10:549–58.

Whitney, T. M. 1975. Introduction to calculators. In *Introduction to Computer Architecture,* edited by H. S. Stone, first edition, chapter 3, pp. 76–135. Chicago: SRA.

Whitney, T. M.; Rode, F.; and Tung, C. 1972. The powerful pocketful: an electronic calculator challenges the slide rule. *Hewlett-Packard Journal*, June 1972, pp. 2–9.

Wilkes, M. V. 1951. The best way to design an automatic calculating machine. Manchester University Computer Inaugural Conference, July 1951, pp. 16–18.

———. 1964. Lists and why they are useful. *ACM Proc. of the 19th National Conf.*, August 1964, Philadelphia, pp. F1-1 through F1-5.

———. 1969. The growth of interest in microprogramming: a literature survey. *Computing Surveys* 1:139–45.

Wirth, N. 1969. On multiprogramming, machine coding, and computer organization. *Communications of the ACM* 12:489–98.

———.1971. The programming language Pascal. *Acta Informatica* 1:35–63.

Wirth, N., and Hoare, C. A. R. 1966. A contribution to the development of ALGOL. *Communications of the ACM* 9:413–32.

Wirth, N., and Weber, H. 1966. EULER: a generalization of ALGOL, and its formal definition: part I. *Communications of the ACM* 9:13–25.

Wortman, D. 1972. A study of language directed computer design. Ph.D. thesis, Stanford University.

Wulf, W. A., and Bell, C. G. 1973. C.mmp—a multi-mini-processor. *AFIPS Conf. Proc., 1972 FJCC* 41 (part II):765–77. Montvale, N.J.: AFIPS Press.

Yaney, D.; Nelson, J.; and Vanskike, L. 1979. Alpha-particle tracks in silicon and their effect on dynamic MOS RAM reliability. *IEEE Trans. on Elec. Devices* ED-26:10–16.

Young, L. H. 1967. Uncalculated risks keep calculator on the shelf. *Electronics,* March 6, 1967, pp. 231–34.

Index/Glossary

Access time: the time delay between a request to memory for a datum and the response by the memory with that datum; 210–1

Accumulator, 8

Adder: a circuit that produces the sum of two operands; 4, 8, 12–3, 48
floating-point, 83
ones' complement, 47, 48
signed-magnitude, 39
two's complement, 47, 48

Adder-subtractor: a circuit that can produce either the sum or difference of two operands; 48, 49

Addition, 35–49, 438–40
diminished-radix complement, 42–4
floating-point, 81
nondecimal, 36
ones' complement, 46
radix-complement, 41–5
signed-magnitude, 38
two's complement, 44

Additive inverse (of a number): that number which when added to the original number yields zero; 38

Address: an integer that uniquely identifies a specific memory cell in a memory system;
bubble storage, 263
disks, 254–5
multiplexed, 236–7
random-access memory, 217
tapes, 251

Addressing modes. See Address modification

Address modification: the ability to compute the address of an operand at the point of execution of an instruction; 9, 14–5, 161, 165, 171, 175–7

Address range, 166

Address space: the set of (virtual) addresses that a given task can generate; 607. See also Address range

ALGOL: a high-level computer language; 9, 320

ALGOL-68 heap, 350

ALGOL-W, 337

Algorithm: a sequential description of a computation in which each basic step is executable by a computing device; 8, 14–5

Algorithmic state machine (ASM): a design aid for control unit design in synchronous digital systems, 115

Alignment, 627, 636. See also Boundary alignment

Allison, D. R., 98

ALLOCATE (in PL/I), 348

Amdahl Corporation, 635, 638
470-V/6 characteristics, 206, 465

APL (A Programming Language), 460, 479

Applications software: programs written for specific end-use applications; 195

Arbiter: a hardware device that selects among several concurrent requests for a resource and determines which shall be honored; 637